Texts and Monographs in Computer Science

AF786662

Texts and Monographs in Computer Science

Suad Alagić
Relational Database Technology

Suad Alagić and Michael A Arbib
The Design of Well-Structured and Correct Programs

S Thomas Alexander
Adaptive Signal Processing: Theory and Applications

Michael A Arbib, A J Kfoury, and Robert N Moll
A Basis for Theoretical Computer Science

Michael A Arbib and Ernest G Manes
Algebraic Approaches to Program Semantics

F L Bauer and H Wossner
Algorithmic Language and Program Development

Kaare Christian
The Guide to Modula-2

Edsger W Dijkstra
Selected Writings on Computing: A Personal Perspective

Nissim Francez
Fairness

Peter W Frey, Ed
Chess Skill in Man and Machine, 2nd Edition

R T Gregory and E V Krishnamurthy
Methods and Applications of Error-Free Computation

David Gries, Ed
Programming Methodology: A Collection of Articles by Members of IFIP WG2.3

David Gries
The Science of Programming

A J Kfoury, Robert N Moll, and Michael A Arbib
A Programming Approach to Computability

E V Krishnamurthy
Error-Free Polynomial Matrix Computations

Franco P Preparata and Michael Ian Shamos
Computational Geometry: An Introduction

Brian Randell, Ed
The Origins of Digital Computers: Selected Papers

Arto Salomaa and Matti Soittola
Automata-Theoretic Aspects of Formal Power Series

Jeffrey R Sampson
Adaptive Information Processing: An Introductory Survey

J T Schwartz, R B Dewar, E Dubinsky, and E Schonberg
Programming with Sets: An Introduction to SETL

William M Waite and Gerhard Goos
Compiler Construction

Niklaus Wirth
Programming in Modula-2

Programming with Sets

An Introduction to SETL

J.T. Schwartz
R.B.K. Dewar
E. Dubinsky
E. Schonberg

With 31 Illustrations

Springer-Verlag New York Berlin Heidelberg
London Paris Tokyo

J.T. Schwartz
R.B.K. Dewar
E. Schonberg
Computer Science Department
Courant Institute of
Mathematical Sciences
New York University
New York, NY 10012
U.S.A.

E. Dubinsky
Department of Mathematics
and Computer Science
Clarkson University
Potsdam, NY 13676

Series Editor
David Gries
Department of Computer Science
Cornell University
Ithaca, NY 14853
U.S.A.

Library of Congress Cataloging in Publication Data
Programming with sets.
(Texts and monographs in computer science)
Includes index.
1. SETL (Computer program language)
I. Schwartz, Jacob T. II. Series.
QA76.73.S4P76 1986 005.13'3 86-20386

Softcover reprint of the hardcover 1st edition 1986

Typeset by Asco Trade Typesetting Ltd., Hong Kong.

9 8 7 6 5 4 3 2 1

ISBN-13: 978-1-4613-9577-5 e-ISBN-13: 978-1-4613-9575-1
DOI: 10.1007/ 978-1-4613-9575-1

Preface

The programming language SETL is a relatively new member of the so-called "very-high-level" class of languages, some of whose other well-known members are LISP, APL, SNOBOL, and PROLOG. These languages all aim to reduce the cost of programming, recognized today as a main obstacle to future progress in the computer field, by allowing direct manipulation of large composite objects, considerably more complex than the integers, strings, etc., available in such well-known mainstream languages as PASCAL, PL/I, ALGOL, and Ada. For this purpose, LISP introduces structured lists as data objects, APL introduces vectors and matrices, and SETL introduces the objects characteristic for it, namely general finite sets and maps.

The direct availability of these abstract, composite objects, and of powerful mathematical operations upon them, improves programmer speed and productivity significantly, and also enhances program clarity and readability. The classroom consequence is that students, freed of some of the burden of petty programming detail, can advance their knowledge of significant algorithms and of broader strategic issues in program development more rapidly than with more conventional programming languages.

The price that very-high-level languages pay for their expressive power is a certain loss of efficiency. SETL should therefore be regarded, not as a tool for production-efficiency programming, but as a vehicle for rapid experimentation with algorithms and program design, and as an ideal vehicle for writing "one-shot" or infrequently used programs whose efficiency is of little consequence. It is also an effective tool for prototyping large systems for purposes of design validation and early customer exposure, systems which if important enough can then be translated into more efficient versions written in programming languages of lower level. Experience with SETL will show that it is efficient enough for a surprising variety of purposes; nevertheless, it is still expensive to run and will remain so until the newest generation of high-performance microcomputers becomes generally available. In spite of this, SETL is a good vehicle for *discussing* program-efficiency issues, since it allows a stepwise approach to these issues, algorithm design being chosen first and data structures which realize them being chosen second. It will also be seen that the data structure representation sublanguage of SETL, described in Chapter 10, is a powerful conceptual tool aiding such "programming by stepwise refinement."

Fairly polished versions of SETL are currently available on the DEC VAX, IBM/370, SUN workstation and APOLLO. The systems running on all these machines are close to identical, all being produced from a common system source by transporting an underlying systems-implementation language from machine to machine.

This book is intended for people who want to write programs in SETL. It does not assume knowledge of any other programming language and is therefore suitable for use in an introductory course. We attempt to explain most of the mathematical concepts which play a role in SETL programs, almost all of which are in fact quite elementary. However, we do assume that the reader has a working knowledge of such basic concepts as set, sequence, etc. The knowledge assumed is roughly equivalent to that which would be acquired in a good high school "new mathematics" course, or in the first month of a freshman-level course in discrete mathematics.

We present considerably more material than can be covered in a one-semester introductory course. Chapter 1 provides an introduction to computer programming and a brief overview of the SETL language. (It can safely be ignored by readers who have some previous exposure to programming.) Chapters 2 and 3 introduce the major data objects of SETL, of which sets, maps, and tuples are most characteristic, and describe many of the language's operations. By the end of Chapter 3, the student is in a position to write various interesting one-liners. Chapter 4 then presents various basic control structure notions, qualifying the student to write interesting short programs. Chapter 5 introduces the most important control structures, namely *procedures*.

Chapter 6 gives advice on program development, testing, and debugging, completing what can be considered the elementary part of the book. Chapter 7 describes the backtracking dictions of SETL. The first seven chapters can be covered in a one-semester introductory course and can be skimmed rapidly by any reader reasonably familiar with at least one modern programming language, such as PL/1, ALGOL 68, PASCAL, or Ada.

The remaining chapters present more advanced material, which could be covered in a second programming course. Chapter 8 introduces the directory, program, module, and library mechanisms used to structure large programs. Chapter 9 describes the I/O features of SETL systematically. Chapter 10 presents SETL's data representation sublanguage and reviews various strategic considerations which play a role in data representation choice. Chapter 11 shows the language in action by presenting several more substantial applications of it.

SETL was developed at the Computer Science Department of New York University, by a group of which three of the present authors were members. The language has now been used by students in courses at NYU, Clarkson University, Dickinson College and University of California, Berkeley ranging from the introductory undergraduate to graduate courses in algorithm design. The style and order of presentation adopted in this book reflects some of the pedagogical experience gained in this way, especially at the undergraduate level.

Thanks are due to the many persons who helped to define and develop the SETL system. David Shields has been a mainstay throughout, inventing and implementing many system improvements, and developing documentation from which several of the sections of the book are drawn. Much of the first version of the system was written by Arthur Grand and brought to solidity by Stefan Freudenberger. Thanks are also extended to Edith Schonberg, Micha Sharir, Robert Paige, Kurt Maly, Phillip Owens, Aaron Stein, Earl Draughon, Bernard Lang, Leonard Vanek, Steve Tihor, Hank Warren, and Gerry Fisher, all of whom contributed to the development of the SETL system. Thanks are also due to the members of the NYUADA group, the largest and most persistent users of the SETL system in their experiments in Software Prototyping. Valuable design suggestions were contributed by our colleague Professor Malcolm Harrison and gleaned from his elegant BALM language. Essential thanks are due to the very helpful and hard-working group of summer interns who helped put this manuscript together and remove many of its errors during the summer of 1981: Leonid Fridman, Nathaniel Glasser, Barbara Okun, and Yi Tso. Many thanks to David Berkowitz who was responsible for coordinating the editing and debugging process in its final stages. We also wish to extend thanks to Professor Andrei Ershov and his group at Novosibirsk, who have aided the development and definition of the language from the very first days, Professor Anthony McCann of Leeds University, and Drs. Su Bogong and Zhou Zhiying of Tsinghua University, whose more recent involvement has been most valuable.

Thanks are due to the research administrators who fostered the development of SETL through its early, relatively isolated years. Among these we should particularly like to thank Milton Rose, who launched our development effort during his years at NSF, also Kent Curtis and Tom Keenan of NSF, who fostered it during the period in which the NYU group was struggling toward a reliable and acceptably efficient implementation. Recent support from the Office of Naval Research is making possible an improved implementation of SETL and renewed research in language design; for his support and encouragement we want to thank here Robert Grafton.

The able secretarial work of Allison Sundheim, Marina Lowry, and Yanire

Zayas is gratefully acknowledged: their care, patience, and unflappable good humor in the face of an ever-changing manuscript has been invaluable. The detailed editorial advice of Springer-Verlag added a layer of much-needed polish to this text. To all of them our heart-felt thanks, and of course a full exoneration from whatever errors remain lurking in the text that follows.

Contents

APPENDIX B
Syntax Diagrams

CHAPTER 1

Programming Concepts

1.1 An Informal Overview of SETL

We begin with a very simple example of a SETL program:

```
program sample_program_number_1;
   print(54 + 45);
   print('The difference of twelve and nine is:', 12-9);
   print(55*55);
end;
```

If these instructions are typed and submitted correctly, the computer, after digesting them, will produce the following results:

```
99
The difference of twelve and nine is: 3
3025
```

Of course, programs in SETL are not restricted to dealing with simple numerical quantities and describing simple arithmetic calculations. You will see, for example, that it is easy to manipulate arbitrarily complex tables—tables of names, addresses, and other information such as the following:

```
[['Aldo Gonzalez','45 Ellwood Ave','278-3591','12-12-45',21315],
   ['Jimmy Archibald','1315 Bole St','479-1919','5-31-78',0]],
```

Such tables can be built up, sorted, searched for particular elements or combinations of elements. Extracts and statistical summaries of them can be prepared and printed, etc. All this will be easy to do once you have learned the programming language described in this book, which can handle a table like the preceding one just about as comfortably as it can handle a simple number like 23.

Programming in SETL is simpler than in many other languages because most decisions on details that a programmer is normally required to make and which are not essential to the algorithm being implemented are handled automatically by the SETL system. For example, it is not necessary to supply declarations for the types and sizes of objects that appear in a SETL program. (Such declarations are mandatory in most conventional programming languages.)

Another detail that the programmer can ignore is the length of a *tuple* (i.e., one-dimensional array). The system keeps track of the length, increasing or decreasing it as required.

A much more important feature is the existence in SETL of certain fundamental mathematical constructs that make it relatively easy to represent complex logicomathematical expressions in concise fashion. In SETL the "one-line program" is not the product of obscure programming tricks but, rather, the result of thinking globally about expressions and representing them in concise, clear mathematical notation.

The most important of these constructs concerns finite sets. SETL stands for "SET Language." As its name implies, SETL makes it easy to work with sets as values. The elements of a set can be any SETL values, including other sets. They do not have to be of the same type, and they can be nested to arbitrary levels.

There are two ways in which a set can be specified. One is simply to list the elements, as in

$$\{7, -1, 0, \{2, \text{'Gonzales'}\}, A + B, \{\{\{x\}\}\}, -9\}$$

and the other is to use an expression called a *set former* (see the following example), which constructs a set from other sets in a manner similar to the mathematical language used to define a set.

In addition to the standard operations of the algebra of sets, the operation of *quantification* (existential or universal) is possible. This allows one to program quite complicated expressions rather easily. For example, to program the Boolean statement that every element in a set *s* has property *P* one simply writes:

forall x **in** s | P(x)

A similar syntax is used to iterate through a set as follows:

```
(forall x in s)
      body
end forall;
```

This is a loop which performs "body" for each element x **in** s.

An important construct derived from set theory is the *map*, which is a set, each of whose elements is a tuple of length 2 (*ordered pair*). There are many ways in which the use of a map can drastically reduce the complexity of a program. One example is a table in which the keys are, say, the names of people. In most programming languages it is necessary to code each name to an integer. This artificiality leads to many errors. In SETL a set consisting of all the names forms the domain of a map, say F, and, for example, F('Gonzales') specifies the table entry for Gonzales.

A loop iterating over such a map F can have the following suggestive syntax:

```
(forall y = F(x))
        body
end forall;
```

A final introductory observation is that SETL programs are relatively easy to read. To do so, you need to know the syntax of the language and elementary mathematical notation. Very often comparatively little of the former is required. In fact, it is sometimes possible for someone who knows a little about mathematics and nothing about SETL to read and understand SETL programs at once.

SETL has many other powerful features, and it will take well over a hundred pages to explain them all. Therefore, this short section can only give you a glimpse of some of these features. Nevertheless, before we march forth to explore the terrain systematically, it is worthwhile to preview some details informally. For this purpose, we consider another example. Suppose that the following set of numbers is given:

$$\{13, 11, 45, 0, -16, 21, 85, 46, 80\} \qquad (1)$$

and call it s. The problem we wish to consider is that of finding the *median* of the numbers in s, namely the number which would come halfway between the first and the last element of s if the elements of s were arranged in ascending sequence from lowest to highest, namely as

$$[-16, 0, 11, 13, 21, 45, 46, 80, 85] \qquad (2)$$

(In our example, this median is clearly 21.) If (as in our example) s has an odd number of elements, then the *median* (which is often used in statistics to represent a "typical" member of a set s) can be defined as follows: it is the unique element x of s such that there are as many elements of s which are smaller than x as there are elements of s which are larger than x. If s has an even number of elements (as it would if we dropped the number 85 from our example) nothing lies exactly in the middle, and we could argue about which of the two numbers (e.g., 13 or 21) lying equally close to the middle of an ordered sequence like (2) should be considered the median. To avoid this complication let us agree for the moment that we will only consider sets having an odd number of members. For such sets, the median is simply the number x defined by the following condition:

(*) The number of members of *s* which are less than *x* is equal to the number of members of *s* which are greater than *x*.

In SETL, a set like (1) can be read in (for example, from the keyboard of a computer terminal) simply by writing the command

read(s);

(See page 149 for a description of input data formats). Once having read *s* in, we may want to find, and then print, its median. As with all programming tasks, this can be done in several different ways. If we knew how to arrange the elements of *s* in order, we could simply find this arrangement, take the element which comes in the middle, and print it out. Arranging elements in order is called *sorting*; we will study many techniques for sorting later in this book, and any one of them would put us into position to use this approach to finding the median. However, it still is too early to do anything quite this complex. In fact, it is much more straightforward and more illustrative of an important way SETL can be used to "think globally" and program the definition (*) directly.

In order to do this, we must first be able to construct "the number of members y of s which are less than x." Since SETL makes it easy for us to form sets and allows us to get the number of elements in any set t simply by writing $\#t$, this is easy: we simply form the set of all members y of s which are less than x and then take its number. The set we want can be formed simply by writing

$$\{y \textbf{ in } s \mid y < x\} \tag{3}$$

and its number of elements is therefore

$$\#\{y \textbf{ in } s \mid y < x\} \tag{4}$$

Similarly, the number of elements in s which are greater than x can be written as

$$\#\{y \textbf{ in } s \mid y > x\} \tag{5}$$

Concerning the construct (3), which is known in SETL as a *set former*, we can make the following remarks:

(a) It is written in a fairly standard mathematical notation, which will be familiar to anyone who has studied some mathematics (even grade-school- or high-school-level "new math").
(b) The notation (3) should be read as follows:
  (b.i) The curly brackets surrounding the rest of formula (3), which are sometimes called *set brackets*, are simply read as "the set of."
  (b.ii) The next part, i.e., y **in** s, is read more or less as it stands: as "y **in** s," or perhaps as "**all** y **in** s," thus giving "the set of all y in s."
  (b.iii) The "|" symbol is shorthand for "such that."

(b.iv) The condition following | is standard mathematical notation, which is read as it stands, giving altogether

'the set of all y in s such that y is less than x'

as the English reading of (3), and similarly

'the number of elements in the set of all y in s such that y is less than x'

and

'the number of elements in the set of all y in s such that y is greater than x'

as the readings of (4) and (5), respectively.

We can therefore express the condition (*) which defines the median simply by writing

$$\#\{y \textbf{ in } s \mid y < x\} = \#\{y \textbf{ in } s \mid y > x\} \tag{6}$$

There will exist such an x if and only if the number of elements in s is odd. SETL allows one to test for existence of an x satisfying the condition (6), and to find it if it exists, simply by writing

$$\textbf{exists } x \textbf{ in } s \mid \#\{y \textbf{ in } s \mid y < x\} = \#\{y \textbf{ in } s \mid y > x\} \tag{7}$$

which in English reads roughly

"there exists an element x in s such that the number of elements in s which are less than x equals the number of elements in s which are greater than x"

If the median *exists*, i.e., if the number of elements in s is odd, we want to print it out; otherwise, only a message announcing that s has an even number of elements will be printed. This sort of conditional action, determined by a condition which cannot be evaluated until actual data have been read and examined, is expressed in SETL (as in most other modern programming languages) by an "**if** statement." The meaning of the following **if** statement should be clear:

```
if exists x in s | #{y in s | y < x} = #{y in s | y > x} then
   print('The median is:', x);
else                                                              (8)
   print('No median, the set s has an even number of elements.');
end;
```

Note the following details concerning the command (8):

(i) To produce output printed on paper or displayed on a terminal, the **print** command is used. This can either print a simple message (like the second of the two **print** commands shown) or (like the first **print** command) can be used to print several items, in this case both a message and a quantity that has been calculated elsewhere in the same program (like the x in example (8)).

(ii) The **if** statement appearing in (8) must be terminated by an occurrence of the word **end**.

(iii) The rules of SETL punctuation require both the **print** commands appearing in the preceding example, and the whole **if** statement, to be terminated with a semicolon.

An introductory "header line" and a terminating "trailer line" must be added to (8) before it can be run. Adding these lines, we arrive at the following fully set-up program, which can be used to read any set s of integers and print out the median of s if s has an odd number of members.

```
program find_the_median;
  read(s);
  if exists x in s | #{y in s | y < x} = #{y in s | y > x} then
    print('The median is:', x);
  else
    print('No median, the set s has an even number of elements');
  end;
end program find_the_median;
```

Though simple, this program illustrates several of the most significant features of the SETL language: SETL allows us to define, construct, compare, and in general manipulate sets of values; such sets can be searched to find whether elements exist that satisfy a given property; such sets can also be read and written, and (as we shall see in Chapter 3) modified in a number of ways. We shall see, as our study of the language progresses, that sets and set operations are particularly versatile concepts for problem solving and programming, and that SETL allows its user to solve complex problems with greater ease than that afforded by most other programming languages.

1.2 Advice to the Would-Be Programmer

This section and the next are addressed to the complete novice, whose first contact with computers is about to take place. The reader who has some experience with programming and is familiar with other programming languages may want to skip them.

As will be seen, the SETL language presented in this book furnishes you with many very powerful tools and makes it possible to create new tools by combining more elementary ones into procedures which you yourself can define. Nevertheless, it provides only certain specific facilities, and not, in some magical way, everything that you might want, think it would be convenient to have, or even imagine to be available. You will therefore have to *distinguish carefully between the facilities which the language makes available and those which it does not, learning the nature, form, and especially the purpose of every feature and facility of the language, but also learning what it does not make available directly* (especially if this is something you would like to have and wish it did make available directly). It is as senseless to plan programs that make use of nonexistent programming language features as it is to work out 7-color, 300-thread patterns for a knitting machine that only allows 4 colors and 180 separate threads.

Of course, since the computer is infinitely more flexible than any other kind of machine, it is likely that you can find a way of building up any well-defined facility which you can conceive clearly and describe precisely. However, this can only be done by accurate use of what is provided explicitly in the language (SETL) that you will be using, not by imagining that you can suddenly leap out of its confines. Thus, even to go successfully beyond what is originally present in the language you will have to learn to distinguish accurately between the tools it offers and those which it omits.

Here, an important psychological point needs to be made. To accomplish an operation that some feature of a programming language provides for directly is easy, provided that one recalls the feature and can look up whichever of its details are relevant. But this kind of memorization merely skims the surface of programming. An infinite variety of more complex and interesting operations can also be programmed, but to do so one needs to *decompose* them into more elementary operations which can be carried out more directly, and so on through progressive stages of decomposition, until one reaches operations which can be expressed directly by single commands of the programming language with which one is working. Though helpful hints about how to do this can and will be given, this process of decomposition cannot be accomplished by application of any simple recipe: it involves *problem solving* and *invention*. Now, you will probably find that programming makes unexpectedly strenuous demands on your problem-solving muscles, demands for which your past education has probably given you very little preparation. Indeed, with few exceptions, school courses teach memorization, or at best application of memorized procedures, but not true, no-holds-barred problem solving of the kind you will encounter in learning to program. In history you have learned facts and interpretations, in chemistry more facts, in undergraduate physics you have learned formulas and how to apply them; in mathematics, up to and well into calculus, you have also memorized various procedures and how to apply them. Therefore it may very well be that to become a programmer you will have to master the intellectual art of problem solving for the first time. The following paternal remarks are intended to help you cope with this challenge.

(a) Don't panic. Although some people are better at problem solving than others, the ability to solve problems, like the ability to cook a good spaghetti sauce or dance the waltz acceptably, can be learned by anyone.

Don't let your instructor's problem-solving speed intimidate you. She probably has both talent and years of experience; of course you will need time to catch up with her.

(b) On first facing a problem that you have never solved before, you will feel confused. Again, don't panic. Remember that you are not trying to *remember* a fact which you have forgotten. Rather, you are trying to *search* out, to *devise*, to *discover* something which, for you, is new. The initial confusion (which everybody, even the strongest problem solver, is bound to feel at first) is not the end of your efforts to solve the problem: it is merely the start of the beginning. Don't say to yourself "I don't see the answer; I am confused; I give up." Instead, say "I am in process of wrestling with, and dispelling, the initial confusion which every new problem generates" and fight on. Significant problems, like nuts, have hard shells, and can only be cracked if they are examined closely enough for their lines of cleavage to be found. Pick the problem up, attach yourself to it, and begin to turn it over, searching from all angles for the hints which will unlock it.

(c) Explore the leads which occur to you, combining caution and boldness. Can you see a fragment of the solution? Can you guess one command which will be helpful? Can you solve any part of the problem? Can you see any way of breaking the problem into two or more parts which look easier to solve than the whole problem does? If you have solved some part of the problem, what problem remains? Can you see any way of extending your partial solution to cover more of the problem? If you can't solve the original problem, can you solve some easier problem that has significant similarities to it? If so, can this solution be improved enough to solve the original problem, or at least a problem substantially closer to it? If not, what is the *easiest* similar problem which you cannot solve? Why not? What feature of it prevents solution? What, if anything, can be done about this feature?

(d) Don't give up too easily. Remember that a programming problem, like a jigsaw puzzle, may have to be solved one piece and one clue at a time.

(e) If no progress seems to be possible along a given line of attack, try to find another approach. Sleep on the problem and start afresh with a new approach the next morning.

(f) If a problem seems intractable, go to an appropriate book and look up a solution, or go to a helpful, more knowledgeable person and have the solution explained. But take this help actively, not passively. Ask yourself: What is the key trick that I failed to discover? In what other situations can this new trick be useful? What part of the problem could I have solved with what I knew before; what aspect really requires the new method that has just been explained? Practice using the new method on a few simple examples you make up for yourself and ponder it carefully, to make sure you digest it.

(g) Accustom yourself to dealing with concepts and methods, not with memorized program fragments. Although memorized fragments, like memorized sequences of chess moves, are useful, and even though the experienced programmer may have memorized dozens or hundreds of them, no two situations are exactly the same in programming, any more than they are in chess. Your basic need in learning to program is not to remember programs presented in a book and adapt them slightly to new situations: it is to learn how to invent general logical plans and to master the principles which will allow you to do this, along with the language in which you will have to explain your plans to a computer. General methods, principles, and approaches will retain their usefulness over a wide range of circumstances; ill-conceived attempts to adapt a textbook example to do something it was not designed to do will often be less profitable than wiping the slate clean and starting afresh.

(h) Train yourself to accuracy, but don't be overly afraid of errors. Computers have only a limited capacity to deal sensibly with errors. On the other hand, they are infinitely patient and will give you all the chances you need to remove the errors initially present in your program. Because of the high degree of accuracy with which programs need to be prepared, errors are as omnipresent in programming as clutter in kitchens and sawdust in woodshops. Remember that no one is looking impatiently over your shoulder as you develop a program; you can have all the tries you want, and only your final success counts. One must scribble to write; everything along the way to final success is just scrap paper to be thrown out.

Your aim in dealing with errors should not be to avoid them *fearfully*, but to learn to *recognize* them clearly, *understand* the violations of rule and principle which let them creep in, and *remove* them swiftly. As long as your programs are moving toward correctness, errors are tolerable. Only errors which you do not know how to remove need to be considered major problems.

(i) On the other hand, accumulation of numerous unnecessary errors through gross carelessness or misunderstanding will wind up wasting large amounts of your time as you struggle to remove mistakes that a little more care could simply have avoided. Hence it is really important to *train yourself in accuracy* and to learn to use the programming language to be presented in this book cleanly and grammatically. You will want to *study it closely*, learning its facilities, restrictions, style, and inner rhythms. As your programs evolve toward completion, you will want to *review them carefully and suspiciously*, trying to search out all errors in programming language use or in underlying logic, all hidden defects which might force you to waste time later. As we have said, the programming language to be presented in this book is a kit of powerful tools for your use: you will want to inspect all the tools in this kit and to understand and reflect upon their capabilities, restrictions, and intended use. This will help you to develop into a skilled practitioner able to do everything in the clearest, most direct, most effortless way.

1.3 Programming Steps: How to Run Your Program and Read Its Results

Knitting instructions, recipes, and the like are intended to be executed manually by a person who can at least be trusted to stop if he starts to get into trouble because something is wrong with the instructions. However, programs, like weaving setups for large automatic looms, will be executed at high speed by a machine. If this is not to lead immediately to failure, or still worse to a high-speed outpouring of trash, programs must be planned, set up, and tested carefully before they are released for full-scale execution. This involves a whole series of steps:

(I) One starts with an initial conception: What would be interesting, useful, scientifically or commercially valuable to have? The answers to such questions come from outside the technical field of programming.

(II) Once a goal has been formulated, what patterns of repetition and choice, what ingenious shortcuts allow the desired output to be produced most simply and efficiently? These questions touch upon an area of program and algorithm design that lies outside the scope of this introductory book; however, the many programs presented in the chapters which follow will illustrate some of the numerous techniques for clear and effective design that are available to the knowledgeable programmer.

(III) Once both a goal and a general plan for realizing it have been specified, there begins the detailed work of restating the plan in terms of the specific toolkit of instructions made available by the programming language that one is using. This is the labor of programming per se. As will be seen, the SETL language presented in this book supplies its user with very powerful tools of expression and therefore allows programs to be expressed more easily, simply, and directly than they would be in other, less abstract programming languages. But these tools must be learned carefully and then used accurately: computers enforce a compulsive attention to detail that takes some getting used to. If used accurately, they will allow you to write both short programs, like the examples shown in the preceding section, and sophisticated programs many hundreds or thousands of lines long which realize very complex functions.

(IV) After being typed at a terminal, a program can be submitted to the computer for execution. This will trigger a whole sequence of behind-the-scenes activities, with which you will only be peripherally involved, but of which it is important to have some understanding in order to cope with the various things that can go wrong between the time that your program is first entered into the computer and the time, several seconds to several hours later, when output finally emerges. Though differing somewhat from machine to machine, these steps will generally be more or less as follows:

(i) Your program is passed, as a passive file of *data*, to another group of programs, prestored in the computer. These programs, which the computer's *operating system* collectively comprises share the computer's power among the many users submitting jobs, all of whom require, and will eventually get, a quantum of service from the computer system.

The first thing that the operating system programs do is validate your identity as an enrolled user of the computer. If this check fails, you will be refused service. However, if you pass the operating system's user validation check, the program you have submitted will be entered onto a *pending work queue*, where it will wait, along with work entered by other legitimate system users to be scheduled for future attention by the operating system.

(ii) When your turn to be served further comes up, the first line or few lines of information supplied with your program are examined by the operating system programs running on the computer. These first lines, known typically as *command lines*, serve to tell the operating system, which provides many services to many users and deals with many programming languages, which one of its services you want.

To run a program in SETL, your command line or lines will have to convey the following information to the operating system:

(1) The language to be used (i.e., SETL).
(2) The identity of the SETL program to be processed.
(3) The location of any *input data* which your SETL program needs to read.
(4) The destination to which output produced by your program is to be sent. The preceding two items are usually file names, or they may designate the terminal as the source of data or the destination of the output, or both.
(5) You can supply additional information to select "options" which influence details of your run. Descriptive material concerning these options is found in Chapter 9.

(iii) Assuming now that both your identification and your command lines have proper form, the operating system programs will prepare for the processing and execution of the program which you have supplied. Though this involves many detailed steps, some of which are now described, the two basic actions that the operating system needs to perform are just the following:

(1) The program which you have supplied will be examined, checked for exact conformity to the rules of the SETL language, and, if it passes this check, translated into an internal program form with which the computer can work directly. This first step, checking and translation, is called *compilation*, and the program which carries it out is called the *SETL compiler*. (Note that compilation is necessary because the form of SETL which you

write and submit to the computer is designed for human, not for machine, convenience; it must be translated into a more machine-convenient form before your program can actually be run.)

(2) After translation into appropriate internal form, the instructions given in your program are actually performed, (possibly) producing output. This step is called *execution*, and the program which carries it out is called the *SETL run-time system*.

(iv) Errors can, and often will, be detected during either of the two preceding steps. Grammatical and other relatively "gross" errors in the use of the SETL language will be detected during compilation. Unless you have switched off the *listing* option of the compiler, it will print out and number all the lines of your program exactly as it sees them, and if it detects any grammatical errors it will flag them in the resulting listing of your program, which forms the first part of the output which you receive.

If compilation errors occur in your program, then, as indicated by a message "ABNORMAL TERMINATION" which will appear in the listing, processing of your program will end as soon as the compiler finishes its work; your program will not actually be run. To get further, you must correct all grammatical errors. Once this is done, your program will be listed without comment, and your program will move on, passing, as one says, *into execution*.

Toward the end of your listing (or on the screen of your terminal), there will then appear the output which your program has produced. The three lines of output produced by the sample program on page 1 would look like this:

```
99
The difference of twelve and nine is: 3
3025
```

In looking for this output in your listing it is important to realize that the output is actually preceded by several dozen more lines of standard "boilerplate" which you will grow accustomed to seeing in your output listings and will normally scan over quite rapidly. This additional material appears because the SETL compiler is a large and complex program which actually operates in three phases:

(1) A *parse* (PRS) or *grammatical analysis* phase, which analyzes your program, checking it for syntactic validity and breaking it down into the elementary clauses of which it is composed.

(2) A *semantic analysis* (SEM) phase which takes the collection of elementary clauses produced by the PRS phase, applies additional validity checks to then, and continues the process of transforming your program into an internal form which can be interpreted directly by the computer.

(3) A *code generation* (COD) phase, which completes the translation process begun by SEM.

See Section 1.5 for a description of the standard listings produced by the PRS, SEM, and COD phases of the compiler.

1.3.1 Common kinds of error that occur during program execution

Once the PRS, SEM, and COD phases of the SETL compiler have successfully translated your program into its internal form, it is passed, in this form, to the so-called SETL *run-time* or *execution* system, which then attempts to follow these translated instructions literally. However, several further sources of error can still give your output an appearance totally different from what you expect.

(a) You may have misunderstood what your program is really saying. For example, you may not have realized that suitably placed *print* commands are necessary if any output is to be produced and may have imagined that results are printed merely by virtue of being calculated by your program. In this case, no output at all may appear.

An endless variety of other small logical errors of this sort are possible, and only experience will teach you how to avoid them. Removing errors of this sort is called *debugging*; hints concerning debugging techniques are found in Chapter 6.

(b) Attempts to execute illegal operations are another common consequence of misunderstanding what a program is really saying. Suppose, for example, that your program contains the command

print(x + y);

but that prior instructions have given x the integer value 1 but not defined the value of the variable y. Addition of an integer and an undefined value is illegal, and the SETL run-time system will detect this violation when it attempts to evaluate $x + y$. The run-time system will then generate a *run-time* or *execution error*, and program execution will be terminated immediately (*aborted*). In such a case, your output will end with a *run-time error message*, describing the problem encountered. When this happens, you may want to rerun the program, using some of the additional debugging options described in Chapter 9, to gather additional information about the location and cause of the error.

(c) If the logic of your program is in some way faulty, your program may not reach its termination but may instead *loop endlessly*, in which case it can either produce output forever or produce no output at all. (The program fragment

again: **print**('Hello there'); **goto** again;

illustrates the first of these possibilities.) If your program starts to loop, then the operating system programs (which always, so to speak, lurk in the background, checking on what other programs are doing) might eventually detect the fact that your program is producing an illegally large volume of output or that it has outrun the time quota which the operating system established for it. When this happens, your program will be *forcibly terminated* by the operating system programs, which will write a message explaining what has happened.

You will need to grow familiar with the appearance that your output listing takes on when these various common problems are encountered. Here, for example, is the output that results from mistyping the number 45 in the second line of our sample program as *x5*, in which case it will be interpreted as the name of a variable, which the run-time system will find does not have any assigned value.

```
*** ERROR AT STATEMENT 2 IN ROUTINE S$MAIN
    INCOMPATIBLE TYPES FOR -A- AND -B- IN -A + B-.
```

Note that this message identifies the offending statement, by number, as "statement 2" of your "main" program (in this simple case, all that exists is a main program; in the more complex cases which we will begin to introduce in Chapter 5, both a main program and numerous procedures can exist). Beyond this rather terse statement, no other information is given (however, more information can be produced by using the debugging options described in Chapter 9).

1.4 How to Type a Program: Character Sets

If the terminal with which you are working has all the characters which appear in SETL programs in this book, then you can type your programs exactly as this book will show them. The special punctuation characters required are

<	less than
>	greater than
=	equals sign
(	left parenthesis
)	right parenthesis
'	quotation mark (apostrophe)
,	comma
:	colon
;	semicolon
/	slash
+	plus sign
−	minus sign

$	dollar sign
?	question mark
#	number sign
_	underline
{	left set bracket
}	right set bracket
[	left square bracket
]	right square bracket
|	"such that" symbol

When not all these characters are available, standard substitutions can be used for some of them. These include the following:

{	can be written as	≪
}	can be written as	≫
[	can be written as	(/
]	can be written as	/)
|	can be written as	ST

The remaining characters are replaced if necessary by single characters which type differently. For lists of these character substitutions, you will have to consult implementation-specific information for the computer on which you run your programs.

Some, but not all, SETL implementations make both uppercase (capital) and lowercase (small) versions of all the alphabetic characters available. When this is so, programs can be typed either in capital letters, small letters, or any helpful and pleasing combination of the two. For example, the command

print(3 + 5);

can also be typed as

PRINT(3 + 5);

or as

Print(3 + 5);

or even as

PrInT(3 + 5);

The SETL system always transposes all *keywords* like PRINT appearing in a program into uppercase and works internally with these uppercase versions. Only characters appearing within quotation marks (i.e. in "quoted strings", see Section 2.2.3) are retained in their original lowercase forms. This means, for example, that the statement

PRINT('hello there');

will produce the output

hello there

whereas the statement

```
print('Hello There');
```

will produce the output

```
Hello There
```

Extra blanks are generally ignored and can therefore be used to space out your program text to make it more readable. For example,

```
print(3 + 5);
print(3   +   5);
print(3      + 5      );
```

will all produce the same output, namely

```
8
```

The only places in which blanks are forbidden to appear (or have meaning if they do appear) are within constants, standard keywords, and variable names. For example,

print	cannot be written as	p rint
1000000	cannot be written as	1 000 000
counter_1	cannot be written as	count er_1.

SETL instructions are terminated by semicolons and can be continued over as many lines as necessary. This means that the instruction

```
print(3 + 5);
```

could also be typed as

```
  print
 (
   3
     +
       5);
```

if there were any sensible reason for doing so. See Section 2.2.3 for rules concerning the continuation of a quoted string from one line to the next.

1.4.1 Comments

The appearance of a $ as a separate token on a line (that is to say, not as part of a string within quotes) indicates that whatever follows the $ (up to the end of that line) is a comment, whose sole purpose is to clarify the meaning of the program for a human reader. Comments are ignored by the SETL system, and they do not affect the execution of a program. They are nevertheless indispensable to the programmer. This is because most programs are not just written, but rewritten, modified, maintained, corrected, expanded, and so on, and this requires that the programmer understand fully the meaning and purpose of a program. This meaning is not always deducible from the program itself, and there is no substitute for clear prose to explain what the intent of each piece of the program is. Programming is a social activity: most programs will be read by more than one person; most large programs are written by many people. Comments are an indispensable means of communication among those involved in the design and maintenance of such programs. Thus, you should always add numerous comments to your programs, for your own sake and those of others that might read them.

EXERCISES

1. Find out how to run the program shown on page 1 on your computer, and run it.
2. How could you define the median of a set having an even number of integer members? Modify the program shown in Section 1.1, so as to make it work irrespectively of whether the set of integers supplied to it has an even or odd number of members.
3. Take the median-finding program of Section 1.1 and introduce various typing errors in it. Submit these mangled programs to the SETL compiler and study the resulting error messages. Try to predict what the response of the compiler will be to each error you insert.

1.5 Appendix: More on How to Read Your Output Listing

Here is how the compilation listing of the sample program shown on page 1 would look if it contained two small grammatical errors, namely omission of the comma shown in the third line of the program and replacement by a colon of the semicolon which should end its fourth line:

program sample_program_number_1;

```
1   1   program sample_program_number_1;
2   2   print(54 + 45);
3   3   print('The difference of twelve and nine is:' 12 - 9);
********* ERROR 3: EXPECT RIGHT PARENTHESIS
   PARSING: 45 ) ; PRINT ( 'The difference of twelve and nine is:' 12
                    ---------------------------------------------

4   3   print(55*55):
******** ERROR 9: EXPECT ASSIGNMENT OPERATOR
   PARSING: 'The difference of twelve and nine is:' 12 - 9 ); PRINT
                                                             =----
```

```
5    3     end;
******** ERROR 91: EXPECT VALID STATEMENT
         PARSING: 55 ) : END ; ;
                             =

*** COMPILATION TERMINATED BY UNEXPECTED
    END-OF-FILE***
         PARSING: ) : END ; ; ;
                             =

  NUMBER OF ERRORS DETECTED = 3
ABNORMAL TERMINATION.
```

Note the following concerning this *compilation listing*:

(1) The compiler numbers the lines of your program. Lines are numbered sequentially down the left of the listing. (The compiler inserts these numbers to make lines easier to refer to. *Do not* type in these numbers yourself.)
(2) Just to the right of these *primary line numbers*, there appear other, similar but slightly different, *secondary line numbers*. These secondary line numbers are needed primarily for longer programs consisting of multiple procedures (see Chapter 5), to allow line numbering to be restarted at the beginning of each procedure. (Again, *do not* type in these numbers yourself; the compiler will insert them.)
(3) Following these numbers, the appropriate line of your program appears. These lines constitute the definitive version of your program, as it has actually been seen by the compiler. *Check them carefully*. If they differ *in any way* from what you think you have typed, then a typing error has occurred; this *must* be fixed before you can go any further.
(4) Immediately following each line in which the compiler has detected (or thinks it has detected) an error, there appears a *diagnostic message*, flagged with 8 stars and the word ERROR as in

```
******** ERROR 3: EXPECT RIGHT PARENTHESIS
```

After each such line, there appears a second diagnostic line, starting with the capitalized word PARSING as in

```
PARSING: 45); print ('The difference of twelve and nine is:' 12
```

Parts of this latter line will be underlined, in part with dashes "—," in part with equal signs '=."

The diagnostic or ERROR message that the compiler supplies when it detects or thinks that it has detected an error consists of an error number (-3- in the example given) and a short statement (in our example, "EXPECT RIGHT PARENTHESIS") representing the compiler's *guess* as to what the error was. Concerning this, you must be aware that, although very accurate in its treatment of error-free programs, the compiler has a very limited ability to deal intelligently with errors, and that these statements, which represent rather nearsighted *guesses* only, are frequently wide of the mark. In the preceding example, the compiler guessed (wrongly) that you meant to end the print statement immediately after the first message, i.e., that what you meant to type was

print('The difference of twelve and nine is:');

Making this guess and not finding the -)- which it guesses should be there, the compiler issues the message "EXPECT RIGHT PARENTHESIS." Of course, a person looking at this line would see that putting in a right parenthesis is not a good way to correct the line, since it would still leave the rest of the line, namely "12 − 9" unexplained. With this clue a person would easily make the more illuminating guess that a comma was missing and could then issue a more intelligent message like-MISSING COMMA-. However the compiler is much more myopic and easily confused, and the guesses which it makes when it encounters an error must therefore be taken very skeptically. About all that can be deduced from the appearance of an error message is that the line which it follows probably contains an error. This line should then be examined very carefully to see whether you can spot the error. If in doubt as to what rules of SETL grammar apply, look up the relevant rules in the appropriate part of this book.

The diagnostic line following the line containing eight asterisks (namely the line starting with the word PARSING) which follows the line containing the word ERROR is actually of greater help than the first diagnostic line when you are trying to locate a minor grammatical error. In this line, the word PARSING is followed by the seven last *tokens* (i.e., words, numbers, punctuation marks, or quoted strings) which precede the point at which the compiler was sure that an error had occurred. In our example, program line 3 is followed by the word PARSING, and then by the seven following *tokens*, which you will note occur in the program, just before the point of error:

45	(an integer)
)	(punctuation mark)
;	(punctuation mark)
print	(a 'keyword')
(	(punctuation mark)
'The difference between line and twelve is'	(quoted string)
12	(an integer)

The compiler detected an error just between the last of these two tokens, where, as we know, a comma is missing.

It is normally not too hard to spot a grammatical error by looking carefully over the line to which an error message has been attached and comparing it to the sequence of tokens following the word PARSING appearing in the second line of the error message, especially to the last few tokens of this sequence, which are likely to lie close to the actual point of error. However, this must be done with some caution, since after an error has occurred it may take a few lines of error-free program text for the resulting confusion (which affects the compiler) to dispel enough for additional error messages to become accurate again. This phenomenon, a spurious error message issued in the wake of an initial error, is seen following lines 4 and 5 of our example program. In line 5, the perfectly correct END; has been flagged as an error since, coming as soon after the erroneous line 3 and 4 as it does, it is mistakenly taken as an illegal continuation of line 4 and not as an independent statement.

The manner in which the seven tokens following the word PARSING in the second line of an error message are underlined can also be helpful. Some of these tokens are underlined with hyphens, others with double bars, others not at all. The underlined symbols are those which the compiler is currently inspecting at the moment when a grammatical error is detected. *Reserved words*, which cannot be used as variable names, and also punctuation marks, are underlined with double bars, other tokens with single bars. (This clue is valuable in cases in which you have accidentally used a reserved word as the name of a variable. See Appendix A for a list of all reserved words.)

1.5.1 Missing quotation marks

In line 3 of our example program, we wanted the output to contain the sentence "The difference of twelve and nine is:" in order to label the result. The sentence that we want to print appears between quotation marks and is displayed *as is* by the print command.

If you accidentally omit a quotation mark (apostrophe) from the end of a quoted string, then whatever happens to follow the resulting unmatched quotation mark will be taken as part of a quoted message. In this event the compiler is particularly hard pressed to make sense of your program. To prevent the compiler from simply reading to the end of the program in search of the missing quote, an arbitrary limit of 128 characters is established as the maximum permitted length of a quoted string; so recovery from this kind of error will normally take place a few lines later. When this kind of error occurs it will give a characteristically strange appearance to the list of tokens following the word PARSING in the very next error message; this should tip you off to the fact that the problem is a missing apostrophe.

Comments preceded by dollar signs ('$', see Section 1.4.1) are bypassed by the grammatical analysis process and will never appear in the list of tokens following an error message. This can give such lists a different appearance from the program text to which they refer, especially if many lines (or even pages) of comments have been bypassed.

1.5.2 Other features of the compilation history

In your compilation listing, the lines that we have just been discussing are actually preceded by a largely blank page, containing just a few lines of information such as:

```
CIMS.SETL.PRS(81121)    THU  13 AUG 81  07:00:19  PAGE  1
  PARAMETERS FOR THIS COMPILATION:

  SOURCE FILE: I = _DBCO:[NYUSETL.BERKOWITZ]TST.STL;2.
    LISTING FILE: L = _DBCO:[NYUSETL.BERKOWITZ]TST.LIS;1.
  POLISH STRING FILE: POL = TST.POL.
    AUXILIARY STRING FILE: XPOL = TST.XPL.
  LIST DIRECTIVES: LIST = 1, AT = 1.
  PARSE ERROR LIMIT: PEL = 999. PARSE ERROR FILE:
  TERM = SYS$ERROR:.
  CHARACTER SET: CSET = EXT. MEASUREMENTS: MEAS = 0.
```

Don't pay attention to this material at first: it merely dates the listing and records various standard options which the compiler is using. You will only become concerned with these options (which are described more fully in Chapter 9) when you are working with complex programs or want to secure one or another special effect.

Next you will see

```
   CIMS.SETL.SEM(81121)    THU 13 AUG 81 07:00:22 PAGE  1
PARAMETERS FOR THIS COMPILATION:

POLISH STRING FILE: POL = TST.POL. AUXILIARY STRING FILE:
XPOL = TST.XPL.
BINDER FILE: BIND =  . IND. BIND FILE: IBIND =  .
LITTLE Q1 FILE: Q1 = TST.LQ1. SETL Q1 FILE: SQ1 =  .
SEMANTIC ERROR LIMIT: SEL = 999. SEMANTIC ERROR FILE:
TERM = SYS$ERROR:.
GLOBAL OPTIMIZATION: OPT = 0. DIRECT ITERATION:
DITER = 0.
USER DATA STRUCTURES: REPRS = 0.

     NO ERRORS WERE DETECTED.

     Q1 STATISTICS:
     SYMTAB(279,16383), VAL(242,16343), NAMES(746,16343).
     FORMTAB(52,2047), MTTAB(35,2047).
     CODETAB(23,8191), ARGTAB(33,16383), BLOCKTAB(3,1023).

     NORMAL TERMINATION.
```

This will be followed one page later by similar output produced by the third (COD) phase, namely

```
   CIMS.SETL.COD(81099)    THU 13 AUG 81 07:00:30 PAGE  1
PARAMETERS FOR THIS COMPILATION:

LITTLE Q1 FILE: Q1 = TST.LQ1. SETL Q1 FILE: SQ1 = .
Q2 FILE: Q2 = TST.COD. SAVE INTERM FILES: SIF = 0.
```

CODEGEN ERROR LIMIT: CEL = 999. CODEGEN ERROR FILE:
TERM = SYS$ERROR.
GLOBAL OPTIMIZATION: OPT = 0. BACKTRACKING: BACK = 0.
RUN-TIME ERROR MODE: REM = 2. ASSEMBLY CODE: ASM = 0.
CONSTANTS AREA SIZE: CA = 65535. SYMBOL TABLE SIZE:
ST = 8191.
INITIAL HEAP SIZE: H = 600000.

NO ERRORS WERE DETECTED.

Q2 STATISTICS:
MIN SYMTAB SIZE = 186. MIN CONSTANTS AREA = 47.
MIN DYNAMIC HEAP = 483.
Q2 CODE SIZE = 38. INITIAL HEAP SIZE = 66018.
MIN HEAP SIZE = 1088.
EXEC STATEMENTS = 4. Q2 INSTRUCTIONS = 19.
Q2 FORMAT DATE = 81099.

NORMAL TERMINATION.

As in the case of the PRS phase standard output, all this material merely records various standard options which are being used for compilation. Since both the SEM and (much more rarely) the COD phases of the SETL compiler can detect a few subtle errors in your code which the PRS phase may have missed, you will want at least to glance quickly at this output, to determine whether it ends with the line NORMAL TERMINATION, signifying the absence of error. If not, the presence of errors is indicated. Note however that errors in an earlier phase can cause mistaken error messages to be omitted by a later compiler phase. Thus, unless you have become expert in the use of the SETL system, you will only want to pay attention to error messages generated by the first compilation phase which detects any errors at all.

Note also that the output produced by your program follows *immediately* after the last line of standard material put out by the COD phase. Thus, especially if your program has produced only a few short lines of output, it is very easy to lose sight of its actual output, which may be concealed from your eye by the larger mass of standard material which precedes it. In this case, you may be confused into thinking that no output has been produced. Grow accustomed to looking for output quite carefully. The following shows the actual appearance of output from the sample program on page 1:

CIMS.SETL.COD(81099) THU 13 AUG 81 07:00:30 PAGE 1

PARAMETERS FOR THIS COMPILATION:

LITTLE Q1 FILE: Q1 = TST.LQ1. SETL Q1 FILE: SQ1 = .
Q2 FILE: Q2 = TST.COD. SAVE INTERM FILES: SIF = 0.
CODEGEN ERROR LIMIT: CEL = 999. CODEGEN ERROR FILE:
TERM = SYS$ERROR.

GLOBAL OPTIMIZATION: OPT = 0. BACKTRACKING: BACK = 0.
RUN-TIME ERROR MODE: REM = 2. ASSEMBLY CODE: ASM = 0.
CONSTANTS AREA SIZE: CA = 65535. SYMBOL TABLE SIZE:
ST = 8191.
INITIAL HEAP SIZE: H = 600000.

NO ERRORS WERE DETECTED.

Q2 STATISTICS:
MIN SYMTAB SIZE = 186. MIN CONSTANTS AREA = 47. MIN
DYNAMIC HEAP = 483.
Q2 CODE SIZE = 38. INITIAL HEAP SIZE = 66018. MIN HEAP
SIZE = 1088.
EXEC STATEMENTS = 4. Q2 INSTRUCTIONS = 19.
Q2 FORMAT DATE = 81099.

NORMAL TERMINATION.

99
The difference of twelve and nine is: 3
3025

1.5.3 Review of principal actions which occur when a job is run

The following summary lists all the principal system actions performed on your behalf between first submission of a program and the moment at which output produced by your program appears. Normally all this will proceed smoothly and require little attention on your part. However, trouble can occasionally develop, and then you will need to have at least some idea of all that is going on, if only in order to know whether the problems that have developed trace back to something wrong with your program or to difficulties elsewhere in the system. Recall that when you run the SETL system, there is, behind the scenes as it were, an *operating system* whose purpose is to manage the resources of the machine, provide the services you request, allow the sharing of the SETL system (and others) among several users, and so on. (The operating system is itself a complex collection of programs.) Each of the following steps is managed or triggered by the operating system:

(1) Command line analyzed and verified.
(2) Operating system (temporarily) passes control of computer to PRS phase of SETL compiler program, which reads, analyzes, and validates the SETL program which you have supplied.
(3) PRS phase completes, producing listing as specified by initiating command, including error diagnostics if any errors are detected. The run may end if errors were serious enough. Otherwise a file representing the half-digested version of your program is saved for use by the next (SEM) compiler phase.

(4) Operating system passes control of computer to SEM phase of SETL compiler, which continues analysis and translation of the SETL program that you have supplied.
(5) The COD phase of SETL compiler is then invoked, to complete the translation of your program. Final compilation messages are added to output listing. Control is returned to the operating system, and a file representing the internal, translated version of your program is saved for use by the SETL run-time system.
(6) The SETL run-time system is then activated by the system; it follows the instructions found in the translated version of your program, producing output, and eventually either terminating, aborting if an illegal situation is found, or being forcibly terminated by the operating system if it runs for too long or produces too much output.
(7) If your program is being run interactively from a terminal, the terminal will return to "command mode" to await your next general instruction. If the program is being run in batch mode, the output file will available for editing or printing.

CHAPTER 2

Simple Data Types, Expressions, and Operations

2.1 The Main Classes of Data Objects

SETL allows one to manipulate two main kinds of data items, namely *simple* data items and *composite* data items. The intuitive distinction between these is that composite data items have elements, or components, which are themselves other (simple or composite) data items.

Four of the simple kinds of data items, namely

integers
floating-point numbers
character strings
Boolean values

are very much like those provided in most other programming languages. A fifth kind of data item, called *atoms*, will be a bit less familiar. One special SETL quantity, namely the undefined value, called **om** (for omega, the last letter of the Greek alphabet), is used frequently in SETL programs, and its somewhat unusual properties, akin to those of atoms, will become fully familiar as we go along. In addition to simple data items, SETL provides exactly two kinds of composite objects, namely

sets

and

tuples

The fact that it allows sets to be used freely gives SETL its name "SET-L."

Sets of one particular kind, namely sets of ordered pairs, play particularly important roles and therefore are often referred to by a special name:

maps

These are the types of data supported by SETL. In the rest of the chapter, we will examine how values of the simple types are created and manipulated. We will discuss the operations that are meaningful, and the operators with which we construct expressions of each of these types. In the next chapter, we will do the same for the composite objects.

2.2 Simple Types and Their Constants

To use objects of any of these kinds in a program we often need to be able to write them out directly. For example, to give a variable x the value 3.14159 we may want to write

x := 3.14159;

A value written into a program in this way is called a *constant*, a *constant denotation*, or (by some authors) a *literal*. The rules for the various forms of constants allowed in SETL are described in this section.

2.2.1 Integer constants

Integer constants are written in the standard way, as sequences of decimal digits possibly preceded by a + or − sign. Examples are

0
1066
−50
+35
001616232358

The proper way to write an integer constant can be summarized by means of a diagram, or graph, as in Figure 2.1:

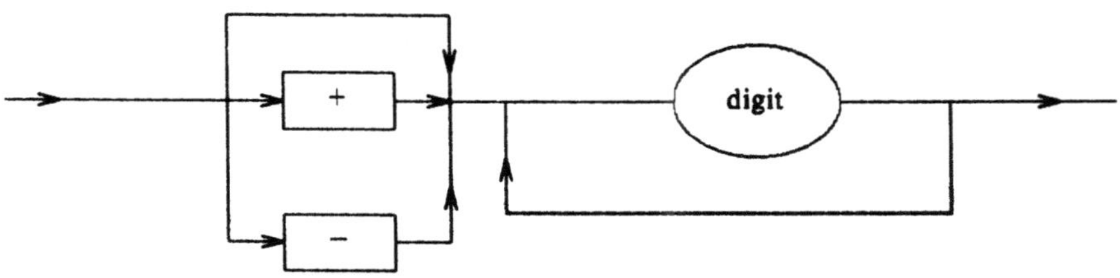

Figure 2.1

This kind of diagram will be used frequently in what follows, to describe precisely the rules of syntax of various constructs of SETL, and we pause briefly to explain the rules of construction of such diagrams, and their meaning.

Such a syntax diagram consists of rounded boxes, square boxes, and paths with arrows connecting these boxes. Each diagram also has an edge that leads into it, and an edge that exits from it. Any path through a diagram that follows the edges in the indicated directions is a valid instance of a language construct. The two kinds of boxes have the following meaning:

(i) A square box denotes a symbol of SETL, which must appear *as is* when used. For example, the + and − signs, the parenthesis, and keywords such as **if**, **loop**, **exists**, and so on.
(ii) Rounded boxes correspond to other language constructs for which a separate diagram is provided. For example, the construct *digit* is described fully by a diagram that lists the 10 digits as valid instances of this construct. A full list of diagrams for SETL is provided in Appendix B. To test your understanding of these, verify that the diagram in Figure 2.1 allows you to write −12345678 as a SETL integer but forbids −12345678−.

2.2.2 Floating-point constants

Floating-point numbers are written in one of the standard notations, namely either in *decimal form* or in *exponent form*. A floating-point number in decimal form is a sequence of decimal digits, followed by a decimal point, followed by a second sequence of decimal digits, and possibly preceded by a + or − sign. The initial but not the final sequence of digits can be omitted. Examples are

```
   0.0
    .3156     (but note that 3. is illegal)
1066.6
 -50.50
 +35.50
   3.1415928
```

A floating-point number in exponent form is a floating-point number in decimal form, immediately followed by the letter *E*, and then by an integer (the exponent). Examples are

```
    1.0E100
31415.9E - 4
    6.0E + 23
```

This last form for real constants corresponds to the ordinary "scientific" notation for decimals; e.g., these three examples would be written in ordinary scientific notation as

$$1.0*10^{100}, \quad 31415.9*10^{-4} \quad \text{and} \quad 6.0*10^{23}$$

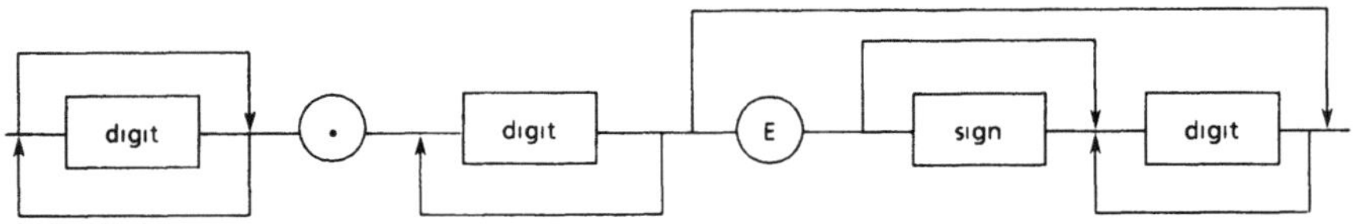

Figure 2.2

The previous description of floating-point constants is summarized by the diagram in Figure 2.2. This diagram makes it clear that any valid floating-point constant must have one digit or more after the decimal point but may have none before it.

2.2.3 String constants

A *string* is an ordered sequence of zero or more characters. To write a string as a constant we enclose it within single quotation marks (i.e., apostrophes) as in the following examples:

‘Brother, can you spare a dime?’
‘*!!—;*!!’
’’

This last example shows the *null string*, i.e., the (unique) string consisting of zero characters. Note that blanks appearing within a string are significant, i.e., are treated in the same way as any other character. Thus, although the number of characters in ‘Hello’ is 5, the number of characters in ‘ Hello’ or ‘Hello ’ is 6, and the number of characters in ‘ Hello ’ is 7.

If the quotation mark (i.e., apostrophe) itself is to appear within a string S it must be written doubled, to indicate that it is part of S and not the end of S. Thus, to write the string Mary’s mom as a constant, we would write

‘Mary’’s mom’

Note that the doubled apostrophe after the letter *y* serves to denote a single apostrophe in the actual string constant.

Any of the characters available in the machine which you are using can be used in a string constant, although SETL programs which are to be run on a variety of different computers should restrict themselves to the characters available on all computers to avoid character-set translation problems.

Sometimes one will need to write a long string constant, so long that it must cross a line boundary. This can be done by ending the first part of the string with a quotation mark (i.e., apostrophe) and then continuing immediately on the next line, with a second quotation mark character to continue the string. This “line break” sequence is called a *string continuation* and is not included in the actual string value of the multiline string constant. This means, for example, that we can write the string assignment statement

x := 'This sentence may be too long to fit into the'
'rest of the line';

in order to assign to x the full 14-word sentence given.

2.2.4 Boolean constants

There are two Boolean values, truth and falsity, in SETL. These are written as **true** and **false**, respectively.

2.2.5 Atoms

Atoms are generated values that can be used to label objects in a SETL program. Atoms are different enough from other data types in their functions and use that we will postpone their discussion until Section 2.5.5. Let us just note that there are no constant denotations for atoms.

2.2.6 **Om**: the undefined value

Om is a special SETL constant that denotes the *undefined* value. The notion of an undefined value may appear paradoxical at first but is in fact exceedingly useful. There are many computations in SETL which under certain circumstances cannot yield a value of any type. These correspond typically to some "nonsensical" calculation such as asking for an element of an empty set, or for the first integer between 2 and 5 which is divisible by 7, and so on. The result of these and similar computations (we shall see later on how to express them in SETL) is the value **om**. **Om** can be used in an assignment statement and in tests (to determine whether a given value is actually undefined) and often serves to indicate that a calculation has reached some end. We will see many examples of its use as we go.

2.3. Variable Identifiers

Most programming languages make it possible to perform calculations and then save their results for reuse later. This is done by *assigning* the results of calculations to a *variable identifier* (sometimes abbreviated simply as *variable*, or as *identifier*). An example is

x := 1 + 2 + 3 + 4 + 5;

which saves the result of the expression 1 + 2 + 3 + 4 + 5 appearing to the right of the *assignment operator* :=, making the result the value of the variable identifier x appearing to the left of this assignment operator. Since the value in question is 15, the command

print(x);

would then print the current value of the variable x, namely 15.

Identifiers are composed of the letters, digits, and the underscore character "_." The first character of an identifier must be a letter. The following are examples of valid identifiers:

x
x23
big1
End_of_Input_flag
set_of_garbage
z123456789
eta_

On the other hand, the following are not valid identifiers:

big 1
x.23
23x

because the first two contain characters other than letters, digits, and underscores (blank in the first case, period in the second), and the third begins with a digit rather than a letter.

Identifiers can be of any length, but they cannot be split between two lines.

Except within quoted string constants, capitalization is ignored by SETL, so that

Big_set
big_set
BIG_SET
big_SET
BIG_sEt

are considered to be identical.

The diagram in Figure 2.3 describes the structure of valid identifiers:

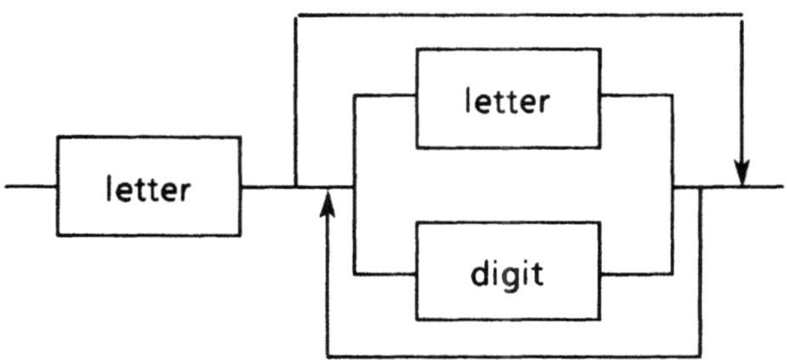

Figure 2.3

The proper choice of identifiers can make an important contribution to the clarity and professionalism of your programs. If you choose identifiers thoughtfully, your program will be easier for others to read and understand, and, equally important, will be easier for you to understand. Careless errors are also less likely to occur, since the inner "rhythm" of a well-chosen set of identifiers will make errors easier to detect when your program is written, typed, and proofread. Here are some useful guidelines for the choice of identifiers:

(a) Choose *mnemonic* identifiers, i.e., identifiers which explain the meaning of the quantities which they represent; e.g., an identifier which represents some sort of upper limit value in a program should be called upper_limit or uplim rather than simply u or L.
(b) Avoid ambiguity in the choice of identifiers and use standard spellings. It is certainly bad practice to have two different identifiers called, e.g., STACK and STAK. It is also bad practice to use variant spellings like STAK, since without noticing it you may slip back to the standard spelling. Use the standard spelling STACK instead.

2.4 Expressions and Statements

The use of *expressions* like those of algebra is one of the main features of SETL. Expressions denote *values*, which can be printed, saved as the values of variables, etc. The following are typical expressions:

```
3 + 5*(7 - 11)

17.0/31.3131 + 19.9

x + y

x1 + x2 + x3 + y1*y2*y3
```

As these examples show, an expression can involve both *constants* and *variables* (also called *identifiers*). Values are given to variables by *assignments*. For example, the following assigns the value 3 to the variable zz1:

```
zz1 := 3;
```

An assignment is written by using the := (colon-equal) sign, sometimes called the *assignment operator*. The assignment is the first type of *statement* that we will use. Statements are the basic building blocks out of which programs are constructed. In this chapter we will only use two types of statements: the assignment statement and the *print* statement, whose purpose is to display (on the screen or on an output listing) the result of a computation. The print statement has the format

```
print(expression1, expression2, ...);
```

that is to say, it consists of the keyword **print**, followed by a list of expressions, enclosed between parentheses and separated by commas. Any number of expressions can appear in a print statement. A print statement that does not include a list of expressions will simply produce a blank line.

Variables can have different values in the course of program execution. To understand the meaning of an expression, the following rule must be kept in mind:

A variable appearing in an expression always stands for its current value.

Thus if we write the statements

```
zz1 := 3;
zz2 := 17;
print(zz1);
print;
print(zz1 + zz2);
```

the current value of the variables zz1 and zz2 at the moment that the *print* instruction is executed will be 3 and 17 respectively, so that the output of this program fragment will be:

```
3

20
```

(Note the blank line separating the two printed values produced by the print statement without argument).

Suppose next that we write:

```
zz1 := 3
zz2 := 17;
print(zz1);
zz1 := 4;
print(zz1 + zz2);
print(zz1);
```

This will produce the output

```
3
21
4
```

because the value of the variable zz1 has been *changed* by the assignment statement "zz1 := 4" after the first print statement but before the second print statement, and because (we say it again) a variable appearing in an expression always stands for its *current* value, i.e., the last previous value given to the variable by any assignment statement. To test yourself, see whether you can tell what output the following sequence of statements will produce:

```
x := 1;
print(x);

s := 2;
print(x);

y := 3;
print(x + y);

x := 0;
print(x + y);

y := 0;
print(x + y);

x := 1;

print(x + x);
y := 1;

print(x + x);
print(x + y);
```

Expressions can be *compounded*; that is, an expression e1 can be substituted for any variable appearing in another expression e2, thereby generating a more complicated but still legal expression. For example, by substituting x + y for z in 2*z, one generates the expression 2*(x + y). Then, by substituting 3*a*b for y in the result, one generates the expression 2*(x + 3*a*b).

As in algebra, the order in which a compound expression containing many operators is evaluated is determined by the "precedences" of the operators involved. For example, multiplication and division are given higher precedence than addition and subtraction and are therefore performed before the latter. The operator precedence rules can be bypassed by using parentheses: subexpressions enclosed within parentheses are always evaluated before any operation is applied to them. For example, 1 + 2*3 has the value 7 because the multiplication 2*3 is performed before the addition, but (1 + 2)*3 has the value 9 since the parentheses force the addition to be performed first.

Both binary operators like the "+" in x + y, and unary operators like the "−" in x + (−y) can appear in expressions. Some operator signs like "−" can designate both binary and unary operators: *unary* if they are preceded by a left parenthesis or by another operator, *binary* otherwise. On the other hand, some operator signs are only used to designate binary operators, and others are used only to designate unary operators. All the (binary and unary) SETL operators will be described in this chapter and in Chapter 3. Section 3.13 contains a table giving the precedences of all operators.

2.5 Operations with Simple Data Types

2.5.1 Integer operators

We begin our systematic description of the SETL operators by discussing those operators that take arguments of integer type. Some of these operators yield a value of the same type, for example, the familiar arithmetic operators of addition, subtraction, multiplication, and division. Another group of integer operators yields a Boolean value: **true** or **false**. This is the case for the comparison operators (greater than, equal to, etc.) These operators are often called *predicates*. Finally, a conversion operator, **float**, allows us to convert an integer into a floating-point quantity.

2.5.1.1 Binary operations on integers

i + j	computes the sum of i and j.
i − j	computes the difference of i and j.
i*j	computes the product of i and j.
i**j	computes i to the jth power. An error results if j is negative or if i and j are both zero.
i **div** j	computes the integer (whole number) part of the quotient of i by j. The fractional part of the quotient is discarded. An error results if j = 0. See the following examples for the way in which i **div** j works if one of i or j is negative.
i **mod** j	computes the remainder left over when i is divided by j. An error results if j = 0. The result is always positive.
i **max** j	yields the larger of i and j.
i **min** j	yields the smaller of i and j.

2.5.1.2 Predicates on integers

i = j	yields **true** if i and j are the same, **false** otherwise.
i /= j	yields **true** if i and j are different, **false** otherwise.
i > j	yields **true** if i is bigger than j, **false** otherwise.
i < j	same as j > i.
i >= j	yields **true if** i is no smaller than j, **false** otherwise.
i <= j	same as j >= i.

Examples of use of these operators are as follows:

print(1 + 1);	yields	2			
print(1 − 1, 1 − 10);	yields	0	−9		
print(1*2, 1*(−2), (−1)*2, (−1)*(−2));	yields	2	−2	−2	2
print(2**3, (−2)**3, 2**0, (−2)**0);	yields	8	−8	1	1
print(1 **div** 3, 2 **div** 3, 3 **div** 3, 4 **div** 3);	yields	0	0	1	1

print(1 **mod** 3, 2 **mod** 3, 3 **mod** 3, 4 **mod** 3);	yields	1	2	0	1
print(7 **div** 3, (−7) **div** 3, 7 **div** (−3), (−7) **div** (−3));	yields	2	−2	−2	2
print(7 **mod** 3, (−7) **mod** 3)	yields	1	2		
print(1 **max** 2, (−1) **max** (−2));	yields	2	−1		
print(1 **min** 2, (−1) **min** (−2));	yields	1	−2		
print(1 = 1, 1 = 2);	yields	**true**	**false**		
print(1 /= 1, 1 /= 2);	yields	**false**	**true**		
print(1 > 1, 1 > 2, 2 < 1);	yields	**false**	**false**	**false**	
print(1 > 1, 1 < 2, 2 < 1);	yields	**false**	**true**	**false**	
print(1 >= 1, 1 >= 2, 2 >= 1);	yields	**true**	**false**	**true**	
print(1 <= 1, 1 <= 2, 2 <= 1);	yields	**true**	**true**	**false**	

Concerning i **div** j and i **mod** j, it is useful to note that for i (and j) positive we always have i = (i **div** j)*j + (i **mod** j), but for i negative this is false, e.g.,

(−7) **div** 3 is −2,

but

(−7) **mod** 3 is 2.

2.5.1.3 Unary integer operators

Unary integer operators compute a result value from a single input i.

+i	has the same value as i.
−i	computes the negative of i.
abs i	computes the absolute value of i.
even i	yields **true** if i is even, **false** if i is odd.
odd i	yields **false** if i is even, **true** if i is odd.
float i	converts the integer i to the corresponding floating-point value. If the conversion causes overflow, which is possible if i has a very large value, then an error results.
random i	returns an integer selected at random from the range from zero to i, including both end points. For example, **random** 5 will give one of the six integers 0, 1, 2, 3, 4, 5. Successive uses of this operator will in general give different randomly selected values.

Examples of these unary operators are as follows:

print(+1, +(−100));	yields	1	−100
print(−1, −(−100));	yields	−1	100

print(**abs** 1, **abs** (−2));	yields	1	2	
print(**even** 1, **even** 2, **even** (−1));	yields	**false**	**true**	**false**
print(**odd** 1, **odd** 2, **odd**(−1));	yields	**true**	**false**	**true**
print(**float** 1, **float** (−1), **float** 2);	yields	1.0	−1.0	2.0
print(**random** 5, **random** 5, **random** 5);	yields	0	4	3

(or some other sequence of integers chosen
independently and at random from the range 0 through 5 inclusive)

print(**random** (−5), **random** (−5), **random** (−5));	yields	−2	0	−4

(or some other sequence of integers chosen
independently and at random from the range 0 through −5 inclusive)

Exercises

1. Which of the following are valid identifiers?
   (a) number_1 (b) number 1 (c) number.1
2. What output will be produced by the following code?

```
program one;

    x := 1; y := 2;
    print(x + y);
    x := 3;
    print(x + y);
    y := x + y;
    print(x + y);

end;
```

3. What is the output produced by the following program?

```
program multiply_x_by_y;

    x := 1; y := 2;
    print(x*y);

end;
```

4. What output will the following code produce?

```
program thr3;

    number := 1;
    Number := 2;
    NUMBER := 3;
    print(number + Number + NUMBER);
    number := number*NUMBER;
    print(number + Number + NUMBER);

end;
```

5. What output will the following code produce?

```
program five;

    number1 := 1;
    Number1 := 2;
    Number_1 := 3;
    print(number1 + Number_1 + Number1);
    number1 := Number1*Number_1;
    print(number_1 + Number1 + Number1);

end program;
```

6. What output will the following code produce?

```
program xs;

    x := 1; y := 2; z := 3; w := 4;
    print((x + y), z*(x + y), z*x + y, w + z*(x + y));
    w := 2;
    print(w + z*x + y, z*y div w, y**(x + y)*z);

end program xs;
```

7. Which of the following are valid expressions?
   (a) x (b) x + y (c) (x + y)**w
   (d) (x + y)**w**w (e) a_1 **div** (x + y)**w**w

8. Evaluate the following constant expressions:
   (a) 2**2 (b) 2**2**3 (c) (2**2)**3
   (d) 2**(2**3) (e) 3 **div** 2 (f) 1 **div** 2
   (g) (1 + 2) **div** 4 (h) (−11) **mod** 5 (i) −11 **mod** 5
   (j) 2**2**3 /= 64 (k) 3 − 0/3 (l) 3 − 0 < 3
   (m) (−35) **min** 1

9. Simplify the following expressions:
   (a) + − + − − x
   (b) − − x
   (c) x **max** y **min** y
   (d) x **max** (y **min** y)
   (e) x **max** x

10. Evaluate the following constant expressions:
   (a) **abs** − 1 + **abs** − 2 (b) **abs** (−**1** + **abs** − 2)
   (c) **abs** (1 **min** − 1) (d) **abs** (1 **max** − 1)
   (e) 1 **max** 2 **min** 3 (f) 1 **max** 2 **max** 3
   (g) 2 + 2 **max** 3 + 3 (h) −2 − 2 **max** −3 − 3

11. Re-express the following expressions in as simple a way as you can, using the **max**, **min**, and **abs** operators:
   (a) x **max** −x
   (b) x **min** −x
   (c) (x **max** 0) + (x **min** 0)
   (d) (x **max** 0) + (−x **max** 0)

2.5.2 Floating-point operators

2.5.2.1 Binary floating-point operators

Binary floating point operators compute a result value from two floating point values, x and y. The binary floating-point operators provided by SETL are as follows:

x + y	computes the sum of x and y.
x − y	computes the difference of x and y.
x*y	computes the product of x and y.
x/y	computes x divided by y. An error results if y is zero, or if the division causes floating-point overflow.
x**i	this variant of the exponentiation operator yields x raised to the integer i. An error results if exponentiation causes floating-point overflow, or if x and i are both zero.
x **max** y	yields the larger of x and y.
x **min** y	yields the smaller of x and y.
x **atan2** y	yields the arc tangent of the quotient x/y. The result is given in radians.

2.5.2.2 Predicates on floating-point values

x = y	yields **true** if x and y are equal, **false** otherwise.
x /= y	yields **true** if x and y are unequal, **false** otherwise.
x > y	yields **true** if x is greater than y, **false** otherwise.
x < y	same as y > x.
x >= y	yields **true if** x is at least as large as y, **false** otherwise.
x <= y	same as y >= x.

2.5.2.3 Unary floating-point operators

+x	yields x.
−x	yields the negative of x.
abs x	yields the absolute value of x, i.e., yields x if x is positive, −x if x is negative.
fix x	yields the integer part of x, dropping its fractional part.
float i	yields a floating-point quantity numerically equal to i, where i is an integer.
floor x	yields the largest integer which is not larger than x. (See the following examples for the rule which applies if x is negative).
ceil x	yields the smallest integer which is at least as large as x. (See the following examples for the rule which applies if x is negative).
exp x	yields e**x, where e is the base of natural logarithms.
log x	yields the natural ("base e") logarithm of x. An error results if x is zero or negative.
cos x	yields the cosine of x, which is assumed to be given in radians.

sin x	yields the sine of x, which is assumed to be given in radians.
tan x	yields the tangent of x, which is assumed to be given in radians.
acos x	yields the arc cosine of x; the result is given in radians. An error results if x does not lie between −1.0 and +1.0.
asin x	yields the arc sine of x; the result is given in radians. An error results if x does not lie between −1.0 and +1.0.
atan x	yields the arc tangent of x; the result is given in radians.
tanh x	yields the hyperbolic tangent of x.
sqrt x	yields the square root of x. An error results if x is negative.
random x	yields a floating-point value which is randomly distributed over the range from zero to x including zero but excluding x. Note that successive calls to this function will return distinct, independently chosen random quantities.
sign x	yields one of the integer results −1, 0, or +1 depending on whether x is negative, zero, or positive.

Examples of some of these operators are as follows:

1.1 + −1.1	yields	0.0
1.1*1.1	yields	1.21
1.1**2	yields	1.21
1.1**2.0	yields	1.21
1.1 = 1.11	yields	**false**
1.1 = 1.10	yields	**true**
1.1 **max** 1.1001	yields	1.1001
1.1 **min** 1.101	yields	1.1
+1.1	yields	1.1
− −1.1	yields	1.1
abs −1.1	yields	1.1
print(fix 1.1, **fix** −1.1)	yields	1, −1
print(floor 1.1, **floor** −1.1, **floor** −1.0)	yields	1, −2, −1
print(ceil 1.1, **ceil** −1.1, **ceil** 1.0)	yields	2, −1, 1
print(float 1, **float** −1, **float** 0)	yields	1.0, −1.0, 0.0

The forms in which floating-point constants can be written are described in Section 2.1.1.

Note that for floating-point numbers x and y, the use of the predicates x = y and x /= y can be a bit tricky since rounding effects might cause (0.5 + 0.5) = 1.0 to yield **false** and 1.0 = 1.0000000000000000001 to yield **true**. Keep in mind the fact that floating-point values can always turn out to have values slightly different from the exact values that you may expect.

2.5.3 String operators

Binary string operators compute a result value from two inputs, at least one of which is a string. Some of these operators take two strings as their arguments, others take a string and a positive integer as their arguments. Some of these operators are predicates and perform string comparisons analogous to the integer comparisons discussed previously.

In what follows, *s* and *ss* are always strings; *i* and *j* are integers.

The string operators are the following:

$s(i)$	computes the *i*-th character of the string *s*; the result is a one-character string. If *i* is negative, an error results; if *i* is greater than the length of *s*, then the value **om** is returned.
$s(i..j)$	this *string slice* operator computes and returns the substring of *s* which extends from its *i*-th through its *j*-th characters, inclusive. If $i = j + 1$, a null string is returned. See Table 2.1 for a description of the treatment of other marginal and exceptional cases for this operator. (Note that this operator actually has three, rather than two, arguments.)
$s(i..)$	this computes and returns the substring of *s* which extends from its *i*-th character through the end of *s*, inclusive. See Table 2.1 for a description of the treatment of marginal cases of this operator.
$s + ss$	concatenates the two strings *s* and *ss*.
$i*s$	concatenates *i* successive copies of the string *s*. If $i = 0$, then $i*s$ is the null string. If $i < 0$ then an error results.
$s = ss$	yields **true** if *s* and *ss* are identical, **false** otherwise.
$s /= ss$	yields **true** if *s* and *ss* are distinct, **false** otherwise.
$s > ss$	yields **true** if *s* comes later than *ss* in standard alphabetical order, **false** otherwise. (Note that this operation, as well as the other string comparisons $s < ss$, $s >= ss$, $s <= ss$, are implementation-dependent, as they depend on an assumed alphabetical order of characters (*collating order*). Of course, alphabetic characters will always have their standard order, but the relative order of punctuation marks, and also the way in which alphabetics compare to numerics, may differ from implementation to implementation.)
$s < ss$	yields **true** if *s* comes earlier than *ss* in standard alphabetic order, **false** otherwise.
$s >= ss$	yields **true** if *s* either is identical with *ss* or comes later in standard alphabetic order, **false** otherwise.
$s <= ss$	yields **true** if *s* either is identical with *ss* or comes earlier in standard alphabetic order, **false** otherwise.

s **in** *ss* yields **true** if *s* occurs as a substring of *ss*, **false** if not.
s **notin** *ss* yields **false** if *s* occurs as a substring of *ss*, **true** if not.

To give examples of these operators, we shall suppose that the value of *s* is the string "ABRA," and that the value of *ss* is the string 'CADABRA'. Then

print(ss(1), ss(4));	yields	C A
print(s(1..2), s(2..4), s(2..2));	yields	AB BRA B
print(s(1..0));	yields	the null string
print(s(1..), s(2..), s(3..), s(4..));	yields	ABRA BRA RA A
print(s(5..));	yields	the null string
print(s(5));	yields	**om**
print(s + ss);	yields	ABRACADABRA
print(3*s);	yields	ABRAABRAABRA
print(s > ss, ss > s);	yields	**false** **true**
print('AA' > 'A', 'A' > ");	yields	**true** **true**
print('AA' < 'A', 'A' < ");	yields	**false** **false**
print(s **in** ss, ss **in** s);	yields	**true** **false**

The unary string operators compute a value from a single input. These operators are

#s yields the number of characters in the string *s*.
abs s here *s* must be a one-character string, or an error results. If *s* is a single character, then **abs** *s* returns the internal integer code for this character. **Abs** and **char** are inverse operators.
char i here *i* must be an integer which can be the internal code of some character *c*. If this is so, then **char** *i* yields the single character *c* (i.e., a one-character string). Otherwise, an error results. (The range of integer values used as character codes is implementation-dependent.)
str x *x* is any SETL object. **str** *x* is a string that is the printable form of the value of *x*.

Table 2.1 shows the way that the string extraction operators *s*(*i*), *s*(*i*..), and *s*(*i*..*j*) behave in various marginal cases.

To each string extraction operator there corresponds a *string assignment* operator that modifies the string section which the corresponding extraction operator would retrieve. These string assignments are indicated by writing either s(i), s(i..), or s(i..j) to the *left* of the assignment operator ":=." For example, if *s* is a string, we can modify the section of it extending from its

Table 2.1. Behavior of String Operators in Marginal Cases

Operator	Condition	Effect
$s(i)$	i negative or zero	causes error
$s(i)$	$i > \#s$	yields **om**
$s(i..)$	i negative or zero	causes error
$s(i..)$	$i = \#s + 1$	returns null string
$s(i..)$	$i > \#s + 1$	causes error
$s(i..j)$	i negative or zero	causes error
$s(i..j)$	$i > j + 1$	causes error
$s(i..j)$	j negative	causes error
$s(i..j)$	$j > \#s$	causes error
$s(i..j)$	$i = j + 1$	returns null string

second to its fourth character (inclusive) by writing

$$s(2..4) := x; \qquad (1)$$

where x is any string. The expression x need not be a string of length 3, so that the assignment operation (1) can lengthen s (if x has length greater than 3) or shorten it (if x has length less than 3). Similar remarks apply to the string assignment operation

$$s(i..) := x;$$

which is treated exactly as if it read

$$s(i..\#s) := x;$$

However, the right-hand side of the simple string assignment

$$s(i) := x;$$

must be a single character, because $s(i)$ denotes the i-th character of string s, not a substring of s.

For examples of all this, suppose that $s1, s2, \ldots, s7$ are seven variables, all having the string value "ABRACADABRA" initially. Then the following assignments produce the indicated results.

```
s1(3..5) := 'XXX';       $ now s1 =  ABXXXADABRA
s2(3..4) := 'XXXXXX';    $ now s2 =  ABXXXXXXCADABRA
s3(3..4) := 'X';         $ now s3 =  ABXCADABRA
s4(3..4) := '';          $ now s4 =  ABCADABRA
s5(7..) := 'XXX';        $ now s5 =  ABRACAXXX
s6(7..) := '';           $ now s6 =  ABRACA
s7(1) := 'Y';            $ now s7 =  YBRACADABRA
```

To summarize, the three string assignment operators are

$s(i) := x;$ x must be a single character, and i must be an integer and lie between 1 and $\#s$; otherwise an error results. This modifies the i-th character of s.

$s(i..j) := x;$ i must be an integer at least equal to 1 and at most equal to $j + 1$ or an error results. j must also also be an integer and cannot exceed $\#s$. The section of s between i and j is made equal to x, which may expand or contract s. Note that if $i = j + 1$, x will be inserted into s immediately before its i-th position. The case $i = \#s + 1, j = \#s$ is legal and adds x to the end of s.

$s(i..) := x;$ this is treated exactly as if it read $s(i..\#s) := x$. Thus i must be an integer which is at least 1 and at most $\#s + 1$.

As an example of the case $i = \#s + 1$, note that if $s1$ and $s2$ are both initially equal to "ABC", then both the assignment

$$s1(4..3) := \text{'XXX'};$$

and the assignment

$$s2(4..) := \text{'XXX'};$$

give "ABCXXX" as the value of $s1$ and $s2$, respectively.

2.5.4 Boolean operators

Boolean operators compute a Boolean result from one or two input Boolean quantities c, cc. That is, both the inputs of these operations and their results must be one of the two Boolean values **true** and **false**. These operations are generally used to combine results produced by prior comparisons or other tests; i.e., they typically appear in contexts such as

if(i > j **and** j > k) **or** (k > j **and** j > i)...

The binary Boolean operators supported by SETL are as follows:

c **and** cc yields **true** if both c and cc are **true**, **false** otherwise.

c **or** cc yields **true** if at least one of c and cc is **true**, **false** otherwise.

c **impl** cc This is the *logical implication* operator and yields **true** except when c is **true** and cc is **false**. That is, if either c is **false**, or cc is **true**, then c **impl** cc yields **true**. But if c is **true** and cc **false**, then c **impl** cc yields **false**.

The only unary Boolean operator provided is

not c yields the logical opposite of c, i.e., **false** if c is **true**, **true** if c is **false**.

In using these operations one will often make use of various well-known rules of logic like those called *De Morgan's rules.* For example since

(not c) **or** (**not** cc)

is **true** if either c or cc is **false**, but is **false** if both c and cc are **true**. It is equivalent to

not (c **and** cc).

Various other equivalences between Boolean expressions are

not (c **or** cc)	is equivalent to	(**not** c) **and** (**not** cc)
not (c **impl** cc)	is equivalent to	c **and** (**not** cc)
c **impl** cc	is equivalent to	(**not** c) **or** cc
not (**not** c)	is equivalent to	c

These and other related logical equivalences can often be used to simplify Boolean expressions that occur in programs. For example, since

c **or** ((**not** c) **and** cc)

is **true** if and only if at least one of c and cc is **true**, it simplifies to

c **or** cc

Thus, instead of writing

if i > j **or** ((**not** i > j) **and** k > j)...

in a program we can simplify this to

if i > j **or** k > j...

Other useful relationships of this sort appear in Exercises 1 through 8.

2.5.4.1 Boolean equivalences

A *tautology* is a Boolean expression E which evaluates to **true** no matter what Boolean values are given to the variables appearing in E. An *equivalence* is a statement of the form E1 = E2 which evaluates to **true** no matter what values are given to the variables appearing in it. For example, the expression

A **or** (**not** A)

can be seen to be true regardless of the value of the Boolean value of A, because (A **or** B) is true if either A or B is true, by the definition of **or**, and either A or **not** A must be true, for any value of A. Thus A **or** (**not** A) is a tautology, or a universally valid Boolean equivalence. To prove that a given expression is a tautology, we build a *truth table* that lists, for each possible set of values of the variables appearing in the expression, the value of each of the subexpressions and that of the whole expression. For this case we have the following table:

A	not A	A or (not A)
true	**false**	**true**
false	**true**	**true**

EXERCISES

The following exercises list various tautologies and Boolean equivalences, which you are asked to prove either by an exhaustive list of or by appropriate mathematical reasoning. In a later section we will see how to write a simple program that builds the truth table of a given expression.

1. Prove the equivalence (A **or** B) = (B **or** A).
2. Prove the equivalence ((A **or** B) **or** C) = (A **or** (B **or** C)); also prove ((A **and** B) **and** C) = (A **and** (B **and** C)).
3. Prove the equivalence (A **and** A) = A, also (A **or** A) = A.
4. Prove the equivalence (A **and** (B **or** C)) = ((A **and** B) **or** (A **and** C)), also (A **or** (B **and** C)) = (A **or** B) **and** (A **or** C).
5. Prove the equivalence (A **or** ((**not** A) **and** B)) = (A **or** B).
6. (De Morgan's rules). Prove that (**not** (A **and** B)) = ((**not** A) **or** (**not** B)), also (**not** (A **or** B)) = ((**not** A) **and** (**not** B)).
7. Prove that **not** (**not** A) = A. Using this fact and the results proved in Ex. 6, show that

   (A **and** B) = (**not** ((**not** A) **or** (**not** B))),

   (A **or** B) = (**not** ((**not** A) **and** (**not** B))).
8. Prove the following equivalences: (A **and true**) = A, (A **and false**) = **false**, (A **or true**) = **true**, (A **or false**) = A.

2.5.5 Operations with atoms

Mathematical constructions occasionally make use of abstract *points* which have no particular properties other than their identity. For example, in dealing with graphs we generally regard them as abstract collections of points (or *nodes*) connected by edges (see Figure 2.4).

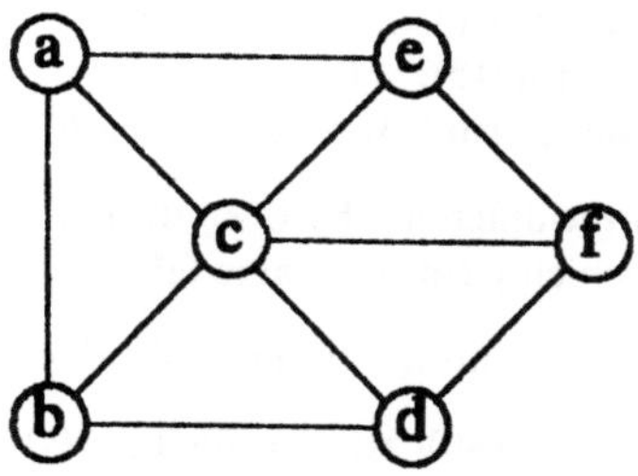

Figure 2.4 A Graph: Six Nodes Connected by Edges.

In this case, to make a new copy of a graph we need a supply of new points. What these points are is of no significance as long as they can be generated in a way which guarantees that all newly generated "points" are definitely distinct from all such "points" previously encountered.

To handle situations of this sort, SETL provides a special kind of object called an *atom*, or for emphasis a *blank atom*. These objects can be members of sets or components of tuples, but very few other operations act on these atoms. In particular, there is only one way of producing objects of this kind: namely, by calling a special, built-in, and argument-free (i.e., *nullary*) function written as

newat

Each time a program invokes this construct, it yields a new atom, distinct from all previously generated atoms. The only operations involving a pair of atoms, a and aa, are

a = aa	yields **true** if a and aa are the same, **false** otherwise.
a /= aa	yields **true** if a and aa are different, **false** otherwise.

EXERCISES

1. Write a program that will read a floating-point number x and print the number of decimal positions of x which will lie to the left of the decimal point when the number is printed in standard decimal formal. For example, if 1.23E − 4 is read, 0 should be printed; when 25.6E + 5 is read, 7 should be printed.

2. Which of the following operations will cause an error?

   (a) 2.2/(1.1 + 1.10 − 2.200)
   (b) −2.2* − 2.2**2.2
   (c) (−2.2)**2.2
   (d) **float**(−2)*2
   (e) (−2.2 **max** 2.2)** − 2.2
   (f) (−2.2 **min** 2.2)**2.2
   (g) **sqrt**(−2 **max** 2)

3. Test the following Boolean expressions to see if they yield **true** or **false**:

   (a) 1.0 = 2.0 − 1.0
   (b) 2.0 = **sqrt**(4.0)
   (c) **sin**(**asin**(0.5)) = 0.5
   (d) **sin**(0.5)***sin**(0.5) + **cos**(0.5)***cos**(0.5) = 1.0

   Determine the size of the difference between the left- and the right-hand sides of each of these equations which yields the value **false**.

4. Which of the following statements are true for all values of the variable x?

   (a) **abs**(**float**(x)) = **float**(**abs**(x))

   (b) **fix**(**float**(x)) = **float**(**fix**(x))

(c) **floor**(x) <= **fix**(x)

(d) **ceil**(x) >= **fix**(x)

(e) **exp**(**log**(x)) = x

(f) **log**(**exp**(x)) = x

5. For what positive values of x is **cos**(x) closest to 0.0? What is the value of **asin**(1.0)? Check your answers by computer evaluation.

6. How small is the sum **sin**(x) + **sin**(x + 3.1415928)? (Evaluate it at the points x = −3.1415928, 0.0, 3.1415928, etc.) Can you find a constant c such that **sin**(x) + **sin**($x + c$) is smaller than **sin**(x) + **sin**(x + 3.1415928) for several values of x?

7. Square the quantity x := 2.0/**sqrt**(4.0) repeatedly to see how its higher powers behave. How many squarings are required to calculate x**1024?

8. Run the following programs and see what results they produce.

   (a) x := 2.0; (**for** n **in** [1 ... 100]) x := x*x; **print**(n, x); **end**;

   (b) x := 0.5; (**for** n **in** [1 ... 100]) x := x*x; **print**(n, x); **end**;

9. Write a short program which would work perfectly if perfectly accurate floating-point arithmetic were performed but which fails catastrophically because of small inaccuracies in the computer representation of floating-point quantities.

CHAPTER 3

Compound Data Types and Operators

3.1 Sets and Set Denotations

Sets in SETL are finite collections of arbitrary SETL values. These values, called the *members* (or *elements*) of the set, are themselves data items of any SETL type. To write a set denotation, we simply list the members of the set, with commas between successive members, within the set brackets "{" and "}". Three examples are

{1, 2, 3, 4}
{'Tom', 'Dick', 'Harry'}
{TRUE, FALSE}

The first of these is the set of all integers between 1 and 4; the second is a set of three strings, namely, 'Tom', 'Dick', and 'Harry'; the third is the set consisting of the two possible Boolean values **true** and **false**.

The *null* or *empty set*, i.e., the (unique) set having no members at all, is a legal SETL value. It is written as follows:

{ }

Any legal SETL value (with the sole exception of the undefined value **om**) can be a member of a set. Examples illustrating this are

{1, **true**, 'Tom'}
{1, **true**, 'Tom', {3}}

The first of these two examples is a perfectly legitimate set whose three members are the integer 1, the Boolean value **true**, and the string 'Tom'. The second has four elements, the integer 1, Boolean value **true**, the string 'Tom', and the set $\{3\}$, i.e., the *singleton set* whose sole member is the integer 3. This shows that sets need not be homogeneous, i.e., are not restricted to having members all of the same kind, and that sets can be members of other sets. Note also that the *integer* 3 is *not* a member of the set {1, **true**, 'Tom', {3}}, but that the *set* $\{3\}$, which is quite a different thing, is. A more complex example illustrating this same fact is

$$\{1, \{2\}, \{\{3\}\}, \{\ \}, \{5, 6\}\}. \qquad (1)$$

This is a set of five members, namely the integer 1; the set $\{2\}$, whose sole member is the integer 2; the set $\{\{3\}\}$, whose sole member is the set $\{3\}$; the null set $\{\ \}$; and the set $\{5, 6\}$ consisting of the integers 5 and 6. Note that in this example the integer 3 is neither a member nor a member of a member of set (1); rather, it is a member of a member of a member of that set.

As ordinarily in mathematics, set values never contain duplicate members, and the members of a set have no implied order. Thus the set $\{1, 1\}$ and $\{1\}$, both of which are legal, designate exactly the same set, namely the set whose sole element is the integer 1. Similarly, $\{1, 2\}$ and $\{2, 1\}$ designate the same set, namely the set whose members are the integers 1 and 2. For a more complex example, note that

$$\{1, 2, \{3, 4\}\}$$

and

$$\{\{4, 3\}, 2, 1\}$$

designate the same set, namely the set whose three elements are the integers 1 and 2 and the set $\{3, 4\}$ (not to be confused with $\{1, 2, 3, 4\}$, which is a set of four elements, namely the integers 1 through 4).

Since the elements of a set are not considered to have any particular order within the set, it is incorrect to speak of the first, second, or last element of a set. That is, it is incorrect to speak of the string 'Tom' as the first element of the set

{'Tom', 'Dick', 'Harry'}

or to speak of the string 'Harry' as its last element, since this same set can as well be written as

{'Harry', 'Tom', 'Dick'}

and

{'Dick', 'Tom', 'Harry'}

In working with sets, one must always remember that their elements have no particular order, and that they are all distinct. This can actually simplify matters because in problems involving a collection of data whose order is irrevelant, the programmer has fewer details to worry about.

3.1.1 Some useful sets of integers

Sets whose elements are successive integers, such as

$$\{1,2,3,4,5,6,7\}, \qquad \{-3,-2,-1,0,1,2,3\}$$

arise often enough that a special notation is provided for them. To describe the set of all integers lying in the range M to N inclusive, where M and N are integers, we write

$$\{M..N\}$$

The two dots (not three, and not commas!) stand for all the integers $M + 1$, $M + 2$, and so on up to $N - 1$. Sets of integers of the form

$$\{1,3,5,7,9\} \qquad \text{or} \qquad \{10,5,0,-5,-10,-15\}$$

that is to say, sets that represent an arithmetic progression, are also useful enough to be given their own notation in SETL: We represent such sets by giving the first, second, and last element of the progression, as follows:

$$\{1,3..9\} \qquad \{10,5..-15\}$$

Note again the use of two dots to indicate the middle part of the sequence. These notations will be used frequently in what follows.

When sets are printed, their elements can appear in any arbitrary order. For example,

print({1..10});

might be expected to produce {1, 2, 3, 4, 5, 6, 7, 8, 9, 10}. However, if you try it out, you will see the following appear:

{4, 5, 6, 7, 1, 2, 8, 3, 9, 10}

(or some other permutation of the integers from 1 to 10). This emphasizes again the fact that the elements of a set have no particular order; the set {1..10} contains the integers in the range 1..10, but the internal representation of this set in the machine is independent of the way in which the set is written in the text of the program. In fact, printing the same set at various times may display its elements in different orders each time.

3.2 Tuples

In contrast to sets, *tuples* (sometimes also called *vectors*) in SETL are finite *ordered* sequences of arbitrary elements. To write a tuple denotation, we list its successive components, in order, within the tuple brackets '[' and ']'. Components in such a list are separated by commas. Three examples are

[1, 2, 3, 4]
['Tom', 'Dick', 'Harry']
[**true**, **false**]

The components of a tuple, as distinct from the elements of a set, do have a definite order within the tuple. Thus a tuple is a quite different kind of object from a set, even though the components of the tuple may all be elements of the set, and vice versa. For example, note that

[1, 2, 3, 4] and {1, 2, 3, 4}

are regarded in SETL as entirely different objects, and, indeed, as objects of entirely distinct types; the first is a *tuple*; the second is a *set*. Note also that [1, 2, 3, 4] and [2, 1, 3, 4] are *different* objects, since the components of a tuple are considered to have a specific order and two tuples are only equal if they have the same components *in the same order*; however, the sets {1, 2, 3, 4} and {2, 1, 3, 4} are the same, since a set, as distinct from a tuple, is defined by the *collection* of its elements, *not* by their order.

Tuples, like sets, need not be homogeneous; i.e., the components of a tuple need not all be of the same type. Tuples can have sets as their components and sets can have tuples as their members. Indeed, sets and tuples can be nested within each other to arbitrary depth as members and components, permitting construction of a great variety of data objects. Examples are

(1) [1, 'Tom', {'Dick'}, ['Harry']]

(2) {1, 'Tom', ['Dick'], {'Harry'}}

(3) [1, {'Tom', ['Dick', 'Harry']}]

The first of these constants represents a *tuple* of four components, which, in order, are the integer 1, the string 'Tom', the singleton set {'Dick'}, and the one-component tuple ['Harry']. The second represents a *set* of four elements, which (in no particular order) are the integer 1, string 'Tom', the one component tuple ['Dick'], and the singleton set {'Harry'}. The third represents a tuple of just two components, namely the integer 1, followed by the two-element set {'Tom', ['Dick', 'Harry']}. We can therefore assert that the string 'Harry' is the first (and only) component of the fourth component of the tuple (1); that 'Harry' is also a member of a member of the four-element set (2); and finally that 'Harry' is the second component of a member of the second component of the tuple (3).

Another example of a perfectly legal though highly nested SETL construction is

{{{{ }}}}

This designates a set (let's call it *s*), and the empty set is the only member of the only member of the only member of *s*.

The presence of repeated tuple components, as distinct from repetition of set elements, is significant and leads to distinct tuple values. For example, the three tuples

['Tom'], ['Tom', 'Tom'], and ['Tom', 'Tom,' 'Tom']

are all distinct; the first has just one component and is of length 1; the second is of length 2; and the third is of length 3 and has three components. Its first, second, and third components are all defined, and each of them is the string 'Tom'. In contrast, the constants

{'Tom'}, {'Tom', 'Tom'}, and {'Tom', 'Tom', 'Tom'}

designate the same set, which has just one element, namely the string 'Tom'. Since tuples, as distinct from sets, are considered to have a definite order, it *does* make sense to refer to the first, second, ..., last component *of a tuple*. For example, the first component of

['Tom', 'Dick', 'Tom', 'Tom']

is the string 'Tom'; its last (also fourth) component is also 'Tom'; its second component is 'Dick'.

There is a (unique) *null* or *empty tuple*, which is written as

[ ]

This plays much the same role for tuples that the important null set, i.e., { }, plays for sets.

3.2.1 Some useful tuples of integers

Tuples whose components constitute an arithmetic progression can be written in a special SETL notation similar to that used for sets of integers. The tuple construct

$$[M..N]$$

where M and N are integers, describes the tuple whose components are the integers M, $M + 1$, $M + 2$, and so forth, up to N. If N is less than M, this construct is equivalent to the empty tuple.

Similarly, an arithmetic progression of the form

$$M, M + k, M + 2*k, .. N$$

where k is some integer (positive or negative), can be described by writing its first, second, and last component; specifically, the tuple whose components constitute such a sequence can be written as:

$$[M, M1..N]$$

where $M1$, the second term in the sequence, has the value $(M + k)$. For example, the construct [3, 6..600] represents a tuple whose components are the first 200 positive multiples of 3, in increasing order. This construct, and the related set construct

$$\{M, M1..N\},$$

are simple instances of a general numeric iterator construct, which will be discussed in detail in Section 4.3.4.1.

3.3 Maps

In SETL a *map* is simply a set all of whose elements are pairs, i.e., are tuples of length 2. Some properties of maps can be deduced from their structure, i.e., from the fact that all their components are pairs. But maps are important enough to have a number of operations that apply solely to them. We will see that maps are one of the most expressive programming features of SETL and that the proper use of maps is a hallmark of good SETL style. Maps allow us to associate with each other elements of various collections of objects: countries with their capitals, numbers with their cubes, people with their dates of birth, courses with their sets of students, and so forth.

Suppose, for example, that the children in a family, listed in increasing order of age, are

Sue, Tom, Mary, Alphonse.

Suppose that we want to associate each child x in this family with the number of younger sisters that x has. For this purpose, we could use the following map:

$$\{['Sue', 0], ['Tom', 1], ['Mary', 1], ['Alphonse', 2]\}. \quad (1)$$

Similarly, the map

$$\{['Sue', 0], ['Tom', 0], ['Mary', 1], ['Alphonse', 1]\} \quad (2)$$

associates each child x with the number of younger brothers that x has. The map

$$\{['Sue', \{'Mary'\}], ['Tom', \{'Sue', 'Mary'\}], ['Mary', \{'Sue'\}], ['Alphonse', \{'Sue', 'Mary'\}]\} \quad (3)$$

associates each child x with the *set* of sisters of x. Note therefore that *maps can be used to associate values of any type with other values of any other type.*

Another interesting map is

$$\{['Sue', 'Mary'], ['Tom', 'Sue'], ['Tom', 'Mary'], ['Mary', 'Sue'], ['Alphonse', 'Sue'], ['Alphonse', 'Mary']\}. \quad (4)$$

This contains a separate pair associating each child x with *each* of the sisters of x (rather than one pair associating x with the set of *all* the sisters of x as in (3); ((3) and (4) are *different*, but closely related and record much the same information). Since several different pairs in (4) (e.g., ['Tom', 'Sue'] and ['Tom', 'Mary']) have the same first component, (4) is called a *multi-valued map*. Maps for which this does not happen, i.e., in which no two distinct pairs share the same first component, are called *single-valued* maps.

Given a map M, we can form the set of all first components of pairs in M. This is called the *domain* of M and is written

domain M

We can also form the set of all second components of pairs in M, which is called the *range* of M and is written

range M

The following table shows the **domain** and **range** of the maps appearing in examples just presented.

Map number	Domain M	Range M
(1)	{'Sue', 'Tom', 'Mary', 'Alphonse'}	{0, 1, 2}
(2)	{'Sue', 'Tom', 'Mary', 'Alphonse'}	{0, 1}
(3)	{'Sue', 'Tom', 'Mary', 'Alphonse'}	{{'Sue'}, {'Mary'}, {'Sue', 'Mary'}}
(4)	{'Sue', 'Tom', 'Mary', 'Alphonse'}	{'Sue', 'Mary'}

Maps, and the map-related operations of SETL, which will be presented in Section 3.8, are the most characteristic and important features of the language.

3.4 The Size of Composite Objects: The # Operator

One of the most important characteristics of a composite object is the number of elements which it has. SETL provides a single operator to determine the size of sets, tuples, maps, and strings: the "#" operator, called *length, size*, or *cardinality*.

When applied to a string this operator yields its length, i.e., the number of characters it contains; when applied to a tuple, it yields the length of the tuple, i.e., the largest position in the tuple that is occupied by a component whose value is not **om**; and when applied to a set it yields its cardinality, i.e., the number of its elements. For a map, it yields the number of pairs in the map. Thus:

#'Tom' is 3, since 'Tom' has 3 characters

#'Tom is hot' is 10, since 'Tom is hot' has 10 characters (including 2 blanks)

['Tom', 'Dick', 'Harry'] is 3, since this tuple has 3 components

['Tom', 'Tom', 'Tom'] is 3, since this tuple also has 3 components

{'Tom', 'Dick', 'Harry'} is 3, since this set has 3 elements

{'Tom', 'Tom', 'Tom'} is 1, since this set has 'Tom' as its only member

{ } is 0, since the null set has no members

[ ] is 0, since the null tuple has no components

#'' is 0, since the null string contains no characters

{[4, 2], [4, −2] [0, 0]} is 3, because this set (or map) contains three elements (pairs)

Exercises

1. Which of the following objects are the same, and which are different?

(a)	'The'	and	'The'
(b)	'The man'	and	'Theman'
(c)	['The', 'man']	and	['man', 'The']
(d)	{'The', 'man'}	and	{'Man', 'The'}
(e)	{'The man'}	and	{'man The'}
(f)	{'The', 'The', 'man'}	and	{'The', 'man'}
(g)	['The', 'The', 'man']	and	['The', 'man']
(h)	['The', 'man']	and	{'The', 'man'}
(i)	['The', 'man']	and	{'The, man'}

2. Write the size #x of the following strings, sets, and tuples. For each set and tuple, also write the list of all its *integer* elements or components and the size of each of its set, tuple, or string elements or components.

(a)	{1, 2, 2, 'Tom'}
(b)	[1, 2, 2, 'Tom']
(c)	{1, {2, 2}, 'Tom'}
(d)	{1, 1, { }, { }}
(e)	[{ }, [[ ]]]
(f)	'abracadabra'
(g)	'abra cadabra'
(h)	'abra, cadabra'
(i)	{1, 'abra', 'cadabra'}
(j)	{1, 'abra''cadabra'}
(k)	{1, 'abra, cadabra'}
(l)	{1, 'abra', 'cadabra'}
(m)	{1, 'abra'', ''cadabra'}
(n)	{[ ], '', { }, '[ ]', '{[ ]}', '{ }'}

3. Write the size of the first, second, and last component of each of the following tuples:

   (a) [‘Tom’, ‘Dick’, ‘Harry’]
   (b) [‘Tom’, ‘Dick’, ‘Harry’, ‘Tom’]
   (c) [‘Tom’, [‘Tom’], ‘[Tom]’, ‘[ ]’, ”, ””]

4. Indicate whether ‘Tom’ is a member, component, member of component, component of member, component of component, etc., of each of the following sets or tuples:

   (a) [1, ‘Tom’]
   (b) {[‘Tom’, 3], [‘Dick’, 4], [‘Harry’, 5]}
   (c) {{‘Tom’, ‘Dick’, ‘Harry’}}
   (d) [[[[‘Tom’], ‘Tom’], ‘Dick’, ‘Tom’, ‘Harry’]]
   (e) [[‘Tom’, ‘Dick’], ‘Tom’, ‘Harry’]

5. Write a map which indicates the age of each of your brothers and sisters by associating their age with their first name. Write the range and domain of this map.

6. Write a map which associates each component of the tuple [‘Tom’, ‘Dick’, ‘Harry’] with the square of the component length. Write the range and domain of this map.

7. How many maps are there whose domain is {‘Tom’, ‘Dick’} and whose range is {‘Sue’, ‘Mary’}? How many of these maps are single-valued?

8. A map M associates the age of each child in a family with the name of the child. The domain of M is $\{7, 9, 13\}$, and the range is {‘Sue’, ‘Mary’, ‘Tom’, ‘Dick’}. What is interesting about this family?

9. Consider the following map M:

   {[‘Smith’, {[‘Sue’, 11], [‘Jim’, 13]}],
   [‘Jones’, {[‘Albert’, 1], [‘Anna’, 3], [‘Ron’, 9]}],
   [‘Skallagrim’, {[‘Thorolf’, 7], [‘Egil’, 5], [‘Asgerd’, 4]}]}

   What information might this map represent? What is its domain? What is its range?

10. Let S be the set

    {‘Tom’, {‘Dick’, [‘Harry’, ‘Arthur’, {‘Tom’}]}}

    ‘Dick’ is a member a member of S. Match each name in the following list with the manner in which it appears in S:
    (a) Tom
    (b) Harry
    (c) Arthur
        (i) component of member
        (ii) member of component of member
        (iii) member

11. Consider the map M of Exercise 9 as a set. What are all the members of this set? Which of the components of the members of M are sets, and what are the members of these components? What are all the components of the members of all the components of the members of M which are sets? What are all the lengths of all the components of the members of M which are not sets?

12. Write a map which associates each of the Pacific coast states with the name of its state capital.

13. For how many integers between 1 and 100 is $I = 5*\ (I\ \mathbf{div}\ 5)$ true? For exactly which integers is this true? For how many integers between 1 and 100 is $I = (5*I)\ \mathbf{div}\ 5$ true?

3.5 Set Operations and Set Formers

SETL provides several important kinds of set operators, of which the easiest to understand are the built-in, elementary set operations and the set formers. We shall present these constructs in the present section; the even more important map operations are presented in Section 3.8.

3.5.1 Binary set operators

The *binary set operations* compute a result value from two inputs, one or both of which must be a set. These operations are as follows (in what follows, s and ss are always sets, and x can be an object of arbitrary type):

s + ss	computes the *union* of two sets, i.e., the set of all objects which belong either to s or to ss.
s − ss	computes the *difference* of two sets, i.e., the set of all objects which belong to s but not to ss.
s*ss	computes the *intersection*, or common part, of two sets, i.e., the set of all objects which belong to both s and ss.
s **mod** ss	computes the *symmetric difference* of two sets, i.e., the set of objects that are either in s or ss, but not in both. Equivalent to s + ss − (s*ss)
k **npow** s	here k must be a nonnegative integer. This operation yields the collection of all subsets of s which contain exactly k elements. An error results if k is negative. So we don't have to remember which of the arguments must be a set, and which an integer, both possibilities are allowed: we can write indifferently s **npow** k or k **npow** s.
s **with** x	produces a set whose members are the members of s, with x inserted (if x is not already a member of s). Equivalent to s + {x}.
s **less** x	produces a set whose members are the members of s, with x removed (if necessary, i.e., if x is a member of s). Equivalent to s − {x}.

The following set operators are *predicates*; i.e., they perform a test and yield a Boolean value:

x **in** s	tests x for membership in the set s. The value **true** is produced if x is a member of s, **false** otherwise.

x **notin** s	tests x for nonmembership in the set s. The value **true** is produced if x is not a member of s, **false** otherwise.
s = ss	tests s and ss for equality, yielding **true** if s and ss have exactly the same members, **false** otherwise.
s /= ss	tests s and ss for inequality, yielding **false** if s and ss have exactly the same members, **true** otherwise.
s **incs** ss	tests ss for inclusion within s, yielding **true** if every member of ss is also a member of s, **false** if ss has any member which is not also a member of s.
s **subset** ss	tests s for inclusion within ss, yielding **true** if every member of s is also a member of ss, **false** if s has any member which is not also a member of ss.

Examples of use of these binary set operators are the following:

print({1,2} + {'Tom','Dick'});	yields	{1 2 'Tom' 'Dick'}	
print({ } + {1,2},{ } + { });	yields	{1 2}	{ }
print({1,2,3} − {1,4}, {1,2,3} − { });	yields	{2 3}	{1 2 3}
print({1,2,3} − {3,1,2});	yields	{ }	
print({ } − {1,2,3});	yields	{ }	
print({1,2,3}*{2,5,3});	yields	{2 3}	
print({1,2}*{3,4});	yields	{ }	
print({ }*{3,4});	yields	{ }	
print({{1},2,3} − {1,2,3});	yields	{{1}}	
print({{1},{2,3}} − {1,2,3});	yields	{{1} {2 3}}	
print(1 **in** {1,2,3},{1} **in** {1,2,3});	yields	**true**	**false**
print({ } **in** { },{ } **in** {{ }});	yields	**false**	**true**
print(1 **notin** {1},{ } **notin** { });	yields	**false**	**true**
print({1,2,3} **with** 5);	yields	{1 2 3 5}	
print({1,2,3} **with** 1);	yields	{1 2 3}	
print({1,2,3} **less** 1, {1,2,3} **less** 4);	yields	{2 3}	{1 2 3}
print({1,2,3} = {3,2,1});	yields	**true**	
print({ } = [ ],{ } = {{ }});	yields	**false**	**false**
print({1,2} /= {2,1}, {1,2,2} /= {1,2});	yields	**false**	**false**

print(2 **npow** {1, 2, 3});	yields	{{1 2} {2 3} {1 3}}	
print({1} **incs** { }, { } **incs** {1});	yields	**true**	**false**
print({1, 2} **incs** {1, 2});	yields	**true**	
print({2, 2, 2} **subset** {1, 2});	yields	**true**	

3.5.2 Unary set operators

Unary set operators compute a result value from a single set input *s*. The unary set operators are as follows:

#s	yields the number of (distinct) elements of the set s.
pow s	yields the set of all subsets of s (which is also called the *power set* of s; hence the name **pow**).
random s	yields a randomly selected element of s. Successive uses of **random** s will yield independently selected elements of s.
arb s	Yields an arbitrarily selected element of s. **arb** s means "some element of s; I don't care which." It differs from **random** s in that the latter, when called repeatedly, yields eventually each element of s, but there is no such regularity to **arb**. (Depending on the particular SETL implementation used, successive evaluations of **arb** s may or may not yield the same element of s). If s is the empty set, **arb** s yields **om**.

Examples of these unary operators are as follows:

print(# {2}, # {2, 2, 2, 2});	yields 1 1
print(# {1, 2, 3, 4, 1, 2, 3, 4, 40});	yields 5
print(**pow**{1, 2});	yields {{ } {1} {2} {1 2}}
print(**arb**{1, 2, 3}, **arb**{1, 2, 3});	yields 1 1 (or possibly 2 2 or 3 3)
print(**arb**{1, 2, 3}, **arb**{3, 1, 2});	can yield 1 2 (even though {1, 2, 3} = {3, 2, 1} yields **true**)
print(**random**{1, 2, 3}, **random**{1, 2, 3});	(possibly) yields something like 2 1

Of course, the basic construct

$$\{x1, x2, \ldots, xk\}$$

which forms a set by enumerating its elements explicitly is also a (multi-argument) set operator. The $x1, x2, \ldots, xk$ appearing in this construct can be arbitrary expressions. As several of the preceding examples show, this construct can form a set of fewer than k elements. For example, if x has the value $\{1, 2\}$ and y the value $\{1\}$, then $\{x, y, x + y\}$ is the two-element set $\{\{1, 2\}, \{1\}\}$

As already noted, the set of all integers in the range from m to n (inclusive) can be written as

$$\{m..n\}$$

and the set of all integers n, $n + k$, $n + 2k$, etc., up to m can be written

$$\{n, n + k..m\}$$

In this last form, the "step" k can be negative, and $n + k$ need not actually be a sum but can be any arbitrary expression. For example,

print(3, 6 − 1 .. 10}) yields{3 5 7 9}

If the m in $n..m$ is less than n, then the null set results. Similar rules apply to {n, n + k .. m}, for example,

print({3, 5 .. 1})	yields	{ }
print({3, 2 .. −3})	yields	{3 2 1 0 −1 −2 −3}
print({3, 2 .. 4})	yields	{ }
print({3, 3 .. 5})	yields	{ }

Section 4.3.4 examines these constructs in greater detail.

Many interesting mathematical relationships connect the set operators presented in this section. For example, the values of (s*$s1$) **subset** s, and ($s1$ + $s2$)*$s3$ = $s1$*$s3$ + $s2$*$s3$ are always **true**. Other relationships of this sort appear in the exercises following Section 3.13.

3.5.3 Set former expressions

Sets are the basic data objects of SETL, and the language provides a number of ways of constructing them. We have seen already in Section 3.1 that sets can be constructed by listing their elements and enclosing the list between set brackets. More generally, sets can be constructed by enumerating their elements, be they constants, variables, or expressions. For example, the set expression

$$\{x, y, x + y, [\ ]\}$$

describes a set whose elements are the value of the variable x, the value of variable y, the expression $(x + y)$, and the null tuple. Such sets *constructed by enumeration* can contain any number of expressions of any type.

In mathematics, the most powerful and general way of forming a set is simply to define it by stating a characteristic property of its elements. We will now describe the method for doing this in SETL, which uses a notation almost identical to mathematical language. The standard mathematical notation for this construction is

$$\{x \mid C\} \tag{1}$$

read "the set of all x having the property C," or equivalently "the set of all x such that C." C must be an expression that yields a Boolean value. For example in mathematics one commonly writes

$$\{x \mid x < 0\} \tag{2}$$

which is read "the set of all x such that $x < 0$." (As this example shows, the Boolean expression C of (1) will generally depend on the variable x.)

It should be noted that this standard method of describing a set in mathematics uses a shortcut which omits any explicit specification of the range of values for the variable x, what is often called the *universal set*. This omission is not permitted in SETL, and that is the only difference between the SETL method of constructing a set and mathematical notation. Thus the following construct is used in SETL:

$$\{x \textbf{ in } s \mid C\}. \tag{3}$$

Here s is a set which has been constructed earlier, either by enumeration as described or by a previous instance of (3). It follows that s itself must be finite, and thus all sets constructed in SETL are finite. The construct (3) is the basic SETL set former.

Several important generalizations of the construct (3) are used in mathematics and also allowed in SETL. Suppose, for example, that s is a set of numbers. Rather than simply forming the set (3), we may want to form a set of numbers obtained from (3) by applying some common transformation to all its elements, for example, by squaring them. To form this set, we are allowed to write

$$\{\mathrm{x*x: x} \textbf{ in } \mathrm{s} \mid \mathrm{C}\}$$

which can be read "the set of all values x squared, for all x ranging over the set s which are such that C." The general form of the more powerful kind of set former is

$$\{e\text{: } x \textbf{ in } s \mid C\} \tag{4}$$

In (4), e can be any expression, s any set valued expression, C any Boolean-valued expression. We can read (4) as "the set of all values e, formed for those x in s for which C has the value **true**." Usually both e and C will depend on the value of x, i.e., on the various values of the members of s.

This reading of the notation (4) suggests a further generalization, which again is used in standard mathematics and is also legal in SETL. Specifically, there is no reason why in forming a set like (4) we should only allow one variable x to range over one set s. Instead, we can allow any number of variables to range over any number of sets. The notations

$$\{\mathrm{e: x} \textbf{ in } \mathrm{s1, y} \textbf{ in } \mathrm{s2} \mid \mathrm{C}\} \tag{5a}$$
$$\{\mathrm{e: x} \textbf{ in } \mathrm{s1, y} \textbf{ in } \mathrm{s2, z} \textbf{ in } \mathrm{s3} \mid \mathrm{C}\} \tag{5b}$$

etc., express this more general construction. Note that (5b) can be read as "x ranging over $s1$, y independently ranging over $s2$, z ranging (again independently) over $s3$, but only in combinations x, y, z for which C has the value **true**."

Subsequently we will see that even further generalizations of the set former constructs (3), (4), (5a), (5b), etc., are allowed. But, even as they stand, these constructs are extremely powerful, as the following interesting examples will illustrate. We begin by considering the problem of printing out prime numbers, for example, all prime numbers in a given range, let us say the range {1 ... 100}. We remind the reader that positive numbers like 6 = 2*3, 9 = 3*3, 4 = 2*2 which are the product of two smaller numbers are called *composite*, and that numbers larger than 1 which are not composite are called *prime*; examples of primes are 3, 5, 7, 11, 13, 17....

It is easy to express the set of all composite numbers up to 100 using a set former (of type (5b)), namely as

{i*j: i **in** {2..10}, j **in** {2..50} | i*j < 101}. (6)

Since the prime numbers we want are exactly the elements of {2..100} which do not belong to the set (6), we can print them out simply by writing

print({2..100} − {i*j: i **in**{2..10}, j **in**{2..50} | i*j < 100});

Sometimes the condition *C* appearing in (4), (5a), and (5b) is unnecessary. For example, given a set *s* of numbers we may simply want to form all the squares of numbers in *s*. In such cases one is simply allowed to drop the condition *C*, i.e., to write {*e*: *x* **in** *s*}, read "the set of all values *e* formed for *x* in *x*." Similarly, we can write

{e: x **in** s1, y **in** s2},
{e: x **in** s1, y **in** s2, z **in** s3}, etc.

For example, we can write the set of all pairs *x*, *y*, where *x* ranges over *s*1 and *y* ranges over *s*2, as

{[x, y]: x **in** s1, y **in** s2}.

(In mathematics, this set is called the *Cartesian product* of *s*1 and *s*2, after René Descartes, the inventor of coordinate geometry.) Using these abbreviated set formers we can print the sets of primes already considered more simply; for example, we can print the primes up to 100 by writing

print({2..100} − {i*j: i **in**{2..10}, j **in**{2..50}})

Mathematicians who study prime numbers are often interested in primes having particular forms, for example, primes *p* which are one more than a multiple of 4, or three more than a multiple of 4. Since the set of all numbers (greater than 1) up to 100 which are one more (respectively, three more) than a multiple of 4 can be expressed as

{4*n + 1: n **in**{0..24} | 4*n + 1 < 101}

and

{4*n + 3: n **in**{0..24} | 4*n + 3 < 101}

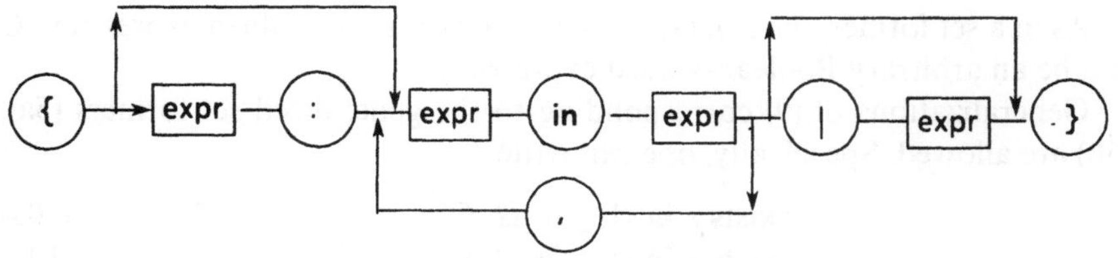

Figure 3.1 Set Former Diagram

respectively, we can print the set of primes (up to 100) which are 1 more than a multiple of 4 by writing

print({4*n + 1: n **in**{1..24} | 4*n + 1 < 101}
    − {i*j: i **in**{2..10}, j **in**{2..50} | i*j < 101});

and the corresponding set of primes which are 3 more than a multiple of 4 by writing

print({4*n + 3: n **in**{0..24} | 4*n + 3 < 101}
    − {i*j: i **in**{2..10}, j **in**{2..50} | i*j < 101});

The various forms of the set former described are summarized in the syntax diagram in Figure 3.1. Other kinds of set formers also exist and will be described later.

3.5.4 Existential and universal quantifiers

Very often, the key to a mathematical problem is to determine whether there exists any object x satisfying a given condition C. Similarly the key to a programming problem often lies in finding such an x if it exists, and if we know where to look for it, i.e., if we know the set of objects among which x might be found. Using set formers, it is easy to express the condition that there should exist an x in s satisfying C. We have only to write

{x **in** s | C} /= { }. (7)

or in words, "the set of elements of s which satisfy C is not empty." Moreover, if the condition (7) is satisfied, we can easily obtain such an x by extracting it from the nonempty set we have just constructed:

arb{x **in** s | C}. (8)

Since the test (7) is so important and common, a special abbreviation is provided for it, namely

exists x **in** s | C. (9)

This is a Boolean-valued expression, yielding exactly the same value as (7). Moreover, if it yields the value **true**, it will set x to the value of (8), i.e., to some value satisfying C. If (7) is false, then the variable x in (8) gets the value **om** (just as **arb** { } is **om**).

As in a set former, the *s* in (9) can be an arbitrary set-valued expression; *C* can be an arbitrary Boolean-valued expression.

Generalizations of (9) corresponding to the generalized set formers (5a), (5b) are allowed. Specifically, one can write

exists x **in** s1, y **in** s2 | C (10a)
exists x **in** s1, y **in** s2, z in s3 | C (10b)

etc., where *s*1, *s*2, .. are arbitrary set-valued expressions and *C* a Boolean expression. The constructs (10a) and (10b) search the set of all *x* in *s*1, *y* in *s*2, ... for values satisfying the condition *C*. If such values are found, then (10a) (or (10b)) yields the value **true** and the variables *x*, *y*, ... are set to these values. Otherwise (10a) (or (10b)) yields the value **false** and *x*, *y*, .. get the value **om**.

The constructs (9), (10a), (10b), etc., are called *existential quantifiers* or *existentially quantified expressions.*

The existential quantifier allows us to express naturally the common query, Does there exist an object in a certain collection which satisfies a given criterion? A related query, which is also very common in programming contexts, is the following: Do *all* the objects in a collection satisfy some stated criterion? Such queries are expressed in SETL by means of constructs such as the following:

forall x **in** s | C (11a)
forall x **in** s1, y **in** s2 | C (11b)
forall x *in* s1, y **in** s2, z **in** s3 | C (11c)

which make use of the keyword **forall**. These constructs which are called *universal quantifiers* are closely related to existential quantifiers. The three cases just given are equivalent to:

notexists x **in** s | (**not** C) (12a)
notexists x **in** s1, y **in** s2 | (**not** C) (12b)
notexists x **in** s1, y **in** s2, z **in** s3 | (**not** C) (12c)

respectively. For example, (11c) searches the set of all *x* in *s*1, *y* in *s*2, *z* in *s*3 for values such that the condition *C* takes on the value **false**. If none exists then (11c) returns the value **true** (and the variables *x*, *y*, *z* take the value **om**). However, if values satisfying **not** *C* exist, then (11c) returns the value **false** (and the variables *x*, *y*, *z* take on values (in *s*1, *s*2, and *s*3, respectively) fulfilling the condition **not** *C*). The keywords **exists** and **forall** are quantifiers. By using quantifiers we can write a simpler and more readable set former representing the set of all primes up to 100. Specifically, an integer *n* is prime if there exists no smaller integer *m* (other than 1) which divides *n* evenly, i.e., such that *n* **mod** *m* = 0. Hence

print({n in{2..100} | ((**not exists** m **in**{2..n − 1} | n **mod** m = 0)
    and (n − 1) **mod** 4 = 0});

will print all the primes up to 100 which are one more than a multiple of 4, and

print({n **in**{2..100} | ((**not exists** m **in**{2..n − 1} | n **mod** m = 0)
and (n − 3) **mod** 4 = 0)});

will print the set of all primes up to 100 which are 3 more than a multiple of 4.

As we have said, the existential quantifier (9) returns exactly the same value as the expression (7). However, the quantifier calculates this value more efficiently than (7) would, since to evaluate (9) the SETL system will search systematically through the elements of *s* but stop searching and return the value **true** as soon as an *x* satisfying *C* has been found, whereas to evaluate (7) it would always search through the *whole* of *s* building up the set {*x* **in** *S* | *C*} and only test it for emptiness after it had been evaluated fully.

3.5.4.1 A remark on bound variables in compound set formers and quantifiers

The variables *x*, *y*, *z* occurring in (9), (10a–b), (11a–c), and (12a–c) are called *bound variables*, since the evaluation of each quantified expression proceeds by giving to *x*, *y*, and *z* the values of successive elements of the sets *s*1, *s*2, etc., i.e., *binds* them to successive values of their respective domains. Quantifiers (or set formers) such as (10a–b), (11b–c), or (12b–c) involving more than one bound variable cause multiple iterations, e.g., in evaluating

exists x **in** s1, y **in** s2 | C

x is given successive values from the set *s*1, and then for each of these values of *x*, *y* is given all possible values from *s*2. For this reason, the expression *s*2 in (10a) is allowed to depend on the bound variable *x*, but *s*1 must be independent of *y*. Similarly, in

exists x **in** s1, y **in** s2, z **in** s3 | C

*s*3 can depend on both *x* and *y*, *s*2 can depend on *x* but not *z*, and *s*1 cannot depend on either *y* or *z*. Similar rules apply to universal quantifiers and to set formers.

3.5.5 Some illustrative one-statement programs

So far only a few of the commands available to the SETL programmer have been described, so that we cannot yet show any substantial programs. However, the mechanisms that have been described are powerful enough to allow various interesting single-statement programs to be written. In this section, we collect a few such programs.

3.5.5.1 More about prime numbers

As noted in the preceding section, an integer is called *prime* if it is not exactly divisible by any smaller (positive) integer other than 1.

To form the set of all prime numbers up to 100 we can use the one-line program idea given in the preceding section, which simply prints a set former:

```
print({n in{2..100} | not exists m in{2..n - 1} | (n mod m) = 0});
```

The output of this single-statement program is

{2 3 5 7 11 13 17 19 23 29 31 37 41 43 47 53 59 61 67 71 73 79 83 89 97}

(Note however that since sets are not ordered the elements of this set will actually be printed in some arbitrary order.)

Mathematicians who study prime numbers are sometimes interested in finding not all the primes in a given range, but only those which have various special properties. For example, a prime n is said to belong to a *prime pair* if both n and $n + 2$ are primes. (Note that, since all primes except 2 are odd, we cannot expect both n and $n + 1$ to be prime, because if n is a prime then $n + 1$ will be even, hence not a prime.) To find all prime pairs up to 100 we can simply write

```
print({n in{2..100} |
            (not exists m in{2..n - 1} | (n mod m) = 0)
                 and (not exists m in{2..n + 1} | ((n + 2) mod m) = 0)});
```

The output of this program is

{3 5 11 17 29 41 59 71}

indicating that the only such twin-prime pairs are

[3, 5], [5, 7], [11, 13], [17, 19], [29, 31], [41, 43], [59, 61], [71, 73],

Sometimes one is interested in primes which satisfy particular quadratic equations, for example, primes n of the form $n = k**2 + 1$. Since if n is not larger than 100, any integer k solving this equation would have to be smaller than 10, we can find all the primes of this form just by writing

```
print({n in{2..100} | (not exists m in{2..n - 1} | (n mod m) = 0)
              and(exists k in{0..10} | n = k*k + 1)});
```

Similarly, to find all the primes up to 100 which have the form $2k**2 + 3$ we can write

```
print({n in{2..100} | (not exists m in{2..n - 1} | (n mod m) = 0)
              and(exists k in{0..10} | n = 2*k*k + 3)});
```

the output of the first of these programs is

{2 5 17 37}

and the output of the second program is

{3 5 11 53}

3.5.5.2 Integer right triangles

The famous theorem of Pythagoras states that the length h of the hypotenuse of a right triangle and the lengths a and b of its two sides are related by the equation $a^2 + b^2 = h^2$. Whole-number solutions of this equation are useful to people who make up elementary mathematics exams and want to invent problems that have whole number answers. Examples of such *integer right triangles* are 3, 4, 5 and 5, 12, 13. The following single-statement program finds all integer right triangles a, b, h for which a is less than b and both are less than 30. We let b range over the set {1..30} and a range over the set {1..b − 1}. To find if $a*a + b*b$ is a perfect square, we simply search for an integer h whose square is equal to that sum. The possible range of h is from 1 to $a + b$ (approximately: can you give a more precise range for it?). In the program that follows we eliminate all triangles for which a and b have a common divisor, since these are simple multiples of smaller integer right triangles.

```
print({[a, b, h]: b in {1..30}, a in {1..b - 1} |
            (exists h in {2..a + b} | (a*a + b*b = h*h)) and
        not exists d in {2..b - 1} | ((b mod d) = 0 and (a mod d) = 0)});
```

The output of this program is

{[3 4 5][5 12 13][8 15 17][20 21 29][7 24 25]}.

It is not hard to prove mathematically that there exist infinitely many different integer right triangles.

3.6 Tuple Operations and Tuple Formers

We have mentioned repeatedly that sets are unordered and can never have duplicate or undefined members; tuples are ordered and can have both duplicate and undefined components. For example,

[1, 0, 1, 0, **om**, **om**, 1, 0]

is a perfectly legal tuple; its first, third, and seventh components are all 1, while its fifth and sixth components are undefined. In spite of this very fundamental difference between sets and tuples, the binary and unary operators on tuples that SETL provides are similar to corresponding set operators. In addition, SETL allows tuple formers that construct tuples in the same manner that set formers build sets. The syntax of tuple formers is similar to that of set formers. In fact, all set-forming expressions can be transformed into tuple forming expressions by replacing the set brackets with tuple brackets.

3.6.1 Binary tuple operators

Binary tuple operators compute a result value from two inputs, one or both of which must be a tuple. The binary tuple operators are as follows (in what follows, *t* and *tt* are always tuples, and *x* can be an arbitrary value):

t + tt	concatenates tt to the end of t.
n*t	here, n must be an integer. This forms n copies of t and concatenates them end to end, to form a tuple n times as long as t. If n = 0, then the null tuple (i.e., [ ]) is obtained; if n < 0, an error results.
t*n	if n is an integer, this is equivalent to n*t
t **with** x	yields a new tuple identical to t except that x is appended to it as an additional final component

The following are predicates on tuples:

x **in** t	yields **true** if x equals one of the components of t, **false** otherwise.
x **notin** t	yields **false** if x equals one of the components of t; **true** otherwise.
t = tt	yields **true** if all components of t are identical to the corresponding components of tt, **false** otherwise.
t /= tt	yields **true** if some component of t differs from the corresponding component of tt, **false** otherwise.

A tuple is considered to extend from its first component to its last defined component, i.e., its last component different from **om**. That is, all tuples can be regarded as having an indefinitely long sequence of trailing **om** components (standing for the arbitrary number of components that may be added to it), but the identity of the tuple is given by its defined components only. In particular, when a tuple is printed its trailing **om** components are not displayed. For example,

[**om**, **om**, **om**, **om**]	is printed as [ ]
[1, **om**, 2, **om**]	is printed as [1, **om**, 2]
[1, **om**] **with om**	is printed as [1]

Some examples of the binary tuple operators are

print([1, 2] + [3, 4])	yields	[1 2 3 4]
print([1, 2] **with** [3, 4]);	yields	[1 2 [3 4]]
print(2*[1, 2], [1, 3]*2);	yields	[1 2 1 2] [1 3 1 3]
print(1 **in**[1, 2, 3], [1, 2]**in**[1, 2, 3]);	yields	**true false**
print(**om in**[1, 2, 3], **om in**[1, **om**, 3]);	yields	**false true**
print([1, 2] = [2, 1], [1, 2, 1, 2] = [1, 21, 2]);	yields	**false false**
print([1, 2, 1, 2] /= [1, 2, 1, 2, 1], [1, 1] /= [1, 1, 1], [1] /= [1, **om**]);	yields	**true true false**
print({ } /= [ ]);	yields	**true**

3.6.2 Unary tuple operators

Unary tuple operators produce a value from a single tuple operand. The unary tuple operators are

#t	yields the index of the last non-**om** component of t
random t	yields a component of t picked at random from its first to its last non-**om** component. All components, including **om** components in this range, have an equal chance to be picked. Note that successive uses of **random** t will generally yield different, independently chosen random components.

The following are examples of the unary tuple operators.

print(# [3], # [ ], # [1, **om**]);	yields 1 0 1
print(# [1, **om**], # [**om**, 1], # [1, 1, 1]);	yields 1 2 3
print(# [1, **om**, **om**, **om**, **om**, 1]);	yields 6
print(# [1, **om**, **om**, **om**, **om**]);	yields 1
print(# [1, 2, 3, 4], # [1, 2, [3, 4]], # [[1, 2, 3, 4]]);	yields 4 3 1

print(**random**[1, 2, 3], **random**[1, 2, 3], **random**[1, 2, 3], **random**[1, 2, 3]);

(probably) yields something like 2 1 2 3

3.6.3 Other tuple operators. Indexing and slicing

As for sets, so for tuples the construct

[x1, x2, . . . ,xk]

forms a tuple by enumerating its elements explicity. The various *xj* appearing in this construct can be arbitrary expressions. If some of the *xj* appearing at the end of this construct evaluate to **om**, then a tuple of length less than k will be formed. For example, if t has the value [1, **om**, **om**, 2], then

$$[t(4), t(3), t(2), t(3)]$$

forms the tuple [2, **om**, **om**, **om**], i.e., the tuple [2], whose length is of course 1.

As was discussed in Section 3.2.1 the tuple of integers ranging from n to m (inclusive) can be written as

$$[n\,..\,m]$$

and the tuple of integers n, $n + k$, $n + 2k$, etc., up to m can be written

$$[n, n + k\,..\,m].$$

In this last form, the "step" k can be positive (producing an ascending sequence) or negative (producing a descending sequence). The quantity $n + k$ need not actually be a sum but can be any integer-valued expression. If the m

in $[n..m]$ is less than n, then the null tuple results. Similarly, if $m = m1$, then $[m, m1..n]$ will yield the null tuple. Similar rules apply to $[n, n + k..m]$. For example,

print([3, 5 . . 1]);	yields	[ ]
print([3, 2 . . − 3]);	yields	[3 2 1 0 − 1 − 2 − 3]
print([3, 2 . . 4]);	yields	[ ]
print([3, 3 . . 5]);	yields	[ ]

Tuple indexing, slice, and assignment operators are similar to the string slice and assignment operators described in Section 2.5.3. The indexing and slice operators are as follows (we assume as before that t designates a tuple):

t(i) yields the *i*-th component of the tuple t. If i is zero or less, an error result; if i exceeds the index of the last non-**om** component of t, then t(i) yields **om**.

t(i . . j) yields the section or slice of t extending from its *i*-th through its *j*-th components, inclusive. If i is zero or negative, or if i exceeds j + 1, an error results. If i = j + 1, then t(i . . j) always yields the null tuple. If i exceeds the last non-**om** component of t, then a null tuple is returned.

t(i . .) yields the section or slice of t extending from its *i*-th through its last non-**om** component, inclusive. This operator is equivalent to t(i . . #t). Thus if i is zero or negative, or if i exceeds #t + 1, an error results. If i = #t + 1, then t(i . .) yields the null tuple.

To give examples of these operators, we assume that *t* is the tuple [10, **om**, 30, **om**, 50, **om**, 70]. Then:

print(t(1), t(2), t(3));	yields	10 **om** 30	
print(t(7), t(8));	yields	70 **om**	
print(t(2 . . 5), t(2 . . 6));	yields	[**om** 30 **om** 50]	[**om** 30 **om** 50]
print(t(2 . . 8));	yields	[**om** 30 **om** 50 **om** 70]	
print(t(3 . . 2));	yields	[ ]	
print(t(8 . . 11));	yields	[ ]	
print(t(3 . .), t(8 . .));	yields	[30 **om** 50 **om** 70]	[ ]
print(t(9 . .));	results in an error		

It should also be noted that if the *i*-th component of *t* is itself a tuple or a string, then further indexing of *t*(*i*) is possible. Suppose, for example, that *t* is the following tuple of tuples of strings:

[['Tom', 'Dick', 'Harry'], ['Peter', 'Paul', 'Mary'], ['Mutt', 'Jeff']]

Then:

```
print(t(2));                           yields [Peter Paul Mary]
print(t(2) (3));                       yields Mary
print(t(2) (3) (1));                   yields M
print(t(2..3));                        yields [[Peter Paul Mary] [Mutt Jeff]]
print(t(2..3) (2..));                  yields [[Mutt Jeff]]
print(t(2..3) (2..) (1));              yields [Mutt Jeff]
print(t(2..3) (2..) (1) (2..));        yields [Jeff]
print(t(2..3) (2..) (1) (2..) (1) (2)); yields e
```

The tuple assignment operators are as follows (we assume as before that the values of *t* and *tt* are tuples):

t(i) := x; modifies the *i*-th component of the tuple t, setting it equal to the value of x. If i is zero or negative, an error results. If i exceeds the index of the last non-**om** component of t, then t will be extended with as many **om** components as necessary, and then its *i*-th component will be set equal to x. (Therefore the assignment t(i) := x can increase the length of t by any amount up to i)

t(i..j) := tt; modifies the section of t extending from its *i*-th through its *j*-th component, setting this section equal to the components of tt. If i is zero or negative, or if i exceeds j + 1, an error results. If i = j + 1, then the components of tt will be inserted into t immediately before position i. If i exceeds the index of the last non-**om** component of t, then t will be extended with as many **om** components as necessary, and then tt will be appended.

t(i..) := tt; this assignment is equivalent to t(i.. #t) := tt. Thus it modifies the section of t extending from its *i*-th component to its last non-**om** component, setting it equal to the components of tt. If i is zero or negative, or if i exceeds #t + 1, an error results. If i = #t + 1, then the components of tt are appended to the end of t.

To give examples of these operators, suppose that *t*1, *t*2, ..., *t*22 all have the value [1, 2, 3, **om**, **om**, 6]. Then,

```
t1(2) := om;                $ now t1 = [1, om, 3, om, om, 6]
t2(4) := 40;                $ now t2 = [1, 2, 3, 40, om, 6]
t3(8) := 70;                $ now t3 = [1, 2, 3, om, om, 6, om, 70]
t4(9) := om;                $ now t4 = [1, 2, 3, om, om, 6]
t5(2..4) := [om, 30, 40];   $ now t5 = [1, om, 30, 40, om, 6]
t6(2..2) := [20];           $ now t6 = [1, 20, 3, om, om, 6]
t7(2) := 20;                $ now t7 = [1, 20, 3, om, om, 6]
```

```
t8(2) := [20];               $ now t8 = [1, [20], 3, om, om, 6]
t9(2..2) := [20];            $ now t9 = [1, 20, 3, om, om, 6]
t10(2..1) := [20, om, 30];   $ now t10 = [1, 20, om, 30, 2, 3, om, om, 6]
t11(6..5) := [20, om, 30];   $ now t11 = [1, 2, 3, om, om, 20, om, 30, 6]
t12(1..0) := [20, om, 30];   $ now t12 = [20, om, 30, 1, 2, 3, om, om, 6]
t13(8..9) := [20, om, 30];   $ now t13 = [1, 2, 3, om, om, 6, om, 20, om, 30]
t14(5..5) := [20, om, 30];   $ now t14 = [1, 2, 3, om, 20, om, 30, 6]
t15(5..5) := [20, om, om];   $ now t15 = [1, 2, 3, om, 20, 6]
t16(4..5) := [ ];            $ now t16 = [1, 2, 3, 6]
t17(2..3) := [20];           $ now t17 = [1, 20, om, om, 6]
t18(2..4) := [20];           $ now t18 = [1, 20, om, 6]
t19(6..) := [ ];             $ now t19 = [1, 2, 3]
t20(5..) := [50, 60, 70, 80]; $ now t20 = [1, 2, 3, om, 50, 60, 70, 80]
t21(7..) := [50, 60, om, 80]; $ now t21 = [1, 2, 3, om, om, 6, 50, 60, om, 80]
t22(8..) := [20, om, 30];    $ results in an error
```

Repeatedly indexed tuple (and map) assignments such as

$$t(i)(j\,..\,k)(1) := tt;$$

are possible in some cases; see Section 3.12 for a general discussion of these assignments.

3.7 Tuple Formers; Simple Tuple and String Iterators

The construct

[e: x **in** s | C] (1)

reads "the tuple of all values assumed by the expression *e* as *x* ranges over the elements of *s* for which the condition *C* has value **true**." It is similar to the set former

{e: x **in** s | C}, (2)

(see Section 3.5.3) except that (2) eliminates duplicates and builds a set, whereas (1) builds a tuple and does not eliminate duplicates. The order in which the components of the tuple (1) are arranged is determined by the order in which iteration proceeds over the elements *x* of the set *s*.

As in the case of set formers, the condition C appearing in (1) need not appear; i.e., one can write

$$[\text{e: x } \mathbf{in} \text{ s}] \tag{3}$$

read "the tuple of all values assumed by the expression e as x ranges over all the elements of s." Moreover, multiple iterations can be used in a tuple formers; i.e., constructs like

$$[\text{e: x } \mathbf{in} \text{ s1, y } \mathbf{in} \text{ s2}] \tag{3a}$$
$$[\text{e: x } \mathbf{in} \text{ s1, y } \mathbf{in} \text{ s2, z } \mathbf{in} \text{ s3}] \tag{3b}$$

etc., are allowed. Again, the order in which the components of (3a) or (3b) are arranged depends on the order in which iteration proceeds over the elements of $s1$, $s2$, etc. For example, in (3a) a complete iteration over $s2$ will always be made each time the variable x advances from one element of $s1$ to the next, and in (3b) a complete iteration over $s3$ will always take place each time the variable y advances from one element of $s2$ to the next.

$$[\text{x } \mathbf{in} \text{ s} \mid \text{C}]$$

is read "the tuple of all x **in** s for which the condition C evaluates to **true**." It is even possible to elide both e and C, thereby writing

$$[\text{x } \mathbf{in} \text{ s}]$$

This simply arranges the elements of the set s in (arbitrary) order as a tuple.

As noted in Section 3.5.3, the *iterator* x **in** s appearing in such constructs as the set former

$$\{\text{e: x } \mathbf{in} \text{ s} \mid \text{C}\} \tag{4}$$

and the existential quantifier

$$\ldots \mathbf{exists} \text{ x } \mathbf{in} \text{ s} \mid \text{C} \ldots \tag{5}$$

iterates over the elements of s, assigning each one of them in turn as the value of x, until the iteration terminates, either because (as in (4)) all elements of s have been processed or because (as in (5)) an element x of s satisfying the condition C has been found. Since iterative constructions and searches of this kind are quite useful, corresponding iterators over tuples and strings are also provided. If t is a tuple, then the iterator x **in** t, which can be used in such contexts as

$$\{\text{e: x } \mathbf{in} \text{ t} \mid \text{C}\} \tag{4a}$$

and

$$\ldots \mathbf{exists} \text{ x } \mathbf{in} \text{ t} \mid \text{C} \ldots \tag{4b}$$

iterates over the components of t, *in order*, from its first component to its last non-**om** component, assigning each component in turn as the value of the variable x, until the iteration terminates for one of the two possible reasons stated. The iteration advances over all components, including **om** components, in turn, but components not satisfying the Boolean condition *C* appearing in (4a) and (4b) are bypassed. We emphasize that, even though the corresponding *set* iterator, e.g.,

...**exists** x **in** s | C

iterates over the elements of the set *s* in some unpredictable, arbitrary order, the tuple iterator (4b) always *iterates over the components of* t *in a known order, namely from first component to last.* Therefore, if the existential search (4b) finds any component *x* of *t* satisfying the condition *C*, it will always find the *leftmost* such component, which will become the value of *x*.

We can iterate over the successive characters of a string in similar fashion. If in (4a) *t* is a string, then (4a) iterates over its characters, *in order*, from its first character to its last, assigning each character in turn as the value of the variable *x*, until the iteration terminates for one of the two possible reasons stated. Characters not satisfying the condition *C* appearing in (4a) are bypassed. Similar remarks apply to the set former (4a) and to universal quantifiers which iterate over strings and tuples.

Note, as an easy application of all this, that the set *s* of all distinct components of a tuple *t* can be formed by writing

{x **in** t}.

If *t* is a string, this same expression will form the set of all its distinct characters.

A more general account of the iterator forms usable in set formers, tuple formers, compound operators, and **for** loops, is given in Section 4.3.

By writing the iterator

x **in** [M..N]

as part of a set former or quantifier we can cause *x* to range over all the integers of the numerical range *M* through *N* inclusive in order. Similarly, by writing the iterator

x **in** [M, M + k..N]

we cause *x* to be iterated over integers lying between *M* and *N*, starting with *M* and proceeding by steps of *k*. This iteration will proceed either in increasing or in decreasing order, depending on whether *k* is positive or negative. (If $k = 0$, the iteration will be terminated as soon as it is attempted.) For example, to find all the vowels in a string which are followed by other vowels and print the corresponding set of all double vowels or *diphthongs*, we can simply write:

```
vowels := {'a', 'e', 'i', 'o', 'u', 'y'};
print({s(i..i + 1): i in [1..#s - 1] | s(i) in vowels and s(i + 1) in vowels});
```

Note that we could have defined vowels as

vowels := 'aeiouy';

because the construct (*a* **in** *b*) will test whether *a* is an element or a component of *b*, if *b* is either a set, a tuple, or a string. Similarly, to find the set of all places in a tuple of integers at which the sign of its component changes from + to − we can simply write

print({i **in** [1 .. #t − 1] | t(i) > 0 **and** t(i + 1) < 0}).

3.8 Map Operations

Sets of a special kind, namely sets all of whose elements are tuples of length 2 (also called *ordered pairs* or simply pairs) have a very special importance in SETL because they can be used to record *associations* between pairs of objects, or between objects and attributes of these objects (for example, between the names of people and their birth dates, between words in one language and words in another, etc.).

Sets of this kind are called *maps*, and the most significant operators of SETL, its *map operators*, apply only to such sets. In this section, we will describe these operators and their use. Let us start by restating that maps are sets, and as such all set operations (union, membership, etc.) apply to maps, without exception.

3.8.1 The image-set operator f{x}.

Suppose that f is a map, i.e., a set of pairs:

$$\{[x1, y1], [x2, y2], \ldots, [xk, yk]\}. \tag{1}$$

Then $f\{x\}$, called the *image set of* f *at the point* x, is defined to be the set of all second components of pairs in f whose first component is x. Using the standard set former, we can write this set as

$$\{y(2)\text{: } y \textbf{ in } f \mid y(1) = x\} \tag{2}$$

The significance of this operation lies in the fact that, if we regard f as representing a certain abstract relationship R, then $f\{x\}$ is precisely the set of all elements which stand in the relationship R to the object x.

Suppose, for example, that f contains the pair $[s, c]$ if and only if s is a student in a particular school and c is a course in which s is registered. Then $f\{s\}$ designates the set of all courses in which student s is registered. Suppose next that g is another map, which contains the pair $[c, s]$ if and only if f contains the pair $[s, c]$. (This map is called the *inverse* of the map f.) Then for each course c, $g\{c\}$ is the set of all students registered.

For a still more specific example, suppose that f is the map

{['Jones', 'Tom'], ['Khalid', 'Leila'], ['Smith', 'Mary'], ['Khalid', 'Fatima']} (3)

Then:

$f\{$'Jones'$\}$ is $\{$'Tom'$\}$;
$f\{$'Smith'$\}$ is $\{$'Mary'$\}$;
$f\{$'Khalid'$\}$ is $\{$'Leila', 'Fatima'$\}$.

Moreover

$f\{$'Chang'$\}$ is the null set, i.e. $\{\ \}$

since no pair beginning with "Chang" is present in the map (3).

In Section 3.3 we introduced the notions of **domain** and **range** of a map. In terms of the image-set operation, their meaning can be restated as follows: the **domain** of f, namely the set of all first components of pairs in f, is also the set of all x for which $f\{x\}$ is different from $\{\ \}$, and the **range** of f, namely the set of all second components of pairs in f, is also the set of all y which belong to at least one set of the form $f\{x\}$.

3.8.2 The single-valued image operator $f(x)$

If the image set $f\{x\}$ contains *exactly one* element y, that is, if $f\{x\}$ is $\{y\}$, then we can also write $f(x)$ for y (rather than **arb** $f\{x\}$). The quantity $f(x)$ (read "f of x") is called the *image* (or sometimes, for additional emphasis, the single-valued image), of the element x under the map f, and we say that the map f *sends x into* $f(x)$. If x is not in the domain of f, so that $f\{x\}$ is empty, or if $f\{x\}$ contains more than one element, then $f(x)$ yields **om**.

This last rule can be understood as follows. If, as before, we regard f as representing an abstract relationship R, then $f(x)$ represents *the unique* element y which stands in the relationship R to x. If x is not in **domain** f, then $f(x)$ is obviously undefined, since *no* element stands in the relationship R to x. If $f\{x\}$ contains more than one element, then $f(x)$ is still undefined, since we cannot tell which one of the several elements of $f\{x\}$ the expression $f(x)$ is supposed to represent. We can only speak of *the* element standing in the relationship R to x if $f\{x\}$ contains exactly one element, in which case $f(x)$ gives a non-**om** value.

For an example of all this, suppose once more that f is the map (3). Then

f('Jones') is 'Tom'; f('Smith') is 'Mary';
f('Chang') is **om**, since 'Chang' is not in the domain of f;
f('Khalid') is **om**, since f{'Khalid'} is a set containing more than one element

A map f is called *single-valued* at x if $f(x)$ is defined but is called *multiple-valued at x* if $f\{x\}$ contains more than one element. The map f is said to be a *single-valued map* (or simply to be *single-valued*) if it is single-valued at each element x of its domain.

Note that maps are also sets (namely sets all of whose elements are tuples of length 2), so that all set operations also apply to maps. In particular, we can form the union, intersection, and difference of maps; add elements to and substract elements from a map using the **with** and **less** operators; evaluate $\#f$ where f is a map, etc. For example, if f and g are both maps, then $f + g$, $f*g$, and $f - g$ are also maps since every element of any one of these sets will be a pair; the same remark applies to f **less** z for any z. Moreover, if f is a map and z is known to be a pair, then f **with** z is still a map since all its elements are pairs. For example, if f is the map (3) and we let $f2$ be f **with** ['Jones', 'Sue'], then $f2$ is still a map; moreover $f2$\{'Jones'\} is \{'Tom', 'Sue'\}, and $f2$('Jones') is **om**.

SETL allows us not only to *evaluate* expressions like $f\{x\}$ and $f(x)$, but also to use such expressions as *assignment targets*. If the value of f is a map, the *map assignment*

$$f(x) := y; \tag{4}$$

is always legal. *The effect of this assignment is to modify* f, and, as the notation (4) is intended to suggest, to modify it in such a way as to cause the value of $f(x)$ to become y immediately after the assignment (4) is executed. This is done by modifying f as follows:

(a) First, all pairs $[x, z]$ whose first component is x are removed from f. (This has the effect of removing x from **domain** f).
(b) Next (if y has a value other than **om**), the single pair $[x, y]$ is inserted into f. Thus f will contain exactly one pair $[x, y]$ whose first component is x, guaranteeing that now $f(x)$ will evaluate to y.
(c) However, if y has the value **om**, then only step (a), but not step (b), is performed. In this case x will simply have been removed from **domain** f, guaranteeing that $f(x)$ will evaluate to **om**.

Rules (a), (b), and (c) tell us that if y /= **om**, then (4) has exactly the same effect as the assignment

f := {z: z **in** f | z(1) /= x} **with** [x, y]; (5a)

while if y = **om**, then (4) has the same effect as the assignment

f := {z: z **in** f | z(1) /= x}. (5b)

The intuitive significance of the assignment (4) can be explained as follows: it directs us to drop any prior association to the element x that is recorded in f, and then to associate x with y (for which we insert the pair $[x, y]$ into f if y /= **om**, but simply leave x without any association if y = **om**). This is exactly the effect of steps (a–c).

For example, suppose again that f is the **map** (3), and that we first perform the assignment

f('Jones') := 'Thomas';

This changes f to

{['Jones', 'Thomas'], ['Khalid', 'Leila'], ['Smith', 'Mary'], ['Khalid', 'Fatima']}

Suppose that the assignment

$$f(\text{'Chang'}) := \text{'Zhong-Tien'};$$

is performed next. In this case, no pairs need to be removed from f, but one pair is added, changing f to

$$\{[\text{'Jones'}, \text{'Thomas'}], [\text{'Khalid'}, \text{'Leila'}], [\text{'Smith'}, \text{'Mary'}], [\text{'Chang'}, \text{'Zhong-Tien'}], [\text{'Khalid'}, \text{'Fatima'}]\}$$

Next, suppose that the assignment

$$\text{f('Cohen')} := \textbf{om};$$

is performed. This will simply remove all pairs with first component "Cohen" from f, but since there are none such, it will actually leave f unchanged. After this, suppose that the assignment

$$f(\text{'Khalid'}) := \text{'Nuri'};$$

is performed. This removes the pairs ['Khalid', 'Leila'] and ['Khalid', 'Fatima'] from f and gives f the value

$$\{[\text{'Jones'}, \text{'Thomas'}], [\text{'Smith'}, \text{'Mary'}], [\text{'Khalid'}, \text{'Nuri'}], [\text{'Chang'}, \text{'Zhong-Tien'}]\}$$

Assignments of the form (4), which change the element y associated with an element x, are generally used for one of three purposes:

(i) to update an attribute $f(x)$ of x;
(ii) to define an attribute of x which has previously been undefined;
(iii) to drop an attribute $f(x)$ that is no longer needed, which we do by executing

$$f(x) := \textbf{om}.$$

Suppose, for example, that a map called *count* is being used to keep track of the number of times that each word x has been seen in a body of text that is being scanned. On encountering a word, we test to see whether it has been seen before; if so, we simply increment its count. Otherwise, we must initialize its count attribute, which will be undefined, to the value 1. This is done by the following code, which uses several map assignment operations.

```
if count(x) = om then          $ word is new.
   count(x) := 1;              $ establish initial count for new word
else
   count(x) := count(x) + 1;   $ increment count if previously seen.
end if;
```

Note that a map assignment $f(x) := y$ begins (see (a)) by attempting to remove a certain set of pairs from f, which assumes that f is already a map. Hence the operation $f(x) := y$ (like the operations $y := f(x)$ and $y := f\{x\}$)

can only be applied *if* f *is already a map*. The question then arises as to how to initialize a map f. This can be done in one of two ways:

(i) If f is initially supposed to be the ("everywhere undefined") map whose domain is null (so that initially $f(x) = \textbf{om}$ for all x and $f\{x\} = \{\ \}$ for all x), we simply write

$$f := \{\ \};$$

This makes f the everywhere undefined map with null domain and null range.

(ii) A map value can be built up directly using a set former, providing that all the elements thus formed are pairs. For example, we can write

$$f := \{[x, \#x]: x \textbf{ in } \{\text{'Tom'}, \text{'Dick'}, \text{'Harry'}\}\};$$

This makes f into the map $\{[\text{'Tom'}, 3], [\text{'Dick'}, 4], [\text{'Harry'}, 5]\}$; i.e., f is a map with domain $\{\text{'Tom'}, \text{'Dick'}, \text{'Harry'}\}$, and f maps each element x in its domain into the length of x.

The *multivalued* map assignment

$$f\{x\} := y; \tag{6}$$

also has meaning in SETL. As the notation (6) suggests, this assignment modifies f in such a way as to cause the value $f\{x\}$ to be y immediately after the assignment (6) is executed. It follows that (6) makes sense only if the value of y is a set. Otherwise the operation (6) generates an error.

The multivalued map assignment (6) is performed as follows:

(a) We first check that f is a map (i.e., a set consisting of pairs only), and that y is a set. If either of these conditions is violated, an error is generated.

(b) All pairs x, y whose first component is x are removed from x. (This has the effect of removing x from **domain** f.)

(c) After this, the set of all pairs $[x, z]$, for all z in y, is added to f. This guarantees that $f\{x\}$ will evaluate to y.

These rules tell us that (6) has exactly the same effect as the assignment

$$\text{f} := \{\text{u: u } \textbf{in} \text{ f} \mid \text{u}(1) \mathrel{/=} \text{x}\} + \{[\text{x}, \text{z}]\text{: z } \textbf{in} \text{ y}\}. \tag{7}$$

Note therefore that if $y \mathrel{/=} \textbf{om}$, the single-valued assignment (4) has exactly the same effect as the map assignment

$$f\{x\} := \{y\}; \tag{8a}$$

if $y = \textbf{om}$, then the effect of (4) is exactly that of

$$f\{x\} := \{\ \}; \tag{8b}$$

The value (5b) given to f by either $f(x) := \textbf{om}$ or by $f\{x\} := \{\ \}$ can also be written in another form, using the map operator **lessf**:

$$\text{f} := \text{f } \textbf{lessf} \text{ x}; \tag{9}$$

which occasionally is more convenient. The expression f **lessf** x means "f less all the pairs in f whose first element is x." Note that (9), like the map assignment operators, applies only to maps and will generate an error if applied to a set f which contains any nonpair elements.

As an example, suppose again that f is the map

{['Jones', 'Tom'], ['Khalid', 'Leila'], ['Smith', 'Mary'], ['Khalid', 'Fatima']} (3)

Then after the assignment

f{'Khalid'} := f{'Khalid'} **with** 'Omar';

f will have the value

{['Jones', 'Tom'], ['Khalid', 'Leila'], ['Khalid', 'Omar'], ['Smith', 'Mary'], ['Khalid', 'Fatima']}

If we subsequently execute the assignment

f{'Jones'} := { };

then f will take on the value

{['Khalid', 'Leila'], ['Khalid', 'Omar'], ['Smith', 'Mary'], ['Khalid', 'Fatima']}

Along with the general set former construct, the map operations $f(x)$, $f\{x\}$, $f(x) := y$, and $f\{x\} := y$ are the most characteristic and important operations of the SETL language. Their importance derives from the fact that they allow arbitrary objects x to appear as *indices*; i.e., any object can appear as the x in a construct like $f(x)$ or $f(x) := y$. Of course, other, lower-level, programming languages, such as PL/1, PASCAL, and Ada, support constructs with exactly the syntax $f(x) := y$ and with a very similar intended use. However, in these other languages, an f used in this way must be an *array* (an object much like a SETL *tuple*), and the x appearing in $f(x)$ or in an assignment $f(x) := y$ must be a *discrete type*, which means an integer or something easily described by an integer. This complicates the manipulation of attributes associated with arbitrary objects x (and attribute manipulation is basic to programming). To manipulate attributes of a noninteger object x (say string or a set) in these other languages, one must first find a way of associating an integer with x and then must use this integer, instead of x itself, whenever the attributes of x need to be used or manipulated. This introduces a layer of artifice into programs, making them less direct, less readable, and more error-prone. This objection applies even to a language as elegant and powerful as APL, which only allows integers (and arrays of integers) to appear as indices. The only well-known languages which support something like the map operations of SETL are SNOBOL (through its TABLE feature) and some versions of LISP.

3.8.3 Some remarks on multivalued maps

When the elements of the range of a map are all of the same type, which is the common case, we often use that type to describe the map. For example, we speak of an integer-valued map f if $f(x)$ is always an integer value. Similarly we say that a map is set-valued if $f(x)$ is always a set.

Set-valued maps can be handled (in SETL) in one of two nearly equivalent styles. Either style is acceptable, and neither has any overwhelming advantage, but they are different, and to avoid error it is important to distinguish clearly between them. These two possibilities are as follows:

(i) A set-valued map f can be represented as a single-valued map whose value $f(x)$ is a set, but
(ii) The same map can be represented by a multivalued map g such that $g\{x\} = f(x)$.

If f is available, then g can be produced by writing

g := {[x, y]: x **in domain** f, y **in** f(x)} (10)

(Note the double iteration: for every element x in the domain of f we obtain the set $f(x)$, and for each element y in this set we add the pair $[x, y]$ to the map g.)

Conversely, if g is available, then f can be produced by writing

f := {[x, g{x}]: x **in domain** g} (11)

Note however that elements x such that $f(x) = \{\ \}$ contribute no pairs to the construction of g in (10). If there are such elements in f, and we perform (10) followed by (11) to recover f, then these elements will have disappeared, and $f(x)$ will now be **om**.

A new pair $[x, y]$ can be added to g simply by writing

g := g **with** [x, y];

The equivalent transformation of f must be written

f(x) := f(x) **with** y;

which is a bit clumsier.

To initialize g to a set of pairs defined by a condition C, one normally writes something like

g := {[x, y]: x **in** s1, y **in** s2 | C}

The corresponding initialization of f, namely

f := {[x, {y **in** s2 | C}]: x **in** s1};

is somewhat heavier.

These small technical differences sometimes lead one to prefer the "g" representation of set-valued maps to the "f" representation.

3.8.4 Two useful map operations

The *inverse* of a map g is the map h such that $[x, y]$ **in** h if and only if $[y, x]$ **in** g. (If g is single-valued, this is equivalent to the condition that $y = h(x)$ if and only if $x = g(y)$). We can produce h from g simply by writing

h := {[p(2), p(1)]: p **in** g};

Here we treat g as a set and iterate over it in the usual fashion. Successive values of the bound variable p are elements of g, namely pairs. We simply reverse the two components of these pairs to construct the elements of the inverse map. This important construction occurs frequently.

The "product" or "composite" of two maps $g1$, $g2$ is the map G such that $[x, y]$ **in** G if and only if there exists a z such that $[x, z]$ **in** $g1$ and $[z, y]$ **in** $g2$. (If $g1$ and $g2$ are both single-valued, this is equivalent to $G(x) = g2(g1(x))$.) To produce G from $g1$ and $g2$, we can simply write

G := {[x, y]: x **in domain** g1, z **in** g1{x}, y **in** g2{z}};

In other words: $g1$ maps each element x of its domain into a set $g\{x\}$; each element z of this set may be mapped by $g2$ into a set $g2\{z\}$; and the composition of the two maps establishes a mapping from x to each one of the elements of $g2\{z\}$.

If $g1$ and $g2$ are single-valued, their composition is expressed more simply by

G := {[x, g2(g1(x))]: x **in domain** g1 | g2(g1(x)) /= **om**};

This *map product* operation is also quite important. For example, if Fa maps each person x onto the father of x, and Mo maps each person y onto the mother of y, then the composite of Mo and Fa maps each person x onto x's paternal grand-mother, while the composite of Fa and Mo maps each x onto x's maternal grand-father.

3.8.5 Multiparameter maps

As noted previously, maps f are used to associate attributes $f(x)$ or sets $f\{x\}$ of attributes with elements x. It is occasionally necessary to deal with attributes $f(x1, \ldots, xk)$ that depend on two or more objects $x1, \ldots, xk$. For this purpose, the generalized map operations

$$f\{x1, \ldots, xk\} \tag{1a}$$

$$f(x1, \ldots, xk) \tag{1b}$$

and the corresponding map assignments

$$f\{x1, \ldots, xk\} := y \tag{2a}$$

$$f(x1, \ldots, xk) := y \tag{2b}$$

are provided. These simply abbreviate

$$f\{[x1,\ldots,xk]\} \qquad (1a')$$

$$f([x1,\ldots,xk]) \qquad (1b')$$

and

$$f\{[x1,\ldots,xk]\} := y \qquad (2a')$$

$$f([x1,\ldots,xk]) := y \qquad (2b')$$

respectively. That is, a *multiparameter* map $f(x1,\ldots,xk)$ of k parameters is regarded simply as a map whose domain consists of tuples of length k. Such a map cannot be used as a function of any smaller number of parameters, since for $j < k$ we will always have $f\{x1,\ldots xj\} = \{\ \}$.

All the map constructs of SETL can be used with multiparameter maps if they are regarded as one parameter maps whose domain elements are tuples. For example, if f is a k-parameter map, then **domain** f will be a set of tuples of length k.

3.9 Compound Operators

Many common calculations on collections of values (sets or tuples) involve the combination of all the elements of this collection by means of some binary operator. For example, if t is a tuple of integers, and we want to compute their average value, we will need first to evaluate their sum, that is to say:

$$t(1) + t(2) + \cdots t(n) \qquad (1)$$

Such computations are common enough that SETL provides a special notation for them. For example, (1) can be written as

$$+/t$$

(read: "plus over t", or "sum over t"). The combination +/ is called a *composite operator*. In this case it is analogous to standard mathematical notation, which would be written:

$$\sum_{i=1}^{N} t(i)$$

For any binary operator *bop*, and any composite object *O*, the notation

$$bop/O \qquad (1a)$$

has the same meaning as the expression

$$e1\ bop\ e2\ bop \ldots bop\ en \qquad (2a)$$

obtained by combining all the elements or components *ej* of *O* together using the binary operator *bop* repeatedly. If *O* contains only one element or component, then the value of (2a) is $e1$, that is to say that single component. If O is empty, then the value of (2a) is undefined, i.e., **om**. For example, if S is the set $\{1..5\}$ then

+/S	yields	15
*/S	yields	120
+/{x **in** S | x < 4}	yields	6
*/[x **in** S | x > 4]	yields	5
+/{x **in** S | x < 0}	yields	**om**

Not all binary operators can be used to construct composite operators: if *a op b op c* is to make sense, then the type of the expression (*a op b*) must also be a valid argument to *op*. The arithmetic operators satisfy this condition, but the comparison operators (for example, >=) do not. Also, binary operations which are not associative (for example, **mod**) may give strange results if used in this context.

In addition to the "prefix" form (1a), composite operators can also be used in "infix" form:

$$x\ bop/O \tag{1b}$$

where x is an expression of a valid type for the operator. (1b) is equivalent to the expression

$$x\ bop\ e1\ bop\ e2\ bop \ldots bop\ en, \tag{2b}$$

where again the ej are all the elements or components of O, and the argument x is used for the first application of *bop*. If O is empty, the value of (1b) is the left argument x.

Here are further examples of use of compound operators:

0 +/ t	yields the sum of all elements of t, 0 if t is null
max/s	yields the maximum element in s, **om** if s is null

If t is a tuple of strings, say ['first', 'next', 'last'], then

+/*t* yields 'firstnextlast'

obtained by concatenating the strings. On the other hand, if S is a set of strings, say {'one', 'another'} then

+/*S* yields 'oneanother', or maybe 'anotherone'

because once again S has no definite ordering, and its elements are chosen in some arbitrary way when computing (1a) or (1b).

If a and b are tuples that represent vectors in some space, then

0 +/ [a(i)*b(i): t **in** [1 .. #a]]

is the *scalar* or *dot* product of vectors *a* **and** *b*. If t is a tuple of integers, then

1*/[x **in** t | x /= 0] (3)

is the product of all the nonzero components of t, or 1 if t is empty. If t is the tuple [0, 2, 0, 2, 5, 2], then the value of (3) is 40. Notice that

$$1*/\{x \textbf{ in } t \mid x \mathrel{/=} 0\} \qquad (3a)$$

which looks very similar to (3), has a different value, namely 10. (Can you see why, before reading further?)

(The reason is that $\{x \textbf{ in } t \mid x \mathrel{/=} 0\}$ is the set $\{2, 5\}$ with no duplicate values, and $[x \textbf{ in } t \mid x \mathrel{/=} 0]$ is the tuple $[2, 2, 5, 2]$. When you want to apply a composite operator over some collection of values, you should examine carefully whether the collection should be represented by a set without duplicate elements, or as a tuple. The results can differ, as the examples demonstrate.)

The compound operator *bop/* can be formed with either the built-in binary operators of SETL or with user-defined binary operators. User-defined binary operators are presented in Section 5.6.2. One can for example introduce an infix operator comp which forms the composite f comp g of two maps, as defined by the formula

$$\text{f comp g} = \{[x, f(y)]\text{: x } \textbf{in domain} \text{ g, y } \textbf{in} \text{ g}\{x\} \mid f(y) \mathrel{/=} \textbf{om}\},$$

then comp/t will form the composite $f1$ comp $f2 \ldots$ comp fn of a sequence $[f1, f2, \ldots, fn]$ of maps, and comp/$[f\text{: } k \textbf{ in } [1 \, .. \, n]]$ will form the *n-th power* of the map f; i.e., the result of taking its composition with itself $n - 1$ times.

3.10 Types and type-testing operators

As we have seen, the possible types of SETL values are **atom, boolean, integer, real, string, set,** and **tuple**. Given a variable x, it is often useful to know what the type of its current value is. This type may change as the result of successive assignments. The built-in unary operator **type** applies to any value or expression and produces its type, as a capitalized string: i.e., for any x with a definite value, type x is either 'ATOM', 'BOOLEAN', 'INTEGER', 'REAL', 'STRING', 'SET', or 'TUPLE'. SETL also provides a set of built-in binary operators called **is_atom, is_boolean, is_integer, is_string, is_set, is_tuple,** each of which yields **true** if applied to an object of the corresponding type, **false** if applied to an object of any other type.

One additional unary *operator*, **is_map**, yields **true** when applied to a set all of whose elements are pairs, **false** otherwise.

The undefined value **om** cannot be expected to have a type, and indeed the expression **type(om)** yields **om** itself. In addition, any of the type predicates, such as **is_set(om) or is_atom(om)**, yields **false**.

3.11 The ? Operator

In certain situations undefined (i.e., **om**) results can be expected to appear, and one will want to replace them by some other default values when they do appear. A typical situation of this kind was described in Section 3.8.2, when counting the number of occurrences of words in a text: it is natural to use

count(*wd*) := count(*wd*) + 1;

to update a map, *count*, representing the number of times each word *wd* has been seen. But then, if *wd* has never been seen before, count(*wd*) will be **om**, and we will want to initialize it to the meaningful default value of 0. To do this we can write as before

if count(wd) = **om then** count(wd) := 0; **end if**;
count(wd) := count(wd) + 1; (1)

However, since constructs like this occur so frequently, the abbreviation *x* ? *y*, which makes them easier to express, is provided. The value of the expression *x* ? *y* is the value of *x*, if this value is defined; else it is the value of *y*. Using this convenient operator, we can write (1) simply as

count(*wd*) := count(*wd*) ? 0 + 1;

As another example, we can construct the composite operator ?/, which when applied to a tuple *T* yields the first component of *T* which is not undefined.

?/[**om**, **om**, {1}, { }, **om**, 3] yields {1}

Exercises

1. Which of the following equations are valid for all tuples t1, t2, t3 and positive integers n, m?

   (a) t1 + t2 = t2 + t1
   (b) t1 + (t2 + t3) = (t1 + t2) + t3
   (c) #(n*t1) = n* #t1
   (d) n*(t1 + t2) = n*t1 + n*t2
   (e) (n + m)*t1 = n*t1 + m*t1
   (f) (n*m)*t1 = n*(m*t1)

   If an equation is not always true, give an example showing a case in which it is false.

2. Given a tuple *t*, write an expression which forms a tuple *t*1 in which every distinct component of *t* occurs exactly once. For example, if *t* is [1, 2, 1, 2, 3, 3], *t*1 should be [1, 2, 3]. Also, write an expression which forms the set of all components of *t* which occur at least twice in *t*.

3. Given a tuple *t*, write an expression which counts the number of non-**om** components of *t*. Also, write an expression that produces a tuple with the same components as *t*, but in reverse order.

4. What are the values of the following Boolean expressions?

   (a) [1, 2, [3, 4]] = [1, 2, 3, 4]
   (b) 3 **in** [1, 2, [3, 4]]
   (c) #[1, 2, **om**, 3, **om**] = 4
   (d) [1, 2, [3, 4], **om**] /= [1, 2, 3, 4]
   (e) [1..4] = [1, 2, 3, 4]

5. The tuple t is [1, **om**, 2, **om**, 3]. Evaluate the following sequences:

(a)	$t(1)$, $t(2)$, $t(3)$, $t(4)$, $t(5)$
(b)	$t(1..1)$, $t(2..2)$, t(3..3), $t(4..4)$, $t(5..5)$
(c)	$t(1..)$, $t(2..)$, $t(3..)$, $t(4..)$, $t(5..)$

6. Write a program which calculates the set of all integers from 2 to 100 which are the product of exactly two primes.

7. The Goldbach conjecture states that every even number greater than 2 can be written as the sum of two prime numbers. Write a one-statement SETL program which verifies that this conjecture is true for the first 100 even numbers.

8. Write a program which prints all the numbers from 2 to 100 together with their prime factorizations. The first three entries printed should be

```
2  [2]
3  [3]
4  [2,2]
```

9. The tuple t is ['Tom', 'Dick', 'Harry', 'Sue', 'Lois']. Write a tuple former whose components are those components of t which contain at least two vowels.

10. Write a tuple assignment of the form $t(i..j) := x$ which will convert the tuple t = [1, 2, 3] to each of the following:

(a)	[4, 5, 6, 7]
(b)	[ ]
(c)	[1, 3]
(d)	[1, **om**, **om**, 3]
(e)	[1, 4, 10, 3]

11. Write a program that reads a tuple t of numbers and prints its three largest components in decreasing order.

12. Changing as few of the elements of the set {[1, 2], [3, 4], [5], [ ]} as possible, produce a set s such that **is_map**(s) evaluates to true.

13. Given a tuple t of integers, write an expression which yields the index of the largest component of t.

14. Assuming that $s1$ and $s2$ are nonnull sets of integers, in what cases do the equations

$$+/(s1 + s2) = +/s1 +/ s2$$

and

$$*/(s1 + s2) = */s1*/s2$$

hold? What happens if $s1$ or $s2$ is null? How can we keep the null case from being exceptional?

15. Write a definition of the sets **domain** f and **range** f using set formers.

16. The inverse inv f of a map f is the set of all pairs $[y, x]$ for which $[x, y]$ belongs to f. Express inv (inv f) in terms of f using a set former.

17. Given a map f, express the set s of all x for which $f(x)$ is different from **om** in terms

of f. What is the relationship between s and **domain** f? In particular, when are s and **domain** f identical?

18. Express the condition

[x, y] **in** f

in terms of the image set $f\{x\}$.

19. Let f denote the set

{[i, j]: i **in** [1 .. 10], j **in** [1 .. 10] | i > j}

What is the domain of f? What is the range of f? For what x is $f(x)$ different from **om**? What is $f\{5\}$? What is $f(5)$? What is the inverse map g (cf. Ex. 16) of the map f?

20. Answer Ex. 19, but for the set f defined by the set former

{[i, i*i]: *i* **in** [−5 .. 5]}

21. Answer the questions in Exercise 19, but for the set f defined by the set former

{[i, i*(i − 1)]: i **in** [−5 .. 5]}

22. The map f has the set of strings 'Tom', 'Dick', 'Harry', 'Louis' as its domain; the map $f1$ has 'Sue', 'Mary', 'Helen', 'Martha' as its domain. Each of these maps sends every string element s of its domain into the length $\#s$ of s. The maps F and $F1$ are the inverses of f and $f1$, respectively (see Ex. 16). Answer the questions in Ex. 19, but for the sets F and $F1$, the union set $F + F1$, and the intersection $F*F1$.

23. Let f be the map

{[i, i*i]: i **in** [−2 .. 2]}

(a) Write a series of map assignments of the form $f(x) := y$ which will make f equal to the null set { }.
(b) Write a series of such assignments which makes inv f single-valued by reducing its domain progressively.
(c) Write a series of such assignments which makes inv f single-valued without ever changing its range.

24. The range of a map is the null set { }. What is the domain of the map? What is the map?

25. The range of a map is defined over (a subset of) {**true**, **false**} and its domain is defined over (a subset of) {1, 2, 3}.
(a) How many elements can the map itself contain?
(b) How many such maps are there?
(c) How many such single-valued maps are there?
(d) How many such maps are there if the domains include all elements of {1, 2, 3}?
(e) How many such maps are there whose range includes both elements {**true**, **false**}?
(f) Write SETL expressions which will evaluate the answers to all these questions.

26. (a) The range of a map is the set {**true**, **false**}. How many elements can the map itself contain?

(b) The domain of a map f consists of the three elements $\{1, 2, 3\}$. How many elements can the map itself contain? If we suppose that f is single-valued, how many elements can the map itself contain, and how many elements can its domain contain?

27. A set s is a subset of every other set. What is s? A map f is a subset of every other map. What is f?

28. Suppose that the variable s has a set value, the variable t has a tuple value, and the variables $s1$ and $s2$ have string values. Write expressions which produce the following quantities:
(a) A tuple whose components are the elements of s, arranged in some order.
(b) A set whose elements are the components of t, with duplicates eliminated.
(c) A tuple whose components are the successive characters of $s1$.
(d) Assuming that $s1$ and $s2$ have the same length, a map from each character of $s1$ to the corresponding character of $s2$.

29. Given two sets $s1$ and $s2$, express $\#(s1 + s2)$ in terms of $\#s1$, $\#s2$, and $\#(s1*s2)$. If $s2$ **incs** $s1$ is **true**, express $\#(s1 - s2)$ in terms of $\#s1$ and $\#s2$.

30. Given two sets $s1$ and $s2$, express the number of single-valued maps f such that **domain** $f = s1$ and **range** $f = s2$ in terms of $s1$ and $s2$.

31. The map part of a set s is the collection of all elements of s which are ordered pairs. Write an expression whose value for any given s is the map part of s. (Make sure that your expression can be evaluated for any value of s, whether or not this value is a set; if s is not a set, your expression should have the value **om**.)

32. The single-valued part of a map s is the set of all pairs in s whose first component is unique. Taking the same precaution noted in Ex. 31, write an expression whose value for any given s is the single-valued part of s.

33. Write an expression which will take any SETL tuple t and generate a map f which indicates how many components of t are of type 'ATOM', 'BOOLEAN', 'INTEGER', etc., and how many components of t are **om**.

34. Generate about a hundred random pairs of tuples, $t1$ and $t2$, of the same length, all of whose components are floating-point numbers. Then count the number of those t's which satisfy the following inequality:

```
(+/[x*x: in t1])*(+/[x*x: x in t2])
        >= abs(+/[t1(i) + t2(i): i in [1.. #t1]])**2.
```

(Be careful not be fooled by small errors in the computation; i.e., a pair of tuples that barely satisfies or fails to satisfy the preceding equality should be considered indeterminate and ignored). What percentage of the tuples tested satisfy this inequality? What do you deduce from this?

35. Build and print out the following sets, letting x vary over 10 floating-point numbers chosen at random from the range of 1.0 to 10.0:
(a) The set of x for which x**0 or x**0.0 is different from 1.0.
(b) The set of x for which x**0 or x**0.0 is different from 1.
(c) The set of all differences **sqrt**(x) − x**0.5.
(d) The set of all differences x**0.5 − x**(1.0/2.0).

(e) The set of all differences $x*x - x**2.0$.
(f) The set of all differences $x**2 - x**2.0$.
(g) The set of all differences $x - (x**3)**(1.0/3.0)$.
(h) The set of all differences $x*x/x - x$
(i) The set of all x such that $\mathbf{sin}(x)**2 + \mathbf{cos}(x)**2 = 1.0$.

3.12 General Form of the SETL Assignment: The Operators **from**, **frome**, & **fromb**

In preceding sections, we have observed that some of the constructs which can appear in an expression, and which retrieve values or parts of values, can also appear on the left hand side of an assignment, allowing the corresponding values to be assigned or modified. For example, when it appears in an expression the expression $f\{x\}$ retrieves the image set of x under the map f, but when it appears to the left of an assignment, as in

$$f\{x\} := e;$$

then the image set of x becomes e. Similarly, when the expression $s(i..j)$ appears in an expression it yields a string or tuple slice, but when it appears to the left of an assignment, as in

$$s(i..j) := e;$$

it causes the value of this string or tuple slice to become e.

Constructs which can appear to the left of an assignment operator can also appear in expressions, and the relationship between left-hand and right-hand appearances (i.e., ordinary appearances within an expression) of any such construct always exhibits an important logical symmetry. Specifically, if *lhs* denotes any construct which, like the constructs $f\{x\}$ and $s(i..j)$, can appear to the left of an assignment, then the effect of the assignment

$$lhs := e;$$

is to assure that immediately subsequent evaluation of *lhs* (within an expression, i.e., in a "right-hand" context) will yield the assigned value e.

The elementary constructs which are allowed to appear to the left of an assignment operator are the following:

(i) A variable identifier x. The assignment

$$x := e;$$

modifies the value of x.

(ii) A tuple-former $[x1, \ldots, xk]$. (Notice that the ellipsis $(\ldots)$ stands for some unspecified number of other components of the tuple. This should not be confused with the SETL substring operation $s(x..y)$).

The assignment

$$[x1,\ldots,xk] := e;$$

where e must be a tuple, modifies the value of each of x1, ..., sk and is equivalent to the series of simple assignments:

$$x1 := e(1);$$
$$x2 := e(2);$$
$$\ldots$$
$$xk := e(k);$$

In such an assignment, any of the xj can be replaced by the dummy symbol "—" (dash), in which case no assignment is performed for this particular xj. (This is the one exception to the general rule that any construct which can appear to the left of an assignment can also appear to its right.) As an example of this, note that the assignment

$$[x, -, y] := [1,2,3]; \qquad (1a)$$

gives x the value 1 and y the value 3. Moreover, the assignment

$$[x, -, y] := [1,2,3,4]; \qquad (1b)$$

has the same effect, since the fact that y occurs as the third component of the tuple on the left of (1b) means that the third component of the right-hand side of (1b) will be assigned to y. For the same reason, the assignment

$$[x, -, y, z, w] := [1,2,3,4]; \qquad (1c)$$

gives x, y, z, and w the respective values 1, 3, 4, and **om**.

(iii) A tuple, string, or map selection $f(x)$. The assignment

$$f(i) := e;$$

modifies component i of f if f is a tuple, character i of f if f is a string, and the value $f(i)$ if f is a map.

(iv) A multiparameter map selection $f(x1,\ldots,xk)$. This is equivalent to $f([x1,\ldots,xk])$, and the assignment

$$f(x1,\ldots,xk) := e;$$

is equivalent to $f([x1,\ldots,xk]) := e$.

(v) A multivalued selection $f\{x\}$. The assignment

$$f\{x\} := e;$$

modifies the set $f\{x\}$.

(vi) A multivalued, multiparameter map selection $f\{x1,\ldots,xk\}$. This is equivalent to $f\{[x1,\ldots,xk]\}$, and the corresponding assignment

$$f\{x1,\ldots,xk\} := e;$$

is equivalent to $f\{[x1,\ldots,xk]\} := e$;

(vii) A string or tuple slice $t(i..j)$ or $t(i..)$. The effect of

$$t(i..j) := e \textbf{ or } t(i..) := e$$

is to modify the portion $t(i..j)$ of the string or tuple. Note that the value of the string or tuple expression e may have a length different from that of the subsection of t which e replaces, so these assignments can increase or decrease length of t. See Section 2.5.3 and 3.6.3, also Table 2.1, for a discussion of marginal cases of these assignments, e.g., $j = i - 1$, and $i = \#t + 1$.

Simple expressions, of any of the types we have just listed, which can appear on the left of an assignment can also be compounded to build up more complex *assignment targets* that are also allowed to appear to the left of an assignment operator. For example, if f and g are maps, t is a tuple, and s is a string, then the assignment

$$[[x, y], f(u), g\{v\}, s(j..)] := e; \tag{1a}$$

is a legal assignment, whose effect is the same as that of the following sequence of assignments:

$$\begin{aligned} x &:= e(1)(1); \quad \$\ \text{The first component of the first component} \\ y &:= e(1)(2); \\ f(u) &:= e(2); \\ g\{v\} &:= e(3); \\ s(j..) &:= e(4); \end{aligned} \tag{1b}$$

Map and tuple component extraction operators can also be compounded; e.g., we are allowed to write $h\{u\}(v)(i)$ if h is a map such that $H1 = h\{u\}$ is also a map such that $H1(v)$ is a tuple whose i-th component can be extracted. The value x that $h\{u\}(v)(i)$ produces is exactly that produced by the sequence

$$\begin{aligned} H1 &:= h\{u\}; \\ H2 &:= H1(v); \\ x &:= H2(i); \end{aligned}$$

where $H1$ and $H2$ are otherwise unused, compiler-generated variables. Compounds of this sort can also be used to the left of assignment operators; for example we can write

$$h\{u\}(v)(i) := e; \tag{2a}$$

This has exactly the same effect as the following sequence, into which the SETL compiler expands (2a):

$$\begin{aligned} H1 &:= h\{u\}; \\ H2 &:= H1(v); \\ H2(i) &:= e; \\ H1(v) &:= H2; \\ h\{u\} &:= H1; \end{aligned} \tag{2b}$$

The general rules used to expand compound assignments can be stated as follows:

(i) An assignment of the form

$$[e1,\ldots,ek] := x \tag{3a}$$

is legal if, for each j between 1 and k, either ej is the sign "—" (dash), or else the assignment

$$ej := y$$

is itself legal. If it is legal, (3a) is expanded into the sequence:

$$\begin{aligned} e1 &:= x(1);\\ &\ldots\\ ek &:= x(k); \end{aligned} \tag{3b}$$

but in (3b) every assignment corresponding to an ej of the form "—" is omitted.

(ii) An assignment of one of the forms

$$e(i) := x; \tag{4a}$$
$$e(i1,\ldots,ik) := x; \tag{4b}$$
$$e\{y\} := x; \tag{4c}$$
$$e\{y1,\ldots,yk\} := x; \tag{4d}$$
$$e(i..j) := x; \tag{4e}$$
$$e(i..) := x; \tag{4f}$$

is legal if and only if e is an expression, other than a tuple former $[z1,\ldots,zk]$, which can appear to the left of an assignment operator, and if in addition the corresponding code sequence

temp_var := e; temp_var(i) := x; e := temp_var; (5a)
temp_var := e; temp_var($i1,..,ik$) := x; e := temp_var; (5b)
temp_var := e; temp_var$\{y\}$:= x; e := temp_var; (5c)
temp_var := e; temp_var$\{y1,..,yk\}$:= x; e := temp_var; (5d)
temp_var := e; temp_var($i..j$) := x; e := temp_var; (5e)
temp_var := e; temp_var($i..$) := x; e := temp_var; (5f)

would be legal. When an operation (4a–f) is legal, it is expanded into the corresponding assignment sequence (5a–f). Of course, the final assignment of each of these sequences may itself require expansion; if necessary, this is performed recursively, leading to expansions like those shown in (1b) and (2b).

3.12.1 Assigning forms of infix operators

Assignments of the form

$$lhs := lhs\ \mathbf{op}\ e; \tag{6}$$

where **op** designates any built-in (or user-defined, see Section 5.6.2) infix operator, and *lhs* designates any simple or compound expression which can legally appear to the left of an assignment operator, are extremely common. In SETL such assignments can be abbreviated as

$$lhs\ \mathbf{op} := e; \qquad (7)$$

For example, we can abbreviate

$$i := i + 1;$$

as

$$i + := 1;$$

and

$$x := x\ \mathbf{max}\ y;$$

as

$$x\ \mathbf{max} := y;$$

3.12.2 Assignment expressions

Simple assignments $x := y$ (and even more complex assignments such as $f\{u\}(v) := y$) can be used as expressions. The value of such an expression is simply its right-hand-side y, but of course evaluation of such an expression always has a side effect; namely it modifies the value of the left-hand side. Because of this side effect, such an assignment is not strictly speaking an expression but can appear anywhere an expression can.

Assignment expressions of this sort are frequently used to abbreviate sequences of assignments which initialize a collection of variables by giving the same value to all of them. For example, the assignment

$$x := y := z := w := 0;$$

which is equivalent to

$$x := (y := (z := (w := 0)));$$

gives all four variables x, y, z, w the value zero. Another common use of assignment expressions is to save the value of quantities that one needs to use just past the point at which they are first evaluated. The code fragment

$$\mathbf{if}\ (x := \mathrm{f(u)} + \mathrm{g(v)})\ \mathbf{in}\ \mathrm{s}\ \mathbf{then}\ \mathrm{f(u)} := \mathrm{x};\ \mathbf{else} \ldots \qquad (8)$$

illustrates this. Since the quantity $f(u) + g(v)$ is needed immediately after the test in which it is first evaluated, the programmer may find it convenient to assign this quantity as the value of an auxiliary variable x, saving reevaluation, and, equally important, abbreviating the program source text. A related example, showing another common use of the assignment expression construct, is

```
if (x := y + z) >0 then
                positives with := x;
    else                                        (9)
                negatives with := x;
    end if;
```

Overenthusiastic use of assignment expressions will lead to a crabbed programming style in which important operations flit by without sufficient syntactic emphasis. This will be bad if it deprives a program's reader of too much of the redundancy on which understanding of the program depends. A good rule of thumb is to use an assignment expression only when the subsequent target variable of the expression is used again within a few lines (less than 5, say) after the assigning expression itself.

3.12.3 Other positions in which assignment targets are allowed

There are a few of the other positions in which variables can occur that resemble the left-hand sides of assignment operators, in that new values are assigned to variables appearing in these positions when the contexts containing them are evaluated. These *assigning positions* are as follows:

(i) The position of *x* in an iterator

```
x in s|...
```

is assigning, since the iterator will assign successive values to *x*. The same remark applies to the position of *x* in an existential quantifier

```
exists x in s|...
```

and in a universal quantifier

```
forall x in s|...
```

This means that in such an iterator, the bound variable need not be a variable name, but can be any valid left-hand side. For example, if m is a map, then we know that in the iterator:

```
p in m
```

the successive values of *p* are tuples of length 2, *p*(1) is in the domain of *m*, and *p*(2) in its range. The components of *p* can be obtained if we write the iterator directly as

```
[x, y] in m
```

Now *x* and *y* are both bound by the iterator; in the course of the iteration, *x* will receive the value of successive elements of the domain of *m*, and *y* the corresponding element in the range. With this notation, the inverse map of m can be written simply as

m_inverse := {[y, x]: [x, y] **in** m};

Of course, the same remark applies to variables appearing in corresponding positions in multiple iterators, as in the case of the variables x, y, and x in

x **in** s, y **in** t, z **in** [1 .. n] | . . .

(ii) The position of x and i in a map, tuple, or string iterator (to be discussed in Chapter 4)

$$x = f(i) \,|\, ..$$

or in a multivalued map iterator

$$x = f\{i\} \,|\, ..$$

is assigning. Of course, the corresponding positions in multiple iterators and in quantifiers are also assigning positions.

(iii) Argument positions in function and procedure invocations corresponding to formal procedure or function parameters (see Chapter 5) that carry the read/write qualifier RW are also assigning positions.

Precisely the same expressions that can appear to the left of an assignment operator are allowed to appear in any other assigning position. Thus, for example, the construction

x + y **in** s | . . .

is illegal, since

$$x + y := e$$

would also be illegal; $x + y$ is not a legal assignment target. On the other hand,

[x, y] **in** s | C (10a)

f(x) **in** s | C (10b)

[[u, v], y] **in** s | C (10c)

are all legal, and have the same respective meanings as the code fragments

(*for* temp_var **in** s) [x, y] := temp_var; **if not** C **then quit**; **end**; (11a)

(*for* temp_var **in** s)f(x) := temp_var; **if not** C **then quit**; **end**; (11b)

(*for* temp_var **in** s) [[u, v], y] := temp_var; **if not** C **then quit**; **end**; (11c)

Much the same remark applies to quantifiers containing iterators in assigning positions, for example, in

. . . **exists** [x, y] **in** s | C(x, y) . . . (12)

The iteration implicit in the existential quantifier (12) will generate successive elements z of s and perform an implicit assignment $[x, y] := z$ before the Boolean expression $C(x, y)$ is evaluated.

As already noted, the position of i in

$$\textbf{(for } \text{x = f(i)} \mid \ldots) \ldots \tag{13a}$$

and in

$$\textbf{(for } \text{x = f\{i\}} \mid \ldots) \ldots \tag{13b}$$

also the positions of $i1, \ldots, ik$ in

$$\textbf{(for } \text{x = f(i1,} \ldots \text{,ik)} \mid \ldots) \ldots \tag{13c}$$

and in

$$\textbf{(for } \text{x = f\{i1,} \ldots \text{,ik\}} \mid \ldots) \ldots \tag{13d}$$

are assigning.

Any expression which can appear to the left of an assignment operator can be substituted for the i in (13a) or (13b), or for any of $i1$ through ik in (13c) or (13d).

$$[x, y] = f([u, v]) \mid C(x, y, u, v)) \tag{14}$$

In (14), the iterator will generate successive elements z of the domain of f and w of its range and then perform implicit assignments $[x, y] := w$ and $[u, v] := z$ before the Boolean expression $C(x, y, u, v)$ is evaluated. Note also that (13c) and (13d) are equivalent to

$$\textbf{(for } \text{x = f([i1,} \ldots \text{,ik])} \mid \ldots) \ldots \tag{15c}$$

and

$$\textbf{(for } \text{x = f\{[i1,} \ldots \text{,ik]\}} \mid \ldots) \ldots \tag{15d}$$

respectively.

3.12.4 The operators **from**, **frome**, and **fromb**

As we will see in coming chapters, a very common model for solving problems involving sets has the following form: construct a set that details the work to be done; then remove some arbitrary element of the set, process it in some fashion, and continue until the set (often called a workpile) becomes empty. This model is also often used with tuples, in cases where the order in which we must tackle the work to be done is important. For this purpose, SETL provides three related operators: **from**, **frome**, and **fromb**. All these of them have an assignmentlike effect. The first of these, namely

x **from** s; (16a)

where s is a set, is equivalent to the following code fragment:

```
x := arb s;     $ Choose any element of s.
s := s less x;  $ Remove it from s.
```
(16b)

Thus the statement (16a) has an effect on both of its arguments: it assigns to the left argument and removes something from the right. The alert reader will easily guess that the left argument of **from** is in an assigning position and can therefore be any valid left-hand side. In fact so is the right-hand side, as (16b) makes clear. For example, if T is a tuple of maps, we might write

```
[f(a), g(b)] from T(x);
```

which is equivalent to

```
p := arb T(x);
f(a) := p(1);
g(b) := p(2);
T(x) less := p;
```

If s is the null set, then the effect of (16a) is to set x to **om** and leave s untouched (there is nothing we can remove from it).

In the case of tuples, it turns out to be useful to be able to specify that the element being removed should come from either the beginning or the end of the tuple. Accordingly, the two operators forms provided are

```
x frome t;   $ take x 'from the end' of t          (17a)
x fromb t;   $ take x 'from the beginning' of t    (17b)
```

The effect of (17a) is to remove the last (non-**om**) component of t and assign it to the variable x. If t is the null tuple, then x becomes **om** and t remains null. The effect of (17b) is to remove the first component of t and assign it to the variable x. If this first component is **om**, then x becomes **om**, but t is reduced in length by 1 (its leading **om** component is removed). If t is null, then x becomes **om** and t remains null.

Like (16a), the forms (17a) and (17b) can be used as expressions. When used in this way they both yield the value assigned to x.

Note that, if t has **om** components immediately preceding its last non-**om** component, then (17a) can decrease the length of t by more than 1. For example, the sequence

```
t := [1, 2, om, om, 3];
x frome t; y frome t;
print(x, y, #t);
```

will produce the output

```
3 2 1.
```

If a tuple is constructed solely by means of the **with** operator, which adds elements to the end of the tuple, and subsequently modified by means of **with** and **frome**, the last element that was added to the tuple is always the first one to be removed from it. Such a structure is known as a "last in, first out," or *lifo*, structure, or more commonly as a *stack*.

Conversely, if a tuple is built by means of **with**, and modified by means of **with** and **fromb**, then the first element that was added to the tuple is always the first one to be removed, and a tuple used in such a fashion is known as a "first in, first out," or *fifo*, structure, or also as a *queue*. If elements are added to a tuple at both ends and removed from either end, the resulting structure is called a *deque*.

3.13 Operator Precedence Rules

The following table shows the precedence rules which determine the order in which the operators in an expression are evaluated. If two operators share a common operand, then the one with the higher precedence is evaluated first. If both operators have the same precedence, then the left-hand one is evaluated first (i.e., operators of a given precedence level are evaluated in a *left-associative* manner.)

Parentheses can be used freely to emphasize or alter the order of operations as determined by this table.

Precedence	Operators
11	:= (*on left side*) *assigning operators* (*on left side*) **from** (*both sides*)
10	*all unary operators except* **not** *and the* **is_***xx operators*
9	**
8	* / **mod div**
7	+ − **max, min**
6	*user-defined binary operators*
5	= /= < <= > >= **in notin subset incs**
4	**not** *and the* **is_***xx operators*
3	**and**
2	**or**
1	**impl**
0	:= (*on right side*) *assigning operators* (*on right side*)

The following examples of equivalent expressions with and without parentheses illustrate the operation of these rules:

$$a + b + c*d$$

is the same as

(a + b) + (c*d).

a + b + := c **div** d

is the same as

a + (b + := (c **div** d)).

a + **ceil** b := c

is the same as

$$a + (\textbf{ceil}(b := c)).$$

EXERCISES

1. Given that t is a tuple, explain the meaning of $?/t$.

2. Write a set former which will produce the set of all proper subsets of a set s, i.e., the set of all subsets $s1$ of s which are different from s.

3. In how many ways can two pairs of parentheses be inserted into the expression

$$1 + 2 - 3*4 \textbf{ div } 5$$

to produce a legal expression? Take 20 of these expressions and write their values. Do the same for

$$1 + 2 - - 3*4 \textbf{ div } 5.$$

4. Express $\#\textbf{pow}(s)$ in terms of $\#s$. Is there any set such that $s = \textbf{pow}(s)$? For what sets is $\#\textbf{pow}(s) = 1$? Is there any set that $\#s = \#\textbf{pow}(s)$? Is there any set such that $\#\textbf{pow}(s) = 2$?

5. Given two sets s and t, their Cartesian product cprod(s, t) is $\{[x, y]: x \textbf{ in } s, y \textbf{ in } t\}$. Express $\#$cprod(s, t) in terms of $\#s$ and $\#t$. If cprod$(s, t) = \{ \}$, what are s and t? Express $\#$cprod(s, t) in terms of $\#$cprod(t, s).

6. Determine the type of the value of x in each of the following code fragments, assuming that the code shown executes without causing any error.

(a)
```
x := z + 1;
```
(b)
```
x := z + '1';
```
(c)
```
x := z - {1};
```
(d)
```
x := z - - [1];
```
(e)
```
read(x);
if x > 0 then print(x); end;
```
(f)
```
x := arb s;
(forall y in s | y > 0) print(y); end;
```
(g)
```
if exists x in s | #x(i..j) < j - i then print(x); end;
```

7. If f is a map and s is a set, then the image set of s under f, sometimes written $f[s]$, is by definition the set $\{y: [x, y] \textbf{ in } f \mid x \textbf{ in } s\}$. The inverse image of s under f, sometimes written f_inv$[s]$, is by definition the set $\{x: [x, y] \textbf{ in } f \mid y \textbf{ in } s\}$. Express $f[s]$ in terms of the sets $f\{x\}$, using a compound operator. What is $f[\textbf{domain } f]$? What is f_inv$[\textbf{range } f]$?

8. Execute the programs

```
[A, A, A] := [1, 2, 3]; print(A);

[A, B, A, B] := [1, 2, 3, 4]; print(A, B);
```

What results do you expect? What is going on?

9. Write expressions which will find the following positions in a string *s*:
   (a) The position of the first occurrence of the letter *a*
   (b) The position of the second occurrence of the letter *a*
   (c) The position of the *n*-th occurrence of the letter *a*
   (d) The position of the last occurrence of *a* that is preceded by no more than five occurrences of *e*

   If the desired occurrences do not exist, your expression should return the value **om**.

10. Write an expression which, given a tuple *t* of integers, forms the tuple *t*2 of all "partial sums" of the components of *t*. That is, the *j*-th component of t2 should be the sum of components 1 through *j* of *t*.

11. A tuple *t* of tuples, all of the same length *n*, can be regarded as an $m \times n$ rectangular array of items. Write a program which rearranges this array by turning it 90 degrees, so that it becomes an $n \times m$ rectangular array of items, represented by a tuple *t*2 of tuples all of length *m*. If this operation is repeated twice, what happens?

12. It can be shown that two set expressions *e*1 and *e*2 involving any number of variables *x*1, ..., *xn* and formed using only the set union, intersection, and difference operations are equal for all possible set values of the variables *x*1, ..., *xn* if and only if they are equal whenever each of these variables has one of the two values { } and {1}. Therefore, we can check a set-theoretic identity like $x*y = y*x$ simply by evaluating

    # {[x, y]: x **in** {{ }, {1}}, y **in** {{ }, {1}} | x*y /= y*x}

    and observing that its value is zero. Moreover since *x* **incs** *y* is equivalent to $x*y = y$, this same technique can be used to check inclusions of the form *e*1 **incs** *e*2. Using this technique, verify that the following set-theoretic identities and inclusions are true for all possible set values of *x*, *y*, and z:

    (a) $(x*y) = (y*x)$
    (b) $(x + y) = (y + x)$
    (c) $((x*y)*z) = (x*(y*z))$, also $((x + y) + z) = (x + (y + z))$
    (d) $((x + y) - z) = ((x - z) + (y - z))$
    (e) $(x*x) = x$, also $(x + x) = x$
    (f) $(x - x) = \{ \}$
    (g) $((x + y)*z) = (x*z + y*z)$, also $((x*y) + z) = ((x + z)*(y + z))$
    (h) $(x + (y - x)) = (x + y)$
    (i) $(x - (y + z)) = ((x - y)*(x - z))$
    (j) $(x*\{ \}) = \{ \}$, also $(x + \{ \}) = x$

3.14 **Om** and Errors

When an illegal operation or an operation having an undefined result is evaluated during the running of a SETL program, one of two possible things will happen. Errors classified (somewhat arbitrarily) as "severe" will cause execution to terminate. In this case, a brief error indication will be placed at the end of the program's output file. Moreover, if the terminal dump option has been switched on (Chapter 9 explains how this can be done), a terminal dump will be written to the dump file specified; valuable hints concerning the cause of error can then be gleaned by examining this dump.

The following errors terminate execution:

(i) Type errors, e.g., an attempt to evaluate

$1 + \{0\}$, $1.0 + 2$, $[0] + \{1\}$, '1' + 2, $s\{y\}$ where *s* is a string or tuple, etc.

(ii) Illegal use of **om**, e.g., attempts to evaluate

{**om**}, f(**om**), **om in** s, s **with om**, **om with** x, etc.

(iii) String or tuple parameters which are out of bounds, e.g., attempts to evaluate

s(0) or s(−1),

where *s* is a string or tuple.

(iv) Illegal file operations, e.g., attempts to manipulate files which have not been opened (see Chapter 9).

(v) Floating-point operations which overflow out of the range of a particular SETL operation, and also conversions of very large integers to floating-point form.

(vi) "Mildly erroneous," deliberately intended, operations whose result is undefined will return the undefined value **om**. These include

(a) selection of an element from an empty set or tuple, as in

x **from** { }, x **from** [ ], x **frome** [ ], or **arb** { }

(b) evaluation of a map at a point at which it is undefined or multiple valued, as in $f(0)$ or $f(1)$, where f is

$$\{[1,1],[1,2]\};$$

also evaluation of an undefined component of a tuple. Since in these cases execution is not immediately terminated, it is possible to test for an **om** result in this case, giving greater semantic flexibility. Some typical constructs exploiting this flexibility are

if (x **from** s) /= **om then**... $ test a set for nullity and extract

if f(x) /= **om then**... $ see if the **map** f is uniquely defined at x

On the other hand, since the legal uses of **om** are severly restricted, unexpected **om** values are likely to force error termination soon after they appear. Consequently, errors of this sort can generally be tracked down pretty easily.

CHAPTER 4

Control Structures

Execution of a SETL program proceeds sequentially, one statement being executed after the other. In the simplest case, the order of execution is simply the order in which the statements are written in the program. For example, consider the following:

```
a := 1;
print('Initially, a =', a);
a := a + 1;
print('Finally, a =', a);
```

In this example, the variable *a* is assigned the value 1; then the first message is printed; *a* is then assigned the value 2; and finally the second message is printed.

Only the simplest computations can be carried out by such straight-line programs. In order to perform more complex calculations, we need to be able to describe *conditional computations*, i.e. computations that are to be executed only when certain conditions are met. We also need to program *repeated computations*, i.e. computations to be executed a number of times (100 times, or for all elements in a set, or until a certain calculation converges, or as long as a certain value has not been reached, etc.).

The order in which these more complex computations are executed is specified in the program text by means of language constructs commonly called *control structures*. In this chapter we will examine the most important control structures of the SETL language, namely: the **if** statement, **case** statement, **loop** statement, and **goto** statement. The **if**, **case**, **goto**, and some variant of the **loop** constructs are commonly found in most modern programming languages and are regarded as the basic tools of "structured programming."

The **loop** construct in SETL is a bit richer than the loop constructs provided by most other languages, and it is specially tailored for the objects that characterize SETL, namely sets, tuples, and maps.

4.1 The if Statement

The **if** statement is used to route program execution along one of several alternate paths, chosen according to some stated condition. An example is

```
if balance > 0 then
    print('Your line of credit is:', balance);
else
    print('you are overdrawn by:', -balance);
end if;
print('Do you want additional information (y/n)?');
```

Here, the condition (i.e. whether the value of balance is positive or negative) determines which of two messages is printed. If the condition being tested is TRUE (i.e., the balance is positive) the statement following the keyword **then** is executed; if the condition is FALSE, the statement following the keyword **else** is executed instead.

After execution of the statements in either branch of the **if** statement, program execution continues from the first statement following the end of the **if**. In the preceding example, after execution of one of the branches of the **if**, the query "Do you want additional information(y/n)?" will be printed.

Any number of statements can appear in either branch of an **if** statement. For example, we can write:

```
if line >= 50 then
    page := page + 1;
    line := 1;
else;
    line := line + 1;
end if;
```

In this case, if the condition—line >= 50—is true, then the assignments to page and line are performed; otherwise,—line—is incremented. The syntax of the form of the **if** statement shown previously is

if *condition* **then**
    group of statements
else
    group of statements
end *optional tokens*;

The construct *condition* denotes any Boolean expression (see Section 2.2.4), i.e., any expression which yields either TRUE or FALSE. The *group of state-*

ments in each branch designates any sequence of executable statements, which can be assignments, control statements such as other **if**s, loops, etc.

The end of the **if** construct is indicated by the keyword **end**, followed optionally by the keyword **if**, and by up to five of the tokens that follow the opening **if**. This convention is particularly useful for clarifying the range of statements governed by **if** statements nested within other **if**'s and is used for other nested control structures as well. The following example illustrates the use of nested **if** statements and displays the convention we have just described for indicating the end of an **if**.

4.1.1 Omitting the else branch of an if statement

Sometimes we want to perform a series of actions when a certain condition is met, but to do nothing if it isn't. In this case it is possible to omit the **else** branch of an **if**

```
if a /= 0 then
    if b**2 > 4.0*a*c then
        discr := sqrt(b**2 - 4.0*a*c);
        print('r1 =',(-b + discr)/2.0*a);
        print('r2 =',(-b - discr)/2.0*a);
    else
        print('Complex roots');
        re_part := -b/2.0*a;
        im_part := sqrt(4.0*a*c - b**2)/2.0*a;
        print('r1 =', re_part, '+i', im_part);
        print('r1 =', re_part, '-i', im_part);
    end if b**2;
    if b /= 0 then
        print('Single root:', -c/b);
    else
        print('degenerate equation: a = b = 0');
    end if b /= 0;
end if a /= 0;
```

statement, as illustrated in the following simple example:

```
if token notin keywords then
    print('Unrecognized operator:', token);
end if;
```

If the condition is true, the statement(s) following the **then** are executed; if the condition is false, the **if** statement does nothing.

4.1.2 The null statement

For reasons of readability, it is often desirable to indicate both branches of an **if** statement, even if one of them is to do nothing. A -do nothing- statement is provided for this purpose. It is written as:

pass;

and causes no computation at all. This allows us to write the previous example as follows:

```
if token notin keywords then
     print('Unrecognized operator:', token);
else pass;
end if;
```

This can also be expressed as

```
if token in keywords then
     pass;
else
     print('Unrecognized operator:', token);
end if;
```

4.1.3 Multiple alternatives in an **if** statement

We often encounter the following programming situation: when the condition of an **if** statement is false, we immediately perform another test to choose among another pair of alternatives, and so on. This can be expressed by means of nested **if**s but can be more clearly stated by "continuing" the **if** statement by means of a special construct to designate subsequent alternatives. In SETL, this is done using **elseif**, as shown in the following example:

```
if month = 'February' then
     if year mod 4 = 0 and year mod 200 /= 0 then
          days := 29;
     else
          days := 28;
     end if year;
elseif month in {'September', 'April', 'June', 'November'} then
          days := 30;
else
          days := 31;
end if;
```

Here, three alternatives are being examined: whether the month is February, or is one of the 30-day months, or is one of the remaining months. Any number of alternatives can appear in this more general **if** construct, whose syntax is

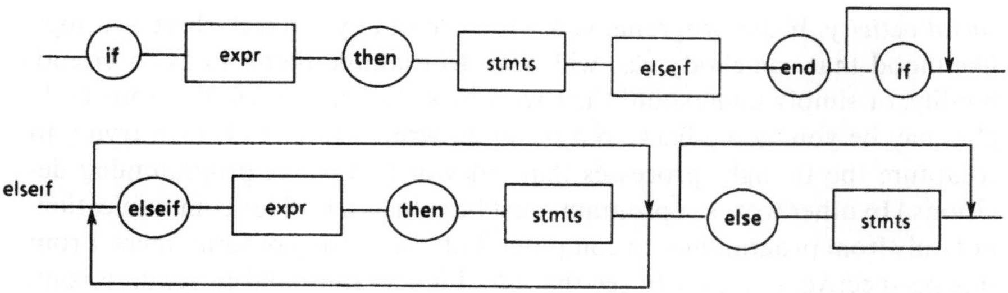

Figure 4.1 **if_Statement Syntax Diagrams**

as follows (see Figure 4.1):

> **if** *condition* **then**
> *group of statements*
> **elseif** *condition* **then**
> *group of statements*
> **elseif**...
> **else**
> *group of statements*
> **end if** *optional tokens*

Note the important syntactic point:

-elseif
is a single word, and it indicates an alternate test within the current **if** statement.

-else if,
on the other hand, indicates that within the **else** branch of the current **if** statement, a nested **if** statement is present, which will need its own closing **end**. Be warned: if you use **else if** when **elseif** should be used, syntax errors, namely "missing **end**" messages, will result.

4.1.4 An important note on indentation and programming style

The physical layout of a SETL program on a printed page (or the screen) is of no concern to the SETL compiler. As long as the syntax of the language is obeyed, the user is free to write successive SETL statements with bizarrely varying indentation, to place several statements on the same line of text, etc. For the human reader, on the other hand, a good choice of program layout can make all the difference between clarity and hopeless muddle. This is particularly true when a program needs to to be read and understood by several programmers. Proper indentation should reflect program structure in such a way as to serve as additional implicit documentation on the intent of a program. The following maxim should be kept in mind: *Programming is a social activity.* If the programs you write are of any interest, there is a high likelihood that somebody else will want to examine them, so as to extend, modify, or simply understand their workings. (Often enough, this somebody else may be you, going back to a program written months before, trying to recapture the thought processes that led you to various programming decisions.) In other words, a program must be seen as a tool for communication, not only from programmer to computer, but also among programmers. From this perspective, it is easy to see that good indentation and program layout, helpful choice of variable names, and ample, carefully considered documentation, are the hallmarks which distinguish the professional programmer's work from that of the amateur.

In the case of **if** statements, it is natural to regard the group of statements in each branch of the **if** as subordinate to the the condition which introduces them. This is clearly reflected in the text if we indent the statements in each branch, with respect to the **if** and **else** keywords, as was done in the preceding examples. An additional rule to follow is to place the **else** in a line by itself, unless the corresponding branch reduces to a single short statement (for example: pass;). The examples in this text follow these rules, as well as other ones which we will mention in connection with other control structures. As is usually the case for rules of style, these should only be regarded as guidelines and suggestions, to be tempered by individual taste. However, some consistent indentation and paragraphing style should be chosen.

4.1.5 The **if** expression

An **if** statement often is used to assign one of several values to a given variable. For example, one may write

if a > b **then** maxab := a; **else maxab** := b; **end if**;

In this case, the **if** expression (also called *conditional expression*) provides a clearer way of achieving the same intent. The syntax of an **if** expression is similar to that of the **if** statement (Figure 4.1). It denotes a value that depends on the outcome of a test (or tests). The general syntax of an **if** expression is

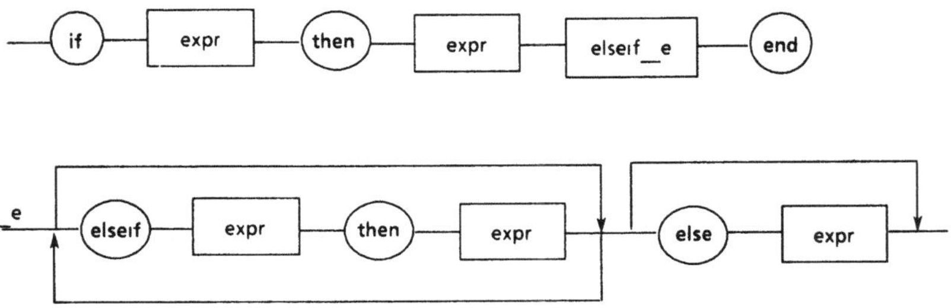

Figure 4.2 Syntax of the **if** Expression

the following:

if
test
then
*expr*1
elseif
*test*2 (1)
then
*expr*2.....
else
exprn
end

This construct may be used in any position where an expression of any other kind would be acceptable. For example the **if** statement (1) can be written as

maxab := **if** a > b **then** a **else** b **end**; (2)

The following are also valid examples of **if** expressions:

print(**if** filler = '' **then** '***' **else** filler + '*' **end**);

print((**if** filler = '' **then** '**' **else** filler **end**) + '*');
distance := distance + (**if** edge = **om then** 0
else length(edge) **end**);

Unlike the **if** statement, the **if** expression must obey the following rules:

(a) In an **if** expression, an **else** part must always be present (to ensure that the expression has a value in all cases).
(b) The terminator of an **if** expression must be a simple **end**, not **end if** or **end if** with extra tokens.
(c) There is no semicolon preceding the keywords **elseif** and **else** in an **if** expression. This is because these keywords are preceded by expressions. In contrast, these same keywords are preceded by semicolons in an **if** statement, because in that case a semicolon terminates the statement previous to the keyword.

If expressions can be nested, as the following rewriting of our 'days in the month' example shows:

days := **if** month = 'February' **then**
(**if** year mod 4 = 0 and year mod 200 /= 0 **then** 29 **else** 28 **end**)
elseif month in {'September', 'April', 'June', 'November'} **then** 30
else 31
end;

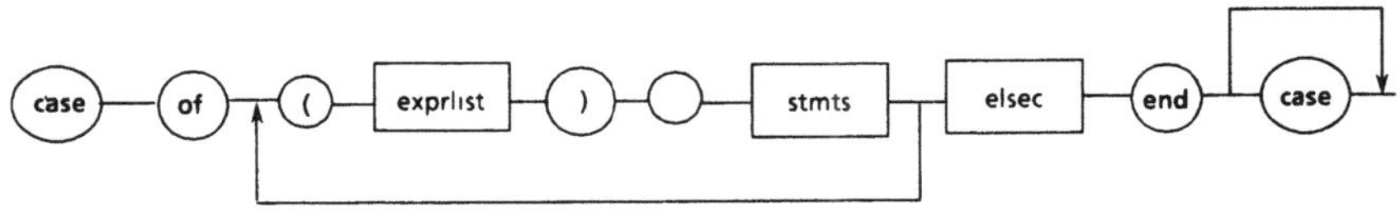

Figure 4.3 **Case-of** Statement Syntax Diagrams

4.2 The **case** Statement

The **case** statement is a generalization of the **if** statement. Whereas the **if** statement controls the flow of execution of a program by choosing between two alternatives, the **case** statement allows us to choose among any number of alternative paths of execution (see Figure 4.3). The **case** statement is available in two forms. Of these, the first and most general is

case of
(test1): statement1
(test2): statement2
(test3): statement3
..
..
(testn): statement*n*
else statement*e*
end;

Each of statement1, statement2.. and statement*e* must be a sequence of one or more statements. Each of the expressions test1, test2.. must be a Boolean expression. Execution of this form of the **case** statement proceeds as follows:

(a) The expressions test1, test2.. are evaluated. If one of them, say testi, yields TRUE, then the corresponding statement, i.e. statement*i*, is executed, and then execution proceeds to the first statement that follows the **case** statement. If several of the expressions test1, test2.. evaluate to TRUE, then any one of them is chosen and the corresponding statement is executed. The **case** statement thus differs from a similar sequence of **if** and **elseif** statements, where the tests are made in sequence.
(b) If none of the tests evaluates to TRUE, then statement*e*, which follows the **else** clause of the statement, is executed. This **else** clause is optional. If the **else** clause is absent, and none of the tests in the **case** statement evaluates to TRUE, the **case** statement is simply bypassed, and execution continues with the first statement that follows it.

It is possible to attach more than one test to a given branch of the **case** by writing:

(test1, test2... testJ): statement*n*

In this case, statement*n* is a candidate for being executed if any one of the tests test1, test2.. yields TRUE.

As a first example of the use of a **case** statement, the following SETL fragment calculates the volume of various geometric figures:

```
case of
    (figure = 'cube'):
        volume := side**3;
    (figure = 'sphere'):
        volume := (4/3)*PI*radius**3;
    (figure = 'cylinder'):
        volume := PI*radius**2*height;
else
        print('Sorry, I don't recognize this figure');
        volume := 0.0;
end case;
```

As this example shows, it is quite common for the tests in a **case** statement simply to test a particular variable or expression for equality with a series of constants. The following second form of the **case** statement simplifies the writing of **case** statements for which this is true (see Figure 4.4):

```
case expr of
  (constant1): statement1
  (constant2): statement2
  .
  .
  (constantn): statementn
else statemente
end;                          $ or more generally end case tokens;
```

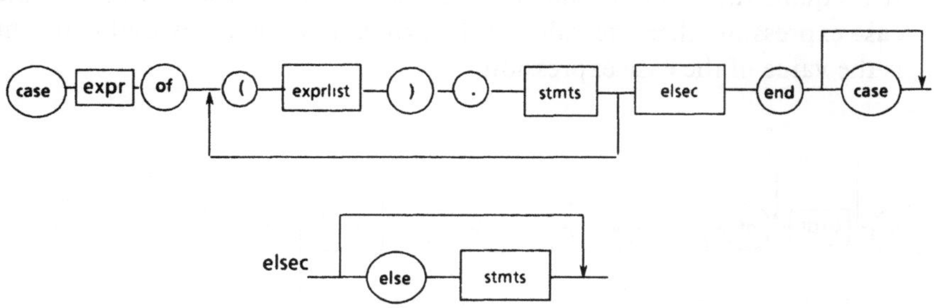

Figure 4.4 **case-expr-of** Statement Syntax Diagram

The expression in the header is evaluated (once) to give a test value. If the evaluation yields one of the constants prefixed to a branch of the case, say constanti, then the associated statement sequence is executed. The **else** sequence is executed if the value of *expr* does not appear as the prefix of any branch of the **case** statement. The **else** sequence can be omitted if no action is to be taken when this happens. As in the first **case** statement form, multiple constants can be attached to one branch by writing

(constant1, constant2, ..., constantn): statements

If this is done, the block will be executed if the value of the expression in the case header equals any of the values constant1, ..., constantn.

4.2.1 The **case** expression

One will sometimes want to use a **case** construct simply to assign one of several alternative values to a variable. This can be done with a **case** statement, for example:

case day of

(Saturday): discount := 0.4;

(Monday, Tuesday, Wednesday, Thursday, Friday):
discount := 0.0;

end case;

In this example, the purpose of the **case** statement is simply to assign an appropriate value to the the variable -discount-. In such situations the **case** expression can be used instead. A **case** expression can appear wherever an expression can appear. Its syntax can be that described by either of the syntax diagrams in Figure 4.5.

Evaluation of a **case** expression closely resembles that of the **case** statement. The execution of a **case** expression of the form (1) proceeds as follows:

(a) The expression following the **case** keyword is evaluated, yielding some value *V*.
(b) If *V* equals the value of one of the constants that mark a branch of the **case** expression, then the value of the expression tagged by that constant is the value of the **case** expression.

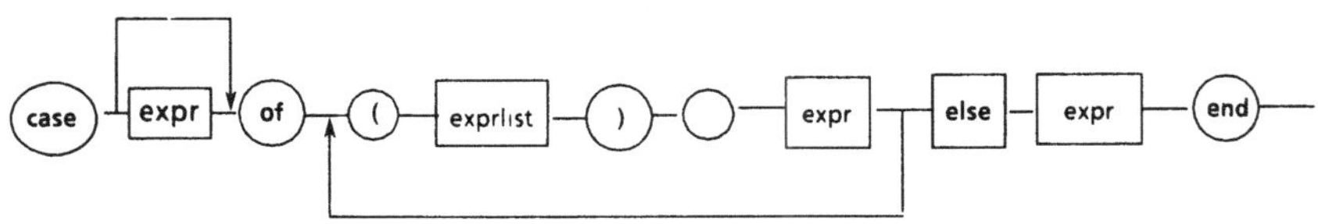

Figure 4.5 **case** Expression Syntax Diagrams

(c) If none of the constants equals V, then the value of the expression following the keyword **else** is the value of the **case** expression.

Using this construct, the preceding example can be rewritten as follows:

```
discount := case day of
                     (Sunday):   0.6,
                     (Saturday): 0.4
            else 0.0

            end;
```

Note that a comma is used to separate successive alternatives of the **case** expression and that no comma appears before the **else** keyword.

The second form of the **case** statement has no expression following the keyword **case**, and in it each case is marked by a list of expressions, each of which must yield a Boolean value. The value of such a **case** expression is the value of the expression tagged by a value of TRUE.

4.3 Loops

Almost every program involves some iteration. Whenever we need to deal with aggregates of data (all the books in a catalog, all the students in a class, all the prime numbers less than 1000, etc.) we need to specify that some computation is to be performed repeatedly. For example, we may want to do the following:

(a) List all the members of a set (for example, all the students registered in a given course).
(b) Modify each component of a tuple (for example, discount all entries in a price list by 10 percent).
(c) Modify selected members of a tuple, for example, raise by 6 percent the tax charged to every Texas resident appearing in a tuple, while leaving unchanged the taxes paid by residents of other states.

We may even want to perform an action repeatedly when no data aggregates are involved. For example:

(d) Perform a series of actions a stated number of times (e.g., print the string -*-*-*-*-*-*- 10 times).
(e) Perform a series of actions as long a a certain condition is true (e.g., to estimate the logarithm (base 2) of a number, we can divide it repeatedly by two as long as the result is greater than 1 and count the number of times the division is performed).
(f) Perform a series of actions until some condition is met (e.g., read input data until an end-of-file is detected).

The first three types of looping are expressed in SETL by using set and tuple iterators. Iterations of type (d) are expressed by using numeric iterators. Types (e) and (f) correspond to **while** and **until** loops, respectively. As we will see subsequently, SETL also allows us to combine all these ways of expressing a repeated calculation into a very general loop construct.

We now start our review of these various loop constructs, beginning with the simplest and most "natural" ones: the set and tuple iterators. We have already encountered various iterator forms when we discussed tuple and set formers. We will now examine these iterators in greater detail.

4.3.1 Set iterators

The *set iterator* is used to specify that a certain calculation is to be performed for each of the elements in a given set. In its simplest form, it reads as follows:

loop for x **in** S **do**

sequence of statements (1)

end *optional tokens*;

The keywords **loop** and **do** can be replaced by left and right parentheses, respectively, and we will often write our iteration loops using this shorter form:

(**for** x **in** S) *sequence of statements* **end** tokens;

The meaning of (1) is as follows:

(a) Obtain the elements of the set S in succession.
(b) Perform the *sequence of statements* repeatedly once for each element of S.
(c) During successive iterations of the loop, assign the value of successive elements of S to variable x.

For example, suppose that S is the following set:

{'Springfield', 'Albany', 'Sacramento', 'Boston'}

Then the loop

```
(for city in S)
        print(city, 'is a state capital.');
end;
```

will produce the following output:

```
Springfield is a state capital.
Albany is a state capital.
Sacramento is a state capital.
Boston is a state capital.
```

The variable x in the construct 'x in S' is called the *bound variable* of the iterator, or simply the *iteration variable* or *loop variable*. As you can see from the example, its name is arbitrary. We chose to call it 'city' in this case but we could have called it 'c', or 'capital_city', or whatever; i.e., exactly the same output would have been obtained with the loop

```
(for c in S) print(c, 'is a state capital.'); end;
```

Each time the *sequence of statements* (also called the *loop body*) is executed, the bound variable is assigned the value of another element of *S*. The loop body is executed exactly as many times as there are elements in *S*. When all elements of *S* have been dealt with, the program moves on to execute the statements that follow the end of the loop.

Consider the following example:

```
Fib13 := {1, 1, 2, 3, 5, 8, 13, 21, 34, 55, 89, 144, 233};
count := 0;

        (for n in Fib13)
            if n mod 3 = 0 then
                print(n, 'is a multiple of 3');
                count := count + 1;
            end if;
        end;
print('There are', count,' multiples of 3 in Fib13')
```

The purpose of this short code fragment is to list the multiples of 3 that appear in the set Fib13 (which happens to be the set of the first 13 so-called Fibonacci numbers). Each element of Fib13 is tested for divisibility by 3 and printed if the test succeeds. A count is kept of the multiples of 3 that we encounter, and this count is printed at the end. The output of this program is

```
3 is a multiple of 3
144 is a multiple of 3
21 is a multiple of 3
There are 3 multiples of 3 in Fib13
```

You may be surprised by the order in which the numbers 3, 144, and 21 appear in the output. Why are they not listed in the same order as in the set Fib13? The reason is of course that sets have no particular ordering, and when we iterate over a set, we don't know in what order its various elements will be obtained. All we know is that we will obtain all of them, in some order, and that is all that matters. (When order matters, we must use tuples instead of sets. More about this later).

The bound variable that appears in a set iterator receives its values from successive elements of the set over which we iterate. When the iteration is complete, that is to say, when all elements of the set have been assigned to the loop variable, the loop variable gets the value **om**. The following loop

```
(for number in {1, 3, 10} + {15, 30})
        print('number is:', number);
end;
```

```
print;
print('Now number is:', number);
```

produces the output:

```
number is:   3
number is:   1
number is:  15
number is:  10
number is:  30
```

Now number is*

Note two points about this example:

(a) We can iterate over any *expression* whose value is a set (i.e., the expression does not have to be a simple variable).
(b) **Om**, the undefined value, is printed as an asterisk ('*').

The reason for calling the loop variable a bound variable should be clear: the values taken by the loop variable are controlled by the iteration mechanism; its successive values correspond to the elements of the set over which we iterate, taken in an order over which the programmer has no control, namely the order in which the elements are stored internally.

The inquiring reader might wonder about the effect of making an explicit assignment to the bound variable in the middle of an iteration or even of making an assignment to the set over which the iteration takes place (the domain of iteration). SETL does not forbid such assignments, although such a practice is not likely to be useful. The SETL system is protected in that such assignments do not affect the way in which the iteration proceeds. For example, consider the following fragment:

```
s := {1,2,3};
(for x in s)   print(x); end;
```

This produces the output

```
1
2
3
```

in some order. Now consider:

```
s := {1,2,3};
(for x in s)
      print(x);
      x := 10*x;
      s with := x;
end for;
print(s);
```

The output of this fragment will be

```
1
2
3
{1,2,3,10,20,30}
```

The assignments to x did not affect the iteration, nor did the modifications to s. It is only on exit from the loop that the modifications are affected. During the iteration, the domain of iteration is kept constant.

4.3.1.1 Conditional set iterators

Consider the following problem: the holdings of a library are described by means of a set catalog and a series of maps: author, subject, and so on. We want to list those books in the catalog whose subject is calculus. This can be achieved by means of the program fragment:

```
(for book in catalog)
   if subject(book) = 'calculus' then
       print(book);
   end if;
end for;
```

The same effect is achieved by the following code:

```
(for book in catalog | subject (book) = 'calculus')
    print(book);
end for;
```

The vertical bar: '|', already introduced in Section 3.5.3, is read 'such that', so that the last iterator can be expressed in English as follows: "iterate over the elements of catalog which are such that their subject is 'calculus.'" In other words, the 'such that' construct appearing in a conditional iterator allows us to specify an iteration over a specified subset of a given set (Figure 4.6).

The general form of the conditional iterator is the following:

(for *name* **in** *set expression* | *Boolean condition*)
statements
end *optional tokens*;

In this construct, *Boolean condition* designates any Boolean expression, i.e., any expression that yields either TRUE or FALSE as its value. The meaning of this construct can be stated as follows:

(a) Iterate over the elements of *set expression* and assign the successive values of these elements to *name*.
(b) After each of these assignments, evaluate the *Boolean condition*. If the condition yields TRUE, perform the *list of statements*. Otherwise, skip directly to the next value of *set expression*.

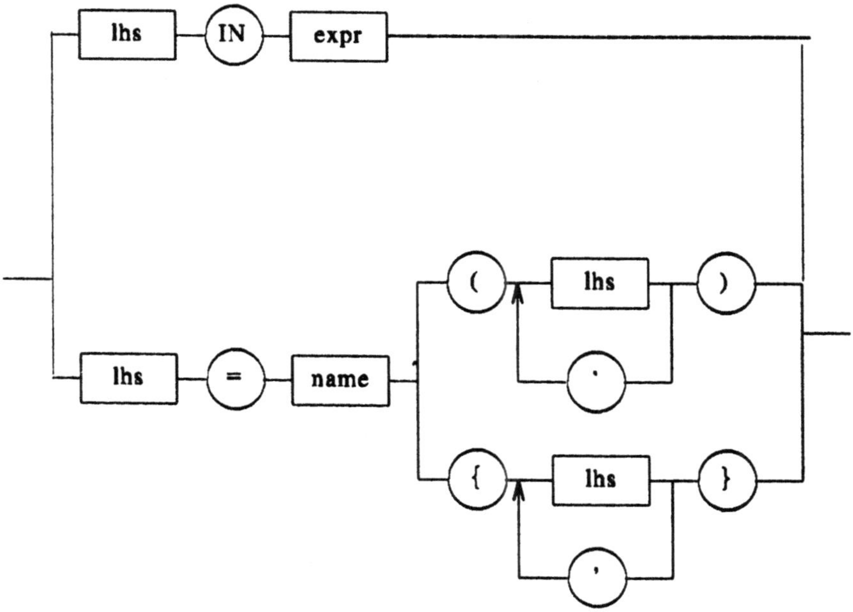

Figure 4.6 Simple Iterator Syntax Diagrams

Typically the iteration variable will appear in the Boolean condition. This is shown in our previous example.

However it is possible, though inelegant, to write a conditional iteration whose Boolean condition does not depend on the iteration variable. For example:

(for x **in** S | true)

is equivalent to:

(for x **in** S)

because the Boolean condition is -true- for all elements of *S*.

The following iteration is less artificial than the preceding example:

(for x **in** S | flag) (2)

where -flag- is some Boolean variable. It selects the elements of *S* according to the current setting of -flag-. This variable may be set elsewhere in the program, perhaps in the body of the iteration loop. However, the intent of (2) is expressed more clearly by the equivalent code

(for x **in** S)
if flag **then**....

which should be preferred to (2) on stylistic grounds.

4.3.2 Tuple iterators

Iterations over tuples can be described in exactly the same manner as iteration over sets. That is, they can be given the following form:

(for *name* **in** *expression* | *Boolean condition*)
statements
end *optional tokens*;

If *expression* is a set expression, the loop is a set iteration. If *expression* yields a tuple, it is a tuple iteration. One significant difference between set and tuple iterators is that for the latter we know the order in which the components of the tuple will be examined by the iteration. Namely, they are produced in order of increasing index. For example,

```
width := [1, 3, 5, 7, 9, 2, 2];
(for w in width) print(w*'*'); end;
```

always produces the following output:

```
*
***
*****
*******
*********
**
**
```

In this example, the iteration variable *w* takes on the values of the components of the tuple -width-, exactly in the order in which they occur: first 1, 3, 5, 7, 9, and finally 2, 2. (Question: what would the picture look like if we had defined width as $\{1, 3, 5, 7, 9, 2, 2\}$?)

If a *Boolean condition* is present, the tuple iterator obeys the same rule as the set iterator: the body of the loop is executed only for those tuple components for which the condition yields true.

4.3.3 String iterators

An iteration over a character string is specified in exactly the same manner as an iteration over a tuple. The following example illustrates this.

```
no_vowels := '';

(for c in 'antidisestablishmentarianism' | c notin 'aeiou')
        no_vowels + := c;
end for c;
print(no_vowels);
```

The output of this loop is the string: 'ntdsstblshmntrnsm'

The action of a string iterator is similar to that of a tuple iterator: successive components (in this case, characters) are assigned to the loop variable, and the body of the loop is executed for those values of the loop variable that satisfy the stated Boolean condition. The characters are iterated over in the order in which they appear in the string, from left to right.

4.3.4 Numerical iterators

An iterative computation is often expressed as follows: 'Repeat the following calculation *N* times'. Here the iterative process does not depend on a data aggregate, such as a set or a tuple, but rather depends on an integer, namely the value of *N*. This is the iterative construct most commonly supported by other programming languages. In SETL, this type of iteration is expressed by a simple variant of the tuple iterator: performing a computation *C* repeatedly *N* times is equivalent to performing *C* once for each one of the integers in the range: 1, 2, 3.. up to *N*. This range of values is described in SETL by writing

```
[1..N]
```

and thus the repeated computation of *C* is expressed as follows:

```
(for i in [1..N])
        C;
end;
```

The construct [1..*N*] looks like a tuple former, and indeed in contexts where a tuple is permissible, it is a valid tuple expression, as we saw in our discussion of tuple formers (Section 3.6). In an iteration this construct designates the range of values taken on by the loop variable in the course of the iteration. Note that an iteration variable appears here, just as it did in set and tuple iterations. This variable takes on the values specified by the range construct, in the order indicated, which is to say from 1 up to *N* in steps of 1.

Because of the importance of numerical iterators in programming, SETL provides a still more general form to describe them. We now proceed to explain this more general numerical iterator form.

4.3.4.1 The general form of the numerical iterator

Any numerical iterator defines the sequence of integer values to be taken on by the iteration variable of a loop. The simple iterator form given previously specifies that the beginning (or lower bound) of the iteration is 1, and the iteration end (or upper bound) is *N*. The step between successive values of the sequence iterated over is 1. In a more general numerical iterator, these three quantities—lower bound, upper bound, and step—can be specified individually. To do so, use the following construct:

[*first*, *second*..*last*] (3)

where first, second, and last are integer-valued expressions. For example,

[1,3..9] specifies the sequence 1, 3, 5, 7, 9
[2,5..17] specifies the sequence 2, 5, 8, 11, 14, 17

As these examples indicate, the sequence iterated over is calculated as follows:

(a) The lower bound is the first expression in the iterator.
(b) The step between successive elements is the difference between the second expression and the first. If the second expression is missing, then, as in the examples of Section 4.3.4, the step is understood to be 1.
(c) Successive elements of the sequence are produced by repeatedly adding the value of the step, until we reach a value exceeding the last expression. (But see the following discussion.)

This description immediately raises three questions:

(i) What happens if the step is negative?
(ii) What happens is the upper bound is not in the generated sequence?
(iii) What happens if the step is zero?

The answer to (i) is what you would intuitively expect, namely, if the step is negative, then the elements of the sequence are produced in decreasing order. In that case, the third expression must be smaller that the first. For example, the iterator

[10,8..0]

specifies the sequence 10, 8, 6, 4, 2, 0 because the step is $8 - 10 = -2$.

This form of the iterator is often used when the elements of a tuple must be processed in reverse order. For example, suppose that the elements of tuple T are numbers sorted in increasing order, and we want to list them in decreasing order, starting from the largest. The following loop will accomplish this:

```
(for i in [#T, #T - 1..1])
        print(T(i));
end;
```

In this example, the first element of the sequence is given by the expression $\# T$; the first value of the iteration variable *-i-* is therefore the index of the last element of T. The next value is $\# T - 1$, from which we conclude that the step for this sequence is -1. The last value iterated over is 1.

Next consider the second question raised, namely, what if the final value appearing in the construct [*first*, *second*.. *last*] is not in the generated sequence? For example, what is the sequence generated by the following iterators:

[1,3..10]

and

[15, 10 . . 1]?

The answer to this question is determined by the following rule: a sequence iterated over is generated by successive additions of the step to the first element. If the sequence is increasing (i.e., if the step is positive) we generate all numbers in the sequence which are smaller than or equal to the last element. If the sequence is decreasing, we generate all the numbers that are larger than or equal to the last element. Thus, for example,

[1, 3 . . 10] specifies the sequence 1, 3, 5, 7, 9
[15, 10 . . 1] specifies the sequence 15, 10, 5

What about [1, 3 . . 1]? According to the rule just stated, we start with 1. The step is 2. The next value in the sequence would be 3, but that is already greater than the stated upper bound of 1. Thus this iterator generates a singleton sequence, whose only element is 1. This leaves one final question: what is the meaning of the iterator if the step of the sequence is zero? In that case, the convention used by SETL is that the iteration is empty, i.e., iterates over no values at all. A loop whose iterator has a step of zero is simply not executed. The following are examples of empty loops:

```
(for I in [1, 1 .. 1000])
            print('This message will never be seen');
end;
(for x in { })
            print('Nor will this one, because { } has no elements');
end;
(for i in [ ])
            print('Need we say more?');
end;
```

The previous rule also answers another lingering question: what is the value of the loop variable on exit from a numerical loop? We saw that in the case of set and tuple iterators, the loop variable became undefined on exit from the loop. In the case of numeric iterators, the value of the loop variable on exit is the first value in the sequence:

first, first + step, first + 2*step . .

that lies outside the specified range. If the step is positive, this means the first value of that sequence that is larger than the stated bound; if the step is negative, it is the first value which is smaller than the bound.

The action of the numerical iterator '**for** i **in** [exp1, exp2 . . exp3]' can also be defined by the following "low-level" code which uses labels and **goto** statements. (The intent of the **goto** statement, which is described fully in Section 4.4, is to indicate the next statement in the program to be executed after the execution of the **goto** itself).

```
            start := exp1;
            step := exp2 - exp1;
            bound := exp3;

            if step = 0 then goto quit_loop; end if;
            i := start;
test_loop:
            if (step > 0 and i > bound) or (step < 0 and i < bound) then
                        goto quit_loop;
            end if;
            i +:= step;
            goto test_loop;
quit_loop:
```

4.3.5 Additional loop control statements: **continue** and **quit**

The **continue** and **quit** statements increase the syntactic flexibility of SETL's loop constructs. Their syntax is simply

continue *optional loop tokens*;

and

quit *optional loop tokens*;

In both cases, the *optional loop tokens* define the loop to which the intended action (continue the iteration or quit altogether) refers. The actions caused by **continue** and **quit** are as follows.

When a **continue** statement is executed in the body of a loop, execution of the rest of the body is skipped, and the iteration proceeds to the next value of the loop variable. Thus, the loop

```
(for x in S | C(x))
      some statements...
end;
```

can be expressed as follows:

```
(for x in S)
      if C(x) then
            some statements..
      else continue;
      end if;
end;
```

Execution of a **quit** statement terminates the execution of a loop and causes execution to continue from the first statement following the end of that loop.

For example, consider the following fragment:

```
sum := 0;
(for x in [1..100])
    sum := sum + x;
    if sum > 10 then quit; end;
end;
print(sum);
```

This code fragment adds the integers in the range 1..100 until the sum obtained is greater than 10. After five iterations through the loop, sum is $1 + 2 + 3 + 4 + 5 = 15$, and at that point the **quit** statement is executed. The value printed is 15, and the 95 iterations that remain are simply not executed.

When they are written without additional tokens, the **continue** and **quit** statements always refer to the innermost loop within which they appear. But these statements also allow an extended form, for example,

continue for x **in** S; (4)

which can be used to indicate which of the several nested loops within which a **continue** (or **quit**) statement like (4) appears, is to be continued. In this example, the loop meant is the innermost loop whose iterator starts with the tokens:

for x **in** S...

The same applies to sequences of tokens following a quit statement.

The **continue** statement might be typically used in a search loop, when an object x satisfying a property $C(x)$ is to be found in some data aggregate S, and then processed in some way. When so used, the body of the loop will include code that tests each element of S for the property C. It may be the case that we can determine that a given element y of S does not have the property C, without completing execution of the loop body. In that case, the **continue** statement allows us to avoid processing y and to proceed to the next element of S. We will see an example of such use later.

Like the **continue** statement, **quit** also typically appears in search loops. However, whereas **continue** bypasses unsuccessful cases, **quit** is used to signal that there is no need to continue with the iteration, either because the search has been successful or because it has become clear that the search will remain unsuccessful even if the remaining elements are examined.

To illustrate the use of these statements let us return to the problem of producing a table of prime numbers. This time, we will write our program as a series of loops. Moreover, we will start with a simple solution to the problem and improve this initial solution in order to develop more and more efficient versions of it. Our initial solution simply restates the definition of prime number: it is a number that has no factors except 1 and itself. In order to determine whether N is prime, we divide N by all numbers smaller than itself. If any of these divisions turns out to have no remainder, N is not prime, and we do not need to continue examining other divisors. If no division is exact,

N is prime. Our first version reads as follows:

```
program primes1;

N := 1000;                              $ The desired range.
primes := [ ];                          $ Sequence to be constructed.

(for num in [2..N])                     $ Examine all numbers in the range

     (for factor in [2..num - 1])       $ Range of its possible divisors

        if num mod factor = 0 then
                                        $ num has an exact divisor. Skip it.

           continue for num;

        end if;
     end for ;
                                        $ If we reach this point, num is a prime.
     primes with := num;

end for:

print('Primes in the range 1 to', N, ':');
print(primes);

end program;
```

This simple program involves many redundant calculations, which we now proceed to discover and remove.

First, note that an even number (with the exception of 2) cannot be a prime number. There is therefore no need to iterate over all numbers in the range [2..*N*]. It is sufficient to consider only the odd numbers in that range. By the same token, these numbers can have only odd divisors. The outer loop should therefore have the range

(for num **in** [3, 5..N])

and the inner one

(for factor in [3, 5..num − 1])

This modification of the initial program makes it four times faster (only half as many operations are performed during each of the two nested levels of iteration).

Next, note that to determine whether -num- is prime, we do not need to examine all its possible divisors: it is sufficient to examine its possible prime divisors, i.e., all prime numbers smaller than it. If we modify the inner iterator accordingly, we obtain the following program:

```
program primes2;

N := 1000; The range.
primes := [2];               $ The first prime.
```

```
(for num in [3, 5..N])
     (for factor in primes)
          if num mod factor = 0 then
               continue for num;
          end if;

     end for;
     primes with := num;
end for;

print('primes in the range 1 to', N, ':');
print(primes);

end;
```

Our next improvement generalizes the observation that allowed us to eliminate all even numbers from consideration: whenever we find a new prime P, we can calculate all the multiples of P in the range $1..N$ and mark them "not primes" so that we do not have to examine them for primality later on. The easiest way of accomplishing this is to keep a set of candidate numbers, from which we remove the multiples of each prime we find. This leads us to an improved program which reads as follows:

```
program primes3;

N := 1000;
primes := [2];
candidates := {3, 5..N};   $ At first, all odd numbers.

(for num in [3, 5..N] | num in candidates)
     (for factor in primes)
          if num mod factor = 0 then
               continue for num;
          end if;
     end for;

     primes with := num;

     $ Now delete all multiples of num from the set of candidates
     (for multiple in [num, 2*num..N])
          candidates less := multiple;
     end for;

end for num;

print('Primes in the range 1 to', N, ':');
print(primes);

end program;
```

This suggests yet another substantial improvement to our program. We notice that whenever we examine -num- for primality, we will have already deleted from (-candidates-) all multiples of prime numbers smaller than -num-. Therefore, -num- is not a multiple of any of them, and it definitely *is* the next prime. In other words, whenever we reach a number in the range 1 .. *N* which is still in the set of candidates, we know that that number is definitely prime, and the loop to find a factor for it is unnecessary. Our program now reduces to the following procedure known as the *sieve of Erastosthenes*:

```
program primes4;

N := 1000;
primes := [2];
candidates := {3,5..N};   $ At first, all odd numbers.

(for num in [3,5..N] | num in candidates)

    primes with := num;

    $ Now delete all multiples of num from the set of candidates

    (for multiple in [num, 2*num..N])
        candidates less := multiple;
    end for;

end for num;

print('Primes in the range 1 to', N, ':');
print(primes);

end program;
```

Several small additional improvements to primes4 can still be made. Let us mention the following simple one: the set *candidates* may become empty before the outer iteration is completed, in which case all subsequent evaluations of the predicate *num* **in** *candidates* will fail. We can bypass these final useless iterations by adding the following statement immediately after the loop that eliminates multiples of the latest prime found:

```
if candidates = { } then quit; end if;
```

When a loop is exited by means of a **quit** statement, rather than after completion of its iteration, then the loop variable retains the value it had just before execution of the **quit** statement. This makes it possible to tell outside of the loop what was the last value of the domain of iteration that was examined. For example, in order to tell whether our last modification to primes4 was particularly useful, we could add the following statement on exit from the outer loop:

```
print('Last number examined:', num);
```

In this case it turns out that 997 is a prime, so that testing to determine whether (candidates = { }) saves us only one check in the iterator.

4.3.6 Map iterators

We have emphasized repeatedly that maps are sets. Hence to iterate over all the elements *p* of a map *f* we can simply write

(for p **in** f)...

In this iteration, the bound variable *p* is assigned successive elements of *f*, that is to say, *ordered pairs*. If within the body of such a loop we wanted to refer to successive elements in the domain of *f*, we could "unpack" *p* by writing

```
(for p in f)
    x := p(1);   $ x is in the domain of f
    y := p(2);   $ y is the corresponding point in the range.
....
```

This same unpacking effect could also be obtained either by placing a tuple assignment of the form

[x, y] := p;

(see Section 3.12) at the start of the body of the iteration or by changing the iteration header itself to read

(for [x, y] **in** f)...

Because of the importance of this type of iteration a still more elegant, maplike alternative notation is provided for it, namely,

(for y = f(x)) (5)

This form of iterator is called a *map iterator*. Note that both the variables *x* and *y* are bound by this iterator: *x* receives successive values taken from the domain of *f*, while simultaneously *y* is set to the corresponding range value *f*(*x*).

For example, suppose that *f* is the following map:

```
{ ['New York', 'Albany'], ['California', 'Sacramento'],
  ['Massachusetts', 'Boston'], ['Illinois', 'Springfield'],
  ['North Dakota', 'Fargo'], ['Idaho', 'Boise']}
```

and that mid_west is the set:

```
{'Kansas', 'Illinois', 'South Dakota', 'North Dakota',
'Michigan', 'Iowa', 'Nebraska'}
```

then the following loop:

```
(for capital = f(state) | state notin mid_west)
    print('the capital of', state, 'is', 'capital');
end for;
```

will have the following output:

The capital of New York is Albany
The capital of Caifornia is Sacramento
The capital of Idaho is Boise
The capital of Massachussetts is Boston

The syntax appearing in (5) can also be used for tuple iterators. If T is a tuple, then the iterator

(for comp = T(i))

assigns the integer values 1, 2.. $\#T$ to *-i-* and simultaneously assigns the values of the corresponding components of T to *comp.* The advantage of this form over the simple tuple iterator is that it makes the index of each component available at the same time as the component. (The use of a syntax like that of map iterators for tuple iterators once again underlines the logical similarity between tuples and maps: tuples are very similar to maps whose domain is a set of integers).

The iterator (5) can be used only for single-valued maps, and the system will generate a run-time error if we attempt to use it on a multivalued map. To iterate over a multivalued map, the following form is provided:

$$(\textbf{for}\ s = f\{x\}) \qquad (6)$$

Like (5), this construct, sometimes called a *multivalued map iterator*, controls both the values of x and s. The variable x receives successive values from the domain of f, and s becomes the corresponding image set of x, that is to say, $f\{x\}$. For example, let f be the map

$$\{[i,j]\text{: i in } [1..4], \text{j in } [1..4] \mid i > j\}$$

Then the iteration

```
(for s = f{x} | odd #s)
    print(s, 'is the image of', x);
end;
```

will produce the following output:

```
{1, 2, 3} is the image of 4
{1} is the image of 2
```

4.3.7 Compound iterators

A compound iterator is a useful shorthand notation t describe nested iteration loops. For example, the code fragment

```
(for x in S1)
    (for y in S2)
        ...
    end;
end;
```

can be written as follows:

```
(for x in S1, y in S2)
    .......
end;
```

Any number of nested loops can be combined in this fashion. A single **end** statement closes all of them. The iterators in a compound iterator are understood to be nested from left to right. The rightmost iterator in the compound is the innermost; its loop variable changes most rapidly.

All iterator forms can appear in a compound iterator: set and tuple iterators, numeric iterators, map iterators. For example,

```
(for x in S, y in [1..x - 1], z = f(t))....
```

Compound iterators can also have a *such that clause*. Such a clause is understood to apply to the innermost iterator in the compound; that is to say, this clause is evaluated for every assignment to the innermost loop variable.

Continue and **quit** statements appearing within a compound iterator apply uniformly to the outermost iterator therein: there is no way to continue or quit any of the inner members of the compound. (If it is necessary to do so, the iterators must be written in the usual nested form).

4.3.8 The general loop construct

Each of the iterators discussed so far generates a sequence of values: the successive elements of a set, the components of a tuple, the characters of a string. We have seen how iteration loops are described by means of such iterators: the body of a loop is executed once for each value that appears in the generated sequence. Different kinds of loop constructs, called **while** and **until** loops, are used to describe computations that repeat until a desired state of affairs is reached, rather than according to some preset sequence of values. For example, we may want to process input data which are to be read from a file, but we may not know how many items are actually present on the file. In this case, we need to express the following intent: "Process the input as long as there is data to process." A second kind of example is furnished by numerical analysis. Many numerical problems have the following general flavor: find a sequence of better and better approximations to a desired value (for example, to the root of an equation) and stop when the answer is 'close enough'. (Close enough usually means that rather than looking for an exact answer, we are satisfied with an answer which differs from the exact one by a very small number, say $1.0\,E - 7$.) In these cases, we generally cannot state in advance how many times the loop body may have to be repeated. For these situations, SETL provides a very general loop construct. The simplest form of this general construct is the *indefinite loop*, whose syntax is as follows:

```
loop do
    statements
end;
```

As with the simpler iterator forms, the keywords **loop** and **do** can be represented by parentheses. Thus, the indefinite loop can also be written:

( ) statements **end**;

An indefinite loop specifies that the loop body should be repeated "forever." This is clearly an overstatement: the computation will have to finish somehow! In fact, an indefinite loop can be terminated either by a **quit** statement, a **continue** statement which refers to an enclosing loop, or a **goto** to a label which is outside the loop body.

The indefinite loop is not used very often, because ordinarily the condition under which it will terminate execution can more clearly be expressed by means of one of two extremely useful loop forms, namely the **while** and the **until loop**. Let us now examine these.

4.3.8.1 The **while** loop

A **while** loop is written as follows:

```
loop while condition do
    statements
end;
```

or equivalently

```
(while condition)
    statements
end;
```

Execution of such a loop proceeds as follows:

The condition is evaluated. If its value is TRUE, then the loop body is executed. After each execution of the body, the *condition* is evaluated anew, and as long as it yields TRUE, the body continues to be executed again. As soon as the *condition* becomes FALSE, looping ends, and execution proceeds with the first statement that follows the loop.

If the first evaluation of the *condition* yields FALSE, then the loop body is not executed at all. It follows that a **while** loop will be executed zero or more times.

Let us look at some examples. As we have already seen, the processing of a stream of data received from input is a typical case. Suppose that we want to read a list of names and print those that start with *A*. We do not know the number of items in the data stream, and it may even be that there are none. Fortunately, the SETL system uses a very simple convention to indicate that data have been exhausted. When we attempt to read data from a file but have reached the end of the file, the **read** statement yields **om**. Thus, the following simple code fragment can be used to handle a stream of input data and stop when the end of the data has been reached:

```
read(name);                $ Get first name from input file.
count := 0;
```

```
(while name /= om)        $ As long as we read something

   if name(1) = 'A' then
        print(name);
        count + := 1;
   end if;

   read(name);            $ Acquire next data item from input.

end while;

print(count, 'names starting with A were found');
```

Note that in this code we execute one **read** statement before the loop, to "prime" the loop, so to speak. Doing this ensures that -name- receives a value before the first evaluation of the **while** condition. If the input file was not empty, then -name- is not **om**, and the body of the loop is executed. If the input file was empty, then -name- is **om**, and the loop is bypassed altogether. At the end of each execution of the loop body, we perform another **read** operation. As long as something is read, the loop will be executed again. As soon as the stream of input data is exhausted, the **read** statement will yield **om**, the **while** condition evaluates to **false**, and execution of the **while** loop will terminate. Program execution will then proceed to the statement following the loop, which in the preceding case is the one that prints the little statistical report on the data.

Our next, more complex example is motivated by the following practical problem. Suppose that the catalog of a school specifies a set of prerequisites for each course that is offered. That is to say, for each course *C*, it specifies a set of courses which the student must take before being allowed to take *C*. Needless to say, the prerequisites of *C* often have further prerequisites of their own, and we will sometimes want to know the full set of courses that have to be taken before *C* is tackled. These include the prerequisites of *C*, the prerequisites of those prerequisites, and so on. Let us assume that the map -prerequisites- contains the standard information that appears in a school catalog, that is to say, the list of immediate prerequisites of each course *C*. Then the desired set can be obtained as follows:

```
P := prerequisites(C);        $ get the 'immediate' prerequisite
                                for the course

all_P := P;                   $ initialize the set we aim to build

(while P /= { })              $ as long as there is some
                                prerequisite that
                              $ has not been processed.

   course from P;             $ take one of them.

   all_P with := course;      $ Add to full set of prerequisites
```

```
P +:= prerequisites(course) - all_P;   $ add all the prerequisites of P to
                                         the set
end while;

print('Before taking', C, 'the following must have been taken');
print(all_P);
```

This example deserves careful study, because it embodies a very common type of program schema, sometimes called the use of a *workpile*. The set *P* originally consists of the immediate prerequisites of *C*. Each of these is placed in all_P, which is to be built up to the full set of prerequisites we are gathering, and each of their prerequisites in turn must be placed in all_P, and also into the set *P*, to see whether further prerequisites are implied by them. The process terminates when we reach courses that have no prerequisites at all (there must be some of those!). The "workpile" set *P* shrinks with each execution of the **from** statement but can increase again with the addition of new prerequisites of the course we have just extracted from *P*. Workpile algorithms of this kind typically involve **while** loops.

4.3.8.2 The **until** loop

The syntax of the **until** loop is similar to that of the **while** loop. We write

```
loop until condition do
    statements
end;
```

or equivalently

```
(until condition)
    statements
end;
```

An **until** loop is executed as follows: The body of an **until** loop is always executed at least once. *After* it is executed the loop *condition* is evaluated. If this yields TRUE, then execution proceeds to the first statement following the loop. If it yields FALSE, the body of the loop is executed again. We can therefore say that the test of a **while** loop is performed *at the beginning* of the loop body, and that the test of an **until** loop is performed *at the end* of the loop body. Note also that the body of an **until** loop is always executed one or more times, in contrast to that of a **while** loop, which may not be executed at all.

As an example, let us consider the problem of finding the smallest number of steps that can take us from one point in a graph to another. In order to tackle this problem we must say a word about graphs, and about the ways in which they are generally described in SETL. A graph consists of a set of vertices, and a set of edges which connect the vertices. Edges of a graph can be represented in SETL by ordered pairs, whose first component is the starting vertex for an edge, and whose second component is the arriving vertex for that

edge. For example, the simple graph

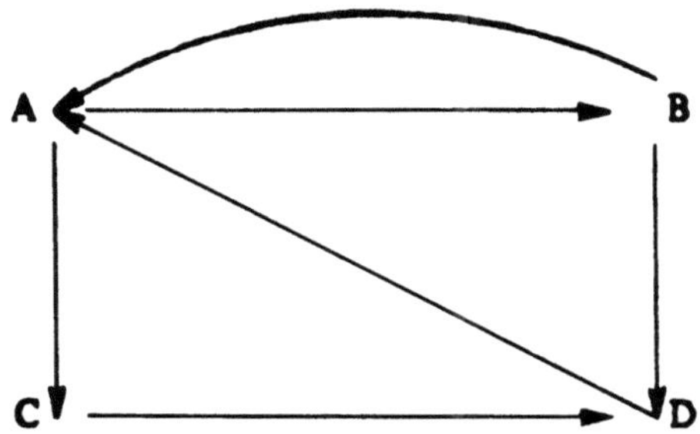

is described by the following set of pairs (i.e., edges):

$$\{[A,B],[B,A],[A,C],[C,D],[B,D],[D,A]\}$$

Since in SETL a set of pairs is at the same time a map, we can also regard this representation as a *successor map* (also called an *adjacency list*) whose domain is the set of vertices of the graph. Then, for each vertex V, the value of the mapping successor$\{V\}$ is the set of vertices that are reachable from V by means of some edge that starts at V. For example, in the graph shown, successor$\{B\}$ is the set $\{A, D\}$, because of the existence of edges from B to A and D.

Using this bit of notation, our problem can be stated as follows: given a graph G, described by its set of edges, and given two vertices s (source) and t (target), find the length of the shortest path between s and t, i.e., the smallest number of edges that must be traversed in order to go from s to t. If we do not know a priori what path to take, we may have to explore a substantial number of paths starting from s, until we find one that reaches t. A possible way of organizing this exploration is to find all the vertices that can be reached from s in one step, two steps, etc., until we reach t. Our problem will therefore be solved by the following:

```
seen := {s};
length := 0;

(until t in seen)
                    $ Add to seen all the vertices that can be reached by
                    $ following one more edge from vertices already reached.
    (for v in seen)
       seen +:= successor{v};
    end for;

    length +:= 1;

end until;
print('There is a path of length', length, 'from', s, 'to', t);
```

Various shortcomings of this code are easily noted: for example, what if our graph is such that there is no path from s to t? As written, the preceding algorithm will iterate indefinitely, and the condition -*t* **in** seen- will never be met; i.e., we will endlessly retrace the edges that lead out of the vertices already reached. In order to prevent this behavior, we can modify our algorithm, so that at each step -seen- contains only those vertices that have not been reached on previous steps. This can be achieved as follows:

```
length := 0;
seen := {s};        $ The set of vertices reached at each step.
reached := {s};     $ The set of all vertices reached so far.
(until t in seen or seen = { })

   $ We collect the new vertices reachable from the latest set,
   $ which were not reached previously.

   seen := +/{successor{v}: v in seen} – reached;

   reached + := seen;

   length + := 1;

end until;

if seen = { } then
print(t, 'is not reachable from', s);
else
   print('There is a path of length', length, 'from', s, 'to', t);
end if;
```

See Section 5.3.1 for a further example continuing this theme.

4.3.8.3 The general loop construct

The indefinite loop, the **while**, and the **until** loop are all special cases of a more general SETL loop construct, whose full rather elaborate, syntax is as follows (see Figure 4.7):

```
loop
   init          $ Loop initialization statements.
   statementi
   doing         $ Step statements at start of loop.
   statementd
```

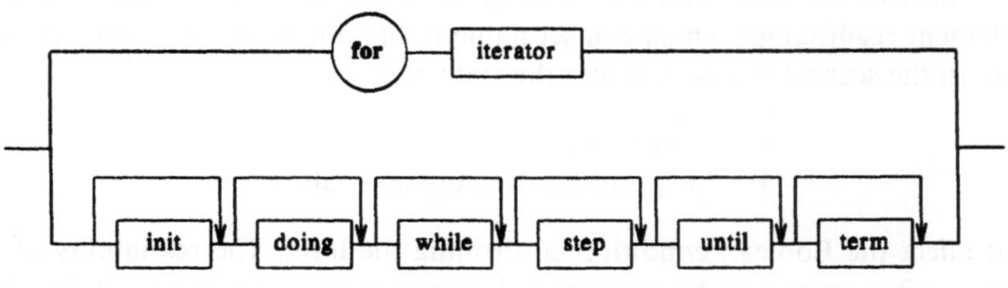

Figure 4.7 General Iteration Syntax Diagram

```
    while          $ Termination test at start of loop.
      testw
    step           $ Step statements at end of loop.
      statements
    until          $ Termination test at end of loop.
      testu
    term           $ Loop termination statements.
      statementt
  do
      statementb   $ Body of loop
  end;             $ Or end loop tokens;
```

Both the iterator and the general loop construct are bracketed by **loop**..**do**. These keywords can be replaced (as we have been doing all along) by parentheses, so that, for example

(**while** X < M **doing** X := X + 1;)

is equivalent to

```
loop
   while X < M
doing X := X + 1;
do
```

You will notice that **while** and **until** clauses are both included in this very general loop form. Its full structure is admittedly complex. However, as you may have surmised from the previous sections, every single clause in this loop construct is optional! If we leave out all of them, we obtain the indefinite loop: **loop do**; The **while** and **until** loops are obtained by keeping only one of the loop clauses. To explain the full construct, we must now describe the purpose of the remaining four clauses in it: **init**, **doing**, **step**, and **term**.

4.3.8.4 The **doing** and **step** clauses

The reader will have noticed that the body of **while** and **until** loops always includes at least one statement that affects the value of the Boolean condition that controls the execution of the loop. In the first example, this was the statement **read**(name); which can set name to **om** and terminate loop execution. In the second example, it was the statements

```
course from P;
P +:= prerequisites(course) - all_P;
```

that affect the Boolean condition controlling the loop. The readability of a loop is often improved by including "housekeeping" actions directly in the loop header, close to the condition that governs loop execution. This can be done using the **doing** and **step** clauses of the loop construct.

(a) If a **doing** clause appears in a loop construct, then the sequence of statements labeled by the keyword **doing** is executed each time execution proceeds through the loop, before the loop body is executed, and also before the **while** condition (if present) is evaluated.
(b) If a **step** clause appears in a loop construct, then the sequence of statements labeled by the keyword **step** is executed each time execution proceeds through the loop, immediately after the loop body has been executed, and before the **until** condition (if present) is evaluated.

For example, using the **doing** clause, the first example in Section 4.3.8.1 can be rewritten as follows:

```
count := 0;
loop while name /= om doing read(name); do
...
end loop;
```

Similarly, the example in Section 4.3.8.2 can be rewritten as follows:

```
length := 0;
seen := reached := {s};

loop step
     reached + := seen;
     length + := 1;
     until t in seen
do

....
end loop;
```

All the the numeric iterators which we examined in Section 4.3.4 can be described by using **while** and **until** statements with **step** clauses. For example, the following loops are all identical in their effect:

```
(for i in [1..100])..end;                          (i)

i := 1;                                            (ii)
(while i <= 100 step i + := 1;)..end while;

i := 1;                                            (iii)
loop until i = 100 step i + := 1; do..end;

i := 0;
(while i <= 99 doing i + := 1;)                    (iv)
...
end while;
```

Choosing between these constructs is a matter of style. If the iterator is numeric, and the associated actions are arithmetic increments, then (1), which is simplest, is preferable. The reader will find it instructive to transcribe the various forms of the numeric iterators into loop constructs that use **while, until, step** and **doing** clauses.

4.3.8.5 The **init** and **term** clauses

The **init** and **term** clauses of the general loop construct allow us to specify initialization actions and termination actions to be performed upon entry and exit from the loop.

(a) If the **init** clause is present, then the sequence of statements labeled by the **init** is executed once before any execution of the loop body, and before evaluation of the **while** clause (if present).
(b) If the **term** clause is present, then the sequence of statements labeled by the **term** keyword is executed once on exit from the block, after evaluation of the **until** clause (if present).

To summarize, the precise effect of the complete loop construct

```
loop init statementi
    doing statementsd while testw step statementss until testu term statementt
do
    statement
end;
```

can be described by the following equivalent sequence of statements:

```
            statementi          $ The init statement.
    start:
            statementd          $ The doing statement.
            if not testw then   $ The while condition.
                goto term;
            end if;

            statement           $ The actual body of the loop.

    step:   statements          $ The step statement.

            if testu then       $ The until condition.
                goto term;
            end if;

                goto start;     $ To continue looping.

    term:
            statementt          $ The term statement.
```

The labels appearing in this code segment also allow us to give a simple definition of **continue** and **quit** statements in a loop construct. The statement

continue;

is equivalent to the statement

```
goto start;
```

and the statement:

```
quit;
```

is equivalent to

```
goto term;
```

4.4 The **goto** Statement

In the example just given, and in the previous chapters, we have several times made use of the notion of a **goto** and the concept of a *label*. It is time to examine this very basic, though rarely used, statement more closely. A **goto** statement changes the flow of program execution in the most direct fashion. When we execute the statement

```
goto there;
```

then execution of the program passes immediately to the statement marked by the label *there*. A SETL label is simply an identifier followed by a colon. Any executable statement can be labeled, and any number of labels can appear before a statement.

```
try_again: read(x);
    if x = om then
        goto have_read_everything;
    end if;
    total := total + x;
    goto try_again;
have_read_everything: print(total);
```

This code should be regarded as inferior (because it is less easy to read) to code which accomplishes the same effect by using a **while** or **until** loop.

The **goto** statement has come to be regarded as a dangerous construct, whose use should be avoided, and some programming languages exclude this statement altogether. While avoiding this puritanical approach, we stress that the **goto** statement is only rarely useful, and that one should strive to describe control flow using the safer constructs described so far: conditionals, **case** statements and loops, but not **goto**'s.

Reservations concerning unrestricted use of the **goto** rest on sound pragmatic grounds. Programs that depend heavily upon the use of **goto**'s are hard to read and to understand, difficult to modify, error-prone, and thus dangerous. Heavy use of labels and **goto**'s obscures the logical structure of a program. In particular, when backward jumps appear in the middle of a large program, their intent is obscure, and the purpose of the code is therefore harder to comprehend.

There are, however, a few cases in which the **goto** statement is useful. The most common of those relates to abrupt exits from a sequence of related code fragments. If they all test for some common kind of error, it may be appropriate to place a label past the end of all these fragments, and to **goto** this label if an error is detected. This is the most common guise in which the **goto** will be seen in this book. Note, however, that ordinarily exit from loops is clearly described by **quit** and **continue** statements, which should always be preferred to **goto**'s and labels.

SETL imposes certain restrictions on the position of labels and of **goto**'s that refer to them. These restrictions are as the following:

(a) A **goto** lying outside a loop construct cannot refer to labels that appear within the body of the loop.
(b) A **goto** can only refer to a label that appears within the same procedure or main program as the **goto**. (See Chapter 5 for a discussion of procedures and main program.)
(c) Label names are local to the procedure in which they appear. (See Section 5.2 for information on scoping rules).

4.5 The **stop** statement

The **stop** statement is used simply to terminate execution when for any reason your program has decided that it should not go on (e.g., when all necessary work has been finished). This statement can be used either in your main program or in any procedure (see Chapter 5). A typical example of its use might be

if workpile = { } **then stop**; **end**;

Of course, your program will always stop by itself when it has executed the last statement of your main program. So no **stop** statement is needed there (even though it does no harm to put one in).

4.6 The **assert** statement

The form of an **assert** statement is

assert expn; (1)

where *expn* designates any Boolean-valued expression. To execute such a statement, the *expn* it contains is evaluated. If the resulting value is **false**, a message of the form 'ASSERTION FAILED AT LINE XXX OF PROCEDURE YYY' is printed, and execution terminates. If **true**, then control passes immediately to the statement following the **assert** statement. More precisely, a **false** assertion will terminate execution if the *check assertions* feature of the SETL execution-time system is switched on. Moreover, if the *confirm assertions* feature of the SETL execution-time system is switched on, then each TRUE assertion will produce a message 'ASSERTION PASSED AT LINE XXX OF PROCEDURE YYY'. (See the discussion in Chapter 9 of the execution-time initial program parameter **assert**.)

Assert statements are ordinarily used in a program for one of two reasons:

(i) To document and to check logical conditions which the programmer knows to be critical for correct functioning of her program. Used in this way, **assert** statements constitute a powerful program debugging aid. See Sections 6.2 and 6.7 for additional discussion of this point.

(ii) To trigger any side effects caused by evaluation of the Boolean -expn- that the statement (1) contains. Note that this -expn- can contain assignments or other subexpressions (such as existential or universal quantifiers) whose evaluation causes side effects. Evaluation of the **assert** statement (1) will always trigger these side effects even if assertion checking is switched off. (See the discussion of initial program parameter **assert** in Chapter 9).

Perhaps the most common case of this second use of the **assert** statement is in constructs of the form

assert exists x **in** s | C(x);

This construct can be used whenever one is certain that the set {x **in** s | C(x)} is non-null, and in this case it will always give *x* a value such that *C*(*x*) is TRUE. A similar, somewhat more elaborate, use of the **assert** statement is shown in

assert (exists x **in** s | C(x)) **or (exists** x **in** s1 | C1(x));

Assuming that the assertion is **true**, execution of this statement will always set *x* either to an element of *s* for which *C*(*x*) is **true** or to an element of *s*1 for which *C*1(*x*) is **true**.

4.7 Programming Examples

4.7.1 An interpreter for a simple language

One of the most typical uses of the **case** statement is programming an interpreter. An *interpreter* is simply a program that executes sequences of commands written in some formalized language. An interpreter works by reading one command at a time, executing it, and then reading the next command, etc. Interpreters serve as an obvious means of creating special-purpose languages, and we will say more about this at the end of this section, but first we will present an example of an interpreter. This will make use of most of the control structures that we have examined so far in this chapter.

We will write an interpreter for the so-called Turtle language used in a popular system for grade-school computer education. The Turtle language consists of a series of commands that control the motion of a "turtle" on a screen or on a sheet of paper. The motions of the turtle generate a picture, and the purpose of the interpreter is to read a series of commands in Turtle language and construct the corresponding picture. The state of the Turtle at any given time is described by its coordinates and its direction of motion. The turtle can be commanded to move forward a certain number of steps, turn left or right, and put its pen down (to draw) or up (to move without drawing a line). The full list of commands and their syntax is the following:

FORWARD N	—Move forward *N* steps.
RIGHT	—Turn right from current direction of motion.
LEFT	—Turn left from current direction of motion.
PEN_UP	—Move without leaving a trace.
PEN_DOWN	—Draw every motion.
DRAW	—Display picture of motions so far.
END	—Terminate picture, draw it, and stop.

For example, the following sequence of commands

```
PEN_DOWN
FORWARD 5
RIGHT
FORWARD 10
RIGHT
FORWARD 5
RIGHT
FORWARD 5
RIGHT
FORWARD 10
DRAW
```

generates the following picture:

```
          *
          *
          *
          *
          *
* * * * * * * * * * *
*         *         *
*         *         *
*         *         *
*         *         *
x         * * * * * *
```

(Turtle starts here)

4.7.1.1 Construction of a Turtle language interpreter

Our interpreter for the Turtle language will consist largely of a simple **case** statement, each of whose options correspond to one command in the Turtle language. That is to say, the basic structure of the interpreter will be as follows:

```
case command of
('RIGHT'): .....
('LEFT'): .....
('FORWARD'): .....
etc.
```

Of course, we have to fill the dotted sections with an exact description of the actions that represent the corresponding motion of the turtle. This requires that we decide on how to represent the picture being drawn, and also the position and direction of motion of the turtle at each step.

First let us examine the matter of picture representation. In order to keep our task simple, we assume that the track of the turtle will be displayed by means of **print** commands. Each **print** statement generates one line of output, and it is reasonable to describe the picture as a sequence of lines. To make matters definite, we must choose the height and width of the picture: We choose size 50 by 50, so that it can fit easily on a simple page of printed output. This size will not change during execution of the program so we just initialize the picture to be an array consisting of 50 strings of length 50, consisting only of blanks:

```
picture := 50*[50*' '];
```

Notice the double use of the replication operation: the expression 50*' ' yields a string of 50 blanks; the brackets around this expression give us a tuple whose only element is such a string; and the outer replication operation yields a tuple with 50 elements, each of which is a blank string.

Of course this is not the only possible way of representing the picture. (Try to think of some alternative representations.) However, we shall see that this choice simplifies the creation and display of the picture.

The position of the turtle at each step is defined by giving a line and a character position on the line. If we think of each line as drawn horizontally across the picture, then the pair [row, column] designates the turtle position. In our simple interpreter the turtle can move in one of four directions, which we can label "NORTH," "EAST," "SOUTH," and "WEST," with the usual (Northern Hemisphere) convention that north is up. We choose to start the turtle on its trek from the lower left-hand corner of the picture, facing north.

Next let us sketch the actions performed upon each Turtle command. The turning commands—RIGHT and LEFT—are the simplest: they change only the direction of motion of the turtle, not its position, and they do not add anything to the picture being drawn. In what follows we have chosen to implement those commands simply by looking up the direction that lies to the right or left of the present direction of motion. This look-up operation uses SETL maps.

The pen commands—PEN_UP and PEN_DOWN—affect neither the position nor the direction of motion of the turtle. We describe their effect by using a Boolean variable called -tracing-, which is interrogated whenever the turtle actually moves.

The only nontrivial command is -FORWARD *N*- where *N* is some positive integer. This command alters the position of the turtle and produces a segment of the picture if the -tracing- indicator is **true**. Clearly the action of FORWARD depends on the current direction of motion. If the turtle faces east, the motion will be to the right, along a line or row. The same is true if the turtle faces west. On the other hand, if the turtle faces north or south, then its motion is along a column, and its row position is altered. The forward statement is therefore best described by a **case** statement. Let -distance- designate the extent of the specified forward motion, and let [new_row, new_col] be the coordinates at which the turtle finds itself after the motion. Then the effect of FORWARD can be described as follows:

```
case direction of

('NORTH'):  new_row  := row - distance;
            new_col  := column;

('EAST'):   new_col  := column + distance;
            new_row  := row;
            .....

            etc.
```

Finally, how is the picture itself to be created? We want to fill in the trajectory described by the turtle by using some printable character, say the asterisk: '*'. After each FORWARD command, we want to place asterisks along the line from [row, column] to [new_row, new_column]. This is simple if the motion is horizontal, i.e., new_row = row, since in this case the line to be drawn is a part of the current row. If we recall that the picture is described by an array of horizontal lines or rows, then it is clear that the line on which the turtle is currently moving is given by picture(row). The motion of the turtle fills a substring of this row, and in the case of eastward motion this can be expressed as follows:

```
picture(row)(col..new_col) := distance* '*';
```

Westward motion is equally simple to describe. North-south motion is a trifle harder to handle. In such a motion, the turtle stays on the same column but crosses several rows. The line it traces has one character on each row traversed. We lay down the line as follows:

```
(for i in [row..new_row])
    picture(i)(column) := '*';
end;
```

We want our interpreter to read any number of turtle commands, and we do not know a priori how many there will be. We therefore enclose our basic case statement in another loop, this one bracketed by the lines:

loop do

and

end loop;

Finally, the statement

stop;

which our interpreter must associate with the **end** command, will terminate interpretation.

```
program turtle;
   right := {['NORTH','EAST'],['EAST','SOUTH'],['SOUTH','WEST'],
            ['WEST','NORTH']}
     $ The map giving the direction to the left of any direction is obviously
     $ the inverse of the -right- map.

       left := {[d1,d2]: [d2,d1] in right};
       picture := 50*[50*' '];

     $ Initially the turtle is at the lower left-hand of the picture, facing north.

       direction := 'NORTH';
       row := 50;
       column := 1;
       tracing := false;
loop do
     $ Main loop of the interpreter.

       read(command);

       case command of

       ('RIGHT'): direction := right(direction);

       ('LEFT'): direction := left(direction);

       ('PEN_UP'): tracing := false;

       ('PEN_DOWN'): tracing := true;

       ('DRAW','END'):
          (for line in picture)
             print(line);

          end;

          picture := 50*[50*' '];
          if command = 'END' then stop; end if;
```

```
('FORWARD'): read(distance);
   case direction of
   ('NORTH'): new_row := (row - distance) max 1;
      new_col := column;

   ('EAST'): new_col := (column + distance) min 50;
      new_row := row;

   ('WEST'): new_col := (column - distance) max 1;
      new_row := row;

   ('SOUTH'): new_row := (row + distance) min 50;
      new_col := column;

   end case;

   if tracing then

      if new_row = row then

$ Find first and last column needed for tracing
         min_col := column MIN new_col;
         max_col := column MAX new_col;
         picture(row)(min_col..max_col) := distance* '*';

      else

$ Find first and last row.
         min_row := row MIN new_row;
         max_row := row MAX new_row;

         (for r in [min_row..max_row])
            picture(r)(column) := '*';
         end;
      end if;
   end if;

   row := new_row;
   column := new_col;

 else print('INVALID COMMAND:', COMMAND);

 end case;

end loop;

end program turtle;
```

Several additional details of this program deserve notice:

(a) Two Turtle commands output drawing: the **draw** command, and the **end** command. It is therefore natural to place both commands in the same **case** tag and to add another simple check, made after the picture has been produced, to determine whether the program should stop.

(b) We all make mistakes, and the interpreter should be prepared to handle less-than-perfect instructions. What should the interpreter do, for example, with the commands

```
FORWAED 10
RIGTH
PIN_UP
```

and so on? In this program we have chosen to notify the user that a command just read is not part of the known set of Turtle commands. This is the purpose of the **else** clause of the **case** statement. A more ambitious program might try to recognize misspellings of the known commands, accept abbreviations for them, accept upper- and lowercase names for commands, and so on. Some of these extensions are pursued in the following exercises.

(c) A different sort of error is exemplified by the command

```
FORWARD 200
```

which attempts to move the turtle beyond the bounds of the picture. In the preceding program, we have made sure that the values of new_row and new_col are always in the range 1 to 50.

(d) The printer is not the best device on which to display a picture. If you run the program as written, you will notice that the separation between successive lines is greater than that between successive characters on a line. As a result the picture looks cramped in the horizontal direction. A more aesthetic result is obtained if we count each horizontal step as two characters, or always add a blank between horizontal characters. This nicety is left to the reader.

4.7.2 Various elementary sorting techniques

Sorting is the problem of taking a set or tuple of items (such as integers, real numbers, or strings) which can be compared to one another and putting them in order. Dozens of interesting ways of using a computer to sort are known, and a few of the more interesting high-efficiency sorting techniques will be presented in later chapters. In this section, we present only some very simple sorting methods, which serve to illustrate various control structures discussed in this chapter. The first and simplest of these, the *bubble sort* method, sorts a tuple. It works simply by scanning the tuple for adjacent components which are out of order and interchanging them if they are found. In this way, larger items "bubble up" to their proper position in the tuple. When no out-of-order pairs remain, the tuple is sorted.

In SETL this is simply

```
(while exists i in [1 .. #t - 1] | t(i) > t(i + 1))
    [t(i), t(i + 1)] := [t(i + 1), t(i)];  $ interchange the items.
end while;
```

This bubble-sort procedure has a number of interesting variants. In one of them, we simply sweep repeatedly through the tuple, interchanging all pairs of adjacent items which are out of order.

If we perform this sweeping operation at least as many times as the tuple has components, all items will be swept into their proper positions, since even if the smallest item originally came last it will have time to move down to the first position in the tuple.

We can express this "sweeping" procedure as

```
(for number of_times in [1 .. # t])
     (for i in [1 .. # t - 1] | t(i) > t(i + 1))
          [t(i), t(i + 1)] := [t(i + 1), t(i)]; $ interchange
     end for;
end for;
```

This can also be put more succinctly as

```
(for number_of_times in [1 .. # t], i in [1 .. # t - 1]) | t(i) > t(i + 1))
     [t(i), t(i + 1)] := [t(i + 1), t(i)];
end for;
```

A very different sorting method is to search repeatedly for the minimum element of a tuple, put it at the end of a new tuple which is being built up, and delete it from the original tuple. This is called the *selection sort* method. It can be written as

```
new_tup := [ ];                          $ initialize tuple to be built up.

(for i in [1 .. # t])

   min_till_now := t(1); min_place = 1;  $ save minimum element
                                         $ scanned, and its location

   (for j in [2 .. # t] | t(j) < min_till_now)

      min_till_now := t(j);              $ save value of newly found
                                         $ minimum
      min_place := j;                    $ save position of new minimum

   end for;

   new_tup with := min_till_now;         $ put minimum element at end
                                         $ of new tuple
   t(min_place .. min_place) := [ ]      $ delete minimum element

end for i;
```

Beyond the methods shown here, you will find that it is instructive to review all the ways you can think of to sort a deck of cards by hand and to express these hand-sorting techniques in SETL.

EXERCISES

1. A set of *Markov productions* is an ordered collection of rules of the form $s1 > s2$, where $s1$ and $s2$ are both character strings, neither of which contains the character ">." The string $s1$ is called the left side of the production $s1 > s2$, and the string $s2$ is called its right side. To apply such a set of productions to a string *s*, one searches through *s*, looking for a substring which coincides with the left-hand side of some production; if any such production is found, this substring is replaced by the right-hand side of the production.

   Write a *Markov production interpreter* program which reads in a set of Markov productions and a string *s* and then applies *n* successive productions to *s*, displaying the result every *m* steps.

2. How would you express a **for** loop of the form

   (**for** n **in** [1..k] | C(n))..

   in terms of a **while** loop? What about **for** loops of the form

   (**for** x **in** t | C(x))...

   and

   (**for** x = t(i) | C(x))...

   where *t* is a tuple?

3. Write a program which will compare two poker hands (each consisting of five cards) and decide which of the two is the winning hand according to the rules of Poker.

4. Explain how the conditional statement

   if C1 **then** block_of_statements_1
   elseif C2 **then** block_of_statements_2
   elseif...
   block_of_statements_n

   can be reexpressed by using **if** statements of the simple form

   if C **then goto** label_j

   but no other conditional statements.

4.8 Reading and Writing Data

Till now we have been using the two basic input-output commands, **read** and **print**, which allow a SETL program to communicate with the rest of the world, informally. It is now time to discuss these commands more systematically. (More elaborate SETL input-output features, such as **reada**, **printa**, **get**, **put**, etc., are described in Chapter 9).

To produce printed output (or, in the case of an interactive run from a terminal, to send output to the terminal), the **print** statement is used. This has the form

print(exp1, exp2, ..., expk);

where each of exp1, ..., exp*k* is an expression. Any valid expression can appear in a **print** statement, and any valid SETL value, including Boolean values and atoms, can be printed. In particular, sets and tuples can be printed. Thus it is perfectly acceptable to write

print(2 + 2, {1, 2, 3}, [{1}, {{2}}, [{3}]], 'HELLO THERE');

The output produced by this **print** statement will look like

4 {3 1 2} [{1} {{2}} [{3}]] HELLO THERE

This example illustrates several details concerning the **print** primitive:

(a) Expressions are evaluated before being printed.
(b) The elements of sets are grouped within set brackets, and tuple components are grouped within tuple brackets. For ease of reading, set elements and tuple components are separated by blanks rather than by commas (even though this can lead to ambiguities when structures containing strings are printed).
(c) Strings are printed without quotation marks; e.g., when we print the constant 'HELLO THERE' only the characters

HELLO THERE

appear in the output file.
(d) Since sets have no particular order when they are printed set elements can appear in any order.
(e) Integers are printed in standard decimal formats. Their representations require a number of characters defined by their size and nature. Floating-point numbers are always printed in exponential form with a fixed number of decimal places; e.g., 2.3 is printed as

2.300000E + 00.

(f) Other kinds of SETL values will be represented by strings formed according to somewhat arbitrary rules. The undefined atom **om** is printed as

*

The Boolean values TRUE and FALSE are printed as #T and #F, respectively. Atoms are represented by strings of the form #nnn, where *nnn* denotes the integer 'serial number' of the atom. Note that these rules inevitably lead to a degree of ambiguity, as shown, e.g., in the output produced by

print([**om**, '*']);
print([TRUE, '#T', FALSE, '#F']);

which is

[* *]
[#T #T #F #F].

(g) Since sets are not printed in any particular order, it can be hard to locate elements in the printed representation of sets, especially large sets.

(h) A single print statement (even a print statement with many arguments) will always try to put all the output which it produces on a single logical line of output. If the value or values to be printed are too large and complex to fit on a single line, they will be printed on as many lines as necessary. When this happens, the points at which one physical line of print ends and the next begins will fall haphazardly, and it can be something of a trial to read the resulting output.

(i) Each print statement starts a new logical line. A parameterless print statement can be used to generate a blank print line. Thus, whereas

print('AA', 'BB', 'CC');

will produce the output

AA BB CC,

the command

print('AA'); **print**('BB'); **print**; **print**('CC');

will produce the output

AA
BB

CC

(j) As illustrated by the preceding examples, successive output items produced by a single print statement are separated by a few blanks but do not start a new line.

The SETL print facility is quite easy to use but does not produce output comparing in elegance with the formatted output generated by programs written in various other languages, especially languages such as PL/I or COBOL, which have a commercial orientation. To produce more elegant formulated output in SETL, it is necessary (albeit easy) to make use of string primitives which the language provides (see Sections 2.5.3 and 5.8). These allow one to build up output strings of arbitrary format and complexity. Note in particular that the **str** operator produces the very same string representation of a value that the **print** command would print but makes this string available as an internal object which can be manipulated by using the string operations which SETL provides. These facilities make it easy to program an arbitrarily complex "pretty print" function in SETL. Such a procedure can indent nested sets and tuples nicely, can sort their elements to make searching easier, etc. Utilities of this kind are well worth developing when large objects need to be printed and inspected repeatedly.

To read input from the standard input file (or, for interactive runs, from the terminal) the **read** statement is used. This has the form

$$\textbf{read}(\text{Lhs1}, \text{Lhs2}, \ldots, \text{Lhsk}), \tag{1}$$

where each of Lhs1, ..., Lhs$k$ is either a simple variable or a more complex expression of the kind which could legally appear on the left-hand side of an assignment statement: see Section 3.12. The statement (1) reads in a sequence of SETL values from the standard input file and makes them the values of Lhs1, Lhs2, ..., Lhsk, respectively. For example, if the next three items in the input file are

```
{1 2 3}
'HELLO THERE'
[{1},2,A],
```

then the command

$$\textbf{read}(x, y, z)$$

will give x, y, and z the respective values $\{1,2,3\}$, 'HELLO THERE', and $[\{1\},2,\text{'A'}]$. This example illustrates several of the following rules governing the **read** primitive.

(i) Successive items in a bracketed SETL value to be read can be separated either by commas or by blanks. For example, to read in the set $\{1,2,3\}$ we can write its external representation either as

$$\{1,2,3\}$$

or as

$$\{1\ 2, 3\}$$

or as

$$\{1\ 2\ 3\}$$

etc.

(ii) Unbracketed items separated by blanks will be read in by successive **read** statements even if they all appear on a single line. None of them will be bypassed, and reading will advance from one line to the next only when more input data are needed to complete the line being read. For example if the first three lines of the input file are

```
1 2 3 4 5 {6 7
   8 9
10},
```

then the commands

read(x, y, z);
read(u, v);
read(w);

will give the variables x through z the same values that they would be given by the following assignments:

x := 1; y := 2; z := 3; u := 4; v := 5; w := {6, 7, 8, 9, 10};

(iii) When read in, *valid identifiers*, i.e., unbroken strings of letters and numbers starting with a letter, will be read as strings even if they are not enclosed in quotation marks. For example, if the input file contains

[A BB C123],

then the command **read**(x) will have the same effect as the assignment

x := ['A', 'BB', 'C123'];

(iv) Other items, namely the Boolean values **true** and **false** and the undefined atom **om** can be read in if they are written in the form in which they would be printed by a **print** command. In particular, **true** and **false** can be read in if they are represented as #T and #F in the input file, and **om** can be read in if it is represented as * in the input file. For example, if the input file contains [*, *, #T, #F, *, *] the command **read**(x) will give x the same value that the assignment

x := [**om**, **om**, **true**, **false**];

would give it. These rules imply that the **read** and **print** operations are almost inverses of each other, i.e., that a file of data written by **print** can almost be read back in by using **read**. Unfortunately, this is not quite the case (however, this perfect inverse relationship does hold for SETL "binary" input-output primitives, namely **getb** and **putb**; see Chapter 9). For example, if the string 'Hello there' is written out using **print** and then read back in using **read**, it will appear as the pair 'Hello' 'there' of successive string items. Moreover, if the string 'Hello!there' is written out using **print** then any attempt to read the result will cause an error, since the unquoted character '!' happens to be indigestible to the **read** primitive. (Also, the external form of an atom is indigestible to the **read** primitive.) Thus **read** and **print** are only inverses to one another if the value being printed and then read back in contains no quoted strings which are not valid identifiers (and also contains no atoms).

As **read** operations are successively executed, an implicit "read position" pointer moves progressively forward in the standard input file, past one SETL value at a time, until eventually the very end of the input file is reached. Thus the input file behaves as a "tape" on which successive SETL values are written and from which they can be read. Even when the end of the input file has been reached, the **read** operation will continue to execute without any errors occurring, but in this case all further values read from the input file will be **om**. Therefore the input file behaves exactly as if its actual contents were followed by infinitely many **oms**. To detect the actual end of input, one must use another SETL primitive operation, represented by the keyword **eof** (end of file). This can be used in expressions just as any other variable is, but its value is always **false** if the last **read** operation executed did not encounter the end of the input file which it is reading. Conversely, **eof** is **true** if the end of the input file was reached by the last **read** statement executed. The value of the quantity **eof** changes as soon as a first attempt is made to read past the end of the input file. For example, if the input file contains just the three items {1} {2} {3}, then the loop

```
(for j in [1..4]) read(x); print(x, eof); end;
```

will produce the output

```
{1}  #F
{2}  #F
{3}  #F
*    #T
```

It follows that to read all data items present in the input and print them out one wants to use a loop which tests the **eof** condition immediately after an item is read, as in the following example:

```
loop do   $ loop to read and echo all items in the input file
    read(x);
    if eof then quit; end;
    print(x);
end loop;
```

If a bracketed item is not properly closed and one attempts to read it, then a run-time error occurs. For example, any attempt to read an input file whose last two lines are

```
{1, 2, 3
'HELLO'
```

or whose last line is

```
{1, 2, 3]
```

is fatal.

4.8.1 Reading data from a terminal

Interactive programs typically take their input from the user terminal. The rules described previously also apply to **read** statements that take their data from the terminal screen: a **read** statement will read as many items as it needs, spread over several lines if need be. If too few items were supplied, the **read** statement simply waits until the full input is supplied. To indicate that the input is complete, always enter a carriage return following the end of the data.

A terminal is a potentially infinite source of data. How is the program to determine that an end of file has been encountered in reading from the terminal? The answer depends on the operating system on which you are running. Special characters are used to indicate end of data, and you should find out the conventions used by the operating system on which your SETL system runs. On DEC systems, the character combination Control-Z marks an end of file, so that entering CTRL-Z will make the **eof** test true.

4.8.2 Character sets

The simple **read** and **print** primitives described in this section get input from the standard input file and send output to the standard output file. If input is to be read from the standard input file the lines of data constituting this file should be supplied following your SETL program (for a batch run) and should be typed in interactively at a terminal (in an interactive run). Other more advanced input-output primitives (described in Chapter 9) allow output to be read from and written to other files. These files are made available to your SETL program in a manner which necessarily depends (to a certain extent at least) on the operating system being used. See Chapter 9 for additional details.

Most SETL implementations use the ASCII character set and thus support the full SETL character set. Systems *not* using ASCII usually require some compromises.

Exercises

1. Write a program which reads a set *s* of integers and prints out a list, in ascending order, of all the members of *s* which are prime.

2. A set of vectors of length *n* and a vector *x* of length *n* are given. Write code which selects the elements of *s* which has the largest number of components in common with *x*.

3. Write a program to read a character string, reverse the order of its characters, and print it out.

4. Write a program that will scan a string of characters containing parentheses, square brackets, and set brackets. Determine whether it is properly bracketed. (A string is properly bracketed if each left bracket or parenthesis is matched by a following right bracket or parenthesis of the same kind. For example, {[ ]} is properly bracketed, but {[}] is not.)

5. Write a program that reads in successive pairs of strings *s*, *t* of the same length and determines whether *t* can be obtained from *s* by substituting for the characters of *s* in some single-valued way. For example, 'ipstf' is obtained from 'horse' by the

A: . -	I: . .	Q: -- . -	Y: - . --
B: - . . .	J: . --	R: . - .	Z: -- . .
C: - . - .	K: - . -	S: . . .	,: -- . --
D: - . .	L: . - . .	T: -	.: . - . - . -
E: .	M: --	U: . . -	;: - . - . - .
F: . . - .	N: - .	V: . . . -	:: --- . . .
G: -- .	O: ---	W: . --	’: . ---- .
H:	P: . -- .	X: - . . -	-: - . . . -

Figure 4.8 Morse Codes for Alphabetic and Special Characters

substitution {['h', 'i'], ['o', 'p'], ['r', 's'], ['s', 't'], ['e', 'f']}, but 'beer' cannot be obtained from 'anna' in this way, since two different characters would have to be substituted for 'a'.

6. (a) Write a program which will translate an arbitrary message into Morse code. The Morse codes for all characters of the alphabet and for the most common punctuation marks are shown in Figure 4.8.
   (b) Write a program which will translate Morse code back into English.

7. A publisher produces books both in hard cover and paperback. Any given book can be either long, medium, or short and can be either elementary or advanced. A short, elementary paperback book sells for $5. Exactly $2 is added to the price of a book if it is in hard cover; medium-length books sell for exactly $1 more, and long books for exactly $3 more, than short books. The price of a book is doubled if it is advanced. Write a small program which will print out all possible categories of books together with their prices.

8. Write a program that will read an integer n and print its successive digits separated by spaces, starting with its leftmost digit.

9. Write a program which can read an arbitrary integer and print it in English. For example, -143 should print as 'minus one hundred forty-three'. Can you do the same for French? For German? For Chinese?

10. Write a program to read in three points x, y, z, each represented by a pair of real numbers, and determine whether these three points
    (a) all lie along a line;
    (b) form the corners of an isosceles or equilateral triangle;
    (c) form the corners of a right triangle.
    Print out an appropriate message in each case.

11. Write a program which will read in a sequence of lines, each containing someone's name, first name first, and print out an alphabetized list of these names, in alphabetic order of last names. Repeat this exercise, but this time print the alphabetized list with last names first.

12. Making use of a map from family names into their probable ethnic origins, write a program which reads a list of names and attempts to guess the ethnic origins of their bearers. Your program should also make use of facts like the following to increase its coverage: names beginning with *Mc* are probably Irish, with *Mac*

probably Scottish; names ending in -*ski* are probably Polish, in *ian* probably Armenian, in *wetz* probably East European Jewish, in *ini* probably Italian, etc. How well does your program guess the family origins of your classmates?

Modify this program so that it uses first names to guess sex. Note here that names ending in -*a* are probably female, etc.

13. A college collects statistics on the members of its entering freshman class. The basic information for each student is a line in a data file, consisting of the following items, in sequence, separated by blanks:

    student's last name, first name, age(in years), sex(M or F),

    marital status (0 = single, 1 = married, 2 = divorced or separated)

    Write a program to print out the following information:
    (i) Percentage under 21 years old
    (ii) Percentage over 21 years old
    (iii) Percentage over 30 years old
    (iv) Percentage male and female
    (v) Percentage of males single, married, and divorced or separated
    (vi) Percentage of females single, married, divorced, or separated

14. An automobile sales agency employs 25 salespersons. Sales records are kept on cards, each card holding the following information, separated by blanks:
    (a) Person's last name
    (b) Make of car sold
    (c) Amount of sale
    (d) Net amount of sale (i.e., total amount minus discount allowed for trade-in)
    Write a program which will read a monthly file of such cards and print out the commission due to each salesperson. The rules determining commissions are as follows:
    (i) Standard commission is 5% on the first $20,000 of net sales, 6% on the next $10,000 of net sales, and 7% on all sales over $30,000.
    (ii) Individual sales totaling more than $10,000 earn a 1% bonus.
    (iii) Sales on which less than $500 trade-in is allowed earn a bonus of one half of 1%.

15. A factory's payroll is prepared from a set of daily time cards and a mapping f giving the hourly wage rate for each employee. Each time card contains an employee's social security number followed by the number of hours worked on a particular day. The mapping f sends each employee social security number into the employee's name, hourly wage rate, and tax withholding rate. Total pay is number of hours worked, times hourly base rate, times $(1 - r)$, where r is the tax withholding rate; however, all hours in excess of 40 are paid at a time-and-a-half rate. Write a program to read a file representing a week's payroll records, and print out a payroll showing employee name, social security number, total pay, tax withheld, and net pay.

16. Suppose that the daily time cards of Ex. 15 are grouped into batches separated by cards which contain only the single digit 0, with the Monday batch coming first, Tuesday next, etc., and that work performed on weekends is paid at a double-time rate. Modify the program of Ex. 15 to handle this rule also.

17. In bowling, a complete game consists of 10 frames. Either one or two balls is rolled in a frame. If all 10 pins are knocked down by the first ball rolled in a frame (this event is called a "strike") the score for the frame is 10, plus the number of pins knocked down by the next two balls rolled. If all 10 pins are knocked down by the two balls rolled in a frame (called a "spare"), the score for the frame is 10, plus the number of pins knocked down by the next ball rolled. Otherwise the score for the frame is the number of pins knocked down by the two balls rolled in the frame. If a spare is rolled in the 10th frame, then you are allowed an extra ball; if a strike is rolled in the 10th frame, then you are allowed two extra balls.

    Write a program which will read a tuple representing the number of pins knocked down by each ball rolled during a game and print out the corresponding score.

18. A telegram is transmitted as a single string of characters, with words separated by blanks but the end of each line marked by a dummy word Z. Write a program which will count the number of words in the actual program. Words with more than eight letters in them are to count as two words.

19. Write a program that will read three strings $s1$, $s2$, $s3$ and then determine whether $s2$ occurs as a substring of $s1$ after all characters in $s3$ have been eliminated from $s1$.

CHAPTER 5
Procedures

A *procedure* in SETL is a sequence of computational steps which have been given a name and which, using one or more data items passed to it for processing, will compute and deliver a value. Most of the built-in SETL operators, for example **max**, which returns the maximum of two values x and y, and **cos**, which returns the cosine of a floating-point number x passed to it, are procedures in this sense. However, since no finite collection will ever exhaust the whole catalog of procedures that a programmer may want to use, it is important to have a way of defining, and then using, as many additional operations as are helpful.

5.1 Writing and Using Procedures

To make the preceding point more convincing, we can consider a simple example. Suppose that the weights of individual eggs in batches coming from a chicken farm are measured daily, thus producing batches of measurements, each of which can be thought of as a set of numbers, e.g.,

$$\{2.7, 2.85, 1.90, \ldots, 1.85\} \tag{1}$$

Suppose that in order to enforce some sort of quality control, various statistical properties are to be reported for each batch, including the weights of the three largest and the three smallest eggs in the batch.

To make this calculation easily, it would be convenient to use a preprogrammed procedure to which a set s like (1) can be passed, and which would then produce a tuple t

$$[1.86, 1.90, \ldots, 2.7, 2.85] \tag{2}$$

such that all the members of s are arranged in increasing order. Since this procedure would simply sort the members of s, it can appropriately be called *sort*. We would like to be able to produce the ordered tuple t from the set (1) simply by writing

$$t := \text{sort}(s). \tag{3}$$

Note that if this can be done, then to print the three largest and three smallest measurements we have only to write

```
print('three smallest measurements are:', t(1), t(2), t(3));
print('three largest measurements are:', t(#t), t(#t - 1), t(#t - 2));
```

Of course, sorting the set s is not hard and can be done by the simple method explained in Section 4.7.2, which is to say, using the code

```
t := [ ];

(while s /= { })
      t with := (x := min/s);                    (4)
      s less := x;
end while;
```

However, what we want is to *package* the code (4), giving it the name *sort* and invoking it by this *name*. By doing this we make it possible to get the effect of the code (4), without having to concern ourselves with its inner workings, simply by writing (3). To "package" bits of code in this way becomes absolutely essential when one is constructing large programs (say a few hundred lines or more). Such large programs can only be built successfully if they are organized hierarchically into a modular collection of subprocedures; typically such a collection will include both high-level functions which simply make use of facilities provided by lower-level functions, and low-level procedures, like the *sort* which we have been discussing, which encapsulate generally useful primitive operations. Like most other programming languages, SETL does provide a facility for defining as many new procedures as you need, and we now proceed to explain how this is done.

To *package* or *encapsulate* the code (4), all we need to do is to enclose it between procedure *header* and *trailer* lines and add a **return** statement. This gives

```
procedure sort(s);
t = [ ];

(while s /= { })
      t with := (x := min/s);
      s less := x;
end while;                                        (5)

return t;

end procedure sort;
```

In (5) the procedure header line is

procedure sort(s); (5a)

This line, introduced by the special keyword **procedure** (which can also be abbreviated as **proc**), opens the procedure (5), gives it a name (in this case, the name *sort*), and also names its *formal parameters* (sometimes simply called *parameters*), i.e., the names of values which will be passed to the procedure whenever it is used (as in (3)), and from which the procedure will calculate the value that it returns. (In (5), the value returned is *t*, and there is only one formal parameter, namely, *s*.) The concluding trailer line

end procedure sort; (5b)

marks the end of the procedure.

Finally the command

return t; (5c)

appearing in (5) both indicates the point at which the procedure computation has finished *calculating the value which it is to produce* and defines the value that the procedure will return.

To *call* or *invoke* the procedure *sort* defined by (5), we have only to write sort(*e*), where *e* can be any set-valued expression (provided that the set members are all integers, or all real numbers, etc.). This automatically calculates and makes available the value returned by the procedure (5). For example, if we write

print(sort({5, 1, 2, 7, 0})); (5d)

the result will be

[0 1 2 5 7]

The expression *e* occurring in such an invocation sort(*e*) of the procedure *sort* is called the *actual parameter*, or *supplied argument, of the invocation*. Whenever evaluation of a procedure invocation like (5d) begins, the value of the actual parameter (or parameters) appearing in it is transmitted to the procedure invoked and becomes the initial value of the procedure's formal parameter (or parameters).

To examine the behavior of SETL function call more closely let us consider an invocation of the procedure, *sort*:

x := sort({5, 1, 2, 7, 0}); (6)

As with all assignment statements, execution of (6) begins with evaluation of its right-hand side. Since *sort* is the name of a procedure, evaluation of the procedure call appearing on the right-hand side of the assignment (6) involves the following steps:

(i) The current value of the actual parameter {5, 1, 2, 7, 0} of the procedure invocation is assigned as the initial value of the formal parameter variable *s* appearing in the procedure header line of the procedure (5).

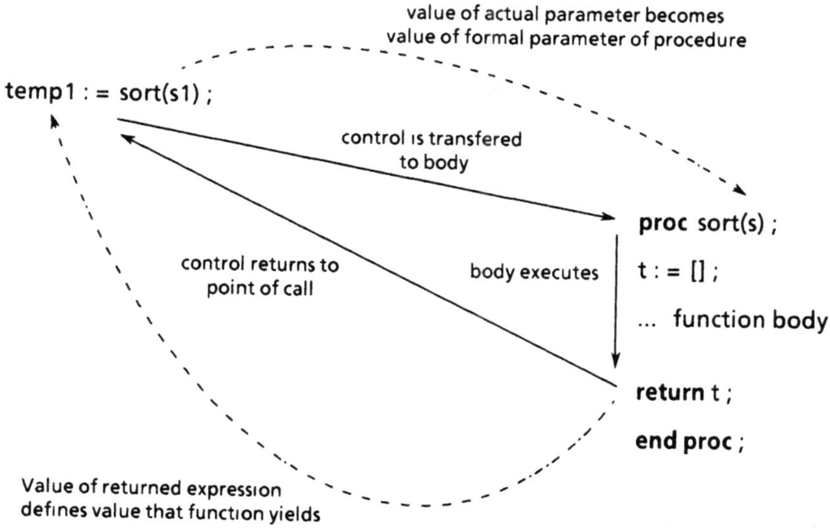

Figure 5.1 Detour and Return in Function Invocations

(ii) Execution of the procedure (5) begins: the statements appearing in the body of this procedure are executed in the ordinary way. Wherever a formal parameter appears, in the body of the procedure, the value of the corresponding actual parameter passed to the procedure is used.

(iii) As soon as a **return** statement is encountered, control is passed back from the procedure (5) to the instruction immediately following the call (6). Just before this happens, the expression following the keyword **return** is evaluated and becomes the value that the procedure (5) yields (e.g., becomes the value of the variable x in (6)).

This "detour and return" action of function invocations is shown schematically in Figure 5.1.

The following analogy should help to clarify the important distinction between the *formal parameters* and the *actual parameters* of a procedure. The formal parameters of a procedure can be compared to the ingredient names in a cookbook recipe. For example, a recipe may say "break an egg into half a cup of flour and stir." The names *egg* and *flour* appearing in such a recipe are *formal names* which stand for all the actual eggs and actual half cups of flour that will be used when the recipe is actually followed. As in the case of a function, new actual items, i.e., a different egg and a different half cup of flour, must be supplied each time the recipe is used, even though the formal names *egg* and *flour* appearing in the recipe remain the same. Continuing this analogy, the text of the recipe can be compared to the body of a procedure, which will yield something (e.g., a cake) when *actual* ingredients matching the *formal* ingredient names to which it refers are substituted.

It is also instructive to consider an example involving two invocations of *sort* with two different parameters:

$$x := \text{sort}(s1) + \text{sort}(s2); \tag{6b}$$

Suppose that $s1$ and $s2$ happen to have the values $\{3, 1, 0\}$ and $\{-3, -1, 0\}$, respectively, when (6b) is executed. Then evaluation of sort(s1) will produce the value $[0, 1, 3]$ and evaluation of sort(s2) will produce the value $[-3, -1, 0]$, so that after (6b) is executed the variable x will have the value $[0, 1, 3, -3, -1, 0]$.

The way this happens is as follows. As with all assignment statements, execution of (6b) begins with evaluation of its right-hand side, i.e., sort(s1) + sort(s2). This is an expression and is evaluated by first evaluating its two subexpressions sort(s1) and sort(s2) and then combining the two resulting values using the "+" operator.

The value of x in statement (6b) will be the same as the value of x resulting from the execution of

```
temp1 := sort(s1);
temp2 := sort(s2);                    (7)
x := temp1 + temp2;
```

As you can see, (7) involves two succesive invocations of *sort*, followed by a use of the "+" operator to combine the two results produced.

The following important rules govern the use of procedures.

(a) The formal parameters that appear in the procedure heading must be valid identifiers, that is to say, they must be variable names; furthermore no two formal parameters can have the same name. For example, both

procedure p1(s*t); (8a)

and

procedure p2(s, t, s); (8b)

are illegal: (8a) because the parameter *s*t* is not a simple variable, and (8b) because the first and the third formal parameters of *p2* are identical. On the other hand, any actual parameter of a function invocation can be an (arbitrarily complicated) expression, and actual parameters can be repeated. For example,

x := sort({x **in** ss | x > 0}); (9a)

is legal if *ss* is a set (and if *ss* were $\{-10, 20, -20, 15, 10\}$ would give x the value $[10, 15, 20]$). Similarly, if dot_prod(x, y) is a function which calculates and returns the dot-product of the two tuples x and y, then

a := dot_prod(u, u); (9b)

is legal (and will put the sum of the squared components of the tuple *u* into *a*).

(b) Each invocation of a procedure must have exactly as many actual parameters as the procedure has formal parameters. (However, it is possible to define procedures for which this rule is relaxed; see Section 5.6.1). When a procedure is invoked, the value of its first (resp. second, third, etc.) actual parameter becomes the value of its first (resp. second, third, etc.) formal parameter. For example, if a procedure whose header line is

```
procedure intermingle(a, b, c);
```

is invoked by

```
x := intermingle ({x in s | x > 0}, {y in s2 | y < 0}, {x in s | x > 0});
```

then *a* and *c* initially get the value {x **in** s | x > 0}, and the value {y **in** s2 | *y* < 0} is transmitted to *b*.

(c) The body of a procedure can contain any number of **return** statements and often will contain more than one. The following code, which simply calculates and returns the maximum of two quantities, exemplifies this remark:

```
procedure my_very_own_max_function(x, y);

if x > y then
    return x;
else
    return y;
end if;

end procedure my_very_own_max_function;
```

If no **return** statement is encountered, execution of the procedure will terminate when and if its trailer line **end proc** is reached, and in this case the undefined value **om** will be returned.[1]

Note that the keyword **return** can be followed by an arbitrary expression. This expression may be complex; in fact, the whole body of the function may simply consist of a single **return** statement and nothing else, as in

```
procedure positive_elements_in(s);
    $ returns the set of positive elements of s

return {x in s | x > 0};

end procedure positive_elements_in;
```

[1] Other programming languages make the distinction between a function which returns a value, and a procedure, which does not. This distinction is not present in SETL: a procedure may or may not return a value.

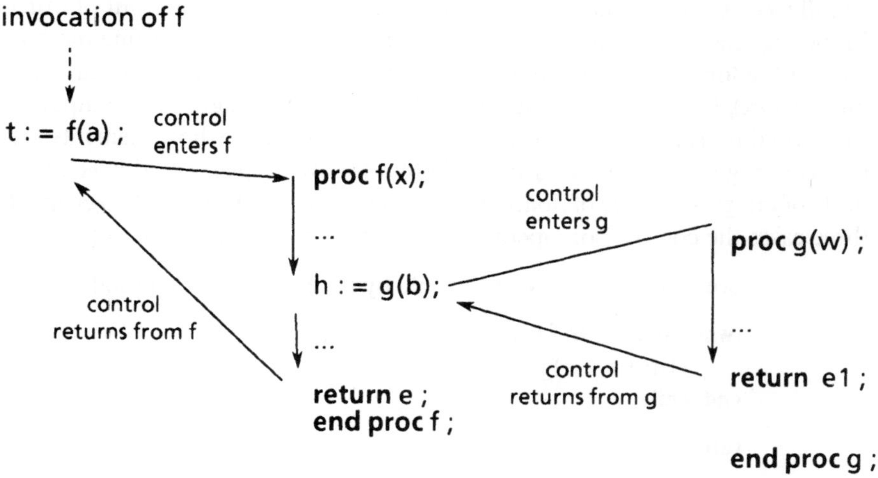

Figure 5.2 Patterns of Control Transfer in Multiple Function Calls.

(d) Procedures can invoke other procedures (including themselves) without restriction. When control is transferred to a procedure *f* which in turn invokes a function *g*, execution will proceed within the body of *f* until an invocation of *g* is encountered, at which point execution of *f* will be suspended and execution of *g* will begin. Thereafter, *g* will execute until a **return** statement is encountered within *g*, at which point *g* will terminate, sending control, and possibly a value, back to *f*. Subsequently, when a **return** statement is encountered in *f*, *f* will itself be terminated, sending control (and a value) back to the procedure from which *f* was invoked. This will lead to patterns of control transfer like that shown in Figure 5.2.

(e) Procedure invocations are themselves expressions and can be used freely as parts of more complex expressions. For example, if *sort* is a function which returns the elements of a set *s* in sorted order as a tuple, and *sum_square* is a function which returns the sum of the squares of the three first elements of a tuple, then we can write

print(sum_square(sort(s)));

to display the sum of the squares of the three smallest elements of *s*.

5.1.1 Some simple sorting procedures

To illustrate the use of procedures, we will now exhibit a variety of procedures for sorting a set or tuple of elements into order. One simple, well-known way of sorting is the so-called bubble-sort method, which, simply stated, operates as follows: as long as there are two adajacent elements that are out of order in the sequence, interchange them. This is not a very efficient sorting method (and in the form presented here it is even more inefficient than the standard bubble sort), but it is one of the simplest to state and program. The input to the procedure is a tuple, and the output is another tuple, whose elements are in increasing order. Note that the code that follows applies equally well to a tuple of integers, a tuple of floating-point numbers, or a tuple of strings: in all three cases the comparison operator ">" defines the desired ordering.

```
proc sort(t);      $ sorts a tuple by the bubble-sort method

(while exists i in [1 .. #t - 1] | t(i) > t(i + 1))
     [t(i), t(i - 1)] := [t(i + 1), t(i)];
end while;

return t;

end proc sort;
```

(The attentive reader will notice that this procedure modifies its own parameter *t* and will wonder whether the value of the actual parameter will be modified when *sort* is invoked. In fact, the value of the actual parameter will not really be affected outside sort; but the rule guaranteeing this will only be stated in Section 5.5. This same remark also applies to several of the procedures presented later in this section.)

As we mentioned, the procedure just shown can be used to sort any tuple of integers, of reals, or of strings. For example, if we write

```
print(sort(['Joe', 'Ralph', 'Albert', 'Cynthia', 'Robert', 'Alfredo']));
```

the result will be

```
[Albert Alfredo Cynthia Joe Ralph Robert]
```

More complex sorting routines than that shown are often needed. One reason for this is that sorting is often used to arrange more complex "records" into an order determined by some common "subfield" of the records. In SETL, such records are typically represented as tuples. Suppose, for example, that a group of students have taken a course in which their grades on a series of homework exercises and examinations have been collected, producing a tuple of tuples having the following form:

```
records := [['Gonzalez, Aldo', 80, 87, om, 73, 90, ..],
            ['Woburn, Linda', 82, 89, 85, 91, 90, 65, ..],
            ['Luciano, Luigi', 80, 81, 75, 79, om, 70, ..],
```

Grades are assumed to be represented by integers, and missed exercises or examinations by occurrences of **om**. One might then want to arrange these records in various orders, e.g.,

(a) Alphabetic order of student names
(b) Order of grade averages, with largest first

(c) Order of grades on midterm examination, largest first
(d) Order of number of exercises not handed in, largest first, etc.

To make it easy to sort these records according to any of their fields, we modify our original sorting procedure, so that it takes two arguments:

(i) The tuple of records to be sorted.
(ii) The record component by which the records must be sorted.

This leads to the following procedure (which, however, does not treat **om** components correctly: see the following discussion).

```
procedure sort1(t, pos);

$ t is a tuple of records (tuples) to be sorted.
$ pos is the index of the component in each record, along which
$ the records are to be sorted in increasing order.

(while exists i in [1 .. #t - 1] | t(i)(pos) > t(i + 1)(pos))

        [t(i), t(i + 1)] := [t(i + 1), t(i)];

end while;

return t;

end;
```

Using this function, we can print the class records in alphabetical order simply by writing

```
(for x in sort1(records, 1))
    print(x);
end;
```

Suppose now that we want to list these records in order of decreasing midterm grades, with students who have missed the midterm coming last. If the midterm is the 11th entry in the record, we may be tempted to sort the records (into increasing order) according to that component and then list them in reverse. The attentive reader will notice that sortl as written will not work in the presence of missing grades: recall the convention that a missed test is marked as **om** in the record. The comparison (**om** > *x*) where *x* is same value is not meaningful, and in fact the SETL system will stop any program at the point at which such a comparison is attempted. As a necessary modification to our sorting procedure, we will therefore replace the comparison that drives the **while** loop, so that a value of **om** is regarded as smaller than any existing grade. Using the "is_undefined" operator, we simply replace *t*(*i*)(pos) by *t*(*i*)(pos) ? (−1). The improved sorting routine then reads

```
procedure sort2(t, pos);

$ T is a tuple of records, some of whose components may be om.
$ pos is the index of the record component along which the records
$ are to be sorted in increasing order.
```

```
    (while exists i in [1.. # t − 1] | t(i)(pos) ? (−1) > t(i + 1)(pos) ? (−1))
      [t(i), t(i + 1)] := [t(i + 1), t(i)];
    end while;
    return t;
    end;
```

With this modification, we can print the desired ordering of records by midterm grades using the following code (recall that a student's name is the first component of his/her record, the midterm grade is the 11th component of the record, and this grade may be undefined):

```
ordered := sort2(records, 11);
(for i in [#ordered, #ordered − 1..1])
    print(ordered(i)(1), ordered(i)(11) ? '**absent**');
end for;
```

5.1.1.1 The main block of a program

A program that makes use of procedures of course includes commands that invoke these procedures. As we have explained, the first function invoked can subsequently invoke any or all of the other functions, but at least one instruction not belonging to any procedure is needed to trigger this first invocation. In a program including one or more procedures, the "directly executed" protion of the program, i.e., everything not included in any procedure, is called the *main block of the program*, or the *main program* for short. This block of instructions has exactly the form of a **program** body, as described in Chapters 2 and 3, and it must precede all procedures. The main program and all the procedures which follow it must be prefixed by a **program** header line of the usual form, and a corresponding trailer line starting with the keyword **end** must follow the last procedure.

For example, a complete program consisting of the *sort* function shown previously and the two fragments of code which invoke it would have the following overall structure:

```
program print_grade_info:   $ program to print student grade records

    read(records);               $ acquire the basic data
    print ('student records in alphabetical order');
    print ('----------------------------------------');

    (for x in sort (records, 1))
       print(x);
    end;

    print('students and mid-term grades, in decreasing grade order');
    print('----------------------------------------------------------');
```

```
    ordered := sort(records, 11);

    (for i in [#ordered, #ordered - 1 .. 1])
       print(ordered(i)(1), ordered(i)(11) ? '**absent**');
    end for;

    proc sort(t, pos);

    $ t is a tuple of records. pos is the position of the record component
      according
    $ to which the records are to be sorted in increasing order.

    (while exists i in [1 .. #t - 1] | t(i)(pos) ? (-1) > t(i + 1)(pos) ? (-1))
          [t(i), t(i + 1)] := [t(i + 1), t(i)];
    end while;

    return t;

    end proc sort;

  end program print_grade_info;
```

Execution of such a program begins at the first statement of its main program block and ends as soon as the last statement of its main program block has been executed (or when a **stop** statement is encountered; see Section 4.5).

5.1.2 A character-conversion procedure

As a next example, we define a procedure that takes a string and returns a similar string in which all lowercase alphabetic characters have been changed into the corresponding uppercase characters. Blanks and punctuation marks are not affected.

```
proc capitalize(s);   $ capitalizes the string s and returns
                      $ the result. Nonalphabetic characters are left alone

small_letters := 'abcdefghijklmnopqrstuvwxyz';
big_letters := 'ABCDEFGHIJKLMNOPQRSTUVWXYZ';
capital_of := {[let, big_letters(i)]: let = small_letters(i)};

                      $ maps each small letter into the corresponding capital.

return +/[capital_of(let) ? let : let = s(i)];

    $ Note that the map capital_of is defined over alphabetic characters
    $ only. Nonalphabetic characters, such as punctuation marks, are not
    $ converted, but left as they are. This is the purpose of the '? let'
    $ expression.

end proc capitalize;
```

A procedure can have any number of parameters, even no parameters. For example, we may want to use a procedure which reads an input string, uses the *capitalize* procedure to capitalize this input, and returns the capitalized result. This function can be written as follows:

```
proc next_line;   $ procedure to read and capitalize a line

read(x);          $ read a quoted string
return if x = om then om else capitalize(x) end;

end proc next_line;
```

To invoke a parameterless procedure of this sort, one must write its name, followed by an empty parameter list. For example, to invoke the *next_line* procedure and print the capitalized string that it returns, we would write

```
print(next_line( ));
```

We emphasize that the empty parameter list, i.e. the "( )" following the name of the parameterless procedure *next_line*, is obligatory.

5.1.3 A package of procedures for manipulating polynomials

As a further illustration of the use of procedures, we give a set of procedures for adding, subtracting, multiplying, and dividing polynomials in a single variable with real coefficients. Such polynomials are ordinarily printed in a standard algebraic form like

$$3.1*x^2 + 7.7*x + 4.5.$$

In the procedures that follow we will assume that a polynomial is represented internally by a SETL map which sends the exponent of each term of the polynomial into the coefficient of that term. For example, the polynomial shown previously would be represented internally by the map

$$\{[2, 3.1], [1, 7.7], [0, 4.5]\}.$$

As in algebra, we simply omit terms whose coefficients are zero.

To add (resp. subtract) two polynomials, we simply add (resp. subtract) the coefficients of corresponding terms. The addition of two polynomials proceeds as follows:

```
proc sum(p1, p2);
  result := { };                $ will contain sum of polynomials

  (for c = p1(e))               $ iterate over terms of first polynomial
    if p2(e) /= om then         $ second polynomial has matching term
      cr := c + p2(e);          $ coefficient of result
      if cr /= 0.0 then         $ term is present
        result(e) := cr;
      end if;
  end for;
```

```
    (for c = p2(e) | p1(e) = om)  $ add terms in second polynomial that are
       result(e) := c;            $ not present in first
    end for;

    return result;
end proc sum;
```

Note that the result of the second loop can be replaced by the following more compact expression.

```
{[e, c]: c = p2(e)|p1(e) = om}
```

We can also abbreviate the first loop by using the "?" operator and obtain the following compact procedure:

```
proc sum(p1, p2);  $ forms the sum of two polynomials
return  {[e, c]: c1 = p1(e) | (c := c1 + (p2(e) ? 0.0)) /= 0.0}
        + {e, c2]: c2 = p2(e)|p1(e) = om};
end proc sum;
```

From this we can write directly the procedure for polynomial difference:

```
proc diff(p1, p2);  $ forms the difference of two polynomials
return  {[e, c]: c1 = p1(e)|(c := c1 - (p2(e) ? 0.0)) /= 0.0}
        + {[e, -c2]: c2 = p2(e)|p1(e) = om};

end proc diff;
```

To multiply two polynomials, we multiply and sum all pairs of their individual terms. Finally, we eliminate terms which turn out to have zero coefficients. This is simply

```
proc prod(p1, p2);  $ forms the product of two polynomials
p := {[e1 + e2, c1*c2]: c1 = p1(e1), c2 = p2(e2)};

return {[e, c]: all_coeffs = p{e}|(c := +/all_coeffs) /= 0.0};

end proc prod;
```

Next, we show how to divide a polynomial $p1$ by a polynomial $p2$. Let $c_1 x^{j_1}$ be the leading term of $p1$, i.e., the term having largest exponent, and let $c_2 x^{j_2}$ be the leading term of $p2$. Then we subtract $(c1/c2)x^{j1-j2}$) times $p2$ from $p1$, to eliminate the leading term of $p1$, and so on repeatedly until all terms of $p1$ with exponents larger than j_2 have been eliminated. The collection of all terms by which $p2$ is multiplied constitutes the terms of the quotient.

```
proc div(p1, p2);                  $ forms the quotient polynomial p1/p2

if p2 = { } then return om; end;   $ this is the case p2 = 0.

e1 := max/[e: c = p1(e)];          $ largest exponent of p1
e2 := max/[e: c = p2(e)];          $ largest exponent of p2

qcoeff := { };                     $ start with an empty quotient
```

```
(for j in [e1 – e2, e1 – e2 – 1 .. 0] | p1(e2 + j) /= 0.0)
     qcoeff(j) := p1(e2 + j)/p2(e2);
p1 := diff(p1, {[e + j, qcoeff(j)*c]: c = p2(e)});

end for;

return qcoeff;                    $ return the map representing the quotient.

end proc div;
```

We note that techniques for manipulating polynomials by computer have been studied very intensively, and that much more efficient methods than those used in these simple illustrative procedures are known. See Knuth, *The Art of Computer Programming*, Vol. 2, for an account of these developments, which go beyond the scope of the present book.

5.2 Name Scopes; Local and Global Variable Names: The **var** Declaration

In writing a long program, which can involve hundreds of procedures, it is irritating, as well as highly error-inducing, to have to remember which variables had been used for which purposes through the whole of a long text. To see this, consider a function invocation imbedded in a **while** loop like

```
i := 0; j := 0;
(while (i + j) < f(j))...                                  (1)
```

and suppose that f is an invocation of a function whose body is found somewhere else in a long program text. It is entirely plausible that, unknown to the author of the code (1), the body of the function f should make use of the convenient variable name i, e.g., in a loop like

```
(forall i in [1 .. #t])...                                 (2)
```

But then, if the i appearing in (1) and the i appearing in (2) were regarded as representing the same variable, the function invocation $f(j)$ which occurs in the **while** loop could change the value of i in ways not at all hinted at by the outward form of the code (1). Were this the case, a programmer wishing to write a loop like (1) would first have to examine the body of the function f, to avoid variable name conflict. This would introduce many highly undesirable interactions between widely separated parts of a lengthy program and make large programs harder to write.

To avoid these very undesirable effects, most programming languages make use of rules which restrict the scope of names. The SETL scope rule is as follows. In the absence of explicit declarations, variables retain their meaning only within a single procedure (or main program). This implies that ordinarily a variable i appearing in one procedure and a variable i appearing in another procedure are treated as distinct. In effect, the SETL compiler (invisibly) applies the following renaming procedure to the program text which it processes:

(a) The main program which begins the program text is numbered zero, and the procedures which follow this main program are numbered 1, 2, .. in their order of occurrence.
(b) Every variable name *xxx* used in the *n*-th procedure, including the names of its formal parameters, is implicitly changed to xxx_n.

As an example, consider the program

```
program example;

    x := {3,0,1,2};
    print(squares(sort({i in x | i > 0})));

    proc sort(s); $ sorts by selection
    t := [ ];

    (while s /= { })
        t with := (x := min/s);
        s less := x;
    end while;

    return t;

    end proc sort;

    proc squares(x);   $ forms and returns the tuple of squares of the
                       $ components of the tuple x

    return [e*e : e = x(i)];

    end proc squares;
end program;
```

Given this program as input, the SETL compiler will implicitly apply the renaming rules (a), (b), and therefore it will really see the following renamed variant:

```
program example;

  x_0 := {3,0,1,2};                           $ main program
  print(squares(sort({i_0 in x_0 : i_0 > 0})));

  proc sort(s_1);                             $ procedure number 1
  t_1 = [ ];

  (while s_1 /= { })
     t_1 with := (x_1 := min/s_1);
     s_1 less := x_1;

  end while;
```

```
    return t_1;
    end proc sort;

    proc squares(x_2);                          $ procedure number 2

    return [e_2*e_2 : e_2 = x_2(i_2)];

    end proc squares;

  end program;
```

As stated previously, rule (b) serves to isolate variables having the same name from each other if they are used in different procedures. Variables used in this way are said to be *local* to the procedures in which they appear.

In some cases, however, we do want a variable used in several procedures to refer to the same object. For example, one or more "major" data objects may be used by all the functions in a related group of functions. To see this, consider the case of a group of functions written as part of an inquiry system to be used by the executives of a bank. This might involve many functions, for example,

```
proc payments(customer_name);   $ returns a given customer's payment
                                $ record

proc tel_no(customer_name);     $ returns a given customer's telephone
                                $ number

proc overdue(ndays);            $ returns set of a customers whose
                                $ payments are more than ndays
                                $ overdue
```

...etc.

All these procedures will have to make use of one or more "master files". (When represented in SETL, these "files" are likely to be sets of tuples representing records, maps sending customer names, or perhaps customer identifiers such as social security or account numbers, into associated records, etc.) Instead of insisting that these master files be passed as parameters to all the procedures that need to use them, it is more reasonable to make them available directly to every procedure, giving them easily recognizable variable names such as *master_customer_file*. To make this possible, SETL provides a special form of statement, called the **var** declaration. By writing

```
var master_customer_file;
```

at the start of the overall **program** in which the listed functions appear, we make *master_customer_file* a *global* variable which designates the same object in all the procedures which reference this variable. The required layout of a program using one or more global variables is shown in the following example:

```
program banking_system;           $ header line for overall program

    var master_customer_file;     $ declaration of global variable
```

```
    $ (additional global variable declarations come here)
    $ (body of 'main' program of banking_system comes here)
    proc payments (customer_name);   $ first procedure
      ...
    end proc payments;
    proc tel_no (customer_name);     $ second procedure
      ...
    end proc tel_no;
    proc overdue (n_days);           $ third procedure
      ...
    end proc overdue;
    $ (procedures come here)
end program banking_system;
```

The statement

var master_customer_file;

appearing first in this example is called a *declaration* rather than an executable statement because it serves to establish the meaning of certain names rather than to trigger any particular calculation.

The general form of a **var** declaration is

var x1, x2, ..., xn;

i.e., it consists of the keyword **var** followed by a comma-separated list of distinct variable identifiers.

Such declaration can appear in one of two positions:

(a) In a **program**, before the program's first executable statement. Variable identifiers appearing in such a declaration are defined to be global variables directly accessible to each following **procedure** in the program. A **var** declaration appearing in this position is called a *global* **var** *declaration*.

(b) In a **procedure** within a program, before the procedure's first executable statement. A **var** declaration appearing in this position is called a *local* **var** *declaration*. Variable identifiers appearing in such a declaration are defined to be local variables accessible only within the procedure. Since variable names not appearing in any **var** declaration are in any case local to the procedures in which they appear, **var** declarations appearing in this position often serve only to document the way in which a procedure uses its variables. However, if the procedure is recursive (see Section 5.4), **var** declarations appearing in it have a more significant effect, which will be described more fully later.

Any number of **var** declarations may appear either at the start of a **program** or within a **procedure**, but all such declarations must precede the first executable statement of the **program** or **procedure** in which they appear. No variable should appear twice in **var** declarations (either global **var** declarations or declarations within a single procedure), nor is it legal for any procedure parameter name to appear in a global **var** declaration. See Chapter 8 for the rules which apply to **var** declarations appearing in **directories**, **modules**, and **libraries** within large SETL programs; see Chapter 7 for an account of the modified **var** declaration used to declare backtracked variables.

A global variable retains its value between invocations of the procedures that use it.

To sum up, there are two ways in which values can be communicated between separate **procedures**:

(i) By being passed as parameters or returned by procedures.
(ii) By direct global communication, i.e., by being the values of variables which have been declared to be global and hence are accessible to more than one procedure.

Method (ii) is powerful, but potentially undisciplined, since it allows procedures to influence each other in ways that their invocations hide. It is therefore good programming practice to avoid using more than a very few declared global variables. Generally speaking, variables should be made global only if

(a) They represent major data objects accessed by more than one of a program's procedures, and their usage is subject to clearly understood rules of style which pervade the entire program.
(b) They represent flags or other conditions that many procedures need to test (e.g., to determine whether particular debugging traces should be produced), but that play no role in the normal functioning of these procedures and are rarely modified.
(c) They need to be shared between procedures that do not call each other and must be kept alive between successive invocations of these procedures.
(d) They represent constants, too complex to be set up conveniently using a **const** declaration (see Section 8.2), which need to be used whenever a procedure is invoked.
(e) They need to be accessible to all logical copies of a recursive procedure (see Section 5.4).

The *capitalize* function appearing in Section 5.1 can be used to illustrate point (d). As written, this forms the map

capital_of := {['a', 'A'], ['b', 'B'], ['c', 'C'], ..., ['z', 'Z']}

each time it is invoked. To do this is of course wasteful of computer time. Using the **const** declaration described in Section 8.2 we would instead declare capital_of to be a constant having this value, but this requires writing out all the elements of const_of explicitly, a nuisance since this involves typing 104 apostrophes, 51 commas, 52 brackets, etc. It is more convenient to declare

var capital_of;

and then to add the instructions

```
small_letters  := 'abcdefghijklmnopqrstuvwxyz';
big_letters    := 'ABCDEFGHIJKLMNOPQRSTUVWXYZ';
capital_of     := {(1, big_letters(i)]: 1 = small_letters(i)};
```

as part of a main program block before the first use of *capitalize*. The *capitalize* function then reduces to the following simple form:

```
proc capitalize(s);

return +/[capital_of(let ? let : let = s(i)];

end proc capitalize;
```

5.3 Programming Examples

5.3.1 The buckets and well problem: a simple artificial intelligence example

The following kind of problem, often called the "buckets and well" puzzle, commonly appears on IQ tests. Suppose that one is given several buckets of various sizes, and that a well full of water is available. To focus on a simple specific case, suppose that just two buckets, a 3-quart bucket and a 5-quart bucket, are given. We are required to use them to measure out exactly 4 quarts of water. Since *exactly* this amount of water is to be measured out, no nonprecise operation is allowed. This means that *only three kinds of operations* can be used in a solution of this problem:

(a) Any bucket can be filled brim-full from the well;
(b) Any bucket can be emptied completely;
(c) Any bucket can be poured into any other, until either the first bucket becomes completely empty or the second bucket becomes brim-full.

As an example, the following is a way of measuring out exactly 4 quarts using only a 3- and a 5-quart bucket.

(i) Fill the 5-quart bucket.
(ii) Pour the 5-quart bucket into the 3-quart bucket (leaving 2 quarts in the 5-quart bucket).
(iii) Empty the 3-quart bucket.
(iv) Pour the contents of the 5-quart bucket into the 3-quart bucket. (Now 2 quarts is in the 3-quart bucket, and the 5-quart bucket is empty).
(v) Fill the 5-quart bucket.
(vi) Pour the 5-quart bucket into the 3-quart bucket, until the 3-quart bucket becomes full. (This leaves exactly 4 quarts in the 5-quart bucket.)
(vii) Empty the 3-quart bucket. (Now exactly 4 quarts has been measured out.)

The fact that it is easy to program a computer to solve problems of this kind might be considered surprising, since such solutions are often considered to require *intelligence.* Nevertheless a systematic approach is not hard to find. The key idea is that of *state.* Specifically, as one moves through the steps of any solution to this kind of problem, the objects being manipulated (in this case, the buckets) will at any moment be in some particular condition. In the case we consider, this *condition* or *state* is determined by the amount of water in each of the buckets. We can represent this state as a tuple, of as many components as there are buckets. Initially, when both buckets are empty, the state is [0, 0]. The *target* state for the example considered is that in which exactly 4 quarts has been measured into the 5-quart bucket; this is represented by the tuple [0, 4]. The state in which both buckets are completely full is [3, 5], that in which the 3-quart bucket is full and the 5-quart bucket is empty is [3, 0], etc. In this representation, the problem solution given by (i–vii) would be represented as the following sequence of states:

[0, 0], [0, 5], [3, 2], [0, 2], [2, 0], [2, 5], [3, 4], [0, 4]

This way of looking at the problem makes it plain that what we need to consider is the set of all possible states, and the manner in which new states can be reached from old. Suppose that the tuple *state* represents the amount of water currently in the buckets, so that state (i) is the amount of water in the *i*-th bucket, and that the tuple *size* represents the sizes of all the given buckets, so that size (*i*) is the capacity of the *i*-th bucket. In the buckets and well problem, only the three manipulations (a), (b), and (c) are allowed. If bucket *i* is poured into bucket *j* until either *i* becomes empty or *j* becomes full, then the amount poured will be

state(i) **min** (size(j)–state(j)).

Hence the following procedure returns the collection of all states than can be reached in a single step from an initially given state:

```
proc new_states_from(state);

   return {empty(state,j): j in [1 .. #state]}
   + {fill(state,j): j in [1 .. #state]}
   + {pour(state,i,j): i in [1 .. #state], j in [1 .. #state]|(i /= j)};

end proc new_states_from(state);

proc empty (state,j);                        $ empties bucket j

   state(j) := 0;
   return state;

end proc empty;

proc fill(state,j);                          $ fulls bucket j

   state(j) := size(j);                      $ the 'size' tuple
                                             $ is assumed to be global
   return state;
```

```
  end proc fill;

proc pour(state, i, j);                        $ pour bucket i into bucket j

  amount := state(i) min (size(j) – state(j)); $ amount that can be poured
  state(i) – := amount;                        $ out of i and into j
  state(j) + := amount;

  return state;

end proc pour;
```

We can now solve our problem by a systematic process of state exploration. We start in the initial *all buckets empty* state to generate all the states that can be reached in one step from this starting state. Then we generate all states that can be reached in one step from these second-level states, etc. States that have been encountered previously are ignored; the ones that remain are precisely those which can be reached from the start in two steps but no fewer. From these, we generate all states which can be generated in three steps but no fewer, and so forth. As we go along, we check to see whether the target state has yet been reached. Eventually, we either reach the target state, thereby solving our problem, or find that no new states can be generated, even though the target state has not been reached. In this latter case, the problem clearly has no solution.

Figure 5.3 illustrates the notion of state search and shows some of the states that come up during search for a solution of our two-bucket example:

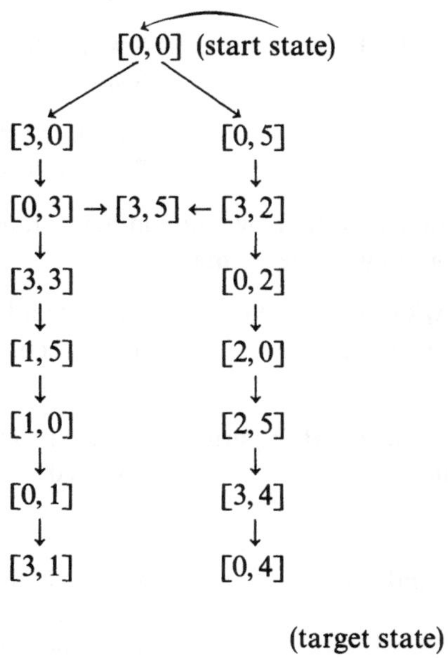

Figure 5.3 States of a Two-Bucket Problem; Bucket Sizes are [3, 5]

Note that in this figure we only show transitions which lead to states that have not been seen before. Other transitions are redundant, since the shortest path from start state to the target state will never pass through the same state twice.

To be sure that we can reconstruct the path from start to target once the target has been reached, we proceed as follows. Whenever a new state *ns* is seen for the first time it will have been generated from some immediately preceding old state *os*. As states are generated, we keep a map came_from which maps each new state *ns* into the old state *os* from which *ns* has been reached. Once the target state has been reached, we can use this map to chain back from the target to the start state. Then the desired solution is simply the reverse of the sequence thereby generated.

The following code implements this state-generation and backchaining procedure. It is deliberately written in a manner that hides all information concerning the structure of states, as well as all details concerning the way in which new states arise from old. This makes it possible to use the same routine to solve many different kinds of state-exploration problems.

```
proc find_path(start, target);            $ general state-exploration
                                          $ procedure.

    came_from := {[start, start]};        $ the start state is considered
                                          $ to have been reached from
                                          $ itself

    just_seen := {start};                 $ initially, only the start
                                          $ state has been seen

    (while just_seen /= { })              $ while there exist newly seen
                                          $ states

      brand_new := { };                   $ look for states that have
                                          $ not been seen before

      (for old_state in just_seen, new_state in new_states_from(old_state)
           |came_from(new_state) = om)

        brand_new with := new_state;      $ record a brand_new state
        came_from(new_state) :=           $ and record its origin
           old-state;

        if new_state = target then goto   $ since problem has been
           got_it; end;                   $ solved

      end for;

      just_seen := brand_new;             $ now the brand-new states
                                          $ define those which have
                                          $ just been seen

    end while;
```

```
  return om;                          $ at this point all states
                                      $ have been explored, and the
                                      $ target has not been found,
                                      $ so we know that no solution
                                      $ exists.

  got_it:                             $ at this point the target
                                      $ has been found, so we chain
                                      $ back from the target to
                                      $ reconstruct the path from
                                      $ start to target

  rev_path := [target];               $ initialize the path to be built
    (while (last_state := rev_path(#rev_path)) /= start)
      rev_path with := came_from(last_state);
    end while;

    return [rev_path(j): j in [#rev_path, #rev_path -1..1]];

end proc find_path;
```

The following main program can be used to acquire a problem specification interactively and to invoke the find_path routine to solve it. Again we hide all problem-specific information in appropriate procedures.

```
program buckets;          $ Hann Xin divides wine

    var size;             $ global variable for storing problem specification

    (while (prob_specs := get_prob_specs( )) /= om)

      [start, target, size] := prob_specs;

      if (path := find_path(start, target)) = om then
        print('This problem is definitely unsolvable');
      else
        print('The following sequence of states constitutes a solution:');
        (for f(x) in path) print(x); end;
      end if;

    end while;

    proc new_states_from(state);

    return {empty(state,j): j in [1.. #state]}
      + {fill(state,j): j in [1.. #state]}
      + {pour(state,i,j): i in [1.. #state], j in [1.. #state]|(i /= j)};

    end proc new_states_from(state);

    proc empty(state,j);   $ empties bucket j
```

```
    state(j) := 0;
    return state;

end proc empty;

proc fill(state, j);        $ fills bucket j

    state(j) := size(j);    $ the size tuple is global
    return state;

end proc fill;

proc pour(state, i, j);                     $ pour bucket i into bucket j

    amount := state(i) min (size(j) -       $ amount that can be poured
        state(j);
    state(i) - := amount;
    state(j) + := amount;

    return state;

end proc pour;

proc find_path(start, target);              $ general state-exploration
                                            $ procedure.
...                                         $ text is on previous page
end proc find_path;

proc get_prob_specs;                        $ acquires and returns
                                            $ specifications of problem

    loop do

    print('Enter a tuple to define bucket sizes, or type "stop" to end:');

        read(x);

        if x = 'STOP' then quit; end;

    print('Enter a tuple of the same length to define first bucket states:');

        read(y);
        if y = 'STOP' then quit; end;

    print('Enter a tuple of the same length to define target of problem:');

        read(z);
        if z = 'STOP' then quit; end;

        data := [y, z, x];

        if exists t = data(i)|(not is_tuple(t) or #t /= #data(1)
        or exists c = t(i)|not is_integer(c) or c < 0) then

    print('Illegal problem specification.'
```

```
        'Please reenter or type "STOP" to halt.');
        continue;                          $ loop, to try again
      else
        return data;
      end if;
      end loop;
    end proc get_prob_specs;
end program buckets;
```

Since the notion of *problem state* used in the foregoing is general and since we have written the find_path procedure and the main program block shown in a manner which insulates them from the details of the problems that they solve, we can use these procedures to handle any path-finding problem of the same general class as the buckets and well problem. Another amusing problem of this kind is the goat, wolf, and cabbage puzzle. In this puzzle, a man, who brings with him a goat, a wolf, and a cabbage, comes to a river which he must cross in a boat just large enough for himself and one but not two of the objects goat, wolf, and cabbage. He can never leave the goat and wolf, or the cabbage and goat, alone together, since in the first case the wolf would eat the goat and in the second the goat would eat the cabbage. How is he to cross the river?

To develop a program to solve this puzzle, we have only to rewrite the *new_states_from* procedure and the parameterless *get_prob_specs* procedure. First, we need to decide on a representation of the states of the puzzle. We can designate the four objects appearing in the puzzle by their initials as 'G', 'W', 'C', and 'M' (man), respectively, and represent each state of the puzzle by a pair $[l, r]$, where l designates the set of all objects remaining to the left of the river, and r designates the set of all objects that have been moved across the river. For example,

[{'G', 'M'}, {'W', 'C'}]

represents the state in which the wolf and the cabbage have been moved across, and the man has returned to the left side of the river to get the goat. The start state is then

[{'G', 'W', 'C', 'M'}, { }]

and the target state is

[{ }, {'G', 'W', 'C', 'M'}]

The *new_states_from* procedure appropriate for this problem can be represented as follows:

```
proc new_states_from(state);
[l, r] := state;   $ 'unpack' state into its 'left' and 'right' portions
  return if 'M' notin l then
        {[l - {'M', x}, r + {'M', x}]: x in l | x /= 'M' and
        is_legal(l - {'M', x})}
      else
        {[l + {'M', x}, r - {'M', x}]: x in r | x /= 'M' and
        is_legal(r - {'M', x})}
      end;
end proc new_states_from;
proc is_legal(s);
  $ verify that goat and cabbage or goat and wolf, are not on same side
  return not ({'G', 'C'} subset s or {'G', 'W'} subset s);
end proc is_legal;
```

5.4 Recursive Procedures

The value $f(x)$ that a mathematical function of an integer, tuple, or set variable takes on for a particular x can often be expressed in terms of the value of the same function for "smaller" argument values x. Several examples of this general principle are

(i) The 'factorial' function $n!$, given by */[*i*: *i* **in** [1 .. *n*]], satisfies the identity

n! = **if** n = 1 **then** 1 **else** n*((n − 1)!) **end**;

(ii) The sum sigma(t) = +/t of all the components of a tuple t satisfies the identity

sigma(t) = **if** #t = 0 **then om elseif** #t = 1 **then** t(1)
else t(1) + sigma(t(2..)) **end**;

(iii) The tuple sort(s) representing the elements of a set s in sorted order satisfies the identity

sort(s) = **if** #s = 0 **then** [ ] **else** [**min**/s] + sort(s − {**min**/s}) **end**

This same function sort(s) also satisfies many other interesting identities. Suppose, for example, that we pick an arbitrary element x from the set s and then divide the remaining elements of s into two parts, the first, L, containing all elements less than x, the second, G, containing all elements greater then x. Then if we sort the elements of L and G and concatenate the resulting sorted tuples, sandwiching x between them, we clearly get a tuple t which contains all the elements of s in sorted order. This shows that the function sort(s) also satisfies the identity

```
sort(s) = if (x := arb s) = om then [ ] else
        sort({y in s: y < x}) + [x] + sort({y in s: y > x}) end;
```

Identities of the kind appearing in the preceding examples are called *recursive definitions*, and the functions appearing in them are called *recursively defined functions*. Such recursive definitions all have the following features:

(a) For certain particular simple or *minimal* values (like $n = 1$ in (i) or $t = [\ ]$ in (ii)) of the parameter variable x of a recursively defined function $f(x)$, the value of $f(x)$ is defined explicitly.
(b) For all other parameter values x, the value of $f(x)$ is expressed in terms of the value that f produces for one or more smaller argument values $x1$, $x2, \ldots xn$. That is, there exists a relationship of the general form

```
f(x) = some_combination(f(x1), f(x2),..,f(xn))
```

(c) Repeated use of the relationship (b) will eventually express any value $f(x)$ in terms of various values $f(y)$ each of which has a parameter y which is minimal in the sense of (a), so that all values $f(y)$ in terms of which $f(x)$ is ultimately expressed are known explicitly.

Any recursive relationship satisfying (a, b, c) gives a method for calculating $f(x)$ for each allowed argument x. Like many other programming languages, SETL allows one to express such recursive calculations very simply and directly, by writing *recursive procedures*, i.e., procedures which invoke themselves. This can be done for each of the three examples given, which then take on the following forms:

```
proc factorial(n);   $ calculates the factorial n!
  return if n = 1 then 1 else n* factorial(n - 1) end;
end proc factorial;

proc sigma(t);       $ calculates the sum of the components of t.
  return if #t = 0 then om elseif #t = 1 then t(1)
      else t(1) + sigma (t(2..)) end;
end proc sigma;

proc sort(s);        $ recursive sorting procedure
  return if s = { } then [ ]
  else [min/s] + sort(s less min/s) end;
end proc sort;
```

These examples illustrate the following general remarks concerning recursive procedures:

(i) Syntactically, recursive procedures have the same form as other procedures. Their only distinguishing trait is that recursive procedures invoke themselves.
(ii) The same name-scoping rules apply to recursive as to other procedures.

Note that a recursive procedure $f(s)$ uses itself but always applies itself to arguments smaller than s; this is why the calculation of f eventually terminates.

A recursive procedure f need not invoke itself directly: It can invoke another procedure g which invokes f, or g can invoke some h which then invokes f, etc. A group of procedures which invoke each other is sometimes called a *mutually recursive family* of procedures, and any procedure belonging to such a mutually recursive family is itself called recursive.

For an example of such a mutually recursive family, consider the problem of defining an overall order for SETL objects, which will allow any two SETL objects to be compared to each other. (Such an order could, for example, serve as the basis for an output routine which alway arranged the elements of sets in increasing order, thereby making it easier to locate elements in large sets when they were printed.) To define such an order, we can agree on the following conventions:

(a) **Om** always comes first, integers before reals, reals before strings, strings before atoms, atoms before tuples, and tuples before sets.
(b) Among themselves, integers and reals are arranged in their standard order, strings in their standard alphabetical order, and atoms in the order of their external printed representations; i.e., if x and y are two atoms then x comes before y if and only if (**str** x) < (**str** y). (Recall that the **str** x operator produces a string identical with the external printed form of the object x; see Section 2.5.3)
(c) Tuples are arranged in lexicographic order, i.e., $t1$ comes before $t2$ if, in the first component in which $t1$ and $t2$ differ, $t1$ has a smaller component than $t2$.
(d) To compare two sets, first arrange their elements in order. This allows them to be regarded as tuples; then apply rule (c).

The following mutually recursive group of procedures implements the ordering strategy we have just described.

```
proc is_bigger(x, y);                        $ return true if x >= y in the
                                             $ order just described

 return if x = y or y = om then true
   elseif x = om then false
   elseif type x /= type y then type_number(x) > type_number(y)
   elseif is_integer(x) then x >= y
   elseif is_real(x) then x >= y
```

```
      elseif is_atom(x) then str x > str y
      elseif is_tuple(x) then lex_compare(x, y)
      else lex_compare(sort(x), sort(y)) end;   $ x and y are sets

end proc is_bigger;

proc biggest(S);                          $ find largest element in S
                                          $ ordering defined by is_bigger.
  big := arb(S);

  (for x ∈ S)
     if is_bigger(x, big) then            $ x may be biggest
        big := x;
     end if;
  end for;
  return big;
end proc;

proc sort(S);
  if S = { } then return [ ];
  else
     b := biggest(S);
     return sort(S less b) with b;
  end if;
end proc sort;

proc lex_compare(t1, t2);                 $ compare two different tuples,
                                          $ in their lexicographic order,
                                          $ components being compared
                                          $ by is_bigger
return exists c1 = t1(i)|is_bigger(c1, t2(i));

end proc lex_compare;

proc type_number(typ);                    $ converts typ, which is the
                                          $ name of a valid SETL
                                          $ type, into an integer

tno := {['INTEGER', 1], ['REAL', 2], ['STRING', 3], ['ATOM', 4,],
['TUPLE', 5], ['SET', 6]};

return tno(typ);

end proc type_number;
```

Until now we have regarded recursive SETL procedures simply as SETL representations of recursive mathematical relationships and have ignored the question of how they are implemented, i.e., how the calculations which they define are actually performed. This is really the best way to look at the matter, since the sequence of steps used to evaluate a recursive procedure can be complex and tricky to follow even when the mathematical relationship on which it is based is simple and easy to understand. Nevertheless one needs to understand how recursive calculations are performed. For example, when an incorrectly programmed recursive procedure malfunctions, one needs to know what is happening in order to diagnose the problem and correct it.

Implementation of recursive procedures, like that of mutually recursive groups of functions, is based upon the following rule. Whenever a procedure f invokes itself, a new logical copy of the procedure is created, initial parameter values are passed to this new logical copy, and execution of this new logical copy begins with its first statement. While the new copy of f is executing, the old copy of the function f, from which the new copy was created, remains in existence, but execution of it is suspended. The new copy can in turn invoke f, thereby creating a third copy of f, which can even go on in the same way to create yet a fourth copy, etc. However, if the recursion has been written correctly, the arguments x passed to the successive copies of f will be getting smaller and smaller. Eventually one of them will get small enough for the corresponding value $f(x)$ to be evaluated directly. Once this happens, the currently active copy of the procedure f will execute a statement

return e;

for some directly evaluable expression e. This will pass the value of e back to the place from which the current copy of f (call it CCF) was invoked. CCF will then become superfluous and will disappear. The immediately prior copy of f will then become active, and when it finishes its execution it will in turn pass a value back to the copy of f from which it has been invoked and disappears, etc. Eventually a value, and control, will be returned to the very first copy of f, and the whole recursive evaluation will be completed as soon as this first copy executes a **return** statement.

As an example of this process of recursive evaluation, suppose that the recursive *sort* routine shown earlier in this section is invoked, and that initially the argument value $\{30, 0, 60, 40\}$ is transmitted to it. This will trigger the following steps of recursive evaluation.

(i) Copy 1 of *sort* begins to evaluate sort($\{30, 0, 60, 40\}$)
(ii) The minimum element 0 is removed from the set s, and *sort* is invoked recursively to evaluate sort($\{30, 60, 40\}$)
(iii) Copy 2 of *sort* begins to evaluate sort($\{30, 60, 40\}$)
(iv) The minimum element 30 is removed from the set s, and *sort* is invoked recursively to evaluate sort($\{60, 40\}$)
(v) Copy 3 of *sort* begins to evaluate sort($\{60, 40\}$)
(vi) The minimum element 40 is removed from the set s, and *sort* is invoked recursively to evaluate sort($\{60\}$)
(vii) Copy 4 of *sort* begins to evaluate sort($\{60\}$)
(viii) The minimum (and only) element 60 is removed from the set s, and *sort* is invoked recursively to evaluate sort($\{\ \}$).
(ix) Copy 5 of *sort* immediately returns [ ] as the value of sort($\{\ \}$) to copy 4 and disappears.

(x) Copy 4 of sort appends the returned value [ ] to [60], returns the result [60] to copy 3, and disappears.
(xi) Copy 3 appends the returned value [60] to [40], returns the result [40, 60] to copy 2, and disappears.
(xii) Copy 2 appends the returned value [40, 60] to [30], returns the result [30, 40, 60] to copy 1, and disappears.
(xiii) Copy 1 appends the returned value [30, 40, 60] to [0], and returns [0, 30, 40, 60], as the final result of the whole recursive evaluation, to the place from which *sort* was first invoked.

The complexity of this sequence of steps underscores the fact that whenever possible a recursive SETL function like *sort* should be looked at as the transcription of a recursive mathematical relationship, in this case, the very obvious relationship

sort(s) = **if** s = { } **then** [ ] **else** [**min**/s] + sort(s **less** **min**/s) **end**

rather than in terms of the sequence of steps required for its evaluation. However, the way in which recursive procedures are evaluated becomes relevant if they are miswritten and consequently malfunction. Certain common pathologies are associated with malfunctioning recursive routines, and one needs to be able to recognize them when they appear. A common error is to write a recursion which does not handle its easy, directly evaluable cases correctly, or which for some reason never reaches a directly evaluable case. If this happens, a recursive procedure will create more and more copies of itself without limit, until the entire memory of the computer on which it is running is exhausted, and a final, 'MEMORY OVERFLOW' error message is emitted.

In somewhat more complex cases, a malfunctioning recursive procedure will loop indefinitely, first creating additional copies of itself, then returning from and erasing these, then again creating new copies of itself, again returning from and erasing these, etc., without any overall progress to termination. Such a *nonterminating recursive loop* is likely to produce much the same symptoms as a nonterminating **while** loop; namely, the program will run on, either with no output or with a flood of repetitive output, until somebody notices that it has outrun its time limit and terminates it forcibly. This situation is most easily diagnosed at an interactive terminal, simply by printing out the parameters transmitted to the recursive function each time it is invoked; this pattern of parameters will fail to show the logical pattern upon which your hopes for eventual termination of the recursion rest.

Having said all this, we now go on to describe another interesting recursive procedure, appropriately called *quicksort*.

5.4.1 The quicksort procedure

This quicksort sorting method works as follows: If the tuple *t* of elements to be sorted has no elements or just one element, we have nothing to do, since an empty tuple or a tuple with just one element is always sorted. Otherwise,

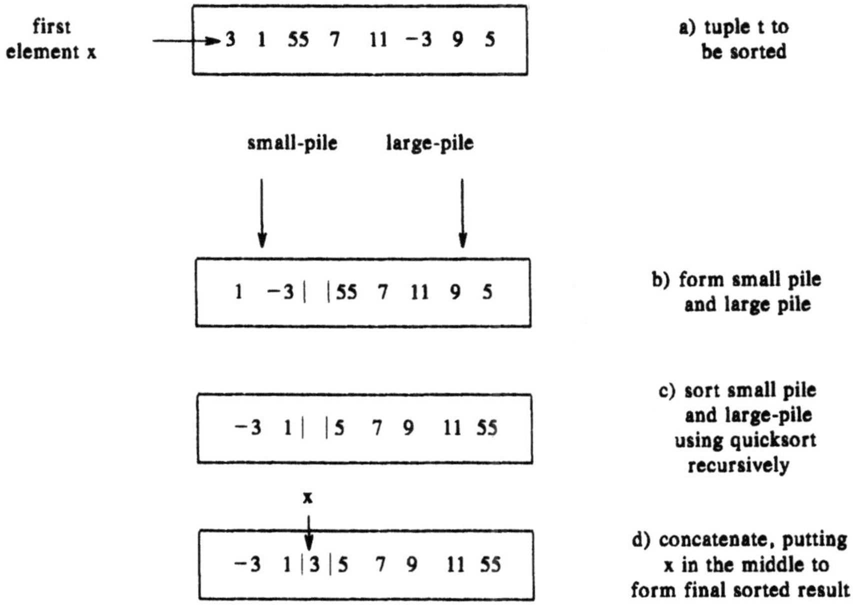

Figure 5.4 Quicksort Procedure

we remove the first element *x* from *t* and divide what remains into two parts, the first ('small_pile') consisting of all those components smaller then *x*, the second ('large_pile') consisting of all those components at least as large as *x*. We then sort these two piles separately. This can most readily be done just by using quicksort itself recursively. Finally, we recombine to get all the original components in their sorted order. This is done by putting the sorted small_pile first, followed by the element *x*, and then followed by the sorted large_pile.

See Figure 5.4 for further explanation of the way in which quicksort works. Code for this procedure can be written as follows:

```
proc quick_sort(t),              $ quicksort procedure, first form

if #t < 2 then return t; end;

x := t(1);                       $ take the first component
small_pile := [y : y = t(i)|y < x];
large_pile := [y : y = t(i)|y >= x and i > 1];

return quick_sort(small_pile) + [x] + quick_sort(large_pile);

end proc quick_sort;
```

By using SETL expression features more strenuously, we can write this whole procedure in just one statement, namely as

```
proc quick_sort(t);   $ quicksort procedure, second form

return if #t < 2 then t
else
   quick_sort([y : y = t(i)|y < t(1)]) + [t(1)]
   + quick_sort([y : y = t(i)|y >= t(1) and i > 1])
end;

end proc quick_sort;
```

5.4.2 Another recursive procedure: mergesort

The quicksort procedure that has just been presented sorts by separating the array to be sorted into two piles which can be sorted separately and then combined. This recursive approach, sometimes called *divide and conquer*, forms the basis for many efficient data-manipulation algorithms. It is often most effective to divide the problem given originally into two halves of nearly equal size. Quicksort does not always lead to this equal division, since random selection of a component x of a tuple t may cause it to be divided into parts [y: y **in** $t \mid y < x$] and [y: y **in** $t \mid y > x$] which are very different in size. For this reason, we will now describe another recursive sorting technique, called *mergesort*, which does begin by dividing the tuple t that is to be sorted into two parts of equal size. This procedure works as follows:

(i) Divide t (at its middle) into two equal parts $t1$ and $t2$, and sort them separately.
(ii) Then merge the two sorted parts $t1$, $t2$ of t, by removing either the first component of $t1$ or the first component of $t2$, whichever is smaller, and putting it first in the sorted version of the full tuple t, after which we can continue recursively, merging the remaining components of $t1$ and $t2$. Code for this procedure is as follows:

```
proc sort(t);   $ recursive merge_sort procedure

  return if #t < 2 then t
                    $ since a tuple of length 0 or 1 is ipso facto sorted
  else merge(sort(t(1..div 2)), sort(t(#t div 2 + 1..))) end;

end proc sort;

proc merge(t1, t2); $ auxiliary recursive procedure for merging

  return if t1 = [ ] then t2
  elseif t2 = [ ] then t1
  elseif t1(1) < t2(1) then [t1(1)] + merge(t1(2..), t2)
  else [t2(1)] + merge(t1, t2(2..)) end;

end proc merge;
```

Instead of programming the *merge* procedure recursively, we can write it iteratively. For this, we have only to work sequentially through the two tuples $t1$ and $t2$ to be merged, maintaining pointers $i1$, $i2$ to the first component of each which has not yet been moved to the final sorted tuple t being built up. Then we repeatedly compare $t1(i1)$ to $t2(i2)$, move the smaller of the two to t, and increment the index of the component that has just been moved to t. This revised merge procedure is as follows:

```
proc merge(t1, t2);            $ iterative variant of merge procedure

  t := [ ];                    $ merged tuple to be built up
  i1 := i2 := 1;               $ indices of first components not yet moved

  (while i1 < #t1 and i2 < #t2)

    if t1(i1) < t2(i2) then    $ move t1(i1) to t
      t with := t1(i1);
      i1 + := 1;
    else                       $ move t2(i2) to t
      t with := t2(i2);
      i2 + := 1;
    end if;

  end while;

  return t + t1(i1..) + t2(i2..);
  $ note that at most one of t1(i1..) and t2(i2..) is non-null

end proc merge;
```

5.4.3 Binary searching: a fast recursive searching technique

If the components of a tuple t are arranged in random order, then to find the component or components having a given value we must search serially through every one of the components of t; clearly no component of t can go unexamined, since this may be precisely the component we are looking for. On the other hand, if the components of t are numbers or character strings, and if they are arranged in sorted order, then, as everyone who has ever looked up a word in a dictionary or a name in a telephone book should realize, a much faster searching procedure is available. The most elegant expression of this searching procedure is recursive and is as follows:

(i) Compare the item x being sought to the middle item t(#t **div** 2) of the sorted tuple t. If x is greater than (resp. not greater than) this middle item, proceed recursively to search for x in the upper (resp. lower) half of t.
(ii) The search ends when the vector in which we are searching has length equal to 1.

In coding this procedure, we maintain two quantities *lo*, *hi*, which are respectively the low and the high limits of the zone of t in which we must still search. When the search procedure is first called, *lo* should be 1 and *hi* should be #*t*. When *lo* and *hi* become equal, we return their common value. If this locates a component of *t* equal to *x*, we have found what we want; otherwise we can be sure that *x* is not present in *t*, i.e., that no component of *t* is precisely equal to *x*.

Recursive code for this searching procedure is as follows:

```
proc search(x, t, lo, hi);
$ binary search for x in t between lo and hi

return if lo = hi then lo
     elseif x <= t(mid := (lo + hi) div 2) then search (x, t, lo, mid)
     else search (x, t, mid + 1, hi) end;

end proc search;
```

It is easy to express this search iteratively rather than recursively: we can write

```
proc search(x, t);          $ iterative form of binary search procedure

  lo := 1; hi := #t;        $ initialize search limits

  (while lo < hi)

      if x <= t(mid := (lo + hi) div 2) then
         hi := mid;
      else
         lo := mid + 1;
      end if;

  end while;

  return lo;

end proc search;
```

Binary searching can be enormously more efficient than simple serial searching. Suppose, for example, that the sorted tuple *t* to be search is of length 1,000,000. Then to search *t* serially several million elementary operations will be required. On the other hand, since 1,000,000 is roughly 2**20, only 20 probes will be required to locate a component of *t* by binary searching. Hence, for sorted tuples of this length, binary searching is roughly 50,000 times as fast as serial searching. This illustrates the vast efficiency advantage that can be gained by proper choice of the algorithm that you will use.

5.4.4 The Towers of Hanoi problem

Among the many different kinds of puzzles that can be bought in toyshops, the Towers of Hanoi puzzle is a classic. This puzzle involves a board with three identical pegs and a set of rings of decreasing size that fit snugly around any of the pegs. As initially set up, the puzzle is as shown in Figure 5.5.

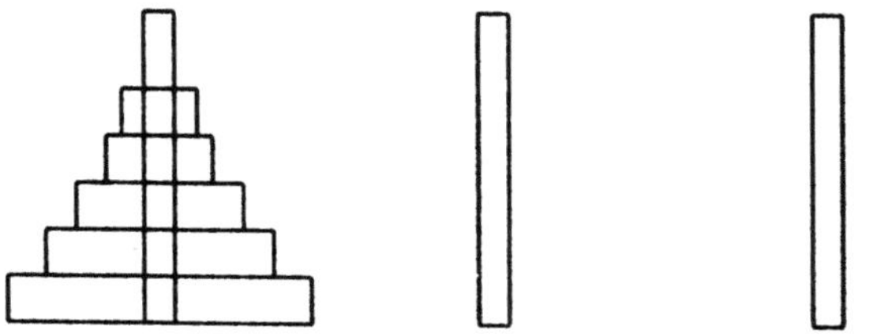

Figure 5.5 The Towers of Hanoi Problem

To solve the puzzle one must move all the disks from the particular peg (peg 1) on which they are originally placed to one of the other pegs (say, to peg 3). However, only one disk can be moved at a time, and it is forbidden ever to place a larger disk on top of a smaller disk.

Recursion gives us an amazingly effective way of writing a solution to this problem. The key idea is this: since a large disk can never be placed atop a smaller, all the disks except the bottom one must be moved to peg 2 before we can move the bottom disk from peg 1 to peg 3. Hence, to move a pile of n disks from peg 1 to peg 3, we must

(a) move a pile of $(n - 1)$ disks from peg 1 to peg 2
(b) move the n-th disk from peg 1 to peg 3
(c) move a pile of $(n - 1)$ disks from peg 2 to peg 3

The following elegant recursive procedure generates the sequence of moves required; each move is represented as a pair $[f, t]$ showing the pegs from which and to which a peg is moved.

```
proc moves(ndisks, fr, to, via);   $ moves n disks from peg fr to peg to

    return (if ndisks = 1 then [[fr, to]]
    else moves(ndisks -1, fr, via, to) + [[fr, to]]
       + moves(ndisks - 1, via, to, fr) end);

end proc moves;
```

5.5 Procedures that Modify Their Parameters

The procedures we have seen so far are given some collection of parameter values and calculate a single result value, which it returns, from them. Occasionally, however, one wants to use procedures in a somewhat different way; namely, one wants to invoke a procedure expressly in order to modify some object that already exists. In this case, such a procedure is invoked for its effect, rather than for the value it delivers. This use of procedures moves us away from the notions of "value" and "expression" and focuses more on the somewhat different notion of *program state*, i.e., the collection of all values that local and global variables have at each moment during a computation. What we will be describing in this section is the way in which procedures are used to modify this program state. There are two ways in which procedures can have this effect: one of them is to modify one or more of their calling parameters; the second is to modify one or more global variables.

This use of procedures is perfectly legal in SETL and is accomplished as follows. A procedure's header line lists its parameters, as for example in

procedure my_proc(x, y, z);

Parameters listed in this way can be modified within the body of the procedure (i.e., within *my_proc*), but parameter values are ordinarily local to the procedure, so that these modifications are not be transmitted back to the point from which the procedure was invoked. For example, if we define the procedure

```
proc change_parameter(x);                    (1a)
x := 0;
return x;
end proc change_parameter;
```

and invoke it by

```
y := 1;
z := change_parameter(y);                    (2)
print('z is:', z, 'y is:', y);
```

then the **print** statement will produce the output

```
z is: 0     y is: 1
```

This reflects the fact that the **return** statement in the **proc** returns the final value of the variable *x* (which is local to the **proc**), but that modifications to the procedure parameter *x* are not transmitted back to the point of invocation and therefore do not affect the value of the actual argument *y* appearing in (2). Thus the argument *y* remains unchanged.

This is the rule which ordinarily applies to **procs**, and which is most appropriate for **procs** used as functions. However, it is possible to bypass this rule, and to create **procs** which do modify one or more of the actual arguments with which they are invoked. To do this, one simply prefixes the qualifier **rw** (meaning *read/write parameter*) to each parameter corresponding to one of these modifiable arguments. Suppose, for example, that we modify the procedure (1a), making it

```
proc change_parameter(rw x);
x := 0;
return x;                                    (1b)
end proc change_parameter;
```

Then the output of the **print** statement in (2) will change to

z is: 0   y is: 0

reflecting the fact that now changes in the value of the parameter x of the procedure (1b) will be transmitted back to the point from which the procedure was invoked.

Procedures whose parameters are qualified in this way will generally not be used as functions that return values (though technically it is legal to use them as functions). Instead, they will ordinarily be invoked simply by writing their names followed by their actual argument lists, as is illustrated by

```
y := 1;
change_parameter(y); print('y is:', y);                (3)
```

which produces the output

y is: 0

Any procedure my_proc($x1,..,xn$) can be invoked in this way, simply by writing a statement of the form

my_proc(a1,...,an); (4a)

where $a1,\ldots,an$ is any list of expressions (called, as usual, the *actual arguments* of the invocation (4a)). An invocation like (4a) is logically equivalent to an invocation

junk_variable := my_proc(a1,...,an); (4b)

where *junk_variable* can be the name of any variable whose value is never used for anything else.

Of course, if the procedure *my_proc* invoked by (4a) does not modify any of its arguments, an invocation like (4a) will generally not be very useful, since none of the arguments $a1,\ldots,an$ will change and since the value returned by *my_proc* is simply thrown away. On the other hand, if the procedure *my_proc* *does* modify its arguments, then the invocation (4a) will trigger corresponding modifications of any arguments which correspond to parameters carrying the qualification **rw**.

Procedures which modify some of their arguments and which are normally invoked in this way are often called *simple-procedures*, as distinct from *functions*, i.e. from procedures which do not modify their arguments and are normally invoked in the manner illustrated by

x := my_proc(a1,...,an);

Since the value returned by a simple-procedure will just be thrown away, the expression e appearing in a statement

return e;

within such a procedure is usually without significance and may as well be

om. SETL allows

```
return om;
```

to be abbreviated simply as

```
return;
```

and this is the form of the **return** statement which is appropriate to use in simple-procedures. Note also that a **return** statement immediately preceding the trailer line of a simple-procedure can be omitted.

Simple-procedures with no parameters can be invoked just by writing their names followed by a semicolon, as in

```
my_simple_proc_without_parameters;   $ invokes procedure with this
                                     $ name.
```

As an example, here is a simple-procedure which "compresses" a tuple by dropping out all of its **om** components:

```
proc compress (rw t);
t := [x in t | x /= om];                    (5a)
end proc compress;
```

(Here we have made use of one of the rules stated previously to save writing a **return** statement just before the trailer line of this **proc**.)

Note that if x initially has the value [1, **om**, **om**, **om**, 2, **om**, 3], then the invocation

```
compress(x);                                (6a)
```

will give x the value [1, 2, 3].

As a matter of style, note also that instead of writing (5a) we could have written a closely related function, namely,

```
proc compress (t);
return [x in t | x /= om];                  (5b)
end proc compress;
```

in which case would have had to write

```
x := compress(x);                           (6b)
```

to get the effect of (6a). The form (6a) is sometimes slightly more convenient to write, and it is this convenience that can induce us to write a simple-procedure rather than a function for some purpose we have in mind.

In addition to the parameter qualifier **rw**, two additional qualifiers **rd** and **wr** are provided. These parameter qualifiers have the following significance:

rd read parameter: can be read and written within its **procedure**, but modifications to it will not be transmitted back to the corresponding actual argument.

rw read/write parameter: can be read and written within its **procedure**, and modifications to it will be transmitted back to the corresponding actual argument.

wr write-only parameter: can be written and will be transmitted back to the corresponding actual argument, but will not be read.

If none of these qualifiers is attached to a particular procedure parameter, the parameter will be treated as if it were qualified with **rd**. Thus **rd** is the default qualifier for otherwise unqualified parameters of procedures.

Next suppose that a procedure called *my_proc* has one parameter *x* which is qualified with **rw** or **wr**. In this case an invocation

```
my_proc(e);                                   (7a)
```

of *my_proc* is translated by introducing an otherwise unused temporary variable (call it *var*), and treating (7a) exactly as if it were

```
var := e;
my_proc(var);                                 (7b)
e := var;
```

The last line indicates that the only forms of expressions which can appear as actual arguments in place of parameters qualified by **rw** or **wr** are those which can legally appear to the left of an assignment operator. (See Section 3.12 for a comprehensive discussion of these assignment targets). This means that the invocations

```
my_proc(3);
```

and

```
my_proc(x + y);
```

are both illegal, since the assignments

```
3 := var;
```

and

```
x + y := var;
```

would both be illegal. On the other hand, the invocations

```
my_proc(t(i));   $ where t is a map or tuple
```

and

```
my_proc([x, y]);
```

are both legal and have exactly the same meanings as

```
var := t(i);
my_proc(var);
t(i) := var;
```

and

```
var := [x, y];
my_proc(var);
[x, y] := var;
```

respectively.

One final, rather esoteric, point deserves mention. Actual argument values are transmitted to a procedure and become the values of its formal parameters immediately upon invocation of the procedure. These values are transmitted by copying; i.e., each parameter receives a logically independent copy of the appropriate actual argument value upon procedure invocation. If the procedure modifies its parameters, it is these copied values that are modified; the original argument values remain unchanged. Moreover, even if the procedure transmits changes in its parameter values back to the point of invocation, these changes are only transmitted when the procedure executes a **return**, at which time an assignment like that appearing in (7b) takes place. These rules are natural enough and normally require little thought. However, examples which show their effects can be contrived. For example, consider the following code, in which the variable *y* is global:

```
program esoteric;

   var x, y;                  $ This declaration makes x and y global
   x := 'initial_val of x,'; y := 'initial_val_of_y';

   manipulate(x, x, y);       $ invoke procedure shown below
   print('y is:', y);

   proc manipulate(u, v, w)

   print('u is', u, 'v is', v);
   $ this will print: u is inital_val_of_x v is initial_val_of_x

   u := 'changed,';

   print('u is', u, 'v is', v);
   $ this will print: u is changed, v is initial_val_of_x

   $ Note that u and v remain different even though the
   $ corresponding actual arguments are the same

   w := 'mangled,';

   print('w is', w, 'y is', y);   $ note that y is global
   $ this will print: w is mangled, y is initial_value_of_y

   $ note that y is still unchanged, even though the change in
   $ w will be transmitted back to y when we return from this procedure

   end proc manipulate;

end program esoteric;
```

Note finally that the last line of output produced by this program, which will be produced by the **print** statement (in line 5 of the program) which immediately follows the invocation of *manipulate*, will be

y is mangled

Exercises

1. Write a procedure whose inputs are a tuple t of integers and a tuple s of integers in increasing order, and which returns a tuple $t1$ of length $\#s + 1$ defined as follows: the first component of $t1$ is the number of components of t which are not greater than $s(1)$; for j between 2 and $\#s$, the j-th component of $t1$ is the number of components of t which are greater than $s(j - 1)$ but not greater than $s(j)$; and the last component of $t1$ is the number of components of t which are greater than the last component of s. Try to make your procedure efficient.

2. "Bags," used in some programming languages, are like sets, but each element of a bag can occur several times (i.e., any specified number of times). In SETL, a bag b can be represented in two obvious ways.
   (a) by a tuple: i.e., the elements of b can be arranged in some arbitrary order and made the components of a tuple; or
   (b) by a map, which sends each element of b into the number of times that it occurs in G.

   Write a pair of procedures that convert between these two different representations of a bag G. Also, write a collection of procedures which extend the following set operations to bags in the most useful way:
   (i) $b1 + b2$, $b1*b2$, and $b1 - b2$ (where $b1$ and $b2$ are bags)
   (ii) x **in** b (where b is a bag and x is arbitrary)

3. The following table describes the tax due on D dollars of taxable income. Write a procedure which, given D, will return the amount of tax due.

Income Over	But Not Over	Tax
\$2,300	\$3,400	14%
3,400	4,000	\$154 + 16% of Amount Over \$3,400
4,000	6,500	314 + 18% of Amount Over 4,400
6,500	8,500	692 + 19% of Amount Over 6,500
8,500	10,800	1,072 + 21% of Amount Over 8,500
10,800	12,900	1,555 + 24% of Amount Over 10,800
12,900	15,000	2,059 + 26% of Amount Over 12,900
15,000	18,200	2,605 + 30% of Amount Over 15,000
18,200	23,500	3,565 + 34% of Amount Over 18,200
23,500	28,800	5,367 + 39% of Amount Over 23,500
28,800	34,100	7,434 + 44% of Amount Over 28,800
34,100	41,500	9,766 + 49% of Amount Over 34,100
41,500	55,300	13,392 + 55% of Amount Over 41,500
55,300	81,800	20,982 + 63% of Amount Over 55,300
81,800	108,300	37,677 + 68% of Amount Over 81,800
108,300	———	55,697 + 70% of Amount Over 108,800

4. Write a program which will read in a sequence of lines, each containing someone's name, first name first, and print out an alphabetized list of these names, in alphabetic order of last names. Repeat this exercise, but this time print the alphabetized list with last names first.

Three Exercises on Permutations

A *permutation* is a one-to-one mapping of a set s of n items into itself. If the set s consists of the integers from 1 to n, then such a permutation can be represented as a vector v of length n such that every integer from 1 to n appears as a component of v. The following exercises concern various properties of permutations.

5. The product prod($v1, v2$) of two permutations $v1$ and $v2$ is the vector v such that $v(i) = v1(v2(i))$ for each i in $\{1 \ldots \# v\}$. The identity permutation e of n integers is the permutation represented by the vector $[1, 2, .., n]$. The inverse inv(v) of a permutation is the permutation such that prod(v, inv(v)) $= e$. Write two SETL procedures *prod* and *inv* which realize these operations. Test them with the help of a procedure rand_perm(n) that generates a different random permutation of the integers from 1 to n each time it is called.

6. Check the following facts concerning permutations by generating a few random permutations and verifying that each fact asserted holds for these permutations. (The routines described in Ex. 5 should be used for this purpose.)
   (a) The product of two permutations is a permutation, and the product of permutations is associative.
   (b) prod(inv(v), v) $= e$ for each permutation v.
   (c) prod(inv(u), inv(v)) $=$ inv(prod(v, u)) for any two permutations u, v of n elements.
   (d) Define power(u, k) to be the product of k copies of the permutation v. Check that power($v, j + k$) $=$ prod(power(v, j), power(v, k)). Check that for each permutation v there exists a positive integer k such that power (v, k) $= e$.
   (e) Is prod(u, v) $=$ prod(v, u) true for every pair u, v of permutations of n items?

7. A simple recursive procedure to generate all the permutations of the elements of a set s is the following:

```
proc permutations(s)
    if s = { } then return [ ];
    else
       return {[x] + P: x in s, P in permutations(s less x)};
    end if;
end proc permutations;
```

It is often more convenient to generate permutations one by one, by successive calls to a generating procedure. For example, a program to generate all permutations (rearrangements) of the integers 1 thru n can be built up as follows. Start with the numbers in the sequence $s = [1..n]$. Then repeatedly find the last element $s(j)$ in the sequence s such that $s(j + 1) > s(j)$. Let $s(i)$ be the last element following $s(j)$ such that $s(i) > s(j)$. Interchange $s(i)$ with $s(j)$, and then reverse the sequence of elements following the j-th position. This gives the next permutation s.

Write this permutation-generation procedure in SETL, and use it to write out the list of all permutations of the integers 1 thru 5. Use this same procedure to create a program which reads in a string of length 5 and prints it out in all possible permutations, but without any repetitions.

8. If a second-order polynomial $P(x) = A*(x**2) + B*x + C$ with integer coefficients A, B, C has a first-order polynomial $M*x + N$ with integer coefficients as a factor, then M is a factor of A and N is a factor of C. Write a procedure which uses this fact to test polynomials like $P(x)$ to see whether they can be factored and that produces the two factors of P if P can be factored. How efficient can you make this factorization procedure?

   Can you devise a similar procedure for factoring third-order polynomials with integer coefficients?

9. A few years ago, tokens on the New York City subway system cost 60 cents. Tokens are sold at change booths. Purchasers normally pay for tokens without saying anything, simply by passing a sum of money to the change booth attendant. Certain sums of money (e.g., $1, which will purchase only one token) are unambiguous. Others, like a $5 bill, are ambiguous, since they will purchase anywhere from one to eight tokens. On the other hand, $5.50 is unambiguous, since the likely reason for adding the last 50 cents is to pay for nine rather than just eight tokens. Write a program which will read a tuple designating a collection of bills and coins, decide whether this is ambiguous or unambiguous, and print out an appropriate response (which might be either 'How many tokens do you want?' or 'Here are *n* tokens').

10. Before Britain began to use decimal coinage, its money consisted of pence, shillings worth 20 pence each, and pounds worth 12 shillings each. Write a procedure to add sums of money represented in this way, reducing the sum to pounds, shillings, and pence. (Sum of money can conveniently be represented as triples.) Write a procedure that will subtract sums of money represented as pounds, shillings, and pence, and which could have been used to make change in predecimal British shops.

11. Write a function whose argument is a tuple t with integer or real coefficients and which returns the positions of all the local maxima in t, i.e., all the components of t which are larger than either of their neighboring components.

Exercises on Recursion

12. The greatest common divisor $\gcd(x, y)$ of two positive integers is the largest positive integer z such that $(x \textbf{ mod } z) = 0$ and $(y \textbf{ mod } z) = 0$. (If x and y are equal, then $\gcd(x, y) = x$). Write procedures each of which calculates $\gcd(x, y)$ efficiently by exploiting one of the following mathematical relationships:

    (a) $\gcd(x, y) = \gcd(x - y, y)$ if $x > y$

    (b) $\gcd(x, 0) = x$ and $\gcd(x, y) = \gcd(x \textbf{ mod } y, y)$ if $x > y$.

    (c) $\gcd(x, y) = 2*\gcd(x \textbf{ div } 2, y \textbf{ div } 2)$ if x and y are both even.
    $\gcd(x, y) = \gcd(x \textbf{ div } 2, y)$ if x is even and y is odd
    $\gcd(x, y) = \gcd(x - y, y)$ if x and y are both odd and $x > y$.

13. Suppose that we make the gcd procedure of Ex. 12 into an infix operator .gcd and then evaluate .gcd/s for a set s. (see Section 5.6.2). What result does this produce? Assuming that $s1$ and $s2$ are non-null sets, is the identity

$$\text{gcd}/(s1 + s2) = (.\text{gcd}/s1).\text{gcd}/s2$$

always true? What will happen if one of $s1$ or $s2$ is null?

14. A rational number, m/n (with integer numerator and denominator) can be represented in SETL as an ordered pair $[m, n]$. Using this representation, write definitions for procedures called rs, rd, rp, and rq, which respectively form the sum, difference, product, and quotient of two fractions. These procedures should reduce fractions to lowest terms, for which purpose one of the gcd procedures developed in Ex. 12 will be found useful.

15. Supposing that fractions have the representation described in Ex. 14, write a procedure which takes a set of fractions and sorts them into increasing numerical order.

16. The following mathematical relationships can be used as the basis for recursive procedures for calculating various mathematical functions. Write out appropriate recursive procedures for each of these functions.
    (a) The value x occurs as a component of a tuple t if and only if it occurs either as a component of the left half of t or as a component of the right half of t.
    (b) The sum of all the components of a tuple t of integers is the sum of the left half of t plus the sum of the right half of t.
    (c) The reverse of a tuple t is the reverse of its right half, followed by the reverse of its left half.

    Think of at least four other relationships of this kind, and write out recursive procedures based on these relationships.

17. The Fibonnacci numbers F(n) are defined as follows:

$$F(1) = F(2) = 1, \qquad F(n+1) = F(n) + F(n-1) \qquad \text{for } n > 1$$

    (a) Write a recursive procedure for calculating $F(n)$.
    (b) Write a procedure which calculates $F(n)$ without using recursion.

18. Write a recursive procedure to calculate the number of different ways that an integer n can be written as the sum of two squares, as the sum of two cubes, and as the sum of three cubes. Print out a table of these values and see whether they suggest any interesting general facts.

19. To compute the power x**n, one can multiply x**m by x**k for any positive integers m and k satisfying $m + k = n$. Write a recursive procedure which uses this fact to determine the minimum number $M(n)$ of multiplications needed to calculate x**n. Print out a table of $M(n)$ for all n from 1 to 100.

20. Take mergesort (Section 5.4.2) and one other recursive procedure, and track their recursive operation by inserting code which computes the level of recursion reached by every invocation of the procedure being tracked. (A global variable should be introduced for this purpose.) Messages like the following should be printed:

    invoking mergesort from recursion level 3
    entering mergesort at recursion level 4, parameter is...
    returning from mergesort to recursion level 3, result is...

21. The correlation corr(u, v) of two vectors u, v of n real numbers is the quotient (u(1) − Mu)*(v(1) − Mv) + ··· + (u(n) − Mu)*(v(n) − Mv)/**sqrt**(VAu*Vav) where Mu and Mv are the means (i.e., average) of u and v, respectively, while VAu and Vav are the variances of u and v, respectively (the variance of a vector v is the sum

of the all squares $v(1) - \mathrm{M}v)^{**}2$, i running from 1 to $\#v$, where Mv is the mean of v). Write SETL procedures which calculate and return this value. Use this procedure to calculate and print the correlation of 10 randomly selected pairs of vectors. What is the largest value that corr(u, v) can possibly have? What is the smallest?

22. Write a procedure which will read a number written in any specified number base from 2 to 36 and convert it to the integer it represents in decimal notation. Numbers in bases below 10 will involve only the digits 0 thru 9; numbers written in larger bases will use the capital letters A thur Z, in increasing order, as additional digits. For example, base 16 numbers will be written by using the characters

0 1 2 3 4 5 6 7 8 9 A B C D E F,

and base 19 numbers will be written by using the characters

0 1 2 3 4 5 6 7 8 9 A B C D E F G H I.

Also, write a procedure which will convert an integer to its string representation in any of these bases. These programs should allow for the fact that an illegal character might occur in a string which is to be converted to an integer.

23. Write a program which can be used to prepare an alphabetized directory of your friends' names, addresses, and telephone numbers. The input to this program is assumed to be a list of multiline entries, each starting with a line having the format

*key,

where *key* designates an alphabetic key which determines the alphabetic position of the given entry. (These keys are not to be printed in the final directory.) For example, two entries might be

```
*Smith
Mary Smith
222 Flowery Way
Ossining, N.Y. 10520
(914)284-1234

*Termites
Acme Exterminators
(Termite Specialists)
(Recommended by Mary)
(202)789-1212
```

24. Write a "personalized letter" generator. The inputs to this program should be a form letter L and a file F containing "addresses" and "variations." The letter L is given as a text containing substrings ***j***, and the file F given as a sequence of items ***s*1***s*2**...***sn*, each *sj* being some "personalizing" string. The expanded form of the letter is produced by inserting the address in an appropriate position and replacing each substring ***j*** in the form L by the string *sj*. For example, if L begins

```
Dear **1**:
    Since only **2** weeks remain before you will graduate from **3**,
...
```

and the first entry in F is

> Ms. Nancy Holman 353 Bleeker St N.Y.C., 10012 NY **Nancy**six**New York University

the "personalized" letter generated will be

> Ms. Nancy Holman
> 353 Bleeker St
> N.Y.C., 10012 NY
>
> Dear Nancy:
> Since only six weeks remain before you will graduate from New York University,...

The "personalized" letters that your program generates should be right-justified and attractively formatted. Try to think of, and implement, features which will improve the utility of the personalized letter generator.

25. Write a procedure which will print a string of up to six characters in "banner" format on your output listing. In this format, each character is printed $1\frac{1}{2}$ inches wide and 2 inches high; the whole banner should also be centered on the listing.

26. The set of distances between the centers of cities x, y directly connected by a road not going through any other city is given by a map dist(x, y). (Whenever dist(x, y) is defined, so is dist(y, x), and of course dist$(x, y) =$ dist(y, x).) Write a program that will use this information to calculate the shortest driving distance between any two cities (whether or not they are connected directly by a road). This information should be printed out as an intercity distance chart of the usual form. Also, print out a chart which describes the shortest driving route between cities by listing the city z that you should drive to first if you want to go from x to z.

27. Write a procedure which, given two tuples $t1$ and $t2$, prints out a list of the number of times each component of $t1$ occurs as a component of $t2$.

28. Write a procedure whose parameters are a string x and a set s of strings and which returns the elements of s which has the largest number of successive character pairs in common with x. How would you structure this procedure if it is to be called repeatedly, always with the same s, but with many different values of x?

29. Write a procedure that determines whether a character C is a letter, digit, blank, or special character. Try to make your code efficient.

30. Manhattan Island was purchased in 1626 for \$24. If instead this money had been deposited in a bank account drawing 6% annual interest, how much would be in the account now?

5.6 Other Procedure-Related Facilities

5.6.1 Procedures with a variable number of arguments

Occasionally one wants to write a procedure or function which can accept a variable number of arguments. One may, for example, want to write a function which sums the value of all its integer arguments, or a procedure which can take any number of arguments, capitalize, and print them. Another example is furnished by SETL's built-in **read** and **print** procedures; the **print** procedure accepts any number of arguments and prints them one after another; the **read** procedure accepts any number of arguments and modifies them all by assigning to them SETL values read from input.

SETL does allow such procedures and functions to be written. To define a function with a variable number of parameters, a header line of the from

proc proc_name(x1, x2, ..., xn(*))

must be used. Hence as before, any proc_name can be used to name the procedure, and *x*1, ..., *xn* are as usual its parameters. However, a procedure declared in this way can be invoked with any number of arguments greater than $n - 1$. All arguments from the n-th onward are then gathered into a tuple which is assigned as the value of the last parameter *xn*. Thus, for example, in the body of the procedure, the references *xn*(1) and *xn*(5) would refer to the n-th and $(n + 4)$-th argument, respectively. Only the last parameter of such a function can be followed by the sign (*) to indicate that it actually represents a list of arguments whose length can vary.

The special reserved symbol **nargs** can be used within the body of such a procedure; its value will be the actual number of arguments with which the function was invoked.

Here, for example, is a modified **print** procedure which accepts any number of arguments and prints them one after another, but which starts a new line whenever it begins printing a set or a tuple, or whenever more than five items have been printed on a single line:

```
proc nicer_print(x(*));

next := 1; $ next item to print

(while next <= nargs)

   if exists j in [next..nargs min (next + 5)]
                  |is_tuple (x(j)) or is_set (x(j)) then

         print_on_line (x(next..j - 1));   $ print simple arguments

         print(x(j));

         next := j + 1;
   else

         print_on_line(x(next..next + 4));
      next + := 5;

   end if;

end while;

end proc nicer_print;
```

```
proc print_on_line(t); $ prints the components of t on one line
    case #t of
        (0):  return;  $ nothing to print
        (1):  print(t(1));
        (2):  print(t(1), t(2));
        (3):  print(t(1), t(2), t(3));
        (4):  print(t(1), t(2), t(3), t(4));
        (5):  print(t(1), t(2), t(3), t(4), t(5));
    end case;
end proc print_on_line;
```

The qualifiers **rd**, **rw**, **wr** can be attached to any of the parameters of a procedure having a variable number of arguments. This is shown in the following example, which gives code for a modified *read* operation which echoes all the information that it reads, i.e., copies this information to the standard output file.

```
proc echo_read(rw x(*));
  (for j in [1..nargs])
      read(y); print(y);
      x(j) := y;
  end for;
end proc echo_read;
```

To use this procedure, we could for example write

```
echo_read(x, y, z);
```

This would read values into *x*, *y*, and *z* in the normal way but would also print the information that it read.

5.6.2 User-defined prefix and infix operators

Procedure names must always be written before their lists of arguments, and these arguments must always be enclosed in parentheses. However, for procedures with two arguments used in expressions, infix notation is generally more convenient; for example, it is more convenient to write

```
a + b
```

than to have to write

```
plus(a, b)
```

and certainly

a + b + c + d

is more convenient than

plus(plus(plus(a, b), c), d).

For this reason, SETL allows its users to define infix operators (and also prefix operators, which however are considerably less useful). The names of such operators must be ordinary SETL identifiers to which the character "." (period) is prefixed. To introduce such operators, a perfectly ordinary function body followed by a trailer line is used, but the header line introducing the operator is changed to

```
op .name(a);    $ to introduce a prefix operator
```

or

```
op .name(a, b);    $ to introduce an infix operator
```

Suppose, for example, that we wish to introduce an operator called *.dot* which forms the dot-product of two vectors of equal length, i.e., the sum of the products of their corresponding components. This can be done as follows:

```
op .dot(u, v);

  If #u /= #v then
    print('tuples of mismatched length', u, v);
    return om;
  else
    return +/[u(i)*v(i) : i in [1 .. #v]];
  end if;

end op .dot;
```

Once this operator has been defined, we can invoke it simply by writing

```
u .dot v
```

Another example is the useful operator *.c*, which forms the composition of two (possibly multivalued) maps (see Section 3.8.4 for an explanation of the meaning of map composition.)

```
op .c(f, g);

  return {[x, y]: x in domain g, z in g{x}, y in f{z}};

end op .c;
```

User-defined infix operators of this kind can be combined with the token ":=" to form assigning operators (see Section 3.12.1). For example, in the presence of the preceding definition we can write

```
f .c := g;
```

to abbreviate the common construct

```
f := f .c g;
```

Moreover, both built-in and user-defined infix operators can be used to form compound operators. For example, we can use the *.c* operator in the following way to write an operator which forms the *n*-th power of a map *f*.

```
op f .to n;

  return if n = 0 then { }        $ the identity map
  else .c/[f : i in [1..n]] end;

end op .to;
```

User-defined prefix operators are less useful than user-defined infix operators, since they cannot appear in either of these convenient contexts. However, by defining a function of one parameter as an operator rather than an ordinary **procedure**, we save what might otherwise be irritating parentheses. For example, if we define a unary operator minus by writing

```
op .minus(u);

return [-x: x in u];

end op .minus;
```

Then the negative of a vector *u* can be formed by writing

```
.minus u
```

If instead of this we made *minus* an ordinary function, we would have to write

```
minus(u)
```

instead.

The arguments of a user-defined infix or prefix operation always carry the implicit qualifier **rd**, so that attempting to give them either of the qualifications **wr** or **rw** is illegal. Attempting to attach the qualifier "(*)" (see Section 5.6.1) to a parameter of an infix or prefix operator is also illegal.

The precedence of any user-defined binary operator is lower than that of any built-in binary operator, with the exception of the following comparators and Boolean operators:

= /= < <= > >= **in notin subset incs and or impl**

Assignments and assigning operators seen from the right also have lower precedence than user-defined infix operators. User-defined unary operators have the same precedence as built-in unary operators (see Section 3.13 for details concerning operator precedence). The following examples illustrate these rules: If .op is a user-defined binary operator, then

```
a + b .op c means (a + b) .op c
b .op c = d means (b .op c) = d
```

b .op c **and** d means (b .op c) **and** d
b .op c + d means b .op (c + d)
a + := b .op c means a + := (b .op c)

5.6.3 Refinements

Procedures play various roles and in particular serve to clarify the logical structure of a complex program by dividing it into subsections whose names hint at their purposes. However, the use of procedures is a bit "heavy" syntactically, in part because procedures require header and trailer lines to introduce them, in part because the variables of a procedure are logically isolated from all other procedures (unless these variables are made global, but then they become accessible to all procedures, which, as pointed out in Section 5.2, is often highly undesirable). This clumsiness discourages the use of small groups of short procedures which need to share many variables among themselves. To fill the need for a facility of this kind, whose use can aid considerably in documenting and clarifying the logical structure of a program, SETL provides a less powerful but easier-to-use alternative to procedures, namely, *refinements*.

A *refinement* is a block of statements which is labeled by an identifier followed by a double colon, as in

```
solve_equation:: x := (-b + sqrt(b*b - 4.0*a*c))/(2.0*a);
```

Within a procedure or a main program block, a refinement can be invoked by using its label as a statement. This is shown in the following example

```
program quadratic;

   input_data;          $ this and the next 2
                        $ lines invoke refinements

   solve_equation;
   output_results;

solve_equation::        $ a first refinement
   x := (-b + sqrt(b*b - 4.0*a*c))/2.0*a;

output_results::        $ a second refinement

   print('Root is', x);

input_data::            $ a third refinement

   read(a, b. c);
   print(a, b, c);
   check_eof;           $ this invokes the fourth
                        $ refinement shown just below

   check_eof::          $ a fourth 'refinement'
```

```
        if eof then print('improper data'); stop; end if;
end program quadratic;
```

This example illustrates the following rules:

(a) All refinements (if any) must follow at the end of the procedure or main program block within which they are used.
(b) Refinements are written one after another but can appear in any order.
(c) A refinement can be invoked anywhere in a procedure or a main program but can be invoked only once. If a section of code is to be invoked more than once, it should be made a procedure rather than a refinement.
(d) Refinements have no parameters. They make use of the same variables as the main program block or procedure *P* to which they belong. Variables used in refinements have the same meaning that they would have in (the block or procedure) *P*. Refinements are executed by inserting the series of statements of the refinement in place of the reference to the refinement.

5.7 Rules of Style in the Use of Procedures

Effective programming depends more on the proper use of procedures than on any other single factor. Your use of procedures should aim to achieve various important stylistic goals:

(a) Procedure are used to "paragraph" programs, i.e., to divide them into manageably short subsections, each performing some easily definable logical function, which can be read and understood in relative independence from each other. Here the key term is independence: it is important to write your procedures in a manner that isolates each of them as much as possible from the internal details of other procedures. Only a small number of well-defined data objects should be passed between procedures. Very few data objects should be shared globally between procedures; sharing is dangerously productive of errors, so that all data object sharing should be carefully planned, should adhere to clearly understood stylistic rules, and must be scrupulously documented. Be sparing in your use of global **var** declarations!
(b) Procedures are also used to abbreviate, i.e., to give frequently used compound constructions a name facilitating their repeated use. This usage will often give rise to short procedures, the shortest of which may reduce to a single **return** statement. Code sequences used more than a very few times should be replaced by short procedures, since such procedures will need to be debugged only once, although repeated code sequences can be repeated incorrectly, and can interact in unanticipated ways with code surrounding them (for example, by accidental overlap of names). These facts make repetition of code sequences dangerous, and their replacement by procedures advantageous.

(c) Procedures define one's conceptual approach to a programming task and are used to clarify and help document programs. If this is done well, a program's topmost procedure will document the main phases of the program and explain the principal data structures passed between its phases. Then each intermediate level procedure will both realize and "flowchart" an important substep of processing. Each bottom-level procedure will realize some well-defined utility operation and will be separately readable.

The narrative commentary that accompanies the program should be organized around the layout of its procedures. Comments concerning overall approach and main shared data objects will accompany top-level procedures, and detailed remarks on particular algorithms will be attached to the low-level subprocedures that implement these algorithms.

(d) Procedures are used to decompose programs into separate parts which have different degrees of generality/specificity, or which have significantly different "flavors" in some other regard. The "buckets and well" example considered in Section 5.3.1 exemplifies this point. In this program, procedures new_states_from, pour, fill, etc., concentrate all details particular to the specific problem being solved, while procedure find_path, which simply realizes a general technique for searching over states and constructing paths, is independent of these details. This separation makes it possible to use find_path to solve other problems of the same kind, simply by replacing new_state_from and its subsidiary routines.

(e) When one is writing a program which addresses a mathematical or application area which makes use of some well-established family of concepts, it can be very advantageous to define SETL representations for all the kinds of objects used in this area and then to write a collection of utility procedures which can be used to apply all the important operations of the area to these objects. These procedures should be written in a way which allows their user to ignore the internal details of the objects representations, making it possible for him to think more as a specialist in the application area rather than as a programmer. This is the important principle of "information hiding": structure your programs in a way which allows the representational details of objects manipulated by the highest-level programs to be concealed from the authors of these programs. (So important is this principle that some modern programming languages include syntactic mechanisms for enforcing it rigorously.) A family of procedures that manipulate objects whose internal representational details are known only to these procedures is sometimes called a *package*. The package of polynomial manipulation procedures shown in Section 5.1.3 is an example; other examples appear in the exercises.

It is worth saying a bit more concerning the paragraphing of code. Elusive errors easily creep into programs whose logic is spread over many lines. For this reason, one should always strive to break programs into independent "paragraphs" no more than 10 or so lines in length. (Longer paragraphs can be used where this is unavoidable, but as these grow to a page or more in size, the likelihood of troublesome multiple errors, as well as the difficulty of understanding what is going on when the code is read subsequently, will rise rapidly.) The three main constructs that can help you to paragraph code adequately are

(i) procedures
(ii) refinements (see Section 8.1)
(iii) the **case** statement

Each procedure and refinement whose integrity is not compromised by an undisciplined use of shared global variables constitutes an independent paragraph of code. Moreover, since only one of its alternatives will be performed each time a **case** statement is executed, the separate alternatives of a **case** statement can be regarded as independent paragraphs. Hence, whenever the body of a procedure extends over more than a few dozen lines, most of this body should consist of one or more **case** statements each of whose alternatives is short. If this is not done, then the rules of good style are being violated; and this violation should either have compelling justification or be removed.

Nesting of loops and of **if**'s also raises interesting stylistic questions. Since iterations will rarely be nested more than three deep, nested iterations can generally be used without significant confusion resulting. When deeper nests start to build up, or the body of an outermost iteration tends to grow long, an effort should be made to relegate parts of its body to one or more separate procedures.

Deep nesting of **ifs** leads very rapidly to confusion. Where at all possible nested **if**'s more than two deep should be replaced by uses of **case** statements, or by segregation of the more deeply nested alternatives into procedures. A third alternative is to "flatten" a deeply nested **if** construct into an **if** construct which is less deeply nested, but in which the alternatives of the original **if**-nest have been combined using the Boolean **and**, **or**, etc. (However, this will tend to generate longish sequences of **elseif**'s.) For example, instead of writing

```
if a > 0 then
    if b < 0 then
        a +:= 1;
    else
        a -:= 1;
    end if;
else
    if b < 0 then
        b +:= 1;
    else
        b -:= 1;
    end if;
end if;
```

it is preferable to "flatten" and write

```
          if a > 0 and b < 0 then
               a +:= 1;
          elseif a > 0 and b >= 0 then
               a -:= 1;
          elseif a <= 0 and b < 0 then
               b +:= 1;
          elseif a <= 0 and b >= 0 then
               b -:= 1;
     end if;
```

Still better, one can use the following **case** statement:

```
case of
   (a > 0 and b < 0):   a +:= 1;
   (a > 0 and b > 0):   a -:= 1;
   (a < 0 and b < 0):   b +:= 1;
   (a < 0 and b > 0):   b -:= 1;
end case;
```

Note than an extended **if**..**elseif**..**elseif**... construct has some of the same paragraphing advantages as an extended sequence of **case** alternatives. However, **if** alternatives are less fully independent than **case** alternatives, since implicit conditions accumulate from each branch of an **if** statement to the next. Some of the confusion which this will cause can be avoided by using auxiliary comments to indicate the conditions under which each branch of an extended **if** will be executed, but it is even safer to use a **case** statement instead.

EXERCISES

The *dot-product* of a pair *u*, *v* of equally long vectors with integer or real coefficients is the sum +/[*u*(*i*)**v*(*i*): *i* **in** [1.. #*v*]].

1. Write a prefix operator .rv *n* which returns a randomly chosen integer-valued vector of length *n* each time it is invoked. Use it and the operator .dot defined in Section 5.6.2 to test the validity of the following statements concerning vector dot-products:

(a)	(x .dot y)	=	(y .dot x)
(b)	(x .dot x)	>=	(**max**/x)*(**max**/x)
(c)	(x .dot y)**2	<=	(x .dot x)*(y .dot y)
(d)	(x .dot y)	<=	(**max**/x)*(**max**/y)* #x

2. The sum of two integer or real vectors *x* and *y* of equal length is [*x*(*i*) + *y*(*i*): *i* **in** [1.. #*x*]], and their difference is [*x*(*i*) − *y*(*i*): *i* **in** [1.. #*x*]]. Write definitions for two **op**'s called .s and .d which produce these two vectors. Proceed as in Ex. 1 to test the following statements:

(a)	((x .s y) .s z)	=	(x .s (y .s z))
(b)	(x .s (y .d x))	=	y

(c) ((x .s y) .dot z) = (x .dot z) + (y .dot z)
(d) ((x .d y) .dot z) = (x .dot z) − (y .dot z)

3. Write a procedure which, given a tuple *t*, calculates a map which sends each component *x* of *t* into the index of the first occurrence of *x* within *t*.

4. The storage space needed to represent a map *f* can sometimes be reduced very considerably by writing *f* in the form *f*(*x*) = *f*1(*x*)? (**if** *x* **in** *s* **then** *f*2(*x*) **else om end**), where *f*1 has a small domain, *s* has a simple representation, and *f*2 is a programmed function. Write a procedure *compress* which, given *f*, *s*, and *f*2, will calculate *f*1. The function *f*2 should be called by *compress*, and it is assumed that user of the *compress* is required to supply code representing *f*2.

5. Write a room assignment program which reads information concerning available rooms and classes needing rooms and generates a room assignment. The first of the two data items read by your program should be a map from room numbers to seating capacities. The second input read by your program should be a tuple of triples, each consisting of a class number (a string of the form *n*.m where *n* is a course number and *m* a section number), number of students, and hour (possible hours are 8, 9, 10, 11, .. up to 20). No two classes meeting at the same hour should be scheduled into the same room. Your program should print out a table, arranged by hour and room, of assignments. Starting with the largest class scheduled to meet in a given hour, each class should be assigned the smallest room into which it will fit. Classes which cannot be scheduled should be appropriately listed. Empty rooms should be indicated in the output table you print.

The next three exercises relate to the earlier exercises on Boolean identities, found in Section 2.5.4.1.

6. A Boolean implication, which we will write as an infix operator *x* .imp *y*, is **true if** either *x* is **false** or *y* is **true**. Thus *x* .imp *y* is equivalent to (**not** *x*) or *y*. Write a SETL **op** definition for this operator, which will be used in the next two exercises.

7. Using the .imp operator defined in Ex. 6 and the method for checking Boolean statements described in Section 2.5.4.1, show that each of the following statements is true regardless of the Boolean values of the variables occurring in it.

(a) (x **or not** y) = (y .imp x)
(b) ((x **and** y) .imp z) = (x .imp (y .imp z))
(c) (x .imp (y or z)) = ((x .imp y) **or** (x .imp z))
(d) ((x .imp y) **and** x) .imp y
(e) (x .imp **not** x). imp **not** x
(f) x .imp (y .imp x)
(g) (**not** x) .imp (x .imp y)

8. None of the following Boolean formulae is valid for all Boolean values of *x* and *y*; each represents a common logical fallacy. Proceeding as in Ex. 7, write a SETL program which will find a case in which each of these formulae evaluates to FALSE.

(a) ((x .imp y) **and** y) .imp x
(b) ((x .imp y) **and** (x .imp z)) .imp (y .imp z)
(c) ((x **or** y) **and** x) .imp **not** y
(d) ((x .imp y) **and not** x) .imp **not** y

9. When a sequence of data items is read by a read statement of the form

read(x, y, .. z),

it will often be appropriate to check the items read to make sure that they have appropriate types and lie in appropriate ranges. For this purpose, the following approach, based upon the notion of "descriptor string," may be convenient:

(a) Capital letters are used in the following way to designate the principal SETL object classes:

Letter	Value	Letter	Value
I	integer	*T*	tuple
R	real	*E*	set
S	string	*A*	atom

(b) The ranges of integers and of real numbers can be constrained. For example, *I* − 100 .. 100 designates an integer belonging to the set {−100 .. 100}, *I*0 .. designates a non-negative integer, *R* − 1.0 .. 1.0 designates a real number lying between −1.0 and +1.0.

(c) The descriptors *T* and *E* can be qualified to show the types of their components or members. For example *T*(*IIR*) describes a tuple of length 3 whose components are an integer, an integer, and a real, respectively; *T.I* describes an unknown-length tuple of integers; *E.T*(*II*) describes a set of pairs of integers.

(d) To describe successive items in a list of variables being read, descriptors are simply concatenated. For example, if three items *x*, *y*, *z*, the first an integer, the second a set of pairs of integers, and the third a tuple of strings, are being read, we would describe it by IE.T(II)T.S..

Write a multiparameter procedure read_check whose first parameter is a descriptor string defining the data expected and whose remaining parameters are the variables whose values are to be read, e.g., in the example appearing in (d). we would write

read_check('IE.T(II)T.S', x, y, z);

The read_check procedure should generate a report if it encounters any data of unexpected form. Of course, the read_check procedure must be foolproof.

10. Modify the read_check procedure of Ex. 9 so that it echoes and labels all data read. For this modified procedure, the sequence of names of the variables being read should follow the data descriptor in the procedure's first parameter. These names should be separated from the data descriptor and from each other by blanks.

5.8 String Scanning Primitives

SETL supports some of the handy string primitives whose use was pioneered in the SNOBOL programming language. These generally have the form

operation_name(scanned_string, pattern_string). (1)

Each of these operations attempts to match a portion of its scanned_string parameter in a manner defined by the pattern_string. If a portion of the scanned_string is successfully matched, it is removed from the scanned_string and returned by the function. If not even the first character of *ss* belongs to *ps*, then *ss* is unchanged and the function (1) yields **om**.

The most often used string primitive is called **span**. The pattern string in this primitive is a sequence of characters. **Span** finds the longest initial segment of the scanned string which consists entirely of characters from the pattern string and breaks it off. If the first character of the scanned string is not in the pattern string, **span** yields **om** (we also say that it fails) and the scanned string is unaffected.

Here are a few illustrations of the action of the **span** primitive; Suppose that *ss* has the value "If, gentlemen." Then

span(ss, 'ABCDEFGHIJKLMNOPQRSTUVWXYZabcdefghij')

has the value 'If' and gives *ss* the value', gentlemen'. Also,

span(ss, 'abcdefghijklmnopqrstuvwxyz')

has the value **om** and does not change the value of *ss*.

The remaining string-scanning primitives provided by SETL are as follows:

any(ss, ps) (2)

breaks off and yields the first character of *ss* if this belongs to *ps*. If the first character of *ss* does not belongs to *ps*, then *ss* is unchanged and the value returned by **any** is **om**. For example, the code fragment

```
ss := 'ABC';
print(ss, any(ss, 'AEIOU'), ss, any(ss, 'AEIOU'), ss);
```

will yield

ABC A BC * BC.

The scanning primitive

break(ss, ps) (3)

scans *ss* from the left up to but not including the first character which does belong to *ps*. This part of *ss* is broken off and becomes the value of the function (3). If *ss* contains no characters not belonging to *ps*, then (3) has the value **om** and *ss* is not changed. If the very first character of *ss* belongs to *ps*, then (3) has a nullstring value and *ss* is not changed.

The scanning primitive

len(ss, n) (4)

has an integer second parameter. If $\#ss >= n$, then (4) yields the value $ss(1\,..\,n)$ and the assignment $ss := ss(n + 1\,..)$ is performed; otherwise (4) yields **om** and *ss* is not changed.

The primitive

$$\textbf{match}(ss, ps) \qquad (5)$$

yields *ps* if $\#ps <= \#ss$ and if $ps = ss(1\,..\,\#ps)$. In this case the assignment $ss := ss(\#ps + 1\,..)$ is performed. Otherwise (5) yields **om** and *ss* is unchanged.

The primitive

$$\textbf{notany}(ss, ps) \qquad (6)$$

breaks off and yields the first character of *ss* if this does not belong to the string *ps*. In the contrary case (6) yields **om** and **ss** is unchanged.

Each of the preceding string primitives is also provided a "right-to-left" form which starts from the right, at the last character of the scanned string, and processes from right to left, rather than from left to right, starting at the first character of the scanned_string as in the cases already considered. The following table shows the right-to-left variant of each of the primitives described previously.

Left-to-Right Variant	Right-to-Left Variant
any(*ss*, *ps*)	**rany**(*ss*, *ps*)
break(*ss*, *ps*)	**rbreak**(*ss*, *ps*)
len(*ss*, *n*)	**rlen**(*ss*, *n*)
match(*ss*, *ps*)	**rmatch**(*ss*, *ps*)
notany(*ss*, *ps*)	**rnotany**(*ss*, *ps*)
span(*ss*, *ps*)	**rspan**(*ss*, *ps*)

Two additional string utilities are provided to make productions of decently formatted string output easier. These are

lpad(ss, n) and **rpad**(ss, n)

The **lpad** primitive returns the string obtained by padding its first argument *ss* out to length *n* (which must be an integer) by adding as many blanks to the left of *ss* as necessary. If $\#ss >= n$, then **lpad**(*ss*, *n*) is simply *ss*. The **rpad** primitive behaves similarly but adds blanks on the right.

5.8.1 Examples of Use of the String Scanning Primitives

5.8.1.1 A simple lexical scanner

One of the first problems that arises when one begins to program a compiler for a programming language (like SETL, BASIC, or any of the other languages with which you may be familiar) is to break the source form of the program into a stream of individual identifiers, constants, and operators (collectively, these items are called *tokens*). The program that the computer will read must be decomposed into these elements before we can determine its meaning. For example, on reading the fragment

'A0 = B1 * C1 + 3.78'

of text, one must break it up into the sequence of symbols

['A0', '=', 'B1', '*', 'C1', '+', '3.78'].

Note that the first of these items is an identifier, the second an operator sign, the last a constant, etc. (Blanks separating tokens are ordinarily eliminated as the source text is scanned).

A procedure which performs this kind of decomposition of strings representing successive lines of program text is called a *lexical scanner*.

It is easy to write a lexical scanner for a simple language using the string scanning operations that we have just described. We will now show how to do this, but to avoid complications, we will suppose that the following rules apply:

(a) The program text to be scanned contains only identifiers, operator signs, integers, floating-point constants, and blanks.
(b) An *identifier* is any string starting with an alphabetic and containing only alphabetic and numeric characters.
(c) Any *special character* (i.e., characters like "+," "−," "," and ":," which are not blank, alphabetic, or numeric) will be regarded as an operator.
(d) An *integer* is a sequence of numerics not followed by a period. A *floating-point number* is a string of numerics including at most one period.

From the string being analyzed, the following procedure repeatedly breaks off a section consisting of a run of blanks, a run of digits, an identifier, or a single "special" character of some other kind. Blanks are ignored. If a run of digits is found, we check to see whether a decimal point and a second run of digits follow. If so, they are concatenated to the run of digits originally found. In each case, a nonblank section broken from *ss* constitutes a token, and it is added to the tuple of tokens which is eventually returned. The code assumes that *num* and *alphanum* are constants which must be initialized as follows:

```
program lexer;                                  $ lexical scan program

  var num, alphanum;                            $ globalise these quantities

    num := '0123456789';
    alphanum := 'abcdefghijklmnopqrstuvwxyz'
     + 'ABCDEFGHIJKLMNOPQRSTUVWXYZ' + '0123456789';

  print(lex_scan('now is the time for all good men 35 35.35 35... ;""'));

  proc lex_scan(stg);                           $ lexical scan routine where the
                                                $ parameter is a string.

  tup := [ ];                                   $ Initialize the tuple to be
                                                $ returned.
```

```
    stg + := ' ';                                   $ Add a terminating blank.
    (while stg /= '')
    token := span(stg,' ')? span(stg, num)? span(stg, alphanum)? len(stg, 1);
                                                    $ Break off a run of blanks, a
                                                    $ number, a variable name
                                                    $ or a single letter.
    if token(1) = ' ' then continue; end;           $ Ignore blanks.
    if token(1) in num then                         $ Test for following '.' and
                                                    $ numerics.
       if match(stg, '.') = '.' then                $ Look for digits following the
                                                    $ decimal point.
          token + := '.' + (span(stg, num)?'');
       end if match;
    end if token;
    tup with := token;                              $ Add token to tuple being
    end while;                                      $ built up.
    return tup;
    end proc lex_scan;
end program lexer;
```

5.8.1.2 A concordance program

The following code generates a *cross-reference listing* or *concordance* of a source text. The source text is assumed to consist of a sequence of strings containing words separated by punctuation marks or blanks. The words present in the source text are printed in alphabetical order, each word being followed by a formatted list of all the lines in which it occurs.

```
program concordance;                            $ concordance generator
var capital_of, alphabetics;                    $ maps small letters to capitals
initialize (capital_of, alphabetics);           $ All upper and lower case
                                                $ alphabetics.
line_number := 0;                               $ Initialize line_number count.
lines_word_is_in := { };                        $ Initialize this to the empty
                                                $ map.
(while (tuple_of_words := break_next_line(line_number)) /= om)
$ break_next_line reads a line of text and decomposes it into the words it
contains by capitalizing them
$ and eliminating punctuation marks.
```

```
(for word in tuple_of_words)
   lines_word_is_in(word) =:
         lines_word_is_in(word)? [ ] with line_number;
end for;

end while;

$ Now sort, putting all words encountered into alphabetical order. This is
  done by using the quicksort
$ procedure described in Section 5.4.1.

(for [word, lines] in sort(lines_word_is_in))
     print(word); arrange(lines);            $ Arrange the line numbers neatly.
end for;

proc break_next_line(rw line_number);    $ Input and scanning routine.

$ This procedure reads a line of input and scans it to break out the words
  which it contains.
$ These words are capitalized and placed in a tuple.

line_number + := 1;                          $ Advance the line number.
read(line);                                  $ Note that to use 'read', the text
                                             $ lines being read must be quoted.

if eof then return om; end;

words := [ ];                                $ Start a new tuple of words.

   (while line /= '')                        $ Until the line has been
                                             $ digested.
   if break(line, alphabetics) = om then     $ Drop any leading nonalphabetic
   quit; end;                                $ characters and quit if there
                                             $ are none.

   $ Some alphabetic characters left.
         words with := capitalize(span(line, alphabetics));

end while;

return words;

end proc break_next_line;

proc arrange(lines);                         $ Routine to print sequence of line
                                             $ numbers.

$ This routine prints up to 10 line numbers per line of the concordance and
  arranges them neatly
$ in fields six characters wide.

(while line /= [ ])                          $ Until all line numbers are
                                             $ processed,
```

```
     group := lines(1..10);                    $ break off a first group of up to
                                               $ ten lines.
     lines := lines(11 min (#lines + 1)..);
     print(12*' '+/[lpad(str 1n, 6): 1n in group]);
end while;

end proc arrange;

proc capitalize(word);                         $ Capitalizes its parameter

Return ''+/[capital_of(let)? let: let in       $ Returning capitalized version
word];

end proc capitalize;

proc sort(s);                                  $ Quicksort procedure, second
                                               $ form
     t := [y: y in s];
     t1 := t(1);                               $ Get first element of unsorted
                                               $ tuple
     return if #t < 2 then t
     else
        sort([y: y = t(i)|y(1) < t1(1)]) + [t1]
        + sort([y: y = t(i)|y(1) >= t1(1) and i > 1])
     end;
end proc sort;

proc initialize(rw capital_map, rw             $ Initialization routine
alphabet_string);

small_lets := 'abcdefghijklmnopqrstuvwxyz';
big_lets := 'ABCDEFGHIJKLMNOPQRSTUVWXYZ';
alphabet_string := small_lets + big_lets;
capital_map := {[small_let, big_lets(i)]: small_let = small_lets(i)};

end proc initialize;

end program concordance;
```

5.8.1.3 A margin justification procedure

Our third example is a *margin justification procedure* which takes a sequence of words separated by blanks and arranges them into lines which fit between left_margin and right_margin with the first nonblank character placed in position left_margin and the last nonblank character placed in position right_margin. Extra blanks are inserted at random positions between the words to force "justification" of the right margin. Procedures of this sort are often used in text preparation programs.

```
proc justify(tuple_of_lines, left_margin, right_margin);
          tuple_of_words := [ ] +/[break_words(line): line in
                                                  tuple_of_lines];
```

```
        (until is_last)

        line_words := break_next_line(tuple_of_words,
                                      right_margin - left_margin + 1);
                $ break_next_line breaks off and returns the tuple of
                  words to be placed on the next line.

        if (is_last := (tuple_of_words = [ ] then

                $ Output last line with no justification.

        print(((left_margin - 1)*' ') +/[word + ' ': word in line_words]);

        else            $ Print justified line.

          spaces :=    $ Calculate vector of extra spaces.
          put_spaces(#line_words, right_margin
                              - ((left_margin - 1) +/[#word + 1: word
                              in line_words]));

          print((left_margin - 1) * ' ' + line_words(1) +
                              +/[(nspace + 1) * ' ' + line_words(i + 1):
                              nspace = spaces(i)]);

        end if;

        end until;
end proc justify;

proc break_words(line);                  $ Breaks line at blanks and returns
                                         $ a tuple of words.

tup := [ ];                              $ Initialize tuple.

(while line /= ' ')

    word := span(line, ' ') ? break(line, ' ') ? match(line, line);
    if word(1) /= ' ' then tup with := line; end;

end while;

return tup;

end proc break_words;

proc break_next_line(rw tuple_of_words, nchars);

$ This procedure breaks off and returns the longest sequence of words that
  will fit into nchars
$ character positions; this sequence is broken off from tuple_of_words.

sum := 0;

(for word = tuple_of_words(i))

    if (sum + := #word + 1) > nchars    $ Too far, back up one word.
```

```
        then
            save := tuple_of_words(1..i - 1);
            tuple_of_words := tuple_of_words(i..);
            return save;
        end if;

end for;

save := tuple_of_words;

tuple_of_words := [ ];                      $ Else this is last line; return
                                            $ all words.

return save;

end proc break_next_line;

proc put_spaces(between_kwords, nblanks);

$ This procedure finds the positions where n blanks are to be placed between
$ k words. The blanks are placed at random for appearance's sake.

space_count := (size := (between_kwords - 1)) * [0];

(for j in [1..nblanks])
        space_count((random (size - 1) + 1)) + := 1;        $ Place a blank.
end for;

return space_count;

end proc put_spaces;
```

5.9 Use of Atoms

Atoms can be made members of sets or tuples (e.g., by the **with** operator) and can be tested for set membership (by the **in** and **notin** operators). Moreover, previously generated atoms which have been put into sets or made into components of tuples can reappear when one iterates over a set or tuple in which they have been placed.

To facilitate debugging of programs which use atoms, the *print* (but not the *read* operation) can be applied to atoms. The internal representation of an atom carries a system-generated integer called its *serial number*; when an atom is printed, the representation of it is placed on the output medium as

#nnn

where *nnn* is the serial number of the atom. Thus, for example, if the very first statement in a program is

print({**newat**: j **in** [10..20]});

the output produced, namely

{#1, #2, #3, #4, #5, #6, #7, #8, #9, #10, #11}

will represent a set of 11 *distinct* atoms.

Another important use of atoms is to represent objects which have a continuing identity, independent of any varying data attributes, associated with them. Consider, for example, the problem of maintaining a simple data base, which keeps track of a few items of data, e.g., name, address, and telephone number for each of a varying group of people.

A given person would of course retain his or her identity if he or she changed address, telephone number, or even name. Since these information items may change, it is not always appropriate to identify a person with a tuple [name, address, tel_no] even if this tuple gives all available information. The most appropriate treatment of such situation may be to represent the person by an atom x and to maintain three maps, called *name*, *address*, and *tel_no*, which map x into the name, address, and telephone number of the person represented by x. Then a name change for person x can be implemented simply by writing:

```
name(x) := new_name;
```

To give a small example of the use of atoms, we shall suppose that a graph G is given as a set of ordered pairs, each pair $[x, y]$ representing a directed edge of G going from node x of the graph to node y of the graph. In graph theory, one often wishes to form new graphs from old by introducing new points and edges that serve to simplify some mathematical argument. Suppose, in particular, that for some reason we wish to introduce two new graph nodes $n1$ and $n2$, and to connect $n1$ to each node of G which is the initial point of an edge in G, and also to introduce an edge $[x, n2]$ for each node x of G which is the second node or "target" of an edge of G. This will define a new graph $G2$ within which the original graph G, with all its edges and nodes, is embedded as a subgraph.

To represent this construction in SETL, it is reasonable to introduce new atoms for the points $n1$ and $n2$. This leads us to the following short and quite straightforward code fragment:

```
n1 := newat;   $ Generate first new point.
n2 := newat;   $ Generate second new point.

               $ Now introduce new edges to build G2.
G2 := G + {[n1, x]: x in domain G} + {[y, n2]: y in range G};
```

5.10 Additional Examples

In this section we collect a few additional examples which illustrate the use of the facilities discussed in this chapter.

5.10.1 Solution of systems of linear equations

Suppose that we are given a system of n linear equations in n unknowns $x1$, $x2, \ldots, xn$. We can suppose that these equations have the form

$$\begin{aligned} a11*x1 + a12*x2 + \cdots + a1n*xn &= b1 \\ a21*x1 + a22*x2 + \cdots + a2n*xn &= b2 \\ \vdots \\ an1*x1 + an2*x2 + \cdots + ann*xn &= bn. \end{aligned} \tag{1}$$

Solution of equations of this kind is one of the most fundamental problems of numerical analysis and has been intensively studied. Without wishing to enter very far into the enormous literature that has developed around this problem, we shall present a simple SETL code for solving such systems of equations. The technique we will use is a variant of the famous (though essentially straightforward) technique introduced by Karl Friedrich Gauss (1777–1855, "The Prince of Mathematicians"). This technique is known as *Gaussian elimination.*

The idea can be summarized as follows: Each equation in the system (1) involves n coefficients $aj1, aj2, \ldots, ajn$. If in any equation all of these coefficients are zero, then the whole left-hand side of the equation is zero, and the whole equation reduces to

$$0 = bj.$$

If the quantity bj occurring on the right-hand side is not zero the original system of equations (1) simply has no solutions. A system of equations (1) which either contains an equation all of whose coefficients $aj1, aj2, \ldots, ajn$ are zero or the steps of whose solution leads to such an equation is said to be *singular*. Singular systems of equations require somewhat special analysis; in what follows, we will avoid this analysis and simply assume that the system (1) which are trying to solve is not singular.

If this is the case, we can take any one of the equations in (1), say the first, and find at least one nonzero coefficient, say $a1j$, on its left-hand side. Then we can form an equivalent but somewhat different system of equations by subtracting $akj/a1j$ times the first equation from the k-th equation for each $k = 2, \ldots, n$. This subtraction eliminates the coefficient akj from all these other equations; i.e., it makes the coefficient akj of the variable xj equal to zero for $k = 2, \ldots, n$. Hence we can regard equations $2, \ldots, n$ as a system of $(n - 1)$ equations for the $(n - 1)$ unknowns $x2, \ldots, xn$. Then, proceeding recursively, we can solve these equations for $x2, \ldots, xn$. Once this has been done, we can substitute the values of $x2, \ldots, xn$ into the first equation, thereby reducing it to a single linear equation in a single unknown. This final equation can then be solved for the remaining variable $x1$ by a single subtraction followed by a division.

We can write SETL code representing this procedure most clearly if we write it recursively. To do this, we will need to use both an outer procedure *Gauss* which sets up initial parameters and an inner "workhorse" procedure

Gauss_solve which performs the actual arithmetic operations. Since the value of the array of coefficients *M* must be accessed and manipulated by all recursively generated invocations of the *Gauss_solve* routine (see Section 5.4), we adopt the (typical) expedient of making it a global variable. Thus the only parameters that need to be passed to Gauss_solve are a set, namely, the set of variables for which a first nonzero coefficient still has to be found, and an integer, namely the number of the next equation to be considered. The *Gauss_solve* routine returns **om** if it encounters a "singular" equation all of whose coefficients are zero; otherwise, it returns a vector giving the values of the variables for which it has solved.

```
const eps = 1.0E - 4                    $ Define a utility real constant close
                                        $ to zero.
var glob_M;                             $ Matrix of equation coefficients.
$ (Note: these declarations must precede the first proc).

proc Gauss(M);                          $ Solves equations by Gaussian
                                        $ elimination.

glob_M := M;                            $ Make original matrix globally
                                        $ available.
glob_soln := [ ];                       $ Initialize tuple of solution values.

return Gauss_solve({1.. #M}, 1);

end proc Gauss;

proc Gauss_solve(var_numbers, next_eqn);

  $ Inner recursion for Gaussian elimination. Var_numbers is the set of all
    indices of variables
  $ still to be processed; next_eqn is the index of the next equation to be
    examined.

if var_numbers = { } then return [ ]; end;
                                        $ No variables, return the empty
                                        $ solution.
row := glob_M(next_eqn);                $ Get the row of coefficients.

if not exists vn in var_numbers | row(vn) > eps then
return om;                              $ Since system is singular.
end if;

(for j in [next_eqn + 1.. #glob_M])

   row_j := glob_M(j);

   subtract := row_j(vn)/row(vn);       $ Multiple of row to be subtracted.

   (for vnx in var_numbers) row_j(vnx) - := subtract * row(vnx); end;

   glob_M(j) := row_j;

end for j;
```

```
$ Now call Gauss_solve recursively to solve for the remaining variables.

if (soln := Gauss_solve(var_numbers less := vn, next_eqn + 1)) = om then
return om;                              $ Since a sigularity has been detected.
end if;

$ Substitute to determine the value of the vn-th variable.

soln(vn) := (row(#row + 1) - /(soln(vnx)*row(vnx): vnx in
var_numbers]))/row(vn);

return soln;

end proc Gauss_solve;
```

It is not difficult to rework this procedure to use iterations rather than recursions. The iterative form of the procedure is shown below. The relationship between the recursive and the iterative form of this code is typical and is worth close study. Note that the iterative form of the procedure must implicitly save information (such as the order in which variables are processed) which the recursive form of the procedure saves implicitly (namely in the multiple procedure invocations which are created when the recursive procedure is executed). This is the reason that the quantity *var_order*, which has no counterpart in the recursive procedure, appears in the iterative variant shown. Aside from this, note that the *Gauss_solve* routine only invokes itself when it is near the point at which it will return; hence the only items of information which need to be saved for use after return from this invocation are *vn* (the number of the variable currently being processed) and *row*. However, *row* is just M(*vn*); thus only *vn* needs to be saved. This explains why we are able to transform the recursive procedure shown previously into the following more efficient iterative procedure. The initial sequence of recursive calls that would otherwise be required is first represented by a "forward elimination" pass over the rows of M, and in which the subsequent sequence of recursive returns becomes an iterative "back-substitution" pass.

```
proc Gauss(M);                          $ Solves linear equations by
                                        $ Gaussian elimination.

  const eps = 1.0E - 4;                 $ Define a constant close to zero.
  soln := [ ];                          $ Initialize solutions to be built.
  var_numbers := {1..n := #M};          $ Initially, all variables need to be
                                        $ processed.
  var_order := [ ];                     $ This tuple will record the order in
                                        $ which variables are processed.
    (for i in [1..n])                   $ Process rows one after another.

      row := M(i);

      if not exists vn in var_numbers | row(vn) >= eps then

        return om;                      $ Since system is singular.
      end if;
```

```
        (for j in [i + 1..n])

        row_ := M(j);
        subtract := row_j(vn)/row(vn);  $ Amount to be substracted.
          (for vnx in var_numbers) row_j(vnx) - := subtract*row(vnx); end;
          M(j) := row_j;

        end for j;

        var_order with := vn;           $ Note variable just processed
        var_numbers less := vn;         $ and exclude it from further
                                        $ processing.

      end for i;

    $ Next we work through the variables in the reverse order from which
      they were initially processed
    $ while calculating their values. Note that at this point the set var_numbers
      has become empty.

    (for i in [n, n - 1..1])

      row := M(i);
      vn := var_order(i);
      soln(vn) := (row(n + 1) -/ [soln(vnx)*row(vnx): vnx in var_numbers]
      /row(vn);
      var_numbers with := vn;

    end for;

    return soln;                        $ Return the formal solution.

  end proc Gauss;
```

5.10.2 An interactive text-editing routine

Our next example will serve to illustrate some of the internal workings of an interactive text editor (though actually the program to be given will support only a few of the features which a full-scale editor would provide, and even these are highly simplified). This editor has the following capabilities:

(a) A vector of strings representing a text file to be edited can be passed to it.
(b) The editor prompts its user for a command by printing "?" and waits for him to respond.
(c) The allowed responses are as follows:
   (i) A response of the form '/ABCD..E/abc..e' makes ABCD..E a member of a collection of *search strings* that the editor maintains and indicates that some of the occurrences of *ABCD..E* in the text file are to be replaced by *abc..e*. Note that here *ABCD..E* and *abc..e* are intended to represent arbitrary strings which need not be of the same length; *abc..e* can even be null. Moreover, the delimiting character,

which we have written "/", can be any character which does not appear in *ABCD..E*.

(ii) A response of the form '/ABCD..E' with just one occurrence of the initial delimiting character indicates that ABCD..E is no longer to be searched for.

(iii) A response of the form '//' indicates that searching is to start again from the beginning of the text file. A response of the form 'done' indicates that editing is complete and triggers a return from the edit procedure.

(iv) A nullstring response searches forward in the text file for the next following occurrence of any search string ABCD..E. If any such occurrence is found, it is displayed on the user's terminal, with a line of underscore characters placed immediately above it to mark its position. After this, another null response will trigger a search, but the response '/' will replace the string ABCD..E that has just been found by the corresponding string abc..e.

```
proc edit(rw text);                          $ Text editor routine.

line_no := line_pos := 1;                    $ Start at the first character of
                                             $ the first line of the text file.

replacement := search_strings := { };        $ Initially no search strings
                                               have been defined.

last_pos := om;                              $ last_pos will be the last
                                             $ character position in a zone
                                             $ located by searching; See the
                                             $ search procedure below.
                                             $ Initially, this is undefined.

first_chars := ' ';                          $ first_chars is a string
                                             $ consisting of the first
                                             $ characters of all search strings.

loop do

  if (r := response( )) = 'STOP' then return;

  elseif r = ' ' then                        $ Search forward from current
                                               position
    search(line_no, line_pos, last_pos, search_strings, first_chars, text);

  $ See the search procedure given below for an account of its parameters.

    if last_pos = om then
      print('**NO STRING FOUND**');
    else
      overbar(line_pos, last_pos, text(line_no));
    end if;
```

```
    elseif #r = 1 then                       $ Try to make replacement.

      if last_pos = om then                  $ Successful search did not precede
                                             $ replacement.

        print('**NO SEARCH POSITION HAS BEEN ESTABLISHED**');
      else                                   $ Perform replacement.
        text(line_no)(line_pos..last_pos) := replacement(text(line_no)
        (line_pos..last_pos));
        print(text(line_no));                $ print the modified line
        last_pos := om;                      $ invalidate the search position

      end if;

    else                                     $ The user's response was at
                                             $ least two characters long.
      c := r(1);                             $ Get first character of this
                                             $ response.

      if not exists i in [2..#r]|c = r(i) then
                                             $ Drop search string.

        replacement(strg := r(2..)) := om;
        search_strings less := strg;

                                             $ Recalculate the 'first-chars'
                                             $ string.

        first_chars := '' +/{x(1): x in search_strings};

      elseif #r = 2 then                     $ '//'; hence restart search at top.

        line_no := line_pos := 1;
        last_pos := om;                      $ Invalidate search position.

    else                                     $ A new replacement is being
                                             $ defined.

        replacement(strg := r(2..i - 1)) := r(i + 1..);
        search_strings with := strg;

                                             $ Recalculate the set of initial
                                             $ characters.

        first_chars := +/{x(1): x in search_strings};
        last_pos := om;                      $ Invalidate any prior search.

      end if not;

    end if;

  end loop;

  end proc edit;
```

```
proc search(rw line_no, rw line_pos, rw last_pos, search_strings, first_chars,
text);

$ This procedure searches forward, starting at a given text line and given
$ character position, for the first position P at which any member of the
$ set search_strings of strings occurs. If such a position is found, then
$ line_no is set appropriately, line_pos is set to P and last_pos is set to the
$ index of the last character matched. If no such position is found, then
$ last_pos becomes om while line_no and line_pos remain the same.

[old_line_no, old_line_pos] := [line_no, line_pos]; $ save to restore

$ If last_pos is not om, indicating that a successful search has just taken
$ place, then the search starts one character after line_pos; this prevents
$ repetitive searching.

if last_pos /= om then line_pos + := 1; end;

search_string := text(line_no)(line_pos..);

(while line_no <= #text)

  (while search_string /= '')

    $ While a portion of the current line remains to be examined.

    if (lead := break(search_string, first_chars)) = om then
    $ No significant character in this line, so go to next line.

    quit;

    else                                   $ See if one of the strings we
                                           $ are looking for is found here.

       line_pos + := #lead                 $ advance the line position

     if exists stg in search_strings|
       match(search_string, stg) /= om then

       last_pos := line_pos + #stg - 1;    $ end of matched zone

    return;

    else                                   $ no match; advance by one
                                           $ character position

      line_pos + := 1;
      search_string := search_string(2..);

    end if;

  end if;

    end while search_string /= '';
```

```
    line_no + := 1;                          $ advance line number
    line_pos := 1;                           $ re-initialise line_pos
    search_string := text(line_no);
end while line_no;
    last_pos := om;                          $ note that search was
                                             $ unsuccessful
    [line_no, line_pos] := [old_line_no, old_line_pos];
end proc search;

proc overbar(lpos, lastpos, line);           $ displays string found
print((lpos - 1)*" + (lastpos - lpos + 1)*'-');
print(line);
end proc overbar;

proc response;                               $ reads user's response
print('?');
get('SYS$INPUT', ln);
return ln;
end proc response;
```

Exercises

1. Write the values which x, y, and z will have after each of the following sequences is executed.

   (a) x := 'abc'; y := **span**(x, 'ABC');

   (b) x := 'abc'; y := **any**(x, 'ABC');

   (c) x := 'abc'; y := **span**(x, 'ab'); z := **rany**(y, 'ab');

   (d) x := 'abc'; y := **break**(x, 'ABC');

   (e) x := 'abc'; y := **break**(x, 'abc');

   (f) x := 'abc'; y := **rbreak**(x, 'ABCabc');

   (g) x := 'abc'; y := **len**(x, 4);

   (h) x := 'abc'; y := **notany**(x, 'ABC');

   (i) x := 'abc'; y := **rnotany**(x, 'ABC');

2. Write a program which will read a string s and will delete all sequences of blank spaces immediately preceding a punctuation mark, insert a blank space immediately after each punctuation mark that is not followed by either a blank or a numeric character.

3. Write a program which prints a set *s* of words in an alphabetized, neatly formatted arrangement; the words printed should be lined up in rows and columns. As many columns as possible should be used, but at least two blank spaces must separate any two words printed on the same line.

4. Modify the lexical scanner procedure of Section 5.8.1.1 so that it returns a pair [toks_and_types, val_map], where toks_and_types is a tuple of pairs [tok, tok_typ], each *tok* being a token appearing in the source text scanned, and *top_typ* is the type (i.e., 'integer', 'floating point', 'identifier', or 'special') of *tok*. The quantity *val_map* should be a map sending the string form of each integer and floating-point number appearing in the sequence of tokens to its value.

5. As written, the lexical scanner procedure of Section 5.8.1.1 always treats the underbar character as a special character and does not allow floating-point numbers like '.3' which begin with a period. Modify this procedure so that it allows underbars within identifiers (but not as the first character of identifiers) and allows floating-point numbers to start with the '.' character.

6. Modify the concordance program shown in Section 5.8.1.2 so that
   (a) all words less than three characters long are omited from the concordance;
   (b) the program begins by reading a list of "insignificant" words, which occur on a sequence of lines terminated by a line containing the string '*****'. It then omits these words from the concordance. (Multiple insignificant words can also occur, separated by blanks, on a single line of the data file listing all the insignificant words).

7. Modify the concordance program shown in Section 5.8.1.2 so that it begins by reading a blank-separated list of words and reports only on the occurrences of words belonging to this list.

8. Modify the concordance program shown in Section 5.8.1.2 so that it reports only on "infrequent" words, i.e., words that occur no more than twice. Words belonging to a specified set *s* of words should be ignored even if they are infrequent. Programs of this kind can be used to locate "suspicious" identifiers in other programs, i.e., identifiers which may have been misspelled or simply forgotten during program composition.

9. The simplified text editor shown in Section 5.10.2 does not protect its user against any of the errors that are likely to occur during a lengthy edit session. Add code which will alleviate this deficiency by implementing the following additional features:
   (a) Demand that '//', rather than any arbitrary string of two identical characters, be used to restart editing from the first line of the file *F* being edited, and that '/', rather than any arbitrary one-character string, be used to trigger a replacement.
   (b) Allow an additional command 'x', which should produce a formatted display of all search strings, with their replacement strings.
   (c) Allow an additional command 'f', which should undo the last correction made. Your system should allow up to five successive changes to be undone using the 'f' command.
   (d) Allow the command '−' to trigger a search backward through the file, i.e., a search from the current character position through earlier positions and lines.

10. Browse through the user's manual of some text editor of medium complexity to become familiar with the various features it provides. Select an interesting one of these features, and modify the text editor code shown in Section 5.8.1.3 so that it implements the feature which you have selected.

11. Modify the character-string search procedure shown in Section 5.10.2 so that it can locate strings which run over from one line to the next. How should the editor program of Section 5.10.2 be modified to allow easy editing of strings of this kind?

12. The function **sin**(x) is the sum of the infinite power series whose n-th term is

((−1)**n)*(x**(2*n + 1))/(2*n + 1)! (n ranges upward from 0).

(a) Let $S5(x)$ and $S10(x)$ denote the first 5 and first 10 terms of this series respectively. Calculate and print the difference $S5(x) - \sin(x)$ and $S10(x) - \sin(x)$ for each value of x from 0.0 to 3.14159 by steps of 0.1. What maximum deviation between $S5(x)$ and $\sin(x)$ do you find? Can you find a constant b such that addition of b to $S5(x)$ reduces this maximum deviation?

(b) Repeat part (a) for cos(x). This is the sum of the infinite series whose n-th term is

((−1)**n)*(x**(2*n))/(2*n)! (again, n ranges upward from 0).

13. Certain types of forests are subject to infestation by budworms. The following rules can be used to model the results of such an infestation. We suppose for simplicity that the forest consists of an n by m rectangular array of trees. In a given year, any tree will be either healthy, infested, or leafless, having been infested the year before. A tree infested one year will be leafless the next year; a tree leafless one year will be healthy the next year. A tree healthy one year will be healthy the next year unless its neighbor to the north, south, east, or west is infested, in which case it will also become infested the next year.

Write a program which will simulate the progress of a budworm infestation obeying these rules. Track the progress of an infestation which starts with just one infested tree, and the progress of an infestation that starts with a row of three infested trees. Your program should print out a diagram of the forest in each of a sequence of years, together with a count of the number of infested, leafless, and healthy trees.

14. Write a procedure which can be used to print a coarse "graph" for any floating-point-valued function f of a floating-point variable x. This should be written as a procedure with floating-point parameters *lo*, *hi* (the lower and upper limit of the values of x for which $f(x)$ will be graphed), lo_range, hi_range (the lower and upper limits of the range of f that will be graphed), and an integer parameter n (the number of lines on the printed output listing that the graph should occupy). Your procedure should call a subprocedure, 'f_to_graph' to obtain the values of the function to be graphed. Vertical and horizontal axes should be printed, with the vertical axis at the extreme left of the output listing. These axes should carry suitable markings to indicate the scale. The x axis should run horizontally.

How would you change this procedure if the x axis is to run vertically down the length of the output listing?

15. Write a procedure which can be used to print a graph showing the values of several functions $f(x)$. The main input to this procedure should be a sequence of tuples t of floating-point numbers all having the same length. Each of these tuples repre-

sents a sequence of values of one function $f(x)$. Two floating-point numbers, *lo* and *hi*, defining the minimum and maximum values of the domain over which the dependent variable x has been evaluated to produce the tuple t, are also given. In addition, there are two more inputs: a character string whose j-th character will be used to print points belonging to the graph of the j-th function, and an integer n indicating the number of lines of the output listing which the graph is to occupy. Your procedure should be written to accept an arbitrary number of tuples t. The scale of the graph should be adjusted to reflect the largest and the smallest values appearing in any of the tuples t. Axes should be printed with scales marked on both the x and y axis. If the tuples t are too long to be displayed with the x axis running horizontally, the graph should be turned 90 degrees so that the x axis runs vertically down the listing.

16. Write a procedure P which can be used to generate a variety of commercial reports in graphical form. The inputs to P should be two tuples, $t1$ and $t2$, of sales or production figures; $t1$ representing the "current year" and $t2$ the "prior year." The third parameter of P should be a two-character string defining the bar chart desired, encoded in the following way:

    'm'—monthly figures desired
    'c' —cumulative monthly figures desired
    'd' —difference between current and previous year desired
    'p' —percentage difference between current and previous year desired

    The 'd' chart should be organized as a series of adjacent pairs of bars showing figures for the current year and the previous year. Axes should be printed with the vertical axis using an appropriate scale and the horizontal axis carrying the names of the months. The 'p' chart requires only a single bar for each month. What other useful features can you design and implement for a program of this kind?

17. Write a procedure which prints "bar charts" or "histograms." The inputs of this procedure should be a tuple t of floating-point numbers and an integer n indicating the number of lines on your listing that the chart is to occupy. A set of bars representing the components of t in graphic form should be printed. The scale of the bars should be adjusted to reflect the largest component and the smallest component of t, and the thickness of the bars should be adjusted to the length of t and the number of columns available on the output listing. Axes should be printed, the vertical axis being scaled. If t is too long for the required number of bars to fit horizontally, the chart should be turned 90 degrees so that the bars of the chart are horizontal.

18. Generalizing the procedure of Ex. 16, write a procedure which prints bar charts with bars which are divided into different "zones" representing different sets of quantities. The main input to this procedure should be a sequence of tuples t of floating-point numbers all having the same length. (But think of a good way to handle the case in which not all tuples have the same length!) The auxiliary inputs to the routine are a character string whose j-th character will be used to print the j-th zone of each bar and an integer n indicating the number of lines that the chart is to occupy on your listing. The procedure should be written to allow an arbitrary number of tuples t as parameters. If the tuples t are too long for the required number of bars to fit horizontally, the chart should be turned 90 degrees so that the bars are horizontal.

19. Write a procedure 'Function_to_Graph' which can be used to print a graph of the "level curves" or "contours" for a floating-point-valued function of two variables x and y, where

$$0.0 <= x <= 1.0$$

and

$$0.0 <= y <= 1.0$$

The procedure should read in the number of contours desired. The printout should identify each contour by marking its outline according to its order from maximum to minimum.

20. Write a translation program which translates French to English word by word. (Warning: such a program will produce extremely mediocre translation.) The program should read a file of lines containing successive blank-separated pairs of French words and their English translations, and then read a French passage to be translated and print out its English translation.

21. Modify the word-by-word translation program described in Ex. 20 so that it becomes interactive, and so that it is prepared for the fact that certain French words might have several possible translations into English. When such words are encountered during translation, a numbered menu of all of them should be displayed, and the user should then have the ability to continue by selecting one of these possible translations.

22. *Pert charts* are used by project administrators to track progress and monitor critical activities in large projects. To set up such a chart, one first reads in a set s of pairs [activity1, activity2] defining the collection of all activities that must finish before any given activity2 can start. One also reads a map T sending each activity to its expected duration. Then one calculates the earliest time that each activity A can finish, and for each such A, the set of all activities whose completion is critical to completing A by this time. Then one can print a list of all activities in order of their completion times. Finally, working back from the last activity, which marks the completion of the whole project, one can calculate the set of all critical activities, that is, all activities which must be completed on time if completion of the whole project is not to be delayed. One can also calculate and print the degree of "slack" available for each activity, i.e., the amount that its completion could be delayed without slowing completion of the whole project.

    Develop a program that calculates this information and prints it out in a set of attractively formatted tables.

23. (Continuation of Ex. 22) Once started, large projects often begin to "slip" because some of their critical activities are not completed on time. Modify the pert program of Ex. 22 to allow it to read a list of activities which have already been started, together with their expected completion times and to produce a new list of critical activities, and a revised table of "slack" for all (started and unstarted) activities. Can you design and implement any additional features which would make this pert program a more useful planning tool, especially if it is to be used interactively?

24. A meteorological station measures the temperature every hour, producing records arranged as a sequence of tuples t, each t having length 24 and representing a day's temperature measurements (the first being taken at midnight). Write a program

which will read these data and print out a record of the highs, lows, and mean temperature for the entire day, and also the highs, lows, and mean temperature for the "daylight" hours (7 A.M. through 6 P.M).

25. The Bureau of Crime Statistics receives annual reports from all cities and incorporated towns, showing the number of major felonies recorded for the year. It then calculates the total number of cities and towns reporting felonies in the ranges 1–100, 101–500, 501–1000, 1001–2000, and more than 2000. Assume that the file of data being read is a set of lines, each of which contains the name of a town and the number of reported felonies, separated by a blank. Write a program for preparing and printing this report.

26. When commands need to be entered interactively at a terminal, it is convenient to allow the shortest unambiguous prefix of any command to serve as an abbreviation for the command. Write a procedure which makes this possible. (Hint: alphabetize the set of allowed commands and locate prefixes by a fast search in this alphabetized list.)

27. Large sets of alphabetic strings which need to be stored can be represented in compressed form by arranging them in alphabetical order. Then all the strings beginning with a particular character, say 'a'., can be preceded by the string '1a', and the initial letter 'a' dropped from all of them. Similarly, if the group of strings beginning with 'a' contains more than two successive strings whose second character is 'b', then the whole group of such strings can be prefixed by the string '2b', and the initial letters 'ab' dropped from all of them. This transformation can be applied to as many initial characters as are appropriate.

    Write a procedure which takes a set *s* of strings, alphabetizes it, and compresses it by using this technique. Write another procedure which takes a set *s* of strings represented in this form and prints *s* in its original alphabetized form.

CHAPTER 6

Program Development, Testing, and Debugging

The normal stages of a program's life cycle are:

(i) Initial conception, formulation of requirements.
(ii) Overall design of a program that will meet these requirements.
(iii) Detailed design and coding.
(iv) Program review, with rework and extension as needed to clarify, simplify, or improve efficiency.
(v) Development of a test plan, testing and debugging, removal of errors, and retest.
(vi) Operational use of program.
(vii) Enchancement and repair during continuing operational use.
(viii) Retirement.

This chapter discusses various key aspects of this program life cycle, providing hints that aim to help the inexperienced programmer to cope effectively with the pragmatic problems normally associated with program design, debugging, and maintenance.

6.1 Bugs: How To Minimize Them

Any error affecting the behavior of a program is called a *bug*. Bugs are inevitable, but a few cardinal rules can help minimize the degree to which they infest your programs.

(i) Know that they will occur. Since any small error, e.g., forgetting a line, typing "−" where "+" is meant, misspelling an identifier or keyword, incorrectly inserting parenthese into an expression, will cause a bug, you must train and discipline yourself to higher levels of logical and typographical accuracy in programming than are required in any other human activity. Be suspicious. Program defensively. Check your programs scrupulously for syntactic and logical correctness, several times if necessary, before you try to run them. If in doubt as to the meaning of any operation or programming language construct, look it up.

(ii) When bugs occur, your problem is to locate, recognize, and remove them. Bugs cannot be located unless you know the programming language with which you are working well enough to recognize problems when you are looking at them. Bugs cannot be eliminated until you have understood them well enough to know why and how they cause the faults that betray their presence. Finding bugs, like finding needles in a haystack, calls for systematic sifting, for careful detective work. A program is a delicate piece of machinery, and it is simple folly to think that you can make it work by kicking it hard in some random way to make its pieces fall into place. Because they involve many submechanisms, all of which must interface correctly if they are to work together properly, programs, like elaborate combination locks, require careful anaylsis and attentive sensing of their hidden internals when they need repair. The novice who tries to fix a malfunctoning program without fully understanding the way in which it is working is attempting a task that is far less hopeful than that faced by someone who tries to open an unfamililiar safe without understanding its workings or combination. "The sequence 33-8-19-27 doesn't work? Then I'll try 23-92-69-46. This doesn't work either? Then maybe 17-51-85-34 will be luckier." A student who allows himself to be drawn into of this sort of thoughtless, random attempt to repair a program will inevitably find that his efforts drag on unsuccessfully, not only till the end of the term or year, but until the end of the solar system, without revealing anything. What is needed instead is a systematic, analytic approach.

(iii) Though programs are almost never entirely bug-free, observance of the rules of good programming style can reduce the density of bugs in your initial program drafts and allow bugs to be found more quickly once testing of your program begins. Finding the right approach to the programming task that confronts you, the right style in which to start writing the code that you need, is of prime importance. To find this "right approach" requires careful consideration of the logical structure of your programming task, with the aim of defining a collection of intuitively transparent operations that work well together and can be used to accomplish this task in as straightforward a way as possible. Code should impress by its clarity, naturalness, and inevitability, all of which make avoidance and exposure of bugs easier, rather than by obscure trickery and impenetrable cleverness. Programs that achieve brevity without sacrificing clarity are most desirable, since lines of code that you never need to write will never contain bugs. Effective brevity is attained by a correct choice of intermediate operations and by systematic use of these operations to produce the program you require. SETL is in itself a powerful programming language, but especially for larger, more complex applications it may be well to program by first inventing a still more powerful language specially adapted to your intended application. Then your initial program draft can be written in this (possibly unimplemented) language, after which it can be transcribed into SETL to make it executable. In this sort of approach, the primitives of your invented language will become the procedures and macros of your SETL code. By using an auxiliary language in this way and by handling its transcription into SETL in as mechanical a style as possible, valuable protection against error is gained. See Sections 5.2 and 8.5 for a discussion of related issues.

(iv) Careful program documentation also serves to expose and eliminate bugs. Good documentation will add an important degree of redundancy to your program. Your code expresses your intent in one way and your comments express the same intent in another. Discrepancies between the two indicate the presence of bugs. Carefully thought-out comments should be added to a program as soon as the code is written. Some comments will in fact be written before the code to which they refer, in order to guide composition of the code. Any additional comments needed to make documentation complete should be added to the code while it is still fresh; this creates an opportunity to review the code, checking it for logical faults. After the whole text, code plus comments, has been constructed and put into proper format, it should be left to "cool" for a few hours or days, after which it should be reviewed attentively and suspiciously. Such a "cooling-off period" will dispel some of the initial misapprehensions which may have crept into a code and thus will allow various systematic errors to be corrected.

(v) As has been said, brevity in coding is desirable, but this should be the kind of brevity that flows naturally from an effective overall approach to the programming task at hand, not the undesirable brevity which comes from stinting redundancy (e.g., by using short, unmnemonic, variable names). Use the features of the SETL language vigorously and eliminate clumsy circumlocutions where direct modes of expression exist, but avoid obscure tricks even where these gain brevity.

(vi) Certain constructions, for example those that perform elementary arithmetic computations to determine positions in strings and tuples (for which "off-by-one" errors can easily occur) are bug-prone and need to be approached with caution. For example, what is the length of a string $s(i..j)$, is it $j - i$, $j - i + 1$, or $j - i - 1$? To ensure that $s(i..j)$ is exactly k characters long, what value do we give j: $i + k - 1$, or $i + k + 1$? Learn to recognize these trouble spots, double-check them when preparing your code, and surround them with **assert** checks when you do use them.

For example, if you write

$$\textbf{assert}\ \#s(i\,..\,j) = j - i;$$

immediately before proceeding on this assumption, your error will be pinpointed immediately; if you omit this check, you may have to find your way back to this error from some obscure symptom. A related idea is to introduce, and use, a collection of standard macros to handle these touchy situations in ways that are more instructive. For example, by introducing the macros (see Chapter 8).

$$\textbf{macro}\ \text{len\_from}\ (i,j);\ j - i + 1\ \textbf{endm};$$

$$\textbf{macro}\ \text{make\_len}\ (i,k);\ i\,..\,i + k - 1\ \textbf{endm};$$

we can accurately extract a string of length k from s starting at character position i by writing

$$s(\text{make\_len}(i,k))$$

and can evaluate the length of $s(i\,..\,j)$ by writing

$$\text{len\_from}(i,j)$$

(vii) As Donald Knuth has remarked, premature optimization is the root of much evil in programming. Compulsive (and ultimately ineffective) attempts to gain minor efficiency advantages often complicate programs and introduce bugs into them. As you compose a program, remember that substantial efficiency advantages will be gained globally by choice of effective algorithms, not locally by compounding of minor advantages.

(viii) Your program test plan should begin to be developed as your program is being written, and a substantial portion of the collection of test- and debug-oriented **print** and **assert** statements that you will use to test your program should be composed and entered as soon as the first draft of the program beings to approach completion. Early attention to your test plan will serve to pinpoint complex program sections that require careful testing. These are also the sections whose logic needs to be inspected most closely before testing begins. See Sections 6.4 and 6.6 for additional discussion of this point.

6.2 Finding Bugs

Even, alas, if you are very systematic and professional, some bugs will creep into your program, and the problem will then be to find and fix them. The following remarks should help you learn how to do this effectively. Debugging always starts with evidence that a program error has occurred somewhere during a program run. The problem in debugging is to work one's way back, from the visible symptom first noticed, to the underlying error. The errors one is looking for can be called the *error sources* or *primal anomalies.* These are the first (incorrectly written) operations or statements which get correct data from what has gone before them but pass data that are no longer correct to what comes after them. They are the instructions at which your program first "runs off the rails." The initial evidence of error that you see may relate only indirectly to these primary error sources. The difficulty of finding the erroneous statements is complicated by the fact that the full history of an extensive computation comprises a vast mass of data, impossible to survey comprehensively. In debugging you must therefore aim to explore as narrow a path as possible, while still finding your way back to one or more primal anomalies.

A good first step, but one that should not be allowed to hold you up too long, is to look closely at whatever fragments of correct output have been produced. If little or no output is correct, then your program may have failed before even the first **print** statement was executed. This hint may help you narrow the bug hunt. On the other hand, if some output is correct, then the program was probably functioning correctly till some point past the statement which produced the last correct output. Find the point in your program at which this output was produced, and see what comes before and after it. Again, this may narrow the hunt. Examine the erroneous output carefully and try to see whether its logical pattern reminds you of any particular section of your program. This also can sometimes yield useful hints concerning the likely location of the bug, especially if different parts of your output data are produced by recognizably different sections of code. If certain items of output that you expect are missing, try to see what evidence there is that all the code that you expected to execute did actually execute: remember that unanticipated data may have caused your program to follow an unexpected path, so that it may have bypassed, or may never have reached, the code sections which were supposed to have produced the output which you are surprised not to see. Evidence of this general kind, analyzed, will in favorable cases point the finger of suspicion at certain narrow program sections. However, in less favorable cases, the available evidence will be ambiguous. In this case, you will need to generate more extensive traces and dumps. This can be done in one of two ways:

(a) By inserting additional **print** statements into your program, to make it print out something of a "motion picture" of what has happened.
(b) By inserting various other checks, especially **assert** statements, which check assumptions on which your program depends, but which you suspect might be failing.

Section 6.6 will have more to say about technique (b), which is related to the general issue of formal program verification. The following more pragmatic hints will help you to apply this technique effectively. It is particularly important to place **assert** statements in sections of code known to involve delicate constructions, especially if (as in the case of the "off by one" bugs considered in the last section) the necessary checks are simple. Since the correct functioning of a program often hinges upon the assumption that key variables will change in a consistent way as iterative execution proceeds (for example, always increasing or always decreasing) it can be useful to save the last previous value of each significant variable *var* and to write checks which compare the last previous value of *var* with its current value. This can be done by introducing an auxiliary variable *last_var* for each *var* and writing an assignment

```
last_var := var;
```

whenever it is desirable to save the last value of *var*. Then checks like

```
assert var = last_var;
or
assert var /= last_var;
or
assert last_var = om or var*last_var = { } and var /= last_var;
```

etc., will all prove useful.

Ultimately, however, the problem with a purely assertion-based debugging technique is that it is not easy to formulate the necessary checks comprehensively enough to make it unlikely that a bug (which probably relates to something that has been overlooked) can slip through.

Hence one must often fall back on method (a), which generates additional raw evidence for inspection. The problem in using this method is to avoid burying yourself in too voluminous a trace of the thousands or millions of events that take place as a program executes. To avoid this danger a carefully planned sequence of probes is necessary. A good idea is to resurvey your program, mentally list its main phases, and determine all the data objects which each phase passes to the next phase. If your program has been well designed, i.e., has been built up from modules interacting with each other in well-structured fashion, there should not be too many of these objects, and then it is reasonable to print them out for inspection. Before inspecting this information, review the logic of your program, and make sure you know just what features you expect to find in values of the variables that you have printed. Try to be aware of every feature on which any part of your program depends. Then check the actual data. If the data printed at the end of a phase looks correct in every detail, then this phase is probably correct. If something strange-looking appears in the data produced by a given phase, although the data supplied to this phase look correct, then there is probably something wrong with the code of this phase.

When this stage of debugging is reached, you will at least have determined which of the several phases of your code contains the error for which you are hunting. At this point, it is a good idea to think over all the evidence that you have examined, and see if any compelling picture of the problem seems to suggest itself. Sometimes the fact that the offending phase has now been located removes enough confusion for the difficulty to be guessed quickly. If not, you will have to carry your tracing to a more detailed level. This is a matter of inserting **print** and **assert** statements more densely into the offending phase, in order to locate the particular subphase that contains the error. As before, this is the subphase to which good data are being supplied, but which is seen to pass bad data along to its successor.

(c) Once the bug location has been pinned down to a program section roughly a dozen lines long, review the logic of these lines. Read them very closely, looking for some misunderstanding which could have produced the anomalous data which you know that this section has generated. Try again to correlate data features with the operations responsible for producing these features. If this doesn't work, take the data supplied to the erroneous subphase, and try to trace the way that the subphase will act on this data, by hand, step by step, until you spot some error.

(d) In most cases, these steps will find the bug without too irritating an expenditure of effort. However, in the stubbornest, fortunately rare, cases, the problem for which you are hunting may still elude clear identification. In these particularly resistant cases one of three causes may be at fault.
   (i) If the algorithm which you are using is complex, you may have misunderstood its logic. It may be that no single line of your code is wrong: rather, its overall pattern may be subtly wrong, causing it to produce the output you see, rather than the results you wrongly expected it to generate. Global logic errors of this sort are often quite confusing. If you come to suspect that a problem of this sort has occurred, you should reason once more through the structure of your program, trying to convince yourself by careful analysis that it is logically sound. Section 6.6 describes the formal rules that underlie reasoning of this sort.
   (ii) There may be nothing wrong: you may simply have misunderstood what output your program was supposed to produce. Or you may have been looking at the wrong phase of a program which really does contain a bug, because you thought that the output of this phase showed some error, while in reality the bug was elsewhere. Or you may not have been running the program you thought you were running, or the version of the program you thought you were running, or your program may have been reading input data different from what you assumed. In such case, take a few minutes to cool off, review the whole situation, including the logic of your program, once more, and start over.
   (iii) Your problem may be caused by a true "system bug," that is, an error, not in your program, but in one of the layers of the software, including the SETL compiler, run-time library, or operating system under which you are running. Concerning bugs of this kind we can say the following:

(iii.a) Don't be too quick to suspect them. Though such problems do crop up from time to time, they are much rarer than errors in your newly written programs. Remember that dozens of people are using the same software systems that you are, and that if the problem afflicting you is a system-level problem, it would affect all of these people. Before you become willing to blame your problem on anything other than a fault in your program, you should always have examined your program with great care, located a section just a few lines long which you can be sure is receiving correct input (because you have printed and inspected its input) and producing bad output (again, you must have printed and inspected this output). Finally, meticulous examination of these few lines, with review of the definition of all the operations these lines involve, of the parenthesization of those lines, and of any applicable rules of operator precedence must give you "courtroom" evidence that the system is not performing according to its specifications. At this point you are almost (but still not quite) in position to report a system problem to the expert in charge of maintaining your copy of SETL system (or of the operating system within which the SETL system runs). Before doing so, however, you should try to simplify the evidence still further, isolating the malfunctioning lines into a malfunctioning program just a few lines long, and then paring this program down still further if possible, ideally to the point at which it contains just three lines: an assignment initialising a very few variables, a single line which obviously does not function as it should, and a print statement which confirms the fact that this line has failed to act in the manner demanded by the rules of SETL. If the system problem which you think lies at the root of your troubles disappears somewhere during this sequence of steps, the cause of your difficulties may not be a system problem at all, but an error or misunderstanding on your part, which your attempts to locate the suspected systems problem may have clarified. In this case, chastened, you should return to your original program, fix the error in it, and continue your debugging. If, however, you do succeed in creating a very short program which gives unmistakable evidence of system malfunction, you should transmit a complete, clean copy of this program to a systems expert. This should be accompanied by a clear explanation of the problem you have pinned down. He will then take steps to fix the SETL system, or to have it fixed.

Note that problems in the SETL system, like problems in your own programs, are most likely to concern marginal, rarely exercised cases. Though the system has been in use for a few years and has been tested fairly extensively, exhaustive testing of so complex a system is simply not possible. (See Section 6.4 for a discussion of some of the issues involved in attempts to test programs comprehensively.)

There are a few cases in which it is reasonable to jump a little more rapidly to the conclusion that a system bug is affecting you. One is the case in which two runs of absolutely identical programs and data yield different results. Another is the case in which insertion into your program of a statement which is harmless by definition changes the behavior of the program significantly. For example, if insertion of a **print** changes your program's flow of control, something is obviously amiss at the system level. This may be evidence that can be reported to an expert immediately (but see the caution extended in (f)).

(e) It should be clear from what has been said that one of the very first things that you will want to trace when you start to analyze a malfunctoning program is the input data it is reading. Always echo this data by printing it out immediately after it is read. Your input data may not be what you think it is, or you may be reading it incorrectly.

(f) Especially if a difficult bug is being pursued, debugging as an activity tends to create an atmosphere of confusion, which grows like a thundercloud as the mind struggles to free itself from the misapprehension which first allowed the bug to slip in. Particularly difficult bugs sometimes make one feel that one is going insane, since the laws of logic seem to be breaking down. To combat this perilous confusion, you must maintain a very deliberate, step-at-a-time, and above all skeptical, attitude while you are debugging. Verify the situation at every turn; look at what really is in your source text rather than trying to remember what was there; print out a record of what your program really is doing rather than guess what is going on. Inexperienced student programmers often come to advisors with old versions of programs they are trying to debug, claiming that "I ran this program on Tuesday, and I made two or three changes that I am sure are harmless, and now it doesn't work." A more experienced programmer, who knows that the only valid evidence to work from is a current, single, untorn listing showing program and output unmistakably together, will only laugh at this.

To reduce the level of your own confusion, it is sometimes helpful to work over your problem with a friend, trying to explain what is going on, and reviewing salient parts of the logic of your program with him, till he begins to understand it. A more expert consultant will often be able to spot the trouble that you have missed, but even if your consultant is less expert than you yourself, you will often find that the very act of explaining the problem lets you spot what is wrong.

(g) Even when a program has once begun to function (and often even when it has been used successfully and intensively over a considerable period), it may still contain bugs, which can lurk within sections of code which are rarely, perhaps almost never, exercised. For this reason, code inserted for debugging should generally not be removed once the bug is found. Don't throw away your crutches: it may become necessary to debug the same program again! Instead of removing debug code, you can *comment it out* by inserting a dollar sign at the start of each line inserted for debugging. (Only inserted lines that never generated any evidence useful for debugging should be wholly removed.) Another technique, particularly useful during extended development and debugging of large programs, is to make the most valuable debug prints and checks *conditional*, by including them in **if** statements containing conditions which are normally false but can be turned on by supplying program initialization parameters. (See Chapter 9 for a discussion of program parameters.) If this is done, it becomes possible to examine the inner working of a malfunctioning program quickly, without having to recompile it all.

6.3 A Checklist of Common Bugs

Certain bugs occur frequently, and the experienced programmer learns to recognize their characteristic symptoms. Here is a checklist of commonly occurring bugs, with some indication of the symptoms they are likely to produce. We only list bugs that would pass through compilation undetected.

Bug	Likely SETL symptom
Variable not given any initial value	"Illegal data-type" error
Incorrect termination of a loop (e.g., count off by 1)	Missing items in data collections, sums or sets too small if loop terminates too soon. "Illegal data-type" error if loop terminates too late
Incorrect limits in string and tuple slices (e.g., count off by 1)	(Similar to incorrect loop termination)
Incorrectly structured **while** loop conditions or bodies, or incorrect initial conditions in **while** loops	Program does not terminate
Incorrect treatment of initial cases in recursions, or bad procedure calls	Program does not terminate, possible memory overflow
Omission of **quit** or **continue** statement	Program "runs on" into code not intended for execution.
Mispelled variables, e.g., AO for A0, Bl for B1, cl for ci	"Illegal data-type" error, possibly no output
Reading unexpected data	Can cause wide variety of effects
Some unanticipated characters encountered by the string-scan operations	Program does not terminate
Failure to set a program switch	Effects can be subtle
Parameters out of order in procedure call	"Illegal data-type" error (generally easy to find)
Shared global variable unexpectedly modified by invoked procedure or function	Efforts can be very subtle, and particularly hard to find if a function is involved, beware of global variables

Variable inadvertently modified by assignment to a variable intended to be different but having the same name	If no data-type error is caused, effects can be subtle
Variables out of order in **read** statement	"Illegal data-type" error (generally easy to find)
Read operations of program inconsistent with data actually present in input file	"Illegal data-type" error (generally easy to find)
Target of an assignment statement misspelled	Effects can be very subtle
Not resetting a counter	Effects can be subtle (see "Incorrect loop termination")
Complex, incorrect combination of Boolean conditions	Effects can be very subtle
Too few or too many parentheses in expressions; misunderstanding of precedence rules	Effects can be very subtle

6.4 Program Testing

Debugging is the process of searching for the exact location of a program error when you know that some error is definitely there. *Testing* is the systematic exercise of a program which you believe might be correct, in an effort to see whether bugs are really absent. If testing shows a bug, debugging starts again. If your tests are not systematically designed, then bugs may go undetected and remain in the program. All one knows about a poorly tested program is that it works in the few cases for which it has been tried; it may fail in many others.

Test design is as important a part of program development as the choice of algorithms and data structures. Development of a test plan should begin while a program is being written. A procedure which is hard to test is apt to be bug-prone, and should be simplified if possible. By keeping testability in mind, you will avoid unnecessarily complex constructions, and produce cleaner, sounder code.

Testing falls into three distinguishable phases, which we will call *first-stage testing*, *second-stage or quality assurance testing*, and *maintainance or regression testing*. *First-stage testing* begins as soon as a program is complete enough for execution to be possible. Its guiding hypothesis is that bugs are present in sufficient numbers to prevent much of the program from working at all. During first-stage testing, one aims to make the main facilities of the program being debugged operable by finding and removing bugs quickly. Quality assurance testing begins when first stage testing ends. It assumes that a few obscure bugs remain in the program to be tested and aims to test systematically enough to smoke them out. Maintainance testing aims to ensure that new bugs are not introduced into old programs during their extension and repair.

6.4.1 First-stage testing

First-stage testing should work through a program "bottom up," first testing the bottom-level procedures which implement the basic operations used by the rest of the program. Once the code realizing these operations has been checked and found to be operable, the testing process will focus on intermediate-level procedures, and once these have been checked one will begin testing the program's main capabilities. Attempts to short-circuit this systematic, level-by-level test procedure by jumping directly to tests of higher program levels are more apt to waste time than to speed things up, since the lower-level causes of higher-level failures will then be hard to understand. For systematic testing, test input will need to be prepared for each procedure to be tested; this should be designed to make the output produced easy to inspect. If any of the procedures being tested make use of difficult or obscure data structures, it may be necessary to develop auxiliary output procedures which print these data structures in formats that clarify their logical meaning. When such procedures become necessary, they should be written and tested immediately.

Perhaps because realism might lead to suicide, programmers are generally overoptimistic concerning the likelihood that a program that they have just written will work right away. Careful preparation of a first-stage test plan serves to counteract this common illusion; the more realistic attitude thereby engendered encourages more careful initial program inspection, and this often reduces the number of bugs present when first-stage testing begins. This is why programs developed cautiously often become operational quickly, whereas programs developed in too optimistic a frame of mind often begin to work only after frustrating and totally unexpected delays.

An effective way of organising tests is to group them into a single procedure called *test_prog*, whose one parameter *s* is a string consisting of test names separated by asteriks. *The test_prog* can then have the following structure:

```
proc test_prog(s)   $ skeleton of test procedure

(while s /= '')
    if span(s, '*') /= om then continue; end;
    if(tn := break(s, '*')) = om then tn := s; s := ''; end;
    print('Beginning Test', tn);
    case tn of
        (put sequence of named tests here)
        else
            print('Unknown test name');
        end case;
end while;

end proc test_prog;
```

To trigger a sequence of tests named test_4, test_2, etc., one has only to write something like test_prog('test_1*test_2* ... '). Later, when first-stage testing is complete, this call, and *test_prog*, can be left in the program *P* that has been tested, but the argument of the test_prog call can be changed so that it reads test_prog(getspp('TEST =/')) (see Chapter 9 for an account of the *getspp* library procedure.) If this is done, no tests will be executed unless *P* is invoked with a command line parameter of the form TESTS = test1*test2...*testn, in which case the named tests will be performed. This approach makes it easy to retest a program in which unexpected trouble has developed. Of course, the test facilities available should be carefully documented at the start of the *test_prog* procedure.

Especially when a long program *P* is being developed, it may be desirable to begin testing before all parts of *P* have been coded (or even designed) in detail. Of course, such an approach will be reasonable only if *P* has a sound, highly modular overall design, and only if the missing sections of *P* have been designed in enough detail so that you can be sure that no inconsistency will develop when they are designed and coded in detail. This mode of organizing development and testing is sometimes called *top-down* testing. It has the advantage of allowing testing and development to proceed in parallel. A related advantage is that it can provide particularly early confirmation of overall design soundness, or, if a design proves to be unsound (say, in terms of human factors, i.e., usability), it can give early warning of trouble.

If a top-down approach to development and testing is taken it will be found useful to provide a standard, multiparameter library routine having the name MISSING_SECTION. Then parts of your program that have not yet been coded can be replaced by invocations

MISSING_SECTION(name_of_missing_section);

where the string-valued parameter -name_of_missing_section- should assign the missing section a name that can be printed. The MISSING-SECTION procedure should also allow optional additional parameters, so that it can be invoked by

MISSING_SECTION('name_of_missing', 'p1 p2 ... pk', p1, ..., pk);

where *p*1, *p*2,.. name various parameters with which the missing section would have to deal or which might explain why it was (perhaps unexpectedly) invoked.

6.4.2 Quality assurance testing

Second-stage (or *quality assurance*) testing should aim to exercise a program comprehensively, in at least the following senses:

(i) It is obvious that parts of your program that have never been executed during debugging may well contain unrecognized errors. The battery of tests you develop should therefore force every line of your program to be executed at least once.

(ii) If your program branches on a Boolean condition, then you will want to supply at least one test case in which the condition evaluates to TRUE, and another in which the condition evaluates to FALSE.

(iii) Improper treatment of extreme values is a common cause of program failure. A program may work for nonnull sets, tuples, or strings, but not for the corresponding null cases; for positive integers n but not if $n = 0$; for integers less than the length of some string, but not for integers equal to this length, etc. It may work when a **while** or a **forall** loop which it contains is entered, but fail if the loop is bypassed entirely.

In preparing a comprehensive collection of tests, you will therefore need to survey your program systematically, listing marginal situations of this kind as exhaustively as you can; then you should prepare at least one test that will force each logically possible situation to occur.

(iv) Once a list of all procedures, loops, branches, code sections, and marginal cases to be tested has been collected and a comprehensive set of tests has been developed, it may be worth preparing a formal test coverage matrix which shows which tests exercise each program feature. A chart of this kind makes it easier to spot cases that have never been tested. It can also help to select tests to be run during regression testing (see the following discussion) and can help to pinpoint program sections to be examined when a test fails. Such a chart will also make it easier to avoid running too many tests all of which exercise the same limited group of program features but never use others. Note that, if regarded as a kind of test, "production" use of a program is subject to this objection; i.e., daily use of a program often exercises only a limited subset of its features. This is why programs that have been in heavy use for extended periods sometimes fail when their usage pattern changes significantly.

(v) Compilers sometimes include features which make it easier to determine the coverage provided by a family of tests. For example, it may be possible to generate a listing of all program statements executed during a sequence of runs, of all branches taken, of all procedures invoked, etc. The DEC VAX SETL measurement facility is not untypical of profiling facilities of this kind. You will want to familiarize yourself with these facilities, since they can help assure that the test sets you develop for your programs are adequate.

(vi) Once developed, test sets become an important adjunct to the programs that they test. Such test sets should therefore be organized in a manner which facilitates their long-term maintainance and reuse. The tests that are available, and the coverage they provide, should be adequately documented.

(vii) Programmers often find it hard to bring sufficient enthusiasm to the task of systematically rooting obscure bugs out of code that they themselves have written. In part, this is a matter of optimism; in part, a result of the mental fatigue which tends to set in at the end of a lengthy code development; in part, a consequence of the difficulty of overcoming the very mind-set which introduced an error in the first place. For all these reasons, it is good practice to make testing of large programs the responsibility of a *quality assurance group* independent of the development group that produced these programs. If this is done, then, knowing that an independent group of programmers will probe their work systematically to find shortcomings, the original development group will be encouraged to simplify their product so as to improve its reliability.

Even where resources do not permit fully independent organization of the activity of program testing, it is well to ensure that every line of a complex program is read and understood by at least two programmers, each of whom will be able to spot problems and suggest tests that the other might have overlooked.

6.4.3 Regression testing

Regression testing is testing routinely applied whenever a previously working program is amended, to ensure that newly introduced code has not caused new errors. Tests which will be used in this way should be written so as to be self-checking, i.e., to produce little or no output if they have run correctly, but to produce copious output pinpointing a problem as closely as possible when an error is detected. This can be done by organizing the tests so that they perform various calculations, always in at least two different but logically equivalent ways. If these paired computations produce the same result, then either no output, or a simple message 'TEST xxx PASSED', should be printed, but if a discrepancy is detected output which shows the discrepancy and displays the values of all variables related to the discrepancy should be printed.

If a chart has been prepared showing the program features exercised by each test (see iv) it can be used when a test fails to suggest what part of the program should be examined first to find the cause of failure. If some one of these program sections has just been changed, it will of course come under immediate suspicion.

6.5 Analysis of Program Efficiency

Up to this point, we have generally ignored one of fundamental issues of programming practice: how much machine resource, i.e., execution time and memory, are actually required to execute a given program. This omission was deliberate, and reflects a basic maxim of programming: *Make it right before you make it fast.* It is now time to repair this omission, and examine two related topics:

(a) The estimation of program efficiency.
(b) The study of means to improve program efficiency by refinement and transformation of a correct but inefficient working program.

Two kinds of machine resources are relevant to the study of program efficiency: execution time and data storage required. In what follows, we will concentrate our attention on the first of these, because in many cases it is time which is critical. Data storage requirements were a pressing concern in the early days of computing, because memory was an extremely expensive hardware component and computers were equipped with only a few thousand words of it. As a result, early programming languages such as FORTRAN included various complex mechanisms for managing the limited memory resources available, which forced the programmer to concern himself with low-level details which were extraneous to the actual application to be programmed. Memory has in the meantime become a much cheaper commodity, and concern with its optimal utilization can in many cases (but by no means all) be left to the machine itself (in the form of some facility for dynamic storage allocation). This is what we will do in most of what follows.

6.5.1 Estimation of program efficiency

It is very easy to use SETL (or any other programming language) to write programs which would take years, or even hundreds or thousands of years, to finish executing. Consider, for example, the code fragment

```
     sum := 0;
(for i in [1..1000])
     (for j in [1..2000])
          (for k in [1..3000])
               (for l in [1..4000])
                                                              (1)
                         sum + := (2*i**3 + j**3 + k**2);

               end for l;
          end for k;
     end for j;
end for i;
```

In this code, fo each successive value *i*, the variable *j* iterates over 2000 different values; for each value of *i* and *j*, the variable *k* iterates over 3000 values; and for each value of *i*, *j*, and *k*, the variable l iterates over 4000 values. Thus, all in all, the innermost statement of the code fragment (1) will be executed 1000 × 2000 × 3000 × 4000 times, i.e., 240 billion times. This statement involves 6 multiplications and 4 additions, so that at least 2.4 trillion elementary arithmetic operations are required to execute the code (1). Even on a computer capable of executing a million arithmetic operations per second (a fairly typical performance figure nowadays) and even if the code (1) were written in a programming language capable of exploiting this raw arithmetic capability to the utmost, 2.4 million seconds would be needed to execute the code (1). Since an hour is about 4000 seconds, this is about 600 hours, i.e., about 24 days. However, since SETL (which pays a price in efficiency for its very high level) is at least 30 times less efficient than this, execution of the SETL code (1) would require more than 2 continuous years of computer time. This makes it quite clear that in writing SETL programs one needs some way of estimating the computational resource which will be consumed to execute the code that one sets down.

6.5.2 The execution time of elementary instructions

Let us begin by describing a basic unit of expense. There is some elementary time interval, which we will call *D*, which is the time it takes to execute the simplest SETL instructions. All instructions consume an amount of time which is some multiple of *D*. The actual value of *D* depends on the computer and on the specific SETL implementation being used and can be anywhere between a millionth to a ten-thousandth of a second. In what follows, estimates of execution times will always be given in units of *D*. We will refer to *D* as the *basic instruction cycle*, or *cycle* for short.

Instructions whose operands are simple data types: integers, floating-point numbers, Booleans, all take roughly one cycle to execute. This includes

Arithmetic operations on integers and floating-point numbers
Boolean operations.
Comparison operations (=,/=, >, <, etc.)

At the level of the actual machine, there may be secondary differences among some of these; for example, a floating-point division is typically slower than an integer addition. In this discussion we can safely ignore these differences, and we shall do so in what follows.

The simple assignment statement

```
v := expr;
```

where *v* is a simple variable name, also takes roughly one cycle to execute (of course, only after the value of expr has been obtained).

6.5.3 Operations on sets

Operations on composite objects (sets, tuples, and maps) fall into two categories: instructions that take a fixed number of cycles, regardless of the size of the object to which they apply, and instructions whose execution time is a function of the size of their arguments. Let us examine each of these categories of set operations.

6.5.3.1 Elementary operations on sets

The following operations on sets can be performed in a constant number of cycles:

Cardinality: $\#S$ takes one cycle to evaluate, regardless of the actual number of elements of S

Membership: (x in S) where x is a simple item (numeric or Boolean) takes typically three to six cycles to evaluate, regardless of the size of the set S

There is nothing obvious about these remarks! You might wonder how the membership test can actually be performed without examining all the elements of S. The answer lies in clever choice of the internal data structures used by the SETL run-time system itself. These structures are discussed in Chapter 10 and we will not say more about them now, except to note that the possibility of using sets as freely as we do in SETL depends in part in the constant execution time required by the membership operation. Note that this constant time behavior applies when x is a simple (nonstructured) value. In general, the membership test x in S takes as long as (or a little longer than) an equality test $x = y$. The relevance of this remark will become apparent in the following section.

Insertion and deletion: For simple objects the operations x **with** S and S **less** x, take a constant number of cycles to execute. Exceptions relate to questions of storage allocation, and will be discussed later. The actual number of cycles needed for insertion of a simple value into a set is about 10–15 cycles.

Map retrieval: To evaluate or to modify $f(x)$, where f is a map and x is a simple value, takes constant time, comparable to the time required for set membership operation. Once again, efficient implementation of this fundamental operation is secured by the use of a sophisticated data structure about which we will say more in Chapter 10.

6.5.3.2 Global operations on sets

Operations that construct composite objects can be expected to take an amount of time proportional to the size of the object they build. This means that set union, intersection, and difference take longer when their arguments are larger. To illustrate this point let us examine the set union operation $S1 + S2$. This is evaluated in several steps:

(i) Initialize by making a copy of $S1$. This can be expected to take a number a steps proportional to $\#S1$.

(ii) Iterate over $S2$, and check each element of $S2$ for membership in $S1$. Whenever an element is found which is not in $S1$, insert it into the union set.

This process is described by the following equivalent SETL fragment:

```
S3 := S1;              $ Initialize result
(for x in S2)          $ Iterate over second set.
  if x notin S1 then
    S3 with := x;                                    (2)
  end if;
end;
```

After code like this has been executed internally, $S3$ will clearly be equal to $(S1 + S2)$. To estimate the execution cost of the loop in (2), we can reason as follows: the loop body is executed $(\#S2)$ times, i.e., once for each element of $S2$. For each such element we perform a membership test and (possibly) a set insertion, both of which take constant time. Therefore the loop takes an amount of time proportional to $\#S2$. The initialization of $S3$ amounts to making a copy of $S1$, which takes a time proportional to the size of $S1$. Putting all of this together, and neglecting small differences between the execution time of membership and insertion operations, we can conclude that the cost of a union operation is proportional to the sum of the cardinalities of the sets involved. This is not an exact statement, but it is sufficiently accurate to convey an idea of the *order of magnitude* of the execution time of this set operation.

We can apply a similar analysis to the set intersection operation $(S1*S2)$. This is evaluated by the SETL run-time system in the following fashion:

(i) Initialize the result to the empty set.
(ii) Determine which one of the two sets has the smaller cardinality (for definiteness, let us say it is $S1$). Then iterate over $S1$, testing each of its elements for membership in $S2$. Insert each element of $S1$ which is also a member of $S2$ into the intersection set being built up. This process corresponds to the following SETL fragment:

```
S3 := { };
(for x in S1)
  if x in S2 then
    S3 with := x;                  (3)
  end if;
end;
```

Using much the same reasoning, we can easily see that the execution time for this fragment is proportional to the cardinality of $S1$, i.e., to the size of the smaller of the two sets entering into the intersection operation.

Set difference, set inclusion, and subset testing operations are performed in similar fashion and can therefore be expected to take an amount of time proportional to the cardinality of one of their arguments.

Other SETL primitives involve similar (implicit) iterations over sets. The most obvious of these is the **print** statement: **print**(S) requires the examination and output of each element of S. Set equality and inequality are more complex examples. To test whether $S1$ and $S2$ are equal, the SETL run-time system performs the following sequence of actions:

(i) Compare the cardinalities of $S1$ and $S2$. If these cardinalities differ, the two sets are distinct.

(ii) If the two sets have the same cardinality, then we must examine each element of one set, and check it for membership in the other set. If an element is found which does not belong in both, we know that the two sets are not equal. If the two sets are equal, each element will have to be examined, and the process of establishing equality will take a time proportional to the common size of $S1$ and $S2$. The internal equality testing process can be described by the following SETL procedure:

```
proc equal(S1, S2);

if #S2 /= #S1 then return FALSE;

else
   (forall x in S1)
      if x notin S2 then return FALSE; end if;
   end;                                                    (4)
   return TRUE; $ All elements are common.

end if;

end proc;
```

We mentioned in the previous section that the membership operation must often perform an equality test involving the object being tested for membership. This means that if $S1$ is a set of sets, and *su* is a set, then the operation

su **in** S1

will take a time proportional to the size of *su*, because it will involve testing *su* and one or more element(s) of $S1$ for equality. It should be clear that when sets of sets of sets of.. are involved on both sides, the membership test operation will become more complex, and the size of the subobjects of $S1$ will have to be taken carefully into consideration.

6.5.4 Operations on tuples and strings

Indexing, i.e., the retrieval or modification of the i-th component of a tuple or string, is the basic operation on indexable objects like strings and tuples. This operation takes a small constant amount of time, typically two to three basic cycles.

On the other hand, *membership testing*, i.e., the operation (x in T) where T is a tuple or string, proceeds by examining all elements of T in succession, in the manner suggested by the following equivalent SETL procedure:

```
proc intuple (x, T);

(forall y = T(i))
   if x = y then return true; end if;
end;                                              (5)

return false;   $ x was not found in T.

end;
```

Given the way that tuples and strings are represented internally, there is no more efficient way to tell a priori where x is found in T, if indeed it is found in T at all. If x is not in T, this will only be ascertained after all elements of T have been examined, and if x is in T, it may be the first, second, ... n-th component. We can say that on the average, half of the elements of T will have to be examined before x is found. This means that a membership test applied to a tuple T can be expected to take a number of cycles proportional to $\#T$. (Compare this with the more advantageous constant time behaviour of membership tests on sets).

If x is itself a structured object, and T is a tuple of such structures, then the equality test in the loop (5) can be expected to be proportional to the size of x. Therefore in this case the membership test (x in T) will take time proportional to ($\#x \times \#T$).

Tuple and string concatenation are analogous to set union: they take a time proportional to the sum of the sizes of the operands, i.e., to the size of the result. Testing tuples and strings for equality is also linear in the size of the operands, as it requires that each component of each object (in the worst case) be examined.

The execution times of the basic SETL operations are summarized in Table 6.1. We can estimate the cost of any straight-line program simply by adding

Table 6.1. Execution Time of Various SETL Primitives

Operation		Time Units
Arithmetic	$i + j$, $i*j$	1
Assignment	$x := y$	1
Indexing	$T(i)$	1
Map retrieval	$M(x)$	5
Set membership	X in S	5
Tuple membership	X in T	#T
Set union	$S1 + S2$	#S1 + #S2
Concatenation	$T1 + T2$	#T1 + #T2
Quantifier	exists X in $S \mid C(x)$	#S × (5 + cost(C)

i, j designate integers, T designates a tuple, S a set, and M a map.

the costs of each instruction in it. However, other issues, discussed in the next section, arise if we go on to examine the more interesting problem of estimating the cost of programs with various loop structures.

6.5.5 The execution time of programs containing loops

Iteration over a set, as for example in

(for x **in** s)... **end**;

or over a map, tuple, or string, as in

(For x = t(i))... **end**;

produces set elements (or map values, tuple components, or string characters) at a rate of one per cycle. Essentially the same remark applies to numerical iterators, like those in (1). Hence to estimate the time required to execute a loop, we have to multiply the number of times the loop will be executed by the (average) time that it will take to execute the body of the loop. An obvious generalization of this rule applies to imbedded loops: if one **for** loop is imbedded within another, then the time required to execute the outer loop is the number of times it will be executed, multiplied by the (average) number of times the imbedded loop will be executed, multiplied by the time required to execute the body of the embedded loop. For example, the double loop

(for i **in** [1..1000], *j* **in** [1..i])... **end;**

will execute in a time roughly equal to 1000×500 multiplied by the amount of time required to execute the loop body, since the embedded loop over j will execute an average of 500 times for each successive value of i. (This number 500 is halfway between the number one of times that j changes when $i = 1$ and the number (1000) of times that j changes when $i = 1000$.)

Since quantifiers and set formers are in effect prepackaged iterations, very similar rules apply to them. An existential quantifier like

...**exists** x **in** s | C(x)... (6)

is evaluated as if it were the following SETL fragment:

```
maybe := false;

(for x in s)
   if C(x) then maybe := true; quit; end if;
end;
```

where *maybe* is an internal variable that holds the Boolean result of the test. This SETL fragment will execute in time equal to the number of items examined, multiplied by the average time required to evaluate the Boolean condition $C(x)$. If the quantifier (6) evaluates to **false**, then all the members of s will need to be examined, so the time required will be #s multiplied by the average time to evaluate C(x). If (6) evaluates to TRUE, then iteration over s will terminate as soon as an x that actually satisfies $C(x)$ is found; since iteration over a set is performed in a somewhat unpredictable order, the number of iterations needed to find such an x should be roughly $\#s/(\#\text{sat} + 1)$, where *sat* is the set of all x satisfying the condition $C(x)$.

Similar remarks apply to set formers and the tuple formers, except that:

(a) Each insertion into a set takes somewhat longer than a simple iterative step, because of the necessity to check for and eliminate duplicate elements, and
(b) The implicit iteration appearing in a set or tuple former like

```
{x in s | C(x)}
```

must always proceed until all the elements of *s* have been examined.

As an application of these rules, note that execution of the harmless-looking code fragment

```
f := { };

(for x in s)
   f(x) := {y in s | (exists z in s | C(x, y, z))};        (7)
end for;
```

involves three nested loops: first the **for** loop which appears explicitly, next the implicit iteration over *s* in the setformer {*y* **in** *s*..}, and then finally the implicit iteration over *s* in the quantifier **exists** *z* **in** *s*... Therefore the number of cycles required to execute (7) is roughly as high as the cube of the number of elements of the set *s*.

6.5.6 The execution time of **while** loops

The possibility that a program can loop forever in an ill-constructed **while** loop should serve to alert us to the fact that analysis of the time required to execute a **while** loop can be much subtler than **for** loop analysis. Of course, some **while** loops are easily analyzed. For example, if the variable *k* is not modified in its body, the loop

```
k := 0;

(while (k + := 1) < n and t(k) /= om)
   ...
end while;
```

where *k* is incremented each time through the loop, behaves in very much the same way as a **for** loop and therefore will terminate after no more than $n - 1$ iterations. On the other hand, consider the loop

```
t := n*[0];

(while exists x = t(i) | x = 0)
   print(t);
   t(i) := 1;                                   (8)
   t(1..i - 1) := (i - 1)*[0];
end while;
```

This begins by generating a tuple $t := [0,0,..0]$ of n zeroes and then repeatedly sets the first nonzero coordinate of t to 1 and all the coordinates preceding this coordinate to zero, thus carrying out a (left-to-right) form of binary counting. The sequence of tuples printed is

$$
\begin{array}{l}
[0,0,0,\ldots 0] \\
[1,0,0,\ldots 0] \\
[0,1,0,\ldots 0] \\
[1,1,0,\ldots 0] \\
[0,0,1,\ldots 0] \\
[1,0,1,\ldots 0], \text{etc.}
\end{array}
$$

and is plainly of length 2^n, in that it generates all binary numbers from 0 to $2^n - 1$. Hence the number of cycles required to execute the **while** loop (8) is at least 2^n, which means that if $n = 50$ the loop will execute for roughly 320 years, even if 100,000 iterations are performed per second!

For a more realistic example of the way in which **while** loops are typically used, consider a particularly simple sorting method, dubbed *flip-sort.*

```
(while exists i in [1.. #t - 1] | t(i) > t(i + 1))
   [t(i), t(i + 1)] := [t(i + 1), t(i)];                (9)
end wile;
```

This searches a tuple t for out-of-order components and interchanges a pair of such components whenever one is found. Plainly the number of cycles required to execute (9) is the average time required to search the tuple t for an out-of-order pair of adjacent components, multiplied by the number of interchanges required to put t in sorted order. Even though precise analysis of these times requires subtle analysis going far beyond the scope of this book, it is not hard to estimate these time requirements crudely. We can guess that, as long as an out-of-order pair exists, one such pair will be found after searching through some fraction of the length of tuple t being sorted; thus evaluation of the existential quantifier appearing in the first line of (9) is estimated to require cn cycles, where c is some constant which we will not attempt to evaluate here and n is $\#t$. Moreover, since each execution of the body of the **while** loop (9) corrects exactly one case in which a pair of elements appears in inverted order, the expected number of times that (9) must iterate to put t into its final sorted order should be roughly equal to the number of pairs of components of t which occur in inverted order. In a random arrangement of the components of t, roughly half the components to the left of a given t(i) should be larger than $t(i)$, and roughly half the components to the right of $t(i)$ should be smaller than $t(i)$. Thus each component $t(i)$ of t should appear in roughly $\#t/2$ inverted pairs, and it follows, since this way of looking at things counts inverted pairs twice, once for each of the components in such a pair that the expected number of inverted pairs in a randomly chosen arrangement of the components of t should be roughly $(1/4)n^2$). Multiplying this expression by cn, representing the estimated time required to evaluate the existential quantifier in the first line of (9), we arrive at

$$\frac{1}{4}cn^3 \tag{10}$$

for the time required to execute flip-sort code on a tuple of length n.

The approximations which we have made in arriving at the estimate (10) are too crude for the constant (c/4) appearing in (10) to be particularly meaningful. (Ex. 9 following Section 6.5 outlines an experimental procedure for estimating this coefficient more accurately.) The significant feature of the estimate (10) is that it tells us that the time required to sort a tuple by the flip-sorting method is proportional to the cube of the length of t, i.e., that sorting a tuple of length 10 by this method should take roughly 120 cycles, sorting a tuple of length 100 roughly 120,000 cycles, and sorting a tuple of length 1000 roughly 120,000,000 cycles. These figures, which are not very favorable, reflect the rapidity with which the cube of n grows as n increases; in the jargon of algorithm analysis, one says that flip-sort is an n *cube algorithm* or *an* $O(n^3)$ *algorithm.* Clearly, any sorting algorithm whose time requirement grows less rapidly than the cube of the length of t will be very much superior to flip sort as a technique for sorting large tuples t.

Let us therefore modify our naive flip-sort algorithm in order to obtain a more efficient sorting method. We begin by noticing that the existential quantifier in (9) forces us to scan the tuple from the beginning, each time we find an out-of-order pair. This is wasteful because an out-of-order element may be out of place with respect to several of its successors, not just one. A better approach is to try to push the winner of each such exchange as far as it will go and go back to the beginning of the tuple only after we have made a full pass over the tuple. This leads to the following:

```
(for j in [1.. #t - 1])
   (for i in [1.. #t - 1])

      if t(i) > t(i + 1) then
         [t(i), t(i + 1)] := [t(i + 1), t(i)];            (11)
      end;

   end;
end;
```

Note that this code will push the largest element in the tuple to the last position the first time the inner loop is executed, the second largest element will be pushed to the second position from the end on the next pass through the inner loop, and so on. Each execution of the inner loop adds one element to the fully sorted portion of *t* which is built up at its end. The outer loop is executed (#*t* − 1) times to ensure that every element of *t* finds its proper place.

A further improvement is possible. Elements that have reached their correct position need not be examined in successive passes because we know that they are in their proper places. We can therefore modify (11) to read as follows:

```
(for j in [1 .. #t - 1])
   (for i in [1 .. #t - j])

         if t(i) > t(i + 1) then
            [t(i), t(i + 1)] := [t(i + 1), t(i)];          (12)
         end if;

   end;
end;
```

The fragment (12) is the bubble-sort method that we examined in Section 5.1.1.

Next let us examine the execution time of (12). Again, let n be #t. The outer loop is executed $(n - 1)$ times. The inner loop is executed $(n - 1)$, $(n - 2), \ldots 3, 2, 1$ times, that is to say, $(n/2)$ times on the average. The body of the inner loop consists of various comparison, indexing and assignment operations, all of which take some constant time c1. Therefore the total execution time of (12) is roughly c1*$(n - 1)$*$(n/2)$ cycles. We therefore can say that the code (12) executes in time proportional to the square of the size of *t*. This is a considerable improvement over our initial flip sort. Several further refinements can be made to (12), but these improvements only affect the constant c1 and do not modify the n^2 behavior that we have just obtained.

The order-of-magnitude analysis that we have just performed is the most frequent and useful kind of algorithm performance analysis. Often it is enough to know what the order-of-magnitude behavior of a program is to estimate whether it is acceptable for the small, medium, large, or very large amount of data that is to be processed.

The transformation that took us from (9) to (12) deserves further discussion. What we did was to remove an existential expression

```
.. exists x in s | C(x)
```

which describes some exhaustive search over *s*, and replace it with a more intelligent search over that set. This shows a fairly typical use of existential quantifiers: they allow us to write a crude specification for some kind of search process, in order to obtain a working algorithm quickly. When time comes to improve the efficiency of that algorithm, we can often replace the existential quantifier with a more precise (and therefore more efficient) search, better adapted to the problem at hand. This stepwise approach to program efficiency is one of the most important principles of good programming practice. Proper use of SETL consists precisely in starting with as condensed and abstract a formulation as can be achieved by use of set formers, quantified expressions, power sets, etc. Once such an abstract program is running, one can then replace these abstract constructs, *in those places where they are unacceptably inefficient*, by more efficient lower-level constructs which make use of sophisticated data arrangements.

6.5.7 Efficiency analysis of recursive routines

The presence of procedure calls adds another dimension to efficiency analysis. To begin with, execution of the procedure call instruction itself has a certain cost. This cost can be divided into a fixed portion and a variable portion. The first part of the cost (on the order of five cycles) does what is needed to remember the point of call (so we can return to it) and start the called procedure. The variable portion of the cost is proportional to the number of actual parameters being passed to the called procedure and can be expected to add two to five cycles per parameter. This indicates that a procedure call involving just a few parameters is as time-consuming as 10 to 15 arithmetic operations.

However, in most cases the important expense is the time the called procedure actually takes to execute. If the called procedure consists only of loops and simple statements, we can estimate its execution time using the techniques sketched in the previous section. On the other hand if the called procedure calls other procedures in turn, or more interestingly calls itself recursively, then the analysis of its efficiency is considerably more subtle. To indicate the kind of reasoning required, and also introduce some useful notation, let us first examine the "quintessential recursive procedure," namely the factorial:

```
proc fact(N);
return if N = 0 then 1 else N*fact(N - 1) end;          (1)
end;
```

Since the factorial of a positive number N is the product of successive integers up to N, an iterative calculation of fact (N) will require N multiplications, i.e., take time proportional to N. It is conventional to indicate this by saying that iterative calculation of fact (N) uses time $O(N)$.

This is also the case for our recursive definition. To establish this, we reason as follows: if N is not zero, execution of fact (N) will require one comparison operation (the test $N = 0$) one multiplication, and one recursive call to fact involving a smaller argument, namely $N - 1$. If we let $T(N)$ designate the time it takes to execute fact when its argument is N, this leads to the following equation:

$$T(N) = 2 + T(N - 1) \tag{2}$$

where the constant 2 corresponds to the two elementary operations noted.

This equation is called a *recurrence relation* for T and defines the value T for each possible argument N, as a function of the value that $T(N)$ takes as an smaller argument. Note that this recurrence parallels the recursive definition of *fact*, in which the value calculated is also defined in terms of another invocation of the same procedure. To solve the recurrence relation means to express $T(N)$ as some explicit function of N. For the recurrence (2), this can be done easily, as follows. The relation (2) holds for arbitrary values of N (except 0), so that substituting N for $N - 1$ in (2) we find that

$$T(N - 1) = 2 + T(N - 2).$$

We can use this to replace $T(N - 1)$ on the right-hand side of (2), which gives

$$T(N) = 4 + T(N - 2)$$

Repeating the same reasoning, we can express $T(N - 2)$ in terms of $T(N - 3)$, and so on. This process ends when we express $T(1)$ as $2 + T(0)$. $T(0)$, that is to say the time required to evaluate the factorial when its argument vanishes, is just the execution time of the test $(N = 0)$ because in that case the procedure does not recurse. Thus $T(0) = 1$. Putting all of this together, we obtain

$$T(N) = 2{*}N + 1 \qquad (3)$$

which indicates that our recursive factorial program also executes in a time proportional to its argument N. The calculation just described neglected the actual cost of the procedure call itself, and that of the return instruction. Taking these into account would modify (3) only by constant factors, i.e., would gives us

$$T(N) = aN + b$$

where the constants a and b are < 10. Hence our conclusion that calculation of fact (N) requires time proportional to N remains correct.

Next let us examine a more complex example of a recursive procedure: the Towers of Hanoi procedure of Section 5.4.4. Recall that the Towers of Hanoi problem is that of moving N rings, stacked in decreasing order of size on a peg A, to a peg B, using some intermediate peg C as a ring holder, and respecting the ordering of the rings, so that a ring never lies over a smaller ring. As seen in Section 5.4.4, the solution is given by means of the following recursive procedure:

```
proc Hanoi(N, fr, to, via);

if N = 0 then return;
else
   Hanoi(N - 1, fr, via, to);
   print('from peg', fr, 'to peg', to);          (4)
   Hanoi(N - 1, via, to, fr);
end if;

end proc Hanoi;
```

Using the same reasoning as before, we can readily establish the following facts:

(a) When the argument N is zero, Hanoi does not recurse but executes a single test and returns.
(b) When N is greater than zero, Hanoi executes a test, a **print** statement, and two recursive calls with argument $(N - 1)$. In other words, the time consumed by the procedure is described by the recurrence relation

$$T(N) = a + 2*T(N - 1) \tag{5}$$

and by the "boundary condition"

$$T(0) = b \tag{6}$$

where a and b are small constants. Once again, we can use this recurrence relation for $T(N)$ to express $T(N - 1)$ in terms of $T(N - 2)$, $T(N - 2)$ in terms of $T(N - 3)$, and so on, until $T(N)$ is expressed only in terms of a and b. These successive replacements look as follows:

$$\begin{aligned} T(N) &= a + 2*(a + 2*T(N - 2)) \\ &= a*(1 + 2) + 4*T(N - 3) \\ &= a*(1 + 2) + 4(a + 2*T(N - 4)) \\ &= a*(1 + 2 + 4) + 8*T(N - 4) \\ &= \ldots \end{aligned}$$

The pattern should be clear: each substitution adds another power of 2 to the coefficient of a, and another factor of 2 to the coefficient of $T(N - i)$, so that this coefficient is always 2^{i-1}. Our calculation stops when $i = N$, at which point we have

$$\begin{aligned} T(N) &= a(1 + 2 + \cdots + 2^{N-2}) + 2^{N-1} \times T(0) \\ &= a(2^{N-1} - 1) + 2^{N-1} \times b = 2^{N-1} \times (a + b) - a \end{aligned}$$

We conclude that procedure Hanoi takes an amount of time which is an exponential function of its input parameter N (the number of rings to be moved). This means that adding one more ring doubles its execution time. Clearly, a procedure with this behavior can only be useful for relatively small values of its argument. (The Buddhist legend from which this problem originates states that 64 such rings are being moved by dedicated monks since the beginning of time, and that the completion of their task will mark the end of the world. The preceding analysis indicates that we need not be too concerned yet about this prospect.)

Procedures are only useful in practice if they do not have the explosive time requirement that the Hanoi procedure illustrates: factorial is linear in its argument, as we saw previously, and the sorting procedures discussed so far are cubic or quadratic in the number of elements to be sorted. Most of the procedures that we use in practice consume time $O(n)$, $O(n^2)$ or $O(n^3)$ at most.

Finally let us analyze the performance of one more simple recursive procedure, namely quicksort, which was presented in Section 5.4.1. This procedure, which can sort any homogeneous set *s* of integers, floating-point numbers, or strings, is simply

```
proc quick_sort(s);
if #s = 0 then return [ ]; end;
x := arb s;                                        (7)
   return quick_sort({y in s | y < x})
  + [x] + quick_sort({y in s | y > x});
end proc quick_sort;
```

Let $T(n)$ be the number of cycles that this procedure will typically require to sort a set of n elements. Building up the two sets which appear in the final **return** statement of (7) will require a number of steps proportional to the size of s, in that a full pass over s is required in each case. Thus the time required to execute (7) is equal to some small constant multiple $c*n$ of the length n of s ($c = 3$ is a fair guess), plus the time required to execute the two recursive invocations of quicksort which appear in the second **return** statement of (7). Since typically the element x chosen from s by the **arb** function of (7) will lie roughly halfway between the largest and the smallest elements of s, each of the two sets $\{y \textbf{ in } s \mid y < x\}$ and $\{y \textbf{ in } s \mid y > x\}$ should contain approximately half the elements of s. Thus, given that $T(n)$ is the time required to sort a collection of n elements by the quicksort method, sorting each of these sets by use of quicksort should require roughly $T(n/2)$ cycles. It follows that $T(n)$ satisfies the recursive relationship

$$T(n) = 2*T(n/2) + c*n \tag{8}$$

The first of the terms on the right of (8) represents the time typically required to execute the two recursive invocations of quicksort appearing in (7), and the term $c*n$ represents all the work needed to prepare for the two invocations.

We solve (8) in the same fashion as in our two previous examples, by substituting the expression (8) for the occurrence of T on the right of (8), which gives

$$\begin{aligned} T(n) &= c*n + 2*c*(n/2) + 4*T(n/4) \\ &= 2*c*n + 4*T(n/4), \end{aligned} \tag{8a}$$

and then substituting (8) for $T(n)$ on the right of (8a) to get

$$\begin{aligned} T(n) &= 2*c*n + 4*c*(n/4) + 8*T(n/8) \\ &= 3*c*n + 8*T(n/8). \end{aligned} \tag{8b}$$

Continuing inductively in this way we will clearly get

$$T(n) = 4*c*n + 16*T(n/16),$$
$$T(n) = 5*c*n + 32*T(n/32),$$

and so forth, until eventually, when the power of 2 in the denominator on the right becomes roughly equal to n (which will happen after $\log n$ steps, where log *n* designates the logarithm of *n* to the base 2), we will find that $T(n)$ is rougly

$$c*n*\log n + n*T(1),$$

i.e., that $T(n)$ can be estimated as the product of a small constant c (still roughly 3), times *n*, times the logarithm of *n*. One therefore says, in the jargon of algorithm analysis, that quicksort is an "*n* log *n*" or "$O(n \log n)$" algorithm.

For *n* at all large and c roughly equal to 3, $c*n*\log n$ will be vastly smaller than the cube or even the square of *n*. For example, for $n = 1000$, $n**3$ is 1,000,000,000, $n**2$ is 1,000,000, whereas $c*n*\log n$ is only 30,000. Therefore quicksort can be used to sort large amounts of data, which could not be sorted in any reasonable amount of time using flip or even bubble sort. For example, if $\#t = 10{,}000$, and on a computer capable of executing 100,000 of our nominal instruction cycles per second, sorting *t* using the flip-sort method will require approximately 16 hours, bubble sort will take about 20 minutes, whereas quicksort will accomplish the same operation in roughly 4 seconds.

This simple example shows why it is so important to find algorithms whose time requirements do not rise rapidly as the arguments passed to them grow larger. Very considerable efforts have been devoted to the search for such high-efficiency algorithms during the past decade, and a great many ingenious and important algorithms having efficient behaviour have been devised. Most of these algorithms lie beyond the scope of the present introductory work. For basic accounts of this important material, see the References at the end of this chapter.

6.5.8 The cost of copying, or Space is time after all

Some SETL operations, like (*s* **with** *x*) where *s* is a set, and (*t* **with** *x*) where *t* is a tuple, also *s* **less** *x*, *x* **from** *s*, *x* **fromb** *t*, and *x* **frome** *t*, modify a composite object (i.e., a set *s* or tuple *t*) which may be large. The same remark applies to the tuple assignment $t(i) := x$, and to map assignments like $f(i) := x$ and $f\{i\} := x$. The time required to execute these operations will vary dramatically depending on whether or not the large composite argument of the operation needs to be copied.

To understand this important point, note first of all that copying is sometimes logically necessary. Consider, for example, the code

```
s := {1,2,3,4,5,6,7,8,9,10,15,20};
s1 := s;
s with := 25;                                  (1)
s1 less := 2;
print('s =', s);
print('s1 =', s1);
```

The output that this will produce is

```
s =   {1 2 3 4 5 6 7 8 9 10 15 20 25}
s1 =  {1 3 4 5 6 7 8 9 10 15 20}.
```

Since two different values will have been created by the time we reach the final step of (1), it is clear that somewhere along the way to this final step the single set constant assigned to the variable s will have to be copied. This copying can be done when the value of *s* is assigned to the second variable *s*1 in the second line of (1) (copying on assignment), or can be done in the third line of (1), when the value of *s* (but not that of *s*1) is modified by addition of the extra element 25 (copying on modification). Exactly where copying actually takes place will depend on the particular version of the SETL system that you are using, and especially on whether or not this compiler includes an "optimization" phase. But in any case, whenever two variables appear to be sharing the value of a composite object, and one of these variables is modified, the other one must be provided with a fresh copy of that composite object, because in SETL *assigning to one variable never affects another*. Copying a set or tuple with *n* components always requires $O(n)$ cycles. Hence execution of an apparently cheap operation like $t(i) := x$ can require a number of cycles proportional to the length of *t*, if the value of *t* has been assigned to some other variable.

On the other hand, copying is frequently unnecessary, and both the optimizing version of the SETL compiler and the SETL run-time library include mechanisms for avoiding copying when it is not logically necessary. (Since these are implementation-level mechanisms, and fairly complex ones at that, we shall say nothing about how this is done.) When no copying is involved, the operation *s* **with** *x* is only two or so times slower than the membership test *x* **in** *s*, and similar remarks apply to the other operations in the group we have been considering. For example, the assignment $t(i) := x$ can be done in just one of our nominal "cycles," and in the same circumstances map assignment is roughly five times as slow.

This is but one symptom of the fact that the storage management which the SETL system performs contributes to the total execution time of a program. This contribution will be small if the objects manipulated by the program do not change size very frequently, but can be very substantial if large objects are constantly created, shared, updated, and then discarded. Programming techniques that avoid storage management costs are known and studied in data-structure courses, for which a number of excellent texts exist. Such data structures can be constructed in SETL, and the next section gives one example of such, namely the linked list. In this text we have largely ignored the subject of data structures of this type, in accordance with the tenet of high-level programming which states that the burden of storage management is best left to the system. The gains in ease of programming thereby attained are well worth the execution costs incurred. Nevertheless, the fact that storage management can become expensive should be kept in mind. Note also that in some circumstances, such as in the programming and control of real-time devices (i.e., physical equipment such as a motor, a cardiac monitor, a radar, an air-conditioning system, etc.) where a computer system must respond with minimal delay, *no* hidden execution costs can be allowed, and the programmer must know, within a few milli- or microseconds, the time that a given code sequence will take to execute. Such systems cannot be programmed in SETL or in any other high-level language such as APL or SNOBOL. For such systems, lower-level languages, in which all storage allocation is described in full detail by the programmer, must be used.

SETL provides its user with mechanisms to improve the execution time of set and map operations. These mechanisms make use of sophisticated data structures as described in Chapter 10. Their use also facilitates efficient storage management, thus making it possible to attain an intermediate level of efficiency between "carefree" SETL and programming in a lower-level language. See Chapter 10 for an account of these optional data structuring facilities.

6.5.9 Data structures used for the efficient realization of some SETL primitives: the linked list

As seen in the preceding pages, execution of some of the most important SETL operations, for example, set union and tuple concatenation, requires time proportional to the size of the arguments to which these operations are applied. However, if the programs performing these unions and concatenations use the relevant sets and tuples only in restricted, particularly favorable ways, we can sometimes improve their efficiency very greatly by using alternate, more complex representations for the objects appearing in these programs. Although doing this is something of a violation of the SETL "spirit," which emphasises ease of programming over efficiency of program, SETL can at least be used to explain these efficiency-oriented techniques.

In order to focus our discussion, we have to examine more details of the implementation of the basic SETL types. In this section we will describe the way tuples are actually represented in the SETL run-time system and examine the advantages and disadvantages of this representation. This will allow us to understand the potential advantages of an alternative representation which is efficient in cases where the standard representation for tuples is comparatively expensive. Note that the representations of sets and maps used by the run-time system are considerably more complex than the representation of tuples, so that their description is postponed to Chapter 10.

Internally, that is to say in the memory of the computer on which your program is running, a tuple is represented by a contiguous sequence of cells, or words, that contain the components of the tuple. These components appear in order, so that the first component of the tuple appears in the first of these cells, the second component in the second, etc. For example, if f is the tuple [2, 3, 5, 7, 11], it will be stored in memory as follows:

2	3	5	7	11

The SETL run-time system will always know where the first component of t is found. From this, it can easily calculate the location of the second, third, components of t, and so on: the location of any component $t(i)$ is simply $(i - 1)$

cells after the location of $t(1)$. This is why a tuple is the most efficient way of storing data that is referred to by number, i.e., according to its ordering: when such a collection of data is represented as a tuple, all items in this collection are equally accessible. *Tuples are built for efficient indexing.*

Other operations on tuples are not as easy to perform. Consider

t(2..3) := [ ];

whose purpose is to shorten t by removing two of its components. After this operation is performed, t will be stored as follows:

2	7	11

Thus we now have $t(2) = 7$, $t(3) = 11$, etc. This requires that the components of t that appear after the deleted section be "moved down" two positions. For a long tuple, this can represent a substantial expense. Similarly, operations that enlarge a tuple, by insertion or concatenation, such as

t **with** := 13;
t(1..3) := [1, 2, 3, 4, 5];
t + := [17, 19, 23, 29];

may require that a certain number of elements of t be moved or copied. If there is no room in the portion of memory currently allocated for t for the expansion required by one of the preceding operations, then a larger area will have to be found by the storage manager, into which the whole of t will have to be copied and then modified. We conclude that operations that modify the size of a tuple repeatedly carry a potentially substantial penalty in storage allocation activity. In cases where data are ordered but are not accessed *by number*, i.e. when no indexing operations are performed, and where substantial changes in the size of a tuple will occur, other representations exist that lead to smaller storage allocation and data motion costs. The most familiar among such representations is the chain, or *linked list.*

In the abstract, a *linked list* is a structure in which data are organized according to some linear order, i.e., with a first element, a second one, and so on, and so that it is easy to go from one element to its immediate successor. A tuple is of course an example of a list, but one in which elements are stored contiguously. In general a linked list is not stored contiguously, and the mechanism that takes us from one element to the next must be described explicitly. In SETL we may choose to use a map (call it *next*) which takes us from any element to its successor in the ordering. Then rather than having to use contiguous locations, successive elements of the list can be anywhere. In this case we can think of the location that holds each element of the list as being marked by an arbitrary tag, for which SETL atoms will be used in what follows. The contents of each such location are also described by a mapping (call it *val_of*), so that if C is a cell in this list, val_of(C) is the element stored at C, and next(C) is the cell that contains the next element. In addition we need to have an explicit way of referring to the first element of the list: a variable *comp 1* must be used, whose value is the first cell. Then, all in all, val_of(comp1) is the first element of the list, val_of(next(comp1)) is the value of the second element of the list, etc. The last cell *cn* in the list is distinguished by having no successor, which we express by setting next(*cn*) = **om**.

We are now ready to build and manipulate lists. In order to create a list with a single element *x*, we execute the following fragment:

```
comp1 := newat;          $ Define cell.
val_of(comp1) := x;      $ place element in cell.
next(comp1) := om;       $ First element is currently the last also.
```

In order to add a new element *y* after *x* on this list, we execute the following fragment:

```
new := newat;            $ Define new cell.
val_of(new) := y;        $ Place element in it.
next(comp1) := new;      $ First element now has successor.
next(new) := om;         $ Second one does not.
```

If instead we want to add a new element in front of the list, we execute

```
new := newat;            $ New cell.
val_of(new) := z;        $ And its value.
next(new) := comp1;      $ First element now becomes second.
comp1 := new;            $ And most recent element is first.
```

Note that each invocation of **newat** just represents a way of obtaining a unique marker for each element in the list. Instead of atoms we could have used integers, strings, or indeed any kind of SETL value. We choose to use atoms to emphasize that each cell in the list requires a "name" of some sort, but that this name serves as a place-marker for the value that goes with it and has no other significant relationship to that value.

In order to transform any tuple *t* into this list representation, we can make use of the following procedure:

```
proc into_list(t);
  if t = [ ] then return om;
    end if;
  first := newat;
  cell := first;
  succ := newat;

  (for i in [1 .. #t]);          $ Place tuple component
    val_of(cell) := t(i);        $ Cell for next.
    next_of(cell) := succ;       $ In which next component
    cell := succ;                $ will be stored.
    succ := newat;
  end for;
```

```
        next(cell) := om;              $ Last element.
        return first;                  $ First allocated cell.
    end proc;
```

This procedure returns the first cell of the list, so that by applying the mappings *next* and *val_of* repeatedly we can reach all the elements of the list. We have assumed that *next* and *val_of* are global variables, defined outside this procedure. This is indeed the way in which a program using lists is usually structured: a single *next* mapping is used to describe the chaining of all lists present in the program. The chained representation of a tuple that is obtained from procedure *into_list* can be pictured as follows (Figure 6.1):

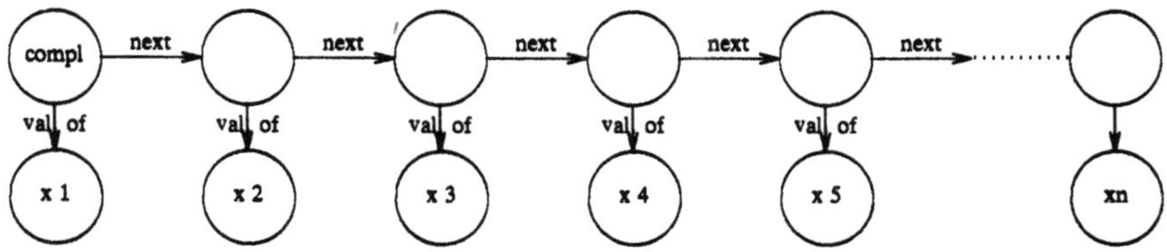

Figure 6.1 A Tuple Represented by a Chained List of Elements

At first sight, representing a tuple in this way may not appear to be such a good idea. Of course, it is not hard to iterate over tuples having this representation: we simply start at *compl* and apply *next* repeatedly to step along, always applying *val_of* to get the component value corresponding to whatever index we have reached. For example, instead of writing

```
                if exists x = t(i) | C(x) then ... else ...            (1a)
```

as we would if *t* were a standard SETL tuple, we would write

```
    i := compl;                        $ Initialize search index

    (while i /= om)
       x := val_of(i);                 $ Value of next element.
       if c(x) then quit while; end;   $ If found, search is successful    (1b)
       i := next(i);                   $ else advance search index
    end while;

    if i /= om then ... else ...
```

Although no less efficient than (1a), the code (1b) is certainly more complex and hard to read. Moreover, accessing a given component *t*(*k*) of *t* is much less efficient in the list representation, since for standard tuples the operation

$$x := t(k)$$

is performed in one or two cycles, whereas if *t* has the list representation we will instead have to count up to *k* as we step through the list, as the following fragment shows:

```
i := compl;
(for j in [1..k − 1])i := next(i); end;
x := val_of(i);
```

whose execution requires at least k cycles; that is to say, indexing operations are not efficient when applied to lists. On the other hand, certain operations that modify the size of tuples can be performed much more rapidly in the list representation than for standard SETL tuples. For example, for a standard tuple the operation which inserts x immediately after the i-th component of t requires time proportional to the length of t, since to create the expanded tuple all of the elements of t will have to be copied into new positions. On the other hand, if t has the list representation, and we know the name *ni* of the cell after which the insertion is to be performed, this operation can be done in just a few cycles, since all we have to do is

(a) create a new atom *ix* to name the cell for the new component value x;
(b) link *ix* at the appropriate position into the list representing t.

Similar remarks apply to the operation $t(i..i) := [\ ]$ which deletes a given component from a tuple in list representation. The following two procedures represent these operations. In writing these procedures, we suppose that a single pair of maps *next* and *val_of* will be used to represent all lists, and that the variables *next* and *val_of* have been declared global. We also suppose that only one logical reference to any of these maps is ever extant, so that no copying (see the preceding section) ever needs to be performed.

```
var next, val_of;                $ Global Variables

next := { };                     $ Initialize to null set
val_of := { };                   $ Initialize to null set

proc insert(x, ni);              $ Inserts x immediately after the list
                                 $ component
ix := newat;                     $ whose cell is ni. Create a new cell ix,
next(ix) := next(ni);            $ and make it the predecessor of next(ni)
next(ni) := ix;                  $ and the successor of ni
val_of(ix) := x;                 $ Place value in cell.
end proc insert;

proc delete(ni);

  $ delete the component immediately following that whose cell is ni
  next(ni) := next(next(ni)?ni);  $ unless ni is the last index in its list make
                                  $ ni's successor the successor of ni's
                                  $ original successor

end proc delete;
```

Provided tuples $t1$ and $t2$ are represented as lists, that $t1$ will not be required after $t1$ and $t2$ are concatenated, and that the name i of the last cell of $t1$ is easily available, the concatenation of $t1$ and $t2$ can also be formed in a number of cycles independent of the length of $t1$ and $t2$. The following procedure, in which we assume that each tuple t in list form is represented by a pair [first, last] consisting of the first and the last cell of t, shows this:

```
proc concat(t1, t2)

[t1_first, t1_last] := t1;        $ unpack the first and
                                  $ last cells of t1
[t2_first, t2_last] := t2;        $ and those of t2

if t1_first = om then             $ t1 is an empty list
   return t2;
elseif t2_first = om then         $ t2 is an empty list
   return t1;
else
   next(t1_last) := t2_first;     $ link the two lists
   return [t1_first, t2_last];
end if;

end proc concat;
```

The mapping *next*, and the variables used to keep track of first and last elements of lists, together define what are called *pointers* in other programming languages.

Quite a few other very useful trick representations of tuples, sets, maps, etc., are known. These representations make use of more complex arrangements of pointers, i.e., internal mappings between elements. If the family of operations applied to a SETL object is appropriately limited, use of an appropriate one of these special representations can be very advantageous. Since further exploration of this very important issue would take us beyond the scope of the present work, we refer the reader to the References at the end of this chapter for additional material concerning the issue of data structuring.

Exercises

1. Write a **while** loop that takes 2**(2**n) cycles to execute, for some n. Write a **while** loop that take 2**(2**(2**n)) cycles to execute. For how many centuries will these loops run, if $n = 100$?

2. If the monks in charge of the Towers of Hanoi began moving the 64 rings in the year 1 million B.C. and if they more one ring per second, when will the world end?

3. By adding a mapping *prev* that takes a given list element to its predecessor in the list, it is possible to iterate over a list forward and backward. Write a procedure to transform a standard tuple into this "doubly-linked" list representation.

4. Write procedures to insert and delete elements from a doubly-linked list.
5. Estimate the cost of the list concatenation procedure of Section 6.5.9. Assuming that a map operation such as next(last) := first; takes five cycles, and that copying a tuple of size n takes $2*n$ cycles, determine the size of $t1$, $t2$ for which the linked representation is preferable to the standard contiguous representation for performing tuple concatenation.

6.5.10 Some techniques for program transformation

The examination of various sorting examples in the previous sections indicates the very general fact that several algorithms, of quite different efficiencies, can usually be found to perform a given task. Several questions then arise:

(a) How can we find the most efficient method or algorithm to perform a computation?
(b) How can we know that it is the most efficient one available?
(c) Given one algorithm which is not the most efficient for the problem at hand, can we modify it in some systematic fashion in order to improve its efficiency, perhaps by transforming it into one of the more efficient algorithms of its family?

The answer to (a) is found in the efficiency analysis which we sketched in Section 6.5. Given two algorithms, we can compare the number of operations they are expected to take in various cases and thus determine which one is preferable. Question (b), namely how do we know that a given algorithm is indeed the best possible for a given task, is much harder, and is the subject of so-called lower-bound analysis. For example, in the case of sorting lower-bound analysis gives the following result: 'When we sort a set of size n by means of comparisons between its elements, $O(n \log n)$ operations are required'. This rigorous mathematical result (which we shall not prove here) shows that quicksort is probably close to the best way to sort, although bubble-sort is definitely not. Unfortunately such lower bounds are known only for a few interesting problems, and in general we have no systematic way of knowing how close to optimal a newly invented algorithm is.

Question (c), namely how can we improve on a given algorithm in order to improve it, is the source of much current research and also of large amounts of programming lore. Some basic techniques for transforming a program into a more efficient one take the form of very general prescriptions, such as

1. Do not evaluate the same expression repeatedly.
2. In particular, if a calculation is performed repeatedly in a loop and yields the same result every time, then perform the calculation once outside the loop, save the result, and use it within the loop.
3. Try to reuse storage occupied by a variable if the value of that variable is not needed any further.
4. When possible, replace recursive calls by iterative loops.

These prescriptions are simple and intuitive and can be expected to be generally useful. They can be applied almost mechanically and in fact can be automated to some extent, so that a clever compiler can apply such prescriptions by itself. In fact, most good compilers perform transformations corresponding to (1) and (2). Reuse of storage, as suggested in (3), is harder to automate, and the application of this rule requires greater ingenuity on the part of the programmer. The removal of recursive calls in favor of iterations has been studied in great detail in the context of languages such as LISP, which use recursion very heavily. We will examine a nontrivial example of recursion removal in a few pages.

In addition to the general rules stated in (1.)–(4.), there are certain optimizing program transformations that apply to very specific program constructs. Catalogs of such transformations can be found in some of the works listed in the References. Here we will only give some simple examples of applications of the rules (1), (2), and (3).

6.5.10.1 The elimination of repeated calculations

The simplest kind of efficiency-improving transformation which we can perform is to identify expressions that are common to several calculations and that can be evaluated once instead of repeatedly. For example, when calculating the roots of a quadratic equation, we may write the following familiar formulae:

```
x1 := (-b + sqrt(b**2 - 4.0*a*c))/(2.0*a);
x2 := (-b - sqrt(b**2 - 4.0*a*c))/(2.0*a);          (1)
```

In this case it is plain that the expression involving the square root is the same for both roots, which makes it possible to rewrite (1) as follows:

```
discr := sqrt(b**2 - 4.0*a*c);
x1 := (-b + discr)/(2.0*a);                          (2)
x2 := (-b - discr)/(2.0*a);
```

Transforming from (1) into (2) saves four arithmetic operations and one square root evaluation and makes the expressions simpler to type. We remark that the expression (2.0*a), which is a common subexpression to $x1$ and $x2$, is still evaluated repeatedly in (2). Replacing the two evaluations by a single one by saving the result in some other variable would eliminate one arithmetic instruction but add one assignment statement and therefore would hardly be a saving at all.

As a less trivial example of removal of redundant subexpressions, consider the evaluation of polynomials at a point. That is to say, given some polynomial

$$a_n x^n + a_{n-1} x^{n-1} + \cdots + a_0 \tag{*}$$

we want to determine its numerical value at some point, e.g., for $x = 10$. If we represent the polynomial by a tuple P containing its coefficients in decreasing order, then we can evaluate the polynomial for $x = c$ by means of the following code:

```
degree := # P − 1;
value := +/[a*c**(degree − i + 1): a = P(i)];          (3)
```

Note that in the loop we evaluate $c^{**}n$, $c^{**}(n-1)$, $c^{**}(n-2)$, etc. These exponentiations are evaluated as repeated multiplications, so that the number of operations performed will be

$$n + (n-1) + (n-2) + \cdots + O(n) = n^2 + O(n) = O(n^2)$$

where the $O(n)$ term takes care of the iteration over P and of a final summation of individual terms. In other words, as written the fragment (3) takes an amount of time proportional to the square of the degree of the polynomial. Substantial improvement can be obtained if we observe that the powers of c can be calculated in increasing order rather than in decreasing order, so that $c^{**}n$ is obtained from $c^{**}(n-1)$ by means of a single multiplication. An improved version is the following:

```
power := 1;
value := 0;
(for i in [# P, # P − 1..1])
   term := power*P(i);                    (4)
   value + := term;
   power* := c;
end;
```

Here the loop is executed n times (where n is the degree of P) and each execution of the loop takes three arithmetic instructions and a few assignments, so that the algorithm is now of order n, rather than n^2. This is a subtantial improvement for large enough n.

Let us note that a similar improvement can be obtained by a different approach, which is several centuries old, and is known as *Horner's rule*. We can rewrite the polynomial (*) by means of successive factorizations:

$$((..(a_n x + a_{n-1})x + a_{n-2})..)) + a_0$$

This suggests the following method for evaluating P:

```
value := 0;
(for a = P(i))
   value := value*c + a;                  (5)
end;
```

Now the loop contains only two arithmetic operations and one assignment. This is certainly superior to (4), and is therefore the method of choice for evaluating polynomials. Note however that (5) was obtained by means of a clever rewriting of the original problem, and the solution was not the result of some systematic transformation rule, but was "pulled out of a hat," as it were. It is appropriate to remember at this point that the development and optimization of algorithms require a healthy dose of inventiveness (guided, to be sure, by a knowledge of existing algorithms and optimization techniques).

6.5.10.2 Reuse of storage and recursion elimination: the case of quicksort

In order to illustrate the kind of program improvement that can be obtained by recursion removal, we will examine in some detail the (by now familiar) quicksort method. In its simplest version, we have described quicksort as follows:

```
proc quicksort (S);

if S = { } then return [ ];
else
   x := arb S;
   lo := {y in S | y < x};
   hi := {y in S | y > x};                         (1)
   return quicksort(lo) + [x] + quicksort(hi);
end if;

end proc;
```

The skeleton of this algorithm consists of two steps: *partition* and *recurse*. That is to say: pick some element of the set to be sorted, and partition the rest of the set into two disjoint sets, corresponding to elements that are smaller (resp. larger) than the partitioning element. Then apply this process recursively to each partition. The two very substantial improvement that can be brought to bear on the efficiency of quicksort are performing the partitioning in place and replacing the recursion with a loop.

Partitioning in Place. To see how to apply this improvement we first observe that after S has been partitioned into lo and hi, the value of S is not used again. This suggests that, instead of building lo and hi at each step as new sets, we may want to reuse the space occupied by S, to place lo and hi in it. How to do this is not immediately apparent: as long as S, lo, and hi are sets, we do not have a simple way of describing how they are actually stored. If however we make them into tuples forming part of a larger tuple, then it is possible to describe them by their size and their starting locations. Suppose S is a tuple of size n, and that the partitioning element which we choose turns out to be the k-th one (in increasing order). Then the locations $1, 2..k-1$ can be used for lo, and the locations $k+1, k+2..n$ can be used for hi. Then, rather than passing lo and hi as tuples in the recursive call, we can instead pass the end points of each and then proceed to partition each subtuple in place as well. (How the partitioning in place is actually performed remains to be discussed.) This leads to the following (tentative) improved version of quicksort:

```
T := [x in S];              $ Initial tuple to be sorted.
quicksort2(1, #T);          $ First call to routine.

proc quicksort2(m, n);

$ Apply quicksort to the portion of T (which is global) between T(m) and
$ T(n) inclusive.
if m >= n then return;      $ Trivial case.
else
   k = partition(m, n);     $ k is the position of the partitioning element

   quicksort(m, k - 1);     $ Elements smaller than it.
   quicksort(k + 1, n);     $ Elements greater than it.
end if;

end proc;
```

In this version of the algorithm, no composite objects are constructed (except for the global tuple T). Each call to quicksort is given an explicit region of T on which to operate. This forces us to mention the indices m, n, k, etc., explicitly, which makes for a longer and less readable piece of code. We must now show that the partitioning itself can be done in place. This is an interesting algorithm in its own right.

Partitioning an Array in Place. The problem is the following: given a tuple t, and an arbitrary element e of t, reorder the elements of t so that all elements $l < e$ appear before e, and all elements $h > e$ appear after e. For simplicity let us assume that e is chosen to be the first element of t. A first thought might be the following: scan t from left to right, and whenever an element $e1 > e$ is found, move it up. But exactly where to? If we are to reorder t in place, then in order not to loose any information, we can only exchange elements. As a moment's reflection will show, the proper way to proceed is the following:

(a) Going from left to right, find an element $e1 > e$, which must therefore appear after e in the desired reordering.
(b) Going from right to left, find an element $e2 < e$, which must therefore appear before e.
(c) Interchange $e1$ and $e2$.
(d) Continue scanning from left to right from the position of $e2$, and from right to left from the position of $e1$, interchanging whenever the next pair of out-of-place elements is found.
(e) Stop when those two scans meet (at the correct location for e).

The following code (which deserves very careful scrutiny) performs this partitioning process:

```
proc partition(i, j);

$ Partition the portion of array T from T(i) to T(j),
```

```
$ using T(i) as the partitioning element e. The procedure plases e at
$ position k, and places all elements smaller than e at positions < k.

e := T(i);            $ Partitioning element.
l := i + 1;           $ Index for left-to-right scan.
r := j;               $ Index for right-to-left scan.

(while l < r)         $ Scans have not met in middle.

   (while T(l) < e)   $ bypass smaller elements.
      l + := 1;
   end while;

   (while T(r) > e)   $ bypass larger elements.
      r - := 1;
   end while;

   $ Now T(l) > e, and T(r) < e. Exchange them if the two scans have not
   $ met yet.
   if l < r then
         [T(l), T(r)] := [T(r), T(l)];

         $ Skip over these two elements which are now in proper place.
         l + := 1; r - := 1;
   end if;

   end while;
   $ Now l >= r. The point at which they cross is the correct position
   $ for the partitioning element. Place it there, and place T(r), which is no
   $ larger than it, at the original position of the partitioning element.
   T(i) := T(r);
   T(r) := e;

   return r;

   end proc;
```

At this point, our first optimization goal has been achieved: we have a quicksort algorithm that works in place, that is to say, without constructing any new composite objects in the course of its execution. This has been achieved by explicitly describing the elementary operations that place each element of the object being sorted at some specified position in a single tuple. In other words, we have deliberately avoided the use of composite objects in the explicit fashion characterizing version (1) of quicksort. Of course, when we avoid manipulation of composite objects, much of the power of high-level languages such as SETL is lost. In fact, our version of quicksort now looks remarkably similar to a PASCAL or an Ada version of the same algorithm. This indicates the relative advantages of these various languages: SETL and other languages that manipulate arbitrary composite objects are the most convenient programming tools and lead most rapidly and with smallest programming effort to correct and lucid versions of algorithms. However, when efficiency considerations become critical, we must often abandon the richer semantic primitives of these languages (or drop to a lower-level language altogether) in order to control the efficiency of every statement we write.

Removing the Recursion from Quicksort. The next step in our improvement of quicksort is to replace the recursive calls within quicksort by some iterative construct which can be expected to be cheaper (recall that a procedure call is as expensive as 10 to 20 arithmetic operations). The skeleton of the recursive version of quicksort is the following:

```
proc quicksort(i,j);
...
   quicksort(i,k - 1);
   quicksort(k + 1,j);
end;
```

Each invocation of quicksort receives some values for *i* and *j* and assigns some value to *k*. Therefore, to eliminate recursive invocations of the procedure, we must save the current values of *i*, *j*, and *k*, because they might be used after we return from the recursive call. This can be achieved by means of a *stack* on which we "pile up" the parameters which we need to preserve. A *stack* is a tuple which is manipulated as follows: elements are added to it at its end and deleted from it from the same end. In other words, the operations that modify a tuple are the following:

```
stack with := x;    $ 'push' operator
z frome stack;      $ 'pop' operator
```

Whenever we perform a recursive call, we use the stack to save whatever needs to be saved, i.e., whatever current values of variables and parameters will be needed after the recursive call. Whenever we return from the recursive call, we obtain, from the stack, all values that we need to resume the computation at the point where we left off. This is in fact what the SETL run-time system does: whenever a recursive call is executed, current values are saved before the (new instance of the) procedure starts executing. However, the run-time system does this in a stereotyped fashion which is often inefficient.

In the case at hand, the two recursive calls are sandwiched between stacking and unstacking operations, whose action corresponds to the following code:

```
proc quicksort(i,j);
  ...
stack with := [i,j,k];   $ Save current values.
quicksort(i,k - 1);      $ Perform recursive call.
[i,j,k] frome stack;     $ Restore current values.
```

```
stack with := [i, j, k];   $ Save them again.
quicksort(k + 1, j);
[i, j, k] frome stack;     $ restore current values.

end proc;
```

(Recall that the stack manipulations are the ones performed by the run-time system.) Several remaining inefficiencies should now be apparent: the most glaring one relates to the fact that the second recursive call is the last statement in the body of quicksort. In other words, there are no computations to be done after the second call, and therefore there is no need to save and restore current values of variables and parameters at this point. A smaller inefficiency is the fact that the second call only requires the values of $k + 1$ and j, so that there is therefore no need to save i either. So in fact we can do with the following:

```
proc quicksort(i, j);
 ...
stack with := [k, j];
quicksort(i, k - 1);
[k, j] frome stack;
quicksort(k + 1, j);

end;
```

At this point, the meaning of the stack should be clear: it allows us to keep track of portions of the tuple T which remain to be sorted. With this understanding, we realize that quicksort will continue calling itself recursively as long as there is some portion of T still unsorted, i.e., as long as there is something left on the stack that indicates some pending invocation of quicksort. Having this insight, we can transform our algorithm into an iterative one that loops as long as the stack is not empty:

```
(while stack /= [ ])

  [i, j] frome stack;          $ Values to work on.
  ....
  stack with := [i, k - 1];    $ to be worked on.
  stack with := [k + 1, j];    $ ditto.

end while;
```

This is still incomplete: as written, each step deletes one pair of indices from the stack and adds two such pairs to it: clearly the stack will grow without bound, and the algorithm never terminates. What prevents this disaster from happening is that successive pairs describe shorter and shorter portions of the tuple being sorted. Whenever $j - i < 2$, there is nothing to sort. Therefore we should only save a pair on the stack if it describes a portion of the tuple of size greater than 1. A final improvement is to save only one pair on the stack and go to work immediately on the other, rather than stacking it and unstacking it at once. In order to keep the stack small, it turns out best to stack the indices of the larger portion to be sorted and go to work on the smaller one. Putting all this together, we obtain the following:

```
proc quicksort(rw T);

$ Optimized version of quicksort procedure. It operates in place, with
$ explicit stack manipulation, and the partitioning process is performed
$ on line.

i := 1;
j := #T;                        $ Initial portion to be sorted is the
                                $ whole of T.
stack := [ ];

loop do
   $ Partition T(i) to T(j).
   l := i + 1; r := j;
   e := T(i);                   $ Partitioning element.

   (while l < r)
        (while T(l) < e) l + := 1; end;
        (while T(r) > e) r − := 1; end;

        if l < r then
           [T(l), T(r)] := [T(r), T(l)];
           l + := 1; r − := 1;
        end if;

   end while < r;

   T(i) := T(r);                $ finish putting partition element in
                                $ place
   T(r) := e;

   $ Save larger partition on stack.
   if r − i > j − r then
      [savei, savej] := [i, r − 1];
      i := r + 1;               $ Work on [r + 1..k]
   else
      [savei, savej] := [r + 1, j];
      j := r − 1;               $ Work on [i..r − 1]
   end if;

   $ Save larger partition only if it is longer than 1.
   if savej − savei > 1 then
      stack with := [savei, savej];
   end;
```

```
        $ Work on smaller partition only if it is longer than 1.
        $ Otherwise take the top pending partition to work on.
        if j - i < 2 then
          if stack = [ ] then              $ Nothing left to do.
            quit;
          else
            [i,j] frome stack;
          end if;
        end if;

      end loop;

      end proc;
```

This is very far from the short and intuitive algorithm with which we started. However, this final version is considerably more efficient than the original. It is in this final form that the quicksort procedure is usually implemented. Moreover, this more efficient version is still incorrect in some details and would have to be touched up to function properly! For example it will not work if *T* contains duplicate elements; moreover, during the partitioning process, it is possible for *l* or *r* to go out of bounds (i.e., *l* may become > #*T*, and *r* may become 0). These problems can be remedied without difficulty (see Exercises). However, their presence is a reminder that optimization is almost invariably accompanied by increased complexity.

Acceptance of the programming burdens that optimization demands is only justified for algorithms that are used often, consume large amounts of resources, or are critical to the overall performance of a system. Clearly, sorting is a frequently used process, and efforts spent in obtaining better sorting algorithms (the subject of much theoretical and pragmatic research in itself) and encoding them well are quite worthwhile. But it is unwise to devote strenuous optimization efforts for algorithms that are not frequently used or are not critical to system performance. In many cases clarity and maintainability are far more important considerations in software design and construction than mere speed. Note however that recent research holds out some promise that it may eventually be possible for sophisticated computer programs to offer substantial assistance in applying optimizations as deep as those described in the present section.

Exercises

1. How could you use the techniques described in Section 6.5 to make nonterminating recursions less likely to occur?

2. The following SETL code is syntactically correct, but very poorly laid out. Put it in a better format, and add appropriate comments.

```
program sort; read(s); t := [ ]; (while s /= { })s less := x := min/s);
t := [x] + t; end; print(t); end;
```

Improve the following program, which is also correct but poorly laid out.

```
program find_palindromes; $ 'Madam Im Adam'
loop do read(x); if x /= om then y := +/[c: c in x | c /= ''];
if y = [y(j): j in [#y, #y - 1..1]] then print(x); end; else
quit; end; end;
```

3. What cases should be run to test the following recursive sort procedure comprehensively?

```
proc sort(s);   $ recursive sort of a set of integers

return if (x := arb s) = om then [ ]
       else sort({y in s | y < x}) + sort({y in s | y >= x})
       end;

end proc sort;
```

Run your tests, and try to estimate how thoroughly they test this code.

4. Suppose that G is a graph represented as a set of ordered pairs. If G contains a cycle C then C can be regarded as a subset of G such that for each x in C there exists a y in C (namely the edge y following the edge x in the cycle C) such that $x(2) = y(1)$. Conversely, if this condition is satisfied, then there must exist a cycle, since starting with any x in C we can find an x' such that $x(2) = x'(1)$, then an x'' in in C such that $x'(2) = x''(1)$, and so on, until eventually we must return to an edge that occurs earlier in the chain $x, x', x'', \ldots$, at which point a cycle will have been formed. This leads to the following program for testing a graph to see whether it has a cycle:

```
program test_for_cycle;   $ tests any graph for the existence of a cycle
read(G);

print(if exists C in pow(G) | forall x in c | exists y in c | x(2) = y(1))
    then 'There exists a cycle'
    else 'There exists no cycle' end);

end program test_for_cycle;
```

Work out a good battery of tests for this program, test it, and try to estimate how comprehensive your tests really are.

5. In the original quick_sort program, change the expression

```
sort({y in s | y < x}) + [x] + sort({y in s | y > x})
```

to

```
sort({y in x | y < x}) + sort({y in s | y > x}),
```

thereby introducing a bug. Then run the erroneous program. What happens? Could you guess the problem from the symptom? What would be a good way of debugging this program?

6. Suppose that the subexpression $[x]$ in Ex. 5 is not omitted but is accidentally mistyped as $[z]$. What will happen? Why? What will happen if it is accidentally mistyped as $[0]$? As $\{x\}$?

7. For debugging purposes, it is useful to have a monadic operator .OUT such that .OUT x always has the value x, but such that "evaluation" of .OUT x prints the value of x. A binary operator s .OUT2 x which returns x but prints both s and x can also be useful. Write definitions for these operators. How might you use them to debug the faulty recursive procedure described in Ex. 5?

8. Each string in the following set consists of characters which are easily mistyped for each other:

   {'1I|l/', '7>', 'L<', 'D0Oo', 'S5s', 'Z7', 'UVuv', '6b', '4 + t*', '_–', 'GC6'}.

   Write an expression that converts this set of strings into a set s consisting of all pairs of letters that are easily confused for one another. Use this set to create a "bugging program" B, which can read the text of any SETL program P, introduce one randomly selected character substitution chosen from P into it, and write the erroneous version of P thereby produced into a file. Collect various short sample programs from your friends, "bug" them using B, and ask your friends to see whether they can spot the error. Then debug these programs, to see how long it takes you to track down the errors which B has introduced. If B is modified so that it never changes characters in SETL keywords, but only in identifiers, how much more elusive do the bugs that it introduces become?

9. Take the bubble-sort procedure described in Section 5.1.1 and the mergesort procedure described in Section 5.4.2, and modify them by inserting code which will count the number of comparisons which they make when used to sort a given vector t. Use these modified routines to sort tuples of length 50, 100, and 200, counting the number of comparisons performed and measuring their relative efficiencies. Try tuples with random components, and also try tuples with only a few components out of sorted order.

10. Suppose that the statement

$$[t(i), t(i + 1)] := [t(i + 1), t(i)];$$

   in the bubble-sort procedure of Section 5.1.1 is replaced by

$$t(i) := t(i + 1); t(i + 1) := t(i); \qquad (*)$$

   What would happen? If we checked the resulting version of bubble_sort by adding

   assert forall i in [1 .. #t – 1] | t(i) <= t(i + 1);

   would the problem introduced by the change (*) be found? What checking assertion could we write to catch the sort of error that (*) introduces?

11. Suppose that in the bubble-sort procedure of Section 5.1.1 we inadvertently wrote [1 .. $\#t$] instead of [1 .. $\#t - 1$]. What would happen? If we wrote [$\#t$ .. 1] instead? If we wrote [1 .. $\#t - 2$]? If we wrote [2 .. $\#t$]?

12. Take the bubble-sort procedure shown in Section 5.1.1 and find at least three errors that might plausibly be made in writing or typing it, any of which would cause the code to loop endlessly. None of these errors should involve changing more than six characters. Take these erroneous versions of bubble sort to friends, and see how long it takes them to spot the errors.

13. Take the mergesort program shown in Section 5.4.2. Then modify it, to produce four different erroneous versions of merge sort, each of which contains one of the following list of common bugs. (Try to make your modifications as plausible, and as hard to spot as possible.)
    (i) Boolean condition stated in reversed form.
    (ii) One branch of an **if** statement omitted.
    (iii) Premature exit from a loop.
    (iv) Input data not checked; data of the wrong type read.

    For each of these erroneous versions estimate the time that would be required to find the error if you did not know where it was. Write a battery of tests sufficient to show that there is something wrong with each of these erroneous programs.

14. Repeat Ex. 13, but for the buckets and well program shown in Section 5.3.1. Produce five erroneous versions of this program, each with one or two plausible errors in every procedure. Devise a debugging plan which could discover most of these errors quickly. In what order does it seem best to test the procedures of this program? Where would it be most useful to place **assert** statements? Try to devise assertions that can be checked quickly, but whose verification will be strong evidence that the program is working as it should.

15. The following version of quicksort contains just one error. What is it?

```
proc quicksort(t);            $ t is assumed to be a tuple of integers

if t = [ ] then return; end;

x := t(1);
t1 := [y: y = t(i) | y < x];
t2 := [y: y = t(i) | y = x];
t3 := [y: y = t(i) | y > x];
quicksort(t1); quicksort(t3);
t := t1 + t2 + t3;

end proc quicksort;
```

16. How many of the errors introduced by the "bugging program" described in Ex. 8 could be found more easily using a program which reads SETL programs and prints out a list of all identifiers appearing only once in them?

17. Write a maintainance test which could be used to check a sort program by comparing its results with those of quicksort. Use this test to verify that the mergesort procedure shown in Section 5.4.2 is correct.

18. Write a SETL system maintainance test which computes 50 set- or tuple-related values in two radically different ways and compares the results obtained. Your test should exploit various set-theoretic identities. For example,

$$\{e(x): x \textbf{ in domain } f\} = \{e(x): [x, y] \textbf{ in } f\} = \{e(x): y = f(x)\}$$

should be true for every map f, and

$$s1*s2 = s1 - (s1 - s2)$$

should be true for every pair of sets.

19. To see what parts of a program have been executed in a series of tests, we can introduce a global variable called *points*, and a *macro*

    macro point(k); points **less** := k **endm**;

    Then if we initialize *points* by writing points := $\{1..n\}$, insert a sequence of statements *point*$(j), j = 1, \ldots, n$ into the code being tested, and print *points* at the end of execution, each remaining member of *points* will represent a section of code that has never been executed.

    Apply this technique to develop a comprehensive set of tests for the text-editing program described in Section 5.10.2. Add tests to your set until the condition *points* = { } is achieved, to make sure that your collection of tests does not leave any section of code unexecuted.

20. *A boundary test* for a program *P* is a systematic collection of tests which exercises *P* in all the legal but extreme cases which *P* is supposed to handle. Work up several such boundary tests for the text-editing program described in Section 5.10.2. Your tests should include items like checks for $0.00, empty transaction files, etc.

21. The text-editing program described in Section 5.10.2 is totally unprotected against bad input. Modify it so that all input is systematically examined for acceptability; your input-examination procedures should check for all remotely plausible input errors. Write an English-language explanation of the input errors for which you check.

22. Take one of your programs, approximately 10 lines long. Strip all comments from it, and then introduce one misprint, to cause a bug (not one that syntax analysis would find). Give the result to a friend (a good friend!) with a 3-line explanation of what the program is supposed to do. See whether your friend can find and fix the error without expending more than an hour's effort.

23. Develop test data for the GCD program outlined in Ex. 12 (following Section 5.5). Your tests should include cases in which the data are zero, negative, etc., and should test all relevant combinations of "extreme" data of this kind.

24. Write the 'MISSING_SECTIONS' procedure described in Section 6.4.

6.6 Formal Verification of Programs

The growing importance of programs to banks, airlines, engineering firms, insurance companies, universities, indeed to all the major institutions of our society, lends an inescapable importance to the question of program correctness. Once a program has been written, how can we be sure that it is correct, i.e., that when given legal input it will always produce the output that its author desires? This is a deep question, whose systematic exploration would take us far beyond the boundaries of the present introductory test. Nevertheless, in order to shed some light on the issues involved, we will use the present section to say something about it.

To begin with, we emphasise that mere program testing, even systematic testing like that described in Section 6.4, can never prove a program's correctness in any rigorous sense. Testing, to repeat an important maxim of the Dutch computer scientist Edsger Dijkstra, can show the presence, but not the absence, of bugs. Though systematic testing is an essential tool of program development, in asserting the rigorous correctness of a program we are asserting that it will run correctly in each of a potentially infinite family of cases. Clearly, no finite sequence of test cases can cover all of them, and so any rigorous assertion that a program functions correctly in all possible cases must rely on some kind of mathematical proof.

The basic raw material out of which such proofs can be built is not too hard to find. When a programmer has written a program and checked it carefully for the first time, why does he believe that it will run correctly? If legitimate, this feeling of correctness must always rest on a comprehensive logical analysis of the conditions that arise as control moves from point to point during the execution of a program.

To show what such analysis involves, we will take a very simple program, namely one which calculates the product of two integers *n* and *m* by adding *n* to itself *m* times. (The basic technique that we will use to prove the correctness of this trivial program is entirely general; however, the mass of technical detail needed to handle more complex examples grows rapidly, and to avoid this it is best to stick to a rudimentary example.) Since it is a bit easier to handle **while** loops than **for** loops, we write our multiplication code as follows:

```
prod := 0;
iterations := 0;

(while iterations /= m)
   prod := prod + n;                          (1)
   iterations := iterations + 1;
end while;
```

To begin to prove this program correct, we must first supplement it by adding a formal statement of what it is that the program is supposed to achieve. This can be done by adding an **assert** statement at the very end of the program, giving us

```
Line1:  prod := 0;
Line2:  iterations := 0;

Line3:  (while iterations /= m)
Line4:     prod := prod + n;                  (2)
Line5:     iterations := iterations + 1;
Line6:  end while;

Line7:  assert prod = m*n;
```

In (2), all lines of the program have been labeled to facilitate later reference. Note that addition of the final **assert** statement is an absolutely necessary preliminary to any attempt to prove anything at all about the program: Until we have stated what a program is supposed to do, we cannot even begin to prove that it does what it is supposed to! This is to say that all rigorous proofs of program correctness are really proofs that two different descriptions of a computation, one a deliberately very high level mathematical statement (like the final line in (2)) of what an algorithm accomplishes, the other a more detailed procedure (like the rest of the code (2)), really say the same thing.

This fundamental principle being understood, we go on to remark that in proving a program correct what one basically needs to do is just to write down the logical relationships between data items upon which the programmer's understanding of his program's behavior rests. However, these relationships must be written down in a sufficiently complete manner and must be expressed formally, using additional **assert** statements.

To see what is involved, let us first analyze program (2) informally. If the author of (2) wished to convince a skeptical colleague that it really does compute the product $m*n$, what facts about (2) would he point out, what more detailed analysis would he offer? The crucial fact upon which program (2) depends is that each time the loop starting at Line 3 begins to repeat, the variable *prod* will be equal to the product of the variable *iterations* by the variable *m*. This is certainly true on the first iteration, since then both *prod* and *iterations* are zero, so we certainly have

$$\text{prod} = \text{iterations}*\text{n} \tag{3}$$

(i.e., $0 = 0*n$) on first entry to the loop. But if (3) is true at the start of k-th iteration, it must also be true at the end of the k-th iteration, since the body of the loop increments *prod* by n and increments *iterations* by 1. Hence (3) remains true during every iteration. Thus, since the loop only terminates when the variables *iterations* and m are equal, (3) implies that prod $= m*n$ at the end of the loop, which is what we wanted to prove.

The argument we have just presented is a satisfactory informal proof of the correctness of the program (2). Nevertheless, it is not quite what we require. In proving that a program is correct, we aim to exclude rigorously the possibility of any small, easily overlooked program bug. For this, merely informal, English-language proof is insufficient, since such proofs are no less likely than programs to contain small errors. Moreover, some of the likeliest errors in programs (for example, counting in a manner that is off by 1) correspond closely to errors that occur frequently in mathematical proofs (for example, starting a mathematical induction at the wrong place or missing one among multiple cases that a proof needs to examine; see Ex. 12 of Section 6.7). Therefore, when we set out to prove a program rigorously correct, we must aim at something more formal and machine-checkable than an ordinary English-language proof of the kind ordinarily found in textbooks.

6.6.1 Formal verification using Floyd assertions: general approach

This observation drives us to a more formal approach, like that devised by Robert Floyd, for proving programs like (2) correct. Floyd's formalism requires us to add **assert** statements to a program P that we are trying to prove correct. These auxiliary **assert** statements, sometimes called the *Floyd assertions* for P, must satisfy two principal conditions:

(a) Enough **assert** statements must be added so that there can exist no indefinitely long path through the program P which does not pass through at least one **assert** statement. Another way of putting this is to say that at least one auxilary **assert** statement must be inserted into every loop in the program P.
(b) Consider any one of these auxiliary **assert** statements. It will have the form

$$\textbf{assert}\ \mathrm{C} \tag{4}$$

where C which can be any Boolean-valued expression, called the *condition* of the **assert** statement. The auxiliary assertion (4) will occur at some specific place in the program P, say, to be specific, immediately after Linej of P. Then we require C to assert every fact about the state of the program's variables that is relevant at Linej, i.e., every fact upon which the correct functioning of P from Linej onward will depend. This important rule ensures that all the essential facts needed for proving the correctness of P are explicitly and formally written down in the auxiliary assertions added to P, and this is what makes a rigorous proof of correctness possible in principle.

Once the required assertions (4) have been added to P, we proceed as follows. Starting either at the first statement of P or at some one of the auxiliary **assert** statements in it, we move forward line by line through the program along every possible path (i.e., every path of control flow, which is to say every path that the program could follow during its execution. All possible paths through P which start at an **assert** statement but do not pass through any other **assert** statement must be considered one after another.) Because (by condition (a)) there are no infinite loops not passing through an **assert** statement, there can exist only finitely many such paths, and each such path will be bounded in length.

Tracing out all such paths q, we will use each of them in the following way to generate a set V of verification clauses. (With one exception, noted in (f), the *verification clauses* associated with a particular path q collect logical relationships between variable values which are certain to hold along q.)

(a) Suppose that the path q starts at an **assert** statement **assert** C, where C is a Boolean formula. Then we begin by putting C into V as its first clause. This simply reflects the fact that C is assumed to be true at the start of q.

(b) If the path q passes through an assignment statement of the form

(A) x := expn;

(where expn can be any expression) we introduce a new variable identifier x' (this identifier simply designates the value which x has after execution the assignment (A)) and add the clause

(B) x′ = expn

to V. Occurrences of x encountered later along the path q (but prior to any subsequent assignment to the same variable x) are then replaced by occurrences of x'. (But at and after any later assignment to x we replace x by yet another new identifier x''.) For example, the sequence of assignments

$$x := x + 1; y := y + 1; z := x + y; x := x + z;$$

would generate the clauses

$$x' = x + 1, \qquad y' = y + 1, \qquad z' = x' + y', \qquad x'' = x' + z'.$$

These rules simply reflect the fact that the new value x' which the variable x takes on immediately after the assignment (A) satisfies the equation (B), and that x retains this value until it becomes the target of a subsequent assignment.

(c) If the path q passes through an assignment of the special form

(C) x := **arb** s;

where s is some set-valued expression, then just as in paragraph (b) we introduce a new name for x, but in this case we add the clause

(D) x′ **in** s

to V. (This reflects the fact that the **arb** operator can select an arbitrary element of s, so that (D) asserts everything we can know about the new value x' given to the variable x by the assignment (C).)

(d) Conditional and unconditional **goto's**: If the path q passes through a control statement of the form

(E) **goto** Label;

then the path q must continue with the statement following the Label that appears in (E), but we add no clause to V at this point, since a simple **goto** does not test any condition or change the value of any variable.

On the other hand, if the path q passes through a control statement of the form

(F) **if** C **then goto** Label; **end**;

then the path q can go on either to the statement immediately following (F) or to the statement following the Label that appears in (F). In the first case, we add the clause **not** C to V; in the second case we add the clause C to V. These rules simply reflect the fact that **not** C must hold if and when q passes through a control statement (F) without the instruction **goto** Label applying, but that C must hold if and when q reaches (F) and the instruction **goto** Label is executed.

(e) The rules for more complex control structures, for example, general **if** constructs, **while** loops, and **until** loops, can be deduced by rewriting them in terms of the more primitive constructs (E) and (F) and then applying the rules stated previously. For example, if q encounters a multibranch **if** statement of the form

(G)
```
if C1 then
   block1
elseif C2 then
   block2
   ...
end if;
```

and then enters block2, it is obvious that we must add the two clauses

not C1, C2

to V. Later, if and when q passes from the last statement of block2 to the first statement following the multibranch **if**, no clause needs to be added to V, since this transition, like (E), counts as an unconditional transfer.

The rules applying to a **while** loop

(H)
```
(while C)
   body
end while;
```

are similar. If and when q passes through the **while** header, either by entering the loop from the statement immediately prior to (H) or by looping back from the final statement of the body of (H), we must add the Boolean clause C to V. On the other hand, if the path q encounters the **while** header but then leaves the loop (H) immediately, we must add the negated clause **not** C to V.

When q encounters the **end while** line in (H) it will go immediately to the loop header standing at the start of (H). Since this is an unconditional transfer we add no clause to V in this case.

When q enters an **until** loop we need not add any clause to V since entry to such a loop is unconditional. However if and when q encounters the **end while** terminating such a loop the action that we must take is a bit more complex. Suppose, to be specific, that the loop in question has the form

(I)
```
(until C)
   body
end until;
```

If, after encountering the **end until** statement, q exits the loop, then plainly we must add the clause C to V. On the other hand, if q encounters the **end until** clause and then loops back and continues with the first statement of the body of the loop, we must add the negated clause **not** C to V.

(f) Eventually, the path q that we are following will end at an **assert** statement

assert C′

Our aim is then to show that C' is necessarily true at the end of q, provided that the assertion C at which q starts (see (a)) is true at the beginning of q, and provided also that program execution does indeed follow the sequence of steps corresponding to q. It is most convenient for this purpose to add the negated condition

not C′

to V. After doing this our aim must be to show that the set V of clauses is inconsistent, i.e., that not all the clauses of V can be true simultaneously. This is equivalent to requiring that, taken all together, the clauses of V, other than its final clause **not** C', imply the condition C'.

(g) To complete the set of rules stated in the preceding paragraphs, we would need rules that tell us how to handle **procedure** definitions and invocations. However, since these rules are somewhat more complex than those stated, we omit them. This means that the rules that we have stated suffice for the formal verification of programs containing no procedure invocations, but not for programs which make use of procedures. This deficiency is not serious—it would not be terribly hard to remedy it, but to do so would take us beyond the limits proper to the present work.

Once we have taken a program P containing **assert** statements and generated the set V of verification clauses corresponding to each path q starting and ending at an **assert** statement (but not passing through any other **assert** statement), we are in position to prove the correctness of P mathematically. To do this, we must prove mathematically that each of the clause sets V which we have generated (i.e., each of the clause sets corresponding to a path q) is inconsistent. Suppose that we can succeed in doing this. We can then note that the clause CI initially placed in V is true by assumption, and that, with the exception of the final clause CF of V (see (f)) all the other clauses inserted into V are true in virtue of the very meaning of the statements which the path q traverses. Hence, by showing that V is inconsistent, we will have shown that if CI is true at the start of q, then CF is true at the end of q. Once this has been demonstrated for every path q through the program P (or, more precisely, every path which connects two **assert** statements but not through any other **assert** statement), it will follow by mathematical induction that every **assert** statement written into P must evaluate to **true** whenever it is reached, provided only that the **assert** statement standing at the very head of P is true at the moment that execution of P begins. (This initial **assert** statement, often called the *input* assertion of P, will normally summarize all the assumptions concerning input data on which the program P relies.) All in all, we will have shown that the truth of every assertion written into P follows from the assumption that its input assertion is true.

It is important to realize that this final step of a formal program verification, i.e., the step of proving that every set V of verification clauses corresponding to a path q between **assert** statements is inconsistent, is a purely mathematical task. That is, when we begin this task we will already have decoupled the work which remains from any entanglement with the control structures and other programming dictions present in the original program P. It is precisely in order to achieve this, i.e., precisely in order to transform our original program-related verification task into a purely mathematical question, that we go to the trouble of reducing the program P to the collection of clause sets V that it generates. Note again that, once all the necessary Floyd assertions have been written into the text of P, generation of the clause sets V using the rules stated is a simple mechanical matter, essentially a matter of systematic variable renaming and extraction of suitable portions of the statements encountered along each of the paths q.

6.6.2 Formal verification using Floyd assertions: an example

To apply the formal verification technique just outlined to the example we considered, we must insert an auxiliary **assert** statement into the **while** loop appearing in the example. We choose to insert this **assert** statement immediately after Line3 of (2). Call this place p. As explained, this added assertion must put on record every condition C which always holds at p and which would appear, implicitly or explicitly, in an informal proof of the correctness of the program (2). Since we have already given an informal proof that this simple program is correct, we already know what the inserted statement should say (namely it should say that (3) is always true at the beginning of an iteration). Such an assertion is easily written and inserted; doing so, we obtain

```
Line1:  prod := 0;
Line2:  iterations := 0;

Line3:  (while iterations /= m)
            assert prod = iterations*n;
Line4:      prod := prod + n;                      (5)
Line5:      iterations := iterations + 1;
Line6:  end while;

Line7:  assert prod = m*n;
```

Writing (5) puts us in position to generate the clause sets needed to verify the correctness of the program we are considering. There are just four paths through this program that need to be taken into account. The first of these is the path running from the start of (5) to the first **assert** statement in (5). By the rules stated, this path generates the clause set

$$\begin{aligned}&\text{prod}' = 0, \text{iterations}' = 0, \text{iterations}' \mathrel{/}= \text{m},\\ &\quad \textbf{not}\ (\text{prod}' = \text{iterations}'*\text{n})\end{aligned} \tag{6}$$

The second path that we need to consider runs from the start of (5), to the **while**-loop header but not into the **while** loop, and then to the final **assert** statement. This path generates the clause set

$$\begin{aligned}&\text{prod}' = 0, \text{iterations}' = 0, \textbf{not}\ (\text{iterations}' \mathrel{/}= \text{m}),\\ &\quad \textbf{not}\ (\text{prod}' = \text{m}*\text{n}).\end{aligned} \tag{7}$$

A third path between **asserts** runs from the **assert** statement following Line3, through the body of the **while** loop, and then back to this same **assert** statement. This generates the clause set

$$\begin{aligned}&\text{prod} = \text{iterations}*\text{n}, \text{prod}' = \text{prod} + \text{n}, \text{iterations}' = \text{iterations} + 1,\\ &\quad \text{iterations}' \mathrel{/}= \text{m}, \textbf{not}\ (\text{prod}' = \text{iterations}'*\text{n}).\end{aligned} \tag{8}$$

The fourth and final path that we need to consider is the one which runs from the **assert** statement following Line3 through the body of the **while** loop, but then exits the loop, passing through Line3 and then going immediately to Line7. The rules stated previously tell us that this path generates the clause set

$$\begin{aligned}&\text{prod} = \text{iterations}*\text{n}, \text{prod}' = \text{prod} + \text{n}, \text{iterations}' = \text{iterations} + 1,\\ &\quad \textbf{not}\ (\text{iterations}' \mathrel{/}= \text{m}), \textbf{not}\ (\text{prod}' = \text{m}*\text{n}).\end{aligned} \tag{9}$$

These are all possible paths not running through any **assert** statement, and hence these are all the clause sets that we need to consider. Once these clause sets have been generated it is easy to prove that each of them is inconsistent. In view of the simplicity of our original example, nothing more than elementary algebra is needed for any of these proofs. In (6), the first two clauses plainly contradict the fourth clause; in (7), the first three clauses contradict the fourth. In (8), the first three clauses contradict the fifth; in (9), the first four clauses contradict the fifth. This completes our formal verification of the program (2).

It is important to note that this formal verification is very close in spirit to the informal, English-language proof of the correctness of (2) that we gave earlier; the formal proof only regularizes and systematizes the informal proof. However, this formalization has the vital effect of making it possible to proceed mechanically, thereby ruling out the possibility of small errors. Strictly speaking, to be quite sure that error is impossible, the clause sets would have to be generated mechanically by an extension of the SETL compiler, and the informal proof of inconsistency which we have supplied for each clause set would have to be checked mechanically. This can be done, but not easily. As already observed, the clause-set generation process that we have applied to the example program (2) is quite general and will apply with much the same ease to any other long or short program which has been decorated with a sufficiently full set of assertions. However, for more complex programs the clause sets generated will not be as simple as (6), (7), (8), and (9). Program (2) involves algebraic operations only, and this is why the clause sets generated from it consist entirely of elementary algebraic formulae. Less elementary programs generally involve both algebraic and set-theoretic operations, and this will cause set-theoretic expressions to appear in the Floyd assertions and hence in the clause sets associated with these programs. (Several programs illustrating this remark appear in the verification-oriented exercises of Section 6.7.) To show that such clause sets are inconsistent is considerably less trivial than to deal with the clause sets arising in the highly simplified example that we have considered. Nevertheless, with care and sufficient effort the proofs required to show clause set inconsistency can always be checked formally after they have been constructed, by using only the tools which formal mathematics and symbolic logic make available. In this sense, the formal **assert** statement-based verification approach that we have described reduces the problem of rigorous program verification to a purely mathematical question, namely, that of proving the inconsistency of certain clause sets written in a formal mathematical notation. This is as far as we will carry our discussion of formal verification, since to discuss the mathematical problems that must then be faced would take us outside the scope proper to an introductory text.

6.7 Formative Influences on Program Development

At this point in our text we have presented programs ranging from the simple to the complex and have discussed both the pragmatic methods used to test programs systematically and the considerably more formal techniques that can be used to prove their correctness rigorously. The present section will discuss a deeper but more amorphous issue; specifically we will try to give some account of the formative influences which shape programs and which determine the features that programs typically exhibit. By gaining some understanding of this fundamental question we can hope to put other important issues such as program design and program testing into a helpful broader perspective.

To understand what underlying forces shape the development of programs, it is well to observe that ingredients of two fundamental sorts enter into the composition of a program. Material of the first kind serves to define user desires and expectations concerning an intended application, for example, the nature of expected input, and of output, including output text formats, graphic output, prompts and warnings issued by interactive systems, and error diagnostics generated by compilers. This material, which often constitutes the overwhelming bulk of a particular application-oriented program, is motivated by user-oriented considerations having an intrinsically nonmathematical character. Material of a second, much more highly algorithmic, kind also appears in programs. This internal program material creates the toolbox of operations which is used to achieve whatever external behavior is desired. Depending on the relative weight of program material belonging to these two categories (*external* and *internal*), a program can be called an *externally motivated* or *internally motivated* program, an *application* or an *algorithm*; one might even say a *superficial* or a *subtle* program.

Looking back over some of the programs presented in earlier chapters, it is easy to apply this distinction. For example, the shortest path code presented in Section 4.3.8.2 is an internally motivated algorithm (though not a very deep one). In contrast, the cross reference program presented in Section 5.8.1.2 of Chapter 5 has very little algorithmic content; most of its details relate to such external matters as the rules which distinguish words from punctuation marks in English text, and one whole procedure, namely *arrange* of this program, is needed only because we want to print lists of line numbers in a neat, easy-to-read tabular arrangement. Other examples are the quicksort procedure of Section 5.4.1 and the mergesort procedure of Section 5.4.2, which are both algorithms whose recursive structure gives them a certain depth in spite of their brevity, and the polynomial manipulation procedures of Section 5.1.3, which are also algorithms, albeit rather easy ones since they are little more than transcriptions into SETL of the ordinary algebraic definitions of polynomial sum, difference, product, etc. On the other hand, the Turtle language interpreter presented in Section 4.7.1 is externally rather than internally determined: this code uses no nontrivial algorithm but merely reflects the rules of the Turtle language in an almost one-to-one manner. The buckets and well program of Section 5.3.1 makes the distinction between internally and externally motivated code particularly clear, since one of its procedures, namely, the crucial *find_path*, is an internally motivated algorithm. All its other procedures are externally motivated, some of these relating to such issues as the acquisition and checking of initial data, although others merely serve to represent the rules of the problem itself.

The basic concepts and notations of mathematics, which SETL makes available as tools of programming, serve very adequately to define the internally motivated, algorithmic parts of programs. We have already seen that SETL's set-theoretic features allow mathematical functions to be described either in a deliberately succinct, "high" style which defines them very directly, or more procedurally by algorithms which compute these same functions, sometimes in surprising, clever, much more efficient ways. We have also noted that useful mathematical operations which are not directly provided by SETL can be built up by writing suitable families of procedures and have emphasized (see our discussion of the family of polynomial-manipulating procedures developed in Section 5.1.3) that such families should be written to hide the internal representational details of the mathematical objects they manipulate, allowing a user to think in terms of these objects (e.g., polynomials) rather than in more primitive set-theoretic terms. By using such approaches, by studying important algorithms carefully, and by consulting the rapidly growing technical literature of algorithms, which by now describes many useful, highly sophisticated ones, you will find that the purely algorithmic side of programming can be brought under a reasonable degree of control.

The externally motivated aspects of programs reflect a considerably more miscellaneous congeries of influences, for example, the physical or administrative structure of real-world systems; the form and sequencing of expected input and desired output; the reactions, including prompts and warnings, expected from interactive systems; and heuristic approaches used to manipulate physical or symbolic objects effectively. How can we come to terms with such varied material?

There has developed a large, though largely administrative, literature concerning the important problem of how to come to terms with external aspects of application design before the start of detailed programming. This is the so-called problem of requirements specification. Concerning the literature devoted to this problem, the astute observer G. J. Myers comments:

> Although no methodology exists for external design, a valuable principle to follow is the idea of conceptual integrity, [i.e.] ... the harmony (or lack of harmony) among the external interfaces of the system.... The easiest way not to achieve conceptual harmony is to attempt to produce an external design with too many people. The magic number seems to be about two. Depending on the size of the project, one or two people should have the responsibility for the external design.... Who, then, should these select responsible people be? ... The process of external design has little or nothing to do with programming; it is more directly concerned with understanding the user's environment, problem, and needs, and the psychology of man-machine communications.... Because of its increasing importance in software development, external design requires some type of specialist. The specialist must understand all the fields mentioned above, and should also have a familiarity with all phases of software design and testing to understand the effects of external design on these phases. Candidates that come to mind are systems analysts, behavioral psychologists, operations-research specialists, industrial engineers, and possibly computer scientists (providing their education includes these areas, which is rarely the case).

Though Myers's general remarks are helpful, it is still important to try to say something more about the organization of externally motivated, applications-oriented programs.

One important possibility in this area is to develop special applications-oriented programming languages whose objects and operations define useful standard approaches to important application areas. Even if such languages remain unimplemented and are not available to be run on any computer, their notations and general conceptual structure can serve as important tools of thought. In particular, in developing an application it may be well to write out a first version of the application in a helpful, even if unimplemented, auxiliary language. This first version can then be translated into SETL by choosing SETL representations for all the kinds of objects appearing in the auxiliary language and writing SETL routines which implement its primitive operations. Used in this way, the auxiliary language serves to tell us what families of operations can work harmoniously together, and into what procedures a SETL application code can most usefully be organized. For this reason, comparative study of numerous disparate application-oriented languages, for example, SNOBOL, GPSS, APL, COBOL, LISP, and PROLOG, is recommended as an intellectual exercise for the would-be programmer.

Another useful suggestion, which plays a role in the design of application-oriented programming languages, is to strive deliberately to write applications by using general mathematical operations rather than tailored special cases of them. Contrasting with this recommended practice, ordinary application-oriented code tends to mix internally and externally motivated program material inextricably; i.e., output details are allowed to control the choice of algorithms, and opportunities to generate output which an algorithm seems to afford are allowed to determine much of what the end user sees. The result is often an inartistic package, which meets user requirements only minimally, and which is full of redundant, hard to maintain, and inefficient algorithmic fragments. By separating external application design from choice and elaboration of internal algorithms much more cleanly, it should be possible to treat these two problems separately and thus to arrive at more satisfactory solutions to both of them.

A related suggestion is to use well-designed, relatively general-purpose application packages as building blocks for the construction of more complex applications. Consider, for example, the problem of designing an interactive system into which formatted commands will be entered to elicit system responses. As part of the design of such a system, command input conventions and command decomposition routines always need to be developed. It may be possible to handle this command input task by adapting a standard text editor very slightly. If this is done, the suitably modified editor will also serve to define and implement command facilities which can be as flexible and successful as the editor itself. This example illustrates the way in which well-designed, flexible application modules can be used, alongside internally oriented mathematical operations, as building blocks for more advanced applications. What is desirable is to familiarize yourself with a library of application-oriented modules which can be used somewhat as one uses a library of algorithms, but with the significant difference that they address more application- and user-oriented issues.

As we have said, much of the text of an applications-oriented program is nothing more than a restatement, in programming language terms, of external facts and rules pertaining to the intended application. Once one has found a way of representing these facts and rules in a form which is as succinct and clear as a well-conceived English language description of these same details would be, one has programmed these external aspects about as effectively as can be expected. Beyond this, the algorithmic content of a highly "external" program will normally be small. However, the following elements will often play some role:

(a) A few genuine but generally rather elementary algorithms may be used. For example, one may want to sort, perform a binary search, or put the data to be processed into some arrangment which makes it easy to locate significantly interrelated groups of data items.
(b) To improve efficiency, one will often apply the process of *formal differentiation* to an application-oriented code. This is the technique of speeding up the calculation of a quantity E that will be required repeatedly by storing its value in a variable value_of_E, which must then be updated whenever any parameter on which E depends is changed. (Whenever this common technique is applied, it tends to complicate the application code, since it replaces a single, integral, often self-explanatory computation of E by multiple scattered, harder-to-fathom updates of value_of_E.) A related technique is to replace direct use of set formers and tuple formers by loops which build these same values. Sometimes this is done in order to combine several such loops, all of which iterate over the same set, into a single loop. For example, in application-oriented code (and even in hand-optimized algorithms) one is less apt to see

```
num_rich_families := #{x in families |
                            family_income(x) >= 100000};
num_middle_families := #{x in families |
   family_income(x) < 100000 and family_income(x) > 5000};   (1a)
num_poor_families := #{x in families |
                            family_income(x) <= 5000};
```

than to see something like

```
num_rich_families := num_middle_families :=
   num_poor_families := 0;

(for x in families)

   if (income := family_income(x)) >= 100000 then
      num_rich_families + := 1;                              (1b)
   elseif income > 5000 then
      num_middle_families + := 1;
   else
      num_poor_families + := 1;
   end if;

end for;
```

The code (1b) arises from (1a) by expansion into loops of the three set formers appearing in (1a), followed by combination of the three resulting loops, and then by the application of a few other rather obvious optimizing transformations. Note that (1b), although much more efficient and not much lengthier than (1a), is not quite as obvious a piece of code; certainly (1b) is less brutally direct than (1a).

Internally motivated code passages, which is to say significant algorithms, use a much wider range of tricks than ordinarily appear in more superficial, application-oriented programs. (It is partly for this reason that it is well to separate internally determined from externally determined code sections: externally oriented code can often be ground out routinely once a good approach has been defined, whereas deeper, internally oriented code needs to be approached much more cautiously, more "by the book"). Formal differentiation, as described previously, also plays a role in the design of internally oriented algorithms.

Another important technique of algorithm design is exploitation of recursive mathematical relationships which express some desired function f of a composite object x in terms of values $f(x1), \ldots, f(xn)$ calculated for one or more smaller subparts xj of x. As noted in Section 5.4, relationships

$$f(x) = g(f(x1), \ldots, f(xn))$$

of this recursive kind underlie such high-efficiency algorithms as mergesort and quicksort.

Beyond these two most common techniques, the ongoing work of algorithm designers has already uncovered many sophisticated techniques which can be used to accomplish a great range of important tasks with remarkable efficiency. Some of these algorithms rest on quite subtle mathematical relationships, whose discussion goes beyond the scope of this book. However, your ability to devise truly effective approaches to programming problems will be strongly conditioned by your familiarity with the rich and growing literature of algorithms, and you are strongly advised to proceed with the study of this material as soon as you have mastered the more basic material contained in this book. A short list of useful collections of advanced algorithms is found at the end of this chapter.

Exercises

1. Into the bubble-sort code shown as (12) of Section 6.5.6, insert code which will count the number of iterations performed.

   Then:

   (a) Measure this number I of iterations for randomly chosen tuples of varying lengths L, and calculate the ratio of I to $L**3$, to estimate the constant C that should appear in the formula $I = C*L**3$ projected in Section 6.5.6. Do the same for quicksort.

   (b) How much more efficient than the bubble-sort method (12) of Section 6.5.6 would you expect quicksort to be, for sorting a tuple of 10 elements? For sorting a tuple of 100 or 1000 elements?

2. Take bubble sort and the mergesort procedure described in Section 5.4.1, and modify them by inserting code which will count the number of comparisons which

they make when used to sort a given vector *t*. Use them to sort tuples of length 50, 100, and 200, counting the number of comparisons performed and measuring their relative efficiencies. Try both tuples with random components, and tuples with only a few components out of sorted order.

3. Use the technique described in Section 6.5 to estimate the time required to sort a vector of length *t* using mergesort and also the time required to search for a specified component in a sorted vector using the binary search algorithm given in Section 5.4.3.

4. What set will be printed by the following code?

```
n := 10;
s := { };
(for i in [1..n]) s with := s; end; print(s).
```

If we changed the first statement to $n := 1000$, for roughly how long would you expect the resulting code to execute?

5. Compare the time required to execute the following codes:

```
n := 500;
s := { };
(for i in [1..n]) s with := 2*i; end;
```

and

```
n := 500;
s := { };
(for k in [1..n]) s with := 2*i, t := s; end;
```

What accounts for the difference?

6. Write a program which will execute the 10 elementary SETL operations which you consider most important, 1000 times each, and which will estimate the time required to execute each such instruction. To estimate the time required just to execute looping operations, your tests should compare loops like

```
(for i in [1..n]) x := y + z; end;
(for i in [1..n]) x := y + z; x := y + z; end;
```

The time difference per iteration is then clearly the cost of executing the additional operation.

7. Take the buckets and well program described in Section 5.3.1 and modify it by inserting code which will count the number of times that every one of its procedures is called and the number of times that every loop in it is executed. This information should be written to a tuple, and a general-purpose routine which prints this information in an attractive format should be designed and implemented.

8. A tuple *t* all of whose components are different from **om** can be represented in the "list" form described in Section 6.5.9, i.e., by a pair $[x1, f]$ such that $x1$ is the first component of *t* and *f* is a map which sends each components of *t* into the next component of *t*. Use an iteration macro to write short codes which convert a tuple *t* from its standard form to this list form and vice versa.

9. Rewrite program (2) of Section 6.6 by introducing labels and **gotos** in place of the **while** loop appearing in this program. More precisely, the **while**-loop header should be replaced by the following labeled statement:

```
Label1: If iterations /= m then goto Label2; end;
```

and the loop trailer **end while** should be replaced by the sequence

```
goto Label1;
Label2:        $ the final assert statement of (2) should follow this label
```

If we transform (2) in this way we can insert the auxiliary assertion

```
assert prod = iterations*n;
```

immediately after Label1. Make this assertion; then generate clause sets as in Section 6.6.1 and prove that the resulting variant of program (2) is correct. How does this proof compare in difficulty to the proof of correctness of program (2) given in Section 6.6.2?

10. A set-theoretic iteration

```
(for x in s)                                   (1)
```

can be rewritten as a **while** loop in the following way: We introduce a new variable *sc* (representing the collection of elements of *s* that have not yet been iterated over.) Then the loop header (1) can be rewritten as a **while** loop header in the following way:

```
sc := s;
(while sc /= { })                              (1')
x := arb sc; sc := sc - {x};
```

(The **end for** corresponding to (1) must be replaced by **end while**.) Applying this technique, prove that if *s* is a set of integers then the program

```
count1 := 0; count2 := 0;
(for x in s)
  if x > 0 then count1 := count1 + 1; end;     (2)
  if x <= 0 then count2 := count2 + 1; end;
end for;
```

gives the variables count1 and count2 final values satisfying the equations count1 + count2 = #*s*. Work out a full set of Floyd assertions for the program, and write out the clause sets generated by these Floyd assertions. A rigorous English-language proof that each of these clause sets is inconsistent should then be given.

11. Assume that *s*1 and *s*2 are two sets. Proceeding as in Ex. 10, prove that the program

```
count := 0;
(for x in s1)
    (for y in s2)
        count := count + 1;
    end for;
end for;
```

gives the variable *count* a final value equal to #*s*1*#*s*2.

12. The following incorrect mathematical proof contains a bug. What typical program bug does it resemble? How likely is it that a proof-bug of this sort would slip through in an (erroneous) proof that some program is correct?

Theorem. *Given any group of n balls, all the balls in the group have the same color.*

PROOF. (By mathematical induction) This is clearly true of $n = 1$. Suppose now that it is true for $m = n - 1$. Given a group of n balls, remove one, call it x. Then by inductive hypothesis the remaining balls all have the same color. Choose one ball in this group, call it y, and replace y by x in the group. This is still a group of m balls, so by inductive hypothesis all the balls in the group have the same color. This shows that x has the same color as all the other balls, so all n balls have the same color, Q.E.D.

6.8 References to Material on Alternative Data Structures: References for Additional Material on Algorithms

Reingold, E., Nievergelt, J., and Deo, N., *Combinatorial Algorithms—Theory and Practice* (Prentice-Hall Publishers, 1977) is an intermediate-level work which presents many useful techniques for generating combinatorial objects, fast searching and sorting, and graph processing. It also discusses the mathematical techniques used to estimate algorithm efficiency and can serve well as a guide to further reading in this important area.

The Design and Analysis of Computer Algorithms by A. Aho, J. Hopcroft, and J. Ullman (Addison-Wesley Publishers, 1975), which is more advanced, contains an excellent survey of many important algorithms, data-structuring techniques, and methods for determining the efficiency of algorithms. This useful book also describes various important techniques for proving upper bounds on the speed with which various quantities can be calculated. The first three volumes of Donald Knuth's famous *Art of Computer Programming* (Addison-Wesley Publishers, 1973) cover several important classes of algorithms (including basic combinatorial algorithms, polynomial manipulation, multiprecision arithmetic, calculation of random numbers, sorting, and searching) very comprehensively. Knuth gives many detailed analyses of algorithm efficiency and is the basic reference for this topic. Borodin and Munro, *Computational Complexity of Algebraic and Numeric Problems* (American Elsevier Publishers, 1975) is a specialized work which presents many algorithms for high-efficiency processing of polynomials and for related algebraic and arithmetic processes.

Numerical algorithms, i.e., algorithms for carrying out numerical computations, including solution of linear and nonlinear equations, calculation of integrals, solution of differential equations, and minimization of functions of several variables, have a very extensive history, which reaches back to the nineteenth century and beyond. A first-class modern inroduction to this classical area of computational technique is found in Dahlquist, Bjorck, and Anderson, *Numerical Methods* (Prentice-Hall Publishers, 1974).

Methods for treating systems of linear equations and inequalities form the content of the area of algorithmics known as *linear programming*. For an account of this interesting and important subject, see D. Luenberger, *Introduction to Linear and Nonlinear Programming* (Addison-Wesley Publishers, 1973).

Many areas of algorithm design have developed very actively during the last few years. One of the most fascinating of these is computational geometry, the body of techniques used for the rapid calculation of solutions to geometric problems. For an introduction to recent work in this area, see M. Shamos and G. Preparata, *Computational Geometry* (Springer-Verlag, 1985).

CHAPTER 7

Backtracking

7.1 Backtracking

Backtracking or *nondeterministic programming* is an ingenious technique useful for solving a very common and important type of search problem. Such problems can be regarded as logical or combinatorial "mazes" which a program must explore in order to find a desired solution point. In favorable cases, one will be able to do this by devising an algorithm which proceeds in relatively direct fashion from an initial position to a solution, along a path involving little or no trial and error. However, some problems are too complex for such algorithms to be available, and it is for these problems that the method of backtracking is most useful. Characteristically, programs for solving these problems encounter situations in which a decision must be made as to which of several alternatives is to be explored next, but in which no clear grounds can be found for making one rather than another decision. A correct decision will lead on to a solution of the problem being explored, but an incorrect decision will wind up in a dead end, and the program will have to revert to the point at which it took its first wrong turning and try an alternative originally ignored. Finding paths through mazes and solving geometric and spatial puzzles like "instant insanity" are obvious examples of this kind of problem.

The backtracking primitives to be described in this section make it easy to program solutions to these problems. Just two primitives, whose power at first seems almost magical, are required. These two primitives, whose workings we will describe in this section, are called **ok** and **fail**, respectively.

Ok is a (parameterless) Boolean-valued function, but one which we can think of as having a very major additional effect. More specifically, wherever **ok** is called, we at once "split" the entire global program into two copies of itself, identical except that **ok** yields the value **true** in one of these copies, and **false** in the other. After splitting, both these copies continue to execute independently and in parallel. If either of these copies subsequently encounters another **ok**, it will split yet again in the same way. If it subsequently encounters an occurrence of our second backtracking primitive **fail** (which is simply a parameterless statement) it will immediately cease execution and disappear. As soon as one of the copies into which the program has split reaches normal termination, all of the other copies disappear. At this point, execution of the program has been completed.

The way in which we really implement this kind of splitting will be described later in this chapter. For the moment, let us simply assume that such splitting is possible, and note how powerful and general its effects are. Suppose, for example, that a program needs to make a simple binary choice, say to perform one of two complex calculations, but that no algorithm for making this choice at that point is known. Then we can simply write

if ok then x := f1(x, y, z); **else** x := f2(u, w, v); **end**;

This creates two copies of our program, one of which executes the invocation of f1, the other one of f2. If one of these copies subsequently encounters the statement **fail** it will simply disappear. Hence (ignoring implementation difficulties) we can concentrate our attention on that lucky copy of the program which eventually finds the problem solution that we are looking for. From the point of view of this lucky copy, **ok** has acted as a magical oracle: when called, it returned one of the possible values **true** or **false**; the value chosen was always such as to steer the program past any lurking occurrence of **fail**.

Note that **ok** can be used to make any kind of choice, to make multiple choices, and to chose among multiple alternatives. For example, consider the following statement:

if ok then return e; **end**;

This splits our program into two, one of which immediately returns with the value *e*, while the other continues executing the section of the program in which the **if** statement appears.

To explore multiple choices, we can for example write

```
if ok then
    if ok then x := north(y); else x := south(y); end;
else
    if ok then x := east(y); else x := west(y); end;
end if;
```

This creates four copies of an initial program, within each of which one of the four functions north, south, east, and west will be invoked.

To choose among still more highly multiple alternatives, we can even write

```
if exists x in s | ok then
    return x;
else
    fail;
end if;
```

where *s* is a set. In this case, the iterative search triggered by the **exists** construct will iterate over all of the elements *x* of *s* in turn. For each such element, **ok** will be evaluated. This will cause a split into two program copies, in one of which *x* will be considered "ok" and will be returned, although in the other copy *x* will have been rejected and the iteration (i.e., the iterative search triggered by the **exists** construct) will continue on to the next element of *s*, again splitting, etc. This will create as many logical copies of the original program as *s* has elements, in each one of which one particular element *x* of *s* will have been selected and returned. (It will also generate a copy in which no *x* is accepted and the **exist** primitive yields **false**; but this copy immediately executes a **fail** and disappears.) This useful backtracking fragment can be embedded in a procedure:

```
proc choose(s);   $ nondeterministic choice procedure

if exists x in s | ok then
    return x;
else
    fail;
end if;

end proc choose;
```

The net effect of a call to choose(s) will be to split the program executing it into as many copies as there are elements in the set (or string, or tuple) *s*; each element (or character, or component) of *s* is the value returned by *choose* in one of these copies.

7.1.1 Implementation of backtracking

To implement the logical splitting implied by the **ok** primitive, one can proceed as follows. Each time **ok** is evaluated, make a complete copy of the state of the program in which it occurs. This should record the value of all variables, the sequence of procedure calls outstanding, the instruction currently being executed, etc. Call all this information an *environment*, and save it somewhere on a stack. Then give **ok** the value **true**, and continue the current computation. If the current computation succeeds in finding the solution it wants and terminates normally, nothing more is necessary. If, on the other hand, it subsequently executes a **fail** and disappears, then retrieve the last environment saved, and restart the computation from the state recorded in this environment, but this time give the **ok** which it is just in process of evaluating the value **false**. (Note that each environment saved contains all the information needed to restart a calculation from a prior point in its history, and that each of these restart points represents a calculation in the very act of evaluating the function **ok**). It is clear that this process of serial exploration will eventually either find the solution being sought or work through the history of all the split computations generated by successive evaluations of **ok**, to discover that all of them **fail**. In this latter case, an error exit is taken, and a diagnostic message is issued:

*** EXECUTED -FAIL- IN PRIMAL ENVIRONMENT

The preceding paragraphs describe something very close to the way in which SETL implements the backtracking primitives **ok** and **fail**. The actual implementation allows the semantics of these operations to be modified slightly, in part to improve their efficiency, in part to allow other, occasionally useful, slightly more complex effects to be obtained. First of all, rather than saving the values of all variables whenever **ok** is executed, the SETL system requires an indication from the user as to which variables should be restored to their previous values after a **fail**. When **fail** is executed, only the values of those variables declared by the user to be backtrack variables are restored. (Of course, the system itself will restore the stack, program counter, internal variables, etc.). The variables which are to be restored to their previous values after a **fail** are declared as in the following example:

var x, y, z: **back**;

In the presence of this (and only this) **back** declaration, the attribute **back** will be attached to the variables *x*, *y*, and *z*, and no others, and only those will be saved and restored on **ok/fail**.

We will illustrate the use of **ok**, **fail**, and the **back** declaration by using them to solve a simple but very well-known combinatorial problem, the so-called eight queens problem, which can be stated as follows:

On an 8 × 8 chess board, place 8 queens (i.e., pieces that move up, down, and diagonally) in such a fashion that no two queens attack each other.

Note that there is no obvious nonbacktracking approach to the problem. However, the backtracking primitives allow it to be solved easily.

We simply place queens successively on the board, in appropriate unattacked squares, until all have been placed. The **ok** primitive is used (as an oracle!) to ensure that we never make the mistake of placing a queen on an inappropriate square. If there were queens still to be placed but no unattacked squares left, we would have to **fail**, but we can take the complacent attitude that the values returned by **ok** will prevent this from ever happening. If for the moment we omit the necessary **back** declaration and postpone writing the simple function which tells us which squares are unattacked, SETL code for solution of the eight queens problem can be written simply as follows:

```
used := { };                          $ the set of board squares which
                                      $ are occupied by a queen

(while # used < 8)                    $ While not all queens have been
                                      $ placed

   possible := safe( );               $ squares which are not under
                                      $ attack

   if exists square in possible | ok then
      used with := square;            $ put queen on one more square
   else                               $ All squares are under attack.
      fail;
   end if;

end while;

print_board;                          $ Display the solution.
```

In order to complete this program, we must

(a) Decide on the variables which must be backtracked.
(b) Choose a representation for the board and specify the function *safe* and the output procedure *print_board*.

The variables which need to be backtracked (i.e., restored to their previous values after a **fail**) are those which will be used before being redefined following some **ok** and which also might be modified after an **ok**. In the preceding code, both *used* and *possible* must be backtracked. The iteration variable *square* need not be saved, because whenever we backtrack it is precisely in order to discard some previously chosen square. Thus, we only need the declaration:

```
var used, possible: back;
var board;
```

The representation of the board, and the nature of the procedures *safe* and *printboard*, are independent of our backtracking schema. For completeness, here is a possible description of these items:

(b1) The board is a set of positions, each position being represented by a pair of coordinates in the range [1..8]. (More economical representations suggest themselves, and you may want to invent some).

```
board := {[i,j]: i in [1..8], j in [1..8]};
```

(b2) The function *safe* iterates over all board positions and discards the ones which are under attack by queens placed in used squares.

```
proc safe;

return {square in board | (not exists queen in used |
            attacks(queen, square))};
end proc safe;
```

Finally, the predicate *attacks*($p1, p2$) establishes whether board positions $p1$ and $p2$ are mutually threatening:

```
proc attacks(p1, p2);

return
  (p1(1) = p2(1))                        or   $ p1 and p2 are on same row.
  (p1(2) = p2(2))                        or   $ or on same column.
  ((p1(1) - p1(2)) = (p2(1) - p2(2)))    or   $ or same upward diagonal.
  ((p1(1) + p1(2)) = (p2(1) + p2(2)));        $ or same downward diagonal.

end proc attacks;
```

The procedure *print_board* is left as an exercise to the reader.

7.1.2 Total failure

In our examples so far, we have assumed that the problem we are tackling actually has a solution. This may not always be the case. For example, how would the queens program behave if we specified a board size which was smaller than the number of queens to place? In such a case, the program would search through all possible positionings of the queens on the existing board and fail on each of them. Eventually, a final failure would be executed, for which no backtracking alternatives exist (all positions having been tried). At this point, the SETL system, having run out of options, would terminate execution in the manner indicated previously, i.e.:

*** EXECUTED -FAIL- IN PRIMAL ENVIRONMENT.

If we do not know a priori whether our problem has a solution or not, we may want to ensure that our backtracking program does not terminate abruptly upon terminal failure, but gives us some information as to the nature of the unsuccessful search (e.g., the number of tries) and perhaps awaits further input; that is to say, we want the program to retain control. This can be achieved by inserting a top-level **ok** to which we will fall back in case a search fails completely. This correponds to the following general backtracking schema:

```
if ok then
    (while not complete(solution))
      possible_move := moves(solution);

      if exists move in possible_moves | ok then
        solution := update(solution, move);
      else
        fail;
      end if;
    end while;
```

```
        display(solution);
        fail;                          $ by failing here we cause the next
                                       $ possible solution to be generated.
else
        print('Problem has no solution');
        ...                            $ Actions upon find failure.
end if;
```

As the following example will show, information about the history of a backtracking computation can be gathered in nonbacktracked variables, i.e., variables that do not appear in a *back* declaration. The values of non-backtracked variables are unaffected by the execution of **ok** and **fail**. An example of a variable that monitors the execution of a backtracking program is the variable *failure* in the tiling program shown in the following section. The variable is used simply to count the number of times **fail** was executed.

7.1.3 Tiling problems

The so-called tiling problem can be stated as follows: given a set of square tiles of various sizes, find whether they can be used to cover a rectangular area of given height and length exactly.

To solve this problem by backtracking, we use the following approach: we keep track of the perimeter of the area which remains to be filled. Initially, this is just the perimeter of the rectangle to be tiled. At each step, the bottom of this perimeter must include a "valley," i.e., a sequence of four vertices whose two middle ones are at a lower height than its first and last.

At each step of our exploration, we insert, into the lower left corner of such a valley, one of the remaining tiles whose width is no greater than that of the valley, update our description of the perimeter of the area which remains to be tiled, and continue.

In the code that follows, the condition that determines the acceptability of a given tile is expressed as a conjunction: we want to find a tile among those remaining which fits (i.e., is not wider than) an existing valley, and which is **ok** (i.e., which will subsequently allow us to place all remaining tiles and complete the solution).

The only data structure of special interest in this program is the perimeter of the area remaining to be filled. It is described as a sequence of points, listed in counterclockwise order, starting from the upper left-hand corner of the area to be tiled. Thus, the original perimeter constitutes a valley, and the first tile to be placed goes in its lower left-hand corner. Each point on the perimeter is described by an ordered pair of coordinates. Further details of the algorithm can be gleaned from the commented code that follows.

```
program tiling_puzzle;

$ This is a backtracking program that finds an arrangement of given set of
$ square tiles to fill in a specified rectangle. The area still to be filled is
$ specified by the global variable perimeter, which is the counterclockwise
$ sequence of vertices of the unfilled space that remains. The algorithm
$ proceeds by finding a valley in the bottom of the empty area into which
$ one of the remaining tiles fits.

    var perimeter,    $ Of area to be tiled.
        placement,    $ Of tiles already used.
        sizes_left,   $ Of available square tiles.
        count,        $ Of tiles in each size.
        corner,       $ Defining valley for next tile.
        next_size:    $ To be tried.
                      back;
var length, height,   $ Dimensions of rectangle to be filled.
        tiling;       $ For display of successive placements.

$ The following macros establish some geometric vocabulary. (See 8.2.)

macro abscissa(i);   perimeter(i)(1)   endm;
macro ordinate(i);   perimeter(i)(2)   endm;

$ Macros describing properties of edges.

macro up(i);       (abscissa(i) = abscissa(i + 1) and
                    ordinate(i) < ordinate(i + 1))   endm;
macro down(i);     (abscissa(i) = abscissa(i + 1) and
                    ordinate(i) > ordinate(i + 1))   endm;

start:
print('enter length, height of area to be tiled');
read(length, height);
print('enter tuple of tiles to be used');
read(tiles);

$ Verify that tiles can cover exactly the specified area.

if +/ [t**2 : t in tiles] /= length * height then
   print('no possible covering with this set');
   goto start;
end if;

perimeter := [[0, height], [0, 0], [length, 0], [length, height]];
placement := [ ];
sizes := {t : t in tiles};
count := {[t, #[t1 : t1 in tiles | t = t1]] : t in sizes};
sizes_left := sizes;

failures := 0;                    $ this variable keeps a count of the
                                  $ number of times we have backtracked
```

```
$ Define the topmost environment to which we will return in case of
$ complete failure.

if ok then
    (while sizes_left /= { })          $ Continue placing tiles.

      $ Find valley in current perimeter: there must be one.

      assert exists corner in [1 .. # perimeter - 2] | down(corner) and
      up(corner + 2);

    if exists next_size in sizes_left | fits(corner, next_size) and ok then

      count(next_size) - := 1;

      if count(next_size) = 0 then
         sizes_left less := next_size;
      end if;

      rebuild(corner, next_size);  $ Fill in perimeter.
      printboard;                  $ Display solution so far.

      else failures + := 1; fail;
    end if exists;
    end while;

      print; print('Solution:'); print; printboard;

else

          print('no solution for this set');
          print('backtracked,' 'failures,' 'times');
end if;

proc fits(c, tile);

$ Determine whether tile fits in the valley defined by the points c, c + 1,
$ c + 2, c + 3 in current perimeter.
$ Note also that we are assuming that all tiles are square.

return
    (abscissa(c + 2) - abscissa(c + 1)) >= tile and

      (height - ordinate(c + 1)) >= tile;

end proc fits;

proc rebuild(i, tile);

$ A valley exists, delimited by points i to i + 3, into which tile fits.
$ Note the placement of the tile at the lower left corner (point i + 1
$ on the perimeter) and update the area which remains to be
$ tiled.

placement with := [perimeter(i + 1), tile];
```

```
$ Calculate the position of the remaining vertices of the tile we have just
$ placed.

p1 := [abscissa(i + 1), ordinate(i + 1) + tile];
p2 := [abscissa(i + 1) + tile, ordinate(i + 1) + tile];
p3 := [abscissa(i + 1) + tile, ordinate(i + 1)];

$ new points on the perimeter of the (partially) filled valley.

new_points := [perimeter(i), p1, p2, p3, perimeter(i + 2)];

$ discard edges of length zero.

if p1 = perimeter(i) then new_points := new_points(3..); end if;

$ eliminate hairpin turns.
if p3(1) = abscissa(i + 2) then
   redundant frome new_points;
   redundant frome new_points;
end if;

$ Check for exact fit.
if p2 = perimeter(i + 3) then
   redundant frome new_points;
   perimeter := perimeter(1..i - 1) + new_points + perimeter(i + 4..);
else
   perimeter := perimeter(1..i + 1) + new_points + perimeter(i + 3..);
end if;

return;

end proc rebuild;

proc printboard;
...
$ Display successive tiling arrangements.

end proc printboard;

end program tiling_puzzle;
```

7.1.4 Other uses of **ok** and **fail**

The **ok** and **fail** primitives are useful in other contexts than those of backtracking programs. We will now describe two such less obvious uses.

7.1.4.1 Combinatorial generators

The generation of a set of combinatorial objects (all the subsets of a set, all the permutations of a sequence, etc.) can often be given a simple description using **ok** and **fail**. We precede the generation of each object from the desired set by an **ok**, and each time the construction of an object is completed, we execute a **fail** to force the generation of another object in the set. As an example of this, consider the problem of generating all the permutations of a set *S*. This can be done as follows: build a sequence by picking elements from *S* in any order; regard each choice of an element among the remaining ones as a backtracking point in order to force all possible choices to be made for a given position in the sequence. We also provide a top-level backtracking point, to which we return when all permutations have been generated. The following code shows the use of this technique:

```
proc permutation_generator(S);

var S, x, perm: back;

perms := { };
perm := [ ];

if ok then                          $ Topmost backtracking point.
  (while exists x in S | ok)
     S less := x;                   $ This element has been used.
     perm with := x;                $ And added to the current perm.
  end while;

  if S = { } then                   $ Add to set of permutations.
     perms with := perm;
  end if;

  $ Now force a different choice.
  fail;
else                                $ All permutations have been generated.
  return perms;
end if;
end proc permutation_generator;
```

7.1.4.2 Failures and exceptions

The **fail** primitive can also be used to exit from a complex calculation in circumstances in which the calculation cannot proceed any further. This mechanism allows a form of error handling which exists in some programming languages under various names (exceptions, on-conditions, etc.) The need for such mechanisms is particularly clear when we consider recursive programs which may uncover an abnormal situation (for example, invalid data) after a number of recursive calls. In such cases, it may become necessary to notify all pending recursive calls that an abnormal situation has arisen, and that the computation should not continue any further. This is a trifle awkward to program in the absence of some exception-handling mechanism. The **ok**/**fail** pair provides a simple mechanism of this type. We can establish a *recovery point* at the top level of a program by writing:

if ok then ...

The code attached to the **else** branch of this conditional statement is executed when a **fail** is performed during program execution (assuming that this is the only **ok** in the program). This code functions as an *exception handler*, and the **fail** is said to *raise the exception.* It is possible to program the handling of several exceptions, i.e., to execute **fail** under diverse abnormal circumstances, and to note in some global variable (accessible to the exception handler) what the nature of the abnormal condition is.

7.1.5 Nondeterministic programs, or it is ok after all

There is another way of looking at the backtracking primitives just described, which adds nothing to the technical details of their workings but sheds a different light on the meaning of backtracking. If we examine the sequence of choices made by a backtracking program which succeeds, then it is clear that those choices were correct: they led to the solution, after all! If we ignore the computer time which has been used, it is immaterial that the program may have come back several times to a certain **ok**, undoing its previous choice and trying something else; eventually, the proper choice was made. From the point of view of the end result, each **ok** was infallible! We can therefore think of the **ok** primitive as an oracle, which will somehow make the right choice when faced with various alternatives. (This explains the name: **ok** rather than a more tentative *try*, for example). It is instructive to think of backtracking programs in this fashion, ignoring the trials and errors which will be executed by the running program, and instead seeing each **ok** as a point at which we have said (to the run-time system): "You choose the right way. I don't know nor care how."

7.1.6 Auxiliary backtracking primitives

SETL provides two additional primitives, **succeed** and **lev**, which allow additional control over the backtracking mechanism.

7.1.6.1 Housecleaning: the **succeed** primitive

Our description of the implementation of the ok primitive should make it clear that a price is paid for each execution of **ok**; namely storage must be used to preserve the value of backtracked variables and other run-time information. This information defines the environment in which an **ok** is executed. The storage utilized by each execution of an **ok** remains in use until execution of a subsequent **fail** brings us back to the environment in which that **ok** was executed. In the case of a program that reaches a solution (or partial solution) after executing an **ok** statement, the storage thus occupied is useless, because we will not fall again into that environment. If space starts to run short, we will want to release this reserved space. This can be accomplished by invoking the **succeed** primitive. When invoked, all the information stored by the most recent execution of an **ok** is erased from the system. Execution of a subsequent **fail** will not return us to the environment of that **ok**, but to some earlier one, if such exists. In other words, **succeed** is a selective way of burning one's bridges behind one. Needless to say, this should only be done if the search has in fact succeeded.

7.1.6.2 Controlling the depth of the search: the **lev** primitive

The computational steps taken by a backtracking program can be seen to form a tree. Each node of this tree corresponds to some (partial) trial version of the solution being built. The descendants of a given node N correspond to the possible sequences of choices the **ok** primitive might make in moving forward from the situation corresponding to N. The root of the tree represents the starting state of the calculation. For example, in the eight queens problem, the root of the tree corresponds to the empty board, the nodes immediately below this node correspond to possible placements of the first queen, etc. In the case of the eight queens program, we can easily see that the full tree to be explored by the program has a height of 8 (counting the root to be at height zero) because there are only 8 queens to be placed. For some backtracking problems, the height of the solution may not have an obvious upper bound, which means that the search may have to perform many tentative guesses (**ok**s) and may have to backtrack correspondingly many times. It is often important to know the current depth of the computation, i.e., the number of **ok**s which have been performed, and to which it may be necessary to backtrack on failure. The value of the system variable **lev** is precisely that number. It is useful, when we happen to know that the solution for which we are searching cannot lie "too deep" in this tree to cut off fruitless searches over unpromising parts of the tree. In such cases, we can, for example, write

if lev > max_level **then fail**; **end**;

Exercises

1. Encoded arithmetic puzzles are a common form of mathematical recreation. In puzzles of this kind, digits are represented by letters of the alphabet, and then an arithmetic relationship is written. For example,

$$\begin{array}{r} \text{SEND} \\ +\ \text{MORE} \\ \hline \text{MONEY} \end{array}$$

To solve the puzzle, one must determine the digit value of each character. Such problems can of course be solved by a backtracking search through all possible assignments of digits to letters, but the following remarks suggest a more efficient approach:

(a) In each digit position, a carry is either present or absent. Depending on the assumptions which we make about carries, each digit position in an enciphered sum leads to one of several equations; e.g., if in the example SEND + MORE = MONEY we assume that carries are present in the second and third digit positions from the right, then we must have $N + R + 1 = E + 10$, i.e., $N + R = E + 9$.

(b) These equations can be used to eliminate as many variables as possible. For example, since the preceding example involves 8 letters and generates 5 equations, we can solve for the digit values of all 5 letters in terms of only 3 of them.

(c) A solution can then be obtained by backtracking through all possible values for the uneliminated letters, and all possible carry patterns. (In the example considered, this will mean that 32,000 possibilities are examined.)

Write a backtracking program along these lines. Your program should be able to solve any encoded addition problem. It should generate all possible solutions. Use your program to solve SEND + MORE = MONEY, and DONALD + GERALD = ROBERT. What modifications to your program are necessary if it is to solve encoded arithmetic puzzles for addition modulo 8?

2. After studying the 8 queens program presented in Section 7.1.1 write a modified, more efficient backtrack program for solving the problem which places queens one after another in appropriate rows of successive columns and exploits the fact that at most one queen can be placed in each row and column. Further modify this program so that it produces all possible solutions of the 8 queens problem but suppresses configurations that can be obtained from a known solution by reflecting the chessboard through one of its axes of symmetry.

3. Write an n bishops program which will place as many bishops as possible on an 8×8 chessboard in such a way that no two bishops attack each other. (Hint: For a somewhat more efficient program than would otherwise result, work through the diagonals of the board in succession, exploiting the fact that no two bishops can be placed on the same diagonal.)

4. Modify the tiling program given in Section 7.1.3 so that it works with rectangular rather than square tiles, where each rectangular tile can be placed either horizontally or vertically, i.e., can be placed in one of two orientations differing from one another by 90 degrees.

5. Write a procedure which uses backtracking to calculate and return the power set POW(s) of a given set s.

6. Let G be a graph, given as a set of ordered pairs, each representing an edge of the graph. A topologically sorted order for G is an ordering of its nodes such that each edge of G goes from a lower-numbered to a higher-numbered node. Write a program that reads in a graph G and then uses backtracking to generate all topologically sorted orders for it.

7. It is often straightforward to eliminate backtracking from simple backtrack programs by using recursion instead of backtracking. When this is done the information required for backtracking is saved in successive calls of a recursive procedure, **ok** is replaced by a recursive call which creates a new invocation rather than a new backtrack environment (cf. Section 7.1.1), and **fail** is replaced by the return of some appropriate value (e.g. **om**).

Apply this idea to develop recursive routines which solve the 8 queens and the tiling problems described in Section 7.1.

CHAPTER 8

Structuring Large SETL Programs

In the present chapter we round out our account of the control structures of SETL by describing certain useful facilities not covered in earlier chapters.

8.1 The **const** Declaration

It is often convenient to use a symbolic name for a constant appearing repeatedly in a program. Among other things, naming a constant and using its name rather than its explicit representation make it much easier to modify your program if modification subsequently becomes necessary. To define constants, one or more constant declarations are used. Generally speaking, such declarations will have the form

const const_name1 = const_expn1,
      const_name2 = const_expn2,
      . . .
      const_namek = const_expnk;   (1)

An example is

const pi = 3.14159,
  two_pi = 6.28318,
  vowels {'A', 'E', 'I', 'O', 'U'};

This example illustrates the following rules:

(i) Each const_namej in (1) must be a valid SETL identifier. By virtue of its appearance in (1), this identifier becomes a *constant identifier*, i.e., a synonym for the constant denotation, const_expnj, that follows it in (1). It retains this meaning throughout the scope of the identifier.

(ii) Each const_expnj appearing to the right of an equals sign in a declaration like (1) must be a valid constant expression. Such expressions are built out of the following:

(a) Elementary constant denotations, each of which designates an integer, a real number, or a quoted string.

(b) Constant identifiers, i.e., identifiers of constants introduced by earlier **const** declarations. For example, it is possible to write

```
const one       = 1,
      two       = 2,
  one_and_two   = {one, two};
```

This is equivalent to

```
      const one1        = 1, two = 2;
const one_and_two       = {1,2};
```

(c) Simple identifiers: an otherwise undeclared identifier appearing within a **const** declaration is treated as an implicitly declared string constant whose value is its capitalized name. For example, in the absence of other declarations, the declaration

```
const colors = {red, green, blue};
```

is equivalent to

```
const colors = {'RED', 'GREEN', 'BLUE'};
```

(d) Compound constant denotations can also appear in **const** declarations. Such denotations are built from elementary constants of the preceding forms (a)–(c) using set and tuple brackets but no other operators. This means that the constructs

```
const complex_thing   = [{'A', 1}, {'B', 2}, {{ }}];

      const let_1     = 'alpha',
            let_2     = 'beta',
          let_map     = {['A', let_1], ['B', let_2]};
```

are all legal, but that the declarations

```
const two_pi    = 2.0*3.14159;
```

and

```
const sixty_blanks    = 60*'  ';
```

are invalid, since they both involve operators other than set or tuple brackets. Note also that a nested construct like

```
const number_name = {[1, one], [2, two], [3, three]};
```

can be used even in the absence of other declarations. Assuming that no other declarations are present, this is exactly equivalent to the declaration

```
const one          = 'ONE',
      two          = 'TWO',
      three        = 'THREE';
number_name        = {[1,'ONE'],[2,'TWO'],[3,'THREE']};
```

(See (c).)

In addition to the **const** declaration form (1), the abbreviated form

const const_name1, ..., const_namek; (2)

is allowed. That is, some or all of the parts '= const_expnj' appearing in (1) can be omitted. An identifier appearing with this elision in a **const** declaration is treated as an implicitly declared string constant, whose value is its capitalized name. For example,

const one, two, three;

is equivalent to

```
const one   = 'ONE',
      two   = 'TWO',
      three = 'THREE';
```

Const declarations can appear in the same place within programs or procedures at which **var** declarations can appear (see Section 5.2).

8.2 Macros

Macros are abbreviations that obviate the need to write similar pieces of code repeatedly; they allow the SETL programmer to introduce and use various convenient shorthand notations for constructs that are used many times in a program. Macros, like procedures, are defined once and can then be used several times.

Macros and **procedures** resemble each other in that both give ways of associating names with bodies of code text and of invoking this code when the name is mentioned. However, when a macro is mentioned in a program after having been defined, the program text which it represents is substituted directly for the invoking occurrence of the macro name; this substitution is called *macro-expansion* and is to be contrasted with the detour-and-return action (see Section 5.1) triggered by a procedure invocation. That is to say, macros make use of a purely textual mechanism; they simply replace the name of the macro by its definition at the point where the name appears. This means that unlike procedures (which can be invoked before their definition has been seen), macros must be defined before they are used; i.e., the definition of a macro must appear physically in a program before the macro is first used.

8.2.1 Macro definitions

Macros in SETL are defined by using one of the following constructs:

```
(1) macro m_name;
      macro-body
    endm;
(2) macro m_name(p_name1, p_name2... p_namek);
      macro-body
    endm;
(3) macro m_name(p_name1 ..., p_namek; gp_name1,..., gp_namej);
      macro-body
    endm;
```

All macro definitions are bracketed with the keywords **macro** and **endm**. The form displayed in (1) is that of a parameterless macro. The construct (2) shows that macros can have parameters. The form (3) includes *generated parameters*.

After a macro has been introduced by one of the preceding constructs, it can be invoked simply by using its name, followed by appropriate parameters. We will now examine the use of these forms, starting from the simplest one, the parameterless macro.

8.2.2 Parameterless macros

Macros without parameters provide for the simplest kind of abbreviation: the name of such a macro simply stands for its macro body, which replaces the macro name whenever this name appears. For example, we can write:

```
(4) macro countup;
        t := t + 1;
        if t > limit then
        errmsg('out of bounds');
        end if
    endm;
```

Following the appearance of definition (4) in a program, module, or procedure, any subsequent appearance of the name *countup*, for example, in the line

```
(5) countup;
```

triggers replacement of (5) by the body of (4), i.e., by the four lines of SETL code shown previously (which of course increment and test the variable *t*).

We note that this replacement is made by the compiler, but it is not shown in the source program listing which the compiler produces. Line (5) appears in the listing as is. However, compilation proceeds as if the macro body of (4) had occurred instead of (5).

Our next example shows that a macro body need not consist of a group of statements, but can be any sequence of tokens, including sequences which are not meaningful in themselves. A useful macro which exploits this fact is

macro find; **assert exists endm**;

This macro can be used as follows:

find x **in** s | c(x);

to describe an existential search in cases where we are certain that a value exists that satisfies the given condition, and we need to find it.

8.2.3 Macros with parameters

Macros with parameters are introduced by macro definitions of the form

```
macro m_name(p_name1,..., p_namek);
   macro-body                                    (1)
endm;
```

Here, *m_name* can be any legal SETL identifier which becomes the name of the macro introduced by (1); p_name1, ..., p_namek, called the formal parameters of the macro, can be any list of distinct identifiers. The *body* of the macro can be any sequence of legal SETL tokens.

After being introduced by a macro definition (1), the macro *m_name* can be invoked simply by using its name, followed by a list of *k* actual arguments, at any place within a program. Suppose, to be specific, that this invoking occurrence is

m_name(arg1,..., argk) (2)

Then the SETL compiler replaces the macro invocation (2) with an occurrence of the *body* of the corresponding macro definition (1), but in this body every occurrence of a formal parameter name *p_namej* will have been replaced by an occurrence of the corresponding argument *argj*. We emphasize again that this is done by replacement of text, and not, as in the case of a **procedure** call, by evaluation of arguments and transmission of their values. This means that the arguments *argj* of macro invocation need not even be complete, evaluable expressions; indeed, they can be arbitrary sequences of keywords, operator signs, constants, or identifiers. (However, since commas are used to separate the successive arguments of a macro invocation, no argument of such an invocation can contain an embedded comma.) This gives macros a syntactic flexibility which procedures do not have and which is sometimes useful. Suppose, for example, that we wish to print out a series of examples illustrating the use of the compound operator in SETL. This could be done directly by using the following code:

```
v := [1,2,3,4,5];

print('Combining the components of v using the operator + gives', +/v);
print('Combining the components of v using the operator*gives', */v);
print('Combining the components of v using the operator max gives',
                                                              max/v);
etc.
```

By using a suitable macro, we can abbreviate this repetitive code, as follows:

```
macro print_op(opsign, op);
print('Combining the components of v using the operator', opsign,
'gives', op/v)
endm;

   v := [1,2,3,4,5];                                              (3)

   print_op('+', +);
   print_op('*', *);
   print_op('max', max);
```

This illustrates the possibility of transmitting an isolated operator sign to a macro as an argument; notice that no corresponding possibility exists for procedures.

For a second example illustrating the syntactic flexibility which sometimes justifies the use of a macro rather than a procedure, consider the common situation in which we need to check repeatedly for erroneous data and return some appropriate error indication if an error is detected. Suppose, to be specific, that these checks need to be made as part of some procedure, and that when an error is detected, we want the procedure to return immediately and to transmit an appropriate numerical error indication. The following macro is suitable for this purpose.

```
macro check(condition, error_no);

    if not condition then return error_no; end                   (4)

endm;
```

After introducing this macro, we can check for errors very simply, e.g., by writing

```
check(a < b, 1);          $ error number 1
...                                                               (5)
check(f(x) /= om, 2);     $ error number 2
... etc.
```

Note that a procedure invocation could not trigger an immediate return in the same convenient way that this macro does.

A syntactic point to be noted is that neither the body of the macro (2) nor the body of (3) ends with a semicolon. This is simply because it is most natural to put the semicolon which terminates an invoked macro body after the macro invocation which triggers insertion of this body (cf. (3) and (4)). Since a substituted body replaces each macro invocation, putting a semicolon both after a macro body and after its invocation would lead (after substitution) to the occurrence of a double semicolon. This is the reason why semicolons are omitted after the last line of the body of the macros (2) and (3).

As a final example, let us mention the oft-used macro which names the last component of a tuple:

macro top(stack); stack(# stack) **endm**;

This macro can be used in expressions as well as in assignments, for example:

x := top(v); top(v) := y + 1;

8.2.4 Macros with generated parameters

In addition to its ordinary parameters and arguments, macros can make use of generated parameters which play the role for macros that local variables play for procedures. To make use of this feature we write macro definitions having the form

macro m_name(p_name1,..., p_namek; gp_name1,..., gp_namen);
macro-body (6)
endm;

The additional parameters gp_name1, ..., gp_namen appearing after the first semicolon in (6) but not in (1) are called *generated parameters*. The programmer does not supply arguments corresponding to parameters of this kind when a macro like (6) is invoked. Instead, one invokes a macro like (6) in exactly the same way as the macro (1). However, when a macro like (6) with generated parameters is invoked, the SETL compiler generates new tokens (of an artificial form that cannot be used accidentally by the programmer) and substitutes them for occurrences of the corresponding generated parameter names in the *body* of (6).

A common use of this option is to generate a supply of fresh variable names when these are required for local use within the substituted body of a macro. Suppose, for example, that we want to write a macro which tests the value of an expression *e* for membership in a given set *s*, and which returns immediately from the procedure invoking the macro in case the test (*e* **in** *s*) fails. Suppose also that in case of failure we want to return both a numerical error indication and the value of the expression *e*. If we write

macro double_check(e, error_no); **if** e **notin** s **then return** [error_no, e];
end endm;

we would not get exactly the desired effect because when this macro is invoked, it will insert the actual argument for *e* in two places, which will lead to repeated evaluation of *e* (notice that *e* appears twice in the body). For example:

```
double_check(f(y) + g(y), 15);
```

would expand into

```
if f(y) + g(y) notion s then
   return [15, f(y) + g(y)];
end;
```

In order to avoid this double evaluation we can use the following macro:

```
macro in_check(e, error_no; temp) $ macro with generated parameter
  if (temp := (e)) notin s then return [error_no, temp]; end          (7)
endm;
```

To invoke this macro we would, for example, write

```
in_check(t + := x, 1);   $ error number 1
...                                                                   (8)
in_check(t + := y, 2);   $ error number 2
...
```

Note that if (as in (8)) an argument expression *e*, causing some side effect, is passed to the macro (7), it becomes essential that the value of *e* should be assigned to an auxiliary variable (the generated parameter *temp*) and that *e* should not be evaluated twice. Note also that each use of (7) will generate a new name for the parameter *temp* so that no accidental interference will occur between invocations of this macro. Finally, note the use of a precautionary extra pair of parentheses around the occurrence of the parameter *e* in the body of (7); these parentheses ensure that the argument transmitted to the macro in place of *e* will be handled as a unit, no matter what its actual syntactic form happens to be.

8.2.5 The lexical scope of macros: macro nesting

The scope within which a macro will be active is determined by the context in which its definition appears. A macro name introduced by a macro definition appearing in a procedure (respectively, a module, program, or library, but outside any procedure) maintains its meaning as a macro throughout this procedure (or program, module, or library), but not past the procedure's end. Note however that the macro can be redefined by a later macro definition appearing in the same procedure (or module, etc.) or can be dropped. (The way in which macros are redefined and dropped is explained in more detail in the discussion that follows.)

Macro bodies can contain invocations of other macros; and macro names can be transmitted to other macros as arguments. For example, suppose that we define the following two macros:

```
macro triple(pa);
    pa, pa, pa
endm;

macro q;
    'hello there'
endm;
```

Then, after expansion, the macro invocation

triple(q)

becomes

'hello there', 'hello there', 'hello there'

This example illustrates the fact that macro expansion is outside-in and recursive. That is to say, the expansion of a given macro body may trigger the expansion of an inner macro invocation.

Macro bodies can also contain embedded macro definitions. For example, the definition

```
macro def_x(pa);
  macro x; pa endm;                (9)
endm;
```

is legal. An embedded macro defintion *imd* becomes active when one invokes the macro *M* in which *imd* is embedded, thus causing the body of *M* to be expanded.

As an example, note that after expansion the sequence

```
def_x('aaa');
x x x
def_x('bbb');                      (10)
x x x
```

becomes

```
'aaa' 'aaa' 'aaa'
'bbb' 'bbb' 'bbb'                  (11)
```

This happens in the following way. The first line in (10) is expanded and, according to the definition (9), becomes the macro definition

macro x; 'aaa' **endm**;

Subsequently the second line of (10) is expanded. It generates the first line of (11). After this, the third line of (10) is expanded into

macro x; 'bbb' **endm**;

This changes the meaning of the macro x, causing the fourth line of (10) to expand into the second line of (11).

8.2.6 Dropping and redefining macros

If a macro is only needed over a limited portion of a program, it is possible to "undefine" it so that the name of the macro can be used for another purpose. To erase a macro definition, one uses the following SETL construct.

drop *macrolist*;

where *macrolist* is a list of macro names, separated by commas. Once a macro has been dropped, it is possible to give it a new definition, or to use its name for any SETL object, without confusion. For example,

```
macro x; print('now you see it') endm;
x;
drop x; $ this drops x from macro-status        (12)
x;
macro x; print('now you don't'); endm;
x;
```

expands into

```
print('now you see it');
x;                                              (13)
print('now you don't');
```

This follows since the first line of (12) makes x a macro equivalent to "now you see it," but then the third line of (12) drops x from macro status, so that the fourth line of (12) carries over unchanged to become the second line of (13). The new definition of x is then seen, invoked, and expanded.

Note that the compiler will see the line

x;

as an invocation of some unspecified procedure x. If no such x exists, the program will of course not execute.

Considerably more elaborate macro features than those we have described are supported by other programming languages, especially by assembly languages. However, high level languages like SETL have less need for complex macro features than do lower-level languages, and thus the macro facility that SETL provides will be found adequate for the use normally made of it. Let us remark that macros, like procedures, perform the useful function of hiding low-level details and thus help make a program more readable and more modular. The information-hiding capability of macros is most useful when we want to shield a program from possible changes in the structure of composite objects which it manipulates. The organization of a data base is a good example. Suppose that a library catalog is to be built. Each book has an entry in the catalog, which includes the title, author, date of publication, subject, and Library of Congress number. The catalog itself can be structured, let us say, as a map whose domain is the set of call numbers, and whose range is a set of tuples of length 5, containing the specified information. In this situation, we may find it appropriate to write

```
macro title(call_number)
   catalog(call_number)(1)
endm;

macro author(call_number)
   catalog(call_number)(2)
endm;
...
```

thereby hiding the tuple structure of the data from its user. This allows us to write

```
if author(x) = 'Barth'...
```

rather than having to recall that the author is stored in the second component of an element of the range of the catalog, etc.

8.3 Programming Examples

Frequently one will be given a map (or programmed function) and an initial element x and will need to iterate over all the elements $y = x, f(x), f(f(x))$, ..., performing some operation repeatedly until an **om** element terminating the iteration is reached. Iterations of this kind can be written as

```
y := x;

(while y /= om)
   body_of_iteration                         (1)
   y := f(y);
end;
```

However, if a program uses many iterations of this kind, it may be worth introducing a macro to abbreviate them. Using SETL's generalized loop construct such a macro can be written as

```
macro orbit(y, x, f);
     init y := x; while y /= om step y := f(y)
endm;
```

This macro enables us to write the loop (1) as

```
(orbit(y, x, f)) body_of_iteration end;               (1a)
```

Note that the iterator introduced in this way can also be used in set formers and tuple formers; e.g., we can write

```
+/[e(y): orbit(y, x, f)]
```

to form the sum $e(x) + e(f(x)) + \cdots$, which includes all terms $e(x), e(f(x)), \ldots$ up to the point at which f first becomes undefined.

Another commonly occurring but somewhat more complex case is that in which a map f is multivalued, and we wish to generate all elements y belonging to any sequence of elements $z_1, z_2, \ldots, z_n$ starting with $x = z_1$ such that $[z_i, z_{i+1}]$ is a member of f for all i in $[1 \,..\, n-1]$. (In mathematics, this set is called the *transitive closure* of $\{x\}$ relative to f). To iterate over the elements of this transitive closure (in some unpredictable order), we can use the following loop, which makes use of two auxiliary variables *to_process* and *seen_already*

```
s := {x}

to_process := seen_already := s;

(while to_process /= { })
   body_of_iteration
   y from to_process;                                  (2)
   to_process + := f{y} - seen_already;
   seen_already + := f{y};

end;
```

This loop can be abbreviated by introducing the following macro

```
macro trans_orbit(y, s, f; to_process, seen_already);
    init to_process := seen_already := s;
    while (to_process /= { })
    step y from to_process;
         to_process + := f{y} - seen_already;
         seen_already + := f{y};
endm;
```

Using this macro, the loop (2) can be written as

```
(trans_orbit(y, {x}, f))   $ y iterates over all the elements
                           $ of the transitive closure of f      (2a)
   body_of_iteration
end;
```

This iterator can also be used in set formers, tuple formers, etc. For example, we can write

```
+/[e(y): trans_orbit(y, s, f)]
```

to sum the expression e over all the points belonging to the transitive closure of s relative to f.

8.4 Programs, Modules, Libraries, and Directories: Structuring Constructs for Large SETL Programs

We have insisted repeatedly on the importance of organizing any program consisting of more than a few dozen lines into logically independent paragraphs, each of which performs a well-defined function in a manner free of close involvement with the details of other paragraphs. We also noted that the procedure, **case** statement, and refinement constructs are the main tools which SETL makes available to aid this kind of paragraphing. In the examples we have seen so far, programs were organized into a main program and a series of procedures. Above a certain size (say 500 lines) additional means of grouping collections of procedures into relatively independent units become necessary. Such collections are called *modules* and *libraries*. Two additional sections, one called the (main) *program* of the overall text being constructed, the other constituting an overall *directory* of the text are also required. In normal usage, each module and library will consist of several dozen procedures and will contain declarations of all variables directly accessible to all procedures of the module or library. The directory, which consists of declarations only, will indicate which of the procedures in each module are available for use in other modules and will declare a set of "program-global" variables that are global to the whole program and available to all procedures in all modules.

In this section, we will describe SETL's extended structuring concepts systematically and will illustrate their use.

8.4.1 Textual structure of complex programs

A *program text* can either be a simple program like those described in the preceding chapters of this book or a complex program. A *simple program* consists of an optional sequence of *declarations*, a *main program* part, and a collection of *procedures*; the role which all of these structures play has already been described in previous chapters. (See especially Chapter 5.) A *complex program* consists of the following items in sequence:

(1) a single *directory*, followed by
(2) a single *program* unit, followed by
(3) a collection of one or more *modules* and *libraries*.

We begin our detailed account of this family of constructs by describing the structure and purpose of module and library units. Each module consists of the following items in sequence.

(i) A *header line*.
(ii) Optionally, a collection of one or more *library items*.

(iii) Optionally, an *access specification*. If present, this will describe the relationship of the module to the other modules present in the same complex program.
(iv) Optionally, a sequence of *declarations*. If present, these will define variables and constants globally accessible to all the procedures in the module *M*, will call for certain initializations, and will specify the manner in which particular variables are to be represented.
(v) A sequence of one or more *procedures*.
(vi) A *trailer line*, which closes the module.

The following example shows all these features except (iii):

```
module logic_analyzer - syntactic_decomposition;
                                           $ header line
libraries lexical_analysis, error_reports;  $ library item
libraries error_tracing, error_reporting;   $ additional library item
var                                        $ declaration of 'module-global'
                                           $ variables
  Formula_grammar, Expression_grammar,

  Analysis_stack;

var                                        $ additional declaration
  Parse_status;                            $ global to module variable

const                                      $ constant declaration
                                           $ (also global to module)
  Expr = 1, Term = 2, Factor = 3;

init                                       $ initialization declaration
  Analysis_stack := [ ], Parse_status = 2*3;

proc parser(x);                            $ first procedure of module

  ...                                      $ body of procedure
end proc parser;

proc special_actions(y),                   $ second procedure of module
  ...                                      $ body of procedure
end proc special_actions;

...                                        $ additional procedures of
...                                        $ module would follow here
end module logic_analyzer - syntactic_decomposition;
                                           $ trailer line
```

This example illustrates the following general rules:

(i) The header line of a module consists of the keyword **module**, followed by a pair of identifiers separated by the sequence space-dash-space. The first of these identifiers is a *directory name*; it names the directory which comes first in the (complex) program containing the modules and must be the same for all modules in a program. For example, the module shown previously would have to follow a directory whose header line was

directory logic_analyzer;

and the other modules in this same (complex) program would have header lines like

module logic_analyzer – propositional_calculus;

...

module logic_analyzer – predicate_calculus;

...

(ii) Each member of the optional sequence of library items which then follow in the module consists of the keyword **libraries**, followed by a comma-separated sequence of library identifiers, each of which names one of the libraries in the complex program (see following discussion) which the module M needs to use.

(iii) The (optional) access specification which can then follow is described later in this section.

(iv) The optional declarations which follow after this have the same structure as the global declarations included in a simple program. **var**, **const**, **init**, and **repr** declarations are all allowed, and can be given in any order. **var** and **const** declarations appearing in this position within the module M specify variables having *module-global namescope*, i.e., variables accessible to all the procedures in M (but to no other procedures).

Libraries have essentially the same structure as modules, except that the header line of a library module begins with the keyword **library**, which is followed by a simple identifier (the library name) rather than a hyphen-separated pair of identifiers, as a standard **module** would be. Moreover, none of the procedures in a library can either access variables or invoke procedures declared outside the library. We can therefore say that, whereas modules constitute the chapters of a complex program outside of which they are not likely to be used, libraries contain self-standing collections of utility routines and are likely to be used in many different programs.

The single *program unit* required in a complex program has much the same structure as a module, except that before the collection of routines which it contains there must occur one or more statements constituting its *main program*. Execution will then begin with the first statement of this main program.

More specifically, a program unit consists of

(i) A header line, consisting of the keyword **program**, which must be followed by the appropriate directory name (see (i)) and then by the name of the program unit itself, these two items being separated by the sequence blank-hyphen-blank, as in

program logic_analyzer – main; ...

(ii) Optionally, a collection of one more library items.
(iii) Optionally, an access specification (just as in a module).
(iv) Optionally, a sequence of declarations (**var**, **const**, **init**, and **repr** declarations, as in a module or a simple program).
(v) The *main program*, i.e., a sequence of one or more executable statements.
(vi) An (optional) collection of one or more procedures.
(vii) A trailer line, terminating the program unit.

Note again that if optional items (ii) and (iii) are omitted, we will have exactly a simple program of the stand-alone sort that could be used without a directory.

Next we describe the structure of a *directory*; this will also explain the structure and purpose of the *directory item* (cf. (iii)) that can be included in any module, library, or program unit. A directory consists of

(i) A header line;
(ii) Optionally, a set of declarations (**var**, **const**, **init**, and **repr** declarations, exactly as in a module or library);
(iii) A single **program** descriptor;
(iv) A sequence of **module** descriptors, one for each module which follows the directory;
(v) A trailer line, which terminates the directory.

These objects are subject to the following general rules:

(i) The header line of a directory consists of the keyword **directory**, followed by an identifier which names the directory, as in

directory logic_analyzer;

As already stated, this identifier must be repeated in all the modules, and also in the main program unit which follows the directory

(ii) The optional **var** and **const** declarations occurring in the directory define the names of program-global variables and constants accessible to (the main program and) all procedures (other than library procedures) in the complex program in which the directory appears. The optional **init** declarations appearing in the directory serve to initialize these program-global variables, and any **repr** declarations appearing in the directory serve to define representations for these variables.

(iii, iv) The program descriptor and module descriptors which come next serve to define the manner in which the program unit and modules which follow the directory are allowed to access the global variables declared in the directory and also determine which procedures in which modules can be invoked by procedures in other modules. The syntactic form of these descriptors is

(for a program descriptor) **program** *directory name—program name*; access specification;
(for a module descriptor) module *directory name—module name*; access specification;

That is, the first part of each such program or module descriptor is identical with the header line of the program or module it describes; but this first part must then be followed by an *access specification*. Such an *access specification* has the following components:

(a) an (optional) item of each of four possible types: **reads**, **writes**, **imports**, and **exports** items.
(b) an (optional) **repr** declaration.

A **reads** (or **writes**) item consists of the keyword **reads** (or **writes**) followed either by a list of names of program-global variables and constants, or by the keyword **all**. This is shown in

reads all;
writes Phase, Subphase;

These items serve to define the program-global variables and constants which are read (or written) by one or more of the procedures in some module (or in the main program of a program unit) of a complex program.

An **imports** item lists and describes all the procedures defined elsewhere which are used within a unit. It consists of the keyword **imports**, followed by a sequence of *procedure descriptors*, each of which is identical to the header line of the procedure being described (but omitting the keyword **proc** or **procedure**). Procedure parameters which are read-only, write-only, or read-write must be declared in the procedure descriptor of an **imports** statement in precisely the same way as they are declared in the header line of the corresponding procedure, i.e., must use **rd**, **wr**, or **rw**, precisely where these occur in the header line. This is shown in the following examples:

```
directory logic_analyzer;
...

module logic_analyzer - propositional_calculus;

imports      b1(x),              $ a one-parameter function
             b2(rw x, rd y),
             b3(x, y, z(*));     $ procedure with variable number of
                                 $ parameters
             ...

module logic_analyzer - predicate_calculus;

imports      a1(x, y, rw z),
             a2;                 $ parameterless procedure
...
```

```
end directory;                      $ directory trailer line

module logic_analyzer - propositional calculus;
...
proc        a1(x, y, rw z);     $ note correspondence with preceding
                                $ declaration
...
end proc    a1;

proc        a2;                 $ parameterless procedure
...
end proc    a2;
...
end module logic_analyzer - propositional calculus; $ trailer line

module logic_analyzer - predicate_calculus;
...
proc        b1(x);              $ a one-parameter function
...
end proc    b1;

proc        b2(rw x, rd y);     $ note correspondence with preceding
                                $ declaration
...
end proc    b2;

proc        b3(x, y, z(*));     $ procedure with variable number of
                                $ parameters
...
end proc    b3;
...
end module logic_analyzer - predicate_calculus;
```

An **exports** item lists and describes all the procedures which a given module makes available for use within other program units or modules. Aside from the fact that the keyword **imports** is replaced by **exports**, it has exactly the same form as an **imports** item and is subject to the same restrictions.

Note that no procedure can be in the **exports** list of more than one module. On the other hand, a procedure defined within a module *M1* but neither exported nor imported by it will be local to the module and can very well have the same name as a different procedure defined in another module *M2*, even if *M2* exports (but *M1* does not import) this procedure.

An access specification occurring in a module, program, or library has the same form, and is subject to the same restrictions, as an access specification in a directory. Such an access specification is used to document the global variable accesses made and the procedures exported and imported by the module, program, or library in which it occurs and is used *only* for documentation, so that if it occurs at all it should be identical with the access specification supplied for the same module or program in the **directory** which precedes it. Since libraries can neither access program-global variables nor **import** procedures from a module or program, an access specification in a library must consist of a single **exports** item only. As with modules, a procedure P defined in a library but not exported by it is local to the library and can have the same name as a different procedure defined in some other library, program, or module.

Note that the libraries imported by a module or program, or by another library, are not listed in the directory which precedes them. Instead, they are listed in a library item within the importing module, program, or library. A module, program, or library $L1$ which lists another library $L2$ automatically imports all the procedures and functions which $L2$ exports.

A concluding note concerning use of these facilities: in subdividing large programs into modules and libraries, one's main aim will be to subdivide the full collection of procedures which constitute it (possibly amounting to many hundreds of procedures altogether) into sensible chapters, each containing procedures which are relatively tightly coupled to each other but which are only loosely coupled to procedures placed in other modules or libraries. Close couplings will develop if procedures share variables globally, or when one procedure makes detailed assumptions about many of the data structures used by another. Procedures should be structured, and partitioned among modules and libraries, in ways calculated to avoid these couplings and to minimize them effectively when they are unavoidable. It is particularly important to avoid accumulation of large numbers of shared global variables at either the **module** or the **directory** (i.e., program-global) level.

Ideally, a **module** should consist of no more than a few dozen procedures and should be considered a candidate for further subdivision when this informal limit is exceeded.

8.4.2 Separate compilation and binding of program subsections

When long SETL programs (i.e., programs more than a few thousand lines long) are being developed, the time required for compilation becomes significant. To have to spend much time recompiling long programs after just a few of their lines have been changed is annoying, and to obviate this annoyance the SETL system allows the modules and libraries of a large program to be compiled separately. Precompiled forms of such modules and libraries (called *Q1*, or intermediate code, files) can then be saved and combined or *bound* with other subsequently compiled program sections, to produce a final, executable, SETL program. Moreover, the SETL compiler can be used to combine several separately produced intermediate code files into one single file of the same

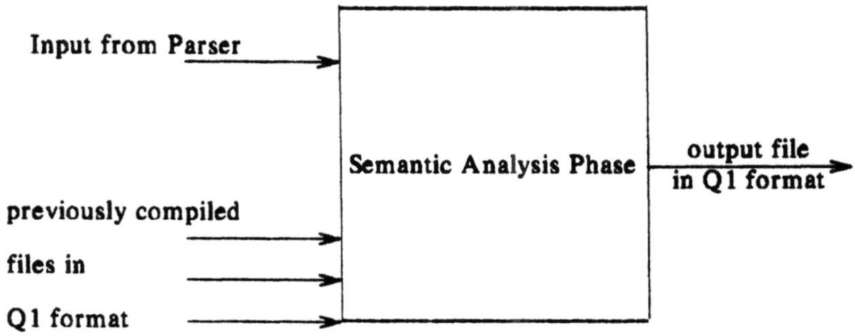

Figure 8.1 Inputs and Outputs of the SETL Compiler When the *bind* Option is used

format, thereby saving part of the expense of repeated intermediate code file binding.

The form of intermediate code saved for subsequent binding is exactly the form of code produced as output by the second (semantic analysis) phase of the SETL compiler (as we have noted earlier, this output is called *Q1 text*). To save this output for subsequent binding, you must either

(a) Run the first two phases of the SETL compiler, without running its third phase.

or

(b) Save the *Q1* file after the third phase (code generation phase) (which otherwise deletes it). To prevent this deletion the control-statement option *save intermediate file* (SIF) must be set. (See 9.4.1.2.)

When several separately compiled modules and libraries, all available in *Q1* format, are being bound together, they are first read in order, and digested by the SETL compiler's second (semantic analysis) phase. After this, the semantic analysis phase reads any additional files representing source code newly parsed by the first compiler phase (the parse phase). All these files are then combined, and a single composite *Q1* format file representing all this input analysis is output by the semantic phase. This output can itself be saved and combined (at a later time) with still other *Q1* format files and with fresh parse output to produce a still longer *Q1* file. Alternatively, a *Q1* format file representing a complete SETL program can be passed to the compiler's code generation phase, to be turned into code and then executed. Figure 8.1 shows the main inputs to and outputs from the compiler's semantic analysis phase when it is used in the manner just outlined to bind separately compiled modules together.

A file in *Q1* format always represents a (parsed and semantically analyzed) sequence of SETL source modules and libraries, in some specific order, and could be produced simply by arranging this source code in appropriate order and compiling it. The rule determining the logical order of modules in a *Q1* format file produced by binding is explained in the following discussion:

The inputs to the compiler's semantic analysis phase are as follows:

(i) Two files, called *pol* and *xpol*, which are passed from the first (parse) phase of the compiler to the semantic analysis phase. Together, these two files represent a SETL source text in parsed form, ready for semantic analysis.
(ii) An additional file, called *bind*. This is a *Q1* format file representing precompiled modules that are to be combined with the newly parsed material represented by the *pol* and *xpol* files.
(iii) If necessary, a third file, called *ibind*. If supplied, the ibind file is simply a list of file names (which should have whatever file name format is required by the operating system under which you are running.) If an *ibind* file is supplied, the files named in it (each of which must be a *Q1* format file) are read one after another by the semantic analysis phase and combined with the *pol*/*xpol* material (i) and the *bind* file (ii), to produce one composite *Q1* format file as output.

The *Q1* format file produced as output by the semantic analysis phase can be regarded as the parsed, semantically analyzed form of a certain SETL source text. This text is exactly what would be obtained by concatenating the following subtexts, in order:

(a) First, the source text corresponding to the *bind* file;
(b) Next, the various source texts corresponding to the successive *Q*1 format files mentioned in the *ibind* file;
(c) Finally, the source text represented by the *pol* and *xpol* files.

Suppose, for example, that we are working with the complex-program 'logic_analyzer' whose structure is shown in the preceding section. This consists of the following principal subdivisions:

> **directory** logic_analyzer;
> ...
> **end directory**;
>
> **program** logic_analyzer – logic_main;
> ...
> **end program**;
>
> **module** logic_analyzer – propositional_calculus; (1)
> ...
> **end module**;
>
> **module** logic_analyzer – predicate_calculus;
> ...
> **end module**;

We could proceed in the following way, via a sequence of separate compilation steps, to produce a version of this program ready for execution:

(i) First, the directory can be compiled, and saved in *Q1* format, let us say in a file called DIRECT.Q1 (here, and in the next few paragraphs, we use file-naming conventions appropriate to the DEC VAX/VMS operating system.)

(ii) Next, the program and the propositional_calculus module can be compiled (separately) and the results of these two compilations stored as two *Q1* format files named MAIN.Q1 and PROPOS.Q1.

(iii) Finally, the predicate_calculus module can be compiled and combined with the precompiled material (i) and (iii). To do this, the final compilation could have the source text of the predicate_calculus module as its SETL source input and in addition have the file DIRECT.Q1 as its *bind* parameter. The *ibind* parameter should then be a file (possible called XTRAQ1.LIS) of file names, which should contain just the following two lines:

MAIN.Q1
PROPOS.Q1

As soon as the semantic analysis phase has finished processing its input, *Q1* format output representing the parsed, semantically analyzed form of the source text (1) will result.

In using the binding mechanisms that have just been explained, the following facts should be noted:

(a) Either of the *bind* and the *ibind* parameters can be omitted, in which case no attempt will be made to read, or to bind in, the corresponding *Q1* files.

(b) If only binding of previously compiled *Q1* format files is desired, pol and xpol files produced by parsing an empty SETL input file can be passed, along with appropriate *bind* and *ibind* parameter files, to the semantic analysis phase of the compiler for binding.

CHAPTER 9

Input/Output and Communication with the Environment

In this chapter, we cover various SETL capabilities that have been ignored in the preceding chapters. These include additional facilities for input/output, for sensing aspects of the environment in which a SETL program is running, and for passing strings or integers as parameters to SETL runs in a particularly convenient way. A full account of all the memory options and listing control commands which can be used to modify various aspects of SETL compilation and execution is given.

9.1 Input-Output Facilities

Although less developed than those of some other languages, the input-output facilities of SETL are adequate for most ordinary applications. Facilities for reading and writing simple string input, structured input representing SETL objects, and input/output using an internal *binary* format which can be handled more efficiently than SETL's structured input are supported. Relatively powerful string facilities available in SETL can also be used to format text that is to be printed.

The SETL I/O operations deal with files of two kinds:

(a) *Text* (also called *coded* files), which can be read, either as sequences of lines (which are read in as simple character strings, using **get**, described later), or as structured encodings of SETL objects (possibly extending over multiple lines; these are read in using **read**).

(b) *Binary* files. These can only be written using **putb** and can only be read using **getb** (see following discussion). These files store SETL objects in an internal representation and are read or written more efficiently than coded files.

All files are treated in strictly *sequential* fashion by the SETL I/O primitives. That is, a file is regarded as a logical sequence (either of strings or of SETL objects) from which input can only be read sequentially, starting with the first item in the file, and reading through the file to its last item, until end-of-file is eventually reached. Read operations are performed by **read**, **reada**, **get**, or **getb**. Output operations (i.e., **print**, **printa**, **put**, or **putb**) always add items to the end of a file, thereby making it longer. At each moment, a given file can only be used either for input or for output, not both, and must be used in one of the two mutually exclusive modes (a) or (b), depending on whether the file contains binary or coded information.

The input-output operations which SETL supports are as follows:

(i) **open**(file, mode). This opens the file specified by its first argument, thereby making the file available for other operations. Both arguments of the **open** operation are strings. The forms acceptable for the first argument are machine-dependent since they are identical with the form of file names as defined by the execution environment. For example, on the DEC VAX running under the VMS operating system, the following file parameters would all be acceptable:

```
open('data.','CODED');                    $ simple file name
open('test.dat','BINARY-IN');             $ qualified file name
open('[dewar.doc]book.txt','CODED');      $ directory name followed
                                          $ by file name
```

The second argument of the **open** function must be one of the following quoted strings:

'BINARY'	(same as BINARY-IN)
'BINARY-IN'	opens file for input by GETB
'BINARY-OUT'	opens file for output by PUTB
'CODED'	(same as CODED-IN)
'CODED-IN'	opens file for input by READ, READA, and GET
'CODED-OUT'	opens file for output by PRINT, PRINTA, and PUT
'PRINT'	opens file for output by PRINT, PRINTA, and PUT Files opened in this manner will include special 'carriage control' characters; see below for details.
'TEXT'	(same as 'CODED-IN')
'TEXT-IN'	(same as 'CODED-IN')
'TEXT-OUT'	(same as 'CODED-OUT')

The **open** *primitive* returns the value **true** if the operation of opening the file succeeds, **false** if this operation fails. Since the **open** operation always involves communication with an underlying operating system, the meaning of success and failure is environment-dependent to a certain degree. Generally speaking, however, opening a file for input will succeed if a file having the name specified in the **open** operation is available in the operating environment and has not already been opened; opening a file for output will succeed if the file has not already been opened. Opening an already opened file causes an error.

(ii) **close**(file). This terminates input/output to a file established by a prior call to **open** and releases the file to the operating environment.

(iii) **get**(file, lhs1, ..., lhsk): This gets successive lines from the specified file and assigns them (as strings) to lhs1, ..., lhsk in turn. (Here and later, lhs1, ..., lhsk must be either simple variables or expressions which can legally occur on the left-hand side of an assignment statement.) Lines read by **get** should not ordinarily be enclosed in quote characters; if quote characters occur in such lines, they will be treated not as string delimiters but as parts of the string being read. For example, if the first two lines of a file 'xxx' are

THIS IS LINE 1
'THIS IS LINE 2'

then the effect of the **get** statement

get('xxx', lna, lnb);

is exactly the same as that of the pair of assignments

lna := 'THIS IS LINE 1';
lnb := '''THIS IS LINE 2''';

If **get** encounters end of data on the file that it is reading, it (like **read**, see Section 4.8) behaves as if it had read an **om**.

To get input from the standard input file, the standard file name 'INPUT' should be used.

(iv) **getb**(file, lhs1, ..., lhsk). This reads successive SETL objects from the specified file and assigns them to lhs1, ..., lhsk in turn. (As in the case of **get**, lhs1, ..., lhsk must be expressions which could legally appear on the left-hand side of an assignment.) In this case, the file being read must be a SETL binary file and must have been opened by the command **open**(file, 'BINARY-IN'). Note that a SETL binary file will almost always have been created by using **putb**.

If **getb** encounters end of data on the file that it is reading, it behaves as if it has read an **om**.

(v) **print**(expn1, ..., expnk). This writes the values of expn1, ..., expnk to the standard output file.

(vi) **printa**(file, expn1, ..., expnk). This is similar to **print**, except that its first argument is the name of a file (of type 'CODED') to which the output produced by this operation is written.

(vii) **put**(file, expn1, ..., expnk). This writes text lines to the file specified by its first argument, which must be of type 'CODED'. The expressions expn1, ..., expnk must evaluate to strings. Each such expression causes a single line to be sent to the specified file.

(viii) **putb**(file, expn1, ..., expnk). This writes the values of expn1, ..., expnk to the specified file, which must be a SETL binary file and must have been opened by the command **open**(file, 'BINARY-OUT'). Here expn1, ..., expnk can be arbitrary SETL values.

Provided that they involve no atoms, values written by **putb** can always be read back in **getb**. (The special rules which govern the handling of atoms by **putb** and **getb** are explained in the following discussion.) Note that the very desirable symmetrical relationship between **putb** and **getb** that this rule reflects does not hold for **printa** and **reada**, simply because strings written by **printa** will not include the quotation marks which **reada** requires. Hence, if you want to write SETL objects to external media for temporary storage and then read them back you must do so by using **putb** and **getb**, rather than **printa** and **reada**.

(ix) **read**(lhs1, ..., lhsk). This reads a sequence of SETL values from the standard input file. (As in the case of **get**, lhs1, ..., lhsk must be expressions which could legally appear on the left-hand side of an assignment.)

If **read** encounters end of data, it behaves as if it had read an **om**.

(x) **reada**(file, lhs1, ..., lhsk). This is similar to **read**, except that its first argument is the name of a file (of type 'CODED') from which the input produced by the **reada** operation will be obtained.

(xi) **eof**. This is a nulladic opertion which yields **true** if the most recent input operation executed (which will be either a **read**, **reada**, **get**, or **getb** operation) reached the end of the file being read; otherwise **eof** yields **false**.

Since every input operation affects the value of **eof**, it may become necessary in some programs to save **eof** values by assigning them explicitly to auxiliary variables.

(xii) **eject**( ) or **eject**(file). This writes a page eject character to the specified file, or, if no file is specified, sends a page eject to the standard output file. The file to which an eject command is directed must either be the standard output file or must have been opened by using the command **open**(file, 'PRINT'). Only files opened in this way can accept carriage-control characters like the "eject" character.

(xiii) **title**( ) or **title**(str). These operations initiate and suspend generation of titles for the standard output file. **title**(str) must have a string-valued argument. **title** causes a page eject on the standard output file and establishes its argument as the title string, which then appears at the head of all subsequent pages (until the title is changed later by another **title** command). Titled pages are numbered sequentially. **title** with no argument disables generation of titles.

Note that if the **put** primitive is used with a file which was opened by an **open**(file, 'PRINT') command and which is intended for printing, the first character of each line of the file printed will be treated as a carriage control character rather than as a normal print character. Characters treated in this way will not be printed, and their presence may cause unexpected page ejects or other undesirable effects. For this reason, the **put** primitive should not be used in place of **print** or **printa** except by programmers familiar with carriage-control conventions.

The **putb** primitive can be used to write atoms to a BINARY file. These atoms can be read back by **getb**. Note however that if a file containing atoms is read in by a program that has just started to run, regeneration of atoms will restart at atom number 1, and hence some of the newly generated atoms may appear to be identical with old atoms obtained from a file via **getb**. To avoid difficulties in this case, it may be necessary to use some annoying artifice, e.g., to begin by generating many "throwaway" atoms, until the last atom present in the data structure read in by **getb** has been bypassed.

The input-output facilities described here can be used to write output interactively to a terminal, as well as to acquire input from a terminal.

9.2 Use of Inclusion Libraries

Carefully crafted procedures that perform common utility functions such as sorting, output formating, and parsing can be used over and over again in SETL programs. SETL supports several features intended to facilitate the use of such standard program libraries. One of these is the LIBRARY feature described in Section 8.4, which makes it possible to bind precompiled collections of library programs into a composite program. In the present section, we will describe a simpler but related facility, which makes it possible to insert sections of source text gathered from an auxiliary *inclusion library* into a SETL program that is about to be compiled.

An inclusion library used in this way must be structured as a sequence of standard SETL source lines, divided into *members* by interspersed lines of the form

. = MEMBER membername (1)

Each such line introduces, and names, a *member* of the inclusion library, which consists of all lines following the line (1), up to the next occurrence of a line beginning with '. = MEMBER'. (Note that the characters . = MEMBER in a header line like (1) must occupy character positions 2 through 9 in the line; the first character in the header line must be blank.) The last member of the inclusion library extends from the header line which introduces it to the very end of the library.

All members of an inclusion library must have distinct member names. To import a member *membername* of an inclusion library into a SETL program text *P* that is to be compiled, a line of the form

.COPY membername (2)

is required. This line must occur in *P* at the point at which the body of the inclusion library member is to be inserted. Like (1), the line (2) must begin in character position 2, following an initial blank. The *membername* in (2) must be identical with the *membername* in the line (1) introducing the text which is to be inserted at (2).

During compilation, each .COPY line of the form (2) is replaced by the body of the member introduced by the corresponding line (1). For example, in the presence of an inclusion library containing the lines

```
 . = MEMBER constants
small_lets := 'abcdefghijklmnopqrstuvwxyz';
big_lets := 'ABCDEFGHIJKLMNOPQRSTUVWXYZ';

 . = MEMBER quicksort
proc quicksort(s);
return if (x := arb s) = om then [ ]
   else quicksort({y in s | y < x}) + [x] + quicksort({y in s | y > x}) end;
end proc quicksort;
```

The source text

```
program something;
 .COPY constants
proc another;
end proc another;
 .COPY quicksort
```

will be compiled exactly as if it read

```
program something;
small_lets := 'abcdefghijklmnopqrstuvwxyz';
big_lets := 'ABCDEFGHIJKLMNOPQRSTUVWXYZ';
proc another;
end proc another;
proc quicksort(s);
return if (x := arb s) = om then [ ]
   else quicksort({y in s | y < x}) + [x] + quicksort({y in s | y > x}) end;
end proc quicksort;
```

The file used as inclusion library during a SETL compilation which makes use of the .COPY feature is specified by the command parameter ILIB. See Section 9.4.1 for additional details.

9.3 Listing-Control Commands

It is possible to alter the form of the listing which the SETL compiler produces by including listing control command lines of the form described here in the source program text. These commands, each of which must always occur on a separate line beginning with the two characters ' .', have no effect on compilation or execution other than to modify the form of the compilation listing. The allowed listing control commands are as follows:

nolist	suspends listing of source text lines
list	resumes listing of source text lines
eject	advances compilation listing to new page
title page_title	This command specifies a page_title which will appear at the top of subsequent pages.

Note that the page title appearing in the preceding command cannot contain the apostrophe character, also that the *at* command parameter described in Section 9.4.1 can be used to request *automatic titling*. If automatic titling is enabled, then each new **procedure** encountered will begin on a new page, which will be given a title derived from the **procedure** header line.

9.4 Environment Operators and SETL Command Parameters

SETL includes several facilities for sensing aspects of a program's external environment and for controlling optional details of compilation and execution. These facilities will be described in this section.

(i) Parameterless built-in functions: The names of the following two functions are keywords: **time** and **date**. The parameterless function

time

yields an integer representing the execution time, in milliseconds, used by the program from the start of execution up to the moment at which the **time** quantity is evaluated. This can be used to monitor the amount of processor time which your program is consuming. The parameterless function

date

yields a string consisting of the current day, date, and clock time, expressed as hours, minutes, and seconds. For example, the result of the command

print(date);

might be

SUN 01 MAR 87 14:493

(ii) Initial program parameters: Integer or string parameters to be transmitted to a SETL program can be included in the operating system command-language line which initiates execution of the program. The precise external form in which these parameters should be given will depend to some extent on the operating system being used. For example, to transmit parameters *P1* and *P2* with values 'YES' and 35 to a SETL program running under the DEC VAX/VMS system, we write

/P1 = YES/P2 = 35 (1a)

If running under the CDC CYBER NOS system we have to write

(P1 = YES, P2 = 35) (1b)

instead, and running under the IBM/370 CMS system we write

(P1 = YES P2 = 35) (1c)

Built-in functions called **getspp** and **getipp** are used to read these program command parameters. For example, to read the values of the string-valued parameter *P1* appearing in the preceding examples and save the value in a variable *x*, we would write

x := **getspp** ('P1 = defval/altval');

where *defval* and *altval* stand for arbitrary string constants. The **getspp** primitive searches the command line which initiated the SETL run for the occurrence of a parameter definition of the form *P1* = abcde, where *abcde* can be an arbitrary string, or if the first occurrence of *P1* in the command line is not followed by an equals sign, simply for an occurrence of the parameter name *P1*. Then

(i) If P1 = abcde occurs on the command line, *x* is given the value abcde.
(ii) Otherwise, if *P1* occurs on the command line, without a value being assigned to it, *x* is given the value *altval*.
(iii) Otherwise *P1* is given the default value *defval*.

The function **getipp** works in exactly the same way, except that it reads integer instead of string parameters, and supplies integer rather than string default values.

Suppose, for an example of all this, that the code

x1 := **getspp**('P1 = LITTLE/BIG'); x2 := **getipp**('P2 = 1/0')

appears in a program being run under the DEC VAX/VMS system. Then the appearance of the following parameter strings on the command line initiating a run of the program would give *x1* and *x2* the values indicated in the following table:

Command-Line Parameter String	*x1 value*	*x2 value*
/P1 = MEDIUM/P2 = 2	'MEDIUM'	2
/P1 = MEDIUM/P2	'MEDIUM'	0
/P1 = MEDIUM	'MEDIUM'	1
/P1/P2 = 2	'BIG'	2
/P2 = 2	'LITTLE'	2
/P2	'LITTLE'	0
(no parameters)	'LITTLE'	1

A typical use of the **getipp** primitive is to switch on debugging or tracing facilities selectively. To do this, one can, for example, introduce a collection of variables called trace1, trace2, ... etc. Debugging prints in your SETL program can then be made conditional on the values of these variables, e.g., by writing statements like

```
if trace13 = 1 then
    print(...);   $ print appropriate debugging information
end if;
```

If the variables trace1, trace2, ... are initialized by statements

```
trace1 := getipp('TRACE1 = 0/1');
trace2 := getipp('TRACE2 = 0/1');
```

then by passing tracej (i.e., tracej = 1) to a run (as a parameter of the command used to bring your SETL program into execution; see Section 9.4.1) one can cause the corresponding trace output to be produced. Note that this will switch on the debug output without your having to recompile the program being debugged.

Facilities very much like **getspp** and **getipp** are used in the SETL implementation, where they support the battery of compiler and run-time options described in the following sections.

9.4.1 Standard SETL command options

The SETL compiler and run-time systems themselves read a variety of command parameters, using the **getipp** and **getspp** facilities of the SETL language. These parameters switch various compilation and debugging features on and off. In describing these parameters, we will use a notation typified by the example 'A = 0/1'; that is, the name of a parameter to be described will be given first, followed by an equals sign, followed by the *default value* that the parameter will be given if its name does not appear in a parameter string followed by a slash, followed by the *alternate value* that the parameter will be given if it is simply mentioned as a SETL command parameter name, but no value is explicitly assigned to it.

A parameter passed to the SETL system can be significant either to the parse, semantic analysis, or code generation phases of the SETL compiler, or to the SETL run-time support library; or to a SETL program containing an invocation of either **getspp** or **getipp**. The list of standard parameters which now follows lists parameters according to the phase of the SETL system to which they are significant.

9.4.1.1 Parse phase options

AT = 0/1 (automatic titling)

This option controls automatic titling of the parse phase output listing. AT = 1 causes each SETL procedure to start a new page on the listing; AT = 0 suppresses this automatic page advance.

CSET = EXT/POR (character set)

This option specifies the character set used in your SETL source. *Por* specifies that only the portable subset of the collection of all possible characters is allowed; *ext* specifies that both the portable set and a wider class of extended character sets are allowed. These character options allow or disallow the following character representations:

<table>
<tr><th></th><th>Portable representation</th><th>Extended representation</th></tr>
<tr><td>Left set bracket</td><td><<</td><td>{</td></tr>
<tr><td>Right set bracket</td><td>>></td><td>}</td></tr>
<tr><td>Left tuple bracket</td><td>(/</td><td>[</td></tr>
<tr><td>Right tuple bracket</td><td>/)</td><td>]</td></tr>
<tr><td>'Such that'</td><td>ST</td><td>| or !</td></tr>
</table>

(The printed characters shown in the table are intended to represent the corresponding ASCII standard internal codes. The actual characters printed or typed for these codes may vary from terminal to terminal, or from one printer to another.)

ETOKS = 5/5 (error tokens)

The value of ETOKS controls the number of tokens listed in parse error diagnostic messages.

I = filename (input file)

The value of I specifies the name of the source file containing the SETL text to be compiled.

ILIB = filename (inclusion library)

As noted in Section 9.2, text from an auxiliary inclusion library can be imported into a SETL program being compiled. The value of ILIB defines the name of this inclusion library.

L = filename (listing file)

The value of *L* specifies the name of the standard listing file to which all compilation phase output will be written.

LIST = 0/1 (list compilation output)

The option LIST = 1 causes a compilation phase listing to be produced; LIST = 0 suppresses this listing.

MLEN = 1000/1000 (macro length)

The value of MLEN defines the maximum number of tokens allowed in a single macro body.

PEL = 1000/1000 (parse error limit)

The value of PEL specifies the parse phase error limit. If more than the specified number of errors are detected by the parse phase, compilation is terminated.

PFCC = 1/0 (write printer carriage-control information)

PFCC = 1 causes the output listing to contain carriage-control information; PFCC = 0 suppresses carriage-control information.

PFLL = 0/0 (line limit)

This command parameter is used in conjunction with PFPL; see the description of PFPL for additional information.

PFLP = 60/0 (lines per page)

The value of PFLP determines the number of lines that will be printed on each output page.

PFPL = 100/0 (page limit)

This parameter, together with PFLL, determines the amount of output that a program will be allowed to produce before being forcibly terminated. The limits imposed are as follows:

PFPL = 0,	PFLL = 0	No output limit enforced.
PFPL = n,	PFLL = 0 $(n > 0)$	A limit of *n* pages or *n**PFLP output lines is imposed.
PFPL = 0,	PFLL = *n* $(n > 0)$	A limit of *n* output lines is imposed.
PFPL = n,	PFLL = *m* $(n > 0, m > 0)$	A limit of *n* pages or *m* output lines is imposed.

POL = filename ('Polish' file name)

This specifies the name of the parsed source file passed by the SETL compiler's parse phase to its semantic analysis phase.

TERM = filename (interactive terminal identification)

The SETL system will normally expect to write certain short messages, generally error and warning messages, to an interactive terminal. If no such terminal is available, or if for any other reason it is desired to write these messages to some other file, then TERM = filename can be used to designate this file. The option TERM = 0 suppresses this "terminal" output.

9.4.1.2 Semantic analysis phase options

BIND = 0/filename (binder file)

This parameter and the associated parameter IBIND (see following discussion) are used to pass separately compiled files in *Q1* format to the semantic analysis phase. If either BIND or IBIND has a value different from zero, the semantic analysis phase will read various *Q1* format files and combine them with newly parsed SETL source input (named by the POL and XPOL parameters to be described) producing a *Q1* format file (named by the Q1 parameter described later). This output file represents the logical concatenation of all its input files in a parsed, semantically analyzed form.

DITER = 0/1 (modifications during iteration are possible)

This option indicates whether the compiler can assume that objects being iterated over in a loop are not modified within the loop. DITER = 0 disallows this assumption and causes the object being iterated over to be copied before an iteration begins; DITER = 1 suppresses these copying operations.

IBIND = filename (auxiliary list of input Q1 files)

This parameter, and the associated parameter BIND (see preceding text) are used to pass separately compiled files in *Q1* format to the semantic analysis phase. The file named by the IBIND parameter should consist of a list of file names, one name per line, these file names having whatever format is appropriate in view of the operating system under which the SETL compiler is running. All the files named in this list of files will be read and bound together into the *Q1* format output file which the semantic analysis phase produces. (See the preceding discussion of parameter BIND.)

L = filename (listing file)

This specifies the name of the standard listing file to which all printable compilation phase output will be written.

OPT = 0/1 (optimization)

Selecting the option OPT = 1 causes a global optimization phase to be executed between the normal semantic analysis and code generation phases. Note that this option has an effect only for implementations which make the SETL optimizer available.

PFCC (carriage control)
PFLL (line limit)
PFLP (lines per page)
PFPL (page limit)

See the previous subsection for details concerning these parameters.

POL = filename ('Polish' file name)

This specifies the name of the "parsed source" or "Polish" file passed from the SETL compiler's parse phase to the semantic analysis phase. (See remarks concerning POL made in the previous subsection.)

Q1 = filename ('Q1' file)

This specifies the name of the preliminary code file passed from the SETL compiler's parse phase to its optimization or code generation phase.

SEL = 1000/1000 (semantic error limit)

The value of SEL specifies the semantic analysis phase error limit. If more than the specified number of errors are detected during the semantic analysis phase, compilation is terminated.

SIF = 0/1 (save intermediate files)

The option SIF = 1 causes the "preliminary code" or *Q1* file produced by the semantic analysis phase to be saved. (See preceeding remarks concerning the parameter *Q*1. Normally this file will be deleted by the compiler's code generation phase.) Note that a file of this sort must be saved if SETL's separate compilation and binder facilities are to be used.

UV = 0/1 (check for undeclared variables)

Selecting the option UV = 1 will cause a warning message to be issued for each variable name used in your program which does not appear in any **var** statement. (This gives a handy way of ensuring that all variables appearing in the program have been documented and of checking against accidental variable-name misspellings.)

9.4.1.3 Code generation phase options

ASM = 0/1 (produce assembler code)

The ASM = 1 option will cause the SETL compiler to produce machine code for the computer on which you are running. ASM = 0 will cause production of a less efficient but generally more compact interpretable code form.

BACK = 0/1 (backtracking enabled)

The BACK = 1 option allows generation of code supporting backtracking and must be selected if the backtracking facilities of SETL are being used.

CA = 0/0 (constants are size)

This code phase parameter is used to control the size of the "constants area," which stores the values of constants appearing in your program. The option CA = 0 sets the constants area size equal to half the initial memory size allocated for your program (see discussion of parameter H). If a positive value less than 1,024 is specified for CA, then this value, multiplied by 1,024, becomes the constants area size; thus CA = 2 is equivalent to CA = 2,048.

CEL = 1000/1000 (code generation error limit)

This specifies the code generation phase error limit. If more than the specified number of errors are detected by the code generation phase, compilation is terminated.

H = 0/0 (heap size)

The value of *H* specifies the initial virtual memory size that will be used when program execution begins. If $H = 0$ is selected, an implementation-dependent default initial memory size is used. If a positive value less than 1,024 is specified for *H*, this value, multiplied by 1,024, becomes the initial memory size; thus $H = 2$ is equivalent to $H = 2{,}048$.

L = filename (listing file)

This option specifies the name of the standard listing file to which all printable compilation phase output will be written.

PFCC (carriage control)
PFLL (line limit)
PFLP (lines per page)
PFLL (page limit)

See subsection 9.4.1.1 for details concerning these parameters.

Q1 = filename ('Q1' file)

This option specifies the name of the preliminary code file passed from the SETL compiler's parse phase to its optimization or code generation phase. See the remarks concerning this parameter in subsection 9.4.1.2.

Q2 = filename ('Q2' file)

This option specifies the name of the interpretable code file passed from the SETL compiler's code generation phase to the run-time support phase when the SETL system is being run interpretively.

9.4.1.4 Run-time support library options

ASSERT = 1/2 (assertion switch)

This parameter can have 0, 1, or 2 as its value. These values have the following significance:

ASSERT = 0	Evaluates all Boolean conditions occurring in ASSERT statements but does not test their values. (Note that evaluation of these conditions may trigger side effects essential to the proper functioning of the program being run.)
ASSERT = 1	Evaluates and tests all assertions. Assertions which fail yield a run-time error.
ASSERT = 2	Evaluates and tests all assertions. A message is printed for each assertion which evaluates to **true**. Assertions which fail yield an error.

H = 0/1 (Heap size)

This command parameter, which specifies the initial (virtual) memory length used during a SETL run, is significant to both the code generation phase of the compiler and the run-time support library. See the account of this parameter in the preceding subsection for additional details.

LCP = 0/1 (list execution time parameters)

The option LCP = 1 causes the values chosen for standard command line options to be listed on the output file at the start of SETL program execution.

LCS = 1/0 (list execution statistics)

The option LCS = 1 causes various standard statistics collected during execution of the program to be printed at the end of SETL program execution.

Q2 = filename ('Q2' file)

This option specifies the name of the interpretable code file passed from the SETL compiler's code generation phase to the run-time support phase when the SETL system is being run interpretively. See the remarks concerning this parameter in subsection 9.4.1.3.

REL = 0/0 (run-time error limit)

The value of REL specifies the run-time error limit. If more than the specified number of errors are detected during SETL execution, then execution terminates.

SB = { }/⟨⟨ ⟩⟩ (set brackets)

The value of SB specifies the characters to be used for printing set brackets.

SNAP = 0/1 (snap dump switch)

The SNAP = 1 option causes an abbreviated dump of recent variable values to be produced when a run-time error is detected. Specify SNAP = 0 to suppress this dump.

STRACE = 0/1 (Statement trace)

Selecting the option STRACE = 1 causes production of a dynamic trace giving the statement number of each statement executed. This option should be used cautiously, since it tends to produce very voluminous output. The statement numbers used are those which appear on the parse phase output listing.

TB = [ ]/( ) (tuple brackets)

The value of TB specifies the characters used for printing tuple brackets.

9.4.1.5 Other options used for system checkout and maintenance

In addition to the command parameters listed, the SETL compiler recognises various other parameters, which are provided for purposes of system checkout and maintenance and are not needed in normal use. Note, however, that you must avoid using the names of these parameters to designate other quantities which your SETL program will read from the control card by using **getipp** and **getspp**.

We list these special parameters with brief indications of their function but give no details concerning them. For more information, consult the SETL Maintenance Manual. The maintenance facilities are activated by the SETL command parameters. A second family of maintenance facilities are activated by inserting special statements of the form

debug dopt1, ..., doptk;

into the text of a SETL program being compiled. Here, dopt1, ..., doptk should be a list of keywords designating debug options. Some of these debug options refer to the parse phase of the SETL system; others to the semantic analysis, code generation, or execution phases. Since the ordinary user will have little reason to concern herself with these options, we list them here in abbreviated fashion only; see the SETL Maintenance Manual for more information.

(i) Parse Phase Debug Options

PTRM0	Disable macro processor trace
PTRM1	Enable macro processor trace
PTRP0	Disable parse trace
PTRP1	Enable parse trace
PTRT0	Disable token trace
PTRT1	Enable token trace
PRSOD	List tokens corresponding to loops and ifs still pending
PRSPD	list polish and xpolish tables
PRSSD	list symbol table

(ii) Semantic Analysis Phase Options

STRE0	Disable entry trace
STRE1	Enable entry trace

STRS0	Disable trace of operator argument stack
STRS1	Enable trace of operator argument stack
SQ1CD	List *Q1* code
SQ1SD	List semantic analysis phase symbol table
SCSTD	List stack used for processing control structures and other nested constructs

(iii) Code Generation Phase Options

CQ1CD	List *Q1* code
CQ1SD	List code generation phase symbol table
CQ2SD	List generated *Q2* code

(iv) Execution Phase Options

RTRE0	Disable trace of entry to run-time library procedures
RERE1	Enable trace of entry to run-time library procedures
RTRS0	Disable statement number trace
RTRS1	Enable statement number trace
RTRC0	Disable code trace
RTRC1	Enable code trace (The code trace prints each internal *Q2* instruction as it is interpreted.)
RTRG0	Disable garbage collector trace
RTRG1	Enable garbage collector trace
RGCD0	Disable dynamic storage dumps during garbage collection
RGCD1	Enable dynamic storage dumps during garbage collection
RDUMP	Dump dynamic storage to file (The file to which an image of dynamic storage is written is specified by a control card parameter: DUMP = filename. The auxiliary maintainance program DMP reformats this file in a readable form.)

Exercises

1. Write a program which will read a sequence of lines constituting an English-language text and print it out after eliminating all multiple blanks and assuring that every punctuation mark (other than hyphen) is followed by exactly one blank.

2. The position on a chessboard is defined by a mapping f which sends every square $[i,j]$ occupied by a piece into the name of the piece occupying it. Pieces are designated by their names, e.g., "pawn," "king," "queen." White pieces are designated by lowercase names, e.g., "pawn." Black pieces are designated by uppercase names, e.g., "PAWN." Write a procedure which prints an attractive visual display of the board position.

3. Given the representation of chessboard position described in Exercise 2, write procedures which will
   (a) return the set of all moves possible for white or black;
   (b) return the set of all white or black pieces threatened with capture;
   (c) return the set of all squares attacked by white or black pieces.

4. When crucial items of information like invoice or customer numbers need to be keyed into a computer system, the possibility of keypunch error is often quite

alarming. To prevent such errors, one often adds "check characters" to the item being keyed in. Such check characters allow miskeyed items to be detected in most cases. If any alphanumeric check character from 0..Z can be used, the following is a convenient way of assigning check characters:

(a) Number all alphanumeric characters, assigning them values lying in the range 0..35.
(b) Go through the characters of the item to be keyed in, from right to left. Multiply the number associated with the j-th item by j, and sum all the resulting integers. Reduce the sum modulo 37, to obtain an integer n.
(c) The check character is the character corresponding to n or is Z if n is 36.

Write a SETL procedure which will apply this check to a string, returning the string if it passes the check, but **om** otherwise.

5. Write a key-entry verification program. This program should begin by reading a file F of lines that are to be verified. Those same lines should then be reentered at the terminal. If a line L reentered has exactly the same form as the corresponding line in the file F, then L should simply be displayed. If not, then the terminal should (if possible) emit a warning audio signal, and the line $L0$ present in the original file F should be displayed along with the $L1$ just entered. Characters which need to be replaced in $L0$ to make L match $L1$ should be marked by displaying appropriate replacement characters under $L1$; characters which need to be deleted should be indicated by displaying a double quote character under $L1$. If one or more characters need to be inserted, they should be displayed in a vertical column under the character of $L1$, after which they need to be inserted. In the event of a difference, the user ought to have the following three options:

   0: accept L0 as correct
   1: accept L1 as correct
   2: re-enter line, and repeat the check.

6. Write a procedure which can be used to display "menus" on the screen of an interactive terminal. The parameter passed to this procedure should be a tuple $[s1, s2, \ldots]$ of strings. As many of these strings as will fit on the screen should be displayed, each accompanied by a number. The user should then type one of these numbers to select the desired item, and the procedure should return the number of the item selected. If something illegal (e.g., an out-of-range integer) is typed, the procedure should return **om**. The display you use should be neatly formatted, in multiple columns if possible, to display as many items as possible on the screen without giving the screen a cluttered appearance. If not all items will fit on the screen, the message

   PRESS RETURN KEY TO SEE ADDITIONAL CHOICES

   should be displayed at the bottom of the screen and appropriate action taken if this key is pressed. (Of course, the feature described by this message should be implemented in a foolproof manner.)

   In such a program, it is sometimes useful to have "secret" options which are known to the expert system user, but not displayed. These can be indicated by negative numbers. Include this feature in your program.

7. Write a program that will read SETL source text and count the number of comments in it. A record should be kept of the number of "short" comments (which

occupy just one line and are followed by a line containing code text) and the number of "long" comments (which occupy several successive lines on which only comments appear.) Two counts of long comments should be kept, namely the number of long comments two to four lines in length, and the number of long comments five or more lines in length. You should also count the total number of lines in the program. Note that every comment starts with a dollar sign ($) character, but that such a character only starts a comment if it is not part of a quoted character string. For exmaple, the first character of the first comment in

x := 'I often think of $"s, $"s, $"s'; $ Not really!

is 'N'. Be sure to handle this rule properly.

8. When punched cards are used to transmit information to a computer system, it is sometimes convenient to pack information densely onto them, without blank spaces between successive information fields. In this case, the size of each information field in a line of characters must be known in advance. Write a procedure P, whose two inputs are a string s of exactly 80 characters representing a punched card being read, and a tuple t representing the "format" of this string, i.e., the size and nature of the successive information fields in it. Each component of t should have the form $[n, k]$, where n is a positive integer designating the number of characters in a particular subfield of s, and k is one of '*I*' (integer), '*S*' (string). The procedure P should return a tuple of converted values, with each value of improper type represented by **om**.

9. To develop a *kwic* (or "key word in context") index for a body T of text, one proceeds as follows:
   (a) A collection of keywords is given.
   (b) The text T consists of a collection of paragraphs, each headed by a "paragraph designator" at most one-third of a line long.
   (c) The paragraphs constituting the text T are scanned for occurrences of any of one the keywords. Whenever a keyword is found, a portion L of the line in which it occurs, two-thirds of a line in total length, is kept, with the keyword as close to the middle of this line section as possible. (Words from preceding or following lines are included if necessary.)
   (d) A designator of the paragraph containing the line is concatenated to L, and the resulting string is added to a collection s of strings.
   (e) When the whole of T has been scanned, the set s of all lines collected is alphabetized according to the keyword each L contains and is printed in alphabetical order, with keyword capitalized.

   Write a program which generates kwic indices of this kind.

10. Write a program P which can be used to scan a mass of English-language text T, counting the frequency of all letter pairs encountered. Use P to scan a few paragraphs of text. Count the total number of pairs encountered and the total number of different pairs. Draw a graph relating number of different pairs encountered to the total number of characters scanned, and use this to estimate the number of different character pairs that you would encounter if you scanned the whole *Encyclopaedia Britannica*.

11. A machine tool company manufactures various kinds of tools, each of which consists of several kinds of parts manufactured by various of its departments.

Information concerning parts requirements is stored as a map

{[tool_name, parts_map], ...}

where each tool_name is the name of a particular tool that the company manufactures, and each parts_map is a mapping from the name of each part used in the manufacture of the tool to the quantity of this part required and the name of the department responsible for manufacturing the part. (Thus parts_map has the form

{[part_name, [number, department]], ...}).

Write a program which will read a list of orders, each having the form

order_name, tool_name, quantity_ordered

and make up a list of parts orders arranged by department. Each parts order generated should be headed by the current date and a department name and should then consist of succesive groups of lines, arranged in alphabetical order by part name. Each such group should start with a line having the form

part_name, total quantity needed

and continue with a sequence of lines having the form

order_number, quantity in order

These latter lines should be arranged by order_number.

The parts order to be sent to a given department can extend over many pages. Every page of this order must be headed by the current date and the appropriate department name, and also by an appropriately positioned caption reading "Page j of n", where n is the total number of pages going to a given department and j runs from 1 to n. The parts order to be sent to a given department should always start at the top of a new page.

12. A spelling error program is one which reads an input text T and produces a list of all the words in T which appear to be misspelled. One way of making this check is to test each of the words in T to see whether it belongs to a standard dictionary D of properly spelled words. Write such a spelling error program. Your program should read two files: one the file T to be checked, which is given as a sequence of text lines; the other a dictionary D, also assumed to be a sequence of lines, each line containing several dictionary words, separated by blanks. The file T can contain capitalized words. The output produced should be a formatted display of all presumably misspelled words.

13. Assuming that the spelling error program described in Exercise 12 is to be run interactively from a terminal, improve it by adding the following features. The program should begin by querying the user for the names of the files T and D. Then it should read and analyze these files as in Exercise 12. The misspelled words in T must then be numbered and displayed on a terminal. After this the program should accept a sequence of commands of the form

    n1correct_spelling1/n2correct_spelling2/

    where each nj is the number of a misspelled word and correct_spellingj is its correct spelling. This sequence of commands is terminated by a command of the form

    STOP,

after which the program should query the user for the name of an output file F into which a corrected version of the input T is to be written. All occurences of misspelled words in T for which correct spellings have been supplied should be corrected, and the corrected text which results written out to F.

14. "Pig latin" transposes words by moving all initial strings of consonants to the end of the word and adding "-ay." If a word begins with a vowel, one simply adds "-ay" to it. The word "a" is changed to "an." For example, the pig latin translation of "John bought a car from Irene" is "Ohnjay oughtbay an arcay omfray Ireneay." Write an interactive program which will read an input text and translate it into pig latin. Your program should handle capitalization and punctuation correctly.

15. Write an interactive program which could be used by a teacher to maintain class grade records. The specifications for this program are as follows. It maintains a list of all the students enrolled in a class. Each student name is mapped into a directory record giving the student's address, telephone number, and any desired additional textual information concerning the student. Each student name is also mapped into a tuple giving the student's grade on a sequence of homework exercises and examinations. Finally, each assignment or examination number is mapped onto a line of text describing the assignment or examination.
The system should accept at least the following commands:

E/student-name	Enroll student with given name
D	Display numbered table of all students
IE	Set up for entering new textual information concerning students
IA	Set up for entering textual information concerning assignments
G/n	Set up for entering new grade information for assignment n
D/n	Display all information concerning student n
n/line-of-text	Enter line of text to information record of student n, or enter comment about assignment n, or enter grade for student n
DA	Display information concerning assignments
DA/n	Display information concerning n-th assignment, including average grade, highest and lowest grade, number of students in each grade quintile, and names of students who have not yet completed assignment.

What other commands would be useful? Design at least three such commands, document them, and include them in your implementation.

16. The "game of life," invented by James H. Conway, models certain elementary biological phenomena. The simulation it embodies takes place on an n by m board. For definiteness, we will suppose that $n = m = 20$. At every step of the simulation, every square on the board is either occupied (by an "organism") or empty. Given such a configuration, the next "generation" of organisms (i.e., the board configuration at the next step) is determined by the following rules:
   (a) If a square is empty but has exactly three full neighbors, it will become full (since an organism will be "born" in it).
   (b) If a full square has four or more full neighbors, it will become empty (since the organism in it will "smother").

(c) If a full square has no neighbor or just one neighbor, it will become empty (since the organism in it will "starve").

Write an interactive program which reads an initial board configuration and then simulates its evolution for a given number of steps.

17. Write an interactive program for use by bank tellers. This program is to maintain a map which sends each client of the bank into his current balance, and another similar map which sends each client into his name, address, and phone number. (Clients are identified by unique "account numbers" issued by the bank). Finally, each client is mapped into a maximum allowed "line of credit" and to the sum currently drawn against this line of credit.

    The program should be such that a teller may call up any or all of the preceding account information given the appropriate account ID number. The following commands should be executable:

E/Customer #	Start new account
IE	Set up for entering new address and phone number
IC	Set up for establishing new credit line
B/Customer #	Display current balance
C/Customer #	Display amount drawn on line of credit
D/Customer #/Dollar amt.	Deposit of funds
W/Customer #/Dollar amt.	Withdrawal of funds

18. Write an interactive program that plays the game hangman. Your program should read the date and time and use this to select a word at random from an internally stored collection of 100 words. The player should then be asked to guess the word, one letter at a time. Each guessed letter present in the word should elicit a display showing all letters guessed so far. If the number of incorrect guesses rises to half the number of letters in the word being guessed, the player loses, and the word should be revealed. Try to write an entertaining program. Your program should keep score of the number of games won and lost.

19. (a) Many large software systems include interactive "help" subsystems which, when entered, allow a tree of helpful information to be traversed. The aim is to make it easier for the system user to locate information which he may require in order to use a system successfully. Use an appropriate variant of the "menu" procedure in Exercise 5 to implement such a help system. When invoked, the help system should begin by reading a file describing part of a graph of nodes, each node representing a state which the system user can reach during his browsing. In each state, the system should display a short paragraph of helpful information and a menu of available subitems. The information which the help system needs should be divided into a set of files, each a few hundred lines in length, which can be read separately as requested by the user. Each such file will contain two maps, which we shall call nodes_map and files_map. Nodes_map has the following format:

$$\{[\text{help\_graph\_node}, [\text{display\_paragraph}, \text{subnode\_menu}]\}$$

The display_paragraph is a tuple consisting of a sequence of lines (strings) to be displayed when help_graph_node is reached. Subnode_menu is a tuple of help_graph nodes, to be displayed as a menu. By selecting an appropriate item of this menu, the user chooses the help system node to which he wishes to advance next. By typing '—', the user retreats to the last help system mode previously examined. The other map, files_map, which is available in a pre-established file which can be read by the help system, simply maps each subnode x referenced by a given file to the name of the file which contains the display_paragraph and subnode_menu information for x.

(b) In order to use the help program we have just described, you will find it convenient to design and implement a "help setup" program which can read a file of text containing all the paragraphs and define all the menus which will appear in the data structures described in (a). This file should also define the manner in which all this information is to be divided into the smaller files which the help system will use. Design and implement this help setup package. Your help setup program should verify that the information passed to it is internally consistent.

20. Write a record-keeping system suitable for daily use in a library. The system should read files of instructions and generate various outputs. Each transaction handled by the system starts with a command line whose first two characters are '**'. The transactions handled are as follows:

```
**E card_number
name
address
telephone_number
```

This transaction enrolls a new subscriber, assigning her the indicated library card number. The card number must be unique, or the transaction will be rejected. The subscriber's date of enrollment should be maintained automatically by the system.

```
**C card_number address
new address
```

This transaction changes the address recorded for a given subscriber. Similar transactions which change the name and telephone number provided for a given subscriber should also be provided.

```
**L card_number
```

This transaction lists, in appropriately sorted order, the information available for a given subscriber, including all books currently charged to the subscriber, with dates of withdrawal, and number of books borrowed in current calendar year.

```
**A
```

This transaction produces an alphabetized list of all subscribers, with addresses and telephone numbers.

```
**B book_number
card_number
```

This transaction charges a book to a customer.

```
**R book_number
```

This transaction notes that a book has been returned.

**Q book_number
Title, Author
Publisher, Publication date

This transaction notes the acquisition of a new book and assigns it a book number. The book number must be unique or the transaction will be rejected. The date of acquisition is noted, internally.

Books can be borrowed for two weeks. Books not returned within a 2-week limit are considered to be overdue. When run, the library record system should produce a warning letter to all subscribers holding overdue books. However, no subscriber should get such a letter more often than once a week. In this dunning letter, books should be listed by title and author. Books for which a previous notice has been sent should carry the additional legend 'SECOND NOTICE', 'THIRD NOTICE', or 'GROSSLY OVERDUE'.

The transaction triggered by

**D

should produce an alphabetized list of all "delinquent" subscribers holding unreturned books for which more than two notices have been sent, with an indication of the number of 'THIRD NOTICE' and 'GROSSLY OVERDUE' books they are holding.

Can you design, and implement, any other useful feature for such a system?

21. Write an interactive "daily reminders" program. This program reads a file of one-line messages, each tagged with a given date, and displays them. Messages displayed are also numbered. The system is to handle the following commands.

—	(Display all reminders remaining from past days)
$+n$	(Display all messages relating to n days from today)
$+$	(Display all future reminders)
$?n$	(Delete reminder n)

Define and implement commands for dealing with the situation in which unmodified execution of a command would display too many messages to fit all at once on your terminal.

22. Write an election forecasting program. The base data for the program should be a map sending each voting precinct into its total of Democratic and Republican votes in the last election, into its state, and into its type: urban, inner city, suburban, and rural.

The program will be run every 30 minutes on election night. As returns come in from various precincts, these will be compared with the returns from same precincts in the last comparable election. If the Democratic and Republican percentages reported for a given type of precinct in a given state are D and R, and the prior Democratic and Republican percentages for the same precinct were d and r, respectively, then the Democratic (or Republican) gain can be estimated as the quotient D/d (or R/r). Use these gain factors to extrapolate the vote for all precincts of the same general character that have not yet reported.

23. It is sometimes hard to use an operating system's interactive facilities without a manual at your elbow, for two reasons:
    (a) The system provides many facilities, and it is hard to remember them all.
    (b) Most operating system commands have numerous parameters and options, whose names and effects are hard to remember.

    Write an operating system command assistance program which will make it easier to compose operating system commands. When invoked, this program should display a numbered menu of all available commands, with one-line comments concerning the purpose of each. When one of these commands is selected (by number) a numbered menu of obligatory and optional command parameters and options should be displayed, with a set of one-line comments on the form and effect of each parameter. The user should then be able to enter parameter values and select options, by number, either on a single line (separated by blanks), or on several successive lines. When he is finished, the command line that he has composed should be displayed. Use an appropriate variant of the "menu" procedure described in Exercise 6 to build up this program.

24. Extend the program described in Exercise 23 so that it allows command language programs to be composed and saved for subsequent use.

25. Write an interactive "perpetual calendar" program. This should handle the following commands:

    month/year (displays calendar for the requested month)
    day/month/year (displays calendar for the week containing the specified day.)

26. If person A makes a taxable payment to person B, he informs the Internal Revenue Service of this fact, giving the amount of the payment and the social security number of person B. Person B is then expected to file a report stating his total income. Write a program which will read a file of lines, each having either the form

    PAYMENT (social security number of recipient) (amount)

    or

    INCOMEREPORT (social security number of person reporting) (amount)

    and will then detect all persons who seem to be concealing more than $200 in income. A list of these persons, with the persons concealing the largest amounts of income coming first, should be printed.

27. A company bills its customers on the fifteenth of each month. Bills fully paid within 14 calendar days of their receipt are granted a 1% discount; bills fully paid within 30 days of their receipt are charged their face amount. Other bills pay a 2% per month interest charge. Write a program which will read two files of records, the first having the form

    BILL bill_number customer_number amount date
    PAYMENT bill_number customer_number amount data

    The program should print a list of all bills for which full payment has not been received, with a statement of the amount still owed on the bill. The "date" entry on each line of the file will be a string: for example, Jan. 9, 1980, would be represented as 1/9/80.

28. Build up an inclusion library containing the following procedures: mergesort (Section 5.4.2) and polynomial package (Section 5.1.3). Using this inclusion library, write a program which reads in a collection of pairs of polynomials represented as vectors, multiplies them, sorts the resulting product polynomials *P* into decreasing order of the values *P(1)*, and then prints them out. Polynomials should be printed in something like their standard representation; e.g., the polynomial read in as [1, 2, 0, 3] should be printed as 3**x**3 + 2*x + 1.

29. This exercise will describe a relatively elaborate page-oriented output facility, which you are asked to program. Your program should be written as a single MODULE.

    The output facility to be programmed will allow a page, which is to be filled with elegantly formatted string text, to be divided into non-overlapping, named areas, which can then be written to separately. To define such a page layout, a multiparameter procedure LAYOUT, with parameters like those shown in

    LAYOUT(field_name_string, field_descriptor_1.., field_descriptor_n);

    is used. The field_name_string parameter is a string, consisting of blank-separated names, each of which names one of the fields whose position and size are defined by a subsequent field_descriptor. The *j*-th name and the *j*-th field descriptor correspond to each other. The nature of any field can be further qualified by appending a qualifier to its name. Attaching a qualifier .R to a field name specifies that incomplete lines written to this field (see following discussion) are to be right-justified; similarly, the qualifier .L specifies left-justification, and the qualifier .C specifies centering.

    Each field_descriptor has the form

    [starting_line, starting_position, width, height]

    Here, starting_line indicates the line number at which a given field is to start (lines are numbered sequentially down the page, beginning at line 1), and starting_position indicates the horizontal position (numbered from position 1 at the extreme left) at which the field is to start. The two final quantities -width- and -height- define the horizontal and vertical dimensions of the field.

    The LAYOUT procedure returns **true** if it detects no inconsistency (e.g., overlapping fields) in the requested layout; but **false** otherwise.

    After defining the layout of fields on a page using the LAYOUT procedure, one can write to any or all of these fields, using a call

    WRITE(field_name_string, s1, s2, ..., sk);

    Here, field_name_string consists of a blank-separated sequence of field names, to which the remaining strings *s*1, *s*2, ... *sk* will be written in sequence. Any field_name in this field_name_string can be qualified by appending one or more characters '*' to it; a single asterisk terminates the current line of the field (moving down one line in this field), and additional asterisks skip one line each.

    The quantity of information already written to a given field, or to the whole page, can be sensed by invoking the function

    AMOUNT(field_name, s).

    Here the parameter *s* indicates what is wanted, specifically *s* = 'LINES' calls for the number of the last-written line of the indicated field, s = 'CHAR' calls for the number of characters already written to this line, and s = 'DESCRIPT' retrieves the descriptor of the field. The simplified invocation

AMOUNT( )

returns the number of the last line written to any field.

Finally, the call

OUTPUT( )

prints the page that prior calls to LAYOUT and WRITE have built. Moreover, it is legal to invoke LAYOUT several times before OUTPUT is called. This allows material to be written to a single page by using several successive layouts.

As you program this package of procedures, you will become aware of various incomplete points in the preceding specifications. Resolve all these ambiguous points in tasteful ways, and then document your decisions carefully, so as to create a detailed user's manual for the "page layout facility" that you will create.

30. Design, and implement, various useful extensions to the page layout facility described in Exercise 29. For example, you may want to allow area names to be qualified with .J in a LAYOUT call, thereby indicating that material written to an area is to be printed in right and left-justified form.

31. Use the page layout facility described in Exercises 29 and 30 to print out the title of a book, and to print the first page of Chapter 1 of the book, with appropriate chapter headings, and with the body of the first page in a two-column format. This first page should include at least one embedded table.

CHAPTER 10

The Data Representation Sublanguage

The *level* of a programming language is determined by the power of the semantic primitives which it provides. The operations provided by the ordinary low-level languages, e.g., languages of the FORTRAN type, all lie close to those elementary operations with a few dozen bits of input and output which computer hardware implements directly. Languages of somewhat higher level, e.g., PL/I, PASCAL, or Ada, supplement these primitives with more advanced pointer-oriented memory management mechanisms and also support recursion; nevertheless, even these languages stay close to operations which can be translated into efficient machine code in relatively obvious ways. SETL aims more radically than any of these languages at simplification of the programmer's task; for this reason it supports use of abstract objects (sets and maps) whose best machine-level representation is not obvious. Of course, many possible representations for objects of this kind are known, but which representation is best will vary from program to program in subtle ways that depend on the specific operations that a program applies to the objects that it manipulates. If the most effective representation of a program's data objects is not chosen, efficiency will suffer, and it is this efficiency barrier that has prevented rapid and widespread adoption of very high level languages like SETL.

If efficiency is an important enough consideration to justify the effort involved, a SETL program can be translated manually into a more efficient version written in a lower-level language such as PASCAL or Ada. A programmer using this approach will soon notice that many (but not all) of the efficiency-enhancing changes made during translation of an original SETL program are stereotyped in character and serve only to make use of advantageous data structures. The SETL facility to be explained in this chapter, namely its *data representation sublanguage*, aims to make it possible to attain efficiency without necessity for laborious translation simply by declaring what data structures (chosen from a library of such structures) are to be used to represent each of the objects appearing in a program. Then elaboration of more efficient code sequences can be left to the SETL compiler. Programming in this style, which begins with a program in which algorithmic actions are represented but data structures are ignored but then subsequently goes on to choose efficient data structures, exemplifies the important general idea of *programming by successive refinement* of an original program text.

SETL's representation sublanguage adds a system of declarations to the core language described in the preceding chapters (which for emphasis we will sometimes call *pure* SETL). These declarations control the *data structures* that will be used to implement an algorithm that has already been written in pure SETL. Ideally no rewriting of the algorithm should be necessary. A pure SETL program to which data structure declarations have been added is called a *supplemented program.* In the absence of error a supplemented program SP must always yield the same result as the pure program PP that it incorporates. (However, if errors or inconsistencies are present, then SP and PP are allowed to abort differently; and certain inconsistencies, detected in SP but not in PP, can cause SP to abort even if PP does not.) Those readers familiar with conventional programming languages will recognize that the representation sublanguage of SETL resembles conventional type declarations. As we shall see, it differs from those in a number of ways.

10.0 Implementation of the SETL Primitives

To implement SETL (or any other language), all its data objects must somehow be represented by sequences of words in the memory of the machine, and all its primitive operations must be represented by using sequences of the high-speed but elementary machine-level operations. We shall now outline the way in which this is done. To do so, it will be convenient to represent data layouts in machine memory diagrammatically. The memory of a computer can be thought of as an array M of words, each able to store a fixed number W of binary bits (zeroes and ones). Such patterns of bits can be interpreted as encodings of integers and hence can be used, when desired, as the indices of other elements of M.

We will picture subareas of the memory array M as sequences of rectangular boxes denoting memory cells, each holding a word. If one memory cell holds a value $M(i)$ which, regarded as an integer j, is the index of the memory cell $M(j)$, then we will sometimes regard $M(i)$ as holding a *pointer* to $M(j)$ and draw an arrow from the box representing $M(i)$ to the box representing $M(j)$, as in Figure 10.1. Where convenient, we will label the picture of a memory cell with an indication of its contents.

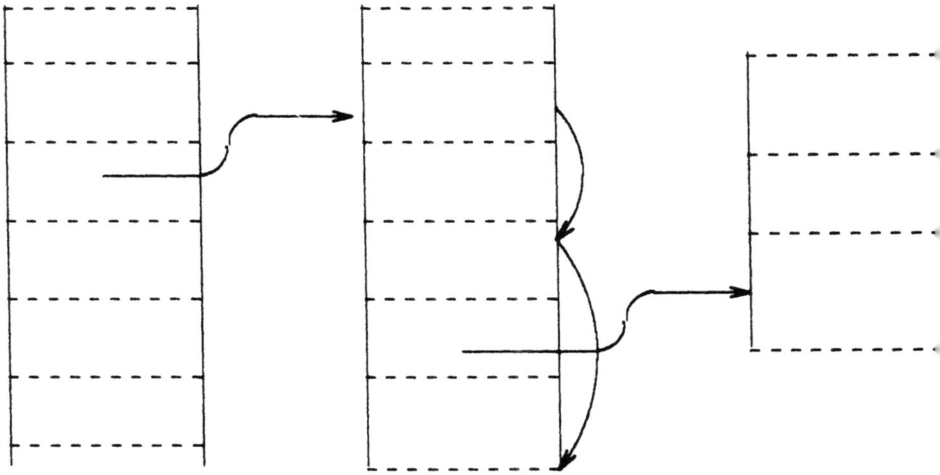

Figure 10.1 Sections of Memory, Showing Cells Which Store the Indices of Other Cells

If the data representation language to be described later in this chapter is not employed, a narrow range of highly standardized data structures will be used to represent SETL data objects. The most significant representations are those of sets, maps, and tuples. Since tuples are simplest, we shall describe their representation first.

10.1 The Standard Representation for Tuples

As for all other SETL data objects, the representation of a SETL tuple begins with a single memory word, *RW*, called the *root word* of the tuple. However, since the group of *W* zeroes and ones which a single machine word can hold are by no means sufficient to represent the (possibly very long) sequence of components of the tuple, this root word simply points to another location in memory, at which the actual representation of the tuple is located (see Figure 10.2). This representation begins with a tuple *header word* which tags the information which follows as a tuple. Next comes a word containing the length of the tuple, after which there follows a succession of root words pointing to the locations holding the representations of the successive components of the tuple. Note that this representation makes it easy and fast to retrieve the i-th component of a given tuple t. Aside from complications caused by error cases, which arise if i exceeds the length of t (or is negative, or is not an integer, etc.) all we have to do is take the integer value contained in the root word *RW*, add $(i + 2)$ to it as an offset, and retrieve the word to which this sum points. How expensive is a tuple retrieval operation? The mechanism we have just outlined takes fewer than 10 machine instructions. However we

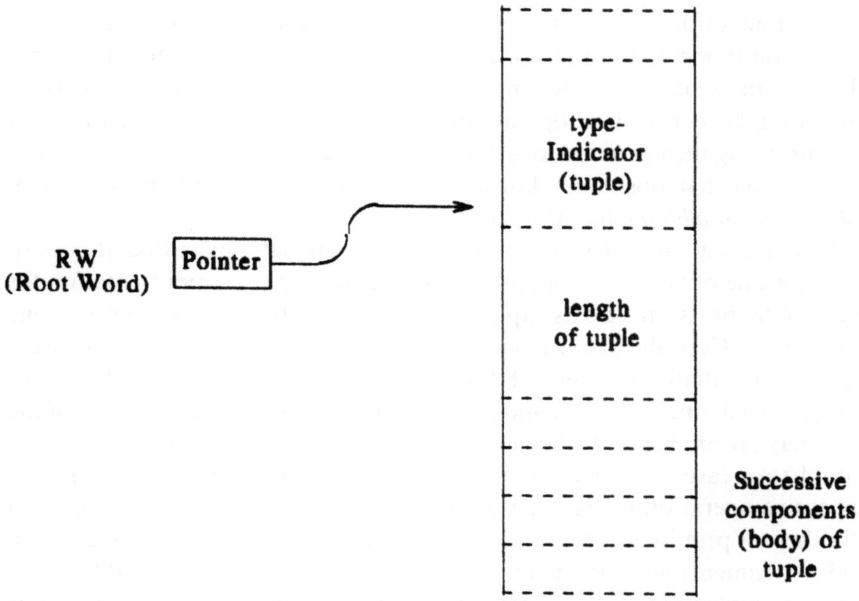

Figure 10.2 Machine-Level Representation of a Tuple

also incur another cost when we evaluate the primitive SETL operation $A(i)$; namely we must check the types of both A and i. More specifically, the following tests must be performed before the i-th element of x is retrieved:

(i) Determine the type of A. A could be a tuple, a string, or a map, or it could have some other type (for which the operation $A(i)$ might be invalid).
(ii) Compare the value of i with the length of A. If $i > \#A$ then $A(i)$ is **om**.

These various tests also require a few dozen machine instructions and therefore add a substantial overhead to the cost of the indexing operation.

10.2 The Standard Representation for Sets

The machine representation of tuples is straightforward and relatively problem-free: a tuple being an ordered sequence of components, can be stored as an ordered sequence of words in memory. When we access a tuple to obtain or modify one of its components, we simply use the index of the desired component to address the component.

Sets are manipulated in a different manner. To see why this is advantageous, consider the basic membership operation such as (x **in** s), which asks whether the current value of x is to be found among the elements of s. Determining this logically involves a search of the elements of s. Searching is also required to implement other basic set operations. For example, when we compute the expression (*s* **with** *x*) we first search *s* to ascertain that the value of *x* is not already contained in *s*, and only if it is not do we perform the insertion operation. In contrast to operations on tuples, which always access components using their position, operations on sets need to locate elements whose value, rather than position, is known. For this reason, sets and maps are often called *content addressable structures.*

Before going on to describe how SETL sets are actually stored, it pays to consider one obvious, though in fact not ideally effective, representation for them: Why not store sets as tuples? The only objection to this choice is one of efficiency. Consider again a membership test (*x* **in** *s*). If the elements of *s* were stored sequentially in some arbitrary order in memory, we would have to compare each one of these elements with *x* to determine the truth value of the membership predicate. If the cardinality of *s* is *n*, then in the worst case it would take case *n* comparisons to compute this predicate, making this an expensive operation if *n* is large. Since the membership operation is basic to all other set primitives (insertion, deletion, union, intersection, map retrieval, and assignment) an efficient membership operation is indispensable to an efficient implementation of sets, and therefore this obvious approach is unacceptably inefficient (for large if not for small sets).

The key to a better representation for sets is the following observation: sets have no a priori order, so that their elements can be stored in any convenient fashion. This suggests that we choose an organization which makes it easy to retrieve an element, given its value. To see how this might be done, suppose first that *s* is a set of alphabetic strings. Then a fairly obvious idea is to store these strings in alphabetic order, in a contiguous sequence of memory locations, and regard this sequence as the representation of the set *s*. This would speed up membership tests because we could then perform a binary search (see Section 5.4.3) to determine where in the set a given string was. Further improvement in performance can be obtained if we keep track of the location at which strings with a given first character begin (very much like the thumbing marks in a dictionary). This would further restrict the range over which we had to search. The actual SETL representation of sets pushes this idea still further, using a data structure called a *hash table* which allows the *value* of a given object *x* to be mapped to a small range of *L* locations in which *x* might be found. In order to apply this technique to sets of elements of arbitrary kinds, we must be able to construct such mappings for objects *x* of any type. The result of applying such a mapping to *x* must be a single location, or a very small range of locations, at which the element *x* will be found if it is present at all. In addition, the data structure we use must allow insertions and deletions to be made easily: note that this is not the case for the alphabetic ordering just suggested. The kind of mapping from values to locations that we will use is called a *hashing function.*

To explain how this data structure works, it is convenient to consider an example, and for specificity's sake we will explain the internal representation

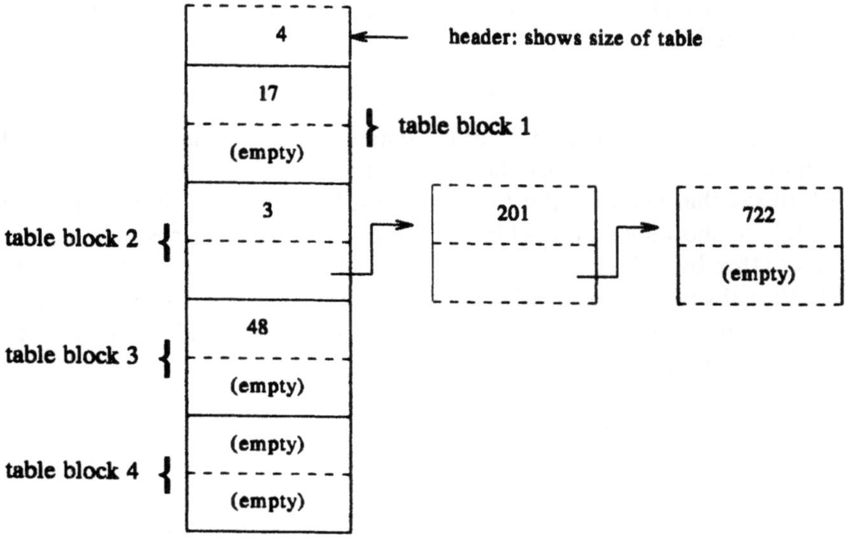

Figure 10.3 Machine-Level Representation of the Set {3, 17, 201, 48, 722}

of a set of integers q. The trick involved in *hashing* is to use the value of q itself to determine the table address at which the set element q will be held. Any function H which converts q into a numerical index to a table of reasonable size can be used: all that is desired is that H should *scatter* the values $H(q)$ in reasonably even fashion over the available table addresses, thus ensuring that we do not attempt to store too many items q in (or near) the same table address. The tables which the SETL implementation uses to represent sets always have a number of entries equal to a power of 2; i.e., 4, 8, 16, 32, etc., table entries are used, depending on the size of the set being stored. The size of the table is adjusted to the size of the set, so that if a set s grows by the addition of new elements, it will eventually be moved to a larger table, and if its shrinks substantially because elements are being removed from it, it will be moved to a smaller table. In this way the SETL implementation ensures that at least half the available entries in the table used to represent a set are occupied, and that table *overloading* (explained in more detail later) never rises to more than two elements per table entry.

In accordance with the preceding remarks, we will suppose that a table of size 4 is being used to represent the five-element set in Figure 10.3. As stated earlier, the standard function $H(q)$ used to map elements to their table positions can be arbitrary, but we want it to *scatter* fairly evenly. This is to say that, given integers $i1$, $i2$.. that are to be placed in a set s, we want the values $H(i1)$, $H(i2)$... to be distributed evenly over the range of table indices, i.e, 1 to 4. Any kind of arithmetic function that yields a number in this range is acceptable as a hashing function. Typically H is some otherwise meaningless sequence of operations, chosen for its simplicity, and for the evenness with which values $H(x)$ will scatter. For example, something like the following might be used:

$$H(q) = ((q + 112)^2 \textbf{ div } 99 \textbf{ mod } 4) + 1$$

(Here we are being suggestive rather than precise; optimal choice of hash functions is a matter that has been studied very extensively, and we do not wish to say that precisely this function is used in the SETL implementation, but only to show something of how a hashing technique works).

Note that by reducing the quantity $(q + 112)^2 \textbf{ div } 99$ modulo 4, we ensure that $H(q)$ always returns a value between 1 and 4, i.e., a number that can be used as an index to an entry in a table of size 4. The exact values that H takes on for the five elements of our set are as follows:

Element q	3	17	201	48	722
Value $H(q)$	2	1	2	3	2

These H values imply that we will store 17 in the first entry of the table representing the set, 48 in the table's third entry, and 3, 201, and 722 in the table's second entry. However, since each table entry can hold no more than one set member, we are forced to place two of these three elements elsewhere. What is done is to place them in separate locations but chain them into a list (called a *clash* list) by means of pointers. The starting location for the clash list containing an element q is simply the hash table location indexed by $H(q)$.

The following examples will clarify the way in which we would use the hash table representation shown in Figure 10.3. If asked to make the test (201 **in** s), where s is the set shown in Figure 10.3, we would calculate $H(201)$, obtaining the result 2, which tells us to examine the second two-word block of the table appearing in Figure 10.3. Upon examining this block, we would note that a chained list L starts in it and would then walk down the list L, looking for the element 201. This will be found when we reach the second element of L. Similarly, if asked to make the test (33 **in** s), we would calculate $H(33) = 1$, and accordingly would examine the first block of the table. It would then be seen that the quantity 33 is not present in this block, and also that the subsidiary *clash* list that could start in this block is empty. This relatively efficient computation would therefore tell us that the value of (33 **in** s) is **false**.

To summarize: when we insert a new element into a set, we calculate its *hash code* in order to determine where in the hash table for S it should be stored. When we perform a membership test on S, we calculate the hash code of the element to know where in the table we must look, and *we use the same hash function each time.*

Maps f are stored in much the same way as sets. (After all, maps are just sets of pairs.) However, the hash code of a pair $[x, y]$ is taken to be the hash code of x, that is, of the domain element of the pair. This makes it easy to find y given x, i.e., to calculate $f(x)$ from x. Figure 10.4 depicts the internal representation of a SETL map; note in particular that the table entries in the

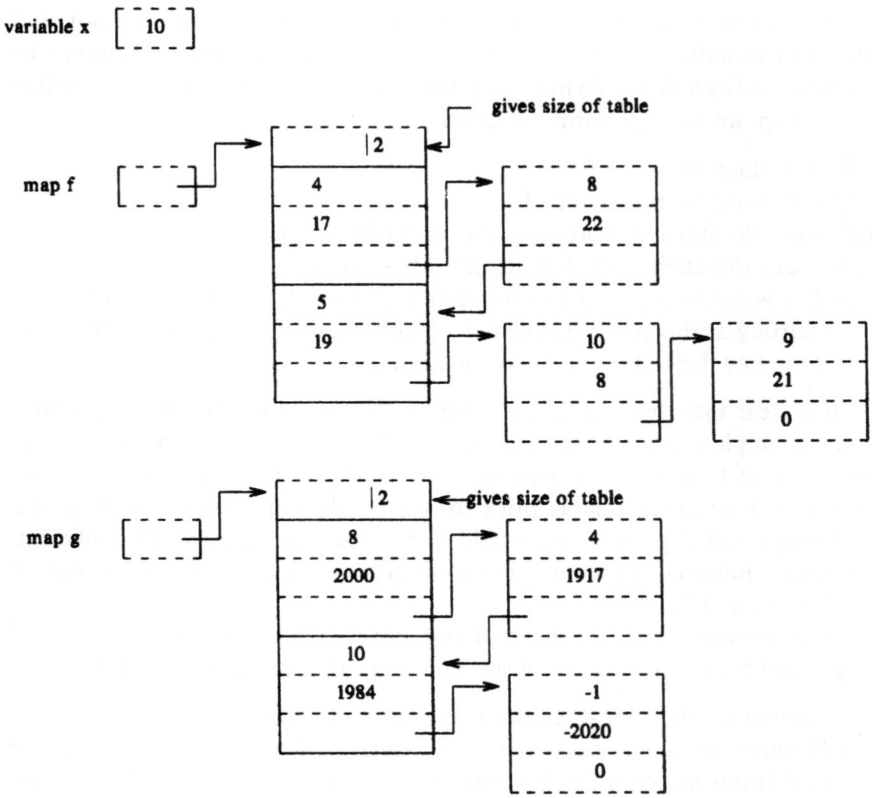

Figure 10.4 Standard SETL Representation of an (Integer) Domain Element x and of Several Maps.

representation of a map are somewhat larger than those used to store elements of sets which are not maps (compare Figure 10.3). We enlarge the table entries in the representation of maps in order to store range elements in immediate proximity to the domain elements to which they correspond. In this example, f and g have the following values:

$$f = \{[4, 17], [8, 22], [5, 19], [10, 8], [9, 21]\}$$

$$g = \{[8, 2000], [4, 1917], [10, 1984], [-1, -2020]\}$$

In working through the last few pages, the attentive reader may have realized that more details have been concealed than revealed. How do we calculate hash values $H(q)$ for quantities q that are not integers? What representation is used for maps that are not single-valued? How do we iterate over sets; how do we test sets for equality? What representation is employed for a set of pairs that is not being used as a map? The SETL implementation, i.e., the SETL run-time support library, must face all these questions and provide effective solutions for them. However, to explain the goals of the data representation language to which this chapter is devoted, we need not, and shall not, describe any of these finer details. All that is important to us can be summarized as follows: To make the basic test (x **in** s), or to evaluate $f(x)$ when f is a map, we must perform the following actions:

(i) Ascertain the type of s (or f)
(ii) Calculate the hash code of x
(iii) Find the starting location of the hash table for s (or f)
(iv) Index this table with the calculated hash code
(v) If x is not found at the position first examined, and there is a clash list starting at this position, examine the elements of this list until either x is found or the end of the list is encountered.

It is clear that this sequence of operations is considerably more expensive than a simple tuple access. Typically, 50 to 100 machine instructions will be executed to complete a standard set membership test or map retrieval. This is not an unreasonable price to pay for the convenience of using sets and maps, but if possible we would like to be considerably more efficient. Gaining additional efficiency is the point of the data structure representation sublanguage of SETL.

The preceding discussion emphasizes two aspects of the execution of important SETL operations on sets and maps that can be considered *costly*:

(a) Each instruction must check the type of its variables.
(b) Hashing must be used to access content addressable objects. These operations are considerably more time-consuming than simple memory references and tuple retrievals.

The data representation sublanguage (DRSL) of SETL, which we will now proceed to describe, allows us to reduce the costs associated with these execution-time activities. This sublanguage gives us a mechanism for adding declarations to a SETL program, declarations which aid the SETL compiler to simplify and in some cases even eliminate expensive computations. The basic ideas used to achieve this are as follows:

(a) In order to reduce expense (a), that is to say, the cost of the type-checking steps that must be performed before a primitive SETL operation is executed, the declarations of DRSL can be used to specify the types that the variables will have at execution time. The types involved here can be *integer*, *boolean*, *string*, *map from integers to strings*, etc. We shall call these declarations *type declarations* for obvious reasons.
(b) In order to reduce the expense associated with hashing operations, we try to avoid repeated rehashing where possible. The DRSL gives us a means to replace repeated rehashing by direct indexing in many cases. The basic idea here is to remember the location of an object after it has been placed in a set or map. The run-time structure that retains this information is called a *base set*, and the declarations that refer to base sets are called

basing declarations. The detailed syntax and semantics of these basing declarations will be described in Section 10.4.

10.3 Type Declarations

We can divide the declarations of the DSRL into two categories: *type declarations* and *basing declarations*. Both of these have the same format, but they are motivated by somewhat different considerations, and basing declarations introduce some rather subtle concepts into the language, discussion of which we will postpone until the next section. In contrast, type declarations are quite straightforward: they describe the types which variables in a SETL program will have at run-time.

However, before specializing our discussion in this way, let us first examine the general syntax and usage of DRSL declarations, also called *representation declarations*, or **repr**s for short. **Repr**s added to a SETL program must be grouped into sequences of declarations bracketed by the keywords **repr** and **end**. Such declarations must appear before any executable statements, and after any declarations for constants and global variables appearing in the same program, module, or procedure. A main program can include a set of **repr** declarations for the global variables declared in a **var** statement, and each procedure can have **repr** declarations for its local variables. We emphasize again that **repr** declarations are optional, and that not all variables in a program or procedure need to be declared. Section 10.8 contains guidelines for the inclusion of **repr**s in a program.

A **repr** clause has one of the following forms:

(1) *name list*: *mode*;
(2) **mode** *name*: *mode*;
(3) **base** *namelist*: *mode*;
(4) **plex base** *namelist*;

where *name list* designates a list of one or more names (identifiers) separated by commas, and *mode* is a type name or a basing descriptor that applies to each of the variables in the list. Clauses of the form (1) are discussed in this section. Mode declarations (2) are examined in the next section, and **repr**s involving bases are discussed in Sections 10.4 and 10.5. An example of (1) is

```
repr
    count, size, left: integer;
    here, there, elsewhere: string;
end;
```

Here the tokens **integer** and **string** are type names; the first **repr** clause declares that the variables *count*, *size*, and *left* will have integer values wherever they appear in the portion of the program which these declarations govern. Similarly, the variables *here*, *there*, and *elsewhere* must be string values wherever they are used. Note that such declarations refer to *all* occurrences of the variables that they name in the same *scope* that they govern. We have seen that, in pure SETL, variables can receive values of different types at various points in the program. In the presence of **repr**s this is no longer the case: values assigned to a variable for which a **repr** is given must *always* have the type that has been declared for the variable. The discipline this imposes on the writer is salutory: one can easily find different names for objects of different types, and it is easier to understand the purpose of a program if the same name is used in the same way wherever it appears.

The systematic list which follows presents most of the modes that can be used in type declarations. Two examples of these *modes*, namely **integer** and **string**, have appeared already. In general, modes can be either *simple* or *compound*. *Simple modes* describe primitive types; *compound modes* describe sets, tuples, and maps. The simple modes allowed in the DRSL are the following:

integer: mode of integers of arbitrary magnitude.

integer *e1 .. e2*: mode of integers constrained to be in the range *e1* to *e2*. Here *e1* and *e2* must be elementary integer-valued expressions involving constants only. Examples and additional details are given later.

real: mode of real numbers.

string: mode of SETL string quantities.

atom: mode of SETL atoms.

The compound modes allowed by the data representation language are as follows:

general: This is the default SETL mode. Quantities declared to have this mode can be arbitrary SETL values.

: The mode symbol '' is simply an allowed abbreviation for **general**.

set($mode_1$): mode of sets all of whose elements are constrained to have mode $mode_1$. Examples showing the use of this construct are given later.

set: allowed abbreviation for **set(general)**.

smap($mode_1$)$mode_2$: mode of single-valued map with domain elements of $mode_1$ and range elements of $mode_2$.

smap($mode_1$): This is simply an allowed abbreviation for **smap**($mode_1$) **general**.

smap: This is simply an allowed abbreviation for **smap(general)general**.

smap($mode_1, .., mode_k$)$mode_r$: mode of single-valued k-parameter map (see Section 3.8.5) with domain elements having mode **tuple**($mode_1, .., mode_2$) (see following discussion) and range elements of $mode_r$.

smap($mode_1, .., mode_k$): abbreviation for **smap**($mode_1, \ldots, mode_k$)**general**.

mmap$\{mode_1\}mode_2$: mode of (possibly) multivalued map with domain elements of $mode_1$ and range elements of $mode_2$.

mmap$\{mode_1\}$: abbreviation for **mmap**$\{mode_1\}$**general**.

mmap: abbreviation for **mmap{general}general**.

mmap$\{mode_1,..mode_k\}mode_r$: mode of possibly multivalued k-parameter map (see Section 3.8.5) with domain elements having mode **tuple**$(mode_1, \ldots, mode_k)$ (see following discussion) and range elements of $mode_r$.

mmap$\{mode_1,\ldots,mode_k\}$: abbreviation for **mmap**$\{mode_1,\ldots,mode_k\}$**general**.

tuple$(mode_1,\ldots,mode_k)$: mode of **tuple** of known length k, whose j-th component is known to have mode $mode_j$.

tuple$(mode_1)$: mode of **tuple** of unknown length, all of whose components are constrained to have mode $mode_1$.

tuple: This is simply an allowed abbreviation for **tuple(general)**.

tuple$(mode_1)(e)$: mode of tuple of unknown length, but of estimated length e, all of whose components are constrained to have mode $mode_1$. Here e must be an elementary integer-valued expression involving constants only.

proc$(mode_1,\ldots,mode_k)mode_r$: mode of k-parameter programmed procedure whose parameters have respective modes $mode_1,\ldots, mode_k$, and which returns a $mode_r$ value.

proc$(mode_1,\ldots,mode_k)$**general**: can also be used to describe non-value-returning procedures whose parameters have respective modes $mode_1, \ldots, mode_k$.

proc: mode of a procedure unconstrained as to mode of arguments and of result value, if any.

op$(mode_1, mode_2)mode_r$: mode of infix operator whose two parameters have respective modes $mode_1$ and $mode_2$, and which returns a $mode_r$ value.

op$(mode_1, mode_2)$: abbreviation for **op**$(mode_1, mode_2)$**general**.

op$(mode_1)mode_2$: mode of prefix operator, with one $mode_1$ argument, which returns a $mode_2$ value.

op$(mode_1)$: abbreviation for **op**$(mode_1)$**general**.

Finally, the qualifier **untyped** can be applied to **integer** and **real** modes. This qualifier indicates that the corresponding mode is a numeric type that can be handled directly by the hardware of the machine, so that no checks on their bounds need to be performed. This makes manipulation of variables with such types particularly efficient. Examples of use of this qualifier are

account: **untyped integer**;
vector: **tuple (untyped real)**;

If the values of such variables are not within the bounds of numeric operations on the machine, the results of any operations involving these variables are undefined.

10.3.1 Mode declarations

The clause

mode ⟨name⟩: mode;

serves to define ⟨name⟩ as a *mode designator*. After such a declaration, the name can be used wherever a mode designator can appear, i.e., in subsequent reprs. For example:

```
mode edge: tuple (node, node);
mode distance: smap (edge) integers;
min_dist, estimated_dist: distance;
e1, e2: edge;
```

Naming modes in such a fashion contributes to program readability and gives a more natural description of the relationships among variables.

10.3.2 An example of the use of type declarations

Next we give a simple example of the use of reprs, which we will apply to one of the prime-finding methods described in Section 4.3.5.

```
program primes;

repr
   prime, next, limit, c: integer;
   prime, candidates: tuple(integer);
   multiples: set(integer);
end;

read(limit);

candidates := [3, 5 .. limit];
primes := [2];
prime := 2;

(while prime ** 2 <= limit)

   prime from b candidates;
   primes with := prime;
   multiples := {prime ** 2};

   (forall c in candidates)

     next := prime * c;
     if next > limit then quit;
     else multiples with := next;
     end if;
   end forall;

   candidates := [c in candidates | c notin multiples];

end while;

primes + := candidates;

print(primes);

end program;
```

In this example, we have supplied type declarations for all variables in the program, including the loop variable *c*. We have not supplied size information for the tuples primes and candidates, because we do not know a priori the number of components that they will have. Note that the variable *limit*, which defines the range in which we want to find primes, gets its value from a **read** statement, and therefore its value is not known to the compiler and cannot be used to declare any variable in the program. That is to say, if we had written the declarations

candidates: **tuple(integer)**(limit);   prime: **integer** 2..limit;

the compiler would reject them on the grounds that *limit* is not a constant.

Our next example concerns graphs. It is the well-known algorithm for determining the shortest distance from one vertex of a graph to all the other vertices.

As before (see Section 4.3.8.2) we regard a graph as consisting of a set of nodes (or vertices) and a set of edges. Each edge is represented by an ordered pair [from, to] of nodes. It is convenient to regard the set of edges as a map: given a node *n*, its image under this map is the set of nodes that are linked to *n* by one edge of the graph. In the program that follows, this map is called *successors*. It is a multivalued map, because several nodes may be reachable from the same *n* by an edge. Each edge has some (positive) assigned length. The length of each edge is represented by a map from edges to integers. The minimum distance from the start vertex to all the other edges, which is the desired output of the program, is a map from nodes to integers. The nodes themselves do not have a particular type: we can use integers to describe them, or strings, or atoms, depending on the application. In the **repr**s that follow, we introduce the mode *node* (see following example for details) and state that *node* can be any type (i.e., general). This allows us to represent program variables in terms of nodes, without having to be any more specific about what a node actually is.

The algorithm works as follows: we construct a set *reached*, whose elements are nodes whose shortest distance to *start* has been determined. Initially *reached* only contains *start*. Each step in the algorithm adds one node to the set *reached*. The node to be added next is chosen as the one whose estimated shortest distance to *start* is the smallest. We estimate the shortest distance from *start* to any node *n* as follows:

(a) If there is an edge from start to *n*, the estimated shortest distance is the length of that edge.
(b) When a node *new* is reached, there may be a path from-start-to-*n* that goes through the node *new* ending with an edge from *new* to *n*. In that case, calculate the distance from *start to n* along that path: it is the minimum distance to *new* plus the length of the edge from *new* to *n*. If this distance is smaller than the previous estimate of the distance to *n*, use this value as the new estimate.

```
program shortest_paths;

var
   successors, length, start, estimate,
   min_distance, min_estimate, reached,
   next, outer, n;

repr

   mode node: general;

   successors: mmap{node}set{node};   $ see preceding comment
   length: smap(node, node)integer;    $ maps each graph edge into its
                                       $ length

   estimate, min_distance: smap(mode)integer;
   $ Maps each node into its estimated idstance from -start-

   min_estimate: integer;              $ shortest estimated distance from
                                       $ -start- to any node not yet
                                       $ processed
   reached: set(node);                 $ set of all nodes reached so far
                                       $ along a path from -start-

   start, next, outer, n: node;

end;

read(length, start);                   $ intially, only -start- has been
                                       $ reached

length + := {[[a, b], d]: [[b, a], d] in length};

$ We represent an undirected graph by giving the distances along each edge,
  in both directions.

successors := { };
(forall [[a, b], d] in length)
   successors{a} with := b;
end forall;

estimate := { };
all_nodes := domain successors + (range successors);

reached := {start};

$ Estimate the distance to the nodes that are adjacent to -start-.

(for next in successors{start})
   estimate(next) := length(start, next);
end for;

min_distance := { };

(while reached /= all_nodes)
   $ Among the nodes that have not been reached yet, find the one
```

```
  $ whose estimated distance to -start- is the smallest.
  min_estimate := min/[estimate(n): n in all_nodes | n notin reached];

   if min_estimate = om then
    print ('Nodes', all_nodes—reached, 'not reachable');
    quit;
   end if;

  assert exists next in all_nodes | estimate(next) = min_estimate;

  $ The minimum estimate is the shortest distance to next, which is now
  $ considered reached.
  reached with := next;
  min_distance(next) := min_estimate;

  $ Update the estimate for all the nodes adjacent to next. A path through
  $ next may yield a shorter distance than that estimated previously.

  (for outer in successors{next})

    if estimate(outer) = om then estimate(outer) := min_estimate +
    length(next, outer);
    else estimate(outer) min := min_estimate + length(next, outer);
    end if;

  end for;

end while;

(for n in all_nodes_| min_distance(n) /= om)
  print('The shortest distance from start to', n, 'is', min_distance(n));
end for;

end program;
```

10.4 Basing Declarations

In Section 10.1 we remarked that the execution of SETL programs is slowed by two kinds of inefficiencies:

(a) Inefficiencies associated with type checking: every SETL operation is preceded by a test to determine the type of its arguments.
(b) Inefficiencies associated with the use of sets and maps: every membership test, every set insertion, every map retrieval or modification requires the calculation of a hash code, followed by a retrieval from a hash table. In what follows we will refer to this sequence of actions as a *hashed search*.

Inefficiencies of type (a) can be corrected by supplementing a SETL program with type declarations, as described in Section 10.3. We therefore turn our attention to the means available to correct inefficiencies of type (b).

We begin with the following obvious remark: many programs that use sets and maps search repeatedly for objects that they need to access. As an example, consider the following typical fragment:

```
S := {....};          $ Some set former expression.
M := { };             $ An empty map.

(for x in S)
   M(x) := g(x);      $ Compute map M, whose domain is S;
                      $ g is some defined function.
end;
```

Note that this code performs two hash searches for every element x of the set S: one when S is built, and the second when M is built (i.e., when an element x of S becomes an element of the domain of M). This situation is fairly typical, and it illustrates the kind of redundancy that we want to minimize.

The following somewhat more subtle example shows another aspect of the problem of redundant hashed searching. Consider a set intersection operation:

```
S3 := S1*S2;
```

The way in which the SETL run-time system computes *S3* is best described by the following code fragment:

```
S3 := { };

(for x in S1 | x in S2)
   S3 with := x;
end;
```

This means that an element which is in the intersection of *S1* and *S2* will be searched for twice: first when it is tested for membership in *S2*, then again when it is inserted into *S3*. Moreover, a hashed search will also have been performed when *S1* was built. Thus, as a single value is inserted into and retrieved from various composite objects, it becomes the object of repeated, redundant searches.

It should be clear at this point that these repeated searches can be eliminated if we somehow *save* the location of objects so that they can be accessed repeatedly without the need to search for them every time. It is also characteristic of the examples presented that some of the objects which play a role in them appear in several hash tables and must be searched for in all of them. This last remark suggests that such objects should be kept in one location, and that every use of the object should make use of a *pointer* to this location, so that no redundant searching will be required.

In other words, if we remember where we leave things, we won't waste time looking for them every time we need them!

To achieve this effect, the data representation sublanguage of SETL uses a special kind of set, called *a base set*, or *base* for short, in which such shared values can be stored.

10.4.1 Base sets

Base sets are special data structures which contain values that are likely to be referenced repeatedly and to be parts of several composite objects (sets, maps, and tuples). Base sets are sets, but sets of a very special nature, which cannot be used in the same way as other sets in SETL. Since they are sets we will speak of the *elements* of a base, but since they are special we will not apply any of the standard set operations to bases: bases are only introduced to minimize the number of hash searches that must be carried out during program execution and to improve the representation of other composite values.

Bases are introduced into a SETL program by means of declarations of the form

base *namelist*; (1)

or

base *namelist*: *mode*; (2)

The form (1) declares that all names in the list are bases whose elements have unspecified type. Form (2) specifies that their elements are of type *mode*.

Examples of the more specific declaration form (2) are

base all_strings: **string**;

base all_nodes, all_records: **atom**;

The *modes* that can appear in (2) include those described in Section 10.3. Additional modes, to be discussed later, arise from the existence of bases themselves. In particular if x is a variable whose value is expected to appear as part of several composite objects, then we can declare x as follows:

x: **elmt** B; (3)

This declaration states that every value assumed by the variable x in the course of program execution will be an element of the base B.

Bases declared in SETL programs are used only to define the modes of based objects. They are never explicitly manipulated by the program and cannot appear in expressions or executable statements. We emphasize again that they serve only to state the existence of significant relationships among actual program objects. These relationships are defined by means of based declarations, and thus, directly or indirectly, in terms of modes of the form (**elmt** B).

The effect of a declaration of the form (3) is the following: whenever the variable x is assigned a new value, this value is automatically inserted as a new element of the base B. The new value is placed in a special structure, called an *element block* of the base B, which contains several pieces of information that pertain to the current value of x. Subsequent references to this value can then use pointers to the element block thereby created.

The information contained in a element block is the following:

(a) The value of the element.
(b) A system-assigned numerical index, which is uniquely associated with this element. In effect, these indices *number* the base elements. We will see later that the existence of this numbering allows us to use particularly efficient representations for certain other based objects.
(c) Several supplementary storage locations can also be allocated in each base block. These can be used to hold information about other sets and maps in which the value represented by the element block appears.

To explain the efficiency gains attainable by the use of based representations, we will first explain the basing declarations that are available for sets and maps. We discuss based maps before based sets, because the efficiency gains obtained for maps are particularly easy to describe.

10.4.2 Based maps

If the domains of several of the maps appearing in a program are expected to overlap (i.e., if these maps are likely to be defined on some of the same values) then it may be appropriate to declare a common domain base for these maps. Similarly, if a set is expected to overlap with the domain of a map, it is often advantageous to specify a common base for the set and the map. This is done for maps as follows. Let B be a base introduced by one of the declarations (1) to (3). Then the declarations

f: **smap(elmt B)** $mode_1$;
g: **smap(elmt B)** $mode_2$;
h: **smap(elmt B)** $mode_3$;

state that f, g, and h are single-valued maps, whose domain elements are elements of the base B, and whose range elements have other specified modes.

The element block structure described in the previous paragraph allows the maps f, g, and h to be represented efficiently, in several ways, called *local*, *remote*, and *sparse*.

10.4.2.1 Local maps

In the element block of B corresponding to a given value x, we can allocate storage to hold the values of $f(x)$, $g(x)$, and $h(x)$. If this is done, the structure of each element block of B will be as follows:

Suppose that f is represented in this way, and that x has been declared to have **elmt** B representation, so that it will be represented by a pointer to an element block. If, during program execution, we need to evaluate $f(x)$ for a value x which is already an element of B, then we can simply retrieve the value of $f(x)$ from the element block for x. This evaluation of $f(x)$ amounts to just one machine-level pointer reference operation and is thus considerably

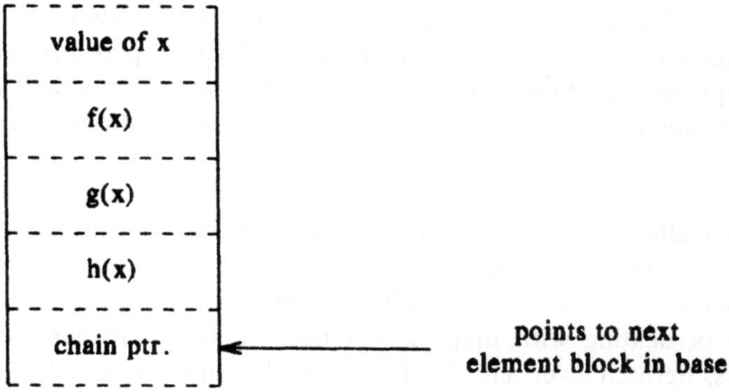

Figure 10.5 A Simple "Element Block" in the Based Representation of Three Maps

faster than a hashed search. Hence representation in the manner shown in Figure 10.5 is the most efficient one to use for maps which are manipulated exclusively by simple storage and retrieval operations.

Because in this representation map values are stored in immediate proximity to the domain value to which they correspond, this map representation is called **local** representation. To ensure that a map is represented as a **local** map, it must be declared as follows:

$$\text{f: } \textbf{local smap(elmt } \text{B) } \textit{mode}; \tag{4}$$

The following figure shows additional details of data structure introduced by the base declaration (1) and by additional declarations of the form (4), on the maps *f* and *g* defined in 10.2. Compare this figure with the structure depicted in Figure 10.4.

Local map representations handle storage and retrieval operations efficiently but are inefficient for some other purposes. For example, the fact that the

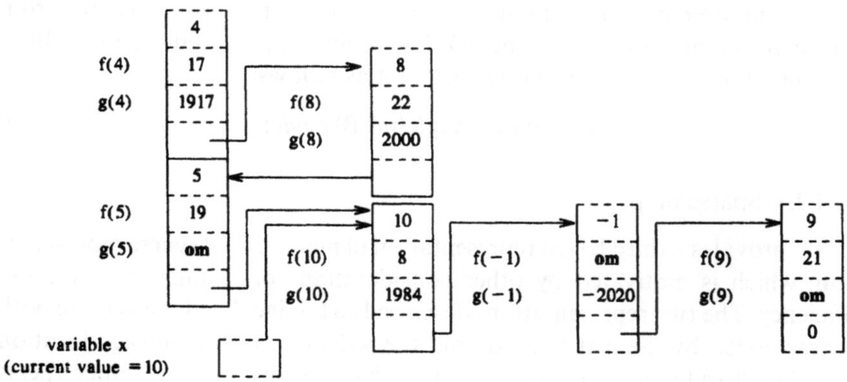

Figure 10.6 Base Table which Stores the Representation of Two Maps *f* and *g*. The Variable *x* Is Represented Here by a Pointer to the Appropriate Block in this Base

range values of a local map are spread over the element blocks of the base maps makes it time-consuming to incorporate a local map as a part of some other composite object (say a tuple of maps.) Building the range of f is also time-consuming if f is represented locally. Moreover, iterations of the form

(for y = f(x))...

will also be inefficient if f is defined for only a few of the elements of its declared base B. This is because such an iteration must examine each element of B to see whether f is defined for it. Thus **local** basing is generally not the ideal way of dealing with maps which need to be made parts of larger composites, iterated over, etc. To handle such situations effectively, other based representations are available.

10.4.2.2 Remote maps

We therefore pass to discussion of a second form of based representation, whose use is advantageous in some of the situations discussed previously, in which **local** based representation leads to inefficiencies. This second form of based representation is called the **remote** based representation. It exploits the fact that each element block in a base contains a numerical index that identifies the value that the block represents. The availability of this numerical index makes it possible to store the range values of a **remote**ly based map f in a tuple t (see Figure 10.8). Suppose, to be specific, that ix is the index stored in the block that holds the value x. Then the value of $f(x)$ is held in the ix-th element of the tuple t. In this case, $f(x)$ is retrieved as follows:

(i) Using the pointer in x, retrieve ix from the element block of x.
(ii) Add ix to the starting address of the tuple t that holds the range of f, retrieve the ix-th component of this tuple, and return its value.

This sequence of operations is considerably faster than a hashed search, even though it is slower than access to a **local** map. (We call this type of map representation **remote** because it stores range elements at some distance from the corresponding domain elements). To specify that a based map is to have remote representation, we simply declare it as follows:

g: **remote smap(elmt** B) *mode*; (5)

10.4.2.3 Sparse maps

SETL provides a third based representation of maps, called **sparse** representation, which is motivated by other considerations of storage and iteration efficiency. The two representations described so far, **local** and **remote**, are both characterized by the fact that to hold the values of $f(x)$, a storage location must be allocated for each element of the base, regardless of whether $f(x)$ is defined or is **om**. In the **local** case, this location is allocated directly in the element block of x; in the **remote** case, this location is the array component location corresponding to the identifying index of x. In both cases, if f is sparsely defined over its base, then a substantial number of storage locations will be wasted. (By *sparsely defined* we mean that $f(x)$ /= **om** only for a small percentage of all the values x in the base of f). For such sparse maps, the third, so-called **sparse**, based representation may be advantageous. To give a map f this representation, we declare it as

f: **sparse map(elmt** B) *mode* (6)

The **sparse** map representation uses a hash table, very much like that used for standard unbased maps. However, the **sparse** map representation does not hold the value of each of its domain elements, but rather represents each domain element x of f by a pointer to the element block in B that represents x. The distinction should be clarified by Figure 10.7, which compares the organization of unbased and sparse maps.

Evaluation of $f(x)$ for a sparse map is distinctly less efficient than for a remote map, but somewhat faster than for an unbased map. As already noted, an important reason for using sparse maps is storage efficiency. Map iteration is an operation that also benefits from the use of the sparse representations. For a local or remote map, the iteration

(**for** y = f(x))

require a full iteration over the base B of map f, which then bypasses the elements of the base for which f is undefined. In other words, the iteration is performed as if it were written:

(**for** x **in** B | (y := f(x)) /= **om**)

If $f(x)$ = **om** for most elements of B it is plain that this iteration will examine a large number of useless elements. If f is represented as a sparse map, its domain is directly available, and no useless elements need to be examined.

The qualifiers **local**, **remote**, and **sparse** can be omitted from a basing declaration. The *default* if all are omitted is **sparse**, that is

f: **smap(elmt** B) *mode* and f: **sparse** smap(elmt B) *mode*

are equivalent.

10.4.3 Based representations for sets

Three types of based representations are available for sets; these representations parallel the ones for maps which we have just described. Based sets can therefore be described as having **local**, **remote**, or **sparse** representations.

(a) Suppose that the following basing declaration is given:

S1, S2, S3: **local set(elmt B)**;

Then *S1*, *S2*, and *S3* are stored internally as follows: in the element block

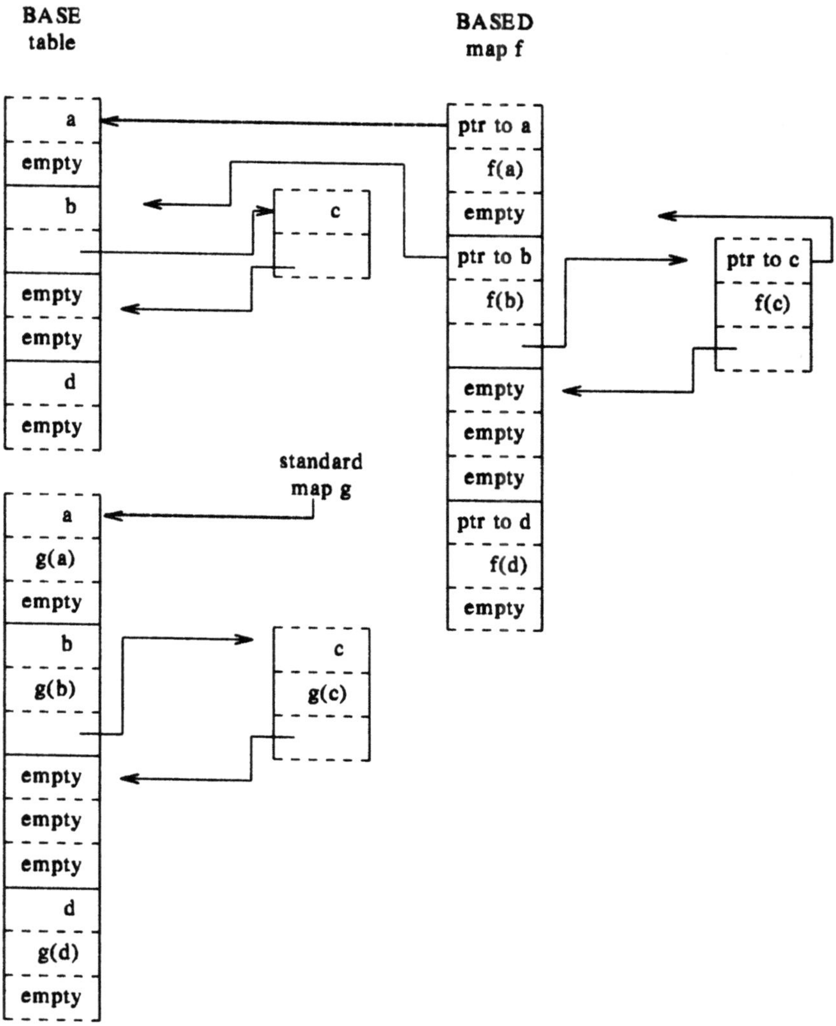

Figure 10.7 Internal Representation of Unbased and of Sparse Maps

of each element x of B, we reserve one bit to indicate the membership of x in $S1$, another bit to indicate membership in $S2$, and so on. These bits, are allocated in fixed locations within every element block of B (see Figure 10.9).

When this representation is used, then the test (x **in** S) and the set operations (x **with** S) and (S **less** x) are handled in a particularly efficient way when x is an element of the base B: in this case, x is represented by a pointer to its element block, and all that is needed is examination or modification of a single bit at a fixed position in that block, which can be

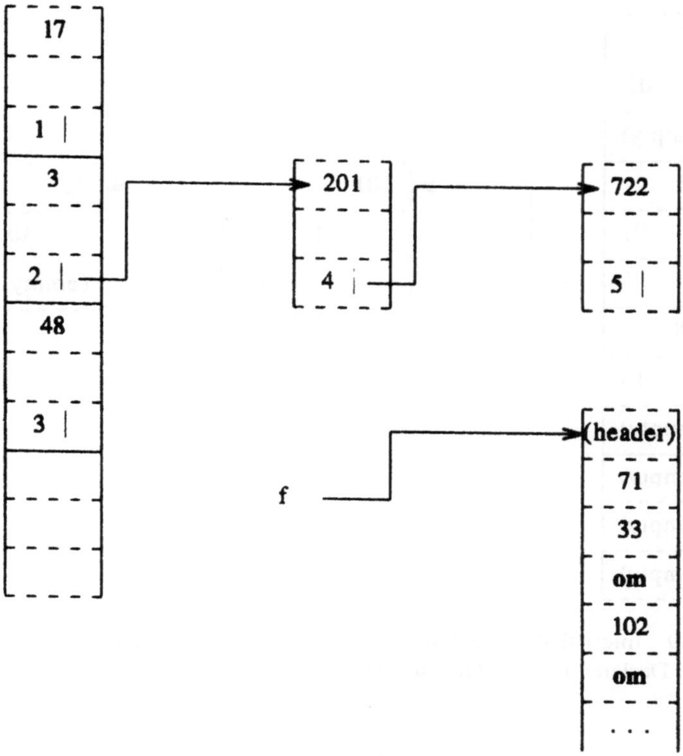

Figure 10.8 Internal Representation of the Map $f = \{[17, 71], [3, 33], [201, 102]\}$ in **remote smap(elmt** *B*) Form. *B* Also Contains the Value 48, But $f(48)$ Is Currently Undefined.

accomplished in very few machine operations. The set representation just described is also storage-efficient, because it uses only 1 bit per element of a based set, in contrast to the several words per element which are required in an (unbased) hash table.

For sets that are constructed and accessed by the preceding operations exclusively, the **local** representation just described is to be preferred over others. However, the drawbacks of this representation are similar to those mentioned for local maps. It is well to discuss the point in more detail. Certain crucial facts affecting the efficiency of based representations derive from particular semantic rules of SETL. As already emphasized, the use of based representations is not allowed to change the meaning of a SETL program: basing declarations can only affect its efficiency. The elaborate machinery of pointers, indices, and bit positions that we have been describing can in no way affect the semantics of the original (undeclared) program to which such declarations may be added. This means in particular that the use of basings must cause no nonstandard side effects. Recall that the semantic definition of SETL requires that the fragment

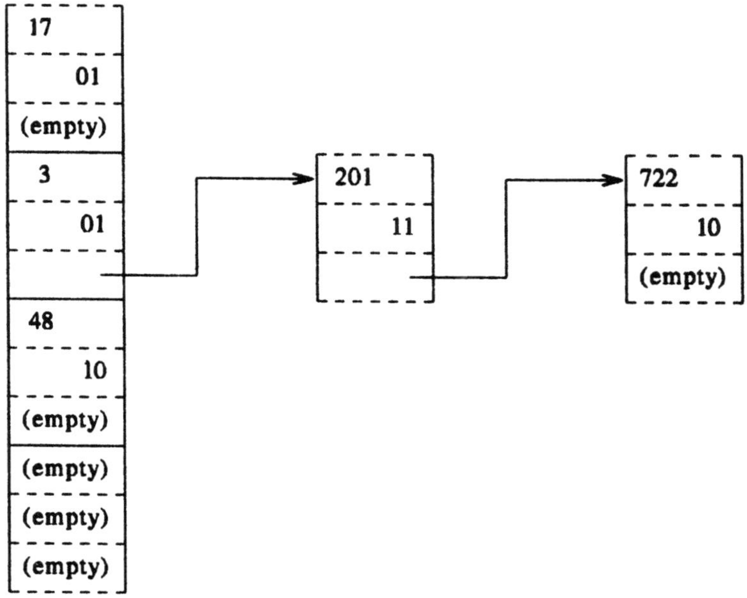

Figure 10.9 Internal Representation of Two Sets *s1* = {17, 3, 201}, *s2* = {201, 48, 722}, Both Declared to Have **local set**(**elmt** *B*) Representation

S1 := {1};
S2 := S1;
S1 **with** := 2;

gives *S2* the value {1}, and that the insertion of 2 into *S1* which follows subsequently does not affect the value of *S2*. The original value is *S2* is preserved because, logically speaking, it is given a "personal" copy of the value {1}, rather than *sharing* this value with *S1*. (In fact this copy is created right before *S1* is modified, but this is an implementation detail). Now if *S1* is a **local** based set and *S2* is not, then producing a copy of *S1* is a potentially expensive process which requires full iteration over the base *B* to extract the elements of *B* which are in *S1*. Furthermore, if *S1* is itself inserted into some composite object, as in

SC **with** := S1;

it must be copied first, in order to prevent accidental sharing of values (and potential modification) between *S1* and the (now anonymous) element of *SC* which holds the value of *S1*. Because of this requirement, **local** sets can become sources of run-time inefficiencies whenever they must themselves be shared. Hence, **local** sets should only be used for sets that only appear in elementary insertion, deletion, and membership tests and that do not become themselves elements or components of larger composite objects.

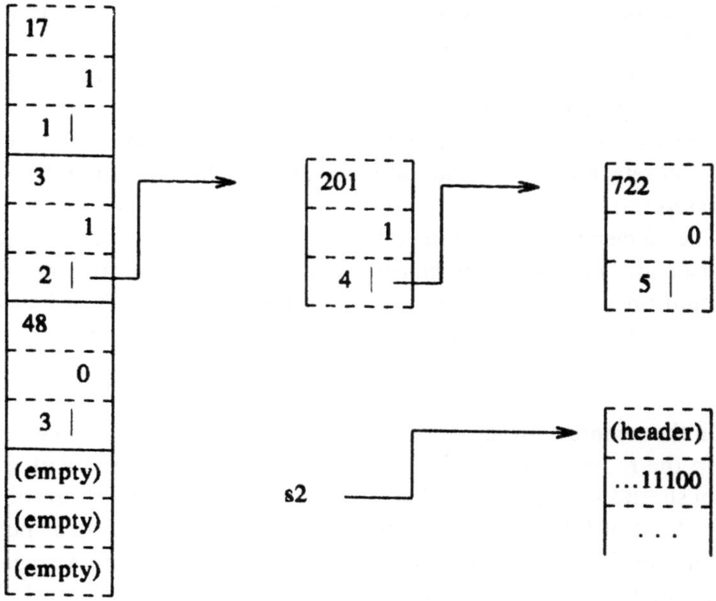

Figure 10.10 Internal Representation of the Sets *s1* = {17, 3, 201} and *s2* = {201, 48, 722}, with Declared Representations *s1*: **local set(elmt** *B*) and *s2*: **remote set(elmt** *B*).

(b) The declaration

R1, R2, R3: **remote** set(**elmt** B);

gives *R1*, *R2*, and *R3* a representation which is particularly efficient for global set operations, i.e., union, intersection, set difference, and set assignment. This representation, which is analogous to the **remote** representation for maps (and which is called the **remote** set representation), makes use of the identifying index present in each element block. More specifically, each of the sets *R1*, *R2*, *R3* appearing in the preceding declaration is represented by a tuple of zeroes and ones, which at the implementation level is actually a sequence of machine bits (see Figure 10.10). These bits are in one-to-one correspondence with the elements of the base *B*: the element block whose index is *i* corresponds to the *i*-th bit in this bit-vector. If the value in element block *i* is an element of the set *R1*, then the corresponding bit in the bit-vector representation of *R1* is on, but otherwise off. The *i*-th position in the representation of *R2* and *R3* is used in the same way to indicate membership of an element of *B* in each of these based sets. If *R1*, *R2*, etc., are given **remote** representation, then the elementary set operations (*x* **in** *R1*, *R1* **with** *x*, *R1* **less** *x*) can be performed in the following manner, assuming as before that *x* is an element of the base *B*:

(i) Retrieve the index *i* of *x* from the element block of *x* in *B*.

(ii) Use this index to access the *i*-th bit in the bit-vector which represents *R1*.

(iii) Return the value of this bit (or modify this bit if a **with** or **less** operation is being performed).

This process is somewhat more time-consuming than the same operation on local sets, but it is considerably faster than the same operation on an unbased set.

The efficiency gains obtained for certain global set operations (union, intersection, etc.) are particularly substantial when the **remote** set representation is used. Suppose, for example, that *R1*, *R2*, *R3* have the representation shown and that we want to evaluate the union

R3 := R1 + R2;

Then the **remote** representation of *R3* can be calculated as follows: the *i*-th bit in the representation of *R3* (corresponding to some element *x* of the base) should be on if *x* is either in *R1* or *R2*, i.e., if the *i*-th bit of *R1* or the *i*-th bit of *R2* is on. The machine-level boolean operation *or* performs exactly this bit-by-bit operation on a full machine word in a single step. Thus, on a 32-bit machine, the **or**-ing of two bit-vectors of size 1000 will take less than 50 machine operations. By contrast, the union of two unbased sets of size 1000 will require 1000 membership tests and up to 1000 hash table insertions. Similarly the intersection operation on remote sets reduces to the machine-level **and** operation, with the same gains in speed. Thus, for large sets on which union and intersection operations are frequently performed, **remote** representations are extremely efficient.

(c) Finally, for representing sets that are relatively sparse (i.e., have a cardinality which is much smaller than that of their base set) and over which iterations are frequently performed, a **sparse** set representation is provided. The declaration

SP1, SP2, SP3: **sparse set(elmt** B);

specifies that SP1, SP2 and SP3 are to be represented by means of hash tables, in which, rather than storing the values of the set elements we keep pointers to these values, i.e., pointers to the element blocks in the base *B* that holds the actual element values.

As in the map case, the qualifiers **local**, **remote**, and **sparse** can be omitted, and **sparse** is the default: If no qualifier appears in a basing declaration for a set, it is equivalent to specifying a **sparse** representation for it.

10.4.4 Basing declarations for multivalued maps

We saw in Section 10.4.2 that declaring a based representation for a single-valued map relates the domain of the map to some base in which the domain elements of the map are automatically inserted. A similar representation is available for multivalued maps; i.e., multivalued maps (which is to say **mmaps**) can be given **local, remote**, or **sparse** representations. Moreover, it is possible to declare a based representation for the range of a multivalued map F. The value of $F\{x\}$ is by definition a set, and therefore the based representation for a multivalued map will generally specify an additional basing which determines the representation of the range sets of F. For example, we can declare

successors: **local mmap(elmt B) remote set(elmt B);**

This declaration specifies that for each x **in** B the image set successors$\{x\}$ is stored in the element block of x, and that this image set is always to be represented as a bit-vector. Similarly, the declaration

successors: **local mmap(elmt B) sparse set(elmt B);**

specifies that the image set successors$\{x\}$ is to be stored as a sparse set, i.e., as a hash table containing pointers to elements of B. Note that the attribute **local** cannot be used for image sets of multivalued maps. This follows from our remarks in Section 10.4.3 on the awkwardness of making local objects into subparts of composite structures.

10.5 Base Sets Consisting of Atoms Only

The based data structure shown in Figure 10.5 serves to support two fundamental operations:

(a) The ability to locate an item x in a base by searching a short list of items, from a starting list position which can be calculated easily once the value of x is known
(b) The ability to iterate over all the elements in the base

Operation (a) is only required when an object x is converted to **elmt** B representation and we need to determine whether x has already been inserted into the base B. Hence, if the only elements ever inserted into B are atoms, and if all of these are created by easily located calls to the **newat** operator, then the searching operation (a) is not required, since each call to **newat** produces a unique object. Hence the blocks constituting such a base can be stored as a simple list. The elements of this list only need to be linked together if iteration over some set having the representation **set (elmt** B**), smap(elmt** B**)**, or **mmap(elmt** B**)** appears in the program. If this is not the case, then no links are necessary; the element blocks of B are then independent.

To allow declaration of these important special cases, the data representation sublanguage allows the keyword **plex** to be prefixed to **base**, as in

B: **plex base**; (1)

If B is a **plex base**, then only atoms can be given **elmt** B representation.

10.6 Constant Bases

A constant set, introduced by a constant declaration (see Section 8.1), as in

const colors = {red, blue, green};

can be used as a base if it is declared as such by writing

base colors;

Elements of such a base *B*, i.e., values *x* having the representation **elmt** *B*, can be represented in a fixed small number *n* of bits. Specifically, *n* must be at least as large as the logarithm of the number #*B* of elements in *B*. Internally, a constant base *B* is represented by a contiguous series of blocks, and an element *x* having the representation **elmt** *B* is represented by a short integer index that locates the block corresponding to *x*. Remote subsets *s* of *B* can then be represented by bit-vectors. In this case, the membership test *x* **in** *s* will be particularly fast if *x* and *s* have the representations **elmt** *B* and **set(elmt** *B*), respectively, since then the representation of *x* is simply the index of the bit in the vector representing *s* which determines the Boolean result of the test *x* **in** *s*. A similar remark applies to maps *f* having the representation **smap(elmt** *B*) or **mmap(elmt** *B*). Moreover, since the internal representation of any value of mode **elmt** *B* can be short, it is possible to pack several **elmt** *B* values into a single machine word. To achieve this, one uses the representation qualifier **packed**, in the manner explained in Section 10.7.

10.7 The Packed Representations

The keyword **packed** can be prefixed to **smap** or **tuple** modes. That is, we can write

f: **packed local smap(elmt** B)mode; (1)
g: **packed remote smap(elmt** B)mode;
h: **packed tuple**(mode);

etc. However, for these constructs to be legal, the mode indicator *mode* shown in (1) must designate some packable mode, i.e., some mode of values which can be represented in less than a full machine memory word. (Note that the machine words of typical present-day computers generally contain between 32 and 64 bits of information. Thus, for example, if a quantity can be represented in just 4 bits, i.e., if it can take on at most 16 different values, then between 8 and 16 quantities of this kind can generally be represented by parts of a single machine word.)

Modes of the two following kinds are packable in this sense:

(i) The mode **elmt** *B*, where *B* is a constant base (see Section 10.6).
(ii) The mode **integer** n1..n2 (see Section 10.3), provided that the interval [*n*1..*n*2] over which integers of this mode range is sufficiently small.

If the mode appearing in a declaration (1) is packable, then the SETL compiler will know how many bits are required to represent values having this mode. It will then be able to store several packable local map values like $f(x)$ (cf. (1)) in a single machine word of the base block of B representing an **elmt** B value x. Moreover, in the vector used to store range values of a **packed remote** map (like the g of (1)), it will be possible to store several map values per machine word. Similarly, several tuple components of a **packed tuple** (like the h of (1)) can be stored per machine word.

This use of packed structures saves memory space, thereby reducing the space needed to run SETL programs. On the other hand, the number of machine cycles needed to run the program will rise slightly, owing to the necessity to convert quantities between their packed and unpacked forms. However, since the cost of such conversion is small (provided that effective representations are chosen for all the variables appearing in a program; see Section 10.8), the storage economy obtainable by packing data where possible can far outweigh the modest execution-time costs which packing incurs.

10.8 Guidelines for the Effective Use of the Data Representation Sublanguage

By adding appropriate data representation declarations to a program, it will often be possible to increase its efficiency substantially. Moreover, a SETL program for which a well-thought-out set of representations has been specified will often constitute a detailed blueprint from which an efficient program in some lower-level language such as PASCAL, PL/I, or Ada can be generated, by straightforward transcription. In this section we will explain the principles governing effective choice of data representation declarations, note some of the restrictions governing the use of the representation sublanguage, and also point out some of the efficiency pitfalls of which you should beware.

As already noted, the main aim of the data representation sublanguage is to speed up functional evaluations $f(x)$ and $f\{x\}$, as well as membership tests (x **in** s), by ensuring that for as many such evaluations as possible x has **elmt** B representation and f has **smap(elmt** B) representation (or **mmap(elmt** B) representation), s has set(**elmt** B) representation, and x and f and s are based on the same base B. On the other hand, to attain a net gain by using this approach, we must be sure that the cost of converting elements x, maps f, and sets s to their based representations does not outweigh the advantage gained by use of such representations. We must also be sure that our choice of representations does not cause excessive object copying to take place.

Objects are converted between different internal representations in the following circumstances:

(i) When a SETL value is read from an external file by a **read** statement and assigned as the value of an identifier x for which some based representation has been declared, the new value of x will be converted, from the standard representation in which it is first read, to the representation declared for x. A reverse conversion takes place whenever a **print** statement is used to move a value x having some specially declared representation to an external file. There is little you can do about conversions of this kind, whose cost is in any case bounded by the amount of input and output which your program performs.

(ii) Whenever a value x having one representation is passed by an assignment $y := x$ to another variable y for which a representation has been declared, x is converted to the form declared for y. A similar conversion takes place whenever x is made part of a composite object y (i.e., a set, tuple, or map), by an assignment $y := y$ **with** x, $y(z) := x$, $y(x) := z$, etc. In these cases, x is converted to the form expected for the part of y which it becomes. For example, in the case of $y := y$ **with** x, if y has been declared to have the representation **set**($mode_1$), then x will be converted to the representation $mode_1$. In the case of $y(z) := x$ (or $y(x) := z$), if y has been declared to have the representation **mmap**(mode)mode′ or **smap**(mode)mode′ (or **mmap**(mode′)mode or **smap**(mode′)mode), then x will be converted to the mode′ form.

(iii) Values extracted from composite objects y will initially have representations deduced from the representation declared for y. For example, if s is declared to have the mode **set(elmt** B), then the iterator **forall** x **in** s... will produce elements of s, each such element initially having **elmt** B format, and assign them successively to x, converting them to the form declared for x if necessary. Similarly, if f is declared to have **smap(elmt** $B1$**)elmt** $B2$ representation, then evaluation of $f(x)$ will require that x be converted to **elmt** $B1$ format, and $f(x)$ will yield a value of mode **elmt** $B2$. If x had some other format immediately prior to the evaluation of $f(x)$, or if we use an assignment $z := f(x)$ involving a variable z that has been declared to have some representation other than **elmt** B, then appropriate conversions will be forced.

(iv) The conversions performed when we execute assignments are also performed in connection with expressions, such as existential and universal quantifiers, having assignment-like side effects, and also in connection with iterators. For example, if s is declared to have **set(elmt** B) representation, but x is declared to have some representation other than **elmt** B, then evaluation of an existential quantifier like

...**exists** x **in** s | C(x)...

will repeatedly extract elements from s (in **elmt** B format) and convert them to the representation declared for x.

(v) Whenever procedures and functions are invoked, their actual arguments are converted to the representations declared for the corresponding formal parameters. Moreover, if a function returns a value having one representation but this value is assigned to a variable for which some other representation has been declared, a conversion will take place.

To minimize these conversions, you need to choose representations for the various data items appearing in your program which make conversion unnecessary. To accomplish this you will need to survey the undeclared form of your program carefully, noting the manner in which each variable is used. The appearance of an assignment $x := y$ will suggest that x and y should be given the same representation; tests x **in** s will suggest that s should have the representation **set**(*mode*), where x has the representation *mode*; map evaluation $y := f(x)$ will suggest that f should have the representations **smap**($mode_1$)$mode_2$ where x has $mode_1$ and y has $mode_2$ representation, etc. Chains of deductions of this sort, together with a bit of reflection about the nature of the various objects which your program is manipulating, will generally lead without undue difficulty to a consistent set of representations avoiding unnecessary conversions. Note that both conversions within single procedures, and conversions of arguments forced when one procedure invokes another, are to be avoided. If there remain some conversions which cannot be avoided, care should be taken that these conversions take place at infrequently executed points in your code.

Exercises

1. Develop an effective set of representation declarations for the buckets and well program shown in Section 5.3.1.

2. Develop an effective set of representation declarations for the Eulerian path procedure shown in Chapter 11.

3. Develop an effective set of representation declarations for the topological sorting procedure shown in Chapter 11.

CHAPTER 11

The Language in Action: A Gallery of Programming Examples

In this, our last chapter, we illustrate the use of SETL by giving a variety of programs which exhibit its features and can serve as useful models of style. Some of the smaller programs present significant algorithms; the larger examples show how more substantial programming problems and applications can be addressed.

11.1 Eulerian Paths in a Graph

A *graph* is a collection of nodes, pairs of which are connected by edges (see Section 4.3.8.2). Graphs come in two varieties, *directed graphs*, each of whose edges has a specified starting node and target node, and *undirected graphs*, whose edges can be traversed in either direction. The most natural SETL representation of a directed graph G is a set of ordered pairs $[x, y]$, each such pair representing an edge with starting node x and target node y. It is convenient to represent an undirected graph G in the same way, but in this case the reversed edge $[y, x]$ belongs to G whenever $[x, y]$ belongs to G. This representation also allows us to regard G as a multivalued map: $G\{x\}$ is the set of nodes connected to x by some edge. The following algorithm makes use of this fact.

Given an undirected graph G, the Eulerian path problem, named after the famous mathematician Leonhard Euler (1707–83), "who calculated as other men breathe," is to traverse all the edges of G exactly once by a single unbroken path p which starts at some node x of the graph and ends at some other node

y (which might be the same as x). We can think of such a path, called a *Eulerian path*, as "using up" edges as it traverses them. Euler used the following arguments to determine which graphs contain paths p of this kind. If a node z along p is different from the starting and ending nodes x and y of p, then immediately after p has reached z along one edge p will leave it along some other edge, and thus p will always use up an even number of the edges which touch any node z of p not equal to x or y. The same remark applies to the starting node x if $x = y$, but if x and y are different then p must use up an odd number of the edges touching x and an odd number of the edges touching y. It follows that a Eulerian path p which traverses all the edges of G just once can only exist if G is connected and either has no nodes x touched by an odd number of edges or has exactly two such nodes x, y; and in this latter case every Eulerian path p must start at one of x, y and end at the other.

Suppose, conversely, that G has either no nodes or exactly two nodes which are touched by an odd number of edges. Then we can construct a Eulerian path p as follows. If every node of G is touched by an even number of edges of G, let x be any node of G; otherwise let x be one of the two nodes x, y of G touched by an odd number of edges. Start the path p at x, and extend p as long as possible by stepping from its endpoint along any edge of G that has not been traversed before. Since we consider an edge to be used up as soon as it is traversed, the construction of p uses up more and more edges of G and therefore must eventually stop. Hence p must be finite. Suppose that p ends at a node y. Clearly all the edges touching y must have been traversed by p, since otherwise p could be extended by some edge. Thus, if the starting node x of p is touched by an odd number of edges, p must end at some other node y which is also touched by an odd number of edges, whereas if x is touched by an even number of edges, then p must return to x and end there. In either case, removing all edges traversed by p from G will leave behind a graph G' each of whose nodes is touched by an even number of edges. If p does not already traverse all the edges of G, then some node z along p will be touched by some untraversed edge. In this case, one can construct a path q by starting from z with this edge and extending q along untraversed edges as long as possible. Since the remarks concerning p apply to q as well, and since q can be regarded as a path in the graph G', and since all of the nodes preceding G are touched by an even number of edges, the path q must both begin and end at z; i.e., q must be a *circuit*. Hence we can insert q into p, thereby constructing a path which first follows p to z, then follows q until q finally returns to z, and then follows the remainder of p to its end. Call this extended path by the same name p. Repeating the construction and insertion of circuits like q as often as possible, we must eventually build up a path p which traverses all the edges of the original graph G.

The two following procedures realize the Eulerian path construction described in the preceding paragraphs. Procedure build_path starts a new path and extends it as far as possible, deleting (from G) the edges traversed by this path; procedure Euler_path installs the path sections returned by build_path into the overall Eulerian path that it constructs and returns.

```
program Euler;                          $ Eulerian path construction
graph := {[1,2],[2,3],[3,4],[4,1],
[4,2]};                                 $ a small graph
print(euler_path(graph +
{[y,x]: [x,y] in graph}));              $ which is undirected.
proc Euler_path(G);                     $ constructs Eulerian path for graph G
  nodes := domain G;                    $ all nodes in the graph.
    if #(odds := {x in nodes | odd(#G{x})}) > 2 then
      return om;                        $ since more than two nodes are
                                        $ touched by an odd number of
    end if;                             $ edges

    $ odds is the set of all nodes of G that are touched by
    $ an odd number of edges

    x := (arb odds)? arb nodes;         $ pick a node of odds if possible;
                                        $ otherwise pick any node of G
    path := [x] + build_path(x,G);

     (while exists z = path(i) | G{z} /= { })
       new_p := build_path(z,G);  $ insert new section into path
       G - := ({[y,x]: [x,y] in new_p} + {e: e in new_p});
       path := path(1..i-1) + new_p + path(i..);
     end while;

    return path;
end proc Euler_path;

proc build_path(x, rw G);               $ builds maximal path section
                                        $ starting at x, and deletes all edges
                                        $ traversed
  p := [ ];

  (while(y := arb G{x}) /= om)          $ while there exists an edge leaving
                                        $ the last point reached

    p with := y;                        $ extend path to traverse the edge
    G - := {[x,y],[y,x]};               $ delete the edge just traversed
    x := y;                             $ step to y

  end while;

  return p;

end proc build_path;

end program euler;                      $ Eulerian path construction
```

11.2 Topological Sorting

Certain problems, of which scheduling problems are typical, require one to arrange the nodes *n* of a graph *G* in a list such that every edge of *G* goes from a node *n1* to a node *n2* coming later in the list. This is called the problem of *topological sorting*. Suppose, for example, that a student must choose the order in which he will take the courses required to qualify as a computer science major, some of which have other courses as prerequisites. Suppose also that we represent the prerequisite relationship as a set *G* of pairs, agreeing that whenever course n_1 is a prerequisite of course n_2, we will put the pair $[n_1, n_2]$ into *G*. Then, mathematically speaking, *G* is a graph; in heuristic terms, $G\{n_1\}$ is the set of all courses for which n_1 is a prerequisite. (Note the connection of the topological sorting problem with the transitive computation of prerequisites described in Section 4.3.8.1.)

To sort a collection of courses topologically is simply to arrange them in any order in which they could actually be taken, given that all the prerequisites of each course *n* must be taken before *n* is taken. To do this we find some course *n* which has no (unfulfilled) prerequisites, put *n* first in the list *L*, drop all edges $[n, n1]$ from *G* (since *n* is no longer an unfulfilled prerequisite), and then continue recursively as long as courses without unfulfilled prerequisites remain. Written as a recursive SETL routine, this is simply

```
proc top_sort1(G, nodes);   $ topological sorting procedure, recursive form
  return if exists n in nodes | n notin range G then
    [n] + top_sort1(G lessf n, nodes less n) else [ ] end;                (1)
end proc top_sort1;
```

Invocation of top_sort1(*G*) will return a tuple *t* consisting of some or all of the nodes of *G*. If it is possible to sort nodes of *G* topologically, then every node of *G* will appear in *t*. This will be the case if and only if *G* admits no cycle of nodes such that

$$n_1 \text{ is prerequisite to } n_2 \text{ is prerequisite to } n_3 \text{ is prerequisite to} \ldots \text{ is prerequisite to } n_k \text{ is prerequisite to } n_1. \quad (2)$$

To see this, note that it is clear that when such a cycle of mutually prerequisite nodes exists, no node in the cycle can ever be put into the tuple *t* returned by (1). Conversely, if a node n_0 belongs to no such cycle, then eventually the code (1) will have processed all the predecessors (i.e., prerequisites) of n_0, and after this (1) must eventually put n_0 into the tuple *t* it returns. This shows that the set of all nodes belonging to any cycle like (2) is simply

nodes − {x **in** top_sort1(G, nodes)},

so that (1) can also be used to test a graph *G* for the presence of cycles.

Like many other *tail recursions*, i.e., recursive procedures which only call themselves immediately before returning, (1) can be rewritten as an iteration (see Section 5.4). Written in this way, (1) becomes:

```
proc top_sort2(G);                    $ first iterative form of topological sort

  nodes := (domain G) + (range G);    $ Here we calculate the set of all
                                      $ nodes; this makes it unnecessary to
                                      $ pass the set of nodes as an additional
                                      $ parameter.

  t := [ ];                           $ initialize the tuple to be returned

  (while exists n in nodes | n notin range G)
                                                                        (3)
    t with := n;
    G lessf := n;
    nodes less := n;

  end while;

  return t;

end proc top_sort2;
```

It is possible to improve the efficiency of (3) very substantially by keeping the current value of the set {*n* **in** nodes | n **notin range** G} available at all times. To do this, we proceed as follows:

(a) For each node *n*, we maintain a count of the number of the predecessors of *n* which have not yet been put into *t*.
(b) When *n* is put into *t*, we reduce this count by 1 for all nodes *n*1 in *G*{*n*}.
(c) If count(*x*) falls to zero, then *x* becomes a member of the preceding set.

These observations, which could be derived step by step from the more general formal differencing principles discussed in Section 6.5, underlie the following revised form of (3):

```
proc top_sort3(G);     $ second iterative form of the topological sorting
                       $ procedure

  nodes := (domain G) + (range G);

  count := { };        $ initialize the count function described previously

  ready := nodes;      $ The following loop will remove elements that have
                       $ any predecessors from ready

  (for [x, y] in G)

    count(y) := (count(y)?0) + 1;
    ready less := y;   $ since y has a predecessor
  end for;
                       $ At this point ready is the set of all nodes without
                       $ predecessors
```

```
    t := [ ];              $ t is the tuple being built up
  (while ready /= { })
    n from ready;
    t with := n;
    (for n1 in G{n})
      if(count(n1) – := 1) = 0 then ready with := n1; end;
    end for;
  end while;
  return t;
end proc top_sort3;
```

It is not hard to see that the preceding code examines each edge of the graph *G* just twice. Thus the time needed to execute this code is linearly proportional to #*G*.

11.3 The Stable Assignment Problem

Suppose that the members of a population of *n* students are applying to a collection of *m* colleges. We suppose also that each student finds a certain collection of colleges acceptable, and that he/she ranks these colleges in order of decreasing preference. Finally we suppose that each college *c* can admit only a given quota *Q*(*c*) of the students who apply to it, and that it is able to rank all the students in order of decreasing preference. We do not suppose that any of these preferences is necessarily related to any other; that is, different students can rank colleges in radically different orders, and different colleges may find quite different types of students preferable.

The problem we consider is that of assigning students to colleges in such a way as to satisfy the following three conditions:

(a) No college accepts more than *Q*(*c*) students;
(b) A college *c* never admits a student *s1* if it has filled its quota *Q*(*c*) and there exists an unassigned student *s2* to whom college *c* is acceptable and whom college *c* prefers to student *s1*.
(c) There is no situation in which student *s1* is assigned to college *c1* and student *s2* is assigned to college *c2*, but both the students involved and the colleges involved prefer to switch; that is, *s1* prefers *c2* to *c1*, *s2* prefers *c1* prefers *s2* to *s1*, *c2* prefers *s1* to *s2*.

This problem was studied by David Gale and Lloyd Shapley (*American Mathematical Monthly*, 1962, pp. 9–15), who gave a simple algorithm for finding an assignment satisifying conditions (a), (b), and (c). The algorithm is just this: Each student applies to his first-choice college. Then each college *c* puts the topmost-ranked $Q(c)$ students who have applied to it on an active list and notifies the others that they have been rejected. All rejected students now apply to their second-choice colleges. Then all colleges rerank their applicants, keep the first $Q(c)$ of these applicants, and again notify the others that they have been rejected. This cycle of reapplication and reranking continues until no rejected students have any more colleges on their list of acceptable colleges.

It is clear that the assignment produced by this procedure satisfies condition (a). Condition (b) is also satisfied, since if *s2* finds college *c* acceptable, he/she will eventually apply to college *c* and can then bump any student *s1* whom *c* finds less acceptable, but will never subsequently be bumped except by a student whom *c* finds more acceptable. Finally, condition (c) is satisfied, since if *s1* prefers *c2* to *c1* he/she must have applied to *c2* before *c1* but been bumped from *c2*'s active list by a student that *c2* prefers to *s1*. But when this happened *c2*'s active list could not have contained any student that *c2* does not prefer to *s1*. Therefore, since the students on college *c2*'s active list never grow any less attractive from *c2*'s point of view, *c2* will never regard any student on its final active list as less desirable than *s2*.

Programmed in SETL, the Gale-Shapley algorithm is as follows.

```
program gale_shapley;  $ Gale-Shapley assignment algorithm

const A, B, CC, D;     $ constants designating colleges

stpref := {[1,[A,B,CC]],[2,[B,CC,A,D]],[3,[CC,A,B]],
[4,[B,A,CC]]};          $ students' choices
colpref := {[A,[1,2,3,4]],[B,[4,3,2,1]],[CC,[2,4,3]],[D,[1,2,4]]};
                        $ colleges' rankings of applicant
quot := {[A,2],[B,1],[CC,1],[D,2]}; $ site of entering class

print(assign(stpref, colpref, quot));

 proc assign(stud_pref, coll_pref, quota);  $ Gale_Shapley stable
                                            $ assignment algorithm

  $ stud_pref maps each student into the vector of colleges he/she finds
  $ acceptable, ranked in decreasing order of preference; coll_pref(c)(s1, s2)
  $ is true if college c finds student s1 preferable to student s2, false otherwise.
  $ The map quata gives the number of students each college will accept.

  colleges := domain quota;
  active := {[c,[ ]]: c in colleges};  $ set up an empty active list for each
                                       $ college

  applicants := domain stud_pref;      $ initialize the pool of applicants

  (for j in [1.. #quota])              $ we may need as many rounds
                                       $ of applications as there are colleges

  new_applicants := applicants;        $ save the set of applicants, which will
                                       $ be iterated over
```

```
  (for s in applicants | stud_pref(s) /= [ ])
   $ each unsatisfied student who has a college to apply to does so

    first_choice fromb stud_pref(s);
    active(first_choice) with := s;
    new_applicants less := s;

  end for s;

  applicants := new_applicants;       $ bring the set of applicants into its
                                      $ new condition

  (for c in colleges | #active(c) > quota(c))
                                      $ drop all 'over quota' applicants

  active(c) := pref_sort(active(c), coll_pref(c));
                                      $ rerank all who have applied
  (for k in[quota(c) + 1 .. #active(c)])
  applicants with := active(c)(k);
                                      $ return student to applicant pool
  end for k;
  active(c) := active(c)(1 .. #active(c) min quota(c));
                                      $ cut back active list

  end for c;

  if not exists s in applicants | stud_pref(c) /= [ ] then
     quit;
  end if;

  end for j;

  return [active, applicants];        $ pattern of assignments is complete

end proc assign;

proc pref_sort(apvect, order);        $ this returns the current group of
                                      $ applicants in the order of the college's
                                      $ choice.
applicants := {x: x in apvect};       $ convert to set

return [x in order | x in applicants];

end proc pref_sort;

end program gale_shapley;             $ Gale-Shapley assignment algorithm
```

11.4 A Text Preparation Program

Text preparation programs aid in the preparation of printed material by arranging text in attractively indented, justified, centered, and titled paragraphs and pages. You may well have used some utility program of this type: they are commonly available under such names as *Script*, *Runoff*, *Roff*, etc. In this section, we will describe the internal structure of a somewhat simplified version of such a program.

Our program, which we will call *prepare*, accepts source text containing embedded command lines as input and reformats the text in the manner specified by the command lines. Command lines are distinguished from text lines by the fact that the former start with a period as their first character, and by the fact that this initial character is followed by a few other characters signifying one of the allowed *prepare* commands, as listed later. In its ordinary mode of operation, *prepare* collects words from the text it is formatting and fills up successive lines until no additional words will fit on the line being filled. Then the line is right-justified and printed. However, commands can also be used to center a line, and lines can be terminated without being filled (we call this action a *break*). Text can also be arranged in several special table formats, as described later.

The *prepare* program treats any unbroken sequence of nonblank characters as a word. An *autoparagraphing* feature, which causes every text line starting with a blank to start a new paragraph, is also available. Margins and spacing are controllable by commands. A *literal* command, which causes following text to be printed exactly as it stands, is available to override the normal reformatting action of *prepare*. Facilities for automatic numbering of sections and subsections are also available. If the activity of *prepare* discloses inconsistencies or errors in the commands presented to it, a file of diagnostic warnings is printed.

The formatting commands supported by *prepare* are listed in the table. However, it will be easier to read these commands if you keep in mind the fact that they sense and manipulate the following variables, which are crucial to *prepare*'s activity:

Variable Name	*Meaning*
Page_horizontal	Horizontal width of paper
Page_vertical	Number of lines on page
Spacing	Current spacing of lines; 1 = single spacing
Left_margin	Current indentation for left margin
Right_margin	Current right indentation for right margin
Old_margins	Saved prior values of margins
Current_line	Line of output text currently being built up
Fill	Controls collection of words into current_line
Justify	Switch controlling right justification of output lines
Line_count	Counts number of lines output so far on current page
Page_number_stack	Stack of page and subpage numbers
Number_pages	Switch for page numbering
Header_number_stack	Stack of section and subsection numbers
Title	Current page title
Subtitle	Current page subtitle
Chapter_number	Current chapter number

The commands supported by the *prepare* system are as follows:

.BR (*BREAK*): causes a break; i.e., the current line will be output with no justification, and the next word of the source text will be placed at the beginning of the next line.

.S n (*SKIP*): causes a BREAK after which *n* is multiplied by the number of spaces between lines. The result is the number of lines skipped. Output is advanced to the top of the next page if there is no room on the current page.

.B n (*BLANK LINES*): causes the current line to be output with no justification, skips *n* line spaces, and then starts output of the current source text. BLANK is like SKIP, except that the space to be left is independent of line spacing.

.FG n (*FIGURE*): leaves *n* lines blank to make room for a figure or diagram. If fewer than *n* lines remain on the current page, text continues to fill this page. Then the page is advanced and *n* blank lines are left at the top of the next page.

.I n (*INDENT*): causes a BREAK and sets the next line to begin *n* spaces to the right of the left margin. The parameter *n* can be negative to allow beginning a line to the left of the left margin. However, a line cannot begin to the left of column 0.

.P n, v, t (*PARAGRAPH*): causes a BREAK and formats the output paragraphs. The parameter *n* is optional and, if present, sets the number of spaces the paragraph is to be indented. The default value for *n* is 5 (*n* can also have a negative value). *v* is the vertical spacing between paragraphs. *v* can range from 0 to 5. (1 denotes single spacing, 2 double spacing, etc.) *t* causes an automatic TEST PAGE (see the TEST PAGE command).

.C n; *text* (*CENTER*): causes a BREAK and centers the following text in the source file. The centering is over column *n*/2 independent of the setting of the left and right margins. If *n* is not given, it is assumed to be the page width.

.NT test (*START INDENTED NOTE*): starts an indented note. This command BLANKS 2, reduces both margins by 15, centers the text (if no text is given, it centers the word "NOTE"), and then BLANKS 1. At this point there follows the text of the note.

.EN (*END INDENTED NOTE*): terminates a NOTE command, BLANKs 2, and reverts the margins and spacing modes to their settings before the last NOTE command.

.PG (*NEW PAGE*): causes a BREAK and an advance to a new page. If the current page is empty, this command does not advance the page. Just like an automatic page advance, this command adds the title (if given) and page numbers on every page.

.TP n (*TEST PAGE*): causes a BREAK followed by a conditional page advance. It skips to the next page if fewer than *n* lines are left on the page. This feature serves to ensure that the following *n* lines are all output on the same page. This command has the form *t* as an optional argument to the PARAGRAPH command.

.NM n (*RESTART PAGE NUMBERING*): starts page numbering. Pages

are normally numbered so there is no reason to issue this command unless page numbering is disengaged. If resumption of page numbering is desired at a certain page, specify *n*.

.NNM (*SUSPEND PAGE NUMBERING*): disengages page numbering. However, pages continue to be counted, so that the normal page number can appear if page numbering is reentered with the NUMBER command.

.CH text (*START CHAPTER*): starts a new chapter using the text as the title of the chapter. This command acts as if the following command string were entered:

.BREAK; *.PAGE*; *.BLANK* 12; *.CENTER CHAPTER n*

The *n* is incremented by 1 automatically. After the CHAPTER *n* is typed on the page,

.BLANK 2; *.CENTER*; *text*; *.BLANK* 3

occurs. This command then resets the case, margins, spacing, and justify/fill modes. It also clears any subtitles and sets the chapter name as the title.

.NC n (*SET CHAPTER NUMBER*): supplies a number (*n*) to be used in a subsequent CHAPTER command. NUMBER CHAPTER would be used when a chapter of a document occupies a source file of its own. In such a case, NUMBER CHAPTER would be the first command of the source file.

.T text (*DEFINE TITLE*): takes the remaining text as the title and outputs it on every page at line 0. The default is no title. If a title is desired, this command must be entered in the source file.

.FT text (*DEFINE FIRST TITLE*): same as TITLE, but used to specify the title to be printed on the first page of the document. This command must precede all text in the source file. Use of the FIRST TITLE command is the only way to print a title line on the first page of the document.

.ST text (*DEFINE SUBTITLE*): takes the remaining text as the subtitle and outputs it on every page. A subtitle appears directly under the page title. The subtitle is not indented, but indentation can be achieved by typing leading spaces.

.SP (*START SUBPAGE NUMBERING*): executes a PAGE with page numbering suspended. The page number is unchanged, but letters are appended to the page number. This permits insertion of additional pages within an existing document without changing the existing page numbering.

.ESP (*END SUBPAGE NUMBERING*): disengages the SUBPAGE command by executing a PAGE command with page numbering resumed.

.HD (*SWITCH PAGE TITLING ON*): causes the page header (title, subtitle, and page number) to be printed.

.NHD (*SWITCH PAGE TITLING OFF*): causes the page header (title, subtitle, and page number) to be omitted. The header lines are completely omitted, so that text begins at the top of the page with no top margin.

.J (*SWITCH ON LINE JUSTIFICATION*): causes a break and sets subsequent output lines to be justified (initial setting). The command increases the spaces between words until the last word exactly meets the right margin.

.NJ (*SWITCH OFF LINE JUSTIFICATION*): causes a break and prevents justification of subsequent output lines, allowing a ragged right margin.

.F (*SWITCH ON LINE FILLING*): causes a break and specifies that subsequent output lines be filled. Sets the justification mode to that specified by the last appearance of JUSTIFY or NOJUSTIFY. FILL adds successive words from the source text until addition of one more word would exceed the right margin but stops before putting in this last word.

.NF (*SWITCH OFF LINE FILLING*): disengages the FILL and JUSTIFY modes. This command is used to permit typing of tables or other manually formatted text.

.LIT (*PRINT FOLLOWING TEXT LITERALLY*): disengages FILL/JUSTIFY to permit printing of text exactly as entered in source file.

.ELI (*END LITERAL TEXT*): used after LITERAL command to re-engage FILL/JUSTIFY.

.LM n (*SET LEFT MARGIN*): sets the left margin to *n*. The *n* must be less than the right margin but not less than 0. The default setting is 0.

.RM n (*SET RIGHT MARGIN*): sets the right margin *n*. The *n* must be greater than the left margin. The default setting is 60.

.PS n.m (*SET PAGE SIZE*): sets the size of the page *n* lines by *m* columns. The default setting is 58 by 60.

.SP n (*SET INTERLINE SPACING*): sets the number of spaces between lines. The *n* can range from 1 to 5. The default setting is 1. SPACING 1 is like single spacing on a typewriter and SPACING 2 is like double spacing. SPACING 2 puts one blank line between lines of text.

.AP (*SWITCH AUTOPARAGRAPHING ON*): causes any blank line or any line starting with a space or tab to be considered as the start of a new paragraph. This command allows normally typed text to be justified without special commands. It does not cause a paragraph if blank lines are followed by a command.

.NAP (*SWITCH AUTOPARAGRAPHING OFF*): disengages the AUTOPARAGRAPH mode.

Now we proceed to give SETL code for our text preparation system.

```
program prepare;          $ text preparation system

var                       $ global variables
  Page_horizontal,        $ horizontal width of paper
  Page_vertical,          $ vertical width of paper
  Spacing,                $ current spacing of lines
  Left_margin,            $ left margin
  Right_margin,           $ right margin
  Autoparagraph,          $ switch for autoparagraphing
  Tuple_of_words,         $ collects words of input for output
  Justify,                $ controls right justification
  Fill,                   $ controls filling of lines
  Line_count,             $ counts number of lines on page
```

```
    Page_number_stack,     $ stack of page & subpage numbers
    Number_pages,          $ switch for page numbering
    Main_title,            $ page title
    Subtitle,              $ page subtitle
    Print_header,          $ controls header printings
    Fill_j_save,           $ saves fill & justify during LIT
    First_page,            $ switch for first page
    Chapter_number,        $ current chapter number
    Page_advance,          $ page advance character
    Margin_save,           $ saves margins during indented note
    Figure_lines,          $ number of lines reserved for figure
    Figure_flag,           $ switch to leave space for figure
    Page_figure_flag,      $ leaves space for figure on top of next page
    Indent_flag,           $ switch for indentation
    Para_indent_flag,      $ switch for paragraph indentation
    Number_blanks,         $ number of spaces to indent
    Paragraph_spacing,     $ current spacing between paragraphs
    Paragraph_indent;      $ number of spaces to indent for paragraph

const                      $ constants designating all commands
  BR, S, B, FG, I, P, C, NT, EN, TP, NM, NNM, CH, NC, T, FT, SB, PG,
  ESP, HD, NHD, J, NJ, F, NF, LIT, ELI, LM, RM, PV, SP, AP, SS, NAP;

const Legal_ops =          $ legal commands
  {BR, S, B, FG, I, P, C, NT, EN, TP, NM, NNM, CH, NC, T, FT, SB, PG,
  ESP, HD, NHD, J, NJ, F, NF, LIT, ELI, LM, RM, PV, SP, AP, SS, NAP};

const Cause_new_line =     $ these commands cause Tuple_of_words to be
                           $ emptied. Text immediately following these
                           $ commands is output at beginning of new line.
  {BR, S, B, I, C, NT, EN, PG, TP, CH, J, NJ, F, NF, LIT, ELI, LM, RM};

$ ************** INFORMATION AND COMMENTS **************

$   The text preparation system's main job is to FILL and/or JUSTIFY the
$ source file. The course of the main procedure depends on these two modes.
$ If both the FILL and JUSTIFY switches are off text is printed in the same
$ format as input. In all other cases words of text are broken out of the input
$ line and placed in a Tuple_of_words. If FILL is off and JUSTIFY is on
$ (i.e., justifying but not filling lines), then the Tuple is printed in justified form
$ immediately after the line of input is processed. If FILL is on then the Tuple
$ is filled until one of the following three cases arises:
$ (1)  a command line is encountered. (a line begining with a period).
$ (2)  a new paragraph is to begin.
$ (3)  end of input.
$ The entire Tuple however is not output at this time. Those words that do not
$ fill the last line of output remain in the Tuple until a specific command that
$ causes a new line is encountered, or until cases 2 & 3.
```

$ NOTE: Only when FILL is on can more than one line of input be read and
$ placed in the Tuple before being output.

$ A major feature of the text preparation system is the "autoparagraph." If
$ the autoparagraph switch is on, (it initially isn't), an input line beginning
$ with a blank causes the Tuple to be emptied, a preset number of lines to be
$ skipped, and a preset number of spaces to be indented. (These numbers are
$ initially set to 5 and 1).

$ PREP.IN should contain the source file. PREP.OUT will contain the
$ output file.

$ Command lines differ from text lines in that they begin with a period.

$ An explanation of some of the subtler uses of some variables follows:

$ Indent_flag/Para_indentflag. Two different flags are used for two situations.
$ Indent_flag is used when the command INDENT is encountered.
$ Para_indent_flag is used in conjunction with the AUTOPARAGRAPH
$ command. Since the INDENT command can be used when
$ AUTOPARAGRAPH is on, two flags are necessary.

$ Figure_flag/Page_figure_flag. When the FG command is encountered
$ Figure_flag is turned on so as to leave a specified number of lines blank
$ the next time the Tuple is output. If there are an insufficient number of lines
$ left on the current page for the figure, blank lines must be left at the top of
$ the next page. Page_figure_flag is turned on in this case.

$ First_page. This switch is on initially and turned off after the first page
$ headers are printed. This switch causes page headers for the first page to
$ be output at the same time as the first words of the Tuple are to be output.
$ First page headers are not printed in the initialization so that commands
$ can be used to change initialization values. This is especially necessary for
$ the following commands;
$ Fill → ON (initialization value)
$ Justify → ON
$ Title → NULL
$ Subtitle → NULL
$ Chapter # → 1
$ Page number switch → ON
$ Page header switch → ON

$ Two major types of error are detected by the program:
$ Justify error. If JUSTIFY is on and FILL is off, too many words in a line
$ of input (initially, greater than 60 characters) or a single word will cause
$ a justify error. This type of error terminates processing.
$ Command error. This is caused by either an invalid command or an error
$ in the command's parameters. In this case the command is ignored and
$ an appropriate message is printed.

```
$ ****  MAIN PROGRAM OF TEXT PREPARATION SYSTEM  ****

initialize;                                  $ initialize all global variables &
                                             $ determine input & output files
loop do                                      $ remain in loop until all text is
                                             $ processed
  get('PREP.IN', line);                      $ read line of input
  if line = om then quit loop; end;          $ end of text input

  if match(line, '.') /= om then             $ a command line
    if (cmd := break(line, '  ')) = om then  $ no parameter
      cmd := line;
      line := om;
    end if;
    if cmd notin Legal_ops then error_proc(cmd); continue loop; end;
    if Fill then print_lines; end;           $ output the text collected
                                             $ in Tuple_of_words in
                                             $ its correct format. Words
                                             $ that remain in the Tuple
                                             $ are those that do not fill
                                             $ last line.
     $ 'command check' checks validity of the command line.
     $ 'handle command' carries out the command.
     command_tuple :=
     command_check(cmd, line);               $ command tuple
                                             $ contains the command
                                             $ and its parameters.

    if command_tuple /= om then handle_command(command_tuple);
    else error_proc(cmd);
    end;
    continue loop do;
  end if match;

  if not (Fill or Justify)                   $ output line as it was read in
    then
     output(line);
    else                                     $ if AUTOPARAGRAPH is on,
                                             $ a blank space at the beginning
                                             $ of the paragraph signals for
                                             $ new paragraph.

     if Autoparagraph and line(1) = '  ' then paragraph; end;
     span(line, '  ');

     (until line = om)                       $ this loop places words
                                             $ of input into Tuple
```

```
        if (next_word := break(line,'   ')) = om then
          next_word := line;
          line := om;
        else
          span(line,'   ');
        end if;
        Tuple_of_words with := next_word;
      end until;

   end if;

   if Justify and not Fill then print_line; end   $ Tuple_of_words is
                                                  $ printed after each line
                                                  $ of text is read

end loop;

finalize;                                         $ finalize system

$ ***************** END OF MAIN PROGRAM *****************

proc initialize;                 $ parameter & file name initialization

$ this procedure initializes all global variables and opens the input & output
  files.

open('PREP.IN','CODED');
open('PREP.OUT','CODED-OUT');
Page_advance := '*';
Page_vertical := 58;             $ default lines per page
Page_horizontal := 60;           $ default spaces per line
Left_margin := 0;                $ default margins
Right_margin := 60;              $ default margins
Spacing := 1;                    $ single spacing
Paragraph_spacing := 1;          $ lines between paragraphs
Paragraph_indent := 5;           $ indentation
Indent_flag := false;            $ switch that controls indentation
Para_indent_flag := false;       $ controls indentation in paragraph
Figure_flag := Page_figure_flag := false;
First_page := true;              $ turned off when first 'page' occurs
Print_header := true;            $ initially on
Main_title := Subtitle := '';
Autoparagraph := false;          $ initially off
Tuple_of_words := [ ];           $ contains words of text to be processed
Page_number_stack := [1];        $ initially on first page
Fill := true;                    $ initially on
Justify := true;                 $ initially on
Line_count := 1;                 $ counts lines on page
Number_pages := true;            $ page numbering switched on
```

```
Chapter_number := 1;                 $ advances with each chapter

end proc initialize;

proc page;                           $ page advance procedure

$ This procedure is invoked whenever output proceeds to a new page. This
$ procedure puts out a line containing a page advance character, then the page
$ number, title, & subtitle if switched on.

put('PREP.OUT', Page_advance);
Line_count := 0;
First_page := false;
if Number_pages then                 $ build up first line with page number
   Number_line := 'PAGE' +/[str Page_number_stack(z) +
   '.': z in[1 .. #Page_number_stack]];
   Number_line := Number_line(1 .. #Number_line - 1); $ drop last
                                                       $ character
   Page_number_stack(#Page_number_stack) + := 1;
   output(Number_line); output('');
end if;
if Print_header then
  center(om, Main_title); center(om, Subtitle);
  output('  ');
end if;
if Page_figure_flag then             $ leave room for a figure
  Page_figure_flag := false;
  blankout(Figure_lines);
end if;
end proc page;

proc output(line);

$ this is the main output procedure of the prepare program.

if First_page then page; end;
nblanks := Spacing;                  $ number of lines to skip

if Figure_flag then
  Figure_flag := false;
  $ if figure can fit on this page, room is left for it. If there is not enough space,
  $ room is left on the top of the next page. Page_figure_flag is used in the
  $ later case.
  if Figure_lines + Line_count + Spacing >= Page_vertical then
    Page_figure_flag := true;
  else nblanks := Figure_lines + Spacing;
  end;
end;
Line_count +:= 1;                    $ counts lines on each page
```

```
put('PREP.OUT', line);
if Line_count >= Page_vertical then page; end;
blankout(nblanks - 1);

end proc output;

proc command_check (cmd, line);          $ breaks command out of line

$ this procedure checks command & parameter validity; it also sends back
$ the command and its parameters in a Tuple.

case cmd of
 (BR, EN, PG, NM, NNM, SP, ESP, HD, NHD,
 J, NJ, F, NF, LIT, ELI, AP, NAP):       $ no parameters
  return [cmd];

 (CH, T, FT, SB):                        $ these commands have
                                         $ one string parameter
  span(line, '  ');                      $ remove blanks
  if line = om then return om; else return [cmd, line]; end;

 (S, B, FG, I, TP, NC, LM, RM, SS, PV):  $ these commands have
                                         $ one integer parameter
  span(line, '  ');                      $ remove blanks
  if (param := integer_check(line)) = om
   then return om;                       $ error encountered
   else return [cmd, param];
  end if;

$ the rest of the commands are now treated separately

(NT):                                    $ has form 'NT text'.
                                         $ If text is omitted the
                                         $ word 'NOTE' is centered

 span(line, '  ');
 if line = om
  then return [cmd, 'NOTE'];
  else return [cmd, line];
 end if;

(C):                                     $ has form of 'C n; text'.
                                         $ n is optional
 span(line, '  ');
 if match(line, ';') = om then           $ integer present
  if (param := integer_check(line)) = om then return om; end;
  span(line, '  ');
  if match(line, ';') = om then return om; end;
  span(line, '  ');
  if line = om then return om; else return [cmd, param, line]; end;
```

```
  else
   span(line,'  ');
   if line = om then return om; else return [cmd, om, line]; end;
  end if;

(P):                                        $ has the form 'P n1 n2'
  span(line,'  ');
  if (param := integer_check(line)) = om then return om; end;
  span(line,'  ');
  if (param2 := integer_check(line)) = om then return om; end;
  return [cmd, param, param2];

end case;
end proc command_check;

proc integer_check(rw line);                $ checks validity of string integer
if (param := span(line,'-0123456789')) = om or (line = '-')
 then return om; end;
if match(param,'-') = om then return num(param);
   else return - num(param); end;
end proc integer_check;

proc num(stg);                              $ converts string to integer

valu := 0;
(for di = stg(q))
 valu := valu*10;
 valu +:= (abs di - abs '0');
end for;
return valu;
end proc num;

proc handle_command(command_tuple);  $ command interpeter

$ this command interpeter handles all prepare commands.

[cmd, p1, p2] := command_tuple;
if (cmd in Cause_new_line) then print_remaining_line; end;

case cmd of

 (BR):                                      $ break command
   return;

 (I):                                       $ indent
   Ident_flag := true;
   Number_blanks := p1 max 0 min (Right_margin - 10);

 (NM):                                      $ resume page numbering
   Number_pages := true;
```

```
(NNM):                                  $ end page numbering
   Number_pages := false;

(NC):                                   $ supply chapter number
   Chapter_number := p1;

(T):                                    $ supply title
   Main_title := p1;

(SB):                                   $ subtitle
   Subtitle := p1;

(SP):                                   $ start subpage
   page;
   Page_number_stack with := 1;         $ begin subnumbers

(ESP):                                  $ end subpage
   page;

 if #Page_number_stack > 1 then         $ drop one level
   junk frome Page_number_stack;
   Page_number_stack(#Page_number_stack) + := 1;
 end if;
(HD):                                   $ print page headers
   Print_header := true;

(NHD):                                  $ end page headers
   Print_header := false;

(J):                                    $ justification
   Justify := true;

(NJ)                                    $ end justification
   Justify := false;

(F):                                    $ fill lines
   Fill := true;

(NF):                                   $ end filling lines
   Fill := false;

(PV):                                   $ lines per page
   Page_vertical := p1;

(LIT):                                  $ suspend fill/justify
   Fill_j_save := [Fill, Justify];
   Fill := Justify := false;

(ELI):                                  $ resume fill/justify
   [Fill, Justify] := Fill_j_save;
```

```
(LM):                                   $ set left margin
  Left_margin := p1 max 0 min (Right_margin - 10);
  Page_horizontal := Right_margin - Left_margin;

(RM):                                   $ set right margin
  Right_margin := p1 min (Page_horizontal + Left_margin) max
  (Left_margin + 10);
  Page_horizontal := Right_margin - Left_margin;

(SS):                                   $ set spacing
  Spacing := p1 max 1 min 5;

(AP):                                   $ start autoparagraphing
  Autoparagraph := true;

(NAP):                                  $ end autoparagraphing
  Autoparagraph := false;

(P):                                    $ set paragraph spacing
  Paragraph_indent := p1;
  Paragraph_spacing := p2;

(S):                                    $ skip n spacings
  if (p1*spacing) + Line_count > Page_vertical then
    page;
  else
    blankout((p1 max 0)*spacing);
  end if;

(B):                                    $ skip in lines
  if p1 + Line_count > Page_vertical then
    page;
  else
    blankout(p1 max 0);
  end if;

(FG):                                   $ leave lines for figure
  Figure_flag := true;
  Figure_lines := p1;

(C):                                    $ center text
  center(p1, p2);

(PG):                                   $ start new page
                                        $ if current is not empty
  if Line_count > 0 then page; end;

(TP):                                   $ start new page if less
                                        $ than p1 lines remain
  if Line_count + p1 >= Page_vertical then page; end;
```

```
 (CH):                                  $ chapter
   chapter(p1);

 (NT):                                  $ indented note
   blankout(2);
   center(om, p1);
   blankout(1);
   Margin_save := [Right_margin, Left_margin, Page_horizontal];
   Left_margin +:= (Page_horizontal div 4);
   Right_margin := Right_margin - (Page_horizontal div 4);
   Page_horizontal := Right_margin - Left_margin;

 (EN):                                  $ end indented note
   blankout(2);
   [Right_margin, Left_margin, Page_horizontal] := Margin_save;

end case;

end proc handle_command;

proc paragraph;

$ autoparagraph procedure. This procedure is called when a space begins a
$ line of input (and AUTOPARAGRAPH is on).

$ first the Tuple_of_words is completely output.

if Fill then print_lines; end;
print_remaining_line;
Para_indent_flag := true;      $ the next time the Tuple is printed
                               $ indentation will be made. (see proc indenter).
blankout(Paragraph_spacing - 1);

end proc paragraph;

proc blankout(nlines);         $ leaves nlines empty. If the end of page
                               $ is reached no more lines are blanked out.
if First_page then page; end;

(for z in [1..nlines])
 Line_count +:= 1;
 put('PREP.OUT', '');          $ outputs a blank line
 if Line_count >= Page_vertical then page; return; end;
end for;

end proc blankout;

proc indenter;

$ if Para_indent_flag or Indent_flag is on, this procedure causes indentation.
$ This is done by adding blanks to the beginning of the first word in the Tuple.
$ Number_blanks contains the number of blanks to be indented.
```

```
if Para_indent_flag and Indent_flag = false then
  Number_blanks := Paragraph_indent;
end;
if Indent_flag of Para_indent_flag then
  Para_indent_flag := false;
  Indent_flag := false;
  If Tuple_of_words = [ ] then quit; end;
  $ remove the word from the Tuple, add blanks to it, then place it back.
  word fromb Tuple_of_words;
  word := ('  '*Number_blanks) + word;
  Tuple_of_words := [word] + Tuple_of_words;
end if;

end proc indenter;

proc print_lines;
$ printing procedure for when fill is on

indenter;

printed_lines := if Fill and Justify
    then fill_justifier( )
    else filler( )              $ Fill on, Justify off
end;
(for line in printed_lines)
    line := ('  '*Left_margin) + line;
    output(line);
end for;

end proc print_lines;

proc filler;                    $ produces output in filled form

filler_lines := [ ];            $ tuple of filled lines
loop do
  temp_line := '';
  nwords := nchar := 0;   $ number of words and of characters
  (for word in Tuple_of_words)
     nchar +:= #word + 1;
     nwords +:= 1;
     if nchar > (Page_horizontal + 1) then goto fillit; end;
     temp_line +:= word + '  ';
  end for;
  return filler_lines;
  fillit: filler_lines with := temp_line;
  (for n in [1..nwords - 1])
     junk fromb Tuple_of_words;
  end for;
end loop;
```

```
end proc filler;

proc fill_justifier;

$ produces output that is filled and justified

justified_lines := [ ];
loop do
   nwords := nchar := 0;
   (for word in Tuple_of_words)
      nchar +:= #word + 1;
      nwords +:= 1;
      if nchar > (Page_horizontal + 1) then goto addit; end;
   end for;
   return justified_lines;
addit: temp_line := put_spaces(nwords - 1,
         Page_horizontal - nchar + #word + 2);
justified_lines with := temp_line;
end loop;

end proc fill_justifier;

proc print_line;

$ printing procedure for when justify is on and fill is off

indenter;
if #Tuple_of_words = 1 then justifier_error; end;
$ one word cannot be justified

nword := nchar := 0;
(for word in Tuple_of_words)
   nchar +:= #word + 1;
   nword +:= 1;
   if nchar > Page_horizontal + 1 then justifier_error; end;
   $ too many words on the input line

end for;
out_line := out_spaces(nword, Page_horizontal - nchar + 1);
output(out_line);

end proc print_line;

proc justifier_error;
output('TEXT PREPARATION TERMINATED DUE TO ERROR
WITH USE OF JUSTIFY');
stop;

end proc justifier_error;

proc put_spaces(nwords, nblanks);
```

```
justified_line := '';
space_count := (size := (nwords - 1))*[1];
(for z in [1..nblanks])
   space_count((random (size - 1)) + 1) +:= 1;
end for;
(for z in [1..size])
   word fromb Tuple_of_words;
   justified_line + := word;
   k := space_count(z);
   (for m in [1..k])
      justified_line +:= '  ';
   end for;
end for;
word fromb Tuple_of_words;
justified_line + := word;
return justified_line;

end proc put_spaces;

proc print_remaining_line;    $ procedure prints remaining line from
                              $ Tuple_of_words

if Tuple_of_words = [ ] then return; end;
temp_line := ('  '*Left_margin);
word fromb Tuple_of_words;
(while word /= om)
   temp_line + := word + '  ';
   word fromb Tuple_of_words;
end while;
output(temp_line);

end proc print_remaining_line;

proc center(n, text);          $ center text on column n

if n = om then n := (Page_horizontal div 2) + Left_margin; end;
k := (n - (#text div 2) - 1) max 0;
line := (k*'  ') + text;
output(line);

end proc center;

proc chapter(text);

$ new chapter is to begin, chapter headers are printed.

Print_header := false;
page;
blankout(3);
center(om, 'CHAPTER' + str Chapter_number);
```

```
Chapter_number + := 1;
blankout(2);
center(om, text);
blankout(3);
Main_title := text;        $ set the title to the chapter text

$ the following are set to their initialization values
Print_header := true;
Subtitle := '';
Spacing := 1;
Justify := true;
Fill := true;
Left_margin := 0;
Right_margin := 60;
Page_horizontal := 60;
end proc chapter;

proc error_proc(cmd);  $ prints out error message
print('ERROR ENCOUNTERED WITH COMMAND', cmd,
'COMMAND IGNORED');
end proc error_proc;

proc finalize;              $ finalize system, first print whats left in the tuple.
if Fill then print_lines; end;
print_remaining_line;
close('PREP.IN');
close('PREP.OUT');
end proc finalize;

end program prepare;
```

11.5 A Simplified Financial Record-keeping System

Next we will give SETL code representing some small part of the operations of a bank, albeit in simplified form. The system to be represented corresponds in a rough way to the "Checking Plus" service offered by Citibank in New York City. Note, however, that the simple code shown does not deal adequately with all the anomalies and error conditions that a full-scale banking system would have to handle, nor does it support all the functions that are actually required. For example, the code we give does not provide any way for customer accounts to be opened or closed. A more ambitious commerical application showing how such matters can be treated would be very instructive, but since the issues that enter into the design of a full-scale commercial system can grow to be quite complex, we will not attempt to discuss the whole interesting range of questions that enter into the design of such systems.

The simplified system which we consider is aware of a collection of *customers*,each of whom has an *account*. A customer's account consists of two parts: a *balance* representing funds available to him, and an *overdraft debit* representing the amount that he has drawn against the Checking Plus feature of his account. This debit is limited for each account not to exceed a given credit_limit, established when the account is opened. The bank pays 5% per annum daily interest on positive balances in checking accounts, and charges 18% per annum daily interest on overdraft debits.

Like most commercial application programs, the following code maintains a *data base*, i.e., a collection of maps which collectively represents the situation with which the program must deal, and reads a *transaction file* whose entries inform it of changes in this situation. Using these files it produces various *output documents*, for example, lists of checks deposited for transmission to other banks, and monthly statements which are mailed to customers.

The transactions supported by our simplified system are as follows:

Transaction	Code	Explanation
deposit	(D)	Customer deposits either cash, a check drawn on another bank, or a check drawn on this bank.
withdrawal	(W)	A customer appears at a teller's booth and attempts to withdraw cash.
payment	(PA)	Customer transfers a stated sum from his available balance to reduce his overdraft debit.
presentation	(P)	Check is presented by another bank for payment.
clear	(C)	Another bank informs this bank that a check has cleared for payment.
return	(R)	A previously deposited check, sent to another bank for payment, is returned either as a bad check or for lack of available funds. (Checks written without sufficient funds cause their writer account to be debited $5.00).
end of day	(DAY)	End of banking day has arrived; daily interest is to be credited/debited to all accounts.

On the last day of each month, an *end_of_day* transaction triggers the production of bank statements which are sent to each customer. On the last day of December, this statement includes an indication of interest charged and interest earned during the year.

Each transaction handled is represented by a single line (string) in the transaction file. This line always starts with a code letter identifying the transaction and for the rest consists of various fields, separated by blanks. The fields expected for the various transactions supported are as follows:

D	customer_number	amount	bank_number account_number (missing if cash deposit)
W	customer_number	amount	teller_terminal_number
PA	customer_number	amount	

P	customer_number	amount	check_number	bank_number
C	check_number			
R	check_number	reason		
DAY				

The global data structures used to support our simplified banking system are as follows:

cust_info	*This map sends each customer_number into the record maintained for the corresponding customer.*	(1)

The components of a customer record are

balance_available	*balance currently available*
balance_deposited	*balance showing checks deposited but not yet cleared*
overdraft_debit	*amount currently drawn against "Checking Plus"*
overdraft_limit	*maximum overdraft allowed*
transactions_this_month	*list of all completed transactions this month*
interest_earned	*total interest earned this year*
interest_paid	*total interest paid for overdrafts this year*
namei	*customer name*
social security number	*customer social security number*
address	*customer address*
telephone number	*customer telephone number*

bank_info	*This map sends the numerical code of each bank from which checks will be accepted into the bank's address information.*	(2)
pending_checks	*When checks deposited are sent along to another bank for confirmation of payment, they are issued unique numerical identifiers. This map sends each such identifier into the transaction to which it corresponds.*	(3)

Having now outlined all the transactions which our simplified banking system will support and listed the principal data structures which it uses, we are in position to give the code itself.

```
program bank_checking;         $ simplified check-processing program
$ ******* DECLARATION OF GLOBAL VARIABLES, MACROS,
$                  AND CONSTANTS *******

var                            $ global variables
```

```
  Cust_info,                  $ maps account number into customer
                              $ record
  Bank_info,                  $ maps bank number into bank address,
                              $ etc.

  Pending_checks,             $ maps each suspended transaction number
                              $ into a detailed transaction record

  This_banks_code,            $ code identifying this bank
  Check_counter,              $ counter identifying checks sent
                              $ to other banks for verification

  Message_list,               $ maps each bank identifier into a list
                              $ of messages to be sent to the bank.

  Bad_transactions,           $ accumulated list of bad transactions
  Transfile,                  $ file of transactions, to be processed
  Last_day;                   $ last day for which 'DAY' operation
                              $ was run

macro customer_items;         $ the vector of items constituting a
                              $ customer's record. Note that all
                              $ amounts are kept as integer numbers
                              $ of pennies.

[balance_available, balance_deposited, overdraft_debit,
  overdraft_limit, transactions_this_month, interest_earned,
    interest_paid, name, sec_no, address, tel_no]

endm;

  const                       $ strings indicating transaction results

    CASH_DEP,                 $ cash deposit
    CASH_WITHDRAWAL,          $ cash withdrawal
    PAYMENT,                  $ payment of check
    CKPLUS_PAYMENT,           $ "checking-plus" payment
    DEPOSIT,                  $ check deposited
    OVERDRAWN,                $ charge for overdrawn check
    NOFUNDS,                  $ funds not available to pay check
    BAD_CHECK;                $ check drawn on nonexistent account

  const                       $ constants designating transaction codes
    D, W, PA, P, C, R, DAY;

  const Transaction_codes = {D, W, PA, P, C, R, DAY};
                              $ constants designating transactions.

  const Involves_customer = {D, W, PA, P};
                              $ transactions whose second
                              $ parameter is a customer number.
```

```
  const Needs_updating = {D, W, PA, P, C, R};
                               $ transactions which modify customer
                               $ record.
  const digits = '0123456789'; $ the decimal digits
  const Annual_rate = 6,       $ interest paid on checking balances
       Overdraft_rate = 18;    $ interest charged on overdrafts
$ ****** MAIN PROGRAM OF BANKING SYSTEM ******
  initialize_system;           $ call initialization procedure
                               $ to read in all required global
                               $ data structures.
loop do
  get('transfile', transaction); $ read next transaction
  if transaction = om then
  quit; end;                   $ all transactions processed
  process_transaction
  (transaction);               $ otherwise process transaction
end loop;
finalize_system;               $ write state of system to output file
print; print; print('END OF TRANSACTION PROCESSING');
proc process_transaction(t);   $ the principal transaction-processing
                               $ procedure.
if (dec := decode_transaction(t))
= om then return; end          $ since transaction is bad.
  [code, number, amount,
  p4, p5] := dec;              $ get fields of transaction.
if code in Involves_customer
then                           $ obtain fields of customer record.
  customer_items := Cust_info(number);
                               $ make balance_available,
                               $ balance_deposited, overdraft_debit,
                               $ overdraft_limit, etc. available.
end if;
case code of
  (D): $ deposit
  if p4 = om then              $ deposit is cash: accept it immediately
    balance_available + := amount;
```

```
        balance_deposited + := amount;
        transactions_this_month with := post(CASH_DEP, amount);

    elseif p4 = This_banks_code then $ check is drawn on this bank

$ We handle a check drawn on this bank as a combination of a 'P' transaction
$ with the transaction (either 'C' or 'R') that responds to this 'P' transaction.
$ For this, it is convenient to allow this procedure to call itself recursively.

        balance_deposited + := amount;

        Cust_info(number) :=
        customer_items;                 $ update balance_deposited

        pending_checks('0') := t;       $ for consistency, note that pending
                                        $ check is drawn on this bank.
        process_transaction('P' + p5 + " + dollar(amount) + '0'
                  + This_banks_code);
        result := Message_list (This_banks_code)(1);
        Message_list (This_banks_code) := [ ];
                                        $ get result and clear message list

        process_transaction(result);    $ process the resulting 'C' or 'R'
        return;                         $ since all steps of transaction
                                        $ are now complete

else                                    $ the check is drawn on another
                                        $ bank. Note, but do not credit,
                                        $ the deposit.

    balance_deposited + := amount;
    identifier := str (Check_counter + := 1);
    Pending_checks(identifier) := t;    $ save transaction for
                                        $ later completion.

    Message_list(p4) with :=            $ send notification to bank
                                        $ on which the check is drawn
      'P' + p5 + " + dollar(amount) + " + identifier +
                 " This_banks_code;

end if;

(W):                                    $ withdrawal

if ok_withdraw(amount, balance_available, overdraft_debit,
      balance_deposited, overdraft_limit) then
   send_teller(p4, 'PAYMENT APPROVED');
   transactions_this_month with := post(CASH_WITHDRAWAL, amount);
else
   send_teller(p4, NOFUNDS);
end if;
```

```
(PA):                                   $ payment of portion of overdraft debit

will_pay :_amount min balance_available min overdraft_debit;

if will_pay = 0 then return; end;       $ bypass transaction if payment 0
balance_available - := will_pay;
balance_deposited - := will_pay;
overdraft_debit - := will_pay;
transactions_this_month with := post(CKPLUS_PAYMENT, will_pay);

(P):                                    $ presentation (for approval)
                                        $ of check by other bank

if(c_info := Cust_info(number)) = om
then                                    $ check is bad
  Message_list(p5) with := 'R' + p4 + 'X' + BAD_CHECK;

                                        $ note: the "reason" parameter is forced
                                        $ into fourth position by the inserted X

 return;                                $ abort transaction
end if;

customer_items := c_info;               $ make fields of customer info available

if ok_withdraw(amount, balance_available, overdraft_debit,
    balance_deposited, overdraft_limit) then

  Message_list(p5) with := 'C' + p4;
                                        $ confirm clearance
  transactions_this_month with := post(PAYMENT, amount);
else
  Message_list(p5) with := 'R' + p4 + 'X' + NOFUNDS;

                                        $ note: the "reason" parameter is
                                        $ forced into fourth position by the
                                        $ inserted X.

                                        $ in this case the customer is charged
                                        $ a $5.00 fee, or whatever smaller
                                        $ amount remains in his account

    charge := 500 min (balance_available + overdraft_limit-
    overdraft_debit) max 0;

    assert ok_withdraw(charge, balance_available overdraft_debit,
    balance_deposited, overdraft_limit);

    transactions_this_month with := post(OVERDRAWN, charge);

  end if;

  (C):                                  $ pending check clears
```

```
   assert(dec := decode_transaction(Pending_checks(number)))/= om;

$ We can make this assertion because the system represented here does not
$ allow customer accounts to be closed. However, this assertion would
$ continue to hold true even in a more realistic system, since in such a system
$ we would not close an account until all its outstanding deposit transactions
$ have been completed.

   Pending_checks(number) := om;  $ drop from pending list
   [-, number, amount] := dec;    $ get customer number and amount
   customer_items := Cust_info(number);
   balance_available + := amount; $ credit to available balance
   transactions = this = month with := post(PAYMENT, amount);

   (R):                           $ spending check fails to clear

   reason := p4;                  $ in this, case the p4
                                  $ field contains the reason
                                  $ for refusal of the check
                                  $ transmitted for approval

   assert (dec := decode_transaction(Pending_checks(number)))/= om;
                                  $ see comment following case(C)

   Pending_checks(number) := om;  $ drop from pending list
   [-, number, amount] := dec;    $ get customer number and amount
   customer_times := Cust_info(number);
   balance_deposited - := amount; $ debit the estimated total
                                  $ of deposits.
   transactions_this_month with := post(reason, amount):
   (DAY):                         $ end of banking day: take end-of-day,
                                  $ and if necessary end-of-month,
                                  $ actions.

   end_of_day;                    $ take end of day actions

   if day_field(daystring(DATE)) = '01' then
      end_of_month;
      end if;

   else                           $ have some system error.
                                  $ take end_of day action,
                                  $ save system, and note error.

      print('SYSTEM ERROR *** ILLEGAL TRANSACTION:', t);

      finalize_system;

      stop;

      end if;
   end case;
```

```
if code in Needs_updating then      $ customer information
                                    $ must be updated
   Cust_info(number) := customer_items;

   print (items(number, customer_items));
end if;
print ('MESSAGE LIST', Message_list);
end proc process_transaction;

proc ok_withdraw(amount, rw bal_avail, rw over_debit, rw bal_deposit,
over_limit);

   $ This auxiliary procedure checks to see whether the stated -amount- can
   $ be withdrawn from an account, by increasing the overdraft debit if
   $ necessary. If so, the balance available, amount provisionally on deposit,
   $ and overdraft debit are appropriately adjusted, and true is returned;
   $ otherwise false is returned.

if amount > (bal_avail + over_limit – over_debit)
then                                    $ no good

   return false;

end if;

bal_avail – := (amt_frm_bal := amount min bal_avail);
bal_deposit – := amt_frm_bal;
                                        $ decrement amount provisionally
                                        $ on deposit
over_debit + := amount—amt_frm_bal;

return true;

end proc ok_withdraw;

proc post(trans_type, amount);

$ This auxilliary routine converts transactions into strings consisting of an
$ amount, a coded indicator of the transaction type, and a date; the result is
$ suitable for printing in a customer's end-of-month statement.

return daystring(DATE) + '   ' + trans_type + '   ' + dollar(amount);

end proc post;

proc decode_transaction(t);             $ decodes string form of transaction

$ This procedure reads the string form of a transaction and decodes it into
$ the various blank-separated fields of which it consists. It verifies that each
$ field has the expected type. If any field is found to be bad, or if any field is
$ missing, then the transaction is posted to a "rejected transactions" list, and
$ this procedure returns om.
```

```
$ Otherwise, a tuple c consisting of the converted fields is returned.

$ Map from transaction type to pattern of fields expected for transaction.
$ See procedure -field_check-, below, for an explanation of the codes
  appearing here.

  const XCABX, XCAX, XCA,
XXAXX, XX, XXXX, X;                        $ checkstring constants

  const Check_strings = {[D,XCABX],[W,XCAX],[PA,XCA],
        [P,XXAXX],[C,XX],[R,XXXX],[DAY,X]};

  savet := t;                              $ save original form of
                                           $ transaction string
  decoded_trans := [ ];                    $ tuple for decoded form of
                                           $ transaction

  nfield := 1;                             $ counter for field number

  check_string := 'T';                     $ check character for first
                                           $ field is 'T'
  t + := '';
                                           $ add blank to capture last field

  (while t /= '' and nfield <= #check_string)

  if span(t,'  ') = om then continue; end;  $ span off blanks

  if (field =: field_check(break(t,'  '), check_string(nfield))) = om then

     Bad_transactions with := savet;
     return om;

  end if;

$ If the first field has just been decoded, use it to determine what further checks
  are necessary.

  if nfield = 1 then check_string := Check_strings(field); end;

     decoded_trans with := field;
     nfield + := 1;

  end while;

$ Check that all required fields, and no others, are present.

  if #decoded_trans = #check_string
     or decoded_trans(1) = D and #decoded_trans = 3 then
     return decoded_trans;
  end;

  Bad_transactions with := t;          $ otherwise missing or
                                       $ superfluous fields
```

```
    return om;

    end proc decode_transaction;

    proc field_check(field, test_char);     $ auxiliary test/convert
                                            $ procedure

$ This procedure checks the -field- passed to it for conformity with the
$ expected field type, which is described by its -test_char- argument.

$ The allowed test_char characters, and their significance, are as follows:

    $ 'T': must be transaction code
    $ 'X': no test required
    $ 'C': must be customer account number
    $ 'A': must be dollar amount
    $ 'B': must be identifier of correspondent bank

$ If the test fails, then om is returned; if the test succeeds, and the field type is
$ 'A', then the field is converted from standard DDDD.CC 'dollars and cents'
$ form to an integer number of cents,

    case test_char of

    ('T'): return if field in Transaction_codes then field else om end;

    ('X'): return field;

    ('C'): return if Cust_info(field) = om then om else field end;

    ('A'): dollars := span(field, Digits)?'';

        if match(field, '.') = om then return om; end;

        cents := span(field, Digits)?'';
        if #cents /= 2 or field /= '' then return om; end;

        return intval(dollars + cents);

    ('B'): return if field /= This_banks_code and Bank_info(field) = om then
    om else field end;

    else

    return om;

end case;

end proc field_check;

proc initialize_system;                      $ system initialization code

$ First we acquire the name of the input file for this run of the banking system,
$ which is supplied as a command-line parameter;

input_file := getspp('OLD = OLD.DAT/OLD.DAT');
```

```
$ Next we read the code for this bank, the pending transaction counter, the
$ master customer file, the bank address file, and the last previous processing
$ date, from the specified input information file.

   open(input_file, 'BINARY');           $ open the input file for reading.
                                          $ (See Section 9.1).

   getb(input_file, This_banks_code, Check_counter, Cust_info,

           Pending_checks, Bank_info, Last_day);

   close(input_file);                     $ now finished with input file;
                                          $ release it (See Section 9.1).

$ Next various subsidiary initializations are performed.

   Bad_transactions := [ ];               $ list of bad transactions is empty

   Message_list := {[bank, [ ]]: x = Bank_info(bank)};
                                          $ start an empty message
                                          $ file for each correspondent bank

   Transfile := setspp('TRANS = TRANS.DAT/TRANS.DAT');
   open('transfile.', 'CODED');           $ open file of transactions

end proc initialize_system;

proc finalize_system;                     $ end-of-run 'dump' procedure

$ First we acquire the name of the output file for this run of the banking
$ system, which is supplied on the command line.

output_file := getspp('NEW = NEW.DAT/NEW.DAT');

   open(output_file, 'BINARY-OUT');       $ open the output file for writing.

$ Next we write the code for this bank, the pending transaction counter, the
$ master customer file, and the bank file to be specified output file

   putb(output_file, This_banks_code, Check_counter, Cust_info,
      Pending_checks, Bank_info, daystring(DATE));

   close(output_file);                    $ now finished with output file;
                                          $ release it(See Section 9.1).

end proc finalize_system;

proc send_teller(terminal_no, msg);

$ In an actual system, this procedure would send the message -msg- to the
$ teller terminal identified by -terminal_no-. Since it is not easy to use SETL
$ to send messages to more than one terminal, we simplify this procedure
$ drastically and simply print -msg-, with an indication of the number of the
$ terminal to which msg should actually be sent.
```

```
  print(msg, 'has been sent to terminal,' terminal_no);

end proc send_teller;

proc end_of_day;                        $ end of day procedure

$ This procedure is called at the end of each banking day. In practice, it would
$ write out a collection of files, including the following:

$ (a) for each bank with which this bank does business, a file of messages, each
$ representing either a

$ (i) confirmation that a check transmitted for approval was actually approved;

$ (ii) rejection of a check, with an indication of the reason for rejection;

$ (iii) request for approval of a check,

$ (b) a list of bad transactions, for visual inspection and possible reentry.

$ We begin by crediting interest payments and making interest charges for all
$ customers.

$ First check to ensure that interest has not already been credited today.

  if daystring(DATE) /= Last_day then

   (for customer_items = Cust_info(number))

     interest_earned + :=
            (earned := (balance_available*Annual_rate) div 36500);
     balance_available + := earned; balance_deposited + := earned;

     $ Next, make charges on the customer's overdraft debit
     interest_paid + :=
            (owed := (Overdraft_debit*Overdraft_rate) div 36500);

$ Draw this interest out of the account if possible. If not enough remains,
$ interest will be charged as an overdraft, even though this causes the actual
$ overdraft to exceed its stated limit.

     if not ok_withdraw(owed, balance_available, overdraft_debit,
       balance_deposited, overdraft_limit)
       then                             $ run an "excess overdraft"

       overdraft_debit + := owed - balance_available;
       balance_deposited - := balance_available;
       balance_available := 0;

     end if;

   Cust_info(number) := customer_items;

   end for;
```

```
end if daystring(DATE);

$ Write a file of messages for each bank with which this bank does business.
   (for bank_inf = Bank_info(code) | code /= This_banks_code)

   write_message_file(bank_inf, Message_list(code));
   Message_list(code) := [ ];        $ clear the message list to avoid resending.

   end for;

$ Write out the file of bad transactions.
   write_bad_transactions(Bad_transactions);
   Bad_transactions := [ ];          $ clear the list of bad transactions

end proc end_of_day;

proc write_message_file(bank_inf, mess_list);

$ In a realistic system, this procedure might write a list of messages to a
$ magnetic tape which was then sent by air express or special courier to one of
$ the banks with which this bank does business. However, in our simplified
$ system, we simply print out a -bank_inf- as a header and follow it by the
$ individual messages of mess_list.

print; print; print(bank_inf); print; print;

(forall m in mess_list) print(m); end;

end proc write_message_file;

proc write_bad_transactions(list);

$ In a realistic system, this procedure might write its list of transactions to an
$ on-line disk file, which would then be scrutinized and manually edited,
$ reference being made if necessary to the original handwritten or typed
$ document which first ordered the transaction. However, in our simplified
$ system, we simply print out the list of bad transactions.

print; print; print('BAD TRANSACTION LIST'); print; print;

(forall m in list) print(m); end;

end proc write_bad_transactions;

proc end_of_month;                   $ end-of-month procedure

$ This procedure, called on the last day of each month, prepares a monthly
$ statement for each customer. If the month is January, a statement of total
$ interest charged/earned appears on the statement, and the accrued interest
$ fields in the customer record are cleared.

if daystring(DATE) =
Last_day then return; end;           $ since statements have already been
                                     $ prepared.
```

```
is_January := (month(daystring(DATE)) = '1');
                                    $ test for January
(for customer_items = Cust_info(cust_number))

  print; print(name, sec_no); print(address);
  print(daystring(DATE)); print;

  (for trans in transactions_this_month) print(trans); end;

  transactions_this_month := [ ];

   if is_January then

     print;
     print('SAVE THIS STATEMENT-IT CONTAINS VALUABLE
     TAX' 'INFORMATION');
     print;
     print('Interest earned:', interest_earned);
     print('Interest paid:', interest_paid);

   end if;

 end for;

end proc end_of_month;

proc dollar(amt);                $ converts numerical amount to dollar

return str (amt div 100) + '.' + if #(cts := str (amt mod 100)) =
2 then cts else cts + '0' end;

end proc dollar;

proc intval(stg);                $ convert string to integer

valu := 0;

(for di = stg(i))
  valu := valu*10;
  valu + := (abs di - abs '0');
end for;

return valu;

end proc intval;

proc day_field(stg);             $ extracts day from date

return stg(1..2);

end proc day_field;

proc daystring(dayt);            $ simplifies full date

dat := DATE;
return dat(9..10) + dat(12..14) + dat(16..17);
```

end proc daystring;

end program bank_checking;

11.6 A Turing-Machine Simulator

Turing machines, named after the famous English mathematician and computer scientist Alan Turing, are the most elementary kind of computer, so elementary that they are not used in any practical way but merely serve as idealized models of computation at its simplest. Used in this way, they play an important role in theoretical investigations of the ultimate limits of computability. A significant fact about these very simple computing mechanisms is that they can be programmed to imitate the action of any other computer; for example, a Turing machine can be programmed to take the text of any SETL program and print out its result.

Turing machines consist of two basic parts: a tape and a read-write head. The tape is a linear array of squares, infinite in both directions. In a tape square, the automaton can print any character chosen from a finite collection called the tape alphabet of the Turing machine. All but a finite number of squares on the tape are always blank. At the start of each cycle of operation of the Turing machine, its read-write head is positioned at one of the tape squares and is in one of a finite collection of possible internal states s. The read-write head then reads the character c held in the square at which it is positioned and performs three actions, all determined by the character c which has just been read and the internal state s of the read-write head:

(i) Some new character c' is written into the tape square at which the read-write head is positioned, replacing the character c that was there;
(ii) The read-write head passes into a new internal state s';
(iii) The read-write head either moves one step right, or one step left or remains where it is.

Plainly, these actions of the Turing machine can be defined by a map action(c, s), whose two parameters are a tape character c and an internal state s, and whose value is a tuple $[c', s', n']$, consisting of the tape character c' that will overwrite c, the new internal state s' of the read-write head, and an indicator n of the direction of head motion, which must be either $+1$ (move right), -1 (move left), or 0 (don't move).

The following procedures read in the description of a Turing machine, check this description for validity, read in the initial contents of the Turing machines's tape, and then proceed to imitate its actions. The tape is represented by a tuple *tape* whose j-th component is the character written in the j-th square. Blank squares contain the blank character. The Turing machine stops when it reaches an internal state s such that action(c, s) is undefined. We assume that the Turing machine description read in initially is a set of quintuples $[c, s, c', s', n']$, each representing an action-map entry $[[c, s], c', s', n]$. This description is checked to verify that the action map it describes is really single-valued. The auxiliary procedure *print_tape* prints the contents of the Turing machine tape after each cycle of operation.

```
program Turing_simulate;                  $ Turing machine simulator

if (atps := read_check( )) = om
then return; end;                         $ illegal specification

[action, tape, position, state] := atps;  $ unpack action table, initial
                                          $ tape, initial position, and
                                          $ initial state

(while (act := action(tape(position), state)) /= om)
                                          $ until stop

  [tape(position), state, n] := act;      $ write new character to tape
                                          $ and change internal state

  if (position + := n) < 1 then           $ moved left to brand-new square

    tape := ['  '] + tape;                $ add blank square at left
    position := 1;                        $ and adjust position pointer

  elseif position > #tape then            $ moved right to brand-new square;
    tape with := '  ';                    $ add blank at right

  end if;

  print_tape(tape, position, state);
end while;

print('Simulation ended. Chapter and state are:', tape(position), state);

proc read_check;                               $ reads and checks action table,
                                               $ tape, initial position, and
                                               $ initial state

macro check(condition, message, quantity);     $ utility macro for input-
 if not condition then                         $ condition checks print
   print(message, quantity);                   $ diagnostic message and
                                               $ offending quantity

   return om;                                  $ as indication of error

 end if

endm;

open('TUR.IN', 'TEXT-IN');
```

```
  reada('TUR.IN', actuples, tape, position, state);
  action := {[[c, s], [c2, s2, n]] : [c, s, c2, s2, n] in actuples};

not_single := false;

  (for im = action{cs} | #im > 1)           $ action is not single-valued

    not_single := true;
    print;
    print('action is indeterminate in condition', cs);
    print('actions could be:');

    (for [c2, s2, n] in im)
      print(c2, s2, n);
    end for;

    print;

  end for;

  if not_single then return om; end;         $ as indication of error in action
                                             $ table
check((bad_cs := {cs: [c2, s2, n] = action(cs)
        | n notin {-1, 1, 0}}) = { },
   'Illegal tape-motion indicators occur for conditions:', bad_cs);

check(is_integer(position), 'Illegal initial position:', position);
check(is_tuple(tape), 'Illegal initial tape:', tape);
check(forall t = tape(i) | is_string(t) and #t = 1,
        'Illegal initial tape', tape);

$ now add extra blanks to the initial tape if necessary

if position > #tape then                    $ extend tape with additional
                                            $ blank squares

  tape + := (#tape - position)*['  '];
else position < 1 then                      $ add extra blank squares to left
  tape := (1 - position)*['  '];
  position := 1;                            $ adjust index of position on
                                            $ extended tape

end if;

return [action, tape, position, state];

end proc read_check;
proc print_tape(tape, position, state);     $ Turing machine tape print
                                            $ utility.

$ This procedure is used to display the state of the Turing machine tape at
$ the end of each cycle of simulation
```

```
const sq = 18, hsq = 9;                    $ one-fourth and one-eighth
                                           screen size
const screen_size = 72                     $ number of characters on
                                           terminal

   topline := screen_size*'_'; topline (4*hsq + 1...4*hsq + 4) :=

   botline := screen_size*'_';

tape_string := (hsq*'  ') +/ tape + (hsq*'  ');
                                           $ convert tape to string and pad
                                           $ with blanks.

tape_string := tape_string(position..position + 2*hsq - 1);

picture := +/ ['|' + t + '  ': in tape_string];
picture(1) := '  ';                        $ remove first vertical bar.

print; print(topline); print(picture + '  ' + str state); print(botline);

end proc print_tape;

end program Turing_simulate;
```

11.7 Huffman Coding of Text Files

The standard ASCII alphabet of computer characters contains 127 characters, each of which is usually represented at the machine level by a sequence of 8 binary bits. If large volumes of English-language text need to be stored, this internal coding, which uses just as much computer memory space to represent a rare character like 'z' as to represent a common character like 'e', is by no means optimal. It is better to represent frequently occuring characters by shorter sequences of bits, even though this forces one to lengthen the internal encoding of less frequent characters, since overall this will diminish the total storage required to store typical texts. An effective method for using variable-length encodings of this kind was described by X. Huffman and has become known as *Huffman coding.* Huffman's technique is to arrange all the characters to be encoded as the terminal nodes of a binary tree, in the manner shown in Figure 11.1. This tree should be set up so that commonly occurring characters appear near its "root" node and rare characters appear at a greater distance from its root.

There will always exist a unique path from the root node of such a tree to each terminal node or "twig" of the tree, and any such path can always be described by a unique sequence of zeroes and ones, where '0' means "take the left branch" and '1' means "take the right branch down the tree. "As the code for a character *c* we can therefore use the binary sequence describing the path

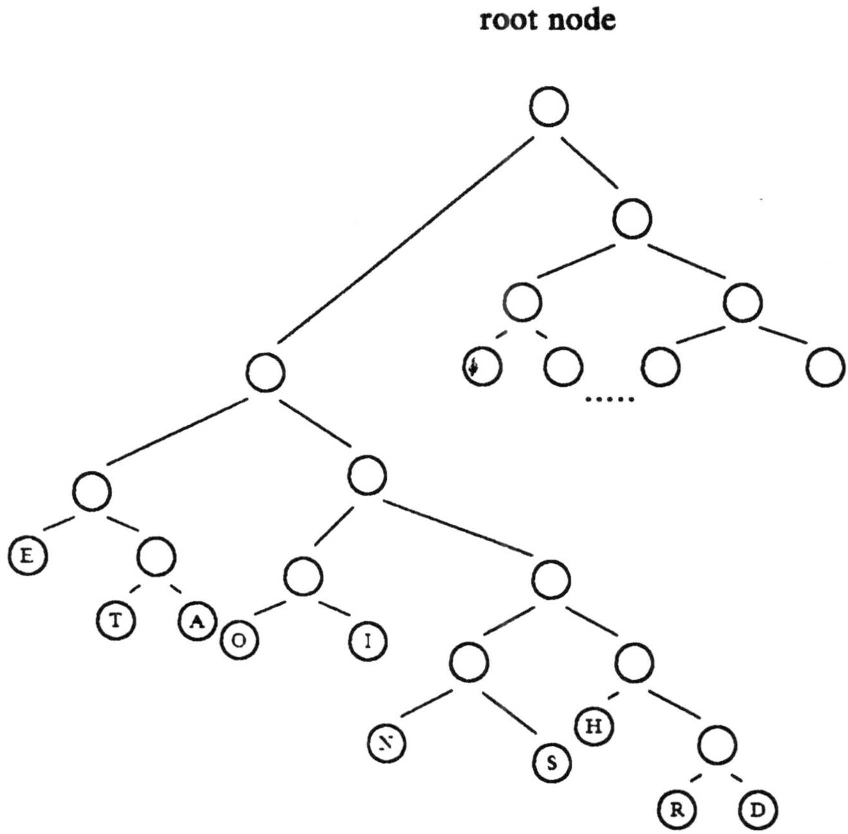

Figure 11.1 Binary Huffman Tree with Characters Attached to its Terminal Nodes.

from the root node of the tree to the terminal node at which *c* is attached. For example, the tree shown in Figure 11.1 would assign the code '000' to 'E', the code '0010' to 'T', the code '0101' to I, etc. To encode a sequence of characters, we simply concatenate the sequences of zeroes and ones representing its individual characters. To decode a sequence *s* of zeroes and ones, we start from the root of the Huffman tree which defines our encoding and use the leftmost bits of *s* to guide us down a path in the tree. As soon as we reach a twig of the tree we add the character attached to this twig to the sequence of decoded characters we are building up. The sequence of bits that led us to this character is then detached from *s*, and we return to the root of the Huffman tree and continue the decoding process using what remains of *s*.

The three routines which follow embody this encoding and decoding technique. The *Huff* procedure takes a character string and encodes it using Huffman's method. *Puff*, which is the inverse of *Huff*, takes the encoded form of a string *s* and recovers the original form of *s*. The third procedure, called *setup*, takes maps *left* and *right* representing a Huffman tree and uses them to initialize various global data objects required by the *Huff* and *Puff* routines. The algorithm uses '1' and '0' to represent bits.

```
program Huffman;                    $ Huffman encode, decode, and setup

var
  H_code,                           $ maps each character into its Huffman code
  H_root,                           $ root node of Huffman tree

  H_left,                           $ maps each node of the Huffman
                                    $ tree to its left descendant

  H_right,                          $ maps each node of the Huffman
                                    $ tree to its right descendent

  H_char;                           $ maps terminal nodes of the Huffman tree
                                    $ to the characters they represent

huff_test;                          $ call test procedure

proc setup(root, left, right, chr); $ auxiliary initialization routine

$ We begin by using the procedure arguments to initialize all but the first of
$ the global variables listed above.

H_left := left; H_right := right;
H_root := root; H_char := chr;

$ Next we calculate H_code(c) for each character c

parent := {[y, x]: [x, y] in
(H_left + H_right)};                $ This maps each tree node to its parent

H_code := { };                      $ begin calculating Huffman codes
                                    $ from tree structure

(for c = H_char(node))              $ chain up to the root, noting how we got
                                    $ there

  bits := '';                       $ initially, path is null

  (while node /= H_root)
    bits := if H_left(par := parent(node)) = node then
      '0' else '1' end + bits;
    node := par;                    $ step up to parent
  end while;

  H_code(c) := bits;                $ record Huffman code for current character

end for;

end proc setup;

proc Huff(stg);                     $ calculates Huffman code for string stg
```

```
return '' +/
[H_code(c): c = stg(i)];          $ concatenate codes of individual characters

end proc Huff;

proc Puff(Huff_stg);              $ decodes a Huffman-coded string

stg := '';                        $ initialize decoded string
node := H_root;                   $ start at Huffman-tree root

(for b = Huff_tg(j))              $ examine binary bits of Huff_stg in order

  node := if b = '0' then H_left(node) else H_right(node) end;

  if (c := H_char(node)) /= om
  then                            $ have reached twig

    stg + := c;                   $ append to decoded portion
    node := H_root;               $ restart at Huffman-tree root

  end if;

end for;

return stg;

end proc Puff;
```

The encoding and decoding procedures shown sidestep the question of how to find the tree that will give us a maximum degree of text compression. Of course, the rule for finding this tree, given the frequency with which each character occurs in the text we are to encode, is Huffman's essential discovery.

His rule is as follows: we begin by finding the two characters *c1*, *c2* of lowest frequency. These are then logically "conglomerated" into a single joint character *c*, of which *c1* and *c2* become the left and right descendants, respectively. We remove *c1* and *c2* from the collection of characters which remain to be processed and replace them by *c*. Continuing this until only one character remains, we will have bulit the Huffman tree.

Represented in SETL, this procedure is as follows:

```
proc Huff_tree(freq);                     $ Huffman tree-build routine
  $ freq is assumed to map all the characters of our alphabet into their
  $ expected frequencies of occurrence.

  $ This procedure returns a quadruple [root, left, right, chr] consisting of the
  $ Huffman tree root, its left and right descendancy maps, and a map chr
  $ which sends each terminal node of the tree into the character attached to
  $ this node.

  $ Since the code which follows will represent tree nodes by character strings,
  $ the chr map is just the identity map on single-character strings and is
  $ conveniently set up right here.
```

```
chr := {[c, c]: c in domain freq};

left := right := { };                     $ initialize the descendancy
                                          $ mappings

(while #freq > 1)

  [c1, freq_c1] := get_min(freq); [c2, freq_c2] := get_min(freq);
  freq(c := (c1 + c2)) := freq_c1 + freq_c2;
                                          $ form "group" character
  left(c) := c1; right(c) := c2;          $ make c1 and c2 descendants of c

end while;

return [arb domain freq, left, right, chr]; $ which is necessarily the tree root

end proc Huff_tree;

proc get_min(rw freq);
  $ This auxiliary procedure finds the character c of minimum frequency,
  $ returns c and its frequency, and deletes c from the domain of freq. Note
  $ that it uses a "dangerous" program construction, legal in SETL, but
  $ certainly not recommended for use in any context which is at all complex;
  $ namely it is a function which modifies the argument with which it is called.

  min_freq := min/[f: f = freq(c)];

  assert exists f = freq(c) | f = min_freq;

  freq(c) := om;                          $ modify the input argument (which
                                          $ is read-write).
                                          $ DANGEROUS!

  return [c, f];

  end proc get_min;

proc huff_test;                           $ test code for Huffman program

order :=
'e taionshrdluqwypfgjkmbvcxz';            $ blank is second most frequent
freq := {[c, 30 - j]: c = order(j)};      $ character in English text.
[root, left, right, chr] := ; huff_tree(freq);

setup(root, left, right, chr);

print(huff('hello there'));
print(puff(huff('hello there')));

end proc huff_text;

end program;
```

Various improvements and extensions of the procedures described in this section appear in Exercises 13–18.

11.8 A Game-playing Program

In this section, we will explore the basic structure of programs which play board games like chess and checkers which involve two players, whom we shall call 'A' and 'B'. The momentary state $s = [p, x]$ of any such game can be defined by giving the position p of the various pieces or counters used in the game, and by stating which of the players, x = 'A' or x = 'B', is to move next. Given any such state s, the rules of the game will determine the moves which are legal and hence will determine the set of all possible new states $s1, \ldots, sk$, exactly one of which must be chosen by the active player, i.e., the player whose turn it is to move. We shall suppose in what follows that the map has_turn(s) determines this player (i.e., has_turn(s) is just x, if as previously s has the form $[p, x]$). We also suppose that the map next_states(s) gives us the set $\{s1, .. sk\}$ of states to which the active player can move.

Any such game will end as soon as certain states, called *terminal states*, are reached. (In chess, for example, these are the states in which one of the players has been checkmated.) For purposes of analysis it is convenient to suppose that when a terminal state s is reached, D dollars are transferred from player B to player A. We can suppose either that the sum D is fixed or that it depends on s. It is actually more convenient to make the latter assumption, and we shall do so, supposing accordingly that we are given a function A_wins(s) defined on all terminal states s, and that when a terminal state s is reached the sum A_wins(s) is transferred from B to A. Plainly A is the winner if $D > 0$, B is the winner if $D < 0$, and the game counts as a tie if $D = 0$. It is convenient to suppose that A_wins(s) = **om** if the state s is not a terminal state; then the condition A_wins(s) /= **om** can be used to test for terminal states.

The three functions has_turn(s) (whose value must be either 'A' or 'B'), next_states(s), and A_wins(s) serve to encapsulate the basic rules of any two-player game we wish to study.

Next, to begin to understand the strategic considerations which determine the laws of effective play, it is useful to extend the function A_wins(s), which is only defined for terminal states, so that it becomes a function A_can_win(s), defined for all states. We do this in the following recursive way:

A_can_win(s) = A_wins(s)?
  if has_turn(s) = 'A' **then max** /[A_can_win(sy): sy **in** next_states(s)]   (1)
    else min /[A_can_win(sy): sy **in** next_states(s)] **end**;

The meaning of this formula can be explained as follows:

(a) If the state s is terminal, the game is over and the amount that A can win is exactly the amount that A has in fact won.
(b) Otherwise, if it is A's turn to move, he will choose the move that is most favorable to him, shifting the game into that state *sy* in next_states(s) for which A_can_win(*sy*) is as large as possible. Conversely, if it is B's turn to move, she will defend herself as well as possible against A's attempts to

win a maximum amount. *B* does this by shifting the game into the state *sy* for which *A*'s attainable winnings are as small as possible. Since *A* wins what *B* loses, and vice versa, this is at the same time the state in which *B*'s winnings are as large as possible.

It is not hard to see that if the function A_can_win defined by (1) is known, and if both players expect their opponents to play with perfect accuracy, player *A* should *always* use her turn to move to a state *sy* such that A_can_win(*sy*) is as large as possible, and player *B* should *always* use his turn to move to a state sy such that A_can_win(*sy*) is as small as possible. To show this, suppose that the sequence of states traversed in the history of a game, from the moment at which it reaches state *s* up to the moment at which the game terminates, is $s = s_1, s_2, \ldots, s_n$. Using (1) it is easy to see that if *A* uses this strategy, A_can_win(s_j) will never decrease, so that by using our recommended strategy *A* guarantees that when the game terminates he will win at least the amount A_can_win(s). Conversely, if *B* uses the strategy we recommend, then formula (1) shows that A_can_win(s_j) will never increase. Hence, if player *A* ever makes a move which decreases the value of A_can_win from *v* to some value *u* which is less than *v*, then after this *B* can prevent him from recovering, i.e., from ever winning more than *u*. If follows that, if *A* gives his opponent credit for playing optimally, *A* must never "give ground" in regard to the function A_can_win, i.e., that when it is his turn to move he should always move to a new state *sy* such that such that A_can_win(*sy*) is as large as possible. (Of course, if he does this, then A_can_win(*sy*) = A_can_win(*s*); see (1)).

Reasoning by symmetry, we also see that *B* should always move to a new state *sy* such that A_can_win(*sy*) is as small as possible.

These considerations indicate that any game-playing program will need to calculate the function (1). However, if the game being analyzed is at all complex, it will not be feasible just to use the recursive definition (1) as it stands, since the tree of possible moves and countermoves which (1) would examine will tend to grow very rapidly. For example, if at every level *A* has just 4 possible moves and *B* has 4 possible countermoves, then 256 different positions can evolve from an initial state *s* after *A* and *B* make two moves each, 64,000 different positions after *A* and *B* have made 4 moves each, and hence the recursion (1) would have roughly 16,000,000 positions to examine if we used it to look ahead through all possible combinations of 6 moves of *A* and 6 countermoves of *B*.

This makes it plain that it is important to accelerate calculation of the function A_can_win as much as we can. Several techniques for doing this have been developed, but we shall only describe one particularly important method of this kind, the *alpha-beta pruning* method. To derive this improvement, suppose that f is a function mapping numbers to numbers, and that f is *monotone*, i.e., has the property that $x \leq y$ implies $f(x) \leq f(y)$. Then since $x \,\mathbf{max}\, y$ is the larger of x and y, it follows that $f(x \,\mathbf{max}\, y) = f(x) \,\mathbf{max}\, f(y)$. Hence

$$\mathrm{f}(\mathbf{max}/[\mathrm{e(x)}\text{: x } \mathbf{in}\text{ s}]) = \mathbf{max}/[\mathrm{f(e(x))}\text{: x } \mathbf{in}\text{ s}] \tag{2}$$

for every set *s* and expression *e*. It is also clear that (2) continues to hold if we replace **max** by **min**. This remark, and (1), make it obvious that the following recursive function calculates the function B(*s*, lo, hi) = A_can_win(s) **min** hi **max** lo:

```
proc B(s, lo, hi);                                                    (3)
if (v := A_wins(s)) /= om then return v min hi max lo; end;
if has_turn(s) = 'A' then
   max_till_now := lo;
   (for sy in next_states(s))
      max_till_now max := B(s, lo, hi);
   end for;
   return max_till_now min hi;
else
   min_till_now := hi;
   (for sy in next_states(s))
      min_till_now min := B(s, lo, hi);
   end for;
   return min_till_now max lo;
end if;
end proc B;
```

Since the quantity returned at the end of the first loop in (3) is max_till_now **min** hi, we can terminate the loop as soon as max_till_now rises to *hi*; and a similar remark clearly applies to the second loop in (3). This crucial observation allows us to rewrite (3) as

```
proc B(s, lo, hi);                                                    (4)
if(v := A_wins(s)) /= om then return v min hi max lo; end;
if has_turn(s) = 'A' then
   max_till_now := lo;
   (for sy in next_states(s))
      if(max_till_now max := B(sy, lo, hi)) >= hi then return hi; end;
   end for;
   return max_till_now;
else
   min_till_now := hi;
```

```
  (for sy in next_states(s))
    if(min_till_now min := B(sy, lo, hi)) <= lo then return lo; end;
  end for;

  return min_till_now;

end if;

end proc B;
```

In the first loop of (4) the quantity max_till_now is never larger than hi or smaller than lo; hence we have

B(s, lo, hi) **max** max_till_now
= A_can_win(s) **min** hi **max** lo **max** max_till_now
= A_can_win(s) **min** hi **max** max_till_now
= B(s, max_till_now, hi).

Similarly, in the second loop of (4) we always have *B*(s, lo, hi) **min** min_till_now = B(s, lo, min_till_now). Moreover, all the recursive calls to *B* appearing in (4) occur in contexts in which *B* can as well be replaced by (*B* **min** hi **max** lo). Hence (v **min** lo **max** hi) can be replaced by v in the second line of (4). These remarks show that the following recursive procedure *B2* satisfies *B2*(s, lo, hi) **min** lo **max** hi = B(s, lo, hi):

```
proc B2(s, lo, hi);                                                  (5)

if(v := A_wins(s)) /= om then return v; end;

if has_turn(s) = 'A' then

  till_now := lo;

  (for sy in next_states(s))

    if (till_now max := B2(sy, till_now, hi)) >= hi then return hi; end;

  end for;

else

  till_now := hi;

  (for sy in next_states(s))
    if(till_now min := B2(sy, lo, till_now)) <= lo then return lo; end;
  end for;

end if;

return till_now;

end proc B2;
```

The fact that the loops in (5) are terminated early, i.e., terminated as soon as till_now rises to hi or sinks to lo, sometimes improves the efficiency of (3) very substantially; this is what we want. Of course, we can exploit the symmetry of *B2* to write it more compactly:

```
proc B3(s, lo, hi);   $ A polished alpha-beta algorithm                    (6)

if (v := A_wins(s)) /= om then return v; end;

if has_turn(s) = 'B' then [hi, lo] := [-lo, -hi]; end;

till_now := lo;

(for sy in next_states(s))
if (till_now max := B3(sy, till_now, hi)) >= hi then return hi; end;
end for;

return if has_turn = 'B' then - till_now else till_now end;

end proc B3(s, lo, hi);
```

If *large* designates any sufficiently large quantity, then *B3*(s, −large, large) will be equal to A_can_win(s). It is convenient to represent such an "infinitely large" quantity by **om**, and also convenient to replace (6) by a recursive procedure yielding the value

```
        if has_turn(s) = 'A' then B2(s, lo, hi) else - B(s, -lo, -hi) end
```

Doing this gives us our next form of the alpha-beta procedure, namely

```
macro reverse(x); if x = om then om else - x end endm;

proc A_can(s, lo, hi);     $ second form of alpha_beta algorithm           (7)

till_now = lo;

(for sy in next_states(s))  $ note that next_states(s) = { } if s is a terminal state

  till_now := if till_now = om then A_can(sy, reverse(hi), reverse(lo))
    else till_now max A_can(sy, reverse(hi), reverse(lo)) end;

  if hi /= om and till_now >= hi then return till_now; end;

end for;

return if (v := A_wins(s)) = om then - till_now
    elseif has_turn(s) = 'A' then v else - v end;

end proc A_can;             $ A_can_win(s) = A_can(s, om, om)
```

A close analysis of algorithm (7) will show that it can be expected to derive the value of the A_can_win function for a tree of moves 2*d* levels deep in roughly the time that algorithm (3) would require to analyze a tree *d* levels deep. However, in spite of this very substantial improvement, complex games will still lead to trees of moves which are so deep and branch so rapidly that full exploration using algorithm (7) is quite impossible. One technique used to cope with this fundamental difficulty is to limit the number of recursive levels explored by using (7). When this limit is reached, we use some ad hoc estimate, called an *evaluation heuristic*, to approximate the value of A_can_win(s). In effect, this approach pretends to replace the full game that we would like to analyze by a truncated game that is played for some limited number L of moves and then terminated with a payoff determined by the evaluation heuristic. To play the full game, we then reanalyze this truncated game each time it is a given player's turn to move and choose the best move in the truncated game as her recommended move in the real game. Assuming that A_estimate(s) is the estimated value of state s to player A, it is easy to modify (7) to incorporate such a limit on the number of levels of move and countermove that will be examined. Doing so, we get

```
macro reverse(x); if x = om then om else - x end endm;

proc Est_A_can_win(s, lo, hi, lim);   $ alpha-beta algorithm
                                      $ with limited search

if (lim - := 1) = 0 then
  return if has_turn(s) = 'A' then A_estimate(s)
     else - A_estimate(s) end;
end if;

till_now := lo;

(for sy in next_states(s))

 till_now := if till_now = om then                                          (8)
  Est_A_can_win(sy, reverse(hi), reverse(lo), lim)

  else till_now max Est_A_can_win(sy, reverse(hi), reverse(lo), lim) end;
if hi /= om and till_now >= hi then return till_now; end;
end for;

return if (v := A_wins(s)) = om then - till_now
     elseif has_turn(s) = 'A' then v else - v end;

end proc Est_A_can_win;
```

11.9 Implementation of a Macroprocessor

In this section we will show how to implement the SETL macro feature described in Section 8.2. The context within which this macroprocessor is to be implemented is assumed to be as follows:

(i) The macroprocessor reads a succession of tokens, obtained by decomposing some input file into successive tokens.
(ii) When the special token **macro** is encountered, a macro definition is opened. This token must be followed by a macro name, which can in turn be followed by a list of formal parameters and generated formal

parameters, in the manner explained in Sections 8.2.3 and 8.2.4. The macro body following such a macro opener is collected and saved in a map *def_of*, which associates each macro name with its list of parameters, its list of generated parameters, and its macro body.

(iii) When a macro invocation starting with a token belonging to the domain of the map *def_of* is encountered, its actual arguments are collected, and the invocation is replaced by a substituted version of the macro body. This substituted text is logically inserted immediately in front of the remainder of the input file and reprocessed by the macro-expansion mechanism, thereby ensuring that macro invocations and definitions embedded within macro bodies will be treated in the manner described in Section 8.2.5.

(iv) The macroprocessor makes various syntactic checks. For example, it checks that the parameters appearing in a macro definition are all distinct, and that each macro invocation has as many arguments as the corresponding macro definition has parameters. If an error is detected, a diagnostic message is printed, and any macro action in progress is simply bypassed.

(v) The macroprocessor is structured as a **module**, which exports just one procedure, namely a parameterless procedure called *next_tok*, which can be called repeatedly to obtain the sequence of tokens representing the input file after macro expansion. When the input file is exhausted, *next_tok* will return **om**. The macroprocessor **module** imports just one procedure, namely a parameterless procedure called *input_tok*. Successive calls to input_tok generate the sequence of input tokens which constitute the macroprocessor's initial input.

```
program macroprocessor;            $ macroprocessor test

var
   gmac_ctr,                       $ counter for generated macro arguments
   def_of,                         $ maps macro names into their definitions
   expanded_toks;                  $ vector of tokens obtained by prior macro
                                   $ expansion

var line_no, line_now, text;       $ globals for reader

const alphanums =
'abcdefghijklmnopqrstuvwxyzABCEDFGHIJKLMNOPQRSTUVWXYZ';

const Illformed_list = 'ILLFORMED MACRO PARAMETER LIST';
                                   $ error message to avoid later trouble in
                                   $ macro arglist
const comma = ',';

   macro check(condition, msg);
      if not (condition) then return err_msg(msg); end
   endm;
```

```
line_now := '';                  $ initially line is empty
line_no := 1;                    $ initialize first line

gmac_ctr := 0;                   $ generated macro argument counter
def_of := { };                   $ initially no definitions
expanded_toks := [ ];            $ initially no prior tokens

text := get_lines('macro.in');   $ read input

(while (wd := next_tok( )) /= om) print(wd); end;

.COPY GET_LINES

proc input_tok;                  $ input reader

span(line_now, ' ');             $ remove blanks

if line_now = '' then
  if line_no > #text then return om; end;
  line_now := text(line_no); line_no +:= 1;
end;

return span (line_now, alphanums)? len(line_now, 1);

end proc input_tok;

proc next_tok;                   $ called to obtain successive tokens in the
                                 $ sequence of tokens generated by macro
                                 $ expansion

loop do                          $ we return to this point whenever macro
                                 $ errors are detected

  if (tok := another_tok( )) = om then return om; end;
                                 $ end of input file encounted

  if (tok /= 'MACRO') and (mdef := def_of(tok)) = om then
                                 $ token is ordinary;
    return tok;
  end if;
  if tok = 'MACRO' then                  $ start new macro definition

   if (parm_list := get_parm_list( )) = om
     or (mac_body := get_macro_body( )) = om then

       continue;                         $ since macro is bad

   end if;

   [mac_name, mac_pars, mac_gpars] := parm_list;
                                         $ get macro name and parameters

   def_of(mac_name) :=
   if mac_body = [ ] then om             $ macro drop
```

```
        else [mac_pars, #mac_gpars,
        template(mac_body, mac_pars, mac_gpars)] end;

   else                                     $ macro invocation

   [mac_pars, n_gpars, mac_template] := mdef;
                                            $ look up macro definition

   if (arg_list := get_arg_list(#mac_pars)) = om
   then                                     $ abort expansion
   continue;                                $ since number of arguments and
                                            $ number of parameters differ
   end if;

   (for n in [1..n_gpars]) mac_pars with := [generated_parm( )]; end;

   $ generate additional parameters as required and replace the macro at the
   $ start of the expanded_tokens vector by its expansion

   expanded_tok :=
    +/ [if is_string (mac_tok) then [mac_tok] else mac_pars(mactok) end:
              mac_tok = mac_template(j)] + expanded_tokens;

   end if tok;

    $ now that macro has been expanded, the top of the loop will try again to
    $ supply the requested token

     end loop;

     end proc next_tok;

proc another_tok;                           $ "token feeder" for macro
                                            $ processor
   $ This returns the token standing at the head of expanded_toks unless
   $ expanded_toks is empty, in which case it calls the "primary" token source
   $ input_tok to get the token to be returned.

return if (tok fromb expanded_toks) /= om then tok
     else input_tok( ) end;

end proc another_tok;

proc get_parm_list;                    $ gets sequence of parameters for
                                       $ macro

   $ The sequence of parameters collected by this procedure must be a
   $ comma-separated list opened by a left paranthesis and closed by a right
   $ parenthesis. If this syntax is violated, or if two parameters are identical,
   $ an error message is printed, and om is returned.

have_parms := false;                   $ flag: No generated parameters yet
```

```
mac_parms := mac_gparms := [ ];   $ initializes parameters and
                                  $ generalized parameters

if (name := namecop := another_tok( )) = om or
      name /= span(namecop, alphanums) then

   print('ILLFORMED MACRO NAME');
   return om;

elseif (tok := another_tok( )) = ';' then

   return [name, [ ], [ ]];          $ no parameters

end;

check(tok = '(', Illformed_list);

(until tok = ')')                 $ until terminating parenthesis

   check((tok := another_tok( )) /= om, illformed_list);
   mac_parms with := tok;
   check((tok := another_tok( )) = comma or tok = ')', illformed_list);

end until;

check(another_tok( ) = ';', Illformed_list);

return [name, mac_parms, mac_gparms];

end proc get_parm_list;

proc err_msg(message);
   $ error message routine: print error message identifying error

   print(message);

   return om;

end proc err_msg;
proc get_macro_body;
   $ collects sequence of tokens up to endm

   body := [ ];

   (while (tok := another_tok( )) /= 'ENDM');
      check(tok /= om, 'MACRO BODY NOT PROPERLY ENDED');
      body with := tok;
   end while;

   return body;

end proc get_macro_body;

proc template(mac_body, mac_pars, mac_gpars);
```

```
    $ This procedure builds the "macro template" stored as the definition of a
    $ macro. The template consists of the string constituting the macro body,
    $ but with every parameter and generated parameter replaced by an integer.

    counter := 0;
    $ start count at zero

    replacement := {[t, (counter + := 1)]: t in mac_pars + mac_gpars};
    $ This maps every macro parameter into its replacement

    return [replacement(t)?t: t in mac_body];

end proc template;

proc generated_parm;
    $ auxiliary procedure to produce generated macro parameters.

    $ The macro parameters generated by this procedure have the form 'ZZZn',
    $ where n is the string representation of an integer.

    return 'ZZZ' + str(gmac_ctr + := 1);

end proc generated_parm;

end program;
```

Exercises

1. A *nondeterministic* Turing machine is a Turing machine TM whose action mapping is not constrained to be single-valued. In addition, one particular internal state of each such machine must be designated as its "failed" state. Such machines can be regarded as describing indefinitely large families of computations which proceed in parallel. More specifically, we start with a given tape, tape position, and internal machine state, as in the case of an ordinary Turing machine. Then, whenever the internal *state* and the *character* under the machine's read head are such that action(character, state) is multivalued (consisting, say, of *n* values), we create as many logical copies of the machine as needed and assign one of them to take each of these *n* actions and continue the computation. This can generate a rapidly expanding set of computations, all proceeding in parallel. If a particular logical copy TM*j* of TM reaches the special "failed" internal state, the particular path of computation which it is following ceases, and TM*j* is simply deleted. As soon as any computation TM*k* reaches an ordinary "stop" condition all other computations are deleted, and the result calculated by this successful logical copy TM*k* of TM becomes the final result of the nondeterministic computation. On the other hand, if all computations TM*k* reach the "failed" internal state, the nondeterministic Turing machine computation is considered to have failed.

   Modify the Turing machine simulation program shown in Section 11.6 so that it can simulate both ordinary and nondeterministic Turing machines.

2. A multitape Turing machine is one which has several separate tapes, with a read-write head on each, whose action on each cycle is determined by its internal state and by the characters found under all of its read-write heads. Modify the

Turing machine simulation program shown in Section 11.6 so that it can simulate multitape Turing machines with any specified number of heads.

3. Can you think of any well-defined computing automaton or computational process whose activity could not be simulated by a SETL program? Review Exercises 1 and 2 before you answer.

4. The macroprocessor shown in Section 11.9 is programmed to imitate the present SETL macroprocessor, which regards every comma in a macro argument list as a separator. For example, if *my_mac* is a macro name, then the invocation

   my_mac(f(x, y), z)

   is considered to have three components, namely

   f(x   y)   z

   This is not the best convention: it would be better to regard commas contained within parentheses or brackets as being invisible to the macroprocessor, so that the macro call shown would be regarded as having just two arguments $f(x, y)$ and z. Modify the macroprocessor so that it behaves in this way.

5. (Continuation of Ex. 4). Especially if the modification suggested in Exercise 4 is made, use of a macroprocessor becomes subject to two dangers:
   (a) If the parenthesis terminating an argument list is missing, much of the body of text following a macro invocation may be swallowed up in what appears to be a very long final argument.
   (b) If the keyword **endm** ending a macro is missing or misspelled, the text following a macro definition may be swallowed up by the macro definition.

   Modify the macroprocessor of Exercise 4 so as to limit each macro argument to 50 tokens and each macro definition to 200 tokens.

Exercises related to the "check processing" system of Section 11.5:

6. Modify the check processing system so that it tracks
   (a) The total dollar volume of transactions handled each day.
   (b) The total dollar credit/debit that the bank using the system has built up against each of its correspondent banks.

   These quantities should be printed out as additional information by the DAY transaction.

7. Modify the check processing system, adding a new transaction DEL which prints out a list of all accounts for which more than a month has gone by without at least 10% of a customer's outstanding overdraft_debit having been paid.

8. Modify the check processing system, adding the following two transactions:
   (a) A transaction *AB* ('abuse') which shows all accounts for which an excess overdraft has accumulated or against which more than 10 "insufficient funds" charges have been made during the current month.
   (b) A transaction *I* ("idle") which shows all accounts against which no checks have been drawn during the past 6 months.

9. Modify the check processing system, adding transactions *O* and *CL* which allow new customer accounts to be opened and closed. Closing of accounts should be

handled carefully: such accounts should be marked as having been closed but should not actually be deleted while there exist outstanding transactions, still to be returned by other banks, that might affect the account which is being closed.

When an account is finally closed, the balance remaining in it should be used to pay off any outstanding overdraft_debit, and a check for the amount remaining in the account after this final payment should be prepared for mailing. How will you handle an account closing when the balance remaining is insufficient to pay off the overdraft debit?

10. Modify the check processing system so that it can add a short advertisement to the monthly statements being prepared for mailing to customers. The text of this advertisement should be supplied by a transaction of the form

advert n

where *n* is an integer, and where this line will be followed by *n* more lines giving the text of the advertisement. This transaction must be run just before the DAY transaction which triggers preparation of monthly statements.

11. If you have a checking account, save the next monthly statement you get from your bank, and scrutinize it carefully. How many of the features of this statement suggest that your bank is using a program similar to the check processing program shown in Section 11.5? What features reveal the use of processing steps that our simplified check processing system does not perform? If you can find any such feature, choose one of them and modify the check processing system to include it.

12. Modify the check processing system so as to make it a model for the activity of several banks. Each of these banks will run the modified check processing system once per day, generating files of messages which are then sent to the other banks in the system and added to the transaction files that these banks will process during their next day's run. Execute your modified program with appropriate inputs so as to simulate several days' activity for the whole "financial system."

13. The degree of compression attained by the Huffman coding procedure shown in Section 11.7 can be increased by using the fact that the probability of encountering a character depends on the character that has just been encountered. That is, we can calculate not one, but a whole family of Huffman trees, one for each high-probability character *c* in our alphabet; this tree should position other characters *d* according to the probability that *d* follows *c*.

    Develop a modified Huffman package which uses these more refined probabilities, and also a modified *Huff_tree* code which calculates all the Huffman trees required.

14. Storing a Huffman tree requires memory space proportional to the size of the alphabet whose characters are attached to the terminal nodes of the tree. If the improved technique described in Exercise 13 is used, such a tree will have to be stored for each character in the alphabet, and the amount of space required for this can grow unpleasantly large (especially if the data compression procedure is to be reprogrammed for a small machine). In this case, the following expedient can be used to reduce the amount of storage required:
    (a) For each character *c*, establish a limit $L(c)$ which will bound the number of nodes used in the modified Huffman tree built from the frequency count

developed for letters following c. This limit should be larger for commonly occurring characters c, smaller for infrequent characters.

(b) For each c, find the $L(c)$ characters which most frequently follow c and "lump" all the other characters into a new character c'. The sum of the frequencies of all these "lumped" characters then becomes the frequency of c'.

(c) Build a Huffman tree for the alphabet of $L(c) + 1$ characters left after step (b). Then let the code of each character not "lumped" into c' be determined as in Exercise 13, but let the code of each character x "lumped" into c' be the concatenation of the normal Huffman code of c' with the standard internal SETL code of c.

Modify the Huffman encode/decode procedures to incorporate this space-saving refinement.

15. If the "Huff" and "Puff" procedures shown in Section 11.7 are really to be used for compressing large texts, we will want them to produce densely packed character strings rather than SETL-level sequences of zeroes and ones. To achieve this without having to abandon SETL in favor of a language in which sequences of bits can be manipulated directly, we can break the sequence of zeroes and ones that "Huff" would most naturally produce into 8-bit sections, each of which is then represented by a single SETL character. Conversely, when decoding, we can first convert each character in the string being decoded into a string of zeroes and ones.

    Modify the Huffman routines shown in Section 11.7 so that they work in this way. Your modified *setup* procedure should construct the extra data structures needed to convert characters into 8-bit sequences of zeroes and ones, and vice versa.

16. The decoding procedure shown in Section 11.7 and further described in Exercise 14 can be accelerated by keeping a map *Decode* which sends the start (say the first 8 bits) of the sequence s being decoded either into a pair $[c, n]$, where c is the first character obtained by decoding s and n is the number of bits of s that represent this character, or into the *node* of the Huffman tree that is reached after walking down the tree in the manner determined by the first 8 bits of s, if these 8 bits do not lead us to a terminal node. Rewrite these routines by incorporating the suggested improvements.

17. The Huffman *setup* procedure shown in Section 11.7 can be made more efficient by saving the sequence of zeroes and ones describing the path from each Huffman tree *node* traversed. This information can be stored at the node. This makes it unnecessary for the *setup* procedure to traverse any edge of the Huffman tree more than once. Rewrite *setup*, incorporating this improvement.

18. The Huff_tree procedure shown in Section 11.7 can be made more efficient by using the treelike structures described in Section 11.7 to accelerate the auxiliary *get_min* procedure. Rewrite *Huff_tree* and *get_min*, incorporating this improvement.

19. In playing a game, one may wish not only to win as much as possible, but also to win in the smallest possible number of moves. A recursion much like formula (1) of Section 11.8 can be used to determine the minimum number of steps which the winning player will need to bring the game to a successful conclusion. Find this recursion, and use it to develop a variant of the "alpha-beta" game-playing

procedure which tells the winning player how to win as rapidly as possible and tells the losing player how to postpone his inevitable defeat as long as possible.

20. The "alpha-beta" game-playing program (see Est_A_can_win, Section 11.8) operates most efficiently if moves likely to return a large Est_A_can_win value are explored first. To guess in advance which moves these are likely to be, one can save the values calculated by Est_A_can_win during each cycle of play and use these values as estimates of move quality the next time it is the same player's turn to move. Write a variant of the Est_A_can_procedure which incorporates this improvement.

APPENDIX A

SETL Reserved Words

The words on the following page have a predefined meaning within a SETL program, and should only be used for their defined purpose. The following keywords appear in the list for historical reasons, and are not otherwise mentioned in this text: **getf**, **getem**, **putf**, **putk**, **setem**, **spec**, and **unspec**.

abs	error	is_real	operator	sign
acos	even	is_set	or	sin
all	exists	is_string	packed	smap
and	exit	is_tuple	pass	span
any	exp	len	plex	sparse
arb	exports	less	pow	spec
asin	expr	lessf	print	sqrt
assert	fail	lev	printa	st
atan	false	lib	proc	statements
atan2	fix	libraries	procedure	step
atom	float	library	prog	stop
back	floor	local	program	str
base	for	log	put	string
boolean	forall	loop	putb	subset
break	from	lpad	putf	succeed
calls	fromb	macro	putk	tan
case	frome	map	quit	tanh
ceil	general	match	random	term
char	get	max	range	then
close	getb	min	rany	time
const	getem	mmap	rbreak	title
continue	getf	mod	rd	trace
cos	getipp	mode	read	true
date	getk	module	reada	tuple
debug	getspp	nargs	reads	type
directory	goto	newat	real	unspec
div	host	not	remote	until
do	if	notany	repr	untyped
doing	impl	notexists	return	val
domain	imports	notin	rewind	var
drop	in	notrace	rlen	where
eject	incs	npow	rmatch	while
elmt	init	odd	rnotany	with
else	integer	of	rpad	wr
elseif	is_atom	ok	rspan	writes
end	is_boolean	om	rw	yield
endm	is_integer	op	set	
eof	is_map	open	setem	

APPENDIX B

Syntax Diagrams

Throughout this text, syntax diagrams are used to describe the grammatical structure of SETL constructs. For convenience, all syntax diagrams are collected in this appendix.

Each diagram describes the structure of a language construct. Each path through a given diagram traces one valid instance of the corresponding construct. The following conventions are used in drawing a syntax diagram:

(a) Syntactic classes are written in lowercase and enclosed in rectangular boxes.
(b) Terminal symbols of the language (delimiters and keywords) are in boldface and enclosed in rounded boxes.
(c) When the presence of a construct in a given diagram is optional (say the declarations in a program) then a path that bypasses the optional construct appears in the graph above that construct. For example, a procedure body includes the following:

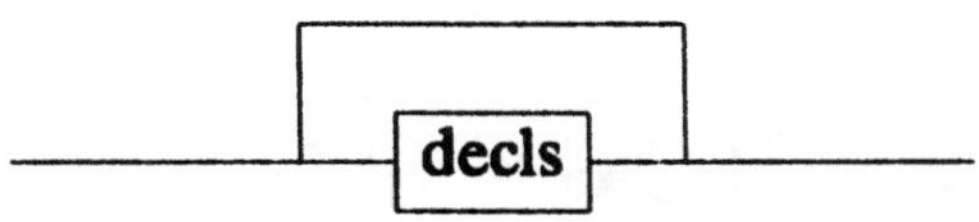

(d) Repetition is indicated by a backward path that passes under the repeated construct. For example, a list of constants is a sequence of one or more constants, separated by commas. The corresponding syntax graph for the construct '*constant list*' is the following:

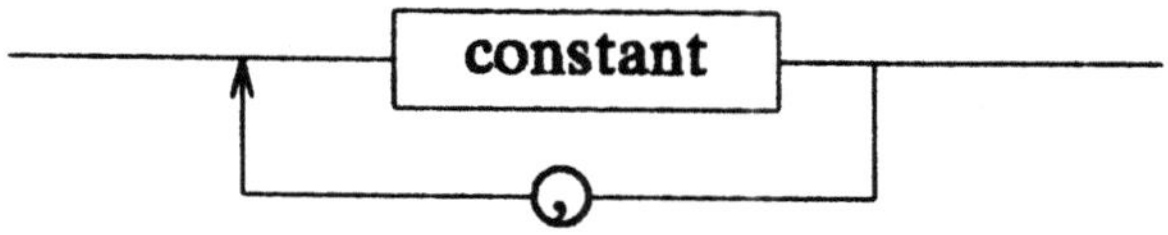

(e) The end of composite statements (loops, **if** and **case** statements) is indicated by the token **end**, optionally followed by one or more of the tokens that start the statement. The ellipsis (...) is used in the syntax diagrams to indicate the presence of such optional tokens.
(f) Unless otherwise marked, horizontal paths go from left and right.

B.1 Lexical Structure

The following graphs describe the structure of the valid tokens of the language.

name

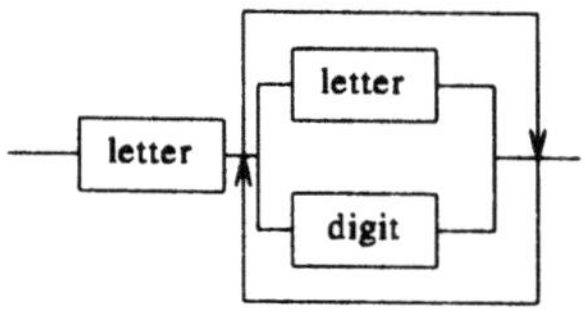

number

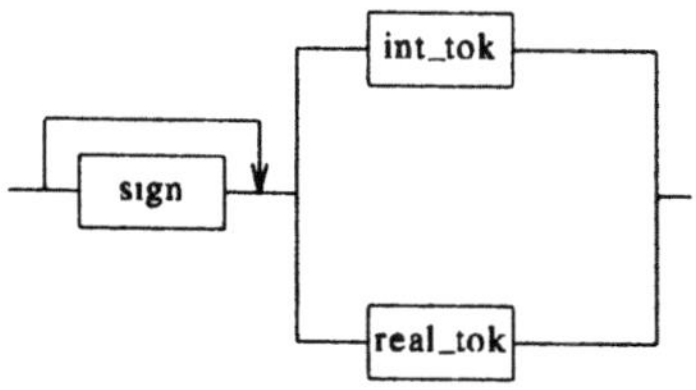

int_tok

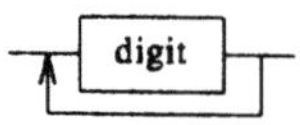

string

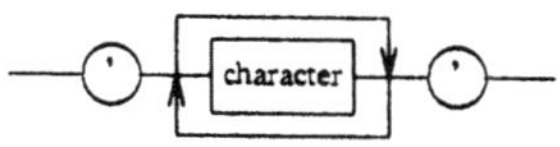

real_tok

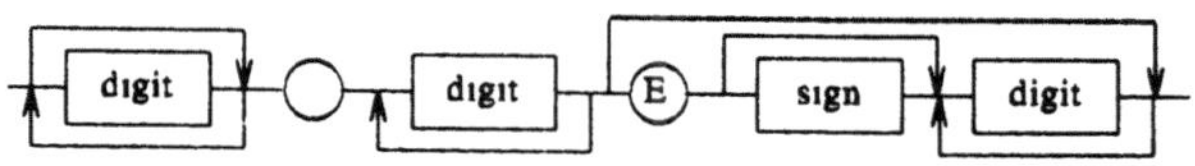

sign

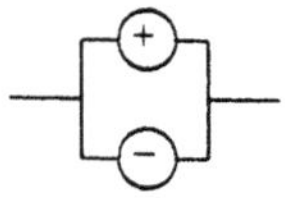

dot_tok

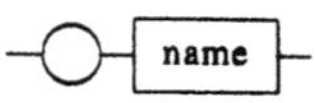

B.2 Program Structure

program

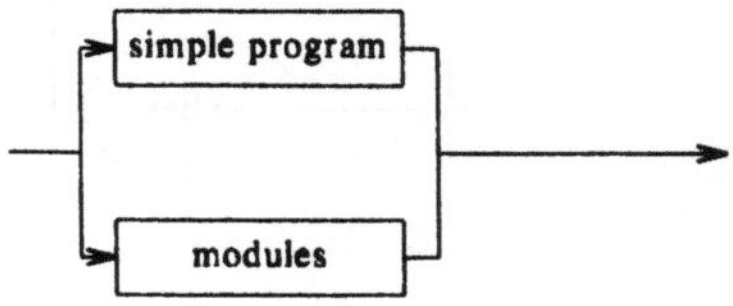

simple program

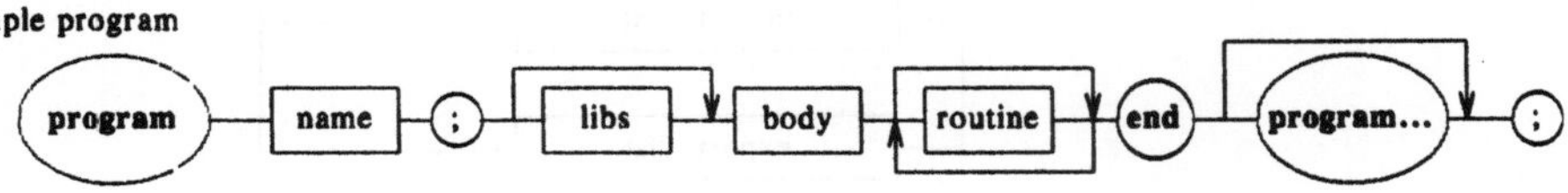

libs

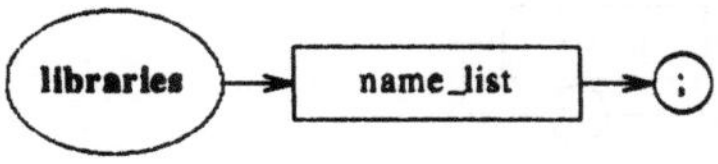

body

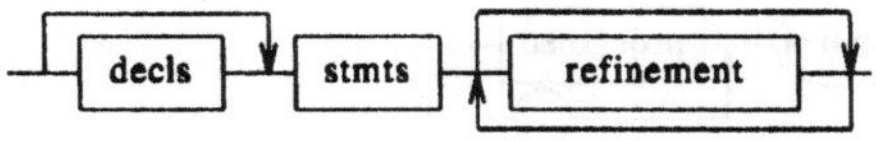

modules

directory_unit

prog_spec

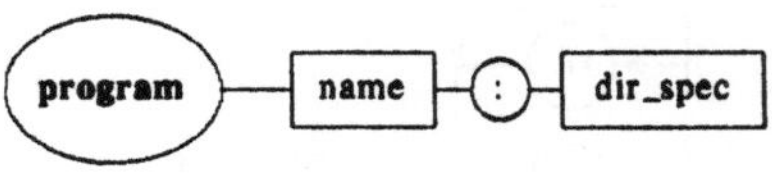

mod_spec

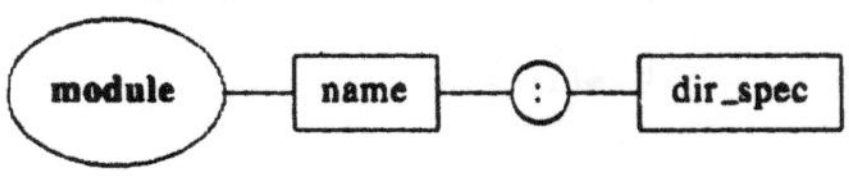

dir_spec

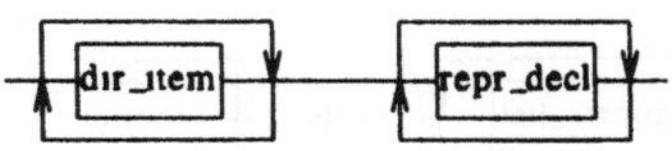

dir_item

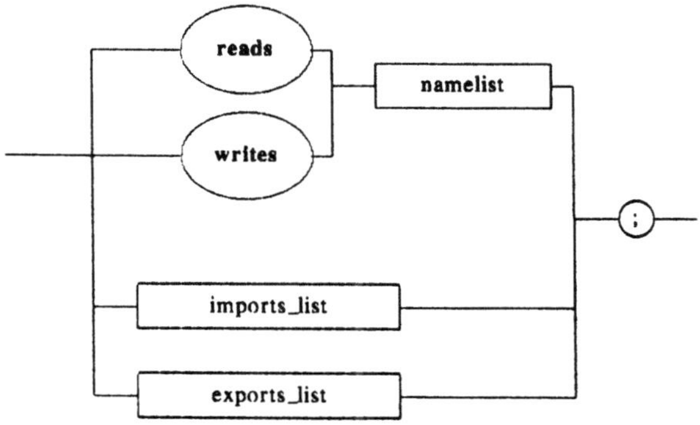

name_list

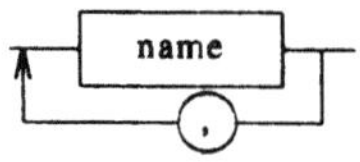

imports_list

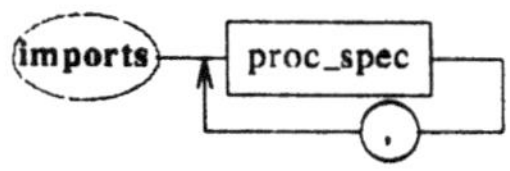

exports_list

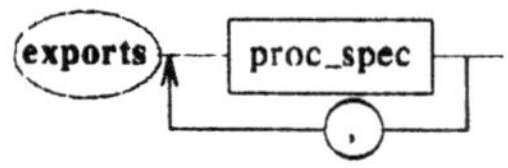

proc_spec

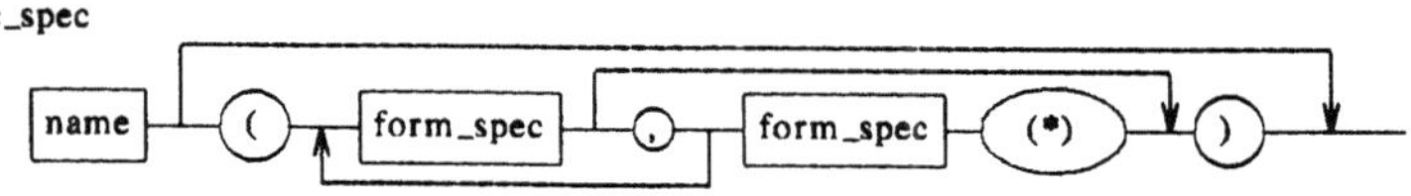

form_spec

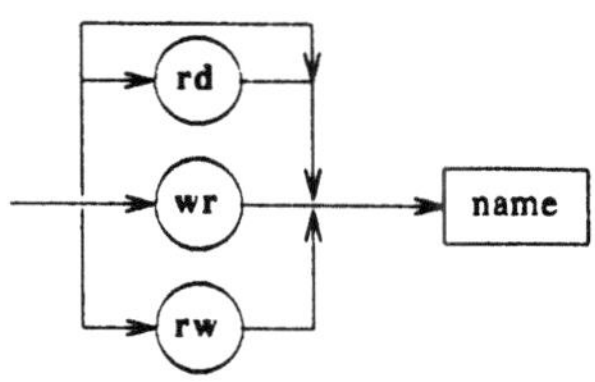

lib_unit

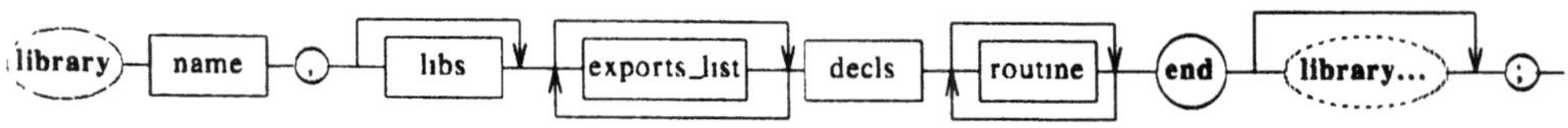

B.3 Declarative Forms

decls

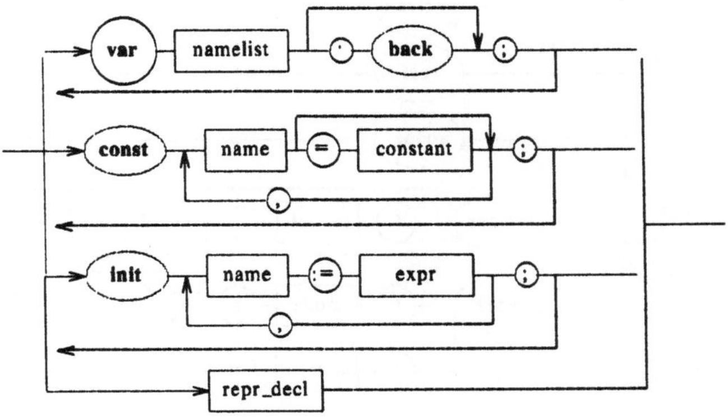

repr_decl

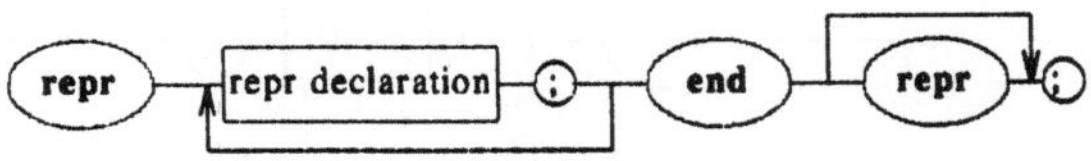

constant

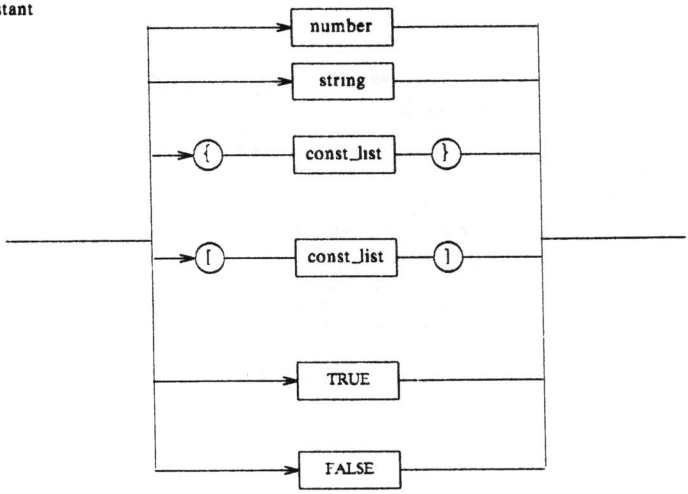

const_list

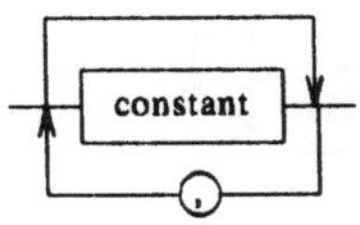

repr declaration

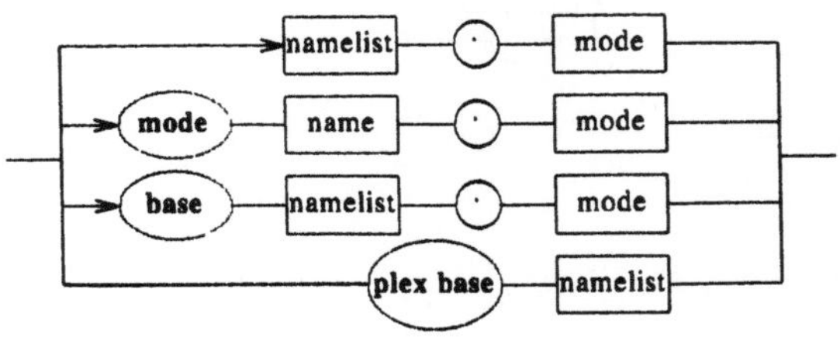

mode

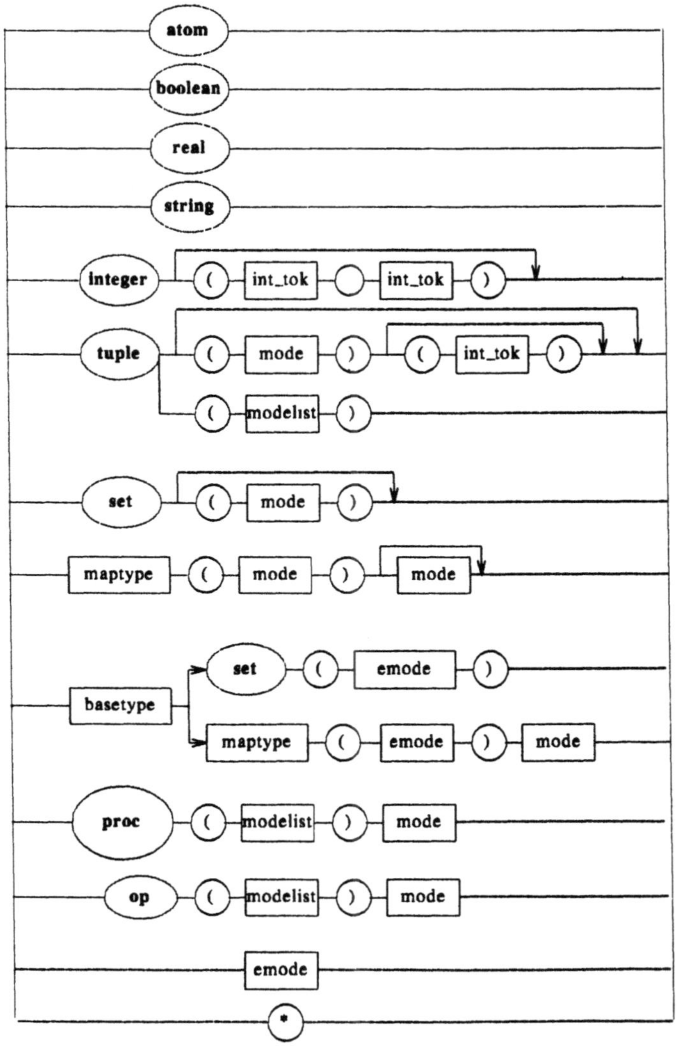

emode

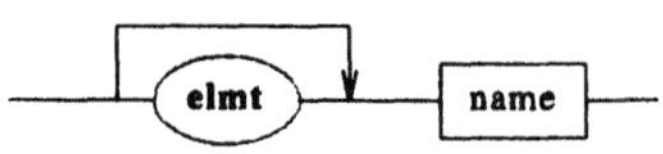

modelist

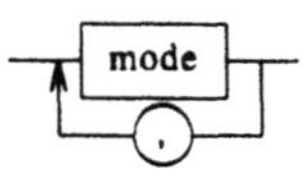

basetype

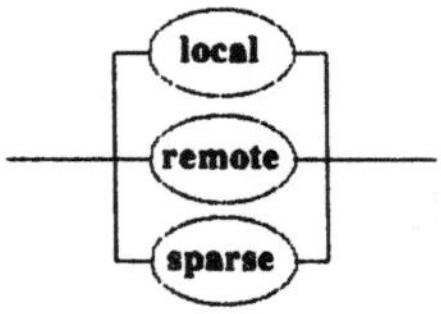

maptype

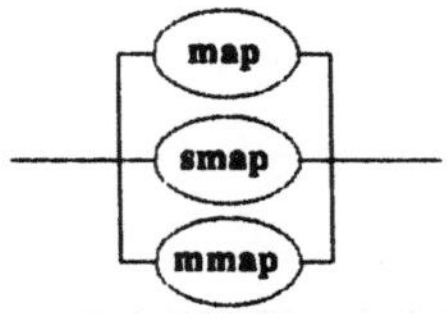

routine

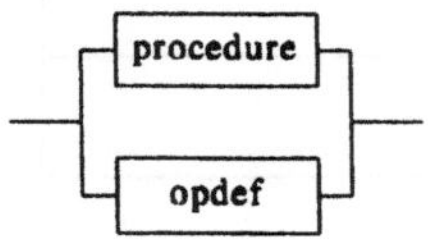

procedure

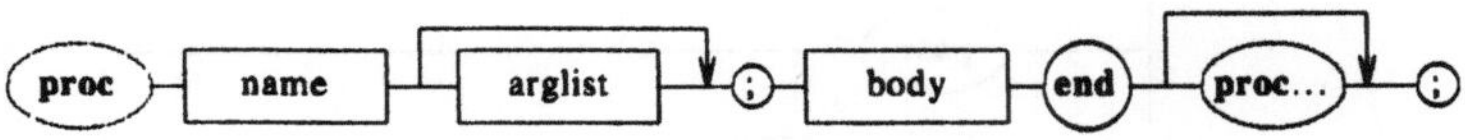

arglist

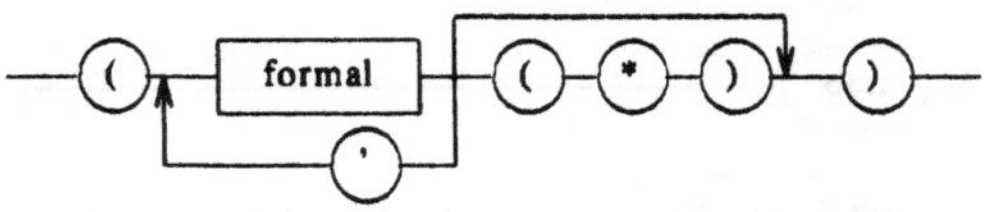

formal

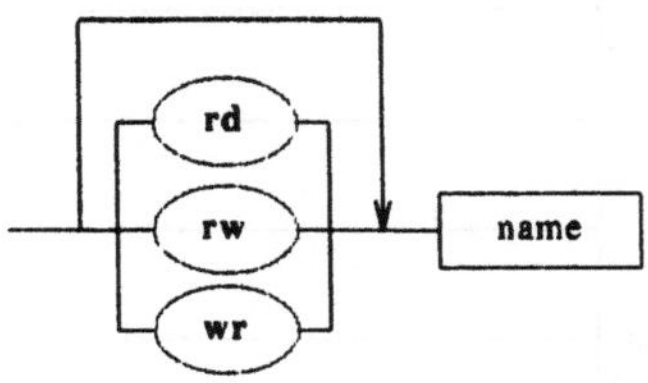

opdef

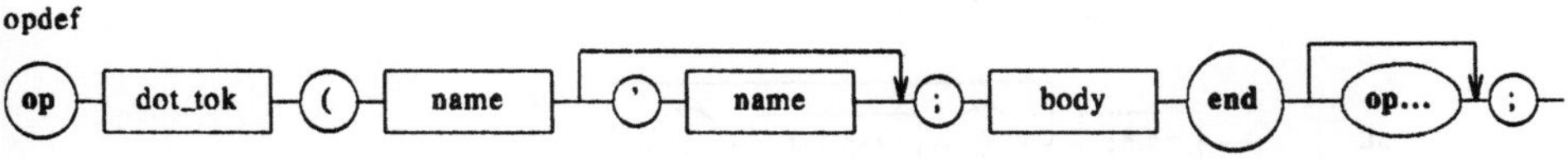

refinement

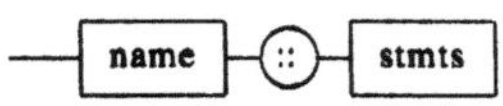

B.4 Statement Forms

stmt

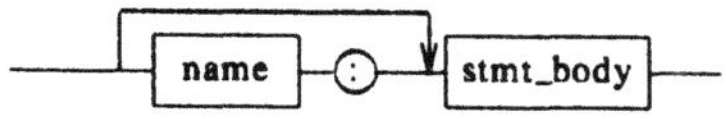

stmts

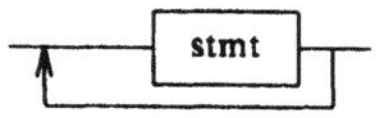

stmt_body

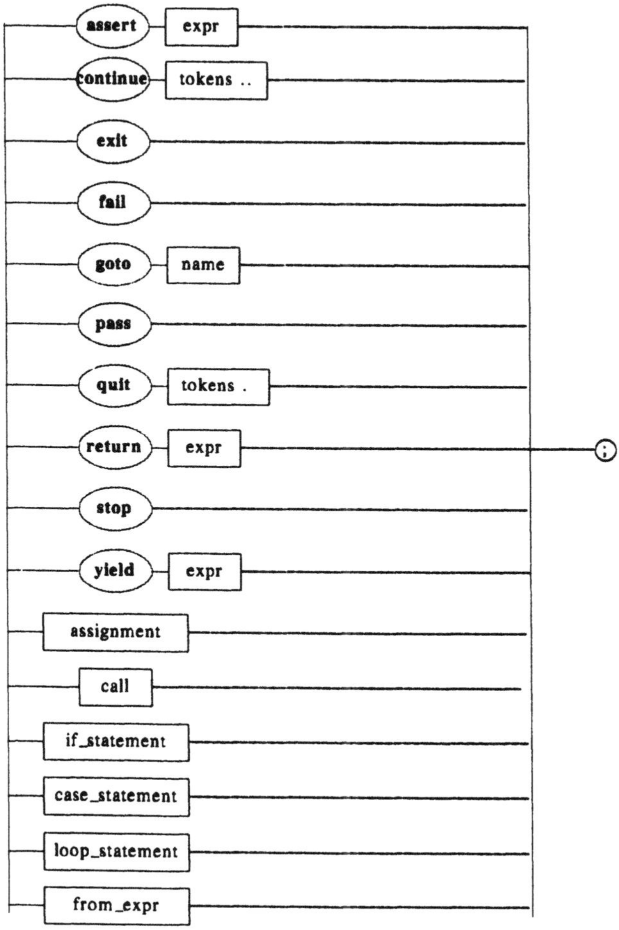

call

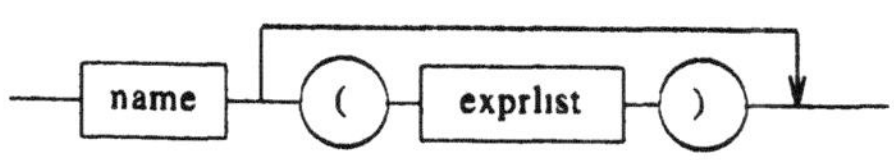

case_statement

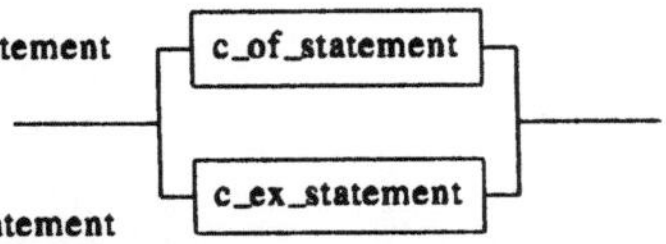

c_of_statement

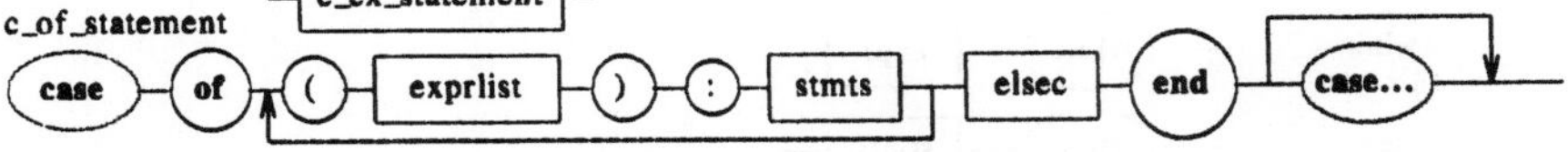

c_ex_statement

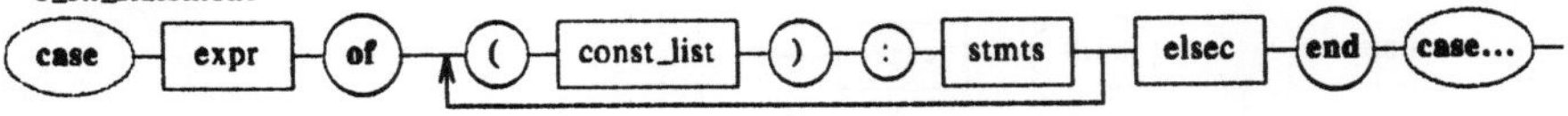

elsec

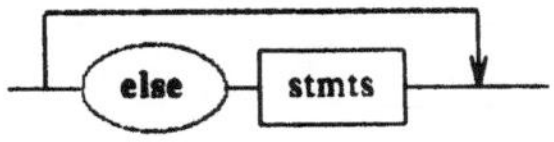

if_statement

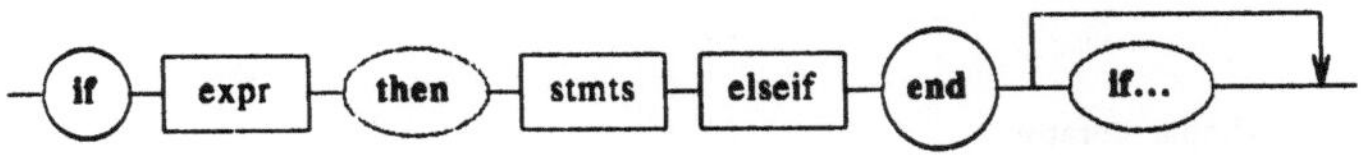

elseif

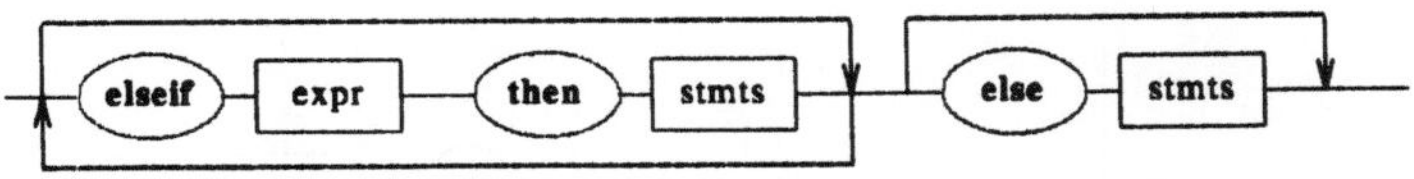

loop_statement

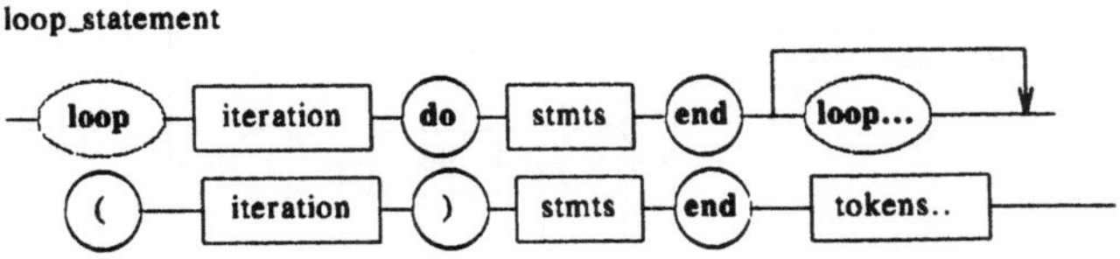

iteration

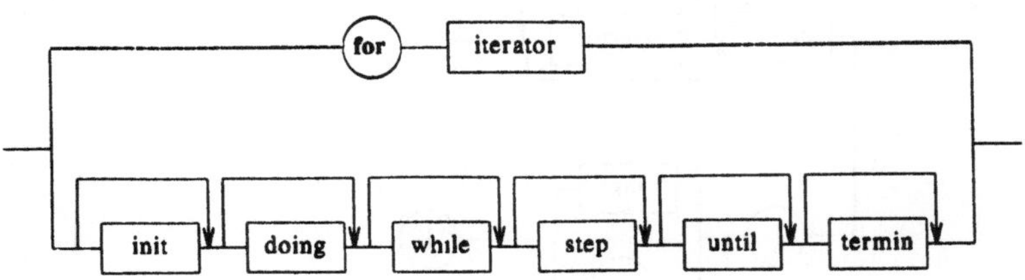

init

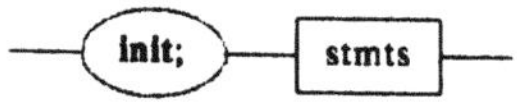

doing

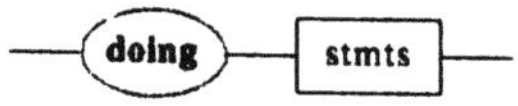

while

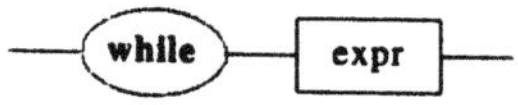

step

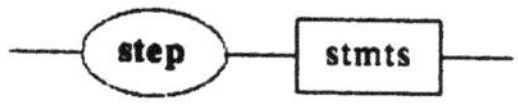

until

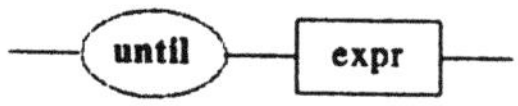

termin

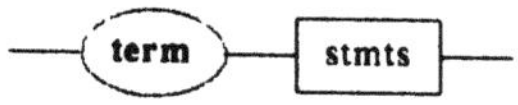

iterator

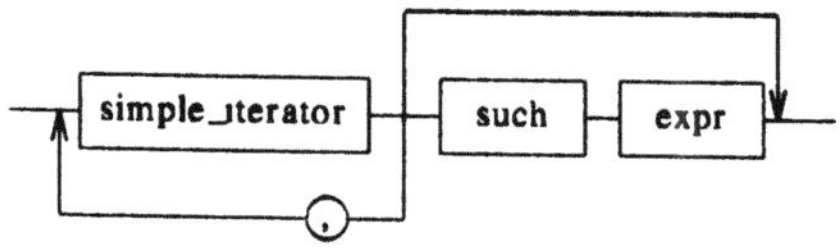

simple_iterator

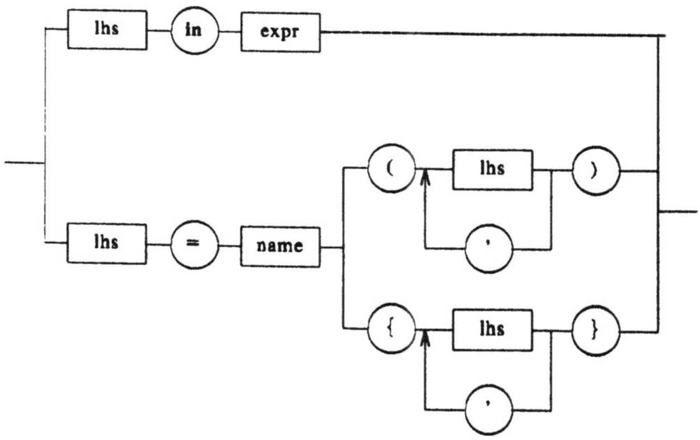

lhs

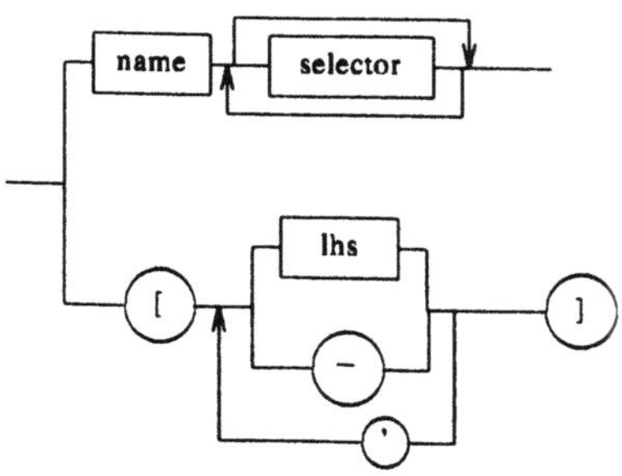

selector

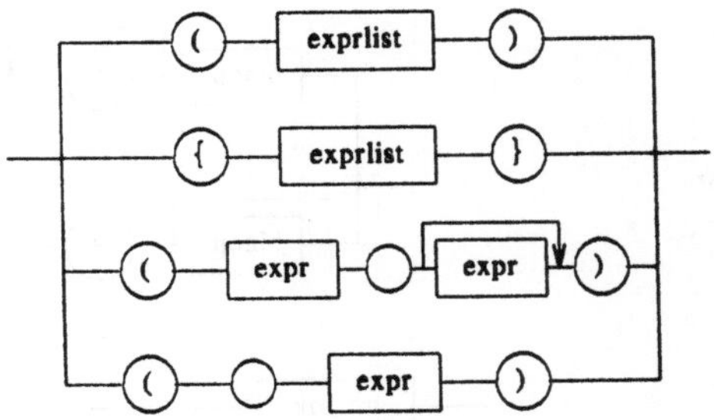

assignment_statement

B.5 Expressions

The following syntax graphs do not fully describe the relative precedence of operators. A complete table of operator precedences is to be found in Section 3.13. The construct *binop* includes the predefined binary operators and the user-defined operators. Similarly, *unop* refers both to predefined and user-defined operators.

expr

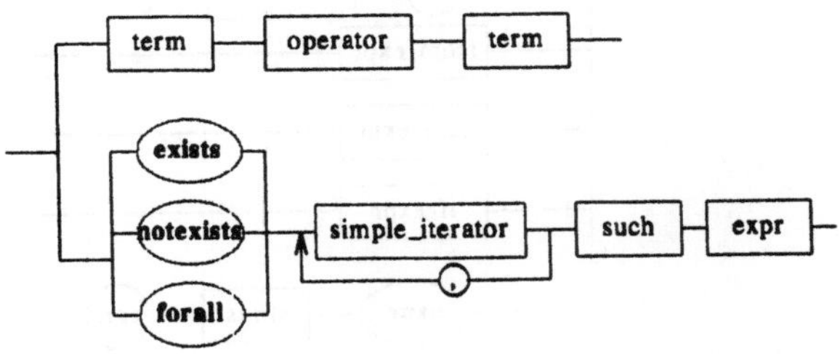

term

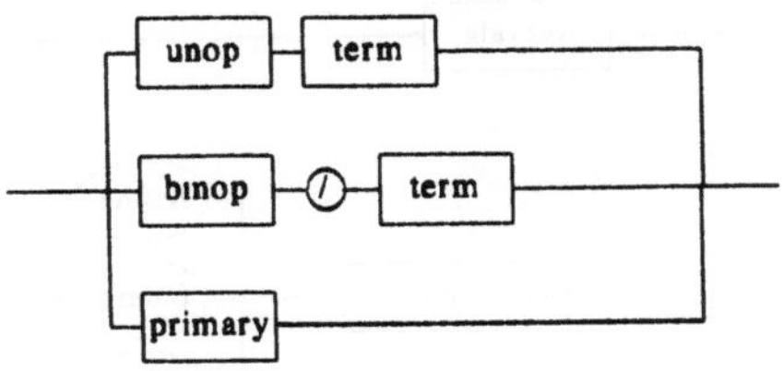

operator

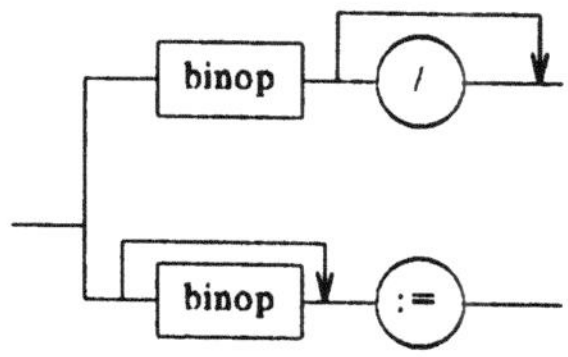

primary

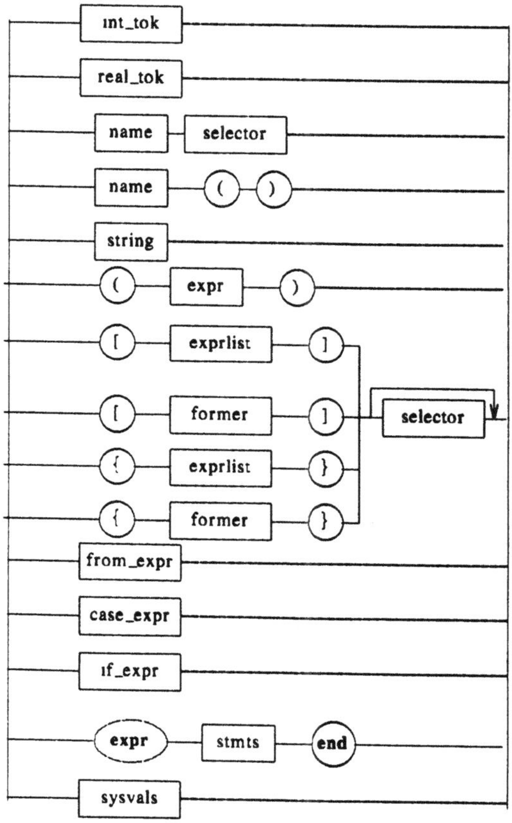

from_expr

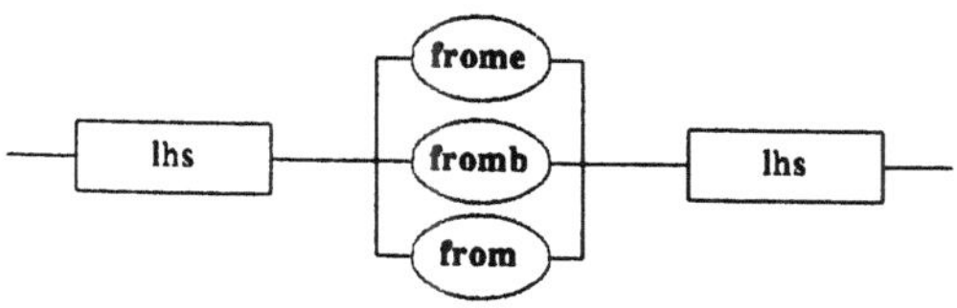

sysvals

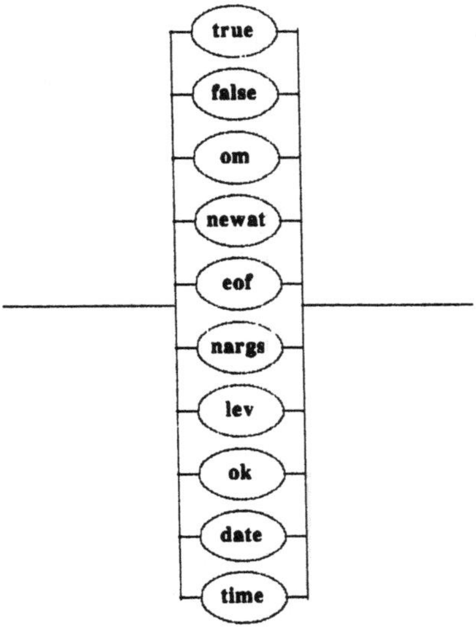

former

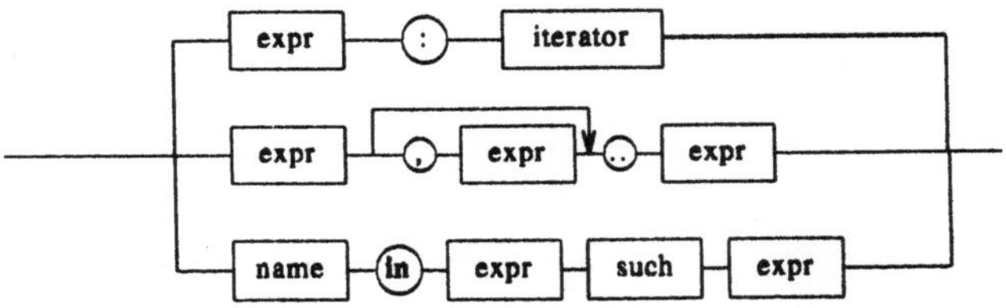

such

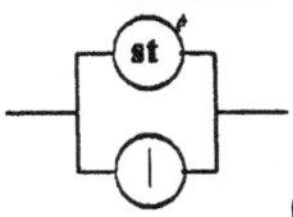

case_expr

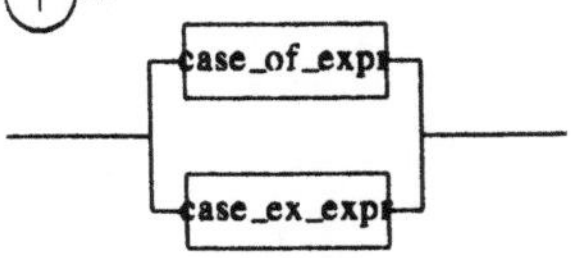

case_of_expr

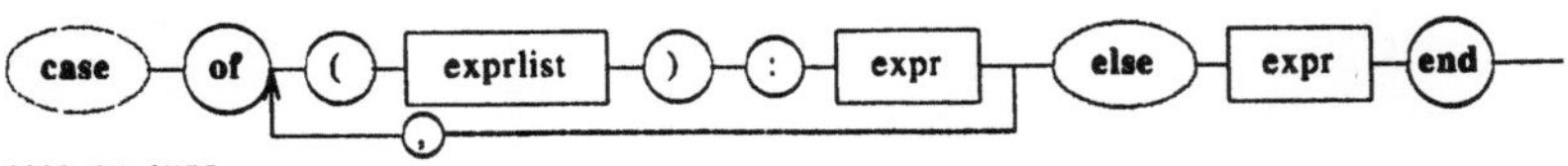

case_ex_expr

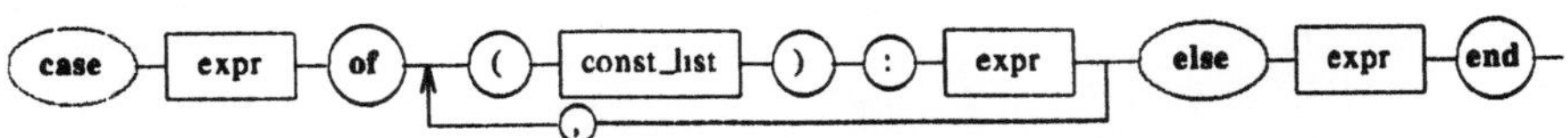

if_expr

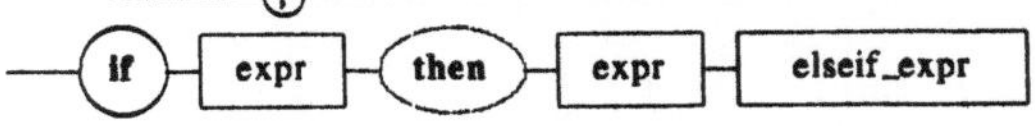

elseif_expr

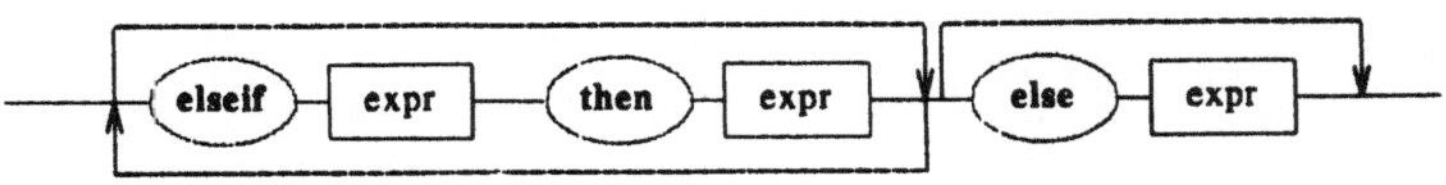

Index

MIX
Papier aus verantwortungsvollen Quellen
Paper from responsible sources
FSC® C105338

If you have any concerns about our products,
you can contact us on
ProductSafety@springernature.com

In case Publisher is established outside the EU,
the EU authorized representative is:
Springer Nature Customer Service Center GmbH
Europaplatz 3, 69115 Heidelberg, Germany

Printed by Libri Plureos GmbH
in Hamburg, Germany